D1757053

SYSTEMS MANAGEMENT FOR INFORMATION TECHNOLOGY AND SOFTWARE ENGINEERING

WILEY SERIES IN SYSTEMS ENGINEERING

Andrew P. Sage

ANDREW P. SAGE and JAMES D. PALMER
Software Systems Engineering

WILLIAM B. ROUSE
Design for Success: A Human-Centered Approach to Designing Successful Products and Systems

LEONARD ADELMAN
Evaluating Decision Support and Expert System Technology

ANDREW P. SAGE
Decision Support Systems Engineering

YEFIM FASSER and DONALD BRETTNER
Process Improvement in the Electronics Industry

WILLIAM B. ROUSE
Strategies for Innovation

ANDREW P. SAGE
Systems Engineering

HORST TEMPELMEIER and HEINRICH KUHN
Flexible Manufacturing Systems: Decision Support for Design and Operation

WILLIAM B. ROUSE
Catalysts for Change: Concepts and Principles for Enabling Innovation

LIPING FANG, KEITH W. HIPEL, and D. MARC KILGOUR
Interactive Decision Making: The Graph Model for Conflict Resolution

DAVID A. SCHUM
Evidential Foundations of Probabilistic Reasoning

JENS RASMUSSEN, ANNELISE MARK PEJTERSEN
and LEONARD P. GOODSTEIN
Cognitive Systems Engineering

ANDREW P. SAGE
Systems Management for Information Technology and Software Engineering

SYSTEMS MANAGEMENT FOR INFORMATION TECHNOLOGY AND SOFTWARE ENGINEERING

ANDREW P. SAGE
School of Information Technology and Engineering
George Mason University
Fairfax, Virginia

A Wiley-Interscience Publication
JOHN WILEY & SONS
New York / Chichester / Brisbane / Toronto / Singapore

Library of Congress Cataloging in Publication Data:

Sage, Andrew P.
    Systems management for information technology and software
engineering / Andrew P. Sage.
        p.   cm.
    Includes bibliographical references (p.   ) and index.
    ISBN 0-471-01583-0
    1. System design.   2. Informative technology.   3. Software
engineering.
QA76.9.S88S24   1995
004.2'1—dc20   94-23585

Printed in the United States of America

10 9 8 7 6 5 4 3 2 1

to LaVerne

Preface

This book discusses some fundamental considerations associated with the engineering of large scale systems, or *systems engineering*. We begin our effort by first discussing the need for systems engineering, and then providing several definitions of systems engineering. We next present a structure describing the systems-engineering process. The result of this is a *lifecycle model* for systems engineering processes. This process may also be called a product line. An organization generally has a number of processes associated with various functional areas of the organization. At a very general level, we may identify processes for research, development, test and evaluation of new and emerging technologies. We may also identify the process for acquisition or production of a system. And, we may speak of a process for planning and marketing. These are the three primary organizational processes that we examine here.

This systems management text discusses important concerns for the trustworthy development of process related approaches for the development of trustworthy systems, especially but not exclusively from the perspective of information technology, information systems engineering, and software systems engineering. The special and dominant focus of the book is the systems management of processes for information technology and software development organizations. This involves a number of very relevant issues associated with systems architectures and integration, quality assurance and management, organizational leadership and learning, process reengineering and process maturity, metrics, software economics, and cost and operational effectiveness analysis for the management of large information technology and software intensive systems.

There are many ingredients associated with the development of trustworthy systems. From a top down perspective, the following ingredients are surely present.

- process development life cycles
- process risk and technical direction for risk management
- metrics for systems management
- metrics for cost and operational effectiveness evaluation, and process cost estimation
- strategic quality assurance and management, or total quality management, and process and product development standards for quality
- organizational cultures and leadership, and process maturity
- reengineering at the level of systems management, process, and product.

These comprise the principal chapters in this book and will follow an introductory chapter that summarizes the book structure, function, and purpose.

Other ingredients could be easily identified. For the most part, however, these seven subject matters can be considered as *top level* supports for the objective of obtaining trustworthy and productive systems engineering products that are of high quality. Although we will be concerned with systems of hardware and software that support a variety of applications, our primary focus will be on information technology and software development areas. While most of our discussions will specifically focus on software, the ultimate applications for the constructs to be described are broader than the very important area of software development.

This text is written both for graduate students and practitioners in industry and government who are concerned with systems engineering, and such related areas as engineering management. It should also have value for other engineering areas that offer courses in systems management, such as in business administration and technology management. Prerequisites for the text are moderate. It will generally be assumed that the reader has a fundamental background common to Bachelor of Science degree recipients in the USA. Perhaps more importantly, some appreciation for the engineering design of large systems is assumed. The book is not specific to any particular engineering specialty. Doubtlessly, the experiences of the author in software systems engineering, decision support systems engineering, information systems engineering, systems management of emerging technologies, and command and control systems engineering have influenced the presentation. However, advanced level courses in these areas are not at all needed for the presentation contained here and what we discuss is ultimately as relevant to construction management, water resource management, and manufacturing management, as it is to information technology and software engineering productivity.

ANDREW P. SAGE

Fairfax Virginia
August 1, 1994

Contents

SYSTEMS MANAGEMENT FOR INFORMATION TECHNOLOGY AND SOFTWARE ENGINEERING

Chapter **1**

An Introduction to Systems Engineering and Systems Management

This chapter provides a perspective on all of systems engineering and, within that, systems management. This is a major challenge for a single short chapter. We believe that some appreciation for the overall process of systems engineering will lead naturally to a discussion of the important role for systems management and the applications of this to information technology and software development processes. Following our introductory comments, we briefly describe the organization of the text.

Here, as throughout the book, we are concerned with the engineering of large scale systems, or *systems engineering* [1]. We are especially concerned with strategic level systems engineering, or systems management. We begin our effort by first discussing the need for systems engineering and then providing several definitions of systems engineering. We next present a structure describing the systems engineering process. The result of this is a *lifecycle model* for systems engineering processes. This is used to motivate discussion of the functional levels, or considerations, involved in systems engineering efforts: *systems engineering methods and tools, systems methodology,* and *systems management.*

Figure 1.1 illustrates the natural hierarchical relationship among these levels. There will be some discussions throughout this chapter and the others on systems engineering methods and systems methodology. Our primary focus, however, is on systems management and technical direction of efforts that are intended to ultimately result in appropriate information technology and software engineering products or services. These products result from an appropriate methodology, an appropriate set of systems engineering methods and tools, and the resulting product line or process effort. These are guided by efforts at systems management as suggested in Figure 1.1, and as we will discuss throughout this text.

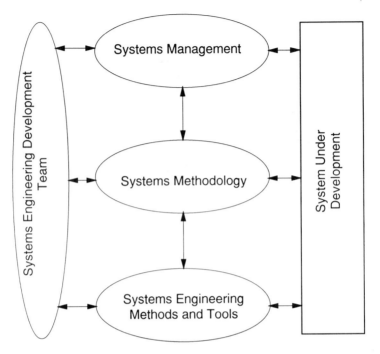

Figure 1.1   Conceptual illustration of the three levels for systems engineering.

1.1   SYSTEMS ENGINEERING

Systems engineering is a management technology. Technology is organization, application, and delivery of scientific knowledge for the betterment of a client group. This is a functional definition of technology as a fundamentally human activity. A technology inherently involves a purposeful human extension of one or more natural processes. For example, the stored program digital computer is a technology in that it enhances the ability of a human to perform computations and, in more advanced forms, to process information.

Management involves the interaction of the organization with the environment. A purpose of management is to enable organizations to better cope with their environments such as to achieve purposeful goals and objectives. Consequently, a management technology involves the interaction of technology, organizations concerned with both the evolution and use of technologies, and the environment. Figure 1.2 illustrates these conceptual interactions.

Information is the glue that enables the interactions shown in this figure. Information is a very important quantity, which is assumed to be present in the management technology that is systems engineering. This strongly couples notions of systems engineering with those of technical direction or systems management of technological development, rather than exclusively with one or more of the methods

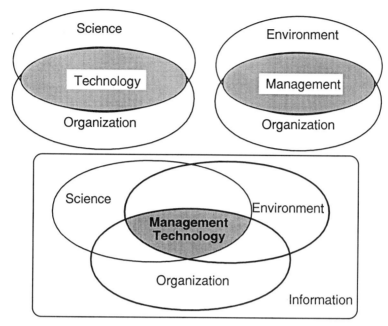

Figure 1.2   Systems engineering as a management technology.

of systems engineering, important as they may be for the ultimate success of a systems engineering effort. It suggests that *systems engineering is the management technology that controls a total system lifecycle process, which involves and which results in the definition, development, and deployment of a system that is of high quality, trustworthy, and cost effective in meeting user needs.* This process-oriented notion of systems engineering and systems management will be emphasized here.

Figure 1.3 illustrates our view that systems engineering knowledge is comprised of the following [2]:

1. Knowledge *perspectives,* which represent the view that is held relative to future directions and realities in the technological area under consideration.

2. Knowledge *practices,* which represent the accumulated wisdom and experiences that have led to the development of standard operating policies for well structured problems.

3. Knowledge *principles,* which generally represent formal problem-solving approaches to knowledge, generally employed in new situations and/or unstructured environments.

Clearly, one form of knowledge leads to another. Knowledge perspectives may create the incentive for research that leads to the discovery of new knowledge principles. As knowledge principles emerge and are refined, they generally become imbedded in the form of knowledge practices. Knowledge practices are generally

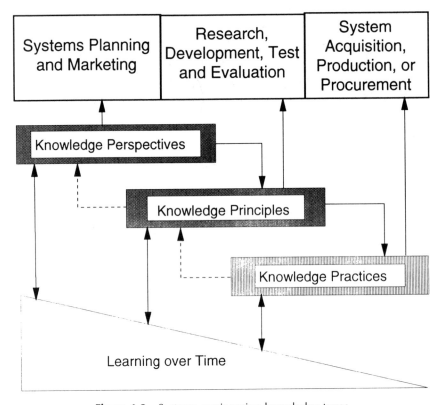

Figure 1.3   Systems engineering knowledge types.

the major influences of the systems that can be acquired or fielded. These knowledge types interact together, as suggested in Figure 1.3, which illustrates how these knowledge types support one another. In a nonexclusive way, they each support one of the principal lifecycles associated with systems engineering. Figure 1.3 also illustrates a number of feedback loops that are associated with learning to enable continual improvement in performance over time. This supports our view, and a major premise of this text, that it is a serious mistake to consider these lifecycles in isolation from one another.

It is on the basis of the appropriate use of these knowledge types that we are able to accomplish the technological system planning and development and the management system planning and development that lead to an innovative product or service. All three types of knowledge are needed. We will soon discuss these three different lifecycles for technology evolution:

System Planning and Marketing

Research, Development, Test and Evaluation (RDT&E)

System Acquisition, Production, or Procurement

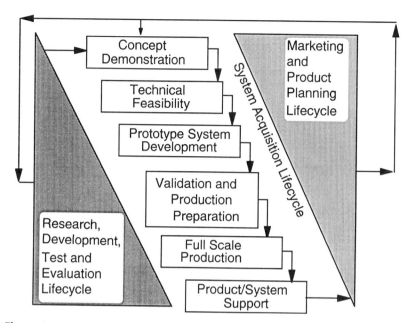

Figure 1.4   Interactions across the three primary systems engineering lifecycles.

These are each generally needed, and each primarily involves use of one of the three types of knowledge. We will discuss these briefly here and will illustrate how and why these make major but nonexclusive use of knowledge perspectives, principles, and practices. Figure 1.4 illustrates interactions across these lifecycles for one particular realization of a system acquisition lifecycle.

It is important when studying a new area to define it. We have provided one definition of systems engineering thus far. It is primarily a structural definition. A related definition, in terms of purpose, is that *systems engineering is management technology to assist and support policy making, planning, decision making, and associated resource allocation or action deployment.* Systems engineers accomplish this by quantitative and qualitative *formulation, analysis,* and *interpretation* of the impacts of action alternatives upon the needs perspectives, the institutional perspectives, and the value perspectives of their clients or customers. Each of these three steps is generally needed in solving systems engineering problems.

1. Issue *formulation* is an effort to identify the needs to be fulfilled and the requirements associated with these in terms of objectives to be satisfied, constraints and alterables (i.e., things that can be changed) that affect issue resolution, and generation of potential alternative courses of action.

2. Issue *analysis* enables us to determine the impacts of the identified alternative courses of action, including possible refinement of these alternatives.

3. Issue *interpretation* enables us to rank order the alternatives in terms of need satisfaction and to select one for implementation or additional study.

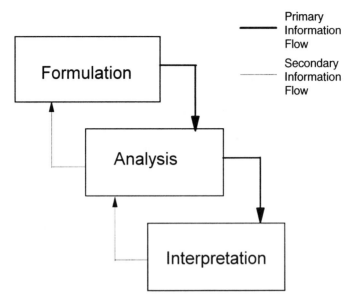

Figure 1.5   Conceptual illustration of formulation, analysis, and interpretation as the primary systems engineering steps.

This particular listing of three systems engineering steps and their descriptions is rather formal. Often, issues are resolved this way. The steps of formulation, analysis, and interpretation may also be accomplished on as "as if" basis by application of a variety of often useful heuristic approaches. These may well be quite appropriate in situations where the problem solver is experientially familiar with the task at hand and the environment into which the task is imbedded [1].

We may apply these systems engineering steps to a variety of situations, which should enable us to develop an appreciation for systems engineering efforts and problem solving. Generally, there is iteration among the steps and they follow, more or less, in the sequence illustrated in Figure 1.5.

The key words in this definition are formulation, analysis, and interpretation. In fact, all of systems engineering can be thought of as consisting of formulation, analysis, and interpretation efforts, together with the systems management and technical direction efforts necessary to bring this about. We may exercise these in a formal sense or in an *as if* or experientially based intuitive sense. These are the stepwise or microlevel components that comprise a part of the structural framework for systems methodology.

In our first definition of systems engineering, we indicated that systems engineers are concerned with the appropriate *definition, development,* and *deployment* of systems. These comprise a set of phases for a systems engineering lifecycle, as illustrated in Figure 1.6. There are many ways to describe the lifecycle phases of the systems engineering process, and we will describe a number of them in Chapter 2. Each of the lifecycle models, and those that are outgrowths of them, are comprised

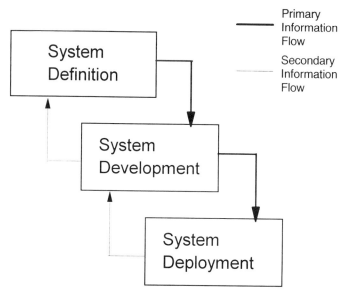

Figure 1.6   Conceptual illustration of the three primary systems engineering lifecycle phases.

of these three phases. For pragmatic reasons, a typical lifecycle will contain more than three phases, as we shall soon indicate.

1.2   THE IMPORTANCE OF TECHNICAL DIRECTION AND SYSTEMS MANAGEMENT

In order to resolve large scale and complex problems, or manage large systems of humans and machines (technology), we must be able to deal with important contemporary issues that involve and require the following:

1. Many considerations and interrelations.
2. Many different and perhaps controversial value judgments.
3. Knowledge from several disciplines.
4. Knowledge at the levels of principles, practices, and perspectives.
5. Considerations involving planning or definition, development, and deployment.
6. Considerations that cut across the three different lifecycles associated with systems planning and marketing, RDT&E, and system acquisition or production.
7. Risks and uncertainties involving future events that are difficult to predict.
8. A fragmented decision-making structure.

9. Human and organizational need and value perspectives, as well as technology perspectives.
10. Resolution of issues at the level of institutions and values as well as the level of symptoms.

The professional practice of systems engineering must use a variety of formulation, analysis, and interpretation aids for evolvement of technological systems and management systems. Clients and system developers alike need this support to enable them to cope with multifarious large scale issues. This support must avoid several potential pitfalls. These include the following 12 deadly systems engineering transgresses.

1. There is an overreliance on a specific analytical method or a specific technology that is advocated by a particular group.
2. There is a consideration of perceived problems and issues only at the level of symptoms and the development and deployment of "solutions" that only address symptoms.
3. There is a failure to develop and apply appropriate methodologies for issue resolution that will allow identification of major pertinent issue formulation elements, a fully robust analysis of the variety of impacts on stakeholders and the associated interactions among steps of the problem solution procedure, and an interpretation of these impacts in terms of institutional and value considerations.
4. There is a failure to involve the client, to the extent necessary, in the development of problem resolution alternatives and systemic aids to problem resolution.
5. There is a failure to consider the effects of cognitive biases that result from poor information processing heuristics.
6. There is a failure to identify a sufficiently robust set of options or alternative courses of action.
7. There is a failure to make and properly utilize reactive, interactive, and proactive measurements to guide the systems engineering efforts.
8. There is a failure to identify risks associated with the costs and benefits, or effectiveness, of the system to be acquired, produced, or otherwise fielded.
9. There is a failure to properly relate the system that is designed and implemented with the cognitive style and behavioral constraints that affect the user of the system, and an associated failure of not properly designing the system for effective user interaction.
10. There is a failure to consider the implications of strategies adopted in one of the three lifecycles (RDT&E, acquisition and production, and planning and marketing) on the other two lifecycles.
11. There is a failure to address quality issues in a comprehensive manner throughout all phases of the lifecycle, especially in terms of reliability, availability, and maintainability.

12. There is a failure to properly integrate a new system together with heritage or legacy systems that already exist and which the new system should support.

All of these may be, and generally are, associated with systems management failures.

The need for systematic measurements is a very real one for the appropriate practice of systems management. The use of the terms reactive measurements, interactive measurements, and proactive measurements may seem unusual. We may, however, approach measurement, and management in general, from at least four perspectives. We first discuss these at the level of product.

1. *Inactive.* This denotes an organization that does not use metrics or that does not measure at all except perhaps in an intuitive and qualitative manner.
2. *Reactive.* This denotes an organization that will perform an outcomes assessment and, after it has detected a problem or failure, will diagnose the cause of the problem and often will get rid of the symptoms that produce the problem.
3. *Interactive.* This denotes an organization that will measure an evolving product as it moves through various phases of the lifecycle process in order to detect problems as soon as they occur, diagnose their causes, and correct the difficulty through recycling, feedback, and retrofit to and through that portion of the lifecycle process in which the problem occurred.
4. *Proactive.* Proactive measurements are those designed to predict the potential for errors and synthesis of an appropriate lifecycle process that is sufficiently mature such that the potential for errors is minimized.

Actually, we may also refer to the systems management style of an organization as inactive, reactive, interactive, and/or proactive. All these perspectives on measurement purpose and on systems management are needed. Inactive and reactive measurements are associated with organizations that have a low level of process maturity, a term we will soon define. As one moves to higher and higher levels of process maturity, the lower level forms of measurement purpose becomes less and less used. In part, this is because a high level of process maturity results in such appropriate metrics for systems management that final product errors, which can be detected through a reactive measurement approach, tend to occur very infrequently. While reactive measurement approaches are used, they are not at all the dominant focus of measurement. In a very highly mature organization, they might be needed only on the rarest of occasions.

Another way to communicate relative to metrics, and quality for that matter, is to indicate that we can talk about metrics at the levels of *systems engineering tools and methods* (Are there bugs in the program?), *systems methodology* (Is the software OK in a verification and validation sense? Are there metrics for configuration management?), and, *systems management* (Are there metrics to identify process maturity? Are there other appropriate management metrics that predict which of several development lifecycles is best in a given situation for a given organization?).

In a very real sense, the metrics corresponding to the three levels mentioned are very *product oriented,* in terms of inspections and quality control of product (product tools and methods metrics); *process oriented,* in terms of lifecycle evolution and configuration management of the product (such as to lead to operational level task quality assurance for the evolving product); and/or *systems management oriented,* in terms of strategic level quality assurance and technical direction of the process.

Note also that these efforts at the three levels are generally also *reactive* (product-oriented metrics that catch bugs in the code of programs and dysfunctional VLSI chips), *interactive* (process-oriented methods that attempt to assure real-time control of quality through operational level assurance at the process level, such as, for example, through verification at each lifecycle phase of the development process), and, *proactive,* in order to yield prospective and predictive control of quality such as to result in a process that can be expected to deliver a trustworthy and high quality operational product with high effectiveness and minimal development cost.

Thus management of the systems engineering process, which we call *systems management,* is very necessary for success. There are many evidences of systems engineering failures at the level of systems management. Often, one result of these failures is that the purpose, function, and structure of a new system are not identified sufficiently before the system is defined, developed, and deployed. These failures generally cause costly mistakes that could truly have been avoided. Failures of definition, development or deployment occur because either the formulation, the analysis, or the interpretation efforts (or all of them perhaps) are deficient at one or more of these phases. A major objective of systems engineering, at the strategic level of systems management, is to take proactive measures to avoid these difficulties.

Now that we have introduced some of the flavor of systems engineering, let us turn to some definitions of the professional area of effort we call systems engineering. There are many of these. As we will see, it is possible to define a term from any of several perspectives or to combine these perspectives. In a great many cases, misunderstandings occur because terms have not been defined clearly.

1.3   DEFINITIONS OF SYSTEMS ENGINEERING

Concerns associated with the *definition, development,* and *deployment* of tools such that they can be used efficiently and effectively have always been addressed, but often this has been on an implicit and "trial and error" basis. When tool designers were also tool users, which was more often than not the case for the simple tools, machines, and products of the past, the resulting designs were often good initially or soon evolved into good designs through this trial and error effort. These phased efforts of definition, development, and deployment represent the macrostructure of a systems engineering framework, as shown in Figure 1.6. They need each to be employed for each of the three lifecycles illustrated in Figure 1.4. And within each lifecycle phase, there are a number of steps, as illustrated in Figure 1.7. Thus we see that our relatively simple description of systems engineering is become more and more complex. Figure 1.8 illustrates how these three steps, three phases, and

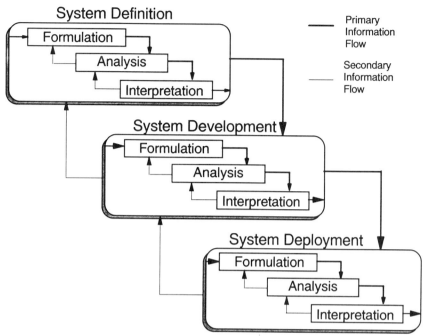

Figure 1.7 One representation of three systems engineering steps within each of three lifecycle phases.

three lifecycles comprise a more complete methodological, or structural, or process-oriented view of systems engineering. Even in this relatively simple methodological framework, which is simultaneously incomplete but relatively complex, we have a total of 27 cells of activity. In a much more realistic view of the steps and phases, as would be the case in actual systems development, we might well have seven phases and seven steps of effort. This yields a total of 147 cells of activity.

In the early days, when the designers of a product were also the ultimate end users, things were even simpler than this 27-cell model. Definition, development, and deployment could often be accomplished on a simple trial and error basis. When physical tools, machines, and systems become so complex that it is no longer possible to design them by a single individual who might even also be the intended user of the tool, and a team is necessary, then a host of new problems emerge. This is very much the condition today. To cope with this, a number of methodologies associated with systems engineering have evolved. Through these, it has been possible to decompose large design issues into smaller component subsystem design issues, to design the subsystems, and then to *build* the complete system as a collection of these subsystems.

Even so, problems remain. There are many instances of failures due to this sort of incomplete approach. Just simply connecting together individual subsystems often does not result in a system that performs acceptably, either from a technological efficiency perspective or from an effectiveness perspective. This has led to the

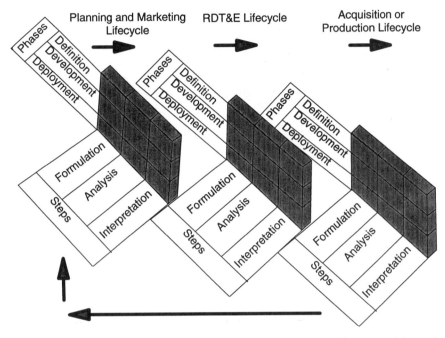

Figure 1.8 Three systems engineering lifecycles and phases and steps within each lifecycle.

realization that *systems integration engineering* and *systems management* throughout an entire system lifecycle will be necessary. Thus contemporary efforts in *systems engineering* contain a focus on tools and methods, on the systems methodology for definition, development, and deployment that enables appropriate use of these tools, and on the systems management approaches that enable the imbedding of systems engineering product and process development approaches within organizations and environments, such as to support the application of the principles of the physical and material sciences for the betterment of humankind.

Figure 1.1 has illustrated this conceptual relationship among the three levels of systems engineering and also shows each as necessary facets, which the various members of a systems engineering team must apply to define, develop, and deploy an evolving system. Each of these three levels—systems engineering methods, systems methodology, systems management—is necessarily associated with appropriate environments in order to assure an appropriate systems engineering process, including the very necessary client interaction during system definition, development, and deployment. The use of appropriate systems methods and tools as well as systems methodology [3,4] and systems management constructs enables system design for more efficient and effective human interaction [5].

System management and integration issues are of major importance in determining the effectiveness, efficiency, and overall *functionality* of system designs. To achieve a high measure of functionality, it must be possible for a system design to be *efficiently* and *effectively* produced, used, maintained, retrofitted, and modified

throughout all phases of a lifecycle. This lifecycle begins with need conceptualization and identification, through specification of system requirements and architectures, to ultimate system installation, operational implementation or deployment,
evaluation, and maintenance throughout a productive lifetime.

In reality, there are many difficulties associated with the production of functional, reliable, and trustworthy systems of large scale and scope:

1. It is very difficult to identify the user requirements for a large system.
2. Large systems are expensive.
3. System capability is often less than promised and expected.
4. System deliveries are often quite late.
5. Large system cost overruns often occur.
6. Large system maintenance is complex and error prone.
7. Large system documentation is inappropriate and inadequate.
8. Large systems are often cumbersome to use and system design for human
   interaction is generally lacking.
9. Individual new subsystems often cannot be integrated with legacy or heritage systems.
10. Large systems often cannot be transitioned to a new environment or mod-
    ified to meet the evolving needs of clients.
11. Unanticipated risks and hazards often materialize.
12. There is no risk management and crisis management provisions.
13. Large systems often suffer in terms of their reliability, availability, and
    maintainability.
14. Large system performance is often of low quality.
15. Large systems often do not perform according to specifications.
16. It is difficult to identify suitable performance metrics for large systems that
    enable determination of system cost and effectiveness.
17. There is often poor communication among program management, designers,
    and customers or program sponsors.
18. System specifications often do not adequately capture user needs and re-
    quirements.

These potential difficulties, when they are allowed to develop, can create many
problems that are difficult to resolve. Among these are inconsistent, incomplete,
and otherwise imperfect system requirements specifications; system requirements
that do not provide for change as user needs evolve over time; and poorly defined
management structures for product design and delivery. These lead to delivered
products that are difficult to use, that do not solve the intended problem, that operate
in an unreliable fashion, that are unmaintainable, and that—as a result—are not
used. Sometimes these failures are so great that operational products and systems
are never even fully developed, much less operationally deployed, before plans for
the product or system are abruptly canceled.

These same studies generally show that the major problems associated with the production of trustworthy systems have more do with the *organization and management of complexity* than with direct technological concerns that affect individual subsystems and specific physical science areas. Often the major concern should be more associated with the definition, development, and use of an appropriate process, or product line, for production of a product than it is with the actual product itself, in the sense that direct attention to the product or service without appropriate attention to the process leads to the fielding of a low quality and expensive product or service.

A functional definition of systems engineering is also of interest and we will provide a simple one here.

Systems engineering is the art and science of producing a product, based on phased efforts that involve definition, design, development, production, and maintenance activities. The system is functional, reliable, of high quality, and trustworthy and has been developed within cost and time constraints.

There are, of course, other definitions. Two closely related and appropriate definitions are provided by MIL-STD-499A and MIL-STD-499B [6].

Systems engineering is the application of scientific and engineering efforts to (a) transform an operational need into a description of system performance parameters and a system configuration through the use of an iterative process of definition, synthesis, analysis, design, test, and evaluation; (b) integrate related technical parameters and ensure compatibility of all physical, functional, and program interfaces in a manner that optimizes the total system definition and design; (c) integrate reliability, maintainability, safety, survivability, human engineering, and other factors into the total engineering effort to meet cost, schedule, supportability, and technical performance objectives.

Systems engineering is an interdisciplinary approach to evolve and verify an integrated and lifecycle balanced set of system product and process solutions that satisfy the customers needs. Systems engineering (a) encompasses the scientific and engineering efforts related to the development, manufacturing, verification, deployment, operations, support, and disposal of system products and processes; (b) develops needed user training equipment, procedures, and data; (c) establishes and maintains configuration management of the system; and (d) develops work breakdown structures and statements of work and provides information for management decision making.

These two definitions attempt to combine structural, functional, and purposeful views of systems engineering. There is a closely related draft (IEEE Standard P1220 [7]) on systems engineering which states that

Systems engineering is the interdisciplinary approach governing the total technical effort required to transform a requirement into a system solution. This includes the definition of technical performance measures, the integration of engineering specialties towards the establishment of a system architecture, and the definition of supporting lifecycle processes which balance cost, performance, and schedule objectives.

This definition specifically recognizes the importance of system architectures in evolving a systems engineering product.

It is generally accepted that we may define things according to either *structure, function,* or *purpose.* Often, definitions are incomplete if they do not address structure, function, and purpose. Our continued discussion of systems engineering will be assisted by the provision of a structural, purposeful, and functional definition of systems engineering. These are based on the three definitions we have provided earlier. Table 1.1 presents these three definitions. Each of these definitions is important and all three are generally needed. In our three-level hierarchy of systems engineering there is generally a non-mutually exclusive correspondence between function and tools, structure and methodology, and purpose and management, as we not in Figure 1.9.

This figure, unlike Figure 1.1, illustrates the reality that there is no truly sharp distinction between these three levels of systems engineering. Structural, functional, and purposeful definitions and discussions will necessarily overlap, since these terms are not mutually exclusive. It is of interest to note in Figure 1.9 that the process, or product line, results from the interaction of systems management and systems methodology. The product is the result of use of a number of methods and tools and systems methodology as it eventuates in a lifecycle process. The product,

TABLE 1.1 Definitions of Systems Engineering

Structure	Systems engineering is management technology to assist clients through the formulation, analysis, and interpretation of the impacts of proposed policies, controls, or complete systems on the need perspectives, institutional perspectives, and value perspectives of stakeholders to issues under consideration.
Function	Systems engineering is an appropriate combination of the methods and tools of systems engineering, made possible through use of a suitable methodology and systems management procedures, in a useful process-oriented setting that is appropriate for the resolution of real-world problems, often of large scale and scope, through development of systems that are of high quality and cost effective.
Purpose	The purpose of systems engineering is information and knowledge organization that will assist clients who desire to develop policies for management, direction, control, and regulation activities relative to forecasting planning, development, production, and operation of total systems to maintain overall quality, integrity, and integration as related to performance, trustworthiness, reliability, availability, and maintainability.

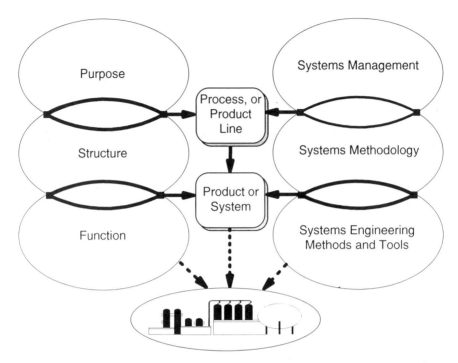

Figure 1.9 Relations between purpose and systems management, structure and systems methodology, and function and methods—and their product and process results.

or system, also results from the process, or product line. Thus it is quite correct to view an abstraction of this figure, as shown in Figure 1.10, in which appropriate systems management results in a process, or product line, and the result of using a systems engineering process is the production of a product. Not explicitly shown here are the interactions across all three levels with the environment. Also not shown in this figure is the fact that there are three lifecycles associated with the process. This does not suggest that the same individuals are associated with all three of these lifecycles, nor even across all phases within a given lifecycle. At a sufficiently high level of systems management, there is doubtlessly this overall responsibility. As in the systems engineering military standards just cited, however, most of the efforts of a given systems engineering team may be associated with the development phase of systems acquisition. Learning over time, such as to enable continuous improvement in quality and effectiveness across all three levels, is shown.

We have illustrated three hierarchical levels for systems engineering in Figure 1.1 and again in Figure 1.9. We now expand on this to indicate some of the ingredients at each of these levels. The functional definition, or lowest level, of systems engineering says that we will be concerned with the various tools and techniques and methods that enable us to design systems. Often, these will be systems science and operations research tools that enable the formal analysis of systems. They can also include specific system design tools and components, such as illustrated in

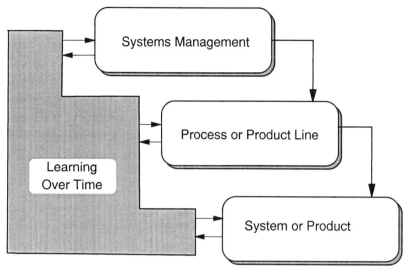

Figure 1.10 Another view of the hierarchical levels of systems engineering.

Figure 1.11. With respect to the information technology and software engineering applications primarily addressed here, these would certainly include a variety of computer science and programming tools or methods. Strictly speaking, it would be more appropriate to refer to these as product level methods. Then we could also refer to systems methodology methods or process methods, and systems manage-

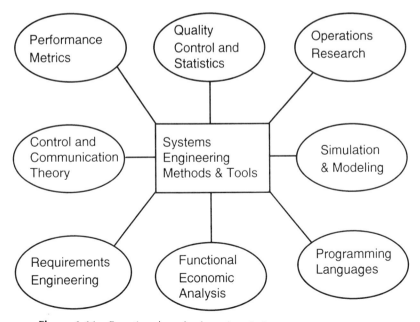

Figure 1.11 Functional methods and tools for systems engineering.

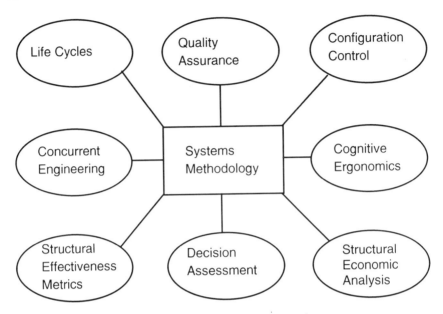

Figure 1.12   Systems methodology and supports.

ment methods. When the term "method(s)" is used alone and without a modifier, we will invariably be referring to product level methods. The specific nature of the most useful methods and tools will depend greatly on the particular lifecycle that is being considered and the particular product, service, or system that is ultimately to be acquired. There are generally many methods and tools, and not just systems engineering methods and tools, that are needed to produce a product or system.

The functional definition of systems engineering also states that we will be concerned with a combination of these tools. In systems engineering, we obtain this combination as the result of using systems methodology. For our purposes, a methodology is an open set of procedures for problem solving. This brings about such important notions as appropriate development lifecycles, operational quality assurance issues, and configuration management procedures, which are very important and are discussed in more detail in Chapter 2. Each of these reflects a structural, or methodological, perspective on systems engineering. Figure 1.12 illustrates some of the process-based methods associated with systems methodology. How to best bring these about will vary from product to product and across each of the three lifecycles leading to that product, system, or service.

Finally, the functional definition of systems engineering states that we will accomplish this in a useful and appropriate setting. This useful setting is provided by an appropriate systems management. We will use the term systems management to refer to the cognitive strategy and organizational tasks necessary to produce a useful process from a systems methodology and design study. The result of systems management is an appropriate combination of the methods and tools of systems engineering, including their use in a methodological setting, together with appropriate leadership in managing system process and product development, to ultimately field

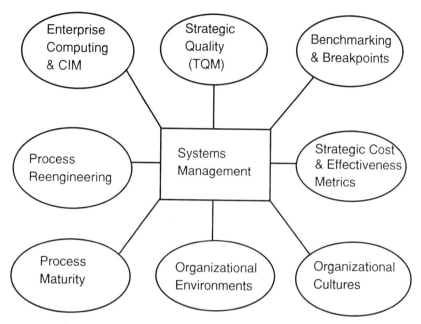

Figure 1.13 Systems management and associated elements.

a system that can be used to resolve issues. There are many interesting concepts associated with systems management, and this is the primary focus of this text, specifically for information technology and software intensive systems. Figure 1.13 illustrates some of the many concerns associated with systems management.

We should note that some of these elements, such as economic analysis, may appear to be at all levels. At the level of the product or systems methods, we use functional economic analysis. This might be associated with cost control of the evolving product. At the level of systems methodology, we would use structural economic analysis, such as associated with a work breakdown structure (WBS). Structured economic analysis would have to do with lifecycle cost and effectiveness determination. Finally, at the level of systems management, we use a number of strategic cost management approaches that deal with strategic positioning in terms of process costs and effectiveness trade-offs. These will enable selection of an appropriate development process, including as a special case the decision not to enter a particular market. Thus economic systems analysis is needed at each of the three systems engineering hierarchical levels. A different form of economic systems analysis is, however, needed. We need to be concerned with these three levels (management, methodology, method), or the somewhat equivalent levels of systems management, process, and product, across the three lifecycles of systems planning and marketing, RDT&E, and system acquisition or production. The particular life-cycle in question, as well as the phase of development, will strongly influence the actual approaches that are appropriate for use at each of these levels. Thus, we see that systems engineering methods support process and systems management, as well as product.

The structural definition of systems engineering tells us that we are concerned with a framework for problem resolution that, from a formal perspective at least, consists of three fundamental steps: (1) *issue formulation,* (2) *issue analysis,* and (3) *issue interpretation.* These are each conducted at each of the lifecycle phases that have been chosen for definition, development, and deployment. Regardless of the way in which the systems engineering lifecycle process is characterized, and regardless of the type of product or system or service that is being designed, all characterizations of systems engineering lifecycles will necessarily involve the following [1,5,8]:

1. *Formulation of the problem,* in which the needs and objectives of a client group are identified and potentially acceptable alternatives, or options, are identified or generated.

2. *Analysis of the alternatives,* in which the impacts of the identified options are identified and evaluated.

3. *Interpretation and selection,* in which the options, or alternative courses of action, are compared by means of an evaluation of the impacts of the alternatives and how these are valued by the client group. The needs and objectives of the client group are necessarily used as a basis for evaluation. The most acceptable alternative is selected for implementation or further study in a subsequent phase of systems engineering.

We emphasize these three steps because of their great importance in systems engineering. Our model of the steps of the fine structure of the systems process, shown in Figure 1.5, is based on this conceptualization. As we shall also indicate later, these three steps can be disaggregated into a number of others.

Each of these steps of systems engineering is accomplished for each of the lifecycle phases. There are generally three different systems engineering lifecycles. Thus we may imagine a three-dimensional model of systems engineering that is comprised of steps associated with each phase of a lifecycle, the phases in the lifecycle, and the lifecycles that comprise the coarse structure of systems engineering. Figure 1.8 has illustrated this across three distinct but interrelated lifecycles, for the three steps and three phases that we have described here. This is one of many possible morphological frameworks for systems engineering.

The words morphology and methodology may be unfamiliar. The word *morphology* is adapted from biology and means a study of form. As we use it, a *methodology* is an open set of procedures for problem solving, as we have noted. Consequently, a methodology involves a set of methods, a set of activities, and a set of relations between the methods and the activities. To use a methodology we must have an appropriate set of methods. Generally, these include a variety of qualitative and quantitative approaches from a number of disciplines that are appropriate for the specific product, service, or system to be acquired. Associated with a methodology is a structured framework into which particular methods are associated for resolution of a specific issue.

Without question, this is a formal rational model of the way in which these three systems engineering functions of formulation, analysis, and interpretation are ac-

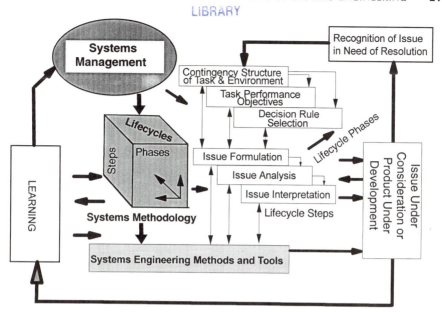

Figure 1.14 Conceptual model of the systems engineering process.

complished. Even within this formal framework, there is the need for much iteration from one step back to an earlier step when it is discovered that improvements in the results of an earlier step are needed in order to obtain a quality result at a later step, or phase, of the systems engineering effort. Also, this description does not emphasize the key role of information and information requirements determination.

Even when these realities are associated with the morphological framework, it still represents an incomplete view of the way in which people do, could, or should accomplish planning, design, development, or other problem-solving activities. The most that can be argued is that this framework is correct in an "as if" manner. We have a morphological box that consists of a number of phases and steps. There is also a third dimension, the lifecycles associated with the systems management, as we illustrated in Figure 1.8 and as further illustrated conceptually in Figure 1.14. This figure shows systems management as exercising strategic management controls over an evolving systems engineering process. The implementation of the process results in the systems engineering product. The term "product" must be interpreted to include "issue" here as, certainly in the systems planning and marketing lifecycle, the product of planning and marketing is a determination of whether RDT&E and/or acquisition of a product or system should be undertaken.

In many, if not most, cases, proper application of one or more technologies is necessary to ameliorate an existing problem or fulfill an existing need through evolution of a definition, development, and deployment of a system. However, the successful application of technology to major problem areas must consider three levels at which solution may be sought [9]—*symptoms*, *institutions*, and *values*—or we may well be confronted with a technological system looking for a problem. This is especially the case when we approach problems only at the level of systems: for example, unemployment, bad housing, inadequate health-care delivery, pollution, or hunger. A technological fix is found that addresses symptoms only and the resulting "solution" creates the illusion that the outpouring of huge quantities of funds to resolve symptoms will actually resolve the fundamental underlying problem. With respect to measurements and management, symptomatic approaches are generally reactive in nature.

Attacking problems at the level of institutions would allow the design of new institutions and organizations to make full and effective use of new technologies. This is generally a major improvement on what results when we consider problem abatement only at the level of removal of symptoms. Measurement and management approaches at the level of institutions are generally interactive and process related.

Of vital importance is the need to also deal with problems at the level of values. Systems engineers serious about resolving major problems must appreciate the significance of human values and be able to identify basic issues in terms of conflicting values. Furthermore, value elements and systems, as well as institutions and purely technological components, must be utilized in determining useful problem solutions. All of this again illustrates the major need for incorporation of systems management approaches into the development of process and product evolvement efforts. Proactive management and proactive measurement are value oriented.

Some necessary ingredients that must exist in order to develop large systems, to solve large and complex problems, to resolve complicated issues, or to manage large systems are associated with the following needs:

1. We need a way to deal successfully with issues involving many considerations and interrelations, including change over time.
2. We need a way to deal successfully with issues in which there are far-reaching and controversial value judgments.
3. We need a way to deal successfully with issues, the solutions to which require knowledge principles, practices, and perspectives from several disciplines.
4. We need a way to deal successfully with issues in which future events are difficult to predict.
5. We need a way to deal successfully with issues in which the environments, external and internal, are difficult to predict.
6. We need a way to deal successfully with issues in which structural and human institutional and organizational elements are given full consideration.

We believe that systems engineering, through empowered systems management, possesses the necessary characteristics to fulfill these needs. Thus systems engineering is potentially capable of exposing not only technological perspectives associated with large scale systems but also needs and value perspectives. Furthermore, it can relate these to knowledge principles, practices, and perspectives such that the result of its application is successful planning and marketing, RDT&E, and acquisition or production of high quality trustworthy systems.

Systems engineering efforts are very concerned with technical direction and management of systems definition, development, and deployment. As we have noted, we call this effort *systems management.* By adopting the management technology of systems engineering and applying it, we become very concerned with making sure that correct systems are designed, and not just that system products are correct according to some potentially ill-conceived notions of what the system should do. Appropriate metrics to enable efficient and effective error prevention and detection at the level of systems management and at the process and product level will enhance the production of systems engineering products that are "correct" in the broadest possible meaning of this term. To ensure that correct systems are produced requires that considerable emphasis be placed on the front-end of each of the systems engineering lifecycles.

In particular, there needs to be considerable emphasis on the accurate definition of a system, what it should do, and how people should interact with it before one is produced and implemented. In turn, this requires emphasis on conformance to system requirements specifications, and the development of standards to ensure compatibility and integrability of system products. Such areas as documentation and communication are important in all of this. Thus we see the need for the technical direction and management technology efforts that comprise systems engineering, and the strong role for process and systems management related concerns in this.

1.4   LIFECYCLE METHODOLOGY FOR SYSTEMS ENGINEERING

As we have noted, systems engineering is the creative process through which products, services, or systems presumed to be responsive to client needs and requirements are conceptualized or specified and ultimately developed and deployed. There are at least 12 primary assertions implied by this not uncommon definition of systems engineering, and they apply to the development of software intensive systems, as well as to hardware and physical systems.

1. Systems planning and marketing are the first strategic level efforts in systems engineering. They result in the determination of whether or not a given organization should undertake a given systems engineering product or service. They also result in a (preliminary) determination of the amount of effort to be devoted to RDT&E and the amount to actual system acquisition or production.

2. Creation of an appropriate process or product line is one result of system planning and marketing.

3. An appropriate process leads to efficient and effective RDT&E, and to the actual system acquisition that follows appropriate RDT&E.

4. The first phase of any systems engineering lifecycle effort results in specifications and architecture for a process or system.

5. Systems engineering is a creative process.

6. Systems engineering activities are conceptual in nature at the initial phases

of effort, for any of the three generic lifecycles, and become operational in later phases.

7. A successful systems engineering product or service must be of high quality and responsive to client needs and requirements.

8. A successful systems engineering product, or service, generally results only from a successful systems engineering acquisition process.

9. An appropriate systems engineering acquisition process is generally the result of successful systems management and appropriate planning and marketing.

10. Appropriate systems engineering efforts need necessarily be associated with systematic measurements to ensure high quality information as a basis for decision making across the three generic systems engineering lifecycles.

11. Appropriate systems engineering efforts are necessarily attuned to organizational and environmental realities as they affect both the client organization and the systems engineering organization.

12. Systems engineering efforts are of necessity interactive; however, they transcend interactivity to include proactivity.

Good systems engineering practice requires that the systems engineer be responsive to each of these 12 ingredients for quality effort. Clearly, not all members of a systems engineering effort are responsible for, and participate in, each and every systems engineering activity.

It is of value to expand on the simple three-phase and three-step model we have used to characterize a framework for systems engineering. Figure 1.15 illustrates a typical sequence of phases—seven in this case. The particular lifecycle chosen here could be a research, development, test, and evaluation lifecycle, or a system acquisition and procurement lifecycle. The particular words chosen are not the most appropriate for a systems planning and marketing lifecycle. However, they could easily be modified to indicate identification of societal needs for a product and development of a product marketing strategy, such that they are appropriate for systems planning and marketing. It is also of interest to compare this lifecycle with the six-phase lifecycle shown in Figure 1.4 for system acquisition. The lifecycle of Figure 1.15 explicitly includes the identification of client needs and the translation of these needs into specifications. These are not explicitly called for in the acquisition lifecycle in Figure 1.4, which is more of a lifecycle for the system development phase of acquisition and production, rather than a more encompassing view of the definition, development, and deployment phases of the lifecycle.

In Figure 1.15, we have identified a phased system engineering lifecycle that consists of seven phases:

1. Requirements and specifications identification.

2. Preliminary conceptual design.

3. Logical design and system architecture specification.

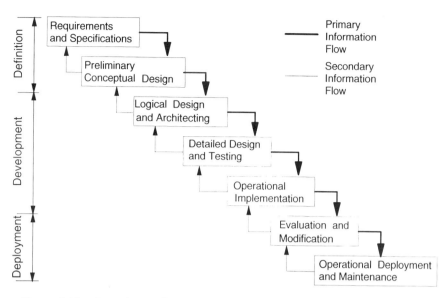

Figure 1.15 One of several possible lifecycle models for systems engineering.

4. Detailed design, production, and testing.
5. Operational implementation.
6. Evaluation and modification.
7. Operational deployment and maintenance.

These lifecycle phases are sequenced in the iterative manner as shown in Figure 1.15. There are many descriptions of systems engineering lifecycles and associated methodologies and frameworks for systems engineering, and we outline only one of them here.

In general, a simple conceptual model of the overall process, for a single lifecycle, may be structured as in Figure 1.16, which illustrates an effort to accommodate the three steps we have described and the seven phases illustrated here. A framework for systems methodology, the middle box in this figure, is represented by a two-dimensional morphological box. In this particular framework, there are 21 activity cells. There should be one or more methods associated with each of these activity cells. Choice of an appropriate mix of methods is an important challenge in systems engineering. One of these morphological box frameworks needs to be associated with each of the three lifecycles that are associated with an overall systems engineering effort, and this would lead to 63 specific activity cells. And this is a simplified model of the process!

If we were to restate the steps of the fine structure as seven rather than three, we would obtain a morphological box comprised of 49 elements. Figure 1.17 illustrates a not untypical 49-element morphological box. This is obtained by expanding our three systems engineering steps to a total of seven. These seven steps, but not the

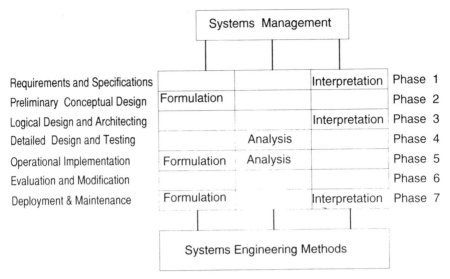

Figure 1.16   The steps, phases, and activity levels in systems engineering.

seven phases that we associate with them, are essentially those identified by Hall in his pioneering efforts in systems engineering [10,11]. They may be described as follows.

Issue Formulation

1. *Problem definition* involves isolating, quantifying, and clarifying the need that creates the problem and describing that set of environmental factors which

	Formulation			Analysis		Interpretation	
	Problem Definition	Value System Design	System Synthesis	Systems Analysis	Alternative Refinement	Decision Making	Planning for Action
Requirements and Specifications							
Preliminary Conceptual Design							
Logical Design and Architecting							
Detailed Design and Testing							
Operational Implementation							
Evaluation and Modification							
Deployment & Maintenance							

Figure 1.17   The phases and steps in one 49-element two-dimensional systems engineering framework.

constrains alterables for the system to be developed. In addition to identifying needs, we need to identify constraints, those facets that cannot be changed, and alterables, those facets that can be changed.

2. *Value system design* involves selection of the set of objectives or goals that guides the search for alternatives. Very importantly, value system design enables determination of the multidimensional attributes or decision criteria for selecting the most appropriate system. There are also known as objectives measures.

3. *Systems synthesis* involves searching for, or hypothesizing, a set of alternative courses of action or options. Each alternative must be described in sufficient detail to permit analysis of the impacts of implementation and subsequent evaluation and interpretation with respect to the objectives. We also need to associate appropriate metrics with each identified alternative or alternative measures.

Analysis

4. *Systems analysis* involves determining specific impacts or consequences that were specified as relevant by the value system. These impacts may relate to such important concerns as product quality, market, reliability, cost, and effectiveness or benefits. Modeling and simulation approaches are often used in systems analysis.

5. *Refinement* of the alternatives refers to adjusting, sometimes by optimizing, the system parameters for each alternative in order to meet system objectives, ideally in a "best" fashion, and to satisfy system constraints.

Interpretation

6. *Decision making* involves evaluating the impacts or consequences of the alternatives developed in analysis relative to the value system. This enables interpretation of these evaluations such that all alternatives can be compared relative to these values. One or more alternatives or courses of action can be selected for advancing to the next step.

7. *Planning for action* to implement the next phase includes communicating the results of the effort to this point. It includes such pragmatic efforts as scheduling subsequent efforts, allocating resources to accomplish them, and setting up system management controls. If we are conducting a single-phase effort, this step would be the final one. More generally, it leads to a new phase of effort.

The specific methods we need to use in each of these seven steps is clearly dependent on the phase of activity that is being completed.

Using a seven-phase and seven-step framework raises the number of activity cells to 49 for a single lifecycle, or 147 when we consider that there are generally three lifecycle phases. A very large number of systems engineering methods may be needed to fill in this matrix, especially since more than one method will almost invariably be associated with many of the entries.

We now describe the seven phases selected here. The requirements and specification phase of the systems engineering lifecycle has as its goal the identification of client, customer, or stakeholder needs, activities, and objectives for the functionally operational system. This phase should result in the identification and description of preliminary conceptual design considerations for the next phase. It is necessary to translate operational deployment needs into requirements specifications so that these needs may be addressed by the system design efforts. Thus information requirements, which are extraordinarily important, and requirements specifications are affected by, and affect, each of the other design phases of the systems engineering lifecycle. We could easily disaggregate this phase into two phases: (1) identification of user level requirements for a system, and (2) translation of these user level requirements into system level specifications.

As a result of the requirements specifications phase, there should exist a clear definition of development issues such that it becomes possible to make a decision concerning whether to undertake preliminary conceptual design. If the requirements specifications effort indicates that client needs can be satisfied in a functionally satisfactory manner, then documentation is typically prepared concerning system level specifications for the preliminary conceptual design phase. Initial specifications for the following three phases of effort are typically also prepared, and a concept design team is selected to implement the next phase of the lifecycle effort. This effort is sometimes called system level architecting [12–14].

Preliminary conceptual system design typically includes, or results in, an effort to specify the content and associated architecture and general algorithms for the system product in question. The primary goal of this phase is to develop some sort of prototype that is responsive to the specifications previously identified in an earlier phase of the lifecycle. A preliminary conceptual design, one that is responsive to user requirements for the system and associated technical system specifications, should be obtained. Rapid prototyping of the conceptual design is clearly desirable for many applications as one way of achieving an appropriate conceptual design.

The desired product of this phase of activity is a set of detailed design and architectural specifications that should result in a useful system product. There should exist a high degree of user confidence that a useful product will result from detailed design, or the entire design effort should be redone or possibly abandoned. Another product of this phase is a refined set of specifications for the evaluation and operational deployment phases of the lifecycle. In the third phase, these are translated into detailed representations in logical form such that system development may occur. A product, process, or system is produced in the fourth phase of the lifecycle. This is not the final system design, but rather the result of implementation of the design that resulted from the conceptual design effort of the last phase. User guides for the product should be produced such that realistic operational test and evaluation can be conducted.

Evaluation of the detailed design and the resulting product, process, or system is achieved in the sixth phase of the systems engineering lifecycle.

Depending on the specific application being considered, an entire systems engineering lifecycle process could be called "design," "manufacturing," or some other appropriate designator, as we have already noted. System acquisition is an often used word to describe the entire systems engineering process that results in an operational systems engineering product. Generally, an acquisition lifecycle involves primarily knowledge practices or standard procedures to produce or manufacture a product based on established practices. An RDT&E lifecycle is generally associated with an emerging technology and involves knowledge principles. A marketing lifecycle is concerned with product planning and other efforts to determine market potential for a product or service and generally involves knowledge perspectives. Generally, this lifecycle is needed to identify emerging technologies chosen to enter an RDT&E lifecycle. It is also needed, particularly in private sector commercial activities, to shape and focus specific configurations for products that are produced or acquired. As we have indicated in many of our discussions, there needs to be feedback and iteration across these three lifecycles and within the phases and steps of a given lifecycle.

Figure 1.18 presents a three-gateway model that has been used to describe the necessary conceptual relation among these three lifecycles [15–17]. Although the systems planning and market planning gateway is shown after, in the sense of being

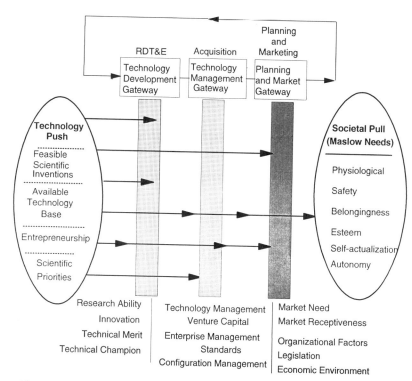

Figure 1.18 A three-gateway model for systems engineering productivity.

to the right, of the other two gateways, much of systems planning and marketing should proceed both RDT&E and acquisition if these latter developments are to be effective, efficient, and to supply useful products and services. Associated with this figure are some incentives associated with technology push and some that are associated with market or societal pull. These latter are based primarily on the Maslow hierarchy of needs [18], after a psychologist who devoted much attention to their study.

Evaluation of systems engineering efforts are very important. Evaluation criteria are obtained as a part of requirements specifications and modified during the subsequent phases of a systems engineering effort. The evaluation effort must be adapted to other phases of the effort such that it becomes an integral and functional part of the overall systems engineering process and product. Generally, the critical issues for evaluation are adaptations of the elements present in the requirements specifications phase of the design process. A set of specific evaluation test requirements and tests are evolved from the objectives and needs determined in requirements specifications. These should be such that each objective measure and critical evaluation issue component can be measured by at least one evaluation test instrument. Evaluation is discussed in some detail in [19] and, to a lesser extent, in [1] and [20].

If it is determined, perhaps through an operational evaluation, that the resulting systems process or product cannot meet user needs, the systems engineering lifecycle process reverts iteratively to an earlier phase, and the effort continues. An important by-product of system evaluation is determination of ultimate performance limitations for an operationally realizable system. Often, operational evaluation is the only realistic way to establish meaningful information concerning functional effectiveness of the result of a systems engineering effort. Successful evaluation is dependent on having predetermined explicit evaluation standards.

The last phase of the systems lifecycle effort includes final acceptance and operational deployment and associated maintenance. Maintenance and retrofit can be defined either as additional phases in lifecycles or as part of the operational deployment phase. Either is an acceptable way to define the system lifecycle and there are many possible systems engineering lifecycles, some of which we will discuss in subsequent chapters.

1.5 INFORMATION TECHNOLOGY AND SOFTWARE ENGINEERING MANAGEMENT, PROCESSES AND PRODUCTS: THE REST OF THE BOOK

This systems management text discusses important concerns for the trustworthy development of process-related approaches for the development of trustworthy systems, especially but not exclusively from the perspective of information technology, information systems engineering, and software systems engineering. The special and dominant focus of the book is the systems management of processes for information technology and software development organizations. This involves a number of very relevant issues associated with systems architectures and integration, quality assurance and management, process reengineering and process maturity, metrics, software economics, and cost and operational effectiveness analysis for the management of large information and software systems.

Software systems engineering [21] is the application of systems engineering design methodologies and process management approaches for the production of trustworthy, high quality software. Here, we introduce systems management approaches for total quality assurance through process-related improvements of information technology and software engineering processes and products.

As we have already noted, there are many ingredients associated with the development of trustworthy systems. From a top–down perspective, the following ingredients are surely present:

1. Systems engineering processes, including process development lifecycles for system acquisition, RDT&E, and systems planning and marketing.
2. Process risk, product development risk, and associated risk management.
3. Systematic measurements.
4. Metrics for cost estimation, and product cost and operational effectiveness evaluation.
5. Strategic quality assurance and management, or total quality management.
6. Organizational cultures, leadership and organizational process maturity, and related systems management issues.
7. Systems reengineering, including reengineering at the level of systems management, processes, and product; methods to implement reengineering, and the resulting needs in enterprise management and integration.

These will comprise the seven remaining chapters in this book and will follow this introductory chapter, which is intended to summarize the structure, function, and purpose of the material to follow.

Other ingredients could easily be identified. For the most part, however, the subject matters listed can be considered as *top level* supports for the objective of obtaining trustworthy and productive systems engineering products that are of high quality. Although we will be concerned with general systems that support a variety of applications, our primary focus will be on those systems that are information technology and software intensive. While most of our discussions will specifically focus on software, the ultimate applications for the constructs to be described are much broader than the very important area of software development in that so very many contemporary systems are very software intensive.

These seven ingredients interact with one another. One of the first efforts in systems management is to identify an appropriate process lifecycle for production of a trustworthy system. As we have already discussed and as indicated in [1] and [20] and in many other sources, this lifecycle involves a sequence of phases. These phases include identification of client requirements, translation of these requirements into (hardware and) software requirements specifications, development of system architectures, detailed design through coding, operational implementation and evaluation, and maintenance of the delivered product. The precise lifecycle that is followed will depend on the client needs. It will also depend on such environmental factors as the presence of existing system components, or subsystems, into which a new system must be integrated, and the presence of existing software modules that may be retrofitted and reused [22] as a part of the new system. This need for system integration [23,24] brings about a host of systems management and, in many cases, legal issues that are much larger in scale and scope than those associated with program development only. In a similar manner, the development of appropriate system level architectures is very important in that efficiency and effectiveness in systems architecting [12–14] influence the ease with which systems can be integrated and maintained and therefore the extent to which an operational system is viewed as trustworthy and of high quality.

Following the identification of an appropriate systemic process development lifecycle, configuration management plans [25] are identified. This involves using the lifecycle and defining a specific development process for the set of lifecycle tasks at hand. Metrics are needed to enable this to be done effectively. These metrics are the metrics of cost analysis or cost estimation [26–28] for systems engineering. They include cost and economic estimation for software [29–32] and information technology based systems [33]. They also include effectiveness analysis or estimation of software productivity indices using various metrics [34–37]. This couples the notion of development of an information technology or software (or other) product into notions concerning the process needs associated with developing this product. It is becoming widely recognized that these metrics must form a part of a process management approach for process, and ultimately product, improvement if substantial progress is to be made [38,39] in such important areas as software testing and evaluation [40]. A study of these process-related subjects without some attempt to place them into the context of application product development or in terms of the lifecycle and configuration management, is less than fully meaningful for specific purposes. Primarily for this reason, we choose to focus on information technology and software system developments here.

Thus our efforts are comprised of eight principal parts, denoted as chapters in the text itself. This introductory chapter begins our efforts. Chapter 2 concerns information technology and software process development lifecycles. It is assumed that readers have prior exposure both to systems engineering and software engineering, such as through some familiarity with [1] or [2], or any of the other excellent works now available in this area in software engineering [41–43], systems engineering [44], or such related areas as software acquisition management [45] and information engineering [46]. Contemporary notions of concurrent engineering and concurrent design of systems [47,48] are of interest here, although we do not emphasize these subjects.

In Chapter 3, we are especially concerned with the subject of risk management. There are a variety of influences on software development risk [49–51] and we will discuss many of these here. Figure 1.19 illustrates some of the many risk management issues and facets that we deal with in Chapter 3. These include risks associated with four facets: technical performance, schedule, cost supportability, and programmatic foundation. We deal with risk management across the many systems engineer-

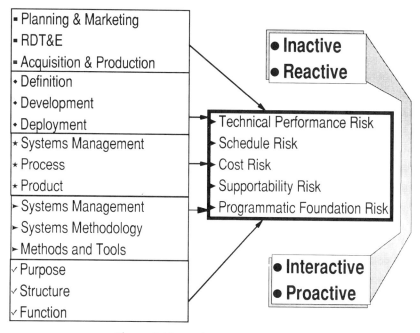

Figure 1.19 Risk management fields.

ing framework elements identified in the figure. Figure 1.20 illustrates a structure for these risk management facets. Of necessity, most of our discussion will be at the operational level involving internal environments [52]. We return to strategic issues associated with risk management in a later chapter.

We discuss quality evaluation metrics and systematic measurement [53–59] in Chapter 4. The purpose of this is primarily process management for information technology and software quality assurance. Since we are often discussing software development that is yet to be undertaken, there are risks and uncertainties associated with this development. There are quality assurance issues associated with information systems and information technology productivity efforts also [60,61].

In Chapter 5, we discuss metrics and systematic measurement for cost assessment, with particular emphasis on metrics at the level of systems management and process. We are particularly concerned with cost estimation and cost and operational effectiveness evaluation. We discuss the variety of methods that have been proposed for estimating software development costs. Most of the models developed to date base software development on estimating the number of lines of program code that will need to be written and the cost per average line of code. Both the number of lines and the cost per line vary significantly with a number of influencing factors. These factors, which act as multipliers in the usual cost algorithms, depend on such variables as the type of software to be developed and the experience of the software development team with the tasks at hand. We will discuss both the constructive cost

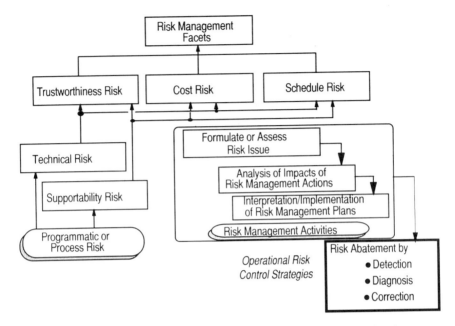

Figure 1.20   Risk management facets at process and product levels.

model (COCOMO) based approach and the function point approach to software cost estimation, as well as extensions of these approaches.

There are other approaches that depend on separate cost estimates for the various phases of the software development lifecycle. These potentially allow independent estimation of the costs of each phase of the lifecycle. In this way, the cost effects of use of reusable software, rapid prototyping, code generators, or computer-aided software engineering (CASE) tools [62,63] can be considered. We also discuss activity based costing (ABC) approaches that lead to activity based systems management.

It then becomes possible to estimate those variables that impact the productivity of the maintenance phase of the lifecycle. This is especially important as many studies suggest that 50% to 80% of an organization's software costs will be for software maintenance, a much larger percentage than expended initially for code development. In principle, it then becomes possible to determine the optimum amount of resources to allocate to client requirements identification [64–67], in terms of reduced marginal economies for additional information obtained. Such approaches allow us to trade off controllable variables in software development to obtain maximum software quality for a given expenditure of resources. Alternately, they enable determination of appropriate management plans, staffing requirements, and cost estimates to produce a software system that meets specified requirements.

Much of the discussion relates to both information technology and software engineering processes and the system management needs to support an effective process. Systems management is also concerned with efforts that relate to organizations and organizational cultures and the engineering and reengineering of organizations for greater productivity. The last four chapters of the book specifically address this aspect of systems management.

In Chapter 6, we get to the nexus of many difficulties relative to innovation and productivity in general, and innovation and productivity relative to information technology and software products and processes. These concern both the development of information technology and software products and services and the use of these. Our efforts are focused both on developer organizations and user organizations.

In almost all of the contemporary discussions of quality, a clear distinction is made between strategic level quality assurance and management, or TQM, and operational level measures of quality. Much of our commentary has related to the former topic, although the latter is clearly needed in order to provide necessary instrumental measures of the former. We will devote significant time to a study of these issues, and how they are strongly influenced by organizational cultures. We will develop these and other related TQM notions [68–70] rather fully in Chapter 6, especially for information technology and software systems development, and with particular focus on the efforts of systems integration organizations.

System or product quality is a major concern today on all fronts, especially as supported by and including software and information technology. Most of the approaches advocated in the past have been at the levels of operational and task management for product improvement. While necessary, these approaches will often not be sufficient. Also required will be efforts at the level of strategic systems management. Systems engineering and information technology based approaches can be used to address issues of quality at the strategic level [71]. This will generally result in a set of strategic quality assurance and management plans and these, in turn, will enhance process quality at the level of systems management or management control. We argue that systems engineering provides a natural companion to strategic quality assurance and management, or total quality management. The concluding portion of Chapter 6 provides a discussion of emerging national and international standards that relate to total quality.

There has been much recent interest in process approaches to strategic quality assurance and management. In addition to the significant interest in manufacturing process improvements in quality and productivity, there has been associated interest in comparable improvements in such intellectual and service industry outputs as software and information technology [72–76]. We turn to a discussion of these issues in Chapter 7.

In Chapter 7, we first provide a very brief summary of efforts associated with organizational structure and leadership. Then we discuss organizational leadership and culture issues associated with quality as well as in a more generic context. Organizational learning and the potential capability for enhanced organizational learning are of major importance here and are discussed also. Each of these topics has direct relevance to organizational maturity issues and the relationship between organizational maturity and process maturity.

It would be of extraordinary interest and value to identify an analogous process maturity assessment instrument that incorporates the organizational culture and leadership issues discussed in the first part of Chapter 7. The concluding part of Chapter 7 discusses this important issue. Of particular importance will be the integration of process maturity models with organizational culture models and the development of approaches for concurrent reengineering of these two facets of system development efficacy.

There are a number of methods that sustain these efforts. The use of benchmarking [77], or breakpoints [78], and the wise use of core competencies potentially enables the organization of an intelligent enterprise and exploitation of radical business change opportunities. This is supported by the creation of an appropriate organizational culture [79], and improvements in process maturity. The overall goal of Chapter 8, which is concerned with what we call systems reengineering, is to study these approaches. In this chapter, we discuss systems reengineering at three levels—organizational systems management, process, and product—that enable the information technology organization to succeed in coping with competition and change.

An important objective in systems management of information technology and software engineering is to improve the efficiency and effectiveness of information management and use. There are at least five strategies that assist in accomplishing this:

1. We should assist in planning for and managing development of an efficient, effective, and integrated systems engineering infrastructure to support information technology and software engineering.

2. We should assist organizational managers, generally at a functional level, to identify ways of doing business through the provision of standard methods and tools for developing improved business practices. Generally, these should be associated with interactive and proactive metrics that represent quantifiable measures of performance, which serve as information supporting enhanced effectiveness and efficiency.

3. We should promote efficiency, effectiveness, and standardization [80] in information technology and software engineering, development, and maintenance. Generally, this will be associated with such macroenhancement approaches as CASE tools, prototyping, and software reuse.

4. We should assist in the systems integration of information technology and software systems within and across each functional area of the user organization.

5. We should promote open systems standards, open systems interconnections (OSI), and open systems architectures [81,82] to allow the use of vendor detached products, in order to facilitate use of commercial off-the-shelf (COTS) software whenever possible, and to facilitate open competition for information technology products and services.

Taken together, they enable enterprise integration and enterprise computing [83] through information technology. This is the sort of effort envisioned in Savage's

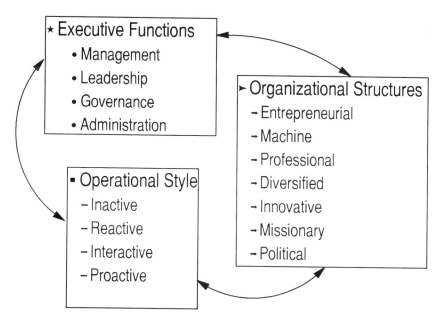

Figure 1.21 Facets of organizations and organizational cultures.

work on *5th Generation Management* [84], in which information technology based approaches to integrate enterprises through human networking are developed, Crosby's effort on *completedness principles* [85], and Peters' recent work *Liberation Management* [86]. To accomplish this well requires systems management professionals with broad scope expertise in knowledge practices, knowledge principles, and knowledge perspectives.

These are strongly related to group and organizational issues. These primarily concern very important and often neglected issues that relate to organizational culture and leadership [87]. These are strongly influenced by a number of facets of organizations and organization cultures, such as illustrated in Figure 1.21. They relate to such important behavioral issues as how leaders create, imbed, and transmit organizational culture and thereby bring about an intelligent enterprise [88] that will enable successful coping with the challenge of organizational change [89] for productivity enhancement. This relates strongly to organizational architectures [90] that result from reengineering the organization [91]. The resulting corporate culture and performance [92] enable the reengineering of work through information technology [93] to result in process innovation and profiting from innovation [94].

Chapters 6, 7, and 8 are very closely related. Chapter 7 is concerned with this subject of organizational culture and leadership for process-related improvements through systems management. It also relates well to managing complexity in high technology organizations [95] through the strategic use of information technology [96]. This is the major subject of Chapter 8. Each of these relate very closely to the total quality management discussions in Chapter 6.

Much of this discussion necessarily relates to group performance in organizations, including information technology and software development organizations. In a group situation, we necessarily must also consider how alliances of people are formed and broken. In an important work that extends their classic works on this subject, March and Olsen [97] indicate that there are two generic types of model of organizational behavior. One of these is the *rational competition model* so familiar to those involved in quantitative systems analysis. The decision-making process can be considered to involve activities of situation assessment and action implementation. This is, of course, the nexus of the rational competition model studied so much in systems engineering and related decision assessment areas.

Coordination styles and the cultural influences that determine organizational behavior in given settings are particularly important in this connection. Henry Mintzberg has become very well known for his studies of management and managerial tasks and several recent works are devoted, in large part, to designing effective organizations. He has indicated [98] that there are six basic coordination mechanisms that describe work coordination approaches in organizations and we will examine these in Chapter 6 as coordination media may be found in any given organization, and some are preferred to others in any given organization.

According to Mintzberg, there are four basically different systems of influence in an organization. *Authority* results from some legally approved power. *Expertise* is a result of officially certified wisdom and power. *Ideology* results from accepted values and beliefs. A *political system of organizational influence* is neither formally authorized nor officially certified. It results from a power base that is not legitimate because the means that are used are not sanctioned, even if the ends promoted are worthwhile. This refers to organizational political power as contrasted with governmental political power, which is both authorized and legitimate.

In the Mintzberg work, seven different forms or structures of organizing follow from this, and we will examine these. They are described in terms of structure, context, preferred strategy, and characteristics of the particular organizing form. A particularly interesting challenge is to determine the ensconced powers needed to enable or inhibit transitions from one of the seven characteristic organizational configuration modes to the other, and which enable an organization to enter into and remain in a healthy state of maturity, or to recover to this state from a state of decline (see Figure 1.22). Mintzberg, in his alluring treatment of organizations, provides some of these. While it would be foolish to suggest that better organizational structure and coordination models and implementations could negate these difficulties, it is also very clear that efforts in this direction are needed to avoid them. Propositions and guidelines to this end are provided in Chapter 7, especially for information technology and software development organizations. Here, we will consider organizational dynamics and evolution over time, and the ways in which organizational culture and leadership influences this evolution.

In another useful work dealing with organizational cultures, Raelin [99] identifies three distinct cultures associated with conflict issues between professionals and managers. Suggestions are given to ameliorate the organizational decay and demise effects of these potential conflict situations, generally through more attention to the

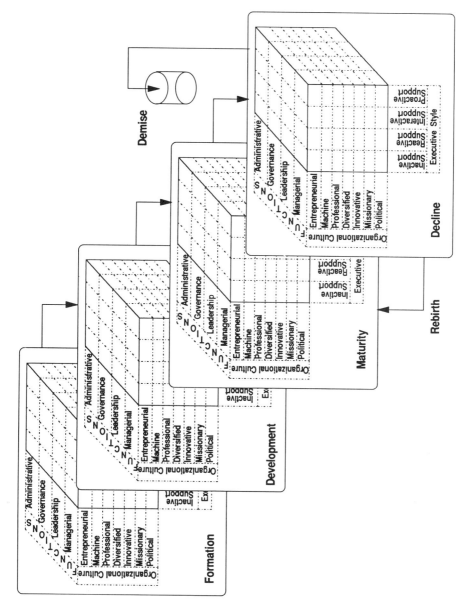

Figure 1.22 Dynamics of organizational growth, maturity, decline, and rebirth.

social culture in the organization. Other major suggestions concern efforts to encourage compatibility between professional and organizational goals. It is generally
suggested that the managers of professionals should themselves be professionals.
This enables much better management understanding of issues at hand and supports
trust in their managers on the part of professionals in the organization. We will be
very concerned with issues such as these in the latter part of our efforts.

In many such situations, there will exist potential conflict between the vision,
which may well not be a shared vision, of organizational leadership and organizational culture. In an insightful work, Wilkins [100] indicates the reality that it is the
organizational character or culture which is the essence of an organization's competitive advantage. Any attempt to impart a new vision on the organization may, unless
very positively orchestrated, result in the organization losing the very substance of
its success.

These notions of organizational culture and evolution over time are not unrelated
to quality issues. In the *Quality Is Free* effort, for example, Crosby [101] identifies
five stages of development of quality maturity. These relate strongly to the subject
of strategic, or total, quality management. We turn to this in Chapter 7 after our
TQM discussions in Chapter 6. Crosby indicates that motivation for quality improvement starts with a study of the "cost of quality." Juran [102] indicates that the
cost of poor quality, defined as the sum of all costs that would disappear if there
were no quality problems, may be a more relevant measure for many purposes.
Feigenbaum [103] incorporates both the *cost of quality* and the *cost of poor quality.*
The central point in this is that quality concerns need to be a part of the overall
systems development effort and associated cost and operational effectiveness evaluation used to support development decisions. Thus our efforts in Chapter 7 relate
closely to the systematic measurement developments in Chapters 4 and 5, as well as
other portions of the text.

There have been several models, in addition to the one by Crosby, that illustrate
related process maturity characterization efforts. In one very popular model that has
been developed for software productivity management efforts, Humphrey [104]
identified five levels of process maturity. There have been a number of extensions of
this initial effort. We will devote some time to study of this process maturity model
and extensions of it for more generic systems engineering process maturity models
in Chapter 7.

Chapter 8 is much concerned with systems reengineering and organizational
improvement through enterprise computing, management, and systems integration.
These will be heavily based on open system integration and architecture concepts
and standardization efforts discussed in Chapter 6. These relate very closely to risk
management (Chapter 3) and systematic measurements (Chapters 4 and 5). Thus
each of the chapters in this work fit together under the general heading of *systems
management.*

A goal in this will be to support developing new knowledge and skills through
information technology [105] and to provide systems engineering and information
technology catalysts for total quality [71]. These will support cognitive systems
engineering [106], generally distributed decision making and cooperative work

[107], integration of organizational processes, strategies for innovation [108], integrating information technology and the organization [109,110], strategic systems planning and development [111,112], and the catalysts for change [113] that enable the creation of successful products, systems, processes, and organizations.

1.6 SUMMARY

This then is the detailed outline for *Systems Management for Information Technology and Software Engineering*. Hopefully you have found this detailed introduction to be rewarding, and that the journey itself will be one of much value and interest. Our discussions to follow will be aimed at a process that we believe will enable effective practice of systems management, especially as it relates to information technology and software engineering organizations. The top level objectives might be stated as the (1) reduction of lead time, (2) reduction of cost, and (3) improvement of quality in the technical direction and management of definition, development, and deployment of modern information technology and software engineering products through the use of systems engineering. This suggests a set of 12 interactive and proactive activities for a process to support implementation of systems management strategies:

1. Identify the present technical direction and management system, including the extent to which the current systems management process is customer driven and supplier driven.

2. Assess the structural and cultural facets of the organization, including its quality culture.

3. Identify and secure a top management commitment to systems management and systems engineering.

4. Create a strategic organizational vision and philosophy that is supportive of systems management.

5. Identify appropriate systems management strategies for the organization under consideration.

6. Identify a management control structure to implement the systems management strategy.

7. Identify education and training needs to accomplish the implementation of systems management and select suppliers of this education and training program.

8. Identify resource needs for implementation of the systems management strategies.

9. Identify quality standards and metrics, in order to ensure continuous quality improvement, and efficiency and effectiveness of the resulting process driven adaptation of systems management.

10. Institutionalize the systems management and systems engineering process

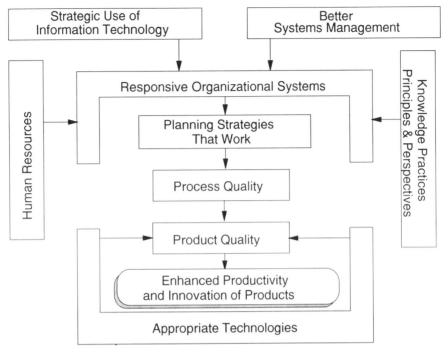

Figure 1.23 Systems management and information technology for process and product quality.

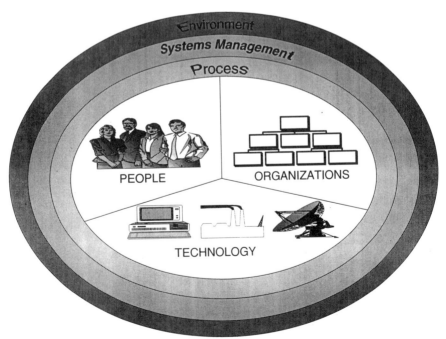

Figure 1.24 Systems engineering as people, organizations, and technology—with a systems management enabled process for environmental compatibility.

such that they become a part of the organization's culture and normal mode of doing business.

11. Monitor and evaluate the results of the systems management implementation.

12. Continue the improvement through the development of more effective and efficient approaches for high quality systems management and systems engineering.

These 12 activities will counteract the 12 deadly sins of systems engineering, which we identified earlier. This is accomplished by proactively adapting the specific systems management process to the organization in question on the basis of actual operating experience with systems engineering. Figure 1.23 illustrates this evolution of product from process, and process from systems management. Together with Figure 1.24, which illustrates the ingredients to be dealt with in a systems engineering study, these provide a fitting summary to these discussions. To set forth some guidelines for this is a principal objective of this book.

REFERENCES

[1] Sage, A. P., *Systems Engineering*, John Wiley & Sons, New York, 1992.

[2] Sage, A. P., "Knowledge Transfer: An Innovative Role for Information Engineering Education," *IEEE Transactions on Systems, Man and Cybernetics*, Vol. 17, No. 5, Sept. 1987, pp. 725–728.

[3] Sage, A. P., *Methodology for Large Scale Systems*, McGraw-Hill Book Co., New York, 1977.

[4] Armstrong, J. E., and Sage, A. P., *An Introduction to Systems Engineering*, John Wiley & Sons, New York, 1995.

[5] Sage, A. P. (Ed.), *System Design for Human Interaction*, IEEE Press, New York, 1987.

[6] MIL-STD-499A and MIL-STD 499B, "Engineering Management Standards," May 1974 and May 1991.

[7] IEEE "Standard for Systems Engineering P1220," Draft Rev. 1.0, IEEE Standards Department, Piscataway NJ, 1993.

[8] Sage, A. P., "Methodological Considerations in the Design of Large Scale Systems Engineering Processes," in Haimes, Y. Y. (Ed.), *Large Scale Systems*, North-Holland, New York, 1982, pp. 99–141.

[9] Chen, K., Ghausi, M., and Sage, A. P., "Social Systems Engineering: An Introduction," *Proceedings of the IEEE*, Vol. 63, Mar. 1975, pp. 340–343.

[10] Hall, A. D., *A Methodology for Systems Engineering*, Van Nostrand, New York, 1962.

[11] Hall, A. D., "A Three Dimensional Morphology of Systems Engineering," *IEEE Transactions on System Science and Cybernetics*, Vol. 5, No. 2, Apr. 1969, pp. 156–160.

[12] Chorfas, D. N., *Systems Architecture and Systems Design*, McGraw-Hill Book Co., New York, 1989.

[13] Beam, W. R., *Systems Engineering: Architecture and Design,* McGraw-Hill Book Co., New York, 1990.

[14] Rechtin, E., *Systems Architecting: Creating and Buidling Complex Systems,* Prentice-Hall, Englewood Cliffs, NJ, 1991.

[15] Sage, A. P., "Systems Management of Emerging Technologies," *Information and Decision Technologies,* Vol. 15, No. 4, 1989, pp. 307–326.

[16] Sage, A. P., "Systems Management for Information Technology Development," in *Expanding Access to Science and Technology; The Role of Information Technologies,* Wesley-Tanaskovic, I., Tocatlian, J., and Roberts, K. H. (Eds.), United Nations University Press, Tokyo, Japan, 1994, pp. 361–405.

[17] Benson, B., and Sage, A. P., "Case Studies of Systems Management for Emerging Technology Development," in W. B. Rouse (Ed.), *Advances in Human Machine Systems Research,* JAI Press, New York, 1994.

[18] Maslow, A. H., *Motivation and Personality,* Harper & Row, New York, 1970.

[19] Adelman, L., *Evaluating Decision Support and Expert System Technology,* John Wiley & Sons, New York, 1992.

[20] Sage, A. P., *Decision Support Systems Engineering,* John Wiley & Sons, New York, 1991.

[21] Sage, A. P., and Palmer, J. D., *Software Systems Engineering,* John Wiley & Sons, New York, 1990.

[22] Biggerstaff, T. J., and Perlis, A. J. (Eds.), *Software Reusability: Volume 1—Concepts and Models, Volume II—Applications and Experience,* Addison-Wesley, Reading, MA, 1989.

[23] Beutel, R. A., *Contracting for Computer System Integration,* Michie Co., Charlottesville, VA, 1991.

[24] Ng, P. A., Ramamoorthy, C. V., Seifert, L. C., and Yeh, R. T. (Eds.), *Systems Integration '92: Proceedings of the Second Intentional Conference on Systems Integration,* IEEE Computer Society Press, Los Alamitos, CA, 1992.

[25] Berlack, H. Ronald, *Software Configuration Management,* John Wiley & Sons, Chichester, UK, 1992.

[26] Sage, A. P., *Economic Systems Analysis: Microeconomics for Systems Engineering, Engineering, Engineering Management, and Project Selection,* North-Holland, New York 1983.

[27] Michaels, J. V., and Wood, W. P., *Design to Cost,* John Wiley & Sons, New York, 1989.

[28] Fabrycky, W. J., and Blanchard, B. S., *Lifecycle Cost and Economic Analysis,* Prentice-Hall, Englewood Cliffs, NJ, 1991.

[29] Boehms, B. W., *Software Engineering Economics,* Prentice-Hall, Englewood Cliffs, NJ, 1981.

[30] Dreger, J. B., *Function Point Analysis,* Prentice-Hall, Englewood Cliffs, NJ, 1989.

[31] Jones, C., *Applied Software Measurement: Assuring Productivity and Quality,* McGraw-Hill Book Co., New York, 1991.

[32] Putnam, L. H., and Myers, W., *Measures for Excellence: Reliable Software On Time, Within Budget,* Prentice-Hall, Englewood Cliffs, NJ, 1992.

[33] Parker, M. M., and Benson, R. J., *Information Economics: Linking Business Performance to Information Technology,* Prentice-Hall, Englewood Cliffs, NJ, 1988.

[34] Conte, S. D., Dunsmore, H. E., and Shen, V. Y., *Software Engineering Metrics and Models,* Benjamin-Cummings Publishing Co., Menlo Park, CA, 1986.

[35] Fenton, N. E., *Software Metrics: A Rigorous Approach,* Chapman and Hall, London, 1991.

[36] Ejiogu, L. O., *Software Engineering with Formal Metrics,* QED Information Sciences, Boston, MA, 1991.

[37] Card, D. N., and Glass, R. L., *Measuring Software Design Quality,* Prentice-Hall, Englewood Cliffs, NJ, 1990.

[38] Grady, R. B., and Caswell, D. L., *Software Metrics: Establishing a Company Wide Program,* Prentice-Hall, Englewood Cliffs, NJ, 1987.

[39] Grady, R. B., *Practical Software Metrics for Process Management and Process Improvement,* Prentice-Hall, Englewood Cliffs, NJ, 1992.

[40] DeMilo, R. A., McCracken, W. M., Martin, R. J., and Passifiume, J. F., *Software Testing and Evaluation,* Benjamin-Cummings Publishing Co., Menlo Park, CA, 1987.

[41] Blum, B. I., *Software Engineering: A Holistic View,* Oxford University Press, New York, 1992.

[42] Pfleeger, S. L., *Software Engineering: The Production of Quality Software,* Macmillan, New York, 1991.

[43] Pressman, R. S., *Software Engineering: A Practitioner's Approach,* McGraw-Hill, New York, 1992.

[44] Thome, B., *Systems Engineering: Principles and Practice of Computer-Based Systems Engineering,* John Wiley & Sons, Chichester, UK, 1993.

[45] Marciniak, J. J., and Reifer, D. J., *Software Acquisition Management: Managing the Acquisition of Custom Software Systems,* John Wiley & Sons, Chichester, UK, 1990.

[46] Martin, J., *Information Engineering: Book I—Introduction, Book II—Planning and Analysis, Book III—Design and Construction,* Prentice-Hall, Englewood Cliffs, NJ, 1989, 1990.

[47] Nevins, J. L., and Whitney, D. E. (Eds.), *Concurrent Design of Products and Processes: A Strategy for the Next Generation in Manufacturing,* McGraw-Hill, New York, 1989.

[48] Carter, D. E., and Baker, B. S., *Concurrent Engineering: The Product Development Environment for the 1990s,* Addison-Wesley, Reading, MA, 1992.

[49] Charette, R. N., *Software Engineering Risk Analysis and Management,* McGraw-Hill, New York, 1989.

[50] Boehm, B. W. (Ed.), *Software Risk Management,* IEEE Computer Society Press, Los Alamitos, CA, 1989.

[51] Bryan, W. L., and Siegel, S. G., *Software Product Assurance: Techniques for Reducing Software Risk,* Elsevier Science Publishing, New York, 1988.

[52] Charette, R. N., *Software Engineering Environments: Concepts and Technology,* McGraw-Hill, New York, 1986.

[53] Vincent, J., Walters, A., and Sinclair, J., *Software Quality Assurance: Volume I—Practice and Implementation, Volume II—A Program Guide,* Prentice-Hall, Englewood Cliffs, NJ, 1988.

[54] Evans, M. W., and Marciniak, J. J., *Software Quality Assurance and Management,* John Wiley & Sons, New York, 1987.

[55] Glass, R. L., *Building Quality Software,* Prentice-Hall, Englewood Cliffs, NJ, 1992.

[56] Dunn, R. H., *Software Quality: Concepts and Plans,* Prentice-Hall, Englewood Cliffs, NJ, 1990.

[57] Hollocker, C. P., *Software Reviews and Audits Handbook,* John Wiley & Sons, Chichester, UK, 1990.

[58] Ould, M. A., *Strategies for Software Engineering: The Management of Risk and Quality,* John Wiley & Sons, Chichester, UK, 1990.

[59] Deutsch, M. S., and Willis, R. R., *Software Quality Engineering: A Total Technical and Management Approach,* Prentice-Hall, Englewood Cliffs, NJ, 1988.

[60] Perry, W. E., *Quality Assurance for Information Systems: Methods, Tools and Techniques,* QED Information Sciences, Boston, MA, 1991.

[61] Umbaugh, R. E. (Ed.), *Productivity Improvement in Information Systems,* Auerbach, Boston, MA, 1993.

[62] Gane, C., *Computer Aided Software Engineering: The Methodologies, the Products, and the Future,* Prentice-Hall, Englewood Cliffs, NJ, 1990.

[63] Lewis, T. G., *CASE: Computer Aided Software Engineering,* Van Nostrand, New York, 1991.

[64] Davis, A. M., *Software Requirements: Objects, Functions and States,* Prentice-Hall, Englewood Cliffs, NJ, 1993.

[65] Kowal, J. A., *Behavior Models: Specifying User's Expectations,* Prentice-Hall, Englewood Cliffs, NJ, 1992.

[66] Dorfman, M., and Thayer, R. H., *Standards, Guidelines and Examples on System and Software Requirements Engineering,* IEEE Computer Society Press, Los Alamitos, CA, 1990.

[67] Thayer, R. H., and Dorfman, M., *System and Software Requirements Engineering,* IEEE Computer Society Press, Los Alamitos, CA, 1990.

[68] Hunt, V. D., *Quality in America: How to Implement a Competitive Quality Program,* Irwin, Homewood, IL, 1992.

[69] Hunt, V. D., *Managing for Quality,* Richard D. Irwin, Homewood, IL, 1993.

[70] Dobyns, L., and Crawford-Mason, C., *Quality or Else: The Revolution in World Business,* Houghton Mifflin, New York, 1991.

[71] Sage, A. P., "Systems Engineering and Information Technology: Catalysts for Total Quality in Industry and Education," *IEEE Transactions on Systems, Man, and Cybernetics,* Vol. 22, No. 5, Sept. 1992, pp. 833–864.

[72] Arthur, L. J., *Improving Software Quality: An Insider's Guide to TQM,* John Wiley & Sons, Chichester, UK, 1993.

[73] Schulmeyer, G. G., and McManus, J. I. (Eds.), *Total Quality Management for Software,* Van Nostrand Reinhold, New York, 1992.

[74] Harrington, H. J., *Business Process Improvement: The Breakthrough Strategy for Total Quality, Productivity, and Competitiveness,* McGraw-Hill, New York, 1991.

[75] Scott Morton, M. S. (Ed.), *The Corporation of the 1990s: Information Technology and Organizational Transformation,* Oxford University Press, New York, 1991.

[76] Keen, P. G. W., *Shaping the Future: Business Design Through Information Technology,* Harvard Business School Press, Boston, MA, 1991.

[77] Liebfried, K. H. J., and McNair, C. J., *Benchmarking: A Tool for Continuous Improvement,* Harper Business, New York, 1992.

[78] Streibel, P., *Breakpoints: How Managers Exploit Radical Business Change*, Harvard Business School Press, Boston, MA, 1992.

[79] Hampden-Turner, C., *Creating Corporate Culture: From Discord to Harmony*, Addison-Wesley, Reading, MA, 1990.

[80] Cargill, C. F., *Information Technology Standardization: Theory, Processes and Organizations*, Digital Press, Bedford, MA, 1989.

[81] Judge, P., *Open Systems: The Guide to OSI and Its Implementation*, QED Information Sciences, Wellesley, MA, 1988.

[82] Wheeler, T., *Open Systems Handbook*, Bantam Books, New York, 1992.

[83] Simon, A. R., *Enterprise Computing*, Bantam Books, New York, 1992.

[84] Savage, C. M., *5th Generation Management: Integrating Enterprises through Human Networking*, Digital Press, Burlington, MA, 1990.

[85] Crosby, P. B., *Completedness: Quality for the 21st Century*, Dutton-Penguin Books, New York, 1992.

[86] Peters, T., *Liberation Management*, Knopf, New York, 1992.

[87] Schein, E. H., *Organizational Culture and Leadership*, Jossey-Bass, San Francisco, CA, 1992.

[88] Quinn, J. B., *Intelligent Enterprise: A Knowledge and Service Based Paradigm for Industry*, Free Press, New York, 1992.

[89] Kanter, R. M., Stein, B. A., and Jick, T. D., *The Challenge of Organizational Change: How Companies Experience It and Leaders Guide It*, Free Press, New York, 1992.

[90] Nadler, D. A., Gerstein, M. S., and Shaw, R. B. (Eds.), *Organizational Architecture: Designs for Changing Organizations*, Jossey-Bass, San Francisco, CA, 1992.

[91] Hammer, M., and Champy, J., *Reengineering the Corporation: A Manifesto for Business Revolution*, HarperCollins, New York, 1993.

[92] Kotter, J. P., and Heskett, J. L., *Corporate Culture and Performance*, Free Press, New York, 1992.

[93] Davenport, T. H., *Process Innovation: Reengineering Work Through Information Technology*, Harvard Business School Press, Boston, MA, 1993.

[94] Howard, W. G. Jr., and Guile, B. R., *Profiting from Innovation*, Free Press, New York, 1992.

[95] Glinow, M. A., and Mohrman, S. A. (Eds.), *Managing Complexity in High Technology Organizations*, Oxford University Press, New York, 1990.

[96] Madnick, S. E. (Ed.), *The Strategic Use of Information Technology*, Oxford University Press, New York, 1987.

[97] March, J. G., and Olsen, J. P., *Rediscovering Institutions: Organizational Basis of Politics*, Free Press, New York, 1989.

[98] Mintzberg, H., *Mintzberg on Management: Inside Our Strange World of Organizations*, Free Press, New York, 1989.

[99] Raelin, J. A., *The Clash of Cultures: Managers Managing Professionals*, Harvard Business School Press, Boston, MA, 1991.

[100] Wilkins, A. L., *Developing Corporate Character: How to Successfully Change an Organization Without Destroying It*, Jossey-Bass, San Francisco, CA, 1989.

[101] Crosby, P. B., *Quality Is Free: The Art of Making Quality Certain*, McGraw-Hill, New York, 1979.

[102] Juran, J. M., *Juran on Leadership for Quality: An Executive Handbook*, Free Press, New York, 1989.

[103] Feigenbaum, A. V., *Total Quality Control*, McGraw-Hill, New York, 1991.

[104] Humphrey, W. S., *Managing the Software Process*, Addison-Wesley, Reading, MA, 1989.

[105] Bainbridge, L., and Quintanilla, S. A. R. (Eds.), *Developing Skills with Information Technology*, John Wiley & Sons, Chichester, UK, 1989.

[106] Rasmussen, J., Pejtersen, A. M., and Goodstein, L. P., *Cognitive Systems Engineering*, John Wiley & Sons, New York, 1994.

[107] Rasmussen, J., Brehmer, B., and Leplat, J. (Eds.), *Distributed Decision Making: Cognitive Models for Cooperative Work*, John Wiley & Sons, Chichester, UK, 1991.

[108] Rouse, W. B., *Strategies for Innovation: Creating Successful Products, Systems, and Organizations*, John Wiley & Sons, New York, 1992.

[109] Walton, R. E., *Up and Running: Integrating Information Technology and the Organization*, Harvard Business School Press, Boston, MA, 1989.

[110] *Information Technology in the Service Society: A Twenty-first Century Lever*, National Academy Press, Washington, DC, 1994.

[111] Boar, B. H., *The Art of Strategic Planning for Information Technology*, John Wiley & Sons, New York, 1993.

[112] Finkelstein, C., *Information Engineering: Strategic Systems Development*, Addison-Wesley, Reading, MA, 1992.

[113] Rouse, W. B., *Catalysts for Change: Concepts and Principles for Enabling Innovation*, John Wiley & Sons, New York, 1993.

Chapter 2

Systems Engineering Process Lifecycles

In this chapter, we continue our introductory discussions in Chapter 1 through the development of some important notions regarding processes of systems engineering, and systems engineering lifecycles for (1) system acquisition or production; (2) research, development, test, and evaluation; and (3) systems planning and marketing. We will also have the opportunity to introduce a number of related issues that will be more fully discussed in subsequent chapters.

Basically, a *process* is a continuous action, or set of activities, designed to serve a particular purpose. For a number of reasons, it is desirable to distinguish a number of phases that, together, comprise a systems engineering process. We will denote the collection of these phases as a *systems engineering lifecycle*. A systems engineering lifecycle prescribes a number of phases that should be followed, generally in an interactive and iterative manner, in order successfully to produce and field a large scale system that meets user requirements.

There have been a number of process models proposed and used for multiphased lifecycle models in systems engineering. Each of them starts, or should start, by capturing user requirements. These user requirements are then converted, in a systems acquisition or production lifecycle, for example, to technological system requirements and systems management requirements that will presumably, when satisfied, produce a product or service that satisfies the customer or user of the product in terms of quality and trustworthiness. The system requirements are next converted into technical system specifications. The system requirements lead to management system requirements that are converted into management controls, or configuration management, specifications. Following the requirements phase(s), there is a conceptual, or architectural, design phase and then a detailed design phase, the result of which is an initial working version of a system. This is evaluated and modified and ultimately produced in sufficient quantity in a high quality and timely manner, to enable ultimate operational deployment of a functionally useful system, a system that fulfills user requirements. Deployment is followed by a maintenance and modification phase and other efforts that together describe an extended systems engineering lifecycle.

This description is an enhanced description of the three-phase lifecycle we discussed earlier. It is particularly suited for systems acquisition. A lifecycle might always be expected to be comprised of three basic phases—*system definition, system development,* and *system deployment*—as we have discussed in Chapter 1, and as indicated in Figure 1.6 and reproduced in an enhanced version as Figure 2.1. This figure shows three generic systems lifecycles and the related interactions with systems management and the customer. For large systems, these three phases illustrated for each lifecycle need expansion into a number of more finely grained phases. This will enable various phases to be better understood, communicated, and controlled in order to support trustworthy systems engineering efforts.

These specific actions that correspond to definition, development, and deployment terms take on somewhat different and definite interpretations for each of the three different systems engineering lifecycles:

Systems planning and marketing

Research, development, test, and evaluation (RDT&E)

Systems acquisition, production, or procurement

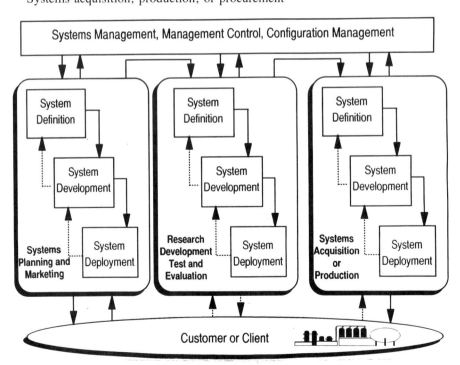

Figure 2.1   Conceptual illustration of the three primary systems engineering lifecycle phases and lifecycles.

It is very necessary that all three of these lifecycles be considered as interrelated, even though responsibility for the details of their implementation may be dispersed throughout an organization. That they are indeed interrelated is evidenced by several objectives that show the needed integration that can occur through high quality systems management and appropriate systems engineering processes.

To achieve the objectives for production of a high quality and trustworthy product or service, we should implement activities for the following purposes:

1. To ensure that the organization has an understanding and appreciation of the market and associated customers or clients.
2. To identify market and customer needs.
3. To identify potentially successful products, systems, and services that fill these needs.
4. To translate these acquisition and market needs into requirements for RDT&E.
5. To ensure RDT&E that is efficiently and effectively planned and performed.
6. To transfer or transition successful emerging technologies from the technology base to the systems acquisition base.
7. To ensure that the RDT&E and system acquisition, or production, efforts of the organization are attuned to the organization's market, technology, and corporate strengths.
8. To establish a risk management program for each of the three primary lifecycles.
9. To ensure that the products of system acquisition, or production, have a high effectiveness, or benefit, to cost ratio.
10. To verify that the products of RDT&E and systems acquisition meet the requirements set forth in systems planning and marketing.

It seems apparent that fulfilling these objectives requires very close systems management from the top levels of organizational management if these transitions and integrations are to be accomplished successfully. The ultimate objectives include acquisition or production or systems and services that have the following attributes:

Superior performance
High quality
Production efficiency and effectiveness
Priced competitively
Compatible with the experiential familiarity and culture of the organization

We will describe some systems engineering lifecycles in this chapter. In addition to some general descriptions, we will emphasize those that are particularly suited for the development of information technology and software engineering products.

Our efforts in this chapter, and throughout the entire text, concern the following:

1. The systems engineering process for major systems and its influences on lifecycle costs and system effectiveness, especially for information technology and software engineering products.
2. Identification of the structure for an appropriate systems development environment and lifecycle, and how constituent activities within this lifecycle environment interact to produce an overall product.
3. Ways in which various technological tools and techniques may improve systems development productivity through configuration management and configuration control.

We will first discuss a variety of different systems engineering lifecycles. Associated with this, we will address ways in which the phases within the lifecycle can be adjusted to take advantage of opportunities to increase the productivity and trustworthiness of systems. We will indicate the role of configuration management and configuration control within this. Most of our initial discussions will focus on lifecycles for RDT&E and systems acquisition and procurement. In the latter part of the chapter we will examine some broader systems management implications of these lifecycles for planning and marketing.

2.1 SYSTEMS ENGINEERING LIFECYCLES: SYSTEM ACQUISITION

In this section, we will describe several lifecycles for systems acquisition, production, or procurement. In each case, we are concerned with the description of steps and phases in a typical lifecycle for acquisition of a major system. Since we are primarily concerned with systems management here, our effort will primarily be concerned with phases, or macrolevel efforts, in the lifecycle. In Chapter 1, we briefly discussed the formulation, analysis, and interpretation steps of the fine, or logic, structure of systems engineering that need to be associated with each phase of the lifecycle. Much more detailed discussions of these issues are provided in [1] and [2].

In the following subsections, we will first review and expand upon our earlier discussions of the three-phase lifecycle, specifically for system acquisition. Then we will examine some more fine grained lifecycles.

2.1.1 Three-Phase Lifecycle

Figure 2.1 illustrates the generic three-phase lifecycle, shown as one of three generic lifecycles for RDT&E, acquisition, and planning and marketing. We will specialize here on efforts involved in systems acquisition. When we use the term acquisition, we will use it as representative of the activities of acquisition, procurement, or production. Often, we will not use the longer expression.

The first phase in the effort is the definition phase. What should happen in the definition phase is very much a function of what has gone on before this phase of system acquisition occurs and how it occurs. If this phase results from an inter-organizational effort at systems planning and marketing, with supporting RDT&E, to develop the requirements for a product, service, or system to be procured or acquired, there will exist a set of requirements for the system that is to ultimately result from the efforts in this lifecycle. In a similar way, if the systems acquisition effort is initiated because of a contract that has been obtained, through open competition or otherwise awarded from outside the systems engineering organization, there will also exist a set of requirements for the system that is to be delivered to the customer or client after it has been successfully procured, produced, or acquired.

In either of these two cases, there is still the need for a definition phase of effort. The major task in this phase is to take this set of user or customer requirements and ultimately convert them into a set of design specifications that can be operationalized to produce the developed product or system. There may, and generally will be, a number of related and ancillary efforts. For example, it will be verify highly desirable to validate the user or customer needs and requirements to be sure that those stated are really what is desired, and to subsequently revise the initial system requirements to more fully satisfy user needs. These requirements will need to be analyzed such that the customer needs, in addition to the resources required and available for acquisition, may be transformed into a set of system level specifications. This will require some high level architecting and preliminary design, perhaps even the construction of a rapid prototype to better enable the user group to specify requirements in terms of ultimate system functionality. Thus the products of the definition phase of system acquisition might be the following:

1. Analysis of the initially supplied set of user requirements.
2. Development of system level architectures, based on the analysis of user requirements and knowledge of the system objective or mission and the environment for use of the system.
3. Definition of a revised set of user requirements, based on these inputs and further communications with system users.
4. Definition of a set of system level specifications that represent a veridical translation of these verified user requirements and objectives.
5. Association of these system specifications with a number of development projects that comprise the system development program that is now ready to be undertaken.

We could describe these activities in the definition phase, by a number of equivalent terms. For example, the words program and project planning could certainly be used to describe these activities. Even here though, a term like a program plan has a different interpretation across the lifecycles of systems planning and marketing, RDT&E, and system acquisition.

After the definition phase—and normally the customer should certify completion of a satisfactory definition phase—the development phase of effort begins. There are several activities that comprise this phase. We need to translate the system specifications and conceptual design, or high level system architectures, into an actual functioning system. The word *functional* is very important here. Among the top level needs in this phase of effort are the need to (1) identify functional requirements and specifications from the system level architectures such that a set of detailed architectures and detailed design requirements are obtained; and (2) develop these functional product or system specifications, generally with interactive and iterative feedback from the system user.

We could describe these activities in a number of related fashions. It would be reasonable that this development effort might well be called synthesis, in that the product to be deployed results from the input to the development phase. Associated with these phasewise efforts will be a number of development management efforts. We will describe the overall effort that includes this as configuration management. Configuration management will be discussed briefly later in this chapter and throughout the text. A much more complete discussion is available in [1] and the references cited therein.

One of the challenges in the system development phase of system acquisition, although it is present in system definition also, is that of determining how much of the technology to be implemented in the operational system to be deployed is to be established and mature technology, and how much of it is to be newly emerged technologies. Some system acquisition or production efforts will be based on very mature technologies only, and no RDT&E effort will be needed. Others will be heavily dependent on RDT&E efforts. Still others will rely on some mix of the emerging technologies that result from satisfactory RDT&E and the mature technologies that are already available. We will discuss this issue in more detail in our later discussions in this chapter.

After completing system development, we undertaken deployment of the procured system(s), products(s), or service(s). Perhaps item(s) might be a suitable generic term that could refer to all of these. There are a number of activities associated with deployment. A systems acquisition contractor involved in deployment will need to (1) install the systems, service(s), or product(s) in an operational setting; (2) conduct operational test and evaluation of the acquired system, such that any difficulties not detected earlier can be detected at this time, the cause of the difficulty diagnosed, and the acquired product corrected such that it performs to the full satisfaction of the customer, (3) maintain the system, including evolving it over time to meet changing user needs; and (4) ultimately retire and replace the system when it no longer is capable of being maintained in a cost effective manner.

A little thought easily convinces us that some activities have been left out of this discussion. Preparation of user manuals and documentation and training of system users have not been explicitly mentioned. They are, of course, included in these activities. The need for systems integration of the new system with existing or legacy systems has not been explicitly mentioned but must also be included. In the activities in each lifecycle phase are appropriate systematic measurements to allow fielding of a high quality system through proactive, interactive, and reactive measurement.

It is not always the case that the systems engineering organization responsible for development will also be responsible for deployment. In many cases it will be responsible for the initial efforts involved in operational test and evaluation, and associated correction efforts if needed, but will not be responsible for maintenance. If an outside organization is responsible for deployment, or some portions of it, there will need to be some very minor modifications to the statements made here.

2.1.2 Seven-Phase Lifecycle for System Acquisition or Product Development

In this subsection, we assume that it has somehow been decided to develop and deploy a product. We assume that the decision has been made relative to who is to do this, and that the requirements for the product to be developed have been identified. The description of the various phases are easily modified to describe more general situations, such as might be encountered in service development, RDT&E, and marketing.

Arthur D. Hall [3,4] reported many years ago a seven-phase lifecycle of this sort. A more recent work by Hall also comments further on this lifecycle [5]. The seven phases of this systems engineering lifecycle are illustrated in Figure 2.2. The phases in this lifecycle and a brief descriptive account of the activities at each phase are as follows.

System Definition

1. *Program planning* is a conscious activity that should result in formulation of the activities and projects supportive of the overall system requirements into more detailed levels of planning. It is the first phase in this lifecycle. The program planning phase must, if it is to be successful, also include identification of system level requirements to the extent that they have not been identi-

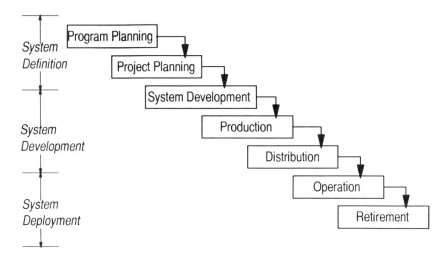

Figure 2.2 The seven phases in the Hall systems engineering lifecycle.

fied from user requirements, and translation of these into the technological system specifications that are planned for later development.

2. *Project planning* is distinguished from program planning by increased interest on the individual specific projects of an overall systems development program in the second phase. The purpose of this phase is to configure a number of specific projects, which together comprise the program, such that system development can begin.

System Development

3. *System design* results in implementation of the project plans through design of the overall system in detail as a number of subsystems, each of which is described by a project plan. This is the first phase of effort that will ultimately translate the system definition into a product. This phase ends with the preparation of detailed architectures, detailed specifications, drawings, and bills of materials for the system manufacturer or builder.

4. *Production,* for manufactured products, or *construction,* for one-of-a-kind systems, is the next phase. It includes all of the many activities that are needed to give physical reality to the desired system. This could involve, for example, using detailed plans and specifications to construct a new building, manufacture a new product, or produce source code for an emerging software product. A number of related efforts would be needed, such as determining the sequence, materials flow, required shop floor layouts, and the establishment of quality control practices. After completion of this phase of effort, we have a systems engineering product that is capable of being fielded or implemented in an operational setting.

System Deployment

5. *Distribution,* or *phase-in,* results in delivering systems engineering products or services to users or consumers. This may involve all kinds of distribution facilities and marketing and sales organizations.

6. *Operations* is the ultimate goal of system deployment. This phase includes such activities as maintenance.

7. *Retirement,* or *phase-out,* of the system over a period of time and replacement by some new system will ultimately occur as the deployed product ages. This is the final phase in this lifecycle.

In this lifecycle, the first phased activity is program planning for production. Program planning is based on a given or established set of requirements. Working with a large scale complex system, either from the initial step of creating the system or from an intermediate step of altering the system, is an activity that can be facilitated by effective planning. Creation of an effective plan generally involves a diverse set of resources and a wide spectrum of disciplines. It is necessary to make a conscious effort to project ideas of what is desired into a framework amenable to tests of reality. Many questions can be asked. Can the past and current states of affairs be measured? Does a need for the proposed solution exist? Are there relevant measures of what is to be planned? Is the time frame realistic? Will the plan be accepted and understood by those who will have to carry it out? Clearly, a program plan cannot be established in the absence of knowledge of user requirements for the system. Thus, as we have noted, program planning must necessarily involve information requirements determination and translation of the user requirements for a system into technological specifications. Even though requirements may be specified initially, it is highly desired that these be validated in program planning. In Section 2.3, we will also discuss some graph-theory-oriented techniques for program planning associated with strategic planning and marketing. These approaches are also useful for information display of planning efforts in other lifecycles and for other phases in all three lifecycles.

Clearly, we could use somewhat different words to describe these phases of the system acquisition lifecycle. For example, the retirement phase includes maintenance, prior to possible system phase-out. As we will soon note in Section 2.4, the particular representation we have used for Figure 2.2 is called a waterfall lifecycle. In this particular figure, there is no explicit way shown to correct deficiencies in one phase that are only discovered in a later phase. We can add some feedback to allow interaction among adjacent phases as shown in Figure 2.3. We can allow for a major amount of interactive and proactive feedback and learning by having a repository of knowledge, and applying this is what we will call an evolutionary manner to influence activities at the several phases. This is indicated conceptually in Figure 2.4, which also allows for the needed influences of the RDT&E and strategic planning and marketing lifecycles. This diagram can be redrawn slightly to become

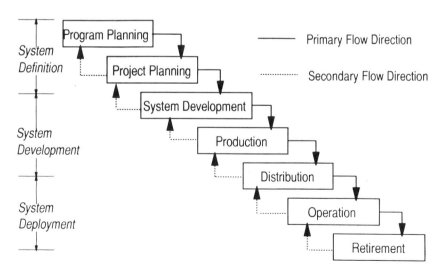

Figure 2.3   The seven phases in the Hall systems engineering lifecycle with feedback and interaction between adjacent phases.

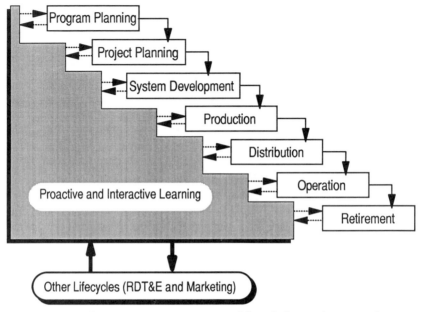

Figure 2.4 Seven phases in systems engineering lifecycle for production with interactive and proactive learning.

a cornucopia or spiral model of systems engineering product evolvement, as indicated by Hall. Spiral-like models have become very popular in software engineering, especially since they allow for a more proactive approach to risk management than is possible through a waterfall model without feedback, as shown in Figure 2.2. We will describe some spiral-like lifecycles in Section 2.4.

2.1.3 22-Phase Lifecycle

We now describe a lifecycle that is comprised of 22 phases. As we will soon see, these phases correspond to the phases in the much simpler appearing three-phase model. Here, we identify a set of phases, initially discussed in [6] and also described in [1], that might exist when one client or stakeholder group, such as a government agency or private company, seeks development by another vendor (to be determined) of a large system. The *system definition* effort, or phase, can be expanded into seven phases. The actors in these phases include system developers, clients for the systems study, and champions or funders of system development efforts.

System Definition

1. *Perception of need* by the customer, or client, or user group.
2. *Requirements definition* of the user group requirements by the user group.

3. *Draft request for proposal* (RFP) by the user group.
4. *Comments on the RFP* by system development industry. The final RFP is typically conditioned by inputs from potential bidders.
5. *Final RFP and statement of work* developed by the user group.
6. *Proposal development,* generally in a competitive manner, by the system development industry. Most proposals will include statements regarding (a) system architecture, (b) selection of approach, and (c) work breakdown structure (WBS). The work breakdown structure, both in terms of the scheduling of system development effort and the nature and timing of the work to be done, is a principal vehicle in which the contractor may display knowledge of system development practices, principles, and perspectives. A systems engineering management plan (SEMP) is often included with a contractor proposal. Sometimes, a tentative SEMP is identified by the contracting agency. Associated with the SEMP is a systems engineering master schedule (SEMS) and at least an initial version of a systems engineering detailed schedule (SEDS).
7. *Source selection* by the customer, client, or user group.

At the end of this phase of effort, a system development contractor has been selected. Formally, this completes the system definition phase of the three-phase system development lifecycle. It enables the start of a number of system development phases. We will describe the system development phase in terms of seven more finely grained phases. It is important to remember that some works consider what we call system development as systems engineering itself. Our definition and interpretation are somewhat broader, although they certainly encompass the system development phase of systems acquisition.

System Development

8. *Development of refined conceptual architectures* by the selected system is engineering contractor, generally at a very high level, such that this effort effectively amounts to program planning.
9. *Partitioning of the system into subsystems* by the systems engineering contractor. An orderly systems engineering process should include systems management efforts that result in configuration management of the evolving systems engineering product. This systems management effort includes partitioning of the entire system so integration and interfacing needs are identified, and such that the need for interfacing and integration is minimized to the extent possible.
10. *Subsystem level specifications and test requirements development* by the systems engineering contractor. A complete systems engineering approach must include means to express and verify subsystem level specifications. These metrics are very important.
11. *Design and development of components* by the systems engineering contractor or potentially by subcontractors. In general, this will include a variety of

hardware and software items, such as (a) major hardware, (b) interfacing hardware, (c) systems software, and (d) application software.

12. *Integration of subsystems* by the systems engineering contractor or possibly one or more subcontractors. This will include integration of (a) hardware, (b) software, and (c) testing practices. An appropriate systems engineering lifecycle must specifically address the systems integration phase of the lifecycle effort. This is generally a far more exhaustive requirement than that of simply linking together a collection of existing subsystems, such as "reused" program modules. The individual technologies that comprise a system must be addressed specifically to ensure ability to facilitate end-to-end tests and performance.

13. *Integration of the overall system* by the system engineering contractor. This will include integration of hardware and software and appropriate integration testing. The considerations here are similar to those in phase 12, with the exception that not all subsystems will be developed at the same technology level or in the same amount of initial detail. thus it will also be necessary to provide for future systems integration efforts.

14. *Development of user training and aiding supports* by the systems engineering contractor. A key concern in this is that the resulting system be flexible, such that new application requirements can be easily and effectively supported.

Following system development, the system is implemented in an operational environment. The final phase of this systems engineering lifecycle begins. Normal operation and maintenance of the system occur. This will normally lead to system evolution over time. This can lead to the need for major proactive modification of existing systems, including retirement of a system and replacement by a new system. At least eight phases of the lifecycle that specifically relate to system deployment can be identified.

System Deployment (Including Operation and Maintenance)

15. *Operational implementation* or *fielding of the system* by the system engineering contractor with support from the user or customer group.

16. *Final acceptance testing* of the implemented system by the user. Acceptance testing will often result in minor adjustments to system operation. Ideally, minor changes can be made and documented in the acceptance environment.

17. *Operational test and evaluation* by the system user or an independent contractor that has been selected for this purpose by the user group.

18. *Final system acceptance* by the client or user group.

19. *Identification of system change requirements* by the user group. As experience with using the system grows, there will be a need for maintenance in order to better adapt the system to its intended use. This maintenance is quite different from "bug fixes" and repair. It includes the need to evolve the

system over time in an adaptive and proactive manner to make it responsive to changing needs and needs that were present initially but unrecognized in the initial set of requirements specifications. Architectural concerns are of major importance here. Better defined system structures make it easier for the user to identify those portions of the system which would need to be changed to effect a desired alteration in system operation. This could tend to minimize requests requiring detailed changes in a large number of sub-system elements. These needs should be addressed as a part of the configuration management process.

20. *Bid on system changes,* or *prenegotiated maintenance support,* by a systems maintenance contractor. Generally, changes will be carried out using the same general approach used to develop the initial system. This will often predispose the user group toward returning to the same contracting source that developed the initial system, or to another one that has the same development tools available.

21. *System maintenance change development* by the maintenance support contractor. Changes will be easier if the "history" of the original system development has been well captured and documented, and if the system is well structured and contains an open architecture.

22. *Maintenance testing by support contractor.* The systems engineering process evolves as a linear sequenced process. Errors in an earlier step of the process may cause errors in a later step. This indicates the need for iteration and feedback from later stages in the process to earlier stages. When potential errors are detected, there should be feedback to earlier activities and appropriate corrective actions taken. Often the only iteration possible is the one of proceeding back to phase 19—system change requirements. If significant defects in the existing system are observed, perhaps brought about by new functional requirements, then iteration back through the entire system acquisition process *may* occur. However, this does not happen often or only happens when very significant performance deficiencies are noted. It is this need for iteration back to any of a variety of earlier phases of a system lifecycle that leads to the need for a look at the overall objectives of the system lifecycle.

This 22-phase description of the systems engineering lifecycle is doubtlessly exhaustive. We have indicated roles for the client or user group, for the systems engineering group or contractor, and potentially for various subcontractors that possess detailed expertise relative to specific technologies. The many phases developed here for the systems engineering, or systems acquisition, lifecycle are illustrated in Figure 2.5. We should note that the lifecycles of Figures 2.2 through 2.4 begin at phase 8 in the lifecycle illustrated in Figure 2.5. A recent text [7] provides an excellent discussion of system architecture and design principles that, for the most part, follow from the extensive lifecycle illustrated in Figure 2.5. This lifecycle is very much patterned after the U.S. Department of Defense (DoD) systems

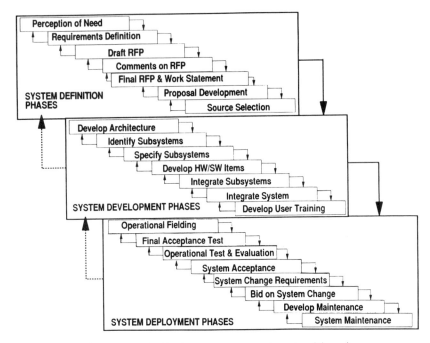

Figure 2.5   A 22-phase systems engineering lifecycle.

engineering lifecycle. We now turn our attention to a description of several versions of this DoD lifecycle.

2.1.4   Defense Systems Acquisition Lifecycle

The lifecycle approach to systems acquisition of the U.S. Department of Defense [8] is illustrated in Figure 2.6. This system acquisition lifecycle is comprised of five primary phases.

0. *Milestone 0—Concept Exploration and Definition/Program Initiation/Mission-Need Decision.* Mission-need is determined and program initiation is approved, including authority to budget the program. A concept-definition analysis is performed. Primary consideration during this initial acquisition phase is given to the following four steps:
   0.1   mission area analysis;
   0.2   affordability and lifecycle costs;
   0.3   feasibility of a modification to an existing system to provide the needed capability; and
   0.4   operational utility assessment.
1. *Milestone I—Concept Demonstration and Validation Decision.* A concept demonstration/validation effort is performed. If successful, the development continues. Primary attention is paid to seven areas of effort:

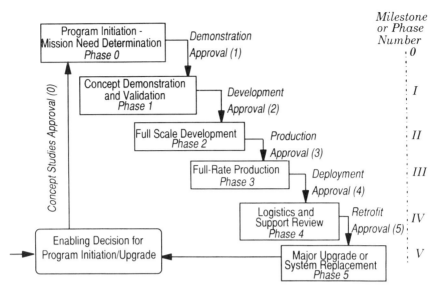

Figure 2.6   The U.S. Department of Defense systems acquisition lifecycle.

1.1   program alternative trade-offs;
1.2   performance/cost and schedule trade-offs, including the need for a new development program versus buying or adapting existing military or commercial systems;
1.3   appropriateness of the acquisition strategy;
1.4   prototyping of the system or selected system components;
1.5   affordability and lifecycle costs;
1.6   potential common-use solutions; and
1.7   cooperative development opportunities.

The efforts in this phase establish broad program cost, schedule, and operational effectiveness and suitability goals and thresholds, allowing the program manager maximum flexibility to develop innovative and cost affective solutions.

2. *Milestone II—Full-Scale Engineering and Manufacturing Development Decision.* Approval for *full-scale development (FSD)* is made at this lifecycle phase. As appropriate, low-rate initial production of selected components and quantities may be approved to verify production capability and to provide test resources needed to conduct interoperability, live fire, or operational testing. Decisions in this phase will precede the release of the final *request for proposals* (RFP) for the FSD contract. Primary considerations in this phase of activity are described by 13 steps. The goal of the steps are to identify:

2.1   affordability in terms of program cost versus the military value of the new or improved system and its operational suitability and effectiveness;

2.2   program risk versus benefit of added military capability;

2.3   planning for the transition from development to production, which will include independent producibility assessments of hardware, software, and databases;

2.4   realistic industry surge and mobilization capacity;

2.5   factors that affect program stability;

2.6   potential common-use solutions;

2.7   results from prototyping and demonstration/validation;

2.8   milestone authorization;

2.9   personnel, training, and safety needs assessments;

2.10   procurement strategy appropriate to program cost and risk assessments;

2.11   plans for integrated logistics support;

2.12   affordability and lifecycle costs; and

2.13   associated command, control, communications, and intelligence (C^{3}I) requirements.

Decisions at this phase result in the establishment of more specific cost, schedule, and operational effectiveness and suitability goals and thresholds than were possible in earlier phases. Particular emphasis is placed on the requirements for transitioning from development to production.

3. *Milestone III—Full Rate Production Decision.* The decision made at this phase regards activities associated with the full rate production/deployment phase. Primary considerations at this phase involve 12 steps, many of which are similar to steps in Milestone II:

3.1   results of completed operational test and evaluation;

3.2   threat validation;

3.3   production cost verification;

3.4   affordability and lifecycle costs;

3.5   production and deployment schedule;

3.6   reliability, maintainability, and plans for integrated logistics support;

3.7   producibility as verified by an independent assessment;

3.8   realistic industry surge and mobilization capacity;

3.9   procurement or milestone authorization;

3.10   identification of personnel, training, and safety requirements;

3.11   cost effectiveness or plans for competition or dual sourcing; and

3.12   associated command, control, communications, and intelligence (C^{3}I) requirements.

4. *Milestone IV—Logistics and Support Review Decision.* The decision process at this phase identifies actions and resources needed to ensure that operations readiness and support objectives are achieved and maintained for the first several years of the operational support phase of lifecycle. Primary considerations at this phase of the lifecycle are:

4.1   logistics readiness and sustainability;

4.2   weapon support objectives;

4.3   implementation of integrated logistics support plans;

4.4   capability of logistics activities, facilities, and training and personnel to provide support efficiently and cost effectively;

4.5   disposition of displaced equipment; and

4.6   affordability and lifecycle costs.

5. *Milestone V—Major Upgrade or System Replacement Decision.* The decision process at this phase encompasses a review of a system's current state or operational effectiveness, suitability, and readiness to determine whether major upgrades are necessary or deficiencies warrant consideration of replacement. Considerations at this phase of the lifecycle are:

5.1   capability of the system to continue to meet its original or evolved mission requirements relative to the current situation;

5.2   potential necessity of modifications to ensure mission support; and

5.3   changes in technology that present the opportunity for a significant breakthrough in system worth.

This phase V of defense systems acquisition is intended to address a system many years, normally 5 to 10, after deployment if the acquisition is *successful*. If there are major flaws, the initially deployed system may not be at all satisfactory and very extensive and perhaps continual maintenance may be required from the day of operational implementation. As is now well known, this has been a particular problem with software acquisition.

There has been much present experience, including some criticism as well, of the defense systems acquisition lifecycle. This lifecycle encompasses the systems engineering lifecycle described in MIL-STD 499A and the forthcoming 499B [9], which generally relate most strongly to phases or milestones II, III, and IV of system acquisition. Our definition of systems engineering is therefore much broader than that defined by MIL-STD 499A and 499B. It encompasses the definition and deployment phase of system acquisition and also includes RDT&E and systems planning and marketing.

This defense systems acquisition cycle is related to, but different from, the various categories of research and development funded by the DoD. There are six categories identified; each are prefixed by the number 6 in the DoD breakdown structure.

6.1   *Research* includes all efforts of study and experimentation that are directed toward increasing knowledge in the physical, engineering, environmental, and life sciences that support long-term national security needs.

6.2   *Exploratory development* includes efforts that are directed toward evaluating feasibility of solutions that are proposed for specific military issues that need applied research and prototype hardware and software.

6.3A   *Advanced technology development* is concerned with programs that explore alternatives and concepts prior to the development of specific weapons systems.

6.3B   *Advanced development* is involved with *proof of design* concepts, as contrasted with development of operational hardware and software. The Milestone I decision, just discussed, occurs during advanced development.

6.4   *Engineering development* results in hardware and software for actual use that is developed according to contract specifications. A program moves from advanced development to engineering development coincident with a Milestone II decision by the Defense Acquisition Board.

6.5   *Management and support* involves the support of specific installations, or those operations and facilities that are required for general research and development use.

2.1.5   Other Lifecycle Models for Systems Acquisition

There are a number of other systems management lifecycle models. The National Society of Professional Engineers, for example, has suggested a six-phase model [10] comprised of the following phases:

Conceptual
Technical feasibility
Development
Commercial validation and production preparation
Full-scale production
Product support

This is the lifecycle we illustrated earlier as the acquisition portion of Figure 1.4.

Some authors suggest a systems engineering lifecycle that encompasses aspects of RDT&E, planning and marketing, and systems acquisition. For example, in the *directed research for product development* model, Gruenwald [11] presented a systems management lifecycle to address new product development objectives. There are seven phases to this lifecycle and they may be described as follows.

1. *Search for opportunity.* To accomplish this phase, compilation of information on the industry, sales data, technology, consumer interests, and the competition is required. The effort is begun by performing an industry analysis, which should include sales volume and trends, basic technology, competition, customer definition, and other pertinent factors such as foreign trade and regulatory restrictions. The next steps are to identify opportunities by defining targets, forecasting rough volume and share, and performing a risk-ratio analysis; to perform a feasibility study and a war-game-like assessment of the competitive reactions; to examine technical hurdles; and to consider legal and policy issues. On the basis of these steps, a decision is made with respect to whether to proceed, that is, to *go* or *no go*.

2. *Conception.* In this phase, we translate market facts into product concepts and customer positioning communications before making commitments to

exhaustive product-oriented and -directed research and development (R&D). There are six steps in this phase, which may be found by consulting the source book cited.

3. *Modeling or prototyping.* This involves bringing proposed new products closer to reality in the form of prototype products and prototype communications. The steps in this phase involve developing descriptors, developing prototypes, and making a go or no go decision for further efforts on the basis of the information obtained from using these prototypes.

4. *Research and development.* This phase covers a number of different activities including checking outside scientific resources and pilot plant production, analyzing the factors necessary to scale up from pilot plant production to full-scale commercialization, conducting controlled tests, and performing feasibility studies. On the basis of the information that results from these steps, a decision is made whether to proceed to the next phase.

5. *Marketing plan.* This involves the development of a marketing plan, and a go or no go decision to proceed to the next phase is made on the basis of the information obtained at this phase.

6. *Market testing.* This phase involves a continuation of marketing to include limited scale introduction of the new product or system.

7. *Major introduction.* This phase expands from the market testing phase if this concludes with a go decision to full scale commercial introduction of the new product or system.

Gruenwald has attempted, through use of this relatively exhaustive lifecycle methodology, to minimize risks and maximize success probability associated with the operational product that is introduced into the marketplace in the final phase in the lifecycle effort.

This is clearly a systems engineering based approach to address new product goals in an organized, phase by phase iterative method. The important decision considerations that are addressed after a possible new product concept has been defined are as follows:

Is there a latent demand for the product?

Can a product be made that will satisfy the market?

Will the entry be profitable and satisfy the corporate charter, as well as other company objectives?

Our preference is to consider this lifecycle of directed research for product development as three separate lifecycles, as we have noted, rather than a single lifecycle that integrates together RDT&E, acquisition, and planning and marketing. This does not invalidate the concept of a single lifecycle; however, it does suggest that many of the phases in a single lifecycle are too highly aggregated and involve too many actors to be easily used for the efforts involved in systems engineering planning and marketing, RDT&E, and system product acquisition. Figure 2.7 illustrates

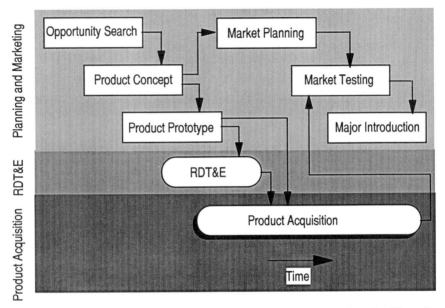

Figure 2.7   Illustration of the need for interaction across systems engineering lifecycles.

the phases in this lifecycle. To make the discussion more applicable to the efforts discussed here, we disaggregate the phase 4 efforts of research and development into two phases—a RDT&E phase and a systems acquisition effort. The major flow patterns for information are illustrated. There are many other information flows not shown here in order to keep the illustration relatively simple. The natural interconnection and interaction across the lifecycles are apparent. As we discussed, some initial portions of systems planning and marketing necessarily occur before RDT&E and acquisition, and after these efforts. Thus we see that systems planning and marketing support RDT&E and acquisition. Planning and marketing also receives support from these two phases, as we have indicated in Figures 1.7 and 1.8.

This illustration provides a natural point for a discussion of Figure 1.18, reproduced as Figure 2.8 and showing a three-gateway model for systems engineering. These gateways correspond to (1) a technology development gateway, grounded primarily on technology "push" and associated RDT&E; (2) a developed technology management gateway, predicated and evidenced primarily on systems acquisition or production; and, (3) a systems planning and marketing gateway.

Technology assessment and forecasting [12–15] are needed for successful determination of appropriate projects for RDT&E in terms of achieving emerged technologies that represent scientific and technological innovations. Market assessment and forecasting are needed to provide perspectives on the societal pull, or demand or receptiveness, for strategic positioning relative to new products, systems, or services.

Together with systems management, technology assessment and forecasting and market assessment and forecasting comprise the basis for technology transfer from

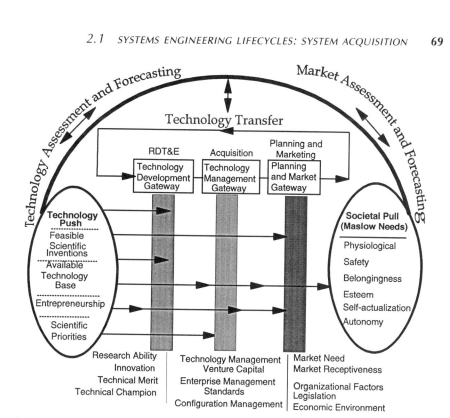

Figure 2.8   Conceptual illustration of technology transfer across three gates for successful systems, products, and services.

embryonic to mature competitive products and services. This is illustrated in Figure 2.8, which shows technology transfer as a bridge across the gap between technology push and demand pull. The major objective in technology transfer is to provide this bridge between the push of technology developers and the pull of technology consumers through the provision of trustworthy products, systems, and services that are of high quality and provide maximum customer satisfaction. This leads us to suggest Figure 2.9 as another way to represent this technology transfer process. It shows systems management strategy at the core of a technological organization's development effort. This leads to the use of technology assessment and forecasting, market assessment and forecasting, and such internal realities associated with the organization as culture, critical core capabilities, and objectives. These lead then to systems management, processes, and product associated with RDT&E, acquisition, and marketing. The major objectives that need to be achieved relative to these three coupled lifecycles are as follows:

1. To identify and implement a strategic level systems management process that will provide for a superior product line process and ultimate product or system.

2. To coordinate and integrate efforts over time by developing appropriate struc-

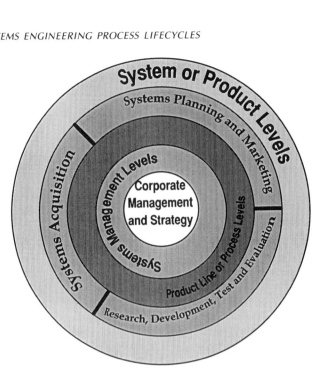

Figure 2.9   Systems management for technology transfer across seamless lifecycle boundaries.

tures and functional tasks across the three lifecycles of RDT&E, systems acquisition or production, and systems planning and marketing, such that organizational purposes are served as efficiently and effectively as possible.

3. To identify, establish, and improve organizational capabilities over time such as to enable achievement of a competitive advantage.

Observations such as this are relatively recent in origin. They suggest a major role for information technology developments as an adjunct and support for systems engineering and systems management improvements. In [16], for example, it is argued strongly that information technology studies and developments extend much beyond the neoclassic engineering of data processing to incorporate intellectual property laws, public and private sector policy considerations, and economic and systems management considerations. Three of the major strategies suggested in this effort relate directly to our efforts here:

1. Redefining the technology base to include information as an essential ingredient.

2. Leading in the development and application, often through technology transfer, of new and emerging technologies.

3. Capturing market share and dominating the commercial production sector.

The major substance of this and other works appears to be that there are indeed strategies that can enhance and restore productivity and quality. Many of these call for efforts and objectives that, when brought to fulfillment, lead to enhanced productivity, such as [17]:

To encourage strong interest in and knowledge of real problems from economic, social, and political perspectives.

To encourage team efforts in the creation of new processes, systems, and products.

To develop the ability to function effectively beyond the confines of a single discipline.

To develop the ability to integrate a deep understanding of science and technology with practical knowledge, including the necessary human and experimental skills and insights associated with market conditions.

There are a variety of ways in which we might conceptualize a model to describe the resulting flow of technological development. In Figure 2.8, we envision gateways that control the development and flow of technology, from either a push or pull standpoint. As noted in this figure, the push of technology is basically scientific in nature in that it includes development of all feasible scientific discoveries. Essentially all studies show that few, if any, successful products emerge only because of technology push [18].

These paragraphs suggest a major integrating role for strategic systems management. The needed integration occurs through technology forecasting and market forecasting such as to enable, in sequence [19], (1) the determination of organizational strategy, and from this (2) the determination of technology strategy, and thence, (3) the determination of appropriate decisions, based on these two strategies, to result in competitive advantage for the organization. A number of related objectives for these three desiderata can be identified. With respect to organizational strategy, it is necessary to identify facets of organizational strategy that are supportive of competitively advantageous technology development. This requires knowledge of the various ways in which technology development and organizational strategy influence and interact with one another. It requires knowledge of the relative trade-offs among process, or product line, improvements and product, or system or service, improvements. With respect to technology strategies, it is necessary to determine the generic processes that will suggest an appropriate blend of newly emerged technologies and established mature technologies within a given product line. This strategy must necessarily be influenced by market considerations and risk management considerations. At the level of the decisions that are made, we must be aware of how best to manage the plethora of risks that are associated with technologies and markets.

Many of the issues associated with these concerns relate to organizational culture, leadership, and performance. We will discuss a number of these in Chapter 7. A number of them also relate to the need for appropriate measurement of critical facets of performance at the levels of product, process, and systems management. A simple reasoning chain clearly illustrates that systems management and measurements are irretrievably interconnected.

1. Organizational success is dependent on management quality.
2. Management quality depends on decision quality.
3. Decision quality depends on information quality.
4. Information quality depends on measurement quality and appropriateness.

High quality and appropriate measurements provide a very befitting and much needed support for systems management.

We will address the subject of systematic measurement in much of our later work, especially in Chapters 4, 5, and 8. In brief, the major objectives of appropriate systems measurements and appropriate use of them in systems management are the following:

- Improved quality of delivered systems and products
- Improved quality of the processes used to develop these systems and products
- Improved predictability of product and system performance
- Improved schedule and cost accuracy and predictability
- Maximized customer satisfaction

This supports systematic measurement, as contrasted with context-free data collection, by enabling the aggregation or fusion of individual pieces of information to provide a corporate level knowledge base. Thus we spend much effort at developing a framework for measurements at the level of product, process, and systems management of process and product. Figure 2.10 illustrates some of the many interconnections involved in, and results obtained from, technological systems management and organizational systems management.

To focus the resources and activities of an organization on the needs and desires of the consumer for a potential new product, one must use market research. Kinnear and Taylor [20] state that the purpose of marketing information input is to narrow decision-making error and to broaden perspectives within which decisions are made. It may be the case that even before a new product development effort is undertaken, one should have a good idea as to the conditions in the market place with respect to the proposed new system, product, or service. Market research can provide this information. It is especially important to note that marketing, as an integrative function, which serves as a primary means for responding to and influencing the environment by providing a product or service that is superior to that of others and which fulfills customer needs, is quite different from advertising, which is publicity and promotion oriented.

It has been often stated that there are three basic components in any marketing research undertaking.

1. It is necessary to make certain that the right marketing research questions are being asked.
2. It is necessary to use marketing research techniques and controls that are appropriate for the issue at hand.

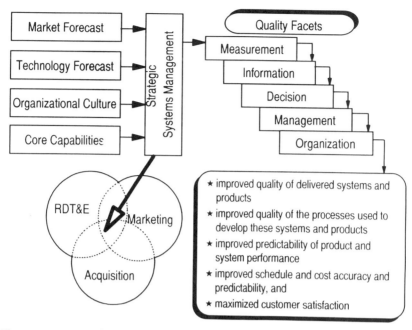

Figure 2.10 Ingredients in quality technology and management system design.

3. It is necessary to present marketing research findings in a clear, comprehensible format that leads to management action concerning such further efforts as research, development, test and evaluation (RDT&E), and system acquisition and support.

Of course, these questions can be restated such that they apply to any phase of the system's lifecycle. These must be given extensive consideration in all three lifecycle phases of development: RDT&E, acquisition, and marketing. Clearly, and as shown in Figure 2.10, marketing is an integral part of an organization's strategy. This must necessarily be associated with knowledge of the present and evolving critical and core capabilities of the organization, culture of the organization, technology forecast and assessment, and market forecast and assessment, if strategic systems management is to be efficient and effective.

This leads to the ultimate observation that the phases in the new product development lifecycle are inexorably linked and that there does need to be a strong coupling, particularly at the strategy development level, among all phases in an enhanced system development lifecycle (SDLC). This enhanced lifecycle includes both the RDT&E lifecycle, the systems acquisition lifecycle, and the planning and marketing lifecycle that we have been discussing here. This is what we have attempted to illustrate in Figure 2.9, which shows a seamless interface across the three lifecycles for systems engineering. It is also what we show in Figure 2.10 from a slightly different perspective. There will often be generally distinct systems management structure associated with each of the often separate organizational functions:

- Systems planning and marketing
- Research, development, test and evaluation
- Systems acquisition or production

A principal task of systems management, at the strategic level, should be to ensure that the management control [21], or systems management, functions associated with each of these lifecycles is well coordinated and integrated.

Let us now examine some specific RDT&E lifecycles. This will be followed by a discussion of systems planning and marketing. Then we will examine some lifecycles specifically proposed for software development. Finally, we conclude our formal discussions of systems engineering lifecycles by returning to a discussion of the need for proper organizational integration across these three lifecycles.

2.2 LIFECYCLES FOR RESEARCH, DEVELOPMENT, TEST AND EVALUATION

New product development, or systems acquisition, is limited by the following:

1. Technological capabilities needed to supply the emerging technologies from RDT&E that are required to produce innovative products and systems.
2. Market knowledge needed to supply information concerning the potential costs and benefits, including risks, associated with large scale acquisition.
3. Systems management capabilities that affect abilities (a) to evolve appropriate processes for acquisition; (b) to supply the needed RDT&E for those emerging technologies, which will make a new product or system competitive; and (c) to supply the needed planning and marketing such that the products and systems that are delivered fill a market need.

When the resulting *technological systems design* and *management systems design* needs are satisfied, there is really only a *push from feasible technological innovations*. There are, of course, approaches that encourage and stimulate technology push [22] and the associated RDT&E. As we have noted, most studies show that market pull is more of a catalyst affecting successful products than is technology push alone. As we have also discussed, technology transfer is necessarily concerned both with technology push and market pull.

For a new system to be developed, there must be an available technology base that supports development. Existing large investments in production facilities may encourage innovations that capitalize this investment. On the other hand, the existence of a large investment in one form of technology may well impede the propensity to allocate resources to an entirely new approach that could make the old approach obsolete. The very fact that there exists one satisfactory way to do something often provides an intellectual bias against thinking about new methods of approach. Thus a successful technology or system developer must be motivated and prepared to demonstrate that a new and potentially innovative approach is *better* in some market-driven, socially acceptable ways. If this is not done, any enthusiasm for technology push-driven accomplishments will likely soon fade over time.

It is possible to characterize existing conditions in an organization along several dimensions relative to development and implementation of a new technology or system. Two questions seem to be of primary importance relative to exploitation of a potential technology development venture. They can be expressed in slightly different form for individuals, groups, and organizations. In generic form, they are as follows:

Which new technology or system development markets should a unit enter?

How should the unit enter these markets so as to maximize the likelihood of success and the reward to be obtained from success, and at the same time to control the risk of failure and the losses to be suffered in the event of a failure?

These can be used as a basis for determination of acquisition and RDT&E strategies.

A potential new technology or systems product can be nurtured by one unit through use of one, or through a combination, of the following two basic approaches: (1) internal development of the technology or system product itself, or (2) venture funding of others to develop the system or product and subsequent acquisition, or transfer, of the technology. In either case, RDT&E is needed if there are nonmature technologies that are desired for incorporation in the product or system and that must be brought to an appropriate state of maturity through an emerging technology development effort. This may be accomplished by either of two approaches: (1) internal RDT&E relative to the emerging technology, or (2) venture funding of others and subsequent acquisition, or transfer, of the developed technology for use in the system to be produced. These lead to important questions affecting acquisition strategies.

There are at least six questions that could be posed relative to how a given organization should go about ultimately obtaining the system in question. In part, the appropriate development strategy depends on an analysis of these six related questions. There are two each for RDT&E, system acquisition, and planning and marketing.

1. How new is the system to be acquired to the organization?
2. How familiar is the organization with the technological development needs affecting the system to be acquired?
3. How new and creative is the RDT&E that needs to be accomplished to obtain the technologies needed for the system to be acquired?
4. How familiar is the organization with the type of RDT&E that needs to be accomplished?
5. How new is the market to the organization?
6. How familiar is the organization with the market?

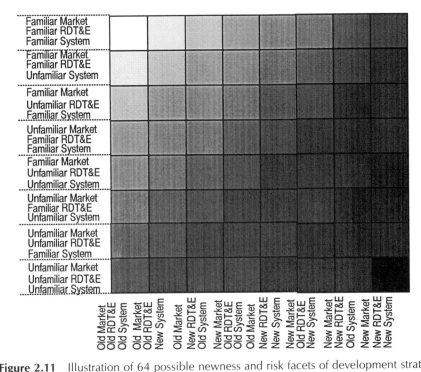

Figure 2.11   Illustration of 64 possible newness and risk facets of development strategies (darker shading indicates increased newness and risk).

The responses to these questions—if we assume binary answers of (1) new or old area of RDT&E, acquisition, and market for the product or system in question; and (2) familiar or unfamiliar RDT&E, acquisition, or market of the organization in question—lead to a $2^6 = 64$ cell selection dimensional matrix, as shown in Figure 2.11.

In reality, binary choice answers are not fully appropriate for questions such as these. We could use the methods of decision analysis and decision assessment [1] to develop an appraisal system, or decision support system [23], that could be used to assist in determination of the readiness of a given organization for adoption of some (or no) strategy for product development.

It seems clear that the easiest product to develop successfully is one that is in the upper left corner of the matrix of Figure 2.11. This corresponds to a situation in which we have an old area for RDT&E, a known system or product, and a well understood market. It also corresponds to a situation in which the organization considering the activity is familiar with the RDT&E, acquisition, and market needs. While this provides the easiest area for entry, and the one in which there is a minimum risk of failure, there is probably also not a great deal of upside potential to be gained. The area in the lower right corner is one with such formidable risks that few would seek to enter under these knowledge conditions. Evaluation of the risk–benefit associated with this sort of situation is a task for strategic level systems management of RDT&E. In a very simplistic manner, we might speculate that those entries just above the main diagonal are such that the risk is moderate and the upside potential is reasonably large.

Also associated with systems management at the strategic level is the development of an organizational learning capability such that the experiential wisdom of the organization relative to various market entry situations is improved. We address some of these concerns here for the specific case of RDT&E. Much of this book relates to these issues, which are very significant ones for obtaining long-term competitive advantage.

These responses indicate the extent to which a specific organization might be able to internally determine solutions to the many potential problems that may eventuate in making a potential new technological system or research capability operational. The term *base technology* and *base market* are used to describe technologies and markets with which a unit is presently concerned in earlier efforts of Roberts and Berry [24], who described appropriate entry strategies for the nine cells that are most supportive of success in development of a new technological product, service, or system for which an RDT&E capability already exists.

A base technology may be defined as a technology that is necessary for organizational functioning, but which offers little competitive advantage since these technologies are generally widespread. A base system or product is one that is comprised of base technologies. A base market is a market that is necessary for organizational functioning but that offers little competitive advantage since there are many organizations active in the market or the present market is saturated. We may generally make incremental improvements over time to a base product and make minor expansions to a base market through derivative or incremental improvements.

Other appropriate terms might be core technologies and core markets. A core technology, or key or critical technology, is one that is most crucial to competitive success through product or system differentiation. A core market, or a key or critical market, is a market where entry is necessary to realize competitive advantage. This is then a next-generation product or next-generation market.

Finally, an emerging technology, or antedating or pacing technology, is one that has potential to alter the entire competitive structure when successful RDT&E leads to a radically new technology that is ultimately implemented in a successful product or system. There is a natural evolution over time here as antedating or revolutionary technologies become core technologies as development continues. When a core or next-generation technology becomes relatively commonplace, it becomes a base technology. This can also be said for markets. Figure 2.12 indicates this evolution over time. A well functioning, high technology organization can be expected to employ a mix of these technology and market modes. Since technologies do mature and become base technologies over time, it is apparent that the most successful organizations need to have the capability of renewal through the successful introduction of new products and systems that evolve from antedating or emerging technologies.

This suggests that organizations must have capabilities at employing core or key technologies. Generally, there are new and emerging technologies that need to be

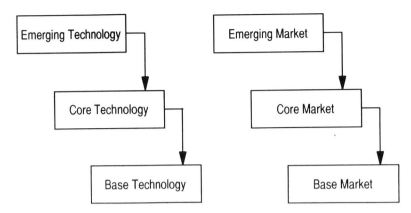

Figure 2.12 Three emergent stages for technologies, products, and markets.

considered for incorporation, generally with older and mature technologies, in a new system acquisition or production effort. Also there will be new markets. *Newness* is the key concern in the matrix entries in Figure 2.10, which indicates a basic 64-cell model of experiential familiarity with research, technology, and market. Certainly, much about many research efforts and the resulting developing technologies will be *new* to an organization considering development. But a potential innovation may involve a *new RDT&E* effort for technology development in a familiar market area for the involved organization. Or the development may involve a *new technology or system,* AND a *new market.* Also, these newness characteristics may exist for the industry in general—or for a nation considering some sort of sponsorship of industrial development. Additionally, there are questions of existing technologies with which a new technology must be integrated, and experiential familiarity with the system integration process can also be expected to vary. Associated with newness is *risk.* All facets of risk cannot be eliminated. Rather than striving for elimination, we should instead strive for applicable understanding and management of a variety of risk elements. Progress is associated with risk management, not risk elimination. We will consider the subject of risk management, in some detail, in our next chapter.

There are other, generally comparable, descriptions of these newness issues. In two excellent works, Wheelright and Clark [25,26] describe internal research and advanced development (R&D) and alliance, or partnered, efforts as needed to produce radically advanced technologies. They categorize the (end) product of these efforts as the result of advanced development. They also describe commercial development projects and programs. They further disaggregate these into the following:

Radical, or breakthrough, projects

Next-generation, or platform, projects

Derivative, or incremental, projects

A radical, or breakthrough, project will result in a new product for the organization and this will generally be associated with a new product line or process. A next-

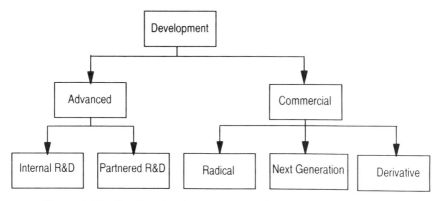

Figure 2.13 The five development types of Wheelwright and Clark.

generation, or platform, project will result in a substantially upgraded product and process that is based on the initial product and process. A portion of this initial product or process may be subject to radical change. A derivative, or incremental, project is one that results in fine tuning and incremental change and associated enhancements to the existing project and product. Figure 2.13 illustrates this conceptualization of the blending of RDT&E and system acquisition efforts according to these various modes of development.

Obviously, these descriptions can be blended. What appears to be a reasonable composite is to describe three levels of products—(1) base products; (2) next-generation, or core, products; and (3) revolutionary, or antedating or emerging, products—and then to note that base products are improved over the short term by derivative technologies and developments. They may be improved over the longer term by next-generation technologies and projects. On a still longer term, base products are improved through revolutionary technologies. By that time, of course, the critical capabilities of what was once a base technology will have undergone very significant change such that the new base product may not easily be recognized as the initial base product.

Another appropriate dimension for consideration is one which represents the type of unit involved in a possible technology or system effort, and the nature of the system itself. Horowitch and Prahalad [27] have identified three ideal organizational modes, and we can easily add a fourth that concerns the individual innovative researcher to obtain:

- The technological innovation process practiced by the individual researcher in an academic or industrial research environment.
- The technological innovation processes found in the system development practices of small, high technology oriented firms.
- The technological innovation processes found in the system development practices of large corporations with numerous products and markets.
- The technological innovation processes found in the system development practices of conglomerates, multipurpose organizations, and transnational multi-sector enterprises that may well have industrial research components.

These could easily be expressed in terms of new system developments. The types of research and technologies and systems most suitable for potential development in each of these four modes of operation will be different, as will the appropriate risk behavior. It would seem reasonable to augment this model to allow consideration of other modes, such as those due to individual entrepreneurs and government development assistance. Also, the taxonomy could be enlarged through consideration of the (potentially very different) roles of the technology or system developer in organizations of four generic sizes: individual, small to midsize, large, and multinational.

Of much importance also will be the type of *organizational culture* and the *coordination structures* or patterns of information flow and decision-making among the individuals and computer systems concerned with technology development. Since we examine these issues at some length in Chapter 7, we will not comment further on this aspect here.

Many have identified strategic purposes for RDT&E. They include the following objectives:

To expand and strengthen an organization's ultimate technological capabilities.

To make existing products and systems more competitive through newly emerged technologies.

To enable the organization to develop new opportunities through innovative products and systems.

The first of these objectives is especially appropriate for an organization whose RDT&E efforts comprise a profit center, with profits generally obtained by marketing the RDT&E capabilities of the organization to outside customers. The second and third objectives serve the system product development organization where a primarily profit center is its systems acquisition efforts, and where RDT&E is intended to support these efforts.

In a recent seminal work describing strategic management of research and development [28], three generations of research and development approaches are identified.

1. *First-Generation Management of Research and Development.*   We call this RDT&E in the terminology used here. It evolved in the middle of the 20th century and is a framework for R&D in which there is virtually no strategic involvement whatever. R&D is regarded as a potentially very necessary overhead item. There is no strategic identification of programs to be undertaken. There is often a culture clash between the research units of an organization and other units. Outside R&D, the view is that "R&D people do not understand organizational and business motivations." The insider R&D view is that "management is equivalent to bureaucracy and that bureaucracy stifles creativity." The inside R&D view is that everything will turn out fine and all that is needed is for management to send more money. The R&D view is that decisions on R&D priorities or targets should be set, if indeed there should be any priority or target setting at all, by R&D people exclusively. Since

anticipated results of the RDT&E efforts are not well defined, there is little effort at evaluation or systematic measurement and whatever effort there is many not be well directed.

2. *Second-Generation Management of Research and Development.* This evolved as a transition between the intuitive style associated with first-generation R&D and strategic, or purposeful, systems management modes. This involves increased communication between the RDT&E units and the rest of the development organization, and associated cooperation in identifying worthy individual RDT&E project efforts. The planning, however, is based primarily on existing core capabilities of the RDT&E groups and the rest of the existing organization. There is little effort to accomplish long-range technology and market forecasting and to position the organization for enhanced success. Often, there is greater reluctance than there should be to secure RDT&E efforts outside of the organization's RDT&E groups, even if this capability might be very useful for desired new products, systems, and services. Systematic measurement of RDT&E efforts is accomplished, but generally on an incremental project by project basis.

3. *Third-Generation Management of Research and Development.* There is much interactive and proactive interaction at the strategic systems management level with the efforts of the RDT&E groups in joint investigations of the structure, function, purpose, timing, and cost of RDT&E efforts to be funded, the balance between internal and external funding of these efforts, and the extent to which externally accomplished RDT&E will be supported. Obviously, different units will have different capabilities and potential contributions with respect to these seven facets of RDT&E support. The setting of RDT&E priorities and targets is in accordance with cost effectiveness analysis principles and the strategic objectives of the organization. Progress is evaluated at appropriate times relative to strategic objectives of the organization through a program of systematic measurements.

In the aforementioned work, the management and strategic context for these three generations of R&D management are established, as is the typical set of operating principles.

As is well known, and definitively established in this work, there is no single "best" generic type of approach to R&D or RDT&E. It is possible to identify at least two generic types of RDT&E: fundamental and applied. Fundamental RDT&E actually involves no DT&E. Applied RDT&E involves a large component of DT&E. We may further disaggregate fundamental RDT&E into curiosity-based fundamental research and directed fundamental research. In a similar way, we can disaggregate applied RDT&E into evolutionary RDT&E and revolutionary RDT&E. Figure 2.14 illustrates this typography of two higher level (fundamental and applied) and four lower level research modes.

1. *Fundamental RDT&E* or *fundamental research* involves a very large **R** and no DT&E at all. This involves scientific exploration into what is now unknown in the hopes of discovery of new knowledge principles. This can vary from curiosity-based undirected fundamental research to directed fundamental research. The objective of

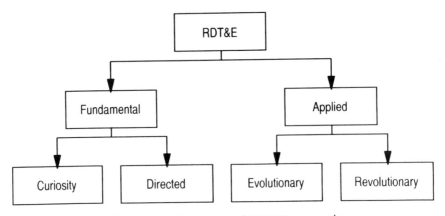

Figure 2.14   Illustration of RDT&E typography.

curiosity research is discovery for the sake of discovery. There can be no question but that some curiosity research has resulted in extraordinarily useful and ultimately pragmatic contributions to knowledge. While the risks associated with failure of the research to satisfy curiosity-driven motivations may be very small, there may be difficulties with purposeful applicability of the results obtained. The objective of *directed fundamental research* is to better position the organization and its personnel in areas projected to have major long-term strategic impact in terms of future competitive advantage. The risks of failure in fundamental directed research are often high, especially when there is not sufficient attention devoted to targeting it to organizational needs and objectives.

   2. *Applied RDT&E* involves a large component of **DT&E**. When there is only a small component of research, generally and almost always of a directed nature, it may be called *evolutionary RDT&E*. The goal of evolutionary or incremental RDT&E is to obtain generally small continual advances in the incorporation of promising emerging technologies into products and systems. Often, evolutionary research is very adroitly orchestrated and is characterized by low risk of failure and reasonable, but modest, returns. *Revolutionary RDT&E* is comprised of large components of research, and large components of development, test, and evaluation. The objective here is to obtain pragmatically results at a quicker pace than might be possible from fundamental research followed by evolutionary RDT&E efforts that are based on the results of the fundamental, directed research. There is often high risk and high potential return from revolutionary RDT&E.

   The major ultimately desired results of RDT&E are high quality, timely systems and products that serve organizational purposes in terms of providing customer satisfaction, competitive advantages, and favorable benefit–risk outcomes. There are necessary resource constraints. These include limited time for delivery, limited finances, limited talent, and risk associated with technologies, markets, and such external realities as government regulations. There are also organizational culture and leadership issues involved. Thus the choice of which RDT&E strategy to follow

RDT&E Modes	Curiosity	Directed	Evolutionary	Revolutionary
Technical Risk of Failure	Very Low	Low	Low, perhaps 0.2 to 0.3 probability	Moderate, 0.3 to 0.4 failure probability
Market Risk of Failure	Very high, perhaps 0.7 to 0.95 probability	Possibly as high as 0.5 to 0.7, risk is a function of organization management	Moderate, perhaps 0.3 to 0.5 probability	Low, 0.2 to 0.3 failure probability
RDT&E Time	Very long	Long	Short	Moderate
Size of Competitive Advantage	Very large if market results are successful	Substantial	Moderate	Large
Duration of Competitive Advantage	Very large, if market results are successful	Substantial	Moderate, but others may imitate	Substantial

Figure 2.15   RDE&E mode attributes.

is not necessarily a simple one. Clearly, it needs to be a third-generation strategy. But the mix of fundamental, evolutionary, and revolutionary RDT&E, which is most appropriate in any given situation, is not necessarily apparent on casual examination.

Figure 2.15 illustrates some of the likely attributes to be expected from these four different RDT&E modes. Figure 2.16 presents comparable information for the various product modes and technology development strategies that result from system acquisition. We will examine the important subject of risk management in Chapter 3 and markets and competitive advantage in Chapter 8.

We now turn our attention to specific systems engineering lifecycles for RDT&E. As with the case in general, we need to have three basic lifecycle phases: definition, development, and deployment. Here, we are talking about an iterative process that involves (1) defining the issues involved in selecting alternatives for RDT&E exploration, (2) development of actual RDT&E results, and (3) deploying successfully tested and evaluated results in operational situations that involve actual system or product acquisition.

We can pose the issues involved as a series of questions.

What are the strategic objectives of the organization?

What are the systems planning and marketing needs to support these objectives?

What are the systems acquisition needs to support these objectives?

What are new and emerging technology needs to support the system acquisition needs?

How can RDT&E best contribute to this need satisfaction?

Product Mode	Antedating	Core or Key	Base
Technology for Improvement	Radical	Next generation	Derivative
Technical Risk of Failure	Moderate, perhaps 0.25 to 0.50	Low, perhaps 0.1 to 0.25 probability	Very low, perhaps 0.01 to 0.1 probability
Market Risk of Failure	Moderate	Low	Moderate to high
Technology Development Time	Long	Moderate	Short
Size of Competitive Advantage	Large, if market results are successful	Moderate	Small to moderate, but decreasing over time
Duration of Competitive Advantage	Large	Moderate	Short

Figure 2.16   Risk and competitive advantages associated with different product modes.

What are the risks and cost effectiveness indices for various RDT&E strategies and targets?

What will the organization support through the results of RDT&E?

How can RDT&E be best integrated with systems acquisition or production and systems planning and marketing?

Each question needs an answer in order to frame an appropriate RDT&E policy.

A systems engineering RDT&E lifecycle for technology identification and assessment, associated research and development, and preliminary implementation or operational deployment is now suggested. The lifecycle is comprised of three major phases, which can be broken into several other more specific phases.

1. *Definition*—technology forecast and assessment and market forecast and assessment:
   (a) *scouting* and identification of requirements and specifications for candidate technologies for research and development;
   (b) *authoritative information documentation* concerning technological, economic, and market need for, and feasibility of, possible research and development technology options;
   (c) *assessment* and evaluation of the technologies and R&D strategies;
   (d) *selection* of appropriate technology for initial research, development, test and evaluation.
2. *Research and development*—as conducted by appropriate specialists in the area concerned, together with preliminary development.

3. *Deployment*—including preliminary operational implementation, test and evaluation:
   (a) *tracking* of the progress of development and implementation concerning all aspects of the candidate engineering technology;
   (b) *supporting* the operational implementation of the technology in ways that are meaningful to the technology itself and the results obtained in the earlier phases of the process;
   (c) *test and evaluation* of the results of the development effort in order to provide information and measurements that aid in supporting to the newly emerging technology;
   (d) *disengaging* from projects that prove to be productive and that have been successfully transferred or that indicate productivity or risk potentials beyond critical thresholds.

These phases can be used to identify and nurture emerging technologies to the point where they might lead to new products and services through a well orchestrated systems acquisition, production, or procurement lifecycle.

The critical attributes of successful technologies and possible RDT&E options should be identified in the initial phases of this systems engineering lifecycle process. Among these attributes are innovativeness, timeliness, risk, supportability, cost effectiveness, marketability, comparative advantage, and profitability of the products, concepts, or services that may result from the technology under consideration, which will or should evolve from the RDT&E effort.

Identification of productive environments for potential emerging technology development and transfer candidates is also a need. It is not difficult to characterize the appropriate environment as one in which a highly motivated group of people are free to pursue potentially unusual ideas, as well as not so unusual ideas. The environment should be one that recognizes and rewards success and that also recognizes the possibility of failure. And there must be a sense of urgency based on the awareness that the utility of any need, idea, or actual product can quickly be outdated. There are a number of considerations that determine the use of RDT&E efforts internal or external to a given organization, and the management structure, function, and purpose for efforts that are undertaken. We will examine many of these in our next chapter. There are also a number of organizational culture and leadership issues that will be discussed, primarily in Chapter 7. Figure 2.17 illustrates the sequencing of these phases; but it does not show the learning that *should* occur as the process is repeated in an iterative manner.

The *scouting and identification of requirements and specification* phase has as its goal the identification of societal and market needs, the translation of these into technology development and/or transfer needs and activities, and identification of the objectives to be achieved by implementation of the resulting technology as a product, process, or system. The effort in this phase should result in the identification and description of preliminary conceptual technology development and/or transfer characteristics that are appropriate for the next phase of the process. It is important to note that it is necessary to translate operational deployment needs into

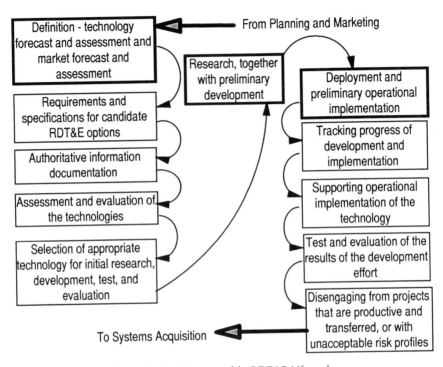

Figure 2.17   One possible RDT&E Lifecycle.

requirements and specifications in order that these needs be addressed by the emerging technology RDT&E efforts that may potentially be undertaken. Thus we see that information requirements determination and associated specifications are affected by, and affect, each of the other phases of the RDT&E lifecycle.

As a result of the scouting and identification of requirements and specifications phase, there should exist a clear definition of alternative technology development and transfer issues such as to permit a decision on whether to undertake the authoritative information documentation and assessment phases. If the scouting effort indicates that marketplace and societal needs can be satisfied in an efficacious manner, then documentation should be prepared concerning specifications that have resulted from this preliminary conceptual first phase of effort. Initial specifications for the following phases of effort should typically also be prepared, as they will be needed in order to do an assessment of candidate technologies.

At the end of this phase, preliminary documentation objectives and plans for the assessment effort are also determined. In general, each phase of effort should always include plans to implement the next phase of the effort.

Authoritative information documentation includes preparation of definitive position papers on each of the identified candidate technologies. This should be accomplished in considerable detail and should encompass all of the important areas of concern that we have just discussed. The authoritative preliminary conceptual design typically results in specification of the content, associated architecture, general design constructs, and research agendas for the product, process, or service that should result from this effort. The primary goal of this phase is to develop conceptualization of a prototype that is responsive to the requirement identified in the previous phase and the organizational and market needs that drive the effort. Preliminary concept papers, prepared according to the requirements specifications, should be obtained from this effort. *Rapid prototyping* is desirable in many cases as an aid in preparing illustrations of likely results. Various feasibility facets, and the potential costs and benefits from the RDT&E effort and the resulting technology, should be investigated as a part of this phase.

The desired product of the *assessment* phase is a set of detailed evaluations of the proposed alternative technology initiatives. There should exist a high degree of evaluator confidence that a useful product, system, or service will result from the detailed technology development and transfer effort that is a by-product of RDT&E, or the entire effort should be redone from phase 1, or possibly abandoned. Another result of this phase should be a refined set of specifications for the supporting and disengaging phases of the effort.

After RDT&E technology development projects are selected and funded, there is need for *tracking* of the efforts of the team that will be engaged in the specific technology development effort. A preliminary development product, design, process, or system is produced at the end of the *supporting* phase of the support process. This will generally not be a final design, but rather the result of implementation of prototype designs and development products. User guides for the product should be produced such that realistic test and evaluation of the results of the effort can be conducted.

Preliminary evaluation criteria are to be obtained as a part of scouting and authoritative information documentation phases, and possibly modified during the following two phases of the effort. A set of specific requirements for *test and evaluation* are evolved from the objectives and needs determined in these earlier phases. These should be such that each objective measure and critical evaluation issue can be measured by at least one test and evaluation instrument or measure. It is important that test and evaluation metrics be interactive and proactive across and throughout the entire RDT&E effort. Of course, there is necessarily a specific phase in the RDT&E lifecycle, after more or less final results are obtained, in which the overall RDT&E product is examined for integrity.

If it is determined, as a result of this test and evaluation phase or earlier, that the emerging technology under development cannot meet technology and marketplace needs, the process reverts iteratively back to an earlier phase, and effort continues with potentially modified objectives and redirected efforts. An important by-product of evaluation is determination of ultimate performance limitations for an operationally realizable technology, and identification of those protocols and procedures for use with the technology that will be most effective in achieving overall goals.

The last phase of the RDT&E lifecycle effort is *disengaging*. This will occur when the technology is ready for transfer to the system acquisition lifecycle for full-scale production and introduction into the marketplace. Alternately, disengaging should occur when consensus is reached that further continued development of the technology will yield little benefit compared to the costs involved in obtaining this benefit.

This systems engineering lifecycle for RDT&E efforts and associated technology development process is doubtlessly extensive and exhaustive. Of course, it needs to be applied with wisdom and maturity. This is particularly the case since exhaustive, time-consuming continual changes in systems requirements may prohibit the lifecycle process from ever being completed. An important advantage of the process just described is that it allows for formal consideration of the interactions among the phases of the effort and attempts to view the "whole" process within a contextually realistic setting. This is necessary because there are many needs to identify potentially innovative technologies at the earliest possible point in the initial research phase such that the development of these emerging technologies can be enhanced and nourished, especially with respect to the potential for their ultimate development into new products, and processes that result in these products. Doing all of this will enable the organization and its people to make existing products better and to make better new products.

Seven strategic planning phases, which also become major ingredients in successful systems engineering for RDT&E, are the following:

1. The identification of an overall strategic plan for the organization.
2. The identification, based on this strategic plan, of RDT&E, acquisition, and marketing objectives and programs that will meet these objectives.
3. The identification of specific projects that are to be covered by the program plan.
4. The identification of a number of representative alternative projects for the RDT&E, acquisition, and marketing programs.
5. The evaluation of these and interpretation within the context of strategic objectives such as to enable selection of a portfolio of suitable alternatives for implementation and appropriate mix of people and disciplinary specialties to ensure success.
6. Identification of incentives that will encourage the foregoing to occur.
7. Identification of the required changes required to implement the projects, and actual implementation of these projects.

A potential difficulty in interpreting some of the commentary presented here is in making the assumption that fundamental research will feed into applied RDT&E, and that this will lead to product or system acquisition and associated manufacturing, and that marketing will then commercialize the resulting products. We must therefore remark that this view of systems management, as illustrated in Figure 2.18, is rather incomplete. It can be significantly improved by realization of the needs for interaction and feedback across the various phases of the lifecycles, and the proactive direction of the overall effort from a strategic position. Figure 2.19 illustrates some of these additional needs.

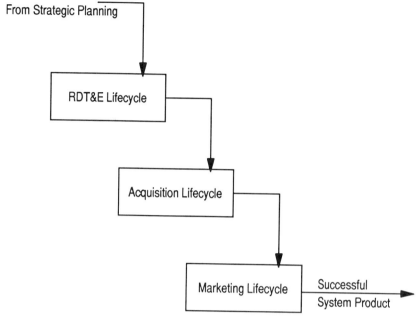

Figure 2.18 Improper linear step-by-step view of innovation through systems management.

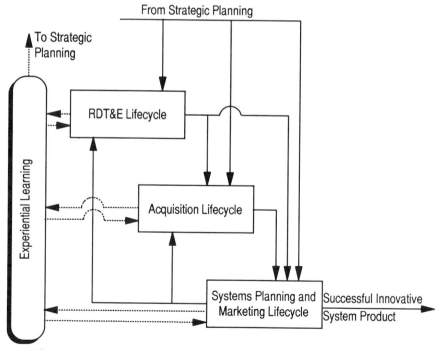

Figure 2.19 The iterative and interactive nature of systems management.

The development of an appropriate lifecycle for RDT&E, new product development, and marketing, as well as the associated systems management processes,
should include strategic quality assurance and management efforts at each of the
lifecycle phases in order to ensure reliability, applicability, and maintainability of
the evolving systems product. We will examine some of these issues later, especially
in Chapters 4 and 6.

We have made a number of comments concerning systems planning and management in our efforts thus far. We now turn our attention to an examination of some
systems engineering lifecycles for this facet of organizational efforts.

2.3   SYSTEMS PLANNING AND MARKETING LIFECYCLES

In this section, we will identify a number of lifecycles for systems planning and
marketing. Also, we continue our discussions of marketing, as one of three lifecycles in systems management.

Systems planning and marketing are intended to ultimately provide requirements
for a system, product, or service that is superior to others that are available. They
are also intended to provide support for development of new systems, products,
and/or services that provide competitive advantages. A major test of whether the
organization is making existing products better, or whether it is providing new and
innovative products, is that the products and services provided should meet customer needs in terms of total quality satisfaction. Thus there is both a technology (or
product or service) ingredient and a market (or customer) ingredient in systems
planning and marketing. As we have noted, this requires technology research and
associated technology forecasting and assessment. It also requires customer and
market research and associated market forecasting and assessment.

There are risks associated with technologies and with markets. Risk management
is needed relative to both technology and market for the successful technology
direction and management that comprises systems engineering. The major risks are
as follows:

External competitive risks or risks associated with poor estimates of the competition relative to a product or service.

   Risks due to competing products and services that may be perceived as yielding equivalent or greater cost effectiveness.

   Risks due to substitute products that, while not entirely comparable to the
   product of an organization, are perceived as suitable substitutes for it.

   Risks due to new products and services, which may be perceived as yielding
   equivalent or greater cost effectiveness.

Customer risks

   Risks due to poor estimates of the demand and market potential for a given
   system, product, or service type.

   Risks due to poor estimates of the perception of the value of our system,
   product, or service.

Risks due to the bargaining power of customers, who may command lower prices or special product functionality and features, because of their size and dominant influence in a given market area.

Risks due to major market segmentation on the basis of demographics, geography, social and cultural perspectives, and behavioral characteristics and the associated difficulty of marketing if the market is not easily segmented.

Technology risks

Risks associated with not anticipating, or falsely anticipating, new and emerging technology breakthroughs.

Risks associated with poor estimation of our ability to develop an emerging technology to the extent needed for incorporation into a system development effort.

Risks associated with the power of technology suppliers to successfully bargain for exorbitant prices for their products if they command a dominant position in a technology sector where there are few, if any, substitutable and equivalent technologies.

Risks associated with technologies and products and services that cannot be "scaled up" to enable upgraded or derived products with enhanced potential.

Compatibility risks associated with not being able to integrate a new system product, or service into an existing or legacy system.

Cost and schedule risks

Risks associated with not being able to afford appropriate marketing efforts.

Risks associated with not being able to afford sales and advertising expenses needed for success.

Risks associated with poor estimates of the cost of technology development efforts and resultant inability to deliver on time, or at all.

Risks associated with poor estimates of the time required for system development, and the resultant inability to deliver on time and within budget.

These risk categories are not at all unique. We will explore other risk taxonomies at pertinent points in our later efforts, especially in the next chapter.

There are, of course, a plethora of risk-related issues. These concern the relative sophistication of both the system's organization and the customer or user group. They concern both the estimated market share currently held by the organization, relative to an existing product, and the estimated growth rate possible for this product if development and maturation of the product continues at a given rate. This is the sort of picture of markets that is considered in classic market analysis efforts. The result of an analysis based on these concerns might lead to an image of four types of product–market–market growth interactions shown in Figure 2.20. This sort of notion can easily be expanded. For example, we can attempt to estimate or measure the market potential for a prospective new product versus the technology potential of the organization. The resulting competitiveness illustration might appear as in Figure 2.21. We provided a similar discussion and illustration previously

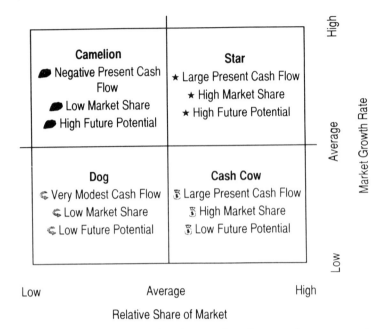

Figure 2.20   Classic market share and market growth rate concepts.

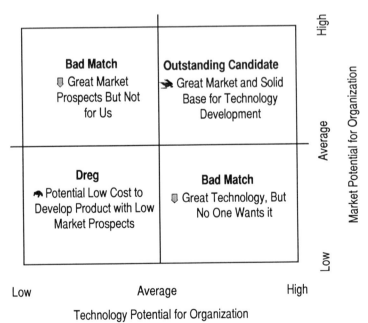

Figure 2.21   Assessment of success potential for technology market mixes.

in terms of the newness matrix of Figure 2.11. In most respects, Figure 2.11 encompasses these latter two figures in that it indicates not only the present state of markets, technology, and products but the familiarity of the organization with these. Further complicating the picture is the presence of errors in estimation associated with these estimates. The subject of human error is an interesting one and a very relevant one for our efforts here. To explore it would, however, take us quite a bit far from much of the rest of this effort. The reader is encouraged to consult Chapter 9 of [1] and especially [29, 30] for a discussion of the many ways in which human and organizational slips, lapses, and mistakes may be committed.

The objectives of systems planning and marketing are as follows:

- To identify potential customers or markets for the products of an organization and their needs as associated with the critical core capabilities of the organization.
- To identify and measure the characteristics of product or system concepts that will potentially fill these needs.
- To indicate the needs for product and technology refinements to meet these needs.
- To introduce prototype products to a selected sample consumer market.
- To manage the actual introduction of the operational product itself.

Measurements are needed to accomplish activities associated with realization of each of these objectives.

Appropriate measurement instruments for marketing include questionnaires, interviews, construction and use of scenarios, and prototyping. These and other approaches are described in [14] and [31, 32]. A number of questions need to be asked. These include the following major questions [33]:

Does the potential opportunity augment and enhance to unique and critical core capabilities of the organization?

Is the potential opportunity one that fits the structure, function, and purpose of the organization?

If the opportunity does not presently fit structurally, functionally, or purposefully, is it appropriate to initiate reengineering efforts to adapt the organization to the opportunity?

Is the opportunity one where the organization can establish and sustain competitive advantage?

How does the organization pursue the potential opportunity in a cost effective manner?

How do these strategic and tactical issues relating to market and organizational issues translate over to strategic, tactical, and operational issues that affect RDT&E, system acquisition or production, and product pricing and sales?

One of the very first efforts in systems planning and marketing is to make an assessment and forecast of technologies and markets relevant to the base and core capabilities and objectives of the organization. Generally, a market forecast and assessment should be associated with a technology assessment and forecast. However, there are important interactions across these two efforts.

In technology forecasting and assessment, we accomplish the following:

1. We identify all distinct technologies and supporting technologies, or subtechnologies, appropriate to the organization and market under consideration. This includes identifying the best features associated with present competitor's products and the technologies that make this value-added possible.

2. We identify the possible future development scenarios and the likely change paths for key technologies.

3. We determine the technologies and likely changes that are most important for increased competitive advantage in the organization.

4. We identify the organization's present capabilities with respect to developing these new technologies, and the likely costs and benefits associated with making these changes.

5. We integrate these findings as the technology forecast and assessment for the organization under consideration.

6. We select a portfolio of technology development strategies, such as to enhance the ultimate competitive advantage of the organization.

7. We implement action plans to bring about these developments, including coordination of the technology development with the market-based efforts that led to identification of the need for a technology forecast and assessment.

We can implement this suggested approach to TF&A for any of the modes for RDT&E:

Fundamental
   Curiosity
   Directed
Applied
   Evolutionary
   Revolutionary

We can also implement it for either of the modes for a product or technology that is a result of emerging technology development:

- Antedating product enhanced through radical technology infusion
- Core or key product enhanced through infusion of next generation technology
- Base product enhanced through infusion of derivative technology

There are a number of appropriate objectives for systems planning and marketing:

1. To provide an applicable framework for evolving planning and marketing strategy and tactics.
2. To assess the situation through exploring the major external forces, including both opportunities and threats, that influence the market in a given sector of activity.
3. To accomplish technical and market forecasting.
4. To identify and define a planning and marketing strategy that is compatible with internal strengths and weaknesses, including fundamental organizational capabilities and culture.
5. To prepare resource allocations for RDT&E, systems acquisition and production, and postproduction marketing efforts that fully implement the deployment phase of system acquisition.
6. To gain internal acceptance for the planning and marketing action plans.
7. To implement marketing tactics concerning product or system pricing, distribution, and communication with potential customers.

Each of these may be cast as phases in the lifecycle of a systems planning and marketing effort. These phases could then be illustrated as in the process model for planning and marketing.

The use of modeling for planning purposes is almost essential for success. In fact, the notion of planning is inevitably associated with the notion of a model. We continue this section by developing some graph theoretic notions related to planning models. These representations are also very useful for communicating the results of a planning effort.

Much intellectual activity, including planning, has been stimulated by, motivated by, or created from attempts to construct a "model" of a system. A simple reasoning process leads to this conclusion.

- We plan in order to better manage the future.
- Future events are necessarily associated with uncertainty and precision.
- We can only develop a perspective on what will likely occur in the future because of some model that we have about how the future will evolve from the present.
- These models may be static or dynamic, and they may well be based on the intuition that comes from much experiential familiarity with an issue, or they may be very formal models appropriate for situations in which there is not much experiential familiarity to use as a guide.

A model is an abstract generalization of an object or system. Any set of rules and relationships that describes something is a model of that thing. When we model systems, we enhance our ability to comprehend their nuances and subtleties, and to understand the relations among the elements internal to the system, and the relations between the system and the external environment into which it is imbedded. A typical result of a systems engineering model is the opportunity to see a system from several viewpoints. A system model may be viewed as a physical arrangement, as a flow diagram, and/or as a set of actions and consequences that can be shown graphically through time as a simplified picture of reality. A set of algorithms, often but not necessarily a set of differential or difference equations, is used to describe a formal model of a system.

Developments and improvements in modeling methodology have become more important as systems have become more complex. Usually, systems evolve as an aggregate of subsystems interacting with one another to create an interdependent whole. Some methods for coping with such interacting subsystems will be discussed in various later efforts in this text. Our major focus is not on the subject of modeling, however, and there are many contemporary efforts that do discuss this subject in depth.

Although models of systems may be constructed at any level, we are particularly concerned here with models and associated forecasting methods for systems planning and marketing. In many organizations, the system for planning and marketing, RDT&E, and system acquisition or production have evolved almost independently of one another. This evolution is a deterrent to overall synergism, in that these subsystems are not coordinated to expend their energy in concert for the organization as a whole. If we understood these subsystems and their interactions more clearly, overall organizational productivity could be potentially enhanced. The complex nature of each of these organizational systems must be understood and their interdependence with one another must be explored and comprehended in order for this to happen. It would therefore seem apparent that a representation of these systems and their interactions will enable increased communication between groups concerned with these systems. A methodology for organizing representations of these seemingly independent subsystems will hopefully diminish the difficulty in envisioning their functioning as an integrated whole.

People have functioned from the beginning of time with mental models of the relationships across elements in systems that are of interest to them. Human comprehension of complex issues is, however, constrained by several underlying limitations.

- There are an infinite number of possible relations among the elements of a complex system.
- Our comprehension of these elements is decidedly finite.
- There are limitations of natural language that affect our ability to fully comprehend the structure, function, and purpose of a large system.
- Our ability to construct models of these systems for better comprehension and understanding is thereby limited.

For these reasons, informal mental models of complex systems usually prove to be inadequate at best in enhancing our understanding of complex large scale issues.

This is also readily apparent when we consider and accept the defects of mental models that result from the aforementioned limitations.

- Mental models are often, but not necessarily, poorly defined in terms of structure, function, and purpose.
- Often, all the elements of a mental model are difficult to identify, and the interaction between elements is not clearly indicated.
- Assumptions needed to define a mental model are often treated as well-fixed and understood elements or relations.
- It is often not easy for us to communicate mental models to others.
- We cannot manipulate mental models effectively in order to determine the sensitivity of the model's output to changes in assumptions.

Each of these defects taken separately creates confusion, but as these defects combine and interact, understanding of complex issues and systems is severely hampered. We postulate that an appropriate systems engineering methodology and framework may be used to transform mental models into forms that are better defined, with clearer assumptions, easier to communicate, and more effectively manipulated.

There are four principal activities involved in construction a formal model of an issue or situation:

1. We need to identify the purpose(s) associated with the modeling effort.
2. We need to identify the functionality associated with these purposes, and the associated relevant problem elements.
3. We need to structure these problem elements.
4. We need to identify the parameters within this structure.

There are also a number of ancillary efforts associated with testing and validating the model in order to assure it as a trustworthy model.

Systems engineering and systems management efforts—either from initial efforts to create an effective process or product line, or intermediate efforts that involve modifying an existing process, or efforts leading to the actual product itself—are efforts that can be facilitated by effective planning, including marketing. Creation of an effective plan is necessary. Several questions are important.

Can the past and current states of organizational concerns relating to the issue at hand be measured?

Does a need for the proposed product or solution exist?

Is there an appropriate technology base to support the RDT&E that is potentially needed?

Are there relevant measures or metrics associated with what is to be planned to realize the product or solution?

Is the time frame realistic?

Will the plan be accepted and understood by those who will have to carry it out?

Responsibility for creating and supervising the conduct of a plan has traditionally rested with management. It is generally accepted that there are seven primary and classic tasks of management.

1. *Planning* comprises identification of alternative courses of action that will achieve organizational goals.
2. *Organizing* involves structuring of tasks that will lead to the achievement of organizational plans, and the granting of authority and responsibility to obtain these.
3. *Staffing* comprises the selection and training of people to fit various roles in the organization.
4. *Directing* refers to the creation of an environment and an atmosphere that will motivate and assist people to accomplish assigned tasks.
5. *Coordinating* involves the integration and synchronization of performance, including the needed measurements and corrective actions, to result in goal achievement.
6. *Reporting* ensures proper information flow in the organization.
7. *Budgeting* ensures appropriate distribution of economic resources needed for goal achievement.

This POSDCORB theory of management is a very common one and is described in almost all classical management texts.

It is quite clear that these functions are not at all independent of one another. As details of these functions are provided in essentially any introductory management guide, we will not pursue these in any further detail here. It is important to note that, collectively, these are the tasks of general enterprise management. They apply to systems management in its planning activities, which involve anticipation of potential difficulties and the identification of approaches for detection of problems, diagnosis of causes, and determination of promising corrective actions. They apply also to systems management and its control activities, which involve controls exercised in specific situations in order to improve efficiency and effectiveness of task controls in achieving objectives.

Planning is a prominent word in much of the foregoing. We can identify three basic types of plans or levels for plans: organizational plans, program plans, and project plans. One of the major differences in these types of plans is the duration of the plans. Organizational plans are normally strategic in nature and can be expected to persist over a relatively long time. Program plans are intended to achieve specific results. For large programs, it is generally desirable to disaggregate the program plans and controls into a number of smaller projects. This leads to a natural hierarchy within the structure of an organization.

In order to conduct these management tasks effectively, one needs a clear statement and understanding of objectives and the interrelations among objectives. Also needed is a method of determining priorities for the objectives based on their relative merit and the costs of implementing them. Thus the need for a value system is evident.

Systems planning and marketing should be innovative processes that necessitate both broad comprehension and understanding on the part of those involved in the activities associated with creating and implementing a plan. Four often-cited key components of planning are (1) definition of the purposes to be obtained and objectives to be served by the plan; (2) identification of current position or situation assessment of the organization with respect to the objectives; (3) assessment of the likely internal and external environmental factors influencing the past, present, and future; and (4) determination and implementation of the best plans and strategic systems management policies.

Definition of objectives or goals that are appropriate for organizational purposes is a normative component of a planning. It involves a statement of what ought to be. Identification of one's current position with respect to these objectives for the planning effort goal is the descriptive component. It involves a "what is" determination. Knowledge of all environmental factors influencing the past, present, and future allows one to establish the planning horizon. It is necessarily associated with time and evolution over time. Determination of the best policy or plans—as based on the objectives, knowledge of the current environment and state of the organization relative to the environment, and assessment of the likely future environment and time frame—is an analytic component of planning. It involves "what to do and how to do it."

These components, illustrated in a slightly different form in Figure 2.22, are clearly applicable to any phase of a systems engineering problem. These are really just a restatement of the three steps of systems engineering: formulation, analysis, and interpretation. Hill and Warfield [34] have introduced several tools that are conducive to the transformation of mental models to a more visible, comprehensible format. The tools are particularly helpful in establishing descriptive scenarios, axiological components of the normative scenarios, and definition of objectives for use in systems planing. The following discussion is based in part on this work.

The descriptive component of a plan involves the existing situation. Elements of the descriptive component of a plan include the major actors or participants in a plan, the roles they play, and the interactions of the environment with the specific program being planned. The normative component, or axiological component, of a plan necessarily reflects a set of values adhered to by those who establish the objectives and purposes for the plan. This set of values may include such elements as costs and benefits, or value, to the unit ultimately served by the product or service being considered, as well as economic benefits and costs that may accrue to the organization itself.

Frequently, the highest level systems planing objectives are axiological in nature and relate to the satisfaction of more than one of the basic human needs that were illustrated in Figure 1.18. These include physiological, security, belonging, self-esteem, realization of potential and self-actualization, autonomy, and aesthetic

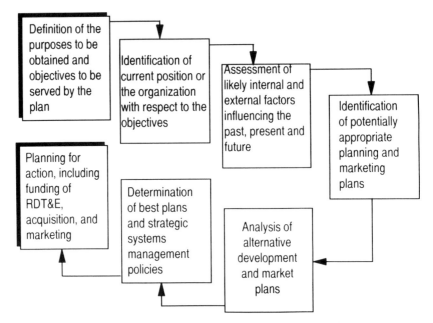

Figure 2.22   Generic steps associated with systems planning.

needs. The systems planning objectives then range from these axiological levels to some objectives that may be quantifiable and measurable. The kinds of systematic measurements that are needed include and may be classed as logical, numerical, probabilistic, and axiological.

The normative component of systems planning consists of a typically verbal description of the desired program state after appropriate plans have been implemented and the associated environment for the organization at a specified set of future points in time. It is this component within which program objectives are defined. The concepts associated with the identification of objectives and purposes for a plan appear to be trivial, but this is not at all so. Two simple facets concerning development of objectives are self-evident.

- If we have a clear idea of what we are trying to accomplish, the chances of accomplishing it are greater.
- We can generally only make meaningful progress toward what we are trying to make progress toward.

It is not clear that these are always addressed in practice. This necessarily associates systems planning, and associated marketing, efforts with the systems engineering and systems management process.

We must be very clear with respect to definition of objectives and their measures, the activity of pursuing the objectives, and the evaluation of results based on agreed-upon objectives and measures. It is usually not at all a trivial matter to establish

Figure 2.23 Hierarchy of systems planning elements.

objectives that can be formulated, organized with respect to structure, evaluated in a purposeful manner, and communicated effectively. A frequent problem in objective identification is the difficulty of recognizing and comprehending relationships between multiple, incommensurate, and conflicting objectives. This problem is usually confronted in trying to establish "higher order" or "lower order" objectives. Another problem in objective setting involves measurement because the numerous facets associated with the trustworthiness and effectiveness of a given program are often very difficult to quantify. In this connection, it is important to recognize that objectives can be posed as activities as well as or even independent of results or events. In a hierarchy we would generally see axiological objectives at the top of the hierarchy, policies (or activities) at the bottom, and various realities in between, as indicated in Figure 2.23. The identification and structuring of objectives or purposes, needs, constraints and alterables, and policies is very important in this regard.

An intent structure, or an objectives structure, enables us to organize and communicate, two of the primary functions of effective management. A major contribution of the intent structure is the use of a definition of an objective that takes the form following:

$$\text{to (action word)} + \text{(object)} + \text{(qualifying phrase)}$$

This form distinguishes between activities and events. If all three portions are contained (action word, object, and qualifying phrase), the general idea of what is being communicated is conveyed for all concerned.

The relationship among numerous objectives is the key to creating a hierarchy of objectives. There are two reasons for placing an objective "below" another in an objective tree or graph.

1. If objective B necessarily must be attained in order to attain objective A, then objective B is placed below objective A in the structure.
2. If objective C, either separately or in combination with other objectives, represents one alternative way of accomplishing objective A, C lies below A in the structure.

An objectives tree or intent structure is most useful as an aid in communication. Its utility as an aid in organizing objectives is enhanced by a number of available approaches such as intent structures and interpretive structural modeling [32,33,35] and structured modeling [36,37].

There are intuitive techniques, such as the why and how technique, for creating an intent structure or objectives tree. Although these intuitive techniques may sometimes lead to difficulties if applied to very complex problems, they are often quite adequate. Consider two scenarios in which we want to create an intent structure of objectives. In the first, objectives have not even been stated and will be created simultaneously with the structure. In the second case, a set of objectives has been defined, but the objectives have not been organized into an intent structure. In the first situation we can postulate an objective and then generate other objectives by asking why we are pursuing this objective or how we can pursue this objective. This results in an iterative sequence of whys and hows. If an intent structure is created in an upward manner, from lower objectives, the why technique is useful. If it is created in a downward direction, the how technique is helpful. Since an objective at any intermediate level can be viewed as a means toward an end at a higher level, intermediate objectives can be viewed as means or ends or both. However, top-level objectives are only ends and bottom-level objectives are only means.

Another intuitive technique for creating an intent structure when objectives are known is the rearrange-and-tape technique. The name describers the technique quite adequately. Objectives are placed on individual cards and arranged in a hierarchy. Upon reevaluation they are successfully rearranged until a satisfactory hierarchy of objectives is arrived at. The why and how relations are useful here also. Figure 2.24 illustrates a relatively simple objectives tree associated with planning for organizational implementation of a total quality management (TQM) system in an organization. We will examine TQM-related issues in Chapter 6.

It is important that an appropriate starting place be found in order to successfully attack an issue that requires determination of a systems plan. When the issue or problem is complex and large in scope, that effort becomes all the more difficult and important. Each phase of systems planning and marketing, regardless of the number of phases used to evolve the planning and marketing strategy, involves *formulation, analysis,* and *interpretation.* It is of particular interest here to discuss the formulation step for systems planning and marketing. This can be described in terms of three related steps: problem definition, value or objective system design, and system synthesis or alternative option generation.

There are several generic products of the problem or issue definition step that are particularly relevant to systems planning and marketing. Basically, we need to accomplish the following.

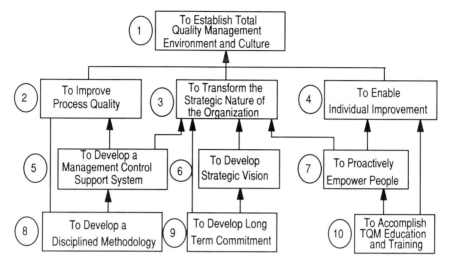

Figure 2.24 Simple objectives tree for total quality management.

Assess the situation associated with systems planning and marketing.

Identify a descriptive scenario, explaining the nature of the problem and how it came to be a problem, and presenting as much history and data as can be prepared with available resources.

Choose an appropriate and well-conceived title for the problem or planning and marketing issue that is in need of resolution.

Determine the customers or clients who will be served by a solution to the problem.

Develop an understanding of what disciplines or professions are relevant to an attack on the problem.

Assess the scope of the problem.

Identify the needs of the customer or client group that are to be resolved by the proposed systems planning and marketing solution.

Identify the constraints that must be associated with appropriate alternative courses of action.

Identify the alterables, or facets of the existing situation that may be changed, which are associated with appropriate alternative courses of action.

These efforts should also be associated with some amount of partitioning of the problem into relevant elements, some isolation of the subjective elements of the problem, a description of interactions among relevant elements of the problem, and a description of how these problem definition variables impact the situation that has been assessed.

Doing this will result in an introduction, background, and discussion of the problem, which ensure that everyone connected with the program has the same understanding of it. Relationships between elements can readily be shown using a

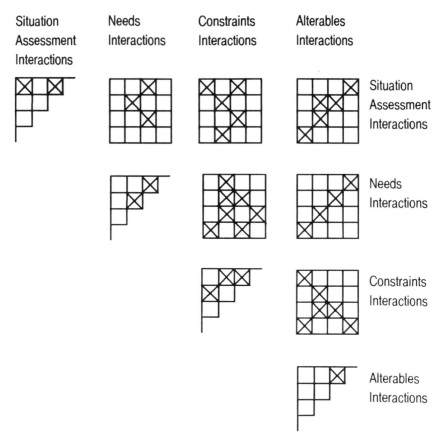

Figure 2.25 Problem definition interactions and linkages.

self-interaction matrix. We can apply this approach to all four of the problem definition variables—situation, needs, alterables, and constraints—to result in the sort of problem definition linkages shown in Figure 2.25. Problem definition, regardless of whether we are discussing systems planning and marketing or any of the other efforts in a systems engineering study, is generally an outscoping activity, as it enlarges the scope of what was originally thought to be the contents of the problem.

Associated with the problem definition effort in issue formulation, we need to accomplish value system design and systems synthesis. An objectives graph or tree for the program in question will be an important end product of this effort. Objectives measures should be given much emphasis as well since they are needed in order to determine success or failure with respect to achieving identified purposeful objectives.

Most philosophers will partition value into two levels called extrinsic (or instrumental) value and intrinsic value. Valuation by money is an example of extrinsic evaluation. Intrinsic values are qualities that are good in themselves and do not depend on anything else for their value. Goodness, truth, happiness, and beauty are classic examples of intrinsic value. Intrinsic values are matters of taste or style. Thus extrinsic values are associated with means used to attain the ends in life, whereas intrinsic values are associated with the basic ends themselves. Interestingly, intrinsic values do not decrease as they are used, but often increase, whereas extrinsic values are diminished as items possessing extrinsic values are consumed. In most traditional business and management planning, extrinsic values are given much more consideration than intrinsic values. This can lead to difficulties as intrinsic values are likely to be much longer lasting. Of course, products with extrinsic value can be used to satisfy intrinsic values.

In complex individual and organizational settings, in both the public and private sectors, a decision maker must frequently allocate resources among alternatives and system elements that compete for the same resources. As we have noted, this is a generally difficult task that is aided by a comprehensive analysis and interpretation effort. Approaches to this end are developed in detail in [1] and [2] and the many references contained in these two efforts. As far as our efforts here are concerned, we need note that value is a relative term, which is associated with various alternatives in a decision analysis problem. The term value system will be used to refer to the set of interacting elements, which provides a basis for decision making.

Value system design is the transformation of the properties of some thing into a format amenable to instrumental or extrinsic valuation. This is inherently associated with measurement, and an inherent part of the value system design portion of an issue formulation effort is to be sure that appropriate measurements are possible.

Allocation of resources represents a value judgment. If we can characterize the value judgment in a manner that relates to human capabilities and human needs, then the judgment is amenable to reasoned criticism. Consider a hypothetical crisis such as black clouds of polluting smoke dominating the environment in a typical industrial small town, which has much of its population employed by the polluting industry. If we dispose of the industry, the workers move on to other areas and the pollution problem is resolved. this solution does not relate to human capabilities and needs, although it rids the town of the pollution. The value judgment implied in the example is specifically a decision to eliminate pollution and thus eliminate much of the town's population. Structurally, there were no alternative solutions postulated and no valuation was exercised, extrinsic or intrinsic. The problem is also approached at the level of symptoms, and not institutions or values. Sadly, this sort of mindless advocacy of symptomatic relief is not at all uncommon.

The conclusion of the process of value judgment is a decision. Decision is the expression of preference for a particular outcome from a class of outcomes. If a value judgment is an expression of preference, a proposed judgment that offers only one outcome must therefore be considered improper and incomplete, since preference implies comparison and this requires two or more class members. In simple cases of decision under complete certainty, there is a one-to-one correspondence between a preferred outcome and an alternative that will result in that outcome. In realistic situations, however, there is no such one-to-one correspondence. The realities of risk, uncertainty, and imprecision assure that the outcome that will result from selecting a chosen alternative is rarely known with precision. This leads to the subject of decision assessment, a subject examined in Chapter 7 of [1] and Chapter 5 of [2] and the references contained therein.

The systems engineer can provide much assistance to support decision making by efforts that involve constructing alternative future scenarios, structuring alternative solutions, developing procedures for reaching decisions, and communication of value judgments. Value judgments are frequently and particularly difficult because such value-related issues are often perceived in the two simultaneous categories— subjective and objective. These are two schools of philosophical thought concerning values and value judgments. The classical subjectivist is the proponent of situational ethics, wherein one reacts dynamically to the perception of the existing situation at the time of decision. An afterthought often expressed when the situation ultimately changes that the best decision at the time was made.

On the other hand, the objectivist admits that feelings are a part, but not the central part, of value judgment. The principal goal of value system design is the capability to cope with subjective issues using objective approaches. In fact, systems engineering methodologies can be exercised in an iterative fashion to arrive at value judgments more palatable to the subjectivist. The objectivistic approach to the value system design portion of program planning consists primarily of identifying values and objectives themselves. It also includes future projections. This identification of an objective, or an associated activity that will lead to objective attainment, suggests that it is possible to obtain value from the attainment of the objective or the pursuit of the activity. Thus selection of some identified objectives, or associated activities, for pursuit and the exclusion of others represents a value claim by the selector. This value claim may be explicit or implicit, depending on whether objectives and activities are identified using analytical or intuitive cognition before being selected for perusal. To explore this further would take us into areas of cognitive ergonomics that are discussed in Chapter 9 or [1] and elsewhere.

Selection of goals or objectives to be pursued represents a claim that these goals have a possibility of value. There is no basis for the belief that priorities established on a subjective basis will necessarily be any better or worse or even different from those established on an objective basis in a given situation. One objective in value system design is defining objectives, obtaining an appropriate structure for them, and ordering them in a hierarchical structure as in Figure 2.24. The same information can be shown on an objective self-interaction matrix as in Figure 2.26. Figure 2.26 contains less information than Figure 2.23 in that subordinations are not shown in the self-interaction matrix of Figure 2.26. Figure 2.27 illustrates the intent structure of Figure 2.24 in directed graph form. Figure 2.27b illustrates what is called a minimum edge adjacency matrix, M, that corresponds to the directed graph of Figure 2.27a. The reachability matrix is the path of length 1 of the directed graph representation of Figure 2.24. Figure 2.27c illustrates the structural model for this directed graph, or reachability matrix. It is obtained from M by the relation

$$R = (I + M)^n$$

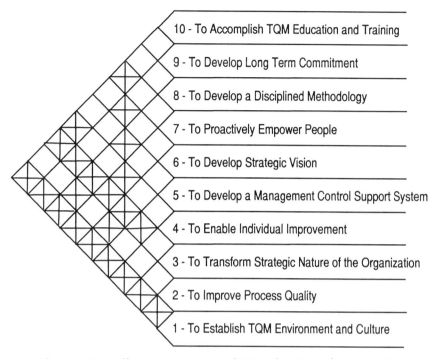

Figure 2.26 Self-interaction matrix of TQM objectives of Figure 2.24.

where I is the identity matrix and n is sufficiently large that R will not change if we replace n by $n + 1$. It is possible to show that n needs to be at most equal to the number of rows or columns in the matrix. There are a large number of graph theoretic results [38,39] that are useful in systems management and software engineering [40,41] and we only present a very small portion of the available results here.

It is also very helpful to relate the objectives to the problem definition linkages of situation aspects, needs, alterables, and constraints. In systems planning, the value system design activity consists of three distinct features:

1. Defining objectives and ordering them in a hierarchical structure.
2. Relating the objectives to needs, constraints, and alterables.
3. Defining a set of measures by which to determine attainment of the objectives.

The ordering of objectives is accomplished using the subordination matrix and the transitive relations "how" and/or "why." Definition of the objectives is obtained from dialogue among relevant parties to the planning endeavor. The needs, alterables, and constraints are obtained from the problem definition step.

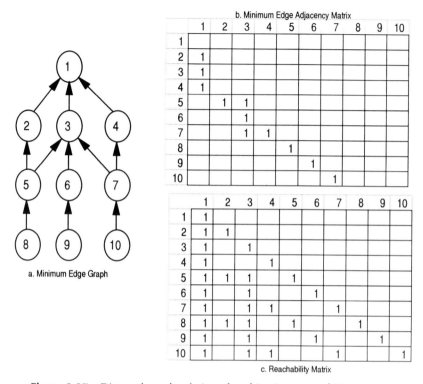

b. Minimum Edge Adjacency Matrix

	1	2	3	4	5	6	7	8	9	10
1										
2	1									
3	1									
4	1									
5		1	1							
6			1							
7			1	1						
8					1					
9						1				
10							1			

a. Minimum Edge Graph

	1	2	3	4	5	6	7	8	9	10
1	1									
2	1	1								
3	1		1							
4	1			1						
5	1	1	1		1					
6	1		1			1				
7	1		1	1			1			
8	1	1	1		1			1		
9	1		1			1			1	
10	1		1	1			1			1

c. Reachability Matrix

Figure 2.27 Directed graph relations for objectives tree of Figure 2.24.

There are several characteristics of a appropriate set of objectives:

Clear and concise, such that they can be widely understood and not misunderstood.

Outcome and results oriented, as contrasted with activity oriented, such that performance and purpose are recognized as the end product.

Appropriate, such that the objectives relate to the situation at hand.

Realistic, such that it is possible to achieve them.

Controllable, such that it is possible to implement alternatives that influence objective attainment.

Measurable, such that it is possible to determine the extent to which the objectives are attained by implemented activities or alternatives.

Thus appropriate measurements are vital and deserve much attention in systems management. This leads us naturally to a discussion of the alternatives that are identified to potentially implement plans and the system synthesis step of issue formulation. While our discussion here relates to planning, these remarks apply to any phase of the three lifecycles.

The system synthesis step is concerned primarily with the answers to three questions.

1. What are the alternative approaches, or courses of action, for attaining each objective?
2. How is each alternative approach described?
3. How do we measure attainment of each alternative approach?

The answers to these three questions lead to a series of activities and a set of activities measures.

The linkages of objectives, activities, activities measures, objective measures, and objectives is the system synthesis portion of planning. The identification of options, option generation, or the creation of the activities is a portion of system synthesis and also involves an application of value judgment. Figure 2.28 presents a

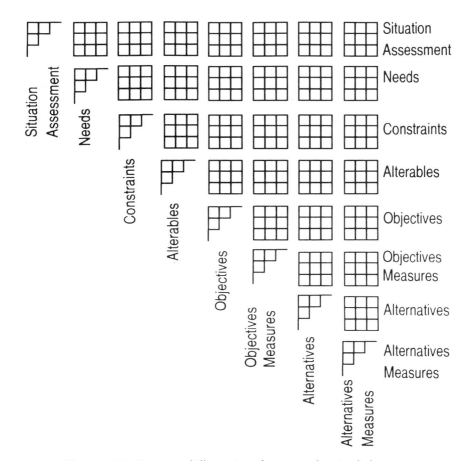

Figure 2.28 Conceptual illustration of systems planning linkages.

very generic set of systems planning linkages, which consist of the planning issue formulation steps associated with problem definition, value systems design, and system synthesis. Needs, alterables, and constraints are represented and linked as they were in the problem definition step. The self-interaction matrix of objectives and their cross-interaction with constraints are a formalized portion of the value system design. The identification, tilting, and structuring of the objectives are other portions of value system design effort that lead to completion of the planning formulation step. The system synthesis step may be created using the approaches we have presented. The objectives measures, activities, and activities measures are developed to satisfy the intentions expressed by the system objectives.

Determination of "a set of measures by which to determine the attainment of objectives" is of much significance and need in systems engineering. The topic of measures is expanded to include the measures of both objectives and activities, as the same discussion is pertinent to both. Selection of relevant sets of measures for objectives and activities is a portion of the value system design and system synthesis steps, respectively. The needs, alterables, constraints, objectives, and activities interaction matrices supply a set of elements with which the measure of objectives and activities can be deduced. A set of objectives measures should be visible to all persons involved in the planning effort.

Figures 2.22 through 2.28 provide many options for the development of relevant systematic measurements. These measures must be relevant to the overall planning objectives or intent, as determined by the objectives structure. If perception of objectives or intent of a complex project is not in conflict with the devised objectives measures, then satisfaction of those tasks associated with the measures is indicative of the success of the program. Systemic planing, by providing well-stated objectives and activities as well as interactions with needs, alterables, and constraints, offers an appropriate approach to the determination and designation of relevant measures of objectives and activities.

This concludes our formal discussion of systems planning and marketing. Clearly, much more could be said and has been said regarding this important subject. Our major goal here has been to illustrate the close interaction needed between the lifecycle of systems planning and marketing and the other lifecycles associated with systems engineering and management. We have also discussed a number of graphical approaches that are useful, especially for the initial phases, of the RDT&E and systems acquisition lifecycles. The result of using these approaches is a detailed and realistic view of the needed efforts at various lifecycle phases.

2.4 EVOLUTIONARY AND INTERACTIVE LIFECYCLE MODELS: SOFTWARE SYSTEMS ENGINEERING LIFECYCLE MODELS

We will now examine some of the evolutionary and interactive lifecycle models that have been proposed, generally for the development of software intensive systems. Although these lifecycles and the associated processes are specifically intended to enable the development of trustworthy software, they are also quite applicable to more general systems engineering development.

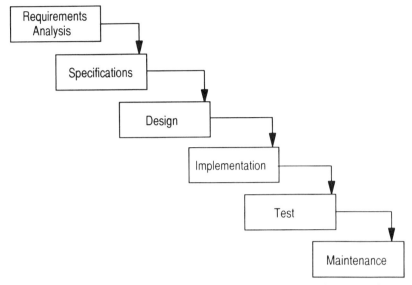

Figure 2.29 Waterfall lifecycle process model for software development of Royce.

2.4.1 Waterfall-Based Process Models

Credit for the introduction of a systems engineering-based lifecycle for use in software development is generally given to Royce [42] and this model is often denoted as a *waterfall model,* doubtlessly because of the geometric orientation used to depict the downward flow of developmental effort. Figure 2.29 presents this particular waterfall model for the software production lifecycle. It embodies existing systems engineering approaches to building large scale software systems.

Since its initial development and use by Royce, many modifications and iterations have been made to the waterfall model concept for software production. Often, the need for iteration and feedback across phases of the lifecycle is recognized. We have indicated this need in our earlier discussions of systems engineering process lifecycles.

Almost all of these modifications to the basic waterfall lifecycle model define five to seven phases for systems engineering software development processes. Boehm [43], for example, has been especially concerned with the economic importance of regularizing the development of software and has further developed and popularized the use of the waterfall lifecycle for software development. He identified an overall set of seven phases for the waterfall software development lifecycle, much as shown in Figure 2.30. In addition to illustrating seven phases and providing a very needed distinction between user needs and requirements and software requirements and specifications, this development process model shows primary information and development flow downward in the neoclassic waterfall patterns and secondary and corrective information flow to enable some iterative development. This similarity to the systems engineering lifecycle modeling construct is quite distinct in this model, as well as in the many others we discuss in this section.

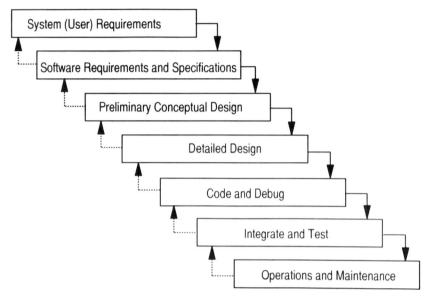

Figure 2.30   Waterfall software development lifecycle process model of Boehm.

The activities to be carried out at each of the seven phases to implement the waterfall software development lifecycle model of Boehm, illustrated in figure 2.30, are as follows.

1. *User and System Requirements Identification.* It is assumed that the software system user group and the systems requirements elicitation group are sufficiently informed about the intended purpose for the new or modified system such that they can identify and develop the system level requirements in sufficiently complete detail that preliminary software requirements can be specified. All this is to be done before preliminary design may be initiated. This phase of effort is very purposefully oriented.

2. *Software Requirements Identification and Translation to Software Specifications.* Development in the software requirements phase focuses on the outcomes of the user and system level requirements identification effort that was carried out in phase 1. This phase is concerned with translating the purposeful requirements identified in phase 1 into structural and functional requirements. Explicit concern is with structure and function in terms of (a) identification of the nature and style of the software to be developed; (b) the data and information that will be required for development and associated structural or architectural frameworks; and (c) the required functionality, performance, and various interfaces that may be needed throughout the remaining phases of software development. Requirements for both the system and the software are reviewed for consistency and then reviewed by the user to be certain that the software requirements faithfully interpret and meet the user-oriented requirements identified in the previous phase. A software require-

ments and specifications definition document is generally produced in this phase. It becomes a technology and management guideline throughout all subsequent development phases, including validation and testing.

3. *Preliminary Conceptual Design.* The software specifications developed in phase 2 are converted into a preliminary and conceptual software product design in this phase. Thus phase 3 is primarily aimed at the further interpretation of the software requirements and specifications in terms of software system level architecture. The product of this phase of software system development is identification and definition of the data structure, software architecture, and procedural activities that must be pursued in the next phase. Data items and structures are described in abstract terms as a guide to the detailed design phase to follow. Instructions that describe the input, output, and processing that are to be executed within a particular module are developed here. Preliminary software design involves representing the functions of each software system in a way that they may readily be converted to a detailed design in the next phase of effort.

4. *Detailed Design.* The effort in the preliminary conceptual design phase results in much insight as to how the system will ultimately work at structural and functional levels in order to satisfy the software system requirements and specifications that were identified in phase 2. Typical activities of the detailed design phase include definition of the program modules and intermodular interfaces, which are necessary precursors to writing source code for the software system under development. Specific attention is directed to data formats in the detailed design phase. Detailed descriptions of algorithms are provided. All inputs to and outputs from detailed design modules must be traceable back to the system and software requirements that were generated in phases 1 and 2. During this phase, the conceptual software design concept is fine-tuned.

5. *Code and Debug.* In this phase, the detailed design is translated into machine-readable code, generally in a high level programming language or perhaps a fourth-generation language. After the software design requirements are written as a set of program units in the appropriate high level programming language, the resulting code is compiled and executed. Generally, "bugs" are discovered, and debugging and recoding take place to ensure the integrity of the overall coding operations of this phase. Automated code generators can sometimes perform all, or a major portion, of this task and produce code almost guaranteed to be bug-free and warranted to satisfy the software specifications that were used as input to the code generator.

6. *Testing and Preoperation.* In this phase, the individual program units are integrated and tested as a complete system in an effort to ensure that the software specifications identified in phase 2, and hopefully the system level requirements specified in phase 1, are satisfied. The testing activities and procedures are primarily concerned with software logic functions. All programming statements should be tested at this phase to determine proper functioning, including whether inputs and outputs are operating properly. After system testing, the software is operated under controlled conditions to verify and validate that the entire package satisfies the software technical specifications, and ideally the system level requirements as well.

7. *Operation, Evaluation, and Maintenance.* This phase of the waterfall lifecycle is often the longest in time, and often the most costly as well. In phase 7, the system is installed at the user location and evaluated, and then put into actual operation. Maintenance is primarily the process of improving the system to accommodate evolving system level requirements as these occur and evolve over time.

These phases normally take place in the sequenced manner described. However, there may be considerable iteration and interaction among the several phases in the lifecycle. Each software development unit would generally adapt the activities in the lifecycle to accommodate such factors as (1) familiarity of the personnel in the software development organization with the software product being developed, (2) detailed needs of users for the software to be developed, and (3) economic, legal, system integration, and scheduling constraints. In an ideal situation, the above phases would be carried out in sequence. When all the phases have been completed, the software product is delivered and ideally performs, as intended by the client, in accordance with the original statement of requirements.

Actually, this purely sequential development rarely happens either for hardware or software development. What usually happens is that one or more phases need to be repeated, as a result of deficiencies in the process that are discovered after initiation of effort. It is easy to see how the need for this arises. As an example, software system development begins with elicitation of an initial set of user requirements. Development proceeds and an initial detailed design results. Upon viewing the results of this detailed software system design, the user discovers that certain requirements were omitted or misunderstood. The software development process than returns to the requirements phase. Further work is needed with the users until they are satisfied that their needs have been met.

As the software product evolves, it is often found that some of the initial requirements cannot be supported by the system because of earlier decisions. The user is involved to help identify a solution for the problem. This calls for revisiting the system requirements phase and tracking the implications of the newly resulting requirements through subsequent system development phases. However, such multiple iterations are seldom fully accomplished, generally because of contractual obligations or due to shortage of time or funds.

Another form of the waterfall software development lifecycle is that used by the U.S. Department of Defense, and denoted DOD-STD-2167-A [44]. A partial representation of this is shown in Figure 2.31. This model splits the system development process into hardware and software development efforts. This occurs as a result of the systems architectural design phase of the lifecycle. In this sense, this DoD standard incorporates some notions of concurrent engineering, a subject of much importance that we will briefly consider in a later chapter. There are a number of configuration management related efforts associated with this lifecycle. Many of them are discussed in Chapter 4 of [1]. The activities at the various phases in this lifecycle are sufficiently well defined by the titles for each phase and we will not discuss them further here.

Standards of this sort are intended to be evolving documents. As of this writing, a

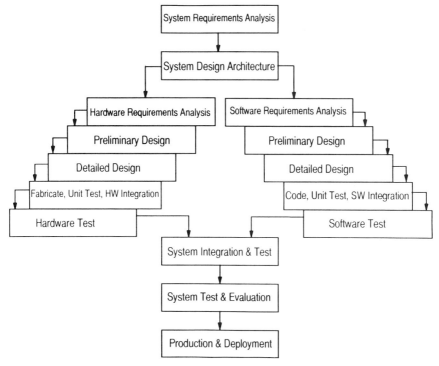

Figure 2.31 The evolving 2167A software development process.

revision to MIL-STD-2167A is in progress. It is known as MIL-STD-SDD [45], and is planned for issues as MIL-STD 498. There are three primary objectives:

1. To create a single DoD software development standard by merging the Defense System Software Development standard DOD-STD-2167A with the DoD Automated Information Systems Documentation Standard DOD-STD-7935A.
2. To ameliorate eight needs often perceived to occur in utilizing DOD-STD-2167A.
   (a) To improve compatibility with both incremental and evolutionary development models.
   (b) To improve compatibility with such nonhierarchical design approaches as those based on object-oriented methodologies.
   (c) To improve compatibility with computer-aided software engineering (CASE) tools.
   (d) To provide enhanced support for document preparation.
   (e) To provide enhanced support for use of reusable software.
   (f) To incorporate software management perspectives.
   (g) To enhance software maintainability and supportability.
   (h) To provide enhanced linkages to systems engineering.

3. To ensure compatibility with evolving DoD standards and directives including those for defense systems acquisition, defense systems acquisition management policies and perspectives, lifecycle management of automated information systems, and configuration and engineering management.

This standard recognizes the existence of three general lifecycle models for software development:

- The *grand design* lifecycle model is one in which there is a single pass through each phase of development. Figures 2.2, 2.29, and, to some extent, 2.31 represent grand design lifecycle models.
- The *incremental* lifecycle model is one in which there is an iterative sequence of builds, with each successive build incorporating more and more of the user requirements, as indicated by the resulting system specifications. The user requirements are initially identified. There are transformed to system level requirements and then to software requirements and specifications. Once established, the software specifications are presumably not subject to modification, except as part of maintenance after the software product has been deployed.
- The *evolutionary* lifecycle model is one in which the software system results from a sequence of iterative builds, as in the iterative lifecycle. However, it is recognized that user needs may well not be captured by system and software requirements and specifications initially. The evolutionary model allows for identification of a refined set of user needs and requirements prior to each successive build.

Figure 2.32 illustrates some of the salient characteristics of these three approaches to systems management of a software development lifecycle.

The determination of the systems management approach to development depends on a risk and operational need analysis of the particular software development opportunity at hand. Our interpretation of the general risks and operational need attribute scores for three systems management approaches for software development are as indicated in Figure 2.33. We will expand on our discussions of risk and risk management in the next chapter.

Lifecycle Model Type	One Pass Specifications Identification	Multiple Iterative Development Cycles	Deployment of Interim Software Products
Grand Design	**YES**	**NO**	**NO**
Incremental	**YES**	**YES**	**POSSIBLY**
Evolutionary	**NO**	**YES**	**YES**

Figure 2.32 Systems management approaches to DOD-STD-SDD lifecycle process.

Risk Item	Grand Design	Incremental	Evolutionary
System Too Large for One Time Build	High	Medium	Low
User Requirements Not Understood Enough to Specify	Medium	Medium	Low
Rapid Changes Expected in Technology	High	Medium	Low
Limited Staff or Budget Availability	Medium	High	Very High
Volatile System Requirements	Very High	High	Medium

Operational Need Item	Grand Design	Incremental	Evolutionary
Need Complete Software System on First Delivery	Medium	Low	None
Need New Software Capability Early	Medium	High	High
New System Must be Phased-in Incrementally	Low	Medium	High
Legacy System Cannot Be Phased-out Incrementally	Medium	Low	None
Legacy System Must Be Phased-out Incrementally	Low	Medium	High
Need Operational Experience to Identify Requirements	Low	Medium	High

Figure 2.33 Risk and operational need analysis to determine appropriate software development management approach.

The 14 technical development phases in the software development lifecycle are invariant across these three approaches to systems management of development: grand design, incremental, or evolutionary. These phases are:

Project planning

Establishing software development environment

System requirements analysis

System design

Software requirements analysis

Software architectural design

Software detail design

Coding and unit testing

Unit integration and testing

Computer software configuration item (CSCI) testing

Computer software configuration item (CSCI) integration and subsequent testing

Software system testing

Preparation for software use and support

Preparation for software delivery

While no specific sequence of these phases is prescribed by the standard, it is quite clear that they will generally flow in the sequence listed.

There are also a number of operational quality assurance activities that are carried out across many of these phases. These management control efforts, carried out as a part of systems management of software development, include the following:

Software product evaluations

Software configuration management

Software process evaluation, including detection, diagnosis, and correction of the development process

Joint technical and management reviews

Other management activities, including

Risk management

Control of security and privacy requirements

Subcontractor management

Interface efforts with the internal verification and validation (IV&N) organization

Identification and use of appropriate software management metrics

Figure 2.34 indicates how we might go about choosing appropriate phases for implementation across the multiple builds that may potentially comprise a particular systems management approach to software development. Regardless of which systems management approach is used, the generic phases are applicable.

There are some variations across the three systems management approaches. For a grand design effort, there would be only one build and each phase would be exercised, as in Figure 2.35. For an incremental or evolutionary approach to systems management, the first two phases would be exercised only once. The other phases might be repeated any number of times depending on how the specific

Activity	Build #1	Build #2	Build #3	Build #4	Build #5
Project Planning					
Establishing Software Development Environment					
System Requirements Analysis					
System Design					
Software Requirements Analysis					
Software Architectural Design					
Software Detail Design					
Coding and Unit Testing					
Unit Integration and Testing					
Computer Software Configuration Item Testing					
CSCI Integration and Subsequent Testing					
Software System Testing					
Preparation for Software Use and Support					
Preparation for Software Delivery					
Software Product Evaluations					
Software Configuration Management					
Process Evaluation and Correction					
Joint Technical and Management Reviews					
Other Management Activities					

Figure 2.34 MIL-STD-SDD framework for phased efforts across multiple builds.

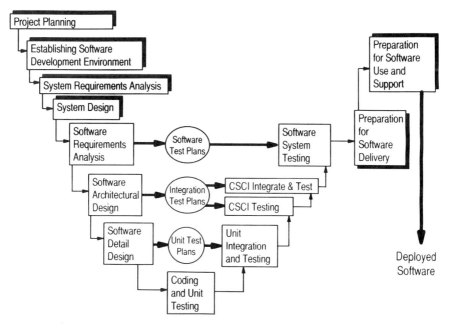

Figure 2.35   Interpretation of the MIL-STD-SDD lifecycle standard.

software development environment is defined. A portion of the third phase might be exercised only once in an evolutionary development environment. Much of the effort in this phase will be interactive in the evolutionary mode of development as a full set of software requirements is identified only as the development process evolves over time.

Also shown in this figure is the way in which the various evaluation and test efforts at the latter portions of the lifecycle evolve naturally from earlier phases in the effort. The shadowed blocks in the figure are not part of the software development effort itself. The first several of these, to the left in the figure, represent efforts involving definition. Those on the right side of the figure correspond to planning for delivery and deployment. Figure 2.36 illustrates those specifically identified management control efforts that comprise the systems management portion of the development efforts for this new standard. This new standard is intended to incorporate such lifecycles as the spiral lifecycle, which is specifically intended to cope with risk management issues in a better fashion than the waterfall lifecycle.

2.4.2 Spiral Lifecycle-Based Processes

The spiral model of the software systems engineering development lifecycle was introduced by Boehm in 1986 [46] and refined somewhat in 1988 [47]. Fundamentally, it represents several iterations of the waterfall lifecycle model with a possible alternative approach to software development at each iteration. For this reason, the spiral lifecycle is often called the incremental lifecycle. At each iteration, new

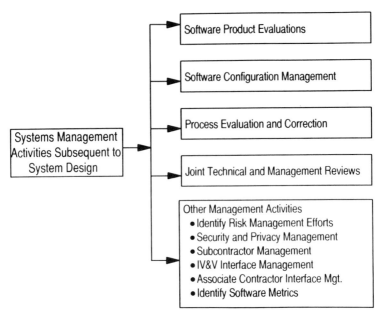

Figure 2.36   Systems management efforts specifically called for in MIL-STD-SDD.

system functionality is added. As also discussed in a previous subsection, we may have an evolutionary lifecycle process in which an effort is made to build most or all of the system on the first build. The first build is generally refined and improved on subsequent builds or iterations. Thus there is a very close relationship between an incremental lifecycle and an evolutionary lifecycle. Both fit under the general heading of an iterative lifecycle. It is the strong belief of this author that these iterations were not, in any sense, intended to be proscribed through general use of the waterfall lifecycle model. The specific focus placed by these iterative spiral-like models on the need for iterative development is very appropriate as well.

Use of a spiral lifecycle is intended to result in a risk-oriented approach to development of software products. Figure 2.37 illustrates some of the central concepts involved. When used as proposed by Boehm, the spiral lifecycle model requires the use of prototyping and also calls for an assessment of the *risk* of continuation of software development at each "cycle" of the development spiral. Only one cycle of fielding a system is shown in this figure. This extension of the conventional waterfall model explicitly incorporates the notion of feedback and iteration across the phases of the development lifecycle. The spiral lifecycle model essentially integrates the waterfall model with notions of incremental modifications needed to incorporate prototyping and risk analysis [48], and with systems management concerns as well.

The cycles or phases of development in the spiral model might well correspond to an individual phase, or a set of connected phases in a waterfall model. The first phase or cycle might correspond to development of a model, or prototype of user and system requirements. The second cycle or phase of development might then be

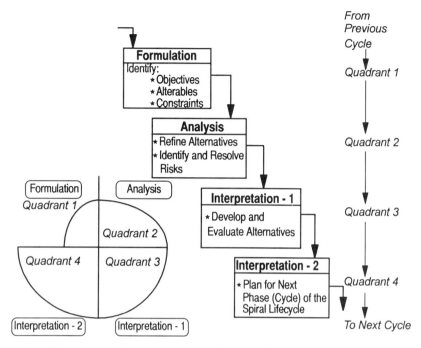

Figure 2.37 Flow activity at each cycle of the spiral lifecycle.

that of determination of software requirements and associated technical specifications. The third cycle might then correspond to preliminary conceptual or architectural design. The fourth cycle or phase of effort might be a final "grand design" one. The architectural or preliminary conceptual-design specifications obtained at the end of the system tree, and potentially modified by the operational prototype constructed in quadrant 2 of the fourth cycle, are used as the specifications for detailed design, code and unit test, integrate and test, and operations and maintenance efforts of the waterfall lifecycle.

The spiral model developments at each phase may be based on use of the three or seven steps of the fine structure of systems engineering, as discussed in Chapter 1. These seven steps follow from the three fundamental steps of formulation, analysis, and interpretation, which are implemented at each of the phases of the system lifecycle. It is convenient to view each cycle in the special model as corresponding to one or more phases of the lifecycle. Thus a phase or a collection of phases comprises a *cycle* or *round* of the spiral lifecycle. The steps undertaken in each round may be described as follows.

Formulation

1.1. We determine the *objectives* of the software to be developed within the particular cycle being considered in terms of such important factors as performance, functionality, and ability to accommodate change.

1.2. We identify the *needs, constraints,* and *alterables* for the particular cycle at hand, such as budgetary constraints and development time specifications. We determine whether an operational need can be satisfied by an identified software development effort, as generally specified by a configuration management plan.

1.3. We identify *alternative* means of satisfying the stated objectives for the particular phase of the product development under consideration through such alternative approaches as buying an existing software product as is, or designing a new software product, or modifying and reusing existing software.

Analysis

2.1. We determine and *evaluate* the alternative impacts in light of the objectives and the constraints. In this step, uncertainties that involve significant risk to the project at the particular phase under consideration will generally be identified.

2.2. We formulate cost effective strategies to address the risk management situation identified in the fourth step, or step 2.1. This may include prototyping, simulation, user interviews, benchmarking, analytic modeling, or a combination of these, as well as other strategies for risk reduction.

2.3. We determine the risk remaining to complete the project and select a sound development strategy that is based on the identified remaining risk. This might include rapid prototyping for areas associated with user interfaces and a waterfall lifecycle approach for interface risk control or for areas where software package development concerns are critical.

Interpretation 1

3.1. The original hypothesis—that an operational need can be satisfied by a software development effort—is tested. This may involve examination of market factors and the effectiveness of the particular software product, for example.

3.2. If the hypothesis tested fails, the development spiral is stopped.

3.3. If the hypothesis tested does not fail, another cycle of spiral development may be conducted until software product implementation and successful operational test and evaluation ultimately result.

3.4. Alternately, if the result of the hypothesis test is satisfactory but considerable risk remains, it may be desirable to disaggregate and partition the development effort through the creation of additional parallel spirals.

3.5. In any case, appropriate plans and schedules are developed, commitment to the plan is obtained, and the resulting plan is executed such that this cycle of development and evaluation of the software product is completed.

Interpretation 2

4.1. More explicit plans for the next cycle of development, if any, are unfolded. These plans for action to implement the next cycle are reviewed and commitment is made to them.

4.2. Systems management reviews are held, updates to various planning documents are made, and resources to implement the next cycle are committed.

The most interesting part of this spiral development lifecycle effort is the interpretation step, which occurs across two quadrants in the spiral lifecycle. Each time the interpretation 2 step is encountered, for each cycle of the spiral model, an assessment is made as to whether to continue or abort the development process. If the risk assessment indicates the project should be continued, another round of the spiral model commences. Otherwise, the development stops, and an evaluation of the entire project is made. As noted, the plan to continue the development may include partitioning the project into smaller pieces for ease of handling, or simply continuing along the path of the spiral model. The decision to proceed may be based on many things, from an analysis of individual design segments to a major review of the overall project requirements.

Figure 2.38 illustrates an activity matrix for the four-phase spiral lifecycle that we have just described. Note that we can easily take phase 4, which is in itself a

		Phases			
		Definition 1 Cycle or Phase 1 *User Requirements and Specifications*	**Definition 2** Cycle or Phase 2 *Software Requirements and Specifications*	**Development 1** Cycle or Phase 3 *Preliminary Concept Design Architectures*	**Development 2 and Deployment** or Phase 4 Final Development and Deployment
Steps	Formulation	Identify Preliminary User Requirements and Specifications	Identify Preliminary Software Requirements and Specifications	Identify Preliminary Conceptual Product Design Architectures	Identify Preliminary Final Development and Deployment Phases
	Analysis	Analysis of Risks and develop User Requirement and Specifications Prototype	Analysis of Risks and develop Software Requirements and Specifications Prototype	Analysis of Risks and develop Preliminary Conceptual Product Design Prototype	Analysis of Risks and develop Final Development and Deployment Prototype of Operations
	Interpretation - 1	Evaluate, Interpret, Select System Specifications	Evaluate, Interpret, Select Software Specifications	Evaluate, Interpret, Select Product Design Specifications	Implement Detail Design, Code, Integrate & Test, & Maintenance
	Interpretation - 2	Plan Software Specification Cycle	Plan Preliminary Development Cycle	Plan Final Development and Deployment Cycle	Plan extended Lifecycle for Software

Figure 2.38 Activity matrix for a spiral lifecycle.

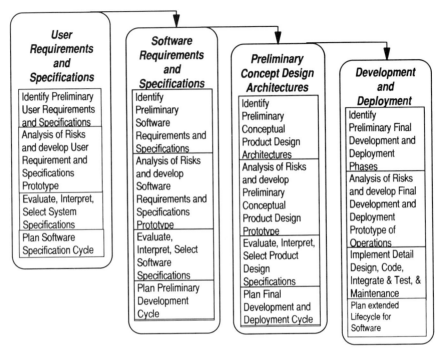

Figure 2.39   Waterfall lifecycle equivalent of the spiral lifecycle.

"grand design" development and deployment effort, and also describe it in terms of any number of subphases. The most likely description would be in terms of the last four phases of the lifecycle model of Figure 2.30. These were the four phases that were aggregated to form this phase. Figure 2.39 illustrates the waterfall lifecycle equivalent of this spiral lifecycle.

One version of the spiral model for a software development lifecycle is shown in Figure 2.40. This corresponds to the description that we have just provided and corresponds to that used by Boehm in his initial discussion of the spiral lifecycle model. Each cycle of the spiral lifecycle model is preceded by an effort and a risk analysis that ultimately results in a different type of prototype, or model, for that cycle of the lifecycle. This allows for an evaluation of *risk* before proceeding to subsequent activities associated with the phases of development of a software product. The opportunity to assess such important risk-related factors as cost, hardware requirements, reliability, and performance enables the software systems engineer to determine whether to continue with development, or to seek an alternative path for development, or to abandon the development process as unfeasible from a risk perspective. Figure 2.40 illustrates the cornucopia-like model used to represent the spiral lifecycle. The spiral model is a generalization and alternate representation of other lifecycle models and is particularly well-suited to incorporating submodels, or *cycles* or *rounds*, within the complete lifecycle effort. Clearly, its use is in no way restricted to software development.

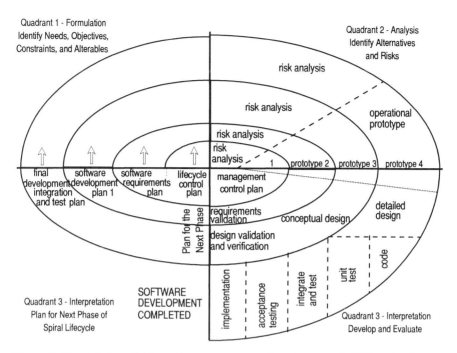

Figure 2.40 Spiral model for software systems engineering waterfall lifecycle of Figure 2.39.

In Figure 2.40, the length associated with the radial dimension is used to conceptually reflect the cost parameter as costs accumulate over the several phases of software development that have been completed at a particular point in the development effort. The angular dimension represents the cumulative progress made in software lifecycle development at any particular phase in the lifecycle. In the spiral model of Figure 2.40, prototypes that offer insight into the development task at hand are introduced. An iterative cycle of risk assessment, prototype construction, evaluation of the resulting product, and formalization of the various lessons that are thereby learned is introduced. This is assumed to continue until it is possible to develop a low-risk system requirements document. In this figure, we illustrate a situation where four prototypes are constructed. The actual number of prototypes that will be needed is a function of the development uncertainty and risk. Once agreement has been reached relative to the system requirements specifications, Boehm suggests using a standard "grand design" form of the waterfall model in order to manage the remaining efforts at final development, integration, and deployment.

Regardless of the specific lifecycle that results from systems management for a given software product development, it is clear that the four quadrants of each cycle are devoted to the following:

1. *Formulation,* in which the most relevant approach for the particular phase or cycle under consideration is identified and defined.

2. *Analysis,* in which risk identification and analysis are conducted to determine an appropriate systems management plan for development.

3. *Interpretation 1,* in which the results of this risk analysis are implemented in the form of a specific set of product development plans that effectively interpret the results of the analysis effort in cycle 2.

4. *Interpretation 2,* in which there are various management reviews and plans for action to implement the next phase or cycle, or to stop further effort if a high quality and trustworthy product has been developed or if further development is deemed somehow inappropriate.

2.4.3 Evolutionary and Other Lifecycle Processes

Since introduction of the waterfall and spiral lifecycle processes into the software development community, there have been a number of modifications to both of them. In this section, we will review and interpret some of these efforts and conclude with a discussion of a process taxonomy.

In an excellent work on software quality and management, Ould [49] identifies four process models.

1. The *V process model* is essentially the "grand design" model we discussed earlier. The term V process model is used because the waterfall lifecycle can be redrawn in a V-like configuration, as we have shown in Figure 2.35. This representation allows us to indicate that this seven-phase lifecycle may be viewed from the perspectives of user, systems architect, and programmer. One should also note that these perspectives are dominantly functional, structural, and purposeful. Figure 2.41 illustrates this V process view of the grand design approach.

2. Ould also identifies a "V process model with prototyping," denoted the *VP process model,* in which a prototype is constructed of the customer perspective, the systems architecture perspective, and the programmer perspective. The VP process model enables more complete treatment of risks and identification of more appropriate risk management strategies, at each of these first three phases. For the most part, this seems equivalent to the initial spiral lifecycle process model. While an illustration of this need not appear necessarily different from that shown in Figure 2.41, it is also possible to show these first three phases as being comprised of a set of phases, or subphases, that together comprise each of these initial three phases. These define, develop, and deploy prototypes for software requirements and specifications, software system level architectures, and detailed design architectures. Our interpretation of this is shown in Figure 2.42.

3. The *evolutionary process model* is one in which a complete, or virtually complete, software system is developed at each of several repetitions of the lifecycle. As we noted before in our discussions of MIL-STD-SDD, it is often the case that a mature specification of user requirements cannot be initially obtained. The major purpose of evolutionary development is to allow for the recognition of this and the resulting development of a refined software system at each successive

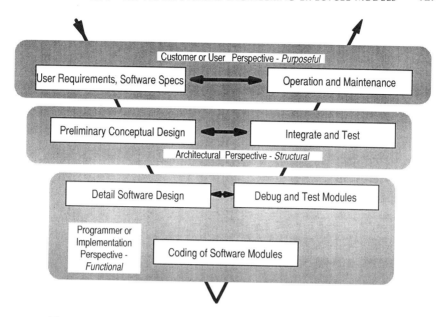

Figure 2.41 Interpretation of the grand design or V process model.

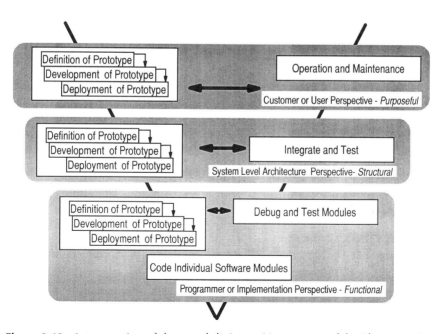

Figure 2.42 Interpretation of the grand design or V process model with prototyping.

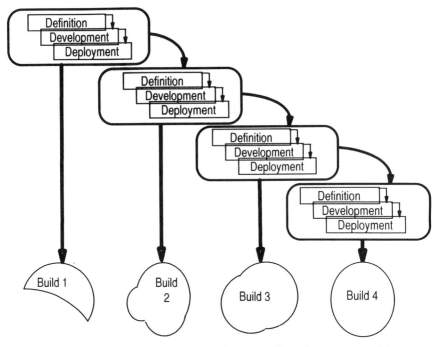

Figure 2.43 Illustration of the evolutionary lifecycle process model.

repetition or iteration of the lifecycle. There is no requirement that each lifecycle process be implemented in the same way in evolutionary development. Figure 2.43 indicates the most salient concepts in evolutionary development.

4. In *incremental development,* a kernel and one portion or increment of the system, *a,* is produced on the first iteration of development. Successive portions are added through iteration until the final incrementally built software system is completed. While the evolutionary lifecycle is intended to produce a potentially incomplete version of the whole system at each phase of development, the incremental lifecycle is one in which an intentionally incomplete version is produced initially and successive additional lifecycles of effort augment this until the whole system results. Figure 2.44 illustrates a conceptual view of the incremental development lifecycle.

Each of these lifecycle models may be thought of as comprised of a number of waterfall lifecycles. The actual development strategies may vary from one lifecycle to another. For example, reusable software may well be a major part of the prototyping strategy for requirements and specifications identifications in one lifecycle, but not in another. There are many activities associated with these lifecycles that are not shown in the illustrative figures. This is especially the case with respect to the numerous configuration management and control efforts that are needed.

One of the major purposes in use of any of these lifecycles is risk management.

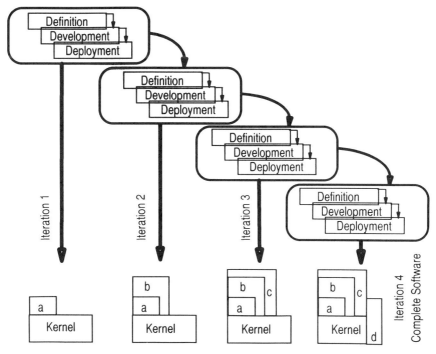

Figure 2.44   Illustration of iterative software process lifecycle.

Risk comes about at each of the three perspectives of development and at the overall systems management level.

- Systems management process risks involve those aspects of risk that are most closely associated with organizational management itself. These risks are associated with process errors in systems planning and marketing, RDT&E, and the acquisition or production process itself. Systems management process risks may be at a purposeful, structural, or functional level. Systems management risks at a purposeful level relate to organizational culture and incentives. Systems management risks at a structural level refer to risks associated with errors in choice of the lifecycle itself. Systems management risks at a functional level relate to the risks associated with the product itself. These product risks also have a purposeful, structural, and functional aspects.
- Product risk at a purposeful level relates primarily to risks associated with requirements and specifications failure.
- Product risk at a structural or architectural level relates primarily to risk associated with faults in the system conceptual design structure or architecture.
- Product risk at a functional level refers primarily to risk associated with human errors in program development.

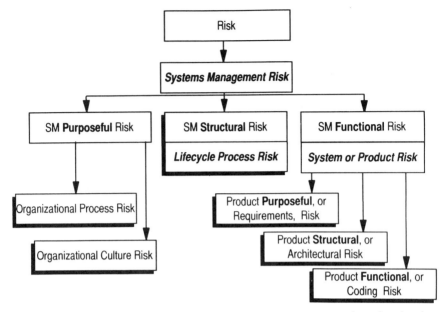

Figure 2.45   Risk taxonomy at systems management, process, and product levels.

Figure 2.45 illustrates this view of risk and risk management. In this figure, we use bold type to indicate the six structural, functional, and purposeful levels for systems management and the system or product. We use boldface italic type to indicate the six lowest level risk categories at which measurements should be taken.

One of the particular uses to which this discussion can be put is the identification of risk management and corrective adjustment approaches to enhance system productivity. These, as our discussions in Chapter 8 indicate, can occur at the levels of:

Systems management reengineering
Systems process reengineering
Product reengineering through
　　Requirements refinement
　　Architectural or conceptual design refinement
　　Detail design and coding refinement

We pay particular attention here to systems management and system processes. Software productivity through product level improvements is addressed, from a systems engineering perspective in [50] and elsewhere.

With respect to this present discussion, we could attempt to identify the structural, functional, and purposeful facets of the systems management process. There seems little to be gained in doing this, and the effort might well be somewhat circular. The detailed structure of the systems management process is just that of the lifecycle being implemented. Instead, it is potentially more relevant to indicate that the lifecycle process is comprised of a number of phases, each with a particular purpose, structure, and function. To achieve the purpose well requires appropriate performers, that the criteria for initiation of a phasewise effort be satisfied, and that criteria for a successful conclusion of the phased effort also be satisfied. The functional components of the process represent the requisite inputs and outputs for each phase. The structural components of the process represent the specific paths through which these inputs are transformed into the outputs.

While we could speak of the risks associated with each of these facets or components, it appears more appropriate to speak of the risk associated with a complete process implementation. Since a process is specified by the components we have just identified—that is,

Purpose
  Participants
  Initiation of effort criteria
  Termination of effort criteria
Function
  Inputs
  Outputs
Structure
  Structural description

and appropriate measurements of these, which provide specific indicators, we can formulate a table with these ingredients and use it as a management control checklist. With appropriate entries, this provides a very useful and rather complete descriptor of each complete phase in the lifecycle. A sample uncompleted checklist is illustrated in Figure 2.46 for a seven-phase waterfall grand design lifecycle. This checklist and its entries are much like those associated with such flowchart methods as the structured analysis and design technique (SADT) and diagrams described in detail by Marca and McGowan [51], or with the entry–task–validation–exit notation suggested by Radice and Philips [52].

The purposeful level has to do with the objectives for the systems management process. The structure of this is very specific to the phase that is being considered. It is highly desirable to augment this taxonomy with other risks and to develop an appropriate evaluation strategy such that it becomes possible to adopt an efficacious risk management strategy. We will expand on and augment these ideas in the next chapter and elsewhere in this text.

There have been a number of related descriptions of essentially the same lifecycles we discuss in this section. The Software Productivity Consortium used the term evolutionary spiral process (ESP) to describe modifications to the spiral lifecycle, which was initially based mostly on a VP development perspective to enable it to also accommodate evolutionary development. The MITRE Corporation has used the term managed evolutionary development (MED) [53] and there are doubtlessly other terms used as well for variations of the basic evolutionary approach.

	User Requirements Software Specifications	Preliminary Conceptual Design	Detailed Software Design	Coding of Software Modules	Debug and Test Modules	Integrate and Test	Operation and Maintenance
Purpose							
Participants							
Initiation of Effort Criteria							
Termination of Effort Criteria							
Inputs							
Outputs							
Structural Description							

Figure 2.46 Checklist for phased efforts in a lifecycle for software acquisition or procurement.

The evolutionary software development lifecycle model is based on the approach of building successively more functional prototypes. This is not a significant departure from the systems engineering approach to software development, as based on the waterfall model. We have indicated how the operational waterfall software development lifecycle may be recast to incorporate spiral, incremental, and evolutionary approaches. The evolutionary, incremental, spiral, and other such approaches can clearly be modeled by an interactive sequence of waterfall models. The concern should not be directed at the level of process in this regard, when it is found that risk management and trustworthiness issues have not been fully considered, but rather at the level of systems management. Thus we would not encourage stopping or getting off the lifecycle [54,55] but would strongly encourage appropriate use of systems management to implement high quality processes, or product lines, that result in high quality products.

2.5 SUMMARY

In this chapter, we have presented a number of lifecycles for systems engineering processes. It is normally very useful to think of a systems engineering process as being described by a number of phases that comprise the time dimension of systems engineering. We have described a number of lifecycle processes and related issues for the following:

Systems acquisition or production
Research, development, test, and evaluation (RDT&E)
Systems planning and marketing

We conclude our discussions with a presentation of some interesting contemporary developments in software systems engineering processes. It is now well known that software has been an especially troublesome area in which to produce trustworthy and cost effective systems. We conjecture that a major reason for this is that software engineering lifecycles are often approached as if they are systems acquisition lifecycles when, in reality, there is so much new development involved that there are many aspects of RDT&E lifecycles that need to be incorporated as well. This particularly manifests itself in the need for significant risk management for software productivity. This is the subject to which we now turn.

REFERENCES

[1] Sage, A. P., *Systems Engineering,* John Wiley & Sons, New York, 1992.

[2] Armstrong, J. E., and Sage, A. P., *An Introduction to Systems Engineering,* John Wiley & Sons, New York, (in press).

[3] Hall, A. D., "Three Dimensional Morphology of Systems Engineering," *IEEE Transactions on Systems Science and Cybernetics,* Vol. SSC 5, No. 2, Apr. 1969, pp. 156–160.

[4] Hall, A. D., *A Methodology for Systems Engineering,* Van Nostrand, New York, 1962.

[5] Hall, A. D., *Metasystems Methodology,* Pergamon Press, Oxford, UK, 1989.

[6] Beam, W. R., Palmer, J. D., and Sage, A. P., "Systems Engineering for Software Productivity," *IEEE Transactions on Systems, Man, and Cybernetics,* Vol. 17, No. 2, Mar. 1987, pp. 163–186.

[7] Beam, W. B., *Systems Engineering Architectures and Design,* McGraw-Hill Book Co., New York, 1990.

[8] U.S. Department of Defense (DoD) Instruction (DoDI) 5000.2, Sept. 1, 1987.

[9] U.S. Department of Defense, MIL-STD-499A and MIL-STD-499B, "Systems Engineering," May 1974 and May 1991.

[10] National Society of Professional Engineers, *Engineering Stages of New Product Development,* NSPE, Alexandria, VA, 1990.

[11] Gruenwald, G., *New Product Development, What Really Works,* NTC Business Books, Lincolnwood, IL, 1985.

[12] Allen, T. J., *Managing the Flow of Technology: Technology Transfer and the Dissemination of Technological Information Within the Research and Development Organization,* MIT Press, Cambridge MA, 1977.

[13] Makridakis, S. G., *Forecasting, Planning and Strategy for the 21st Century,* Free Press, New York, 1990.

[14] Porter, A. L., Roper, A. T., Mason, T. W., Rossini, F. A., and Banks, J., *Forecasting and Management of Technology,* John Wiley & Sons, New York, 1991.

[15] Alic, J. A., Branscomb, L. M., Brooks, H., Carter, A. B., and Epstein, G. L., *Beyond Spinoff: Military and Commercial Technologies in a Changing World,* Harvard Business School Press, Boston, MA, 1992.

[16] Brandin, D. H., and Harrison, M. A., *The Technology War: A Case for Competitiveness,* John Wiley & Sons, New York, 1987.

[17] Dertrouzos, M. L., Lester, R. K., and Solow, R. M., *Made in America: Regaining the Productive Edge,* MIT Press, Cambridge, MA, 1989.

[18] Betz, F., *Managing Technology: Competing Through New Ventures, Innovation, and Corporate Research,* Prentice-Hall, Englewood Cliffs, NJ, 1987.

[19] Monroe, J. G., *Winning in High-Tech Markets: The Role of General Management,*

Harvard Business School Press, Boston, MA, 1993.

[20] Kinnear, T. C., and Taylor, J. R., *Marketing Research,* McGraw-Hill Book Co., New York, 1983.

[21] Anthony, R. N., *The Management Control Function,* Harvard Business School Press, Boston, MA, 1988.

[22] Souder, W. E., "Improving Productivity Through Technology Push," *Research/Technology Management,* Vol. 32, No. 2, Mar. 1989, pp. 19–24.

[23] Sage, A. P., *Decision Support Systems Engineering,* John Wiley & Sons, New York, 1991.

[24] Roberts, E. B., and Berry, C. A., "Entering New Businesses: Selecting Strategies for Success," *Sloan Management Review,* Vol. 26, No. 3, Spring 1985.

[25] Wheelwright, S. C., and Clark, K. B., *Revolutionizing New Product Development: Quantum Leaps in Speed, Efficiency, and Quality,* Free Press, New York, 1992.

[26] Clark, K. B., and Wheelwright, S. C., *Managing New Process and Product Development: Text and Cases,* Free Press, New York, 1993.

[27] Horowitch, M., and Prahalad, C. K., "Managing Technological Innovation: Three Idea Modes," *Sloan Management Review,* Vol. 17, No. 2, Winter 1976.

[28] Roussel, P. A., Saad, K. N., and Erickson, T. J., *Third Generation R&D: Managing the Link to Corporate Strategy,* Harvard Business School Press, Boston, MA, 1991.

[29] Reason, J., *Human Error,* Cambridge University Press, Cambridge, UK, 1990.

[30] Rasmussen, J., Pejtersen, A., and Goodstein, M., *Cognitive Systems Engineering,* John Wiley & Sons, New York, 1994.

[31] Rouse, W. B., *Strategies for Innovation: Creating Successful Products, Systems, and Organizations,* John Wiley & Sons, New York, 1992.

[32] Sage, A. P., *Methodology for Large Scale Systems,* McGraw Hill Book Co., New York, 1977.

[33] Monroe, J. G., *Winning in High Technology Markets: The Role of General Management,* Harvard Business School Press, Boston, MA, 1993.

[34] Hill, J. D., and Warfield, J. N., "Unified Program Planning," *IEEE Transactions on Systems, Man, and Cybernetics,* Vol. 2, No. 5, November 1972, pp. 610–621. Also in Sage, A. P. (Ed.), *Systems Engineering: Methodology and Applications,* IEEE Press, New York, 1977, pp. 23–36.

[35] Warfield, J. N., *Societal Systems: Planning, Policy, and Complexity,* John Wiley & Sons, New York, 1976.

[36] Geoffrion, A. M., "Computer Based Modeling Environments," *European Journal of Operations Research,* Vol. 41, No. 1, 1989, pp. 33–43.

[37] Geoffrion, A. M., "FW/SM: A Prototype Structured Modeling Environment," *Management Science,* Vol. 37, No. 12, 1991, pp. 1513–1538.

[38] Harary, F., Norman, R. Z., and Cartwright, D., *Structural Models: An Introduction to the Theory of Directed Graphs,* John Wiley & Sons, New York, 1965.

[39] Roberts, F. S., *Discrete Mathematical Models: With Application to Social, Biological, and Environmental Problems,* Prentice-Hall, Englewood Cliffs, NJ, 1976.

[40] Steward, D.V., *Systems Analysis and Management: Structure, Strategy, and Design,* Petrocelli, Princeton, NJ, 1981.

[41] Steward, D. V., *Software Engineering: With Systems Analysis and Design,* Brooks Cole, Belmont, CA, 1987.

[42] Royce, W. W., "Managing the Development of Large Software Systems: Concepts and Techniques," *Proceedings WESCON,* 1970, pp. 1–70.

[43] Boehm, B. W., "Software Engineering," *IEEE Transactions on Computers,* Vol. 25, No. 12, Dec. 1976, pp. 1126–1241.

[44] U.S. Department of Defense, *Defense System Software Development,* DoD STD-2167A, June 1985.

[45] U.S. Department of Defense, *Military Standard Software Development and Documentation,* DoD STD-SDD (Draft), Dec. 1992.

[46] Boehm, B. W., "A Spiral Model of Software Development and Enhancement," *ACM SIGSOFT Software Engineering Notes,* Vol. 11, No. 4, Aug. 1986, pp. 14–24.

[47] Boehm, B. W., "A Spiral Model of Software Development and Enhancement," *IEEE Computer,* Vol. 21, No. 5, May 1988, pp. 61–72.

[48] Boehm, B. W. (Ed.), *Software Risk Management,* IEEE Computer Society Press, Washington, DC, 1989.

[49] Ould, M. A., *Strategies for Software Engineering: The Management of Risk and Quality,* John Wiley & Sons, Chichester, UK, 1990.

[50] Sage, A. P., and Palmer, J. D., *Software Systems Engineering,* John Wiley & Sons, New York, 1990.

[51] Marca, D. A., and McGowan, *SADT™: Structured Analysis and Design Techniques,* McGraw-Hill Book Co., New York, 1988.

[52] Radice, R. A., and Philips, R. W., *Software Engineering: An Industrial Approach,* Prentice-Hall, Englewood Cliffs, NJ, 1988.

[53] Reynolds, P. A., Ward, E. S., Gonzalez, P. J., Blyskal, J., Hofkin, R., Garfield, D., and Marple, J., "The Managed Evolutionary Guidebook: Process Description and Applications," Report MTR92W0000251, The MITRE Corporation, McLean, VA, Mar. 1993.

[54] McCraken, D. D., and Jackson, M.A., "Lifecycle Concept Considered Harmful," *ACM Software Engineering Notes,* Vol. 7, No. 2, 1982, pp. 29–32.

[55] Gladden, G. R., "Stop the Lifecycle. I Want to Get Off," *ACM Software Engineering Notes,* Vol. 7, No. 2, 1982, pp. 35–39.

Chapter 3

Risk Management

Systems engineering concepts are directly applicable to the development and integration of management and technological processes that support all major lifecycle functions needed to produce high quality and trustworthy systems. Information is the glue that holds together such functions as research and development, design, production, distribution, maintenance, and marketing in a total quality approach. Systems management deals with such issues as program and project management, technical direction of development, quality management, configuration management, and risk management.

A major purpose of the systems management function is to implement the strategic plan of the organization so as to provide a total quality approach, including associated risk management. In this chapter, we will examine a number of issues related to risk management. Systems engineering processes are inherently subject to risks of a variety of types. When risks materialize, they usually manifest themselves as cost issues, schedule issues, and technological failure issues that impact the product. These risks can be further disaggregated into a number of subordinate risk issues.

It is important to define risk. For our purposes, *risk* is the probability or likelihood of injury, damage, or loss in some specific environment and over some stated period of time. Thus risk involves two elements—probability and loss amount. A related concept is reliability. *Reliability* is the probability that a product or system will perform some specified end user function under specified operating conditions for a stated period of time.

In this chapter, we will examine a number of relevant aspects or risk management, including the effect of such facets as system quality and information requirements. Most of the other chapters also comment on various aspects of risk. Risk and risk management are associated with virtually every facet of systems engineering and systems management. Risk management involves realizing that decisions may lead to future events that cause adverse events; and developing a strategic plan and operational risk abatement tactics to manage and control risks in an acceptable manner. Ideally, we would like to forecast risk possibilities and implement plans to avoid unnecessary risks. We also need strategies to ameliorate the effects of risks that do eventuate. This requires several approaches to risk and risk management.

We can approach risk management in an inactive, reactive, interactive, or proactive manner. These approaches are relatively easily described.

1. In *inactive risk management,* we simply neglect to consider risk issues at all. We just do not bother to address, or even concern ourselves with, the possibility that things may not turn out as we intend. One might easily argue that this is not risk management. We would not disagree but prefer to call it bad risk management.

2. In *reactive risk management,* we attempt postmortem efforts to ameliorate the effects of risks that have materialized. This may involve crisis management efforts to extricate an organization from a significant mess. More often, it is concerned with getting rid of bad or defective products, often in the form of inspections, before they are delivered to consumers. This involves scrap and rework and therefore increased production expenses.

3. In *interactive risk management,* we are concerned with risk throughout each of the various lifecycles of various systems engineering efforts. This means that we pay particular attention to such needs as configuration management and project controls to ensure that each phase of each lifecycle is as risk free as possible in terms of the risk associated with the product of that particular phase.

4. In *proactive risk management,* we plan and forecast risk potentials and then adopt systems management activities for technical direction that control, to the extent possible, risk potentials across all organizational lifecycle processes. Ideally, we manage risk in a manner such that it is very unlikely that any unnecessary risk actually occurs. In this way, we avoid the scrap and rework associated with an exclusively reactive approach to risk management.

It appears clear that we should always approach risk management, to the extent possible, from a proactive perspective. Interactive risk management would generally be of much value, however, in that it will not be possible to prevent all risks from materializing through a proactive approach. Even interactive risk management will not always prevent some products from being defective. On rare occasions, crisis situations will develop even though we have implemented sound proactive and interactive approaches to risk management. Thus there is a role for reactive management, but it surely needs to be augmented and supported by interactive and proactive risk management. We will address this issue in a somewhat more general context in Chapters 6 and 7 when we consider quality management and organizational culture issues.

It is particularly necessary that risk management enables appropriate actions to deal with unfortunate situations that might possibly occur, as contrasted with react-ing to crises after they materialize. This reactive approach is really damage control. If a crisis actually eventuates, damage control is necessary. But, it is better to avoid crises situations, rather then to react to them. Of course it is better to react than not to react. There is virtually no circumstance that warrants an inactive approach to risk management.

Although we will provide a generic definition of risk later, risk can really only be defined in an actionable manner if we have identified organizational objectives and a meaningful set of program plans for the organization as an entity, as well as for specific components of the organization. We must also be able to deal with specific risks that have been identified and quantified, and with very general risks that have yet to be fully identified in terms of their hazard potential. Thus we must necessarily deal with issues that involve "known unknowns," or events with known proba-bilities of occurrence and known values, and "unknown unknowns," or events with imprecise probabilities of occurrences and imprecise specified hazard values. We will discuss all these situations in this chapter.

We can immediately partition risk management into two related components.

- In *risk program planning,* we forecast and assess the potential for risks. This involves formulation, analysis, and interpretation steps. In these we identify possible risks, determine alternative courses of action that will potentially ameliorate the effects of the various risks, determine the impacts of these alternative courses of action on the risks, and then evaluate and prioritize these such that we develop plans to avoid unacceptable risks, and operational risk control or abatement tactics to ameliorate the harmful impacts of those risks that do materialize.

- In *operational risk abatement,* we implement the selected abatement tactics such that we are able to monitor the situation so that we can *detect* an impend-ing risk situation, *diagnose* the cause of the situation, and *correct* it through selection of an appropriate risk abatement alternative.*

Figure 3.1 illustrates the structure of this suggested approach to risk manage-ment. Figure 3.2 expands on this by allowing for reactive, interactive, and proactive approaches to each of these.

We suggest an eight-step approach to the overall risk management strategy that will allow meaningful implementation of the risk management facets illustrated in Figure 3.2. These steps may be described as follows:

1. Provide an adequate support framework for identifying an overall risk man-agement strategy.
2. Analyze the major external forces that influence risk management strategies.

---

*The terms detection, diagnosis, and correction are very much equivalent to the terms formulation, analysis, and interpretation but are more appropriate for the particular case of the operational risk abatement aspect of risk management than these more generic terms.

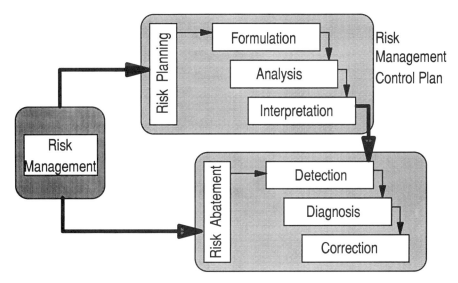

Figure 3.1 Generic lifecycle approach to risk management.

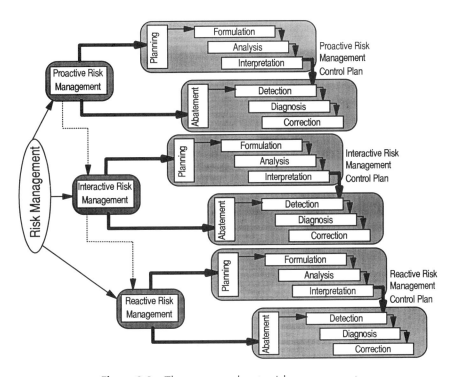

Figure 3.2 Three approaches to risk management.

3. Analyze the basic internal strengths and weaknesses of the organization as they influence risk management strategies, including cultural issues and process maturity issues.
4. Define an appropriate risk management strategy, including program plans for proactive, interactive, and reactive risk management.
5. Prepare budgets and allocate resources to risk management, at all three levels.
6. Communicate the risk management strategies, program plans, and operational risk abatement controls to all concerned parties.
7. Accomplish risk program planning through formulation, analysis, and interpretation efforts. These involve assessment of potential risk situations, the recognition and structuring of high risk areas, and the identification of possible alternative approaches to ameliorating risks through such efforts as project configuration management, work breakdown structures, task scheduling, modeling and analysis of the impacts of risk abatement alternatives, and assessment of these impacts such as to enable selection of appropriate operational risk management plans and tactics.
8. Operationalize the risk management plans through detection, diagnosis, and control efforts.

We will examine these issues in a detailed treatment. Several volumes could be written on the great variety of analytical support methods that potentially enable risk management; we can only present the highlights of some of these approaches here.

3.1 RISK

Certainty is rarely encountered in actual choice-making situations, and risk may be thought of as lack of full control over the outcomes of implementing a particular alternative course of action. Stated somewhat differently, risk reflects lack of full information or certain knowledge about the outcome that will result from implementing an alternative. If we had full information about what would result from implementing an alternative and if there were no uncertainties associated with what would happen, then there is really no risk. This does not suggest, in any sense, that such a risk-free outcome would be a desirable outcome. The outcome might well be free of risk, but it could well be very undesirable.

The traditional approach used to model risky situations employs probability distributions of the outcomes of alternative choices and the associated utilities of these outcomes. Risk and gamble are therefore essentially equivalent expressions. Slovic and Lichtenstein [1], Rowe [2], and many others have proposed that a gamble can be described by its location on four basic risk dimensions: (1) probability of winning, (2) amount to win, (3) probability of losing, and (4) amount to lose. These basic dimensions are assumed to be integrated into a contingency structure for decision making. Decision making, in this case, is a form of information processing. There are a number of other frameworks for the description of risk-

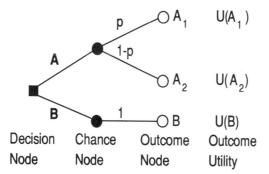

- **Certainty:** p=1, and the utilities of the outcomes are known.
- **Probabilistic Uncertainty:** p is known, 0<p<1, and the utilities are known.
- **Probabilistic Imprecision:** p is imprecise, and the utilities are known.
- **Information Imperfection:** p may be imprecise, the utilities may be imprecise.
- **Conflict:** the values of p and U may be changed by the action of an opponent .

Figure 3.3   Fundamental model of decision risk.

oriented choice making, including mean–variance models, in which risk preference is described in terms of mean risk and risk variance [3]. There are also a number of approaches based on stochastic dominance [4] of one alternative over another. These subtleties, and there are a great many of them, need not concern us here even though they are of importance for detailed risk studies.

Figure 3.3 represents a set of generic decision analysis based graphs of a decision node and the outcome nodes or states that may result from the decision node. Chapters 5 and 7 in [5] and the references contained therein describe the construction of decision trees and other decision structures in some detail. We summarize some of the most salient features here.

It turns out that there are five risk categories for decisions.

1. *Decision under certainty* issues are those in which each alternative action results in one and only one outcome and where that outcome is sure to occur. The decision situation structural model is established and is correct. There are no parametric or structural uncertainties. In other words, $p = 1$ in Figure 3.3. In the situation illustrated in Figure 3.3, we know that selecting option **A** will certainly result in outcome A_1 which has known utility or value $U(A_1)$. Selecting option **B** will result in outcome B with known utility $U(B)$. The optimum decision rule is a simple one. If we prefer utility $U(A_1)$ to $U(B)$, that is, if $U(A_1) > U(B)$, we should select option **A**. If this is not the case, we should select option **B**.

2. *Decision under probabilistic uncertainty* issues are those in which one of several outcomes can result from a given action depending on the state of nature, and these states occur with known probabilities. The decision situation structural

model is established and is correct. There are outcome uncertainties, and the probabilities associated with these are known precisely. The utility of the decision maker for the various event outcomes can be quite precisely established. This is the usual situation addressed in the majority of decision analysis studies. In terms of the structural model illustrated in Figure 3.3, we should select option **A** if and only if the expected utility of option **A** is greater than that for option **B**. Thus we select option **A** if $\{pU(A_1) + [1 - p]U(A_2)\} \geq U(B)$. Otherwise, we select option **B**.

3. *Decision under probabilistic imprecision* issues are those in which one of several outcomes can result from a given action depending on the state of nature, and these states occur with unknown or imprecisely specified probabilities. The decision situation structural model is established and is correct. There are outcome uncertainties, and the probabilities associated with the uncertainty parameters are not all known precisely. The utility of the decision maker for the event outcomes can be quite precisely established. In the situation illustrated in Figure 3.3, for example, we might be given the expression that p is unknown but in the range given by the inequality expression $1 \geq \alpha \geq p \geq \beta \geq 0.5$. We might further know that $U(A_1) = 1.0$, $U(A_2) = 0.0$, and $U(B) = 0.5$. It is now much more difficult to obtain the best decision. However, we do know that alternative **A** will dominate alternative **B** if the minimum value for the expected utility of selecting option **A** is greater than that for selecting option **B**. In this particular case, the expected utility of selecting option **A** is $\{pU(A_1) + [1 - p]U(A_2)\} = p$. The minimum value of p is known to be 0.5 and this is the maximum utility of option **B**, which is 0.50. Here, we can say that option **A** dominates option **B** and should be selected. In more complicated cases, it is nowhere near as easy to obtain the best decision as we suggest here for this simplified example. However, the same general approach is followed.

4. *Decision under information imperfection* issues are those in which one of several outcomes can result from a given action depending on the state of nature, and these states occur with imperfectly specified probabilities. The decision situation model is established but may not be fully specified. There are outcome uncertainties, and the probabilities associated with these are not all known precisely. Imperfections in knowledge of the utility of the decision maker for the various event outcomes may exist as well. In the situation illustrated in Figure 3.3, for example, we might be given the expression that p is unknown but in the range $1 \geq \alpha \geq p \geq \beta \geq 0.5$. We might further know that $U(A_1) = 1.0$ and $U(A_2) = 0.0$. The utility for option **B** is imprecise, potentially due to measurement inadequacy of some sort, and is given by the inequality $0.4 \leq U(B) \leq 0.70$. It is usually even more difficult to obtain the best decision in this case. We do know that alternative **A** will dominate alternative **B** if the minimum value for the expected utility of selecting option **A** is greater than that for selecting option **B**. In this particular case, the expected utility of selecting option **A** is $\{pU(A_1) + [1 - p]U(A_2)\} = p$. The minimum value of p is known to be 0.5. However, the maximum value for $U(B)$ is 0.70. Since this is not less than the minimum expected utility for **A**, we cannot state that decision **A** dominates decision **B**. If the maximum value for $U(B)$ were less than or equal to 0.50, we could have made this statement. In order to determine whether option **A** dominates option **B** and should be selected, we need to obtain higher quality

information in order to reduce the information imprecision. To explore this fully here would take us far afield of where we really wish to go.

5. *Decision under conflict issues* are those in which there is more than a single decision maker, and where the objectives and activities of one decision maker are not necessarily known to all decision makers. Decision under conflict issues may also be viewed as those in which *nature* is augmented or replaced, at least in part, by a not necessarily hostile challenger. We could further subdivide these issues according to information imperfection concerns. We shall not do this, as we will not consider decision under conflict issues in any detail here. They do exist and are the subject for a game theoretic or conflict analysis approach. Often, these result in very difficult analytical problems. Some recent effort [6] has been devoted to developing support systems that are user oriented and allow coping with these decisions under conflict issues.

Problems in category 1 are those for which deterministic principles may be applied. This condition of known states of nature ignores the overwhelming majority of issues faced in a typical private or public sector decision making situation. Many questions can be posed.

How will my customer base or constituency be affected?

What will happen to the cost or quality of my product or service if this solution is implemented?

How will the morale and organization of my workforce be affected?

How does the ever-changing institutional and societal environment bear on this decision?

What are the implications of this decision on other decisions I must make elsewhere in my organization?

It is rare that one can provide responses to questions such as these without bringing forth a number of risk and uncertainty considerations.

Problems in category 5 are game theoretic based problems and will not be considered in this text. The majority of decision assessment efforts have been applied to issues in grouping or category 2, although current approaches to decisions under information imperfections allow solution to some problems in categories 3 and 4 as well. In a category 5 problem, the probabilities may well take on the nature of variables that are alterable by a competitor.

Decision assessment [5] provides us with a framework for describing how people do choose, or ideally could best choose, or should choose, among alternative sources of action when the outcomes resulting from these alternatives are clouded by uncertainties and information imperfections. These are the descriptive, normative, and prescriptive approaches to decision assessment.

Many foundations for decision assessment are available. Behavioral psychology provides us with information concerning both the process and the product of judgment and choice efforts. Systems modeling, at least in principle, provides us with methods that can be used to represent decision situations. Probability theory allows, at least in principle, the decision maker to make maximum use of the uncertain information that is available. Utility theory, at least in principle, guarantees that the choice will reflect the decision maker's preferences if all aspects of the decision situation structural model have been modeled correctly. There are a variety of approaches to normative, prescriptive, and descriptive decision assessment. Most of these rely on what is called utility theory. Peter Fishburn [7,8] has identified 25 different variations, or generalizations, of what we will call expected utility theory. Most of the variations are minor and most lead to relatively similar normative recommendations. These really need not be of concern to us here although they are of importance for a detailed analysis of specialized risk issues.

A risk unit could be defined as the probability per unit time of the occurrence of a unit cost burden. In this sense, risk represents the statistical likelihood of being adversely affected by some potentially hazardous event. Thus risk involves measures of the probability and severity of adverse impacts. Safety may be said to represent the level of risk that is deemed acceptable. Each of these provide illustrations of appropriate use of the term risk [9,10].

By risk to an individual or to an organization, we refer to the possibility that an individual or the organization will be seriously impaired by implementing some alternative course of action. This may result from either the hazards of normal living, such as being struck by lightning, or accidents, such as being shot by a hunter. There are voluntary risks that individuals elect to assume, such as those due to one's own smoking, and involuntary risks that individuals do not elect to assume, such as those due to a nearby power plant or being forced to inhale the smoke of others.

Risk issues fall into several categories, which are not at all mutually exclusive [11]:

1. Technically complex risks that are easily comprehensible only to those very educated in the specific technology.
2. Risks that can be significantly reduced by applying an appropriate technology.
3. Risks that constitute public problems and whose technical components need to be distinguished explicitly from their social and political components, so that responsibilities may properly be assigned.
4. Risks whose possible consequences appear so grave or irreversible that prudence dictates urging of extreme caution, even before the risks are known precisely.
5. Risks that result from technological intrusions on personal freedom, which are made in pursuit of safety.

This list has a clear focus on public sector risk issues. Public sector decision making involving low-probability but high-hazard possible consequences has a number of particularly interesting and difficult aspects [12].

Private sector risk studies [13,14] are similarly complicated. These include aggregation of preferences, limited knowledge, uncertainty, irreversibility, inter-generational effects, distribution of benefits versus risks, counter risks, and second-order intended and unintended consequences. One of the major results of these studies, especially applicable in the private sector, is that decision makers take efforts to avoid risks rather than confront them head on. Another major finding is that managers often view risk as a challenge that they should strive to overcome both through the appropriate exercise of formal knowledge and, in particular, through use of experientially based skills. This has led to other studies of behavioral and cognitive perspectives on risk taking [15]. Some of these are discussed in Chapters 7 and 9 of [5].

There are, of course, a number of risks and risk factors affecting the private as well as public sectors. These include such factors as market structure of a particular industrial sector, impact of financial institutions and their linkages to industrial organizations, prestige and status identification with "advanced" technology development, the role of public sector management in nurturing emerging technologies in the private sector, and the risk management strategies and tactics of decision makers. These factors vary across the nations of the world and across industrial groups within a given nation. Thus we note the complex nature of the trade-offs in issues involving risk and hazard. One of the major needs, in fact, in developing a risk management strategy is that of coping with trade-off issues in an appropriate manner.

There appears little doubt that risk-associated decision making is primarily influenced by responses to two questions.

What are the possible event outcomes of alternative courses of action and their valuation?

How likely is the occurrence of the various event outcomes?

An economically or technologically rational theory of choice typically involves giving numerical measures to these probabilities and values and aggregating these numbers into a single index of merit that a decision maker concerned with risk management should maximize in order to obtain the best risk management strategy. This is technoeconomic rationality [5], and an economic or technologically rational approach to choice making can conveniently be divided into two parts: (1) the proper way to measure probabilities of outcomes and the value measures to be associated with these outcomes; and (2) the proper way to combine these measures. We examine these very briefly here.

In classic gambles, outcomes are simply different amounts of money. These gambles may be modeled in terms of urn models or random number generators with easily determined objective probabilities. Very early theories ignored the value measure part of choice making. Monetary value and objective probabilities were accepted as appropriate measures, and effort concentrated on combining these to create statistically probable monetary returns. This model is of great importance in many applications but is inappropriate in many other cases. Expected monetary value is the basis of many models of economic rationality.

The expected utility model, which is of central importance in modern decision making theories in systems engineering, differs from the expected value model in two respects. First, it substitutes subjective for objective probabilities. Second, it replaces monetary values with the decision maker's subjective utility. The rule of combination, however, is still the same. Subjective utility models form the basis for contemporary technological rationality.

Risk perceptions will depend on the type of risk, the scope of the risk, and the effect of the risk. When risks materialize, risk effects may be completely reversible, perhaps at a very large cost, or totally irreversible, and still perhaps with very large costs. Risk management tasks are complex. It is natural to inquire concerning development of a methodology for risk assessment, and associated choice making, which will allow and encourage explicit risk management approaches. To do this, we turn our attention from these somewhat theoretical, but important, issues to more pragmatic risk management issues.

3.2 RISK MANAGEMENT METHODOLOGY

As we define it, risk management is an approach to managing that is based on identification and control of those areas and events in the systems engineering lifecycle or process that have the potential for causing unwanted change in either the process or product. Risk management requires developing optional plans for managing risk situations that might arise and then implementing the appropriate corrective action plan when a risk has eventuated. Risk management is necessarily concerned with the three generic lifecycles for systems engineering: (1) research, development, test and evaluation; (2) systems acquisition, procurement, or production; and (3) systems planning and marketing. Failures and crisis situations can develop because of risks that materialize in any of these efforts. There are other organizational processes and these need to be subject to risk management as well. These three are the ones of special concern here.

Risk management is concerned with each of the six needs identified in Figure 3.3. We must accomplish strategic risk program planning as a proactive effort through formulation, analysis, and interpretation of potential risk issues. After formulation of the risk issues, we analyze them in order to determine the likely impacts of risks, should they materialize. Next, we interpret the analysis such as to enable strategy evaluation and selection of an operational risk abatement control strategy. This set of risk abatement tactics is implemented through an interactive strategy across all phases of the lifecycle such that we can then detect the presence of potentially hazardous risks, diagnose the cause of these risks, and implement corrective action.

In developing plans for risk management, we (1) assess, identify, and otherwise *formulate* generic risk situations and issues that might arise; (2) *analyze* these generic risk situations; and (3) *interpret* the results of the analysis to enable risk handling through selection of an appropriate risk management and risk control approach to enable both the avoidance of inappropriate risks and the abatement of those that do eventuate.

This first effort in risk management is basically that of risk program planning. The second effort involves risk handling at the operational level, or operational risk abatement of any evolving risk to a systems product as it proceeds through one of the lifecycles. In these operational risk abatement efforts, we accomplish the following.

1. We assess the situation relative to the evolving conditions, identify the appropriate risk management operational plan, and *detect* any developing risk.
2. We *diagnose* the developing risks according to the risk abatement plan.
3. We monitor and control the results by taking *corrective* actions and adjust the system lifecycle efforts accordingly.

Figures 3.1 and 3.2 illustrate these risk management steps and Figure 3.4 illustrates risk management within the overall systems engineering lifecycles as orchestrated through systems management for reactive, interactive, and proactive management. Not specifically shown in this figure are the many opportunities for systematic measurement and the need for systematic measurement in risk management.

The proactive risk management outputs are applied to anticipate problems at the planning level for each of the three lifecycles. The interactive risk management approaches are implemented across each phase of each lifecycle. The reactive risk management approaches are used to indicate, by inspection of the final output

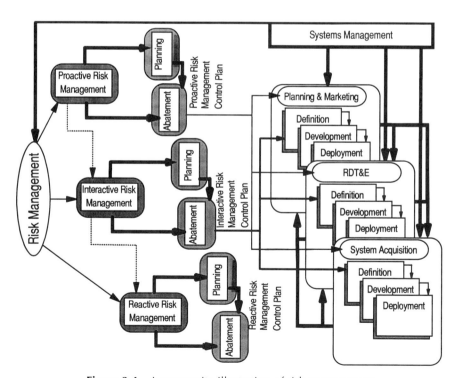

Figure 3.4 A composite illustration of risk management.

product of each of these three phases, those results or products that are unacceptable in terms of defects or other forms of low or unacceptable quality.

For clarity of presentation, we do not show the inputs from reactive management into the lifecycle outputs in Figure 3.4. The correction, at this level, clearly implies much rework and potentially disposal of defective results. As we noted earlier, reactive risk management is really damage control. Damage control is better than no damage control, but it is better to anticipate potential problems and take actions to avoid their materialization, rather than to only react to them. This entire discussion suggests risk management as one of the major ingredients in any approach to total quality management. This is indeed correct, as we will indicate in Chapter 6.

We can easily identify several different types of risk in fielding a new system. For systems acquisition, procurement, or production, the following risks can be identified:

1. *Technical performance risk* results when the fielded system operates in such a manner as to create hazards or poor operating properties. A technical risk may result in societal or other harm that occurs because of poor initial forecasting of technological impacts on society. It is often, but by no means always, preventable by an appropriate systems acquisition lifecycle.

2. *Acquisition schedule risk* results when the intended time for delivery of a fielded system needs to be migrated to some later time.

3. *Acquisition cost risk* results when the anticipated cost of fielding the system increases beyond that forecast.

4. *Fielded system supportability risk* results when the operational system is unsupportable by planned maintenance efforts.

5. *Programmatic foundation risk* is created by events outside the formal control of the systems management process for the particular acquisition lifecycle under consideration. These risks may be due to internal factors, such as difficulties in the RDT&E or systems planning and marketing lifecycles. They may be due to a variety of factors external to the organization.

Figure 3.5 illustrates one possible influence structure among these risk facets.

A number of similar taxonomies of risk factors have been identified [16,17]. The risk elements identified here pertain directly to the product but are significantly influenced by the lifecycle process used in fielding or acquiring the system. This is especially the case with technological performance risk, which will result from an improper lifecycle, or from programmatic foundation risk, which will often result from undetected changes in the external environment.

It is important to note that technical risk, programmatic risk, and support risk are generally the cause of schedule or cost risks. It is these latter two risks that are most often detected in practice prior to actual deployment of the resulting product from the marketing, RDT&E, or acquisition processes. At the time of deployment, the materialization of technical risk is often apparent. Soon after deployment, the materialization of supportability risk becomes known. It is important to be able to

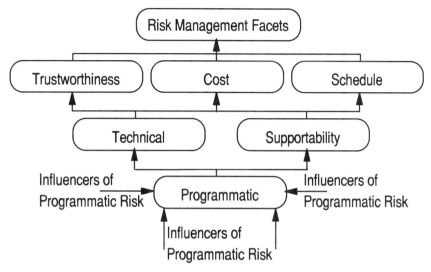

Figure 3.5 Risk management facets for systems acquisition.

diagnose the cause of the detected risk, in order to implement corrective risk management efforts. Ideally, these are more of a proactive and interactive nature than a reactive one. We also note that risks may result from causes internal to a given project or external to it. Also, the risks may be long term or short term in nature. And the magnitude of their impacts may be quite varied.

In many instances, it will be possible to associate a probability of occurrence with a risk. The probability of a given risk may vary from 0, in which case the risk cannot eventuate, to 1, in which case the risk is certain to materialize. In addition, a given risk can have virtually no impact, or the risk may have a catastrophic impact. The importance of a given risk element clearly depends on a blend of the probability of it being realized and the impact that it can have if it is realized. Figure 3.6 illustrates a matrix of risk importance in terms of the probability of the risk materializing and the criticality of the risk element itself. It provides a conceptual illustration of how we might speak of this combination of risk event probability and risk event magnitude. Low risk, moderate risk, high risk, and crisis are the terms used here. There are other categories, and the assumption and use of four risk categories are somewhat arbitrary.

This leads us to the definition we have used here that the risk associated with an event is a combination of the probability of the event occurring and the significance of the impact of the occurrences of this event. A risky event is generally thought of as being undesired, and we will generally maintain this tradition. However, there is nothing at all strictly incorrect about speaking of the risk of a desirable event, especially when we regard risk as the combination of an event occurring and the significance of the risk.

While we have discussed these risk facets in terms of the systems acquisition lifecycle primarily, there seems little question that the same risk factors affect efforts

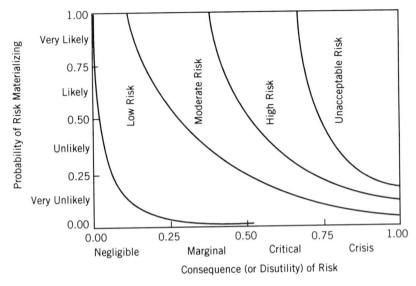

Figure 3.6 Risk management categories.

in the RDT&E lifecycle as well as the systems planning and marketing lifecycle. Of course, the specific meaning of the terms and the likely impact that each of these risks could have will differ across the other two lifecycles. For example, a schedule slippage risk may well not be as critical for the RDT&E lifecycle, as it is for a systems acquisition lifecycle. It could be quite critical for a marketing lifecycle, however. This illustrates the need for risk management issues in those reengineering efforts that are concerned with concurrent engineering and/or fast cycle time approaches. We examine these as part of our reengineering discussions in Chapter 8.

The term "risk" is used in several, often not fully compatible, ways. Our statement that "risk represents the statistical likelihood of being adversely affected by some potentially hazardous event" may suggest that a risky undertaking is always undesired. This is not correct, however. A decision that involves risk is not necessarily an undesirable or inappropriate decision. The risk outcome is bad, but not necessarily the decision itself. We need to carefully distinguish between good and bad decisions and good and bad outcomes. A decision may well be a good one, even though there is some possibility that a bad outcome may result from it. On the other hand, a decision may be a bad one and may result in a good outcome.*

---

*As a bad decision with a good outcome, consider the case of paying $1000 for a lottery that involves flipping a coin and obtaining $1200 if we get a head and nothing if we get a tail. We may well, with $p = 0.50$, get the $1200. This is a good outcome. But the decision is bad, from almost all perspectives, since we pay $1000 for a lottery that has an expected average return of $600. If, however, the lottery purchase price is the same and we now receive $10,000 upon obtaining a head and nothing if we obtain a tail, the decision is a good one from almost all perspectives in that the average return is $5000 and we only have to pay $1000 to buy the lottery. Presumably, we can afford the $1000 loss. If we cannot, the decision to purchase the lottery is bad; we may well receive a rather bad outcome. We should perhaps feel sorrow at

Risk events or risk outcomes always deal with events that are hazardous or otherwise undesirable. Some such events are generally understood to be undesirable in and of themselves. Examples of this would include an outbreak of typhoid fever, an automobile crash, a hurricane, a bolt of lightening, or dying from cancer. We can easily think of organizational hazards and risks that compliment these individual risks. In these cases, one generally refers to the risk of a particular event occurring.

Alternatively, risk may be associated with a decision that is not, in and of itself, undesirable. This might include, for example, a lottery ticket that we have purchased, a delicate brain operation, a bold amphibious military operation, or introduction of an incompletely tested new product into the marketplace. In this case, we generally refer to the risk of a decision, or decision under risk, or decision under probabilistic uncertainty or imprecision. In general, we need to deal with cases of information imperfection in both probabilities and values, and even in the structure of the risk management situation.

The risk event concept necessarily involves probability of harm and amount of harm. This makes it difficult, but not at all impossible, to determine a single number that can be used to characterize or measure risk. In the case of a single number, we would be unable to distinguish whether we were observing a situation in which there were a very small (nearly zero) probability of a very large loss, or a very large (nearly 1.0) probability of a very small loss. There are also other important considerations as well. Time is surely one of these. For example, we may be much more reluctant to take a 0.0001 probability of loss of life tomorrow than a 0.0001 probability of loss of life some time over the next 20 years. This just says that a consequence must be associated with its evolution over time. Such single number measures are possible, and Chapter 7 of [5], Chapter 5 of [18], and many other texts do discuss these in some detail. There are many other important associated considerations which cannot be neglected and these cannot easily and meaningfully be imbedded into this single number.

We note that there are at least two opportunities for imperfect information that are associated with risk. We may lack precise knowledge of the probabilities of the various risky events materializing. In addition, we may well not have precise knowledge of how individuals value the impacts of these risks. As a result, it is often difficult to identify the precise contours of the curves in Figure 3.6, which separate the various risk categories. Clearly, we know that we are in trouble if there is a very high probability of occurrences with very significant damage. Similarly, we know that there are few difficulties associated with events with a very low probability of occurrence and negligible damage. But what about events for which there is a low probability with truly catastrophic damage, or events with moderate probabilities and moderate damage? How much management effort is warranted to

---

receiving a bad outcome, but we should not blame ourselves for making a bad decision. The decision was a good one. On the average, if we could have repeated it many times, we would come out a sure winner. This, of course, explains why no sane organization would offer any number of these lotteries. The "production" cost is very high. It averages $5000 per unit, and the selling price of $1000 is much less than the cost.

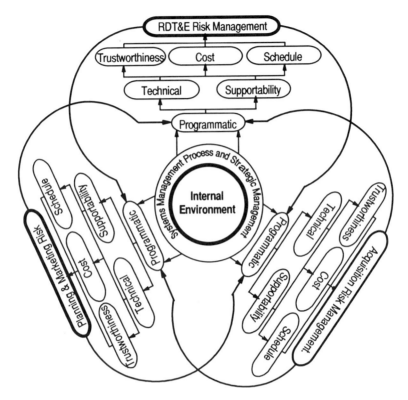

Figure 3.7   Interactions among risk management facets.

alter these risks? These are significant questions, and ones that we wish to posture here.

As we have noted, systems engineering acquisition risks are generally reflected in the failure to deliver a product that is trustworthy, or the failure to deliver the product on time, or the failure to deliver the fielded system within specified costs. Failures can occur with respect to any of the three situations. The product may not be trustworthy. We use trustworthy in a general sense to indicate a product that pleases the customer. A product may fail to be trustworthy because it does not perform as expected, or is not reliable, or is not maintainable, or for a large number of other reasons. It may not be delivered on time. It may not be delivered within allocated costs. Obviously, these are not mutually exclusive possibilities. There are also risk issues associated with functional aspects of the result of a process and risk issues associated with the nonfunctional aspects. As we have noted, Figure 3.7 illustrates the facets of risk management identified here and the risk management activities that are to be used to control them.

We can consider RDT&E and market risks. For the case of RDT&E efforts, we may define a set of five risk management facets. These are similar, in name, to those used for system acquisition or production.

1. *RDT&E performance risk* results when the product of the research and development effort operates in such a manner as to create hazards or poor operating properties. Such an emerged technology generally cannot be used to develop a successful product for ultimate deployment to customers. The RDT&E risk may result in societal or other harm that occurs because of poor initial forecasting of the likely societal impacts of the emerged technology.

2. *RDT&E schedule risk* results when the intended time for delivery of the emerged technology from the RDT&E effort needs to be migrated to some later time.

3. *RDT&E cost risk* results when the anticipated cost of the RDT&E increases beyond that initially forecast and budgeted.

4. *RDT&E supportability risk* results when the product of the RDT&E effort, the presumably emerged technology, is unsupportable or unreliable through the retrofit that generally occurs as a by-product of evaluation efforts.

5. *Programmatic foundation risk* is created by events outside the formal control of the systems management process for the particular RDT&E lifecycle under consideration. These risks may be due to internal factors, such as difficulties in systems planning and marketing lifecycles. They may be due to a variety of factors external to the organization, such as changes in customer requirements for the emerging technology under development, or changes in standards that affect the use of the emerged technology in the systems acquisition or production lifecycle.

We can easily picture a two-dimensional risk management graph for RDT&E, much like that associated with Figure 3.6 for an RDT&E situation. Alternately, we can think in terms of the potential reward that could result from the RDT&E effort. In this case, we would imagine a "reward management relationship," very much like a risk management relationship, such as illustrated in Figure 3.8. Here, we picture the potential reward from the RDT&E effort. Of course, for actual use, a graph like this needs to be quantified in greater detail to include specification of the amount of funding and schedule involved, and the potential market return from the result of the RDT&E effort.

We can identify these same generic risks in systems planning and marketing efforts. These relate to the competitive advantages associated with low price and those associated with product differentiation. They also deal with the scope of the market and other factors we discuss in Chapter 8. Our listing is similar to that used for systems acquisition and production. Market risks may be described as follows:

1. *Technical planning and marketing risk* results when the strategies for postdeployment marketing, RDT&E, and acquisition are such as to create hazards or an immature product. A hazard may exist for the organization in that subsequent effort will not lead to a viable product. It may exist for consumers of the product because it will ultimately be unsafe. Even if this is detected in the RDT&E and/or acquisition lifecycle, there are still hazards to the organi-

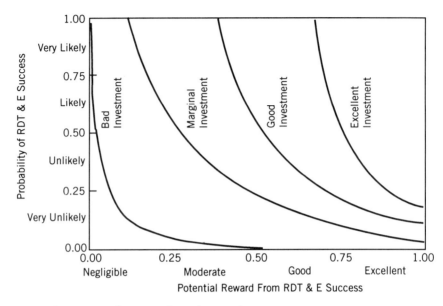

Figure 3.8   The equivalent of a two-dimensional risk curve for RDT&E.

zation because of the fruitless efforts that may be spawned by the initial planning and marketing studies. A technical planning and marketing risk may occur because of poor initial forecasting of the technology or service under consideration.

2. *Systems planning and marketing schedule risk* results when the intended time for delivery of plans for RDT&E and acquisition need to be migrated to some later time.

3. *Systems planning and marketing cost risk* results when the anticipated cost of the planning and marketing effort, including postdeployment marketing, increases beyond that forecast.

4. *Systems planning and marketing supportability risk* results when the resulting efforts are unsupportable, or incapable of realization, by planned RDT&E and/or acquisition efforts.

5. *Programmatic foundation risk* is created by events outside the formal control of the systems management process for the particular systems planning and marketing acquisition lifecycle under consideration. These risks may be due to internal factors, or they may be due to a variety of factors external to the organization.

There have been some attempts to identify risks in planning and marketing of high technology products. In a recent exploratory study [19], ten key potential risk areas were identified:

1. *Inadequately emerged technologies* that, when they are imbedded into a product or system, result in a poor product or system.

2. New systems that are *not an acceptable substitute* for a system they are intended to replace.

3. *Specification drift* due to changing customer requirements during system planning and later development, especially when the requirements volatility is not identified.

4. *Technology leapfrogging,* due to a newly emerged technology being capable of incorporation into a system by competitors and thereby damaging the market potential for a system.

5. A potential lack of *credibility* [20], either on the part of the system itself or the organization itself.

6. *Too lengthy a time scale for projected sales,* which imposes significant cost and cash flow problems.

7. *Inappropriate standards,* either because they are lacking or because they are present and conflict with other standards or across market segments.

8. *Customer "mismanagement" of the system,* which can result in reduced market acceptability due to potentially threatening legal and other issues when presumed harm is done to the customer by the system.

9. *Cost and/or schedule overruns* for the system product, which may nullify initial systems planning and marketing efforts.

10. *Lack of proper infrastructure* to fully implement systems planning and marketing efforts.

These risks have implications not only for marketing and planning but also for the other two product line efforts of an organization, the RDT&E process and the production or manufacturing process.

There are other listings. In a recent work, for example, Rouse [21] identifies 12 marketing risks.

1. Overestimation market potential.

2. Not understanding customer and marketplace values.

3. Entering a market in which there are too many diverse customers needed for success, and where there is great difficulty in reaching this diverse customer base.

4. Not being able to afford the marketing costs needed to assure success.

5. Underestimating the competition.

6. Overestimating our system production capabilities.

7. Overestimating our credibility or standing in the marketplace.

8. Not anticipating new emerging technology breakthrough.

9. Eliminating or cheapening resources for needed RDT&E or system acquisition.

10. Inability of adapting the culture of our organization to that required for the contemplated effort.

11. Not providing for supportability, such that the system can continue to meet customer needs over an extended period of time.

12. Not being able to deliver the system for the price the market will bear and at the price quoted.

The effects of these are lost financial capital, due to the associated poor expenditures in each of the three lifecycles, and personal losses, failures, and frustration. Almost all of these risk issues can be categorized under the general heading of not understanding the marketplace. They also relate to having competitive advantage of either low price or product differentiation, which is not matched to the marketplace. Thus we have adopted an inappropriate competitive strategy. Clearly, these two lists of marketing risk factors are related and can be structured within the framework of the six risk facets identified earlier.

In much of our discussion to follow in this section, we will specifically address the systems acquisition, procurement, or procurement lifecycle. Much of what we have to say is applicable, directly or with minor modifications, to these other two lifecycles.

In the context of systems acquisition, there are five fundamental factors of risk. We have just identified these and it is now desirable to provide a more detailed discussion of them.

1. Technical risk is risk associated with fielding a new system or perhaps a major upgrade to an existing system. Usually a new system or technology is used in the hope of providing enhanced performance in the same environment as a present technology or system, or provision of the same system performance level in a new and more challenging environment. Fundamentally, technical risk results from the demand for greater performance. Generally, technical risk results from immature technologies, or lack of understanding of the impacts of using a given technology that is presumed to be mature. Ordinarily, a product based on an emerging technology involves more risk than one based on an established technology. Technical risk is associated with all elements of product trustworthiness, including functionality, reliability, availability, and maintainability. It can result from difficulties associated with integrating the new system in with legacy, or existing, systems. It is also associated with the fielded system causing harm. This, of course, is a functional deficiency. Structurally and purposefully related risks are also possible. Technical risk may result from requirements volatility. Technical risk exists at all phases of the systems lifecycle and should be addressed by appropriate systems management efforts throughout the systems engineering process. When technical risk materializes, the presumed competitive advantage of the product will be illusory.

2. Acquisition schedule risk results from poor forecasting of the time necessary to field a system or produce a product. Of course, this risk can materialize because of influences outside the control of the systems development organization or causes external to it.

3. Acquisition cost risk results from poor cost forecasting. Again, this can be influenced by factors that are external or internal to the system development organization. Also, technology risks can contribute to cost risks. Cost risk relates strongly to low cost competitive advantage risk.

4. Fielded system supportability risk results when the system proves to be not fully supportable over time. This might result from the lack of an open systems architecture that makes it difficult or impossible to evolve the system over time. It could result from reliability or operational maintainability concerns. Supportability and evolvability needs must be addressed throughout the lifecycle. Fielded system supportability risk affects any competitive advantage associated with product differentiation that is claimed for this nonfunctional aspect of product quality.

5. Programmatic support risk is risk that is associated with activities and events that are formally outside the sphere of influence of the systems acquisition process lifecycle itself but that can exert an influence on the outcome of a given lifecycle process and the resulting systems engineering product. These deficiencies may result from a planned lifecycle that is deficient for the development environment, or from such necessary alterations in the lifecycle as those due to labor strikes, requirements volatility, systems engineering contractor instability, or other causes. They can result from improper outputs from RDT&E and systems planning and marketing that are used as inputs to systems acquisition. There are a number of possible programmatic risks in systems acquisition. Among these are: (a) judgments and decisions made by others, often at higher authority levels, that directly affect the system acquisition program; (b) environmental events that affect the system acquisition program, even though they are not specifically directed at it; and (c) unanticipated changes brought about by imperfect systems management capabilities, such as poor forecasting of market needs or internal RDT&E needs, or poor transitioning from customer requirements to technical specifications for the system to be produced. It would easily be possible to further expand on this listing of programmatic support risks. For example, an inexperienced systems management team may fail to anticipate external environment issues that affect system acquisition. While this is an environmental risk, it may be brought about because of a deficiency in systems management. This will lead to technical risk as well. Programmatic support risk, then, includes those risk occurrences caused by events external to the systems engineering acquisition lifecycle under consideration, and perhaps even outside the organization, and leads to unforeseen problems with the process or the system under development. These may manifest themselves in a loss of competitive advantage through either low production price, which does not materialize, or high product differentiation, which does not materialize. They may manifest themselves as marketplace scope-related difficulties.

As indicated, these five facets of management risk are not at all mutually exclusive, and the occurrence of one risk facet can lead to other risks. In many cases, cost and schedule risks are created when other risks eventuate. Often, the realization of programmatic or environmental risks will result in technical and/or supportability risks, which in turn will lead to cost and schedule risks. The realization of a

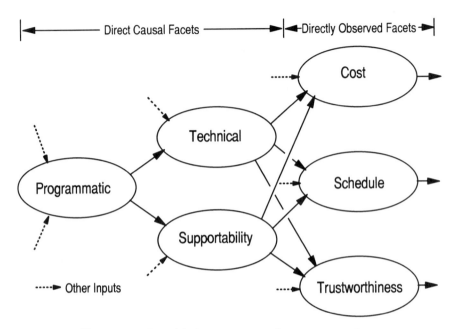

Figure 3.9   Causal linkages among risk management facets.

technical risk, such as poor or low quality system performance, will often lead to programmatic changes that affect system production. The combination of technical risk and supportability risk, with perhaps other inputs as well, leads to trustworthiness risk. This should have perhaps been separately identified as a risk facet. We also discussed competitive advantage risks and competitive scope risks. While these result from and are caused by the more basic risks, these are also additional risk facets that could have been identified.

Others risks could also be identified as well. It is reasonable to ask whether a second-order problem—such as a cost overrun that arises from a primary risk facet, say, a technical risk—is actually a risk in itself. It might be better to call these "associated risks." The practical point is that it is not feasible to calculate the probability or cost of such associated events without reference to the probability of other more primary and causative events. This creates a need for a structuring tool that will support influence relations among probabilistic events. Of course, there are causal feedback loops among these risk facets [5]. Figure 3.9 illustrates some typical causal linkages among these risk facets. Of particular interest is the fact that it shows programmatic risk as a major driver of risk. This influences technical and supportability risks, although there are other inputs that affect these risks, such as a poor lifecycle (for system acquisition in this case). Technical and supportability risks affect the directly observed risks associated with cost, schedule, and trustworthiness. As we indicated earlier in our discussion, the cost and schedule slippage will often be noticed earlier in the acquisition effort than will trustworthiness.

If systems management controls are very well conceived and executed, there should be no risks that are directly due to cost, schedule, supportability, or technology risk facets. That is, there should be no internal causes of risk. But external or environmental risks may still exist and these will potentially result in programmatic support risks. Of course, ideal systems management of acquisition or the other lifecycles cannot be fully realized. This suggests that a major task for proactive systems management is that of determining the root causes of risk, and developing appropriate risk management efforts associated with this knowledge and understanding of risk situations.

Of course, we will never know all we need to know at the appropriate time in order to manage risk completely—that is, to eliminate it. And even what we do know loses its value over time, as circumstances invariably change. We must simply accept the fact that judgments regarding risk must be based on imperfect knowledge. Risk is inherently a present- and future-oriented concept. There are no past risks. The past has occurred and thus is factual, even though we may not know all the facts about past history. Thus lack of historical knowledge may well introduce present and future risks.

We see that there are indeed a large number of risk management ingredients and that Figures 3.1, 3.4, 3.5, and 3.7 have indicated only the top level risk management facets. There have been many studies of how project and process management relate to product success, and they may enlarge our perspective on risk possibilities.

In one such study, Deutsch [22] identifies a number of factors associated with technical performance, business project adversity, intrinsic management power, and operational level management. His hypothesis is that the project adversity factors and management control influence operational level management, and this in turn influences both business performance and technological system performance. This conclusion seems self-evident. The major research issue investigated, however, is the extent to which it is possible for quality management control to overcome intrinsic development program adversity factors. The factors identified by Deutsch, with project adversity being of major importance, are each essentially risk factors. They are as follows:

Technical performance factors
  (a) User satisfaction—the degree to which the users of the system are satisfied by system performance.
  (b) Requirements achieved—the degree to which the requirements for functional, external interface, operational, and quality performance are satisfied.
Business performance
  (a) Cost performance—the variance between projected and actual system costs.
  (b) Schedule performance—the number of months of slippage in key schedule milestones.
Project adversity factors
  (a) Project size and character—complexity of system.

(b) External interface adversity—complexity of interactions with the surrounding external environments.

(c) Business constraints—difficulty of setting realistic schedule projections.

(d) Technology development—degree and extent of new technology development required to field a satisfactory system.

(e) Number of users—number of ultimate users, and diversity of their objectives for the system.

Intrinsic management control factors

(a) Three party dialogue—thoroughness of coordination among user, customer, and contractor.

(b) Requirements priorities—degree of consensus among user, customer, and contractor regarding priority of technical requirements.

(c) Technical scope definition—clarity, scope, and stability of technical requirements.

(d) Risk mitigation—measures taken before a commitment to full-scale development.

(e) Risk monitoring—thoroughness of risk management processes.

(f) External interface control—measures to facilitate interaction with elements external to the system.

(g) Multiple users reconciliation—reconciliation of potentially conflicting technical specifications among user organizations.

(h) Personnel resources—availability and quality of project personnel.

(i) Technological resources—quality and amount of technological resources assigned to the project.

(j) Strategic planning—scope of strategic planning efforts throughout the systems engineering lifecycle.

(k) Management control—scope of the operational level systems management measures.

Operational or task management factors

(a) Business risk management—degree to which management neutralizes the effects of unrealistic cost and schedule projections.

(b) Technical risk management—degree to which management neutralizes the risk of new and emerging technology developments.

(c) External interface management—degree to which management neutralizes the effect of uncertain system interfaces with external elements.

(d) Multiple user needs management—degree to which management neutralizes the effect of potentially conflicting requirements from multiple user organizations.

(e) Problem scope management—degree to which management neutralizes the effects of project size, scope, and complexity.

(f) Planning, feedback, and control—degree to which management integrates strategic planning with operations.

The results of this interesting study provide a relatively strong indication that the system acquisition technical and business performance factors are significantly influenced by the identified systems management factors. It turned out that business risk management and problem scope management were the two factors most heavily correlated to performance, but not by any large amount, for the specific software development projects considered in the study referenced here. Two major risk parameters were determined to be the degree of technology development required for a successful system acquisition effort, and unrealistically optimistic cost and schedule projections. In a more generic sense, many of the factors identified in this study are components of one of the five fundamental risk facets noted earlier: technical risk, acquisition schedule risk, acquisition cost risk, fielded system supportability risk, and programmatic support risk. Clearly, the strategic management approach adapted for quality assurance will strongly influence these.

3.3 ASSESSMENT OF RISK MANAGEMENT FACTORS

We can speak of risk in two ways: the risk associated with a specific course of action and the risk associated with a specific outcome that may follow from selection of an alternative course of action. This relates to the need to discuss, and distinguish between, decisions under risk and risk events or outcomes. Risk assessment may be defined as the procedure by which risk considerations are formulated, analyzed, and interpreted in order to incorporate risk management into decision making. Risk assessments may be performed at an individual group, organizational, or societal level. A risk assessment process may vary from highly intuitive and experiential, to very formal and analytical.

The overall risk assessment process may be partitioned into two levels, as we have discussed. The first supports the development of risk program, or risk strategic management, plans. This is a systems management or management control function. The second supports the actual implementation of these plans for purposes of risk abatement. This is an operational control, or task level, function. Each of these levels involves the formulation, analysis, and interpretation of risk issues. For semantic purposes, and to agree with much past terminology associated with faults and human errors, we use the terms detection, diagnosis, and correction to refer to the specific efforts implemented in operational risk abatement.

Strategic risk management can be separated into components, one involving planning for risk avoidance, in which the desired degrees of risk reduction through risk avoidance are determined, and risk acceptance, in which an effort is made to ameliorate the effect of a given risk even when that risk materializes. It is at the risk program planning level that these plans are developed, and at the risk abatement level that generic plans for risk alleviation or amelioration are implemented.

Our suggested approach to the assessment of risk management factors is based on the three primary steps of systems engineering. As we know, these three steps involve the formulation, analysis, and interpretation of the impacts of action alternatives on the needs and the institutional and value perspectives of stakeholders. Each of these three steps is important in obtaining an understanding of the effects of risky or potentially hazardous activities and event outcomes.

In the risk impact formulation step, a number of elements representing risk factors of a technological innovation are identified, including needs, constraints, alterables, objectives and potential measures of these, and activities and activity measures.

In the analysis step, we forecast the hazards and other consequences of the risk event under consideration. This will include the estimation of the probabilities of occurrence of hazardous outcomes and the impact magnitudes associated with these outcomes, such that subjective interpretation of these in terms of utility becomes possible. Many methods are available, including cross impact analysis, structured modeling, economic modeling, cost–benefit analysis, mathematical programming, optimum systems control, and system estimation and identification theory. There are a large variety of systems engineering tools available and a complete description would require an encyclopedia [23] and more! This is especially true when we recognize the interaction that exists between risk assessment [24,25] and the diverse areas of technology forecasting and assessment [26] and business and public policy. An excellent overview of these areas, together with a number of systems analysis methods and procedures for application to the forecasting and management of technology, is presented in [27].

After formulation and analysis of the risk impacts, we attempt to interpret these impacts. The risk interpretation step will specify individual and group utility for the impacts of the technological innovation. Finally, choice making and plans for action are formulated, based on these interpretations. While estimating risk probabilities, the risk analyst must be careful not to "change" the respondent's perspectives, such as to destroy existing perspectives, create new perspectives, or deepen existing perspectives. Other problems in expressing risk occur when converting risk to cost of risk, assessing the risks of environmental catastrophe, and eliciting estimates of probabilities. A structural model, generally in the form of a hierarchy or tree structure or in an influence form convertible to a tree structure, provides the framework within which risk probabilities are estimated. The risk impact assessment model will be no better than this structural model and aids are very useful to assist in determining and expressing this structure.

There are many risk management factors that lead to information imperfections. These include human error of various types [28,29], improper forecasting of technological impacts, overconfidence relative to technological progress and organizational capabilities, and failure to anticipate environmental and/or cultural changes. Each of these will affect the interpretation of risk, at either the management control or task control level. At the strategic level, effort is directed at a risk program plan that will ameliorate, to the extent possible, both the likelihood of risks materializing and the impact of those that do eventuate.

Among the characteristic ingredients that influence the interpretation of risk events are the following:

The type of consequence—for example, economic, social, technological, organizational, ethical, political, and environmental.

The scope of the risk—for example, voluntary or involuntary, time horizon, spatial or geographic distribution, equity distribution over individuals and groups, controllability, and observability.

The probability of the event—including both the likelihood that a given event will materialize and the confidence that this estimate of probability is sound.

The magnitude of impact of the event—including an assessment of the likely influence that will be felt, including the distribution of this impact over time and space.

The individual, organizational, or societal propensity for risk taking.

Embedded in these characteristic ingredients are the specific risk detection, diagnosis, and correction tasks, if we assume that the risk planning has been accomplished. One of the potential advantages of a systems approach to risk planning and management, and associated risk assessment, is the ability to disaggregate these factors into several strategic steps. These steps involve:

Generic risk issue *formulation,* including some attempt at structuring the various risk management issues and the identification of alternative risk management plans.

Analysis of generic risk management plans, including the determination of probabilities of outcomes for alternative courses of action and associated magnitude of hazards.

Interpretation of these alternative risk management plans to enable selection of a specific risk management plan.

This is followed by specific operational risk abatement efforts.

When risks are assessed, attention is often focused on some particular dimension of risk impact believed to be of preeminent importance for the risk abatement decision. For example, people with very little money and a great fear of losing it in a particular decision situation may focus attention on the amount of money that could be lost and base their decision almost exclusively on this aspect, largely disregarding other information provided. They may choose an option that results in a sure outcome of $1000, rather than accept a risky alternative that might result in an outcome of $10,000 with a probability of 0.95 and an outcome of $0 that is associated with a probability of 0.05. While it might appear to be a very good decision to accept the gamble, it could (with very low probability) produce a very unfortunate outcome and this might well be quite devastating in some circumstances. Risk-taking behaviors, such as this, and the general subject of decision assessment are discussed in [5], and in the many other sources that are referenced therein.

Beliefs about the relative importance of a few risk aspects may derive from previous experience with a similar risk, or from a logical and rational analysis of the decision task, or even from quite irrational fears or prejudices. Whatever a person's beliefs about the relative importance of various risk aspects, our argument is that appropriate risk management techniques involving planning and action should be employed.

When individuals or organizations "voluntarily" take risks, regardless of whether they are for personal pleasure or organizational and competitive advantage, they sometimes appear willing to accept rather high risk levels for rather modest benefits return. Under other circumstances, just the opposite is true, and people will avoid even risks that involve very low probabilities of small losses. There are two parameters affecting choices that help explain this phenomenon. The first is perception of the ability to personally manage risk-creating situations. In "involuntary" situations, when individuals or organizations no longer believe they can personally control or influence their risk exposure, the associated risk exposure is perceived to be more significant than if it were a voluntary risk [30].

A second major aspect is the way in which the risk situation and associated decision are framed. This depends greatly on the model of the risk situation used for judgment and choice. Here we only provide some overall perspective for these models. One of the typical results of a formal risk impact analysis is a model, which indicates possible outcomes of the events under consideration. The outputs from this step serve as inputs to the interpretation step. There are three principal tasks in the interpretation step of risk assessment, regardless of whether we are at the level of risk management planning or risk management abatement.

1. Determine utilities of possible risk management activity outcomes.
2. Evaluate the effectiveness of proposed risk management activities in terms of these utilities and the probability of their being realized.
3. Select appropriate risk management action options that maximize the overall subjective expected utility and plan for implementation of these options.

This completes this step of risk management effort.

Our discussions in this and previous sections, based in part on [31], have indicated the necessity of informed choice making in situations involving risk outcomes. We have indicated that there are many different characteristics of risks. These include individual risks versus organizational or societal risks; voluntary risks versus involuntary risks; high-probability, low-impact risks versus low-probability, high-impact risks; delayed impact risks versus immediate consequence risks; and risks with low-value impacts for many, versus risks with disastrous ramifications for a few. The very different characteristics of risk complicate the process of determining suitable risk management plans and risk abatement efforts. Adding to these complications are issues concerning organizational goods, profit and survival, organizational competitiveness, social equity and justice, and decision-maker responsibility and ethics. Finally, there are concerns with problem structuring and obtaining sufficient and accurate information for decision making. This complicates considerably the notion of acceptable risk, and these have been examined in considerable detail elsewhere [32].

Decisions by management related to risk often face difficulty in acceptance and implementation because of problems in communications. Covello, von Winterfeldt, and Slovic [33], based on their review of the risk communication literature, indicate four important problem areas that affect risk communications:

1. *Message problems,* due to the high level of technological complexity and associated data uncertainties.
2. *Source problems,* which result from a lack of institutional trust and credibility, expert disagreements, and the use of technical bureaucratic language that is often intended to obfuscate rather than to clarify.
3. *Channel problems,* which result from selective and biased reporting that focuses on sensational and dramatic aspects and that contains inaccuracies and distortions.
4. *Receiver problems,* which result from inaccurate and improper risk perceptions, overconfidence in the ability to avoid harm, unrealistic demands for certainty, and potential inability or reluctance to make trade-off decisions.

Four generic efforts are proposed to cope with these difficulties:

1. Information and educational programs.
2. Behavior change to encourage personal risk reduction behavior.
3. Disaster warnings and other emergency information to provide direction and behavioral guidance.
4. Joint problem solving and conflict resolution, so as to involve potentially affected stakeholders in risk management decisions.

While these efforts may appear to deal primarily with public sector issues involving disasters, they have clear individual and private sector organizational implications as well.

Many questions exist pertaining to the proper role of systems management and systems engineering with respect to risk management efforts, as well as to the proper role of the scientist, the domain expert, the enterprise manager, and the public. While risk management efforts cannot eliminate all risk, they can provide advice to clients on how best to allocate resources to maximize utility in the presence of risks.

In this effort, we have emphasized frameworks for risk management, including risk program planning and operational risk abatement. We can identify a large number of system product characterizations that are associated with risk and hazards. These include, but are surely not limited to, those characteristics identified in Figure 3.10.

3.4 RISK MANAGEMENT THROUGH CONFIGURATION MANAGEMENT

Configuration management (CM) is a systems management activity that identifies needed functional characteristics and nonfunctional characteristics of systems or products early in the lifecycle, controls changes to those characteristics in a planned manner, and documents system changes and implementation status. Determination and documentation of who made what changes, why the changes were made, and

System Quality and Risk Attributes

Accurate	Documentable	Precise
	Documented	Reliable
Accessible	Effective	Repairable
Accountable	Efficient	Reusable
Adaptable	Error-tolerant	Robust
Appropriate	Expandable	
	Flexible	Secure
Assurable	Generalizable	Self-contained
Available	Integratable	Survivable
Clear	Interoperable	Testable
Complete	Maintainable	Timely
Consistent	Manageable	Transferable
Correct	Manufacturability	Understandable
Cost to Build	Modifiable	Usable
Cost to Maintain	Modular	User-friendly
Cost to Operate	Operable	Valid
Cost to Purchase	Portable	Verifiable
	Predictable	

Figure 3.10   Some attributes of product or system quality and risk.

when the changes were made are the functional products of CM. CM is a subject of considerable interest in systems engineering management [34,35] and particularly in software systems engineering management [36–39]. Virtually all the CM literature relates to the acquisition or production lifecycle. While it can be adapted to the RDT&E and systems planning and marketing lifecycle, this does not appear to have been done and we do not discuss these aspects of CM here.

There are four essential functions or "baseline" efforts that comprise CM in the initial DoD CM standards [40] and, to a perhaps lesser extent, in the IEEE software CM standards [41] that have served to foster most subsequent developments in this area.

1. *Configuration identification* deals with specifications that characterize the system and the various subsystems or configuration items (CI) throughout the lifecycle. This specification becomes more precise and explicit as activities move to later phases of the lifecycle. Partitioning of a system into subsystems is a systems management and technical direction decision and frequently involves major judgmental concerns.

2. *Configuration control* is concerned with characterization and direction of proposed changes. These may be important changes that affect structure of the product under development and associated costs and schedules. Configuration con-

trol should not affect the purpose of the product being acquired. It should be implemented to improve both the functional and nonfunctional features of the product. Configuration control may result in relatively minor changes that are more in the nature of parametric changes, such as editorial changes in documentation or substitution of functionally equivalent hardware items, that are not associated with structural product modifications.

3. *Configuration status accounting* generally involves use of a management information system (MIS) in order to ensure traceability and tractability of the configuration baseline as it evolves over time. This MIS records changes and provides reports that document these changes. Configuration status accounting should encompass (a) the time at which each baseline came into existence; (b) descriptive information about each CI, including the time of each change; (c) such configuration change information as disapprovals, approvals, and delay decisions; (d) detailed information about each engineering change proposal (ECP) made by the systems engineering contractor, including such information about each change as decision status; (e) status of documentation of the baseline; and (f) deficiencies to a proposed baseline that are uncovered by a configuration audit. Configuration status accounting is primarily a reporting function.

4. *Configuration audits and reviews* are needed to validate achievement of overall system or product requirements. This is done by ensuring integrity of the various baselines, which are interpretations of the requirements at more and more finely grained levels. Most importantly, these make the systems engineering product as visible and understandable as possible. It enhances the traceability of the system as it evolves throughout the acquisition lifecycle. There are three basic kinds of audits in CM, functional configuration audits (FCA), system configuration audits (SCA), and physical configuration audits (PCA). These operational product level audits are performed prior to any proposed major baseline change. There are a number of reviews as well, such as requirements, specifications, and in-progress reviews.

The essential tasks in CM involve identifying the configuration of a system at discrete points in time. Changes to this configuration are controlled and documented such that integrity, tractability, and traceability of the resulting configuration are made transparent throughout the system's lifecycle. CM is the means through which a systems engineering team assures trustworthiness and integrity of the design, development, and cost trade-off decisions that determine performance, producibility, operability, and supportability of the fielded system.

CM efforts begin at the first phase of the lifecycle and extend throughout as the system is made operational. Configuration changes occur throughout the lifecycle. Changes are controlled to ensure cost effectiveness and are documented such that all system users are made aware of the current state of the system.

The concept of baseline management is central to the DoD notion of configuration management. By definition, baselines are designated points in the system's lifecycle where some important features of the system configuration are defined in detail. Configuration control is the primary driver in CM; the identification, accounting, and auditing efforts serve to provide formal evaluations and records of

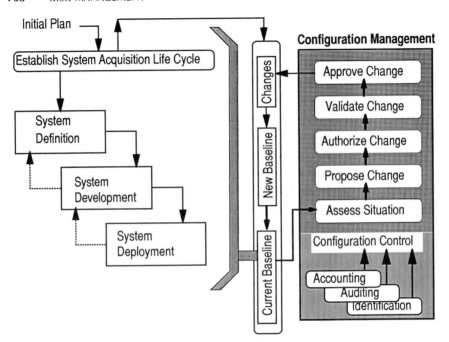

Figure 3.11   Configuration management for operational risk abatement.

control efforts. Figure 3.11 illustrates the major ingredients in CM. There are three formally defined DoD baselines:

1. The *functional baseline* is established at the end of the phase in the lifecycle that deals with concept exploration (CE). The system level requirements specifications define the technical specifications for the program. The functional baseline contains the initially determined system specifications.

2. The *allocated baseline* is comprised of allocated functional specifications for subsystems or projects. Each CI is generally associated with an allocated baseline and it is the allocated baseline that provides the specified basis for the detailed design and development activities in the systems engineering lifecycle.

3. The *product baseline* is established for each project or subsystem and the associated CI. The product baseline generally contains specifications for each project or subsystem. The FCA and PCA serve to verify and validate the subsystems in the CI.

Figure 2.6 may be used to illustrate the point or phase in the system lifecycle at which these baselines are established. The DoD system acquisition lifecycle is shown in Figure 2.6, although we could clearly associate these baselines with any of the systems engineering lifecycles that we have discussed, as well as others. It is important that the many interfaces in the system's lifecycle, which represent interfaces with a great variety of people and products, be properly established. It is especially important that baselines be established at appropriate times. If they are established too early, design and development creativity and the ability to make trade-offs are reduced. If they are established too late, unnecessary and expensive change to partially developed systems will, more often then not, result. This is one of the crises that result from lack of appropriate CM.

There are many alternate baseline possibilities. For example, it may well be appropriate to disaggregate the functional baseline into two baselines.

1. The *user requirements baseline* is established after user requirements for the system to be developed have been established. The initial user requirements baseline would include the original set of user system requirements and associated documentation. Succeeding requirements are incorporated into a modified baseline. This baseline will naturally tend to be very purposefully and functionally oriented.

2. The *system specifications baseline* is established after user requirements have been translated into an initial set of technical system specifications. This baseline will first include the original technical system specifications, for hardware and for software, and will be updated as technical system specifications change.

In a similar way, alternate names for the baselines may be somewhat more appropriate in specific systems acquisition efforts. The allocated baseline is, in essence, a *development baseline.*

3. It is comprised of a *conceptual design baseline* that includes critical design architectures and how these are related to technical specifications.

4. In a similar way, it may be more appropriate to use the term *subsystem design baseline* to describe those portions of the allocated baseline that are identified later in time.

These baselines would describe task performance requirements for each subunit of hardware and software that comprise the projects in what the DoD calls the Systems Engineering Management Plan (SEMP) and the Configuration Management Plan (CMP).

Further disaggregation may be desirable. The product baseline is generally a *deployment baseline* that is established to control the latter portions of the lifecycle. It may be desirable to associate additional baselines with these phases. The operational implementation and maintenance portions of the systems engineering lifecycle are often very critical in the production of trustworthy systems. Thus it may well be worthwhile to separate baselines for operational implementation and/or maintenance. Definitions for such baselines follow.

5. A *systems integration baseline* may be used to assist in management of the operational implementation needs for interoperability and architectural compatibility across new and existing systems.

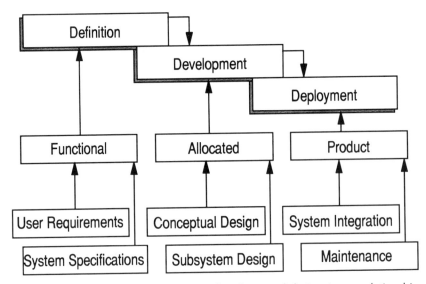

Figure 3.12 Configuration management baselines and their primary relationships to the systems acquisition lifecycle.

6. A *maintenance baseline* may be appropriately established at the time of operational deployment of a system in order to better manage maintenance and other enhancement and evolution efforts.

Figure 3.12 illustrates the relationships among these two baseline sets.

We will now discuss some pragmatic management issues associated with CM. The Configuration Control Board (CCB) is generally headed by, or responsible to, a configuration manager. For small programs, one person might well perform CM functions. For very large programs, a number of people will be needed. The CCB is a part of this team, and the other persons in the CM office are, in effect, staff members for the CCB. It is generally necessary for the client or customer for a systems acquisition effort to be represented on a CCB. Configuration control management efforts may therefore be a significant part of an overall systems acquisition effort. CM efforts need proper configuration also.

Baseline control is a very important function of CM. There are necessary trade-offs that must be made in baseline control. The principal challenge is to ensure the maximum flexibility possible to the extent that this aids in the acquisition of trust-worthy functional systems. On the other hand, the baseline must be safeguarded against unauthorized change. Major tasks in this are associated with risk management and ensuring system integrity. Every proposed baseline change must be thoroughly tested in order to verify both that the intended change produces desired results and that the change does not simultaneously degrade some other functional or nonfunctional capability of the product.

This is not at all an easy task. If, for example, there are *n* subsystems, we need to do much more than ensure that a change made in one of them does not influence operations of the other $n - 1$ subsystems. There is a problem of second-order changes as well. It may turn out that a change in one subsystem does not formally produce a change in behavior of any other subsystem. It may also turn out that a change in a second subsystem also does not produce a change in the behavior of the other $n - 1$ subsystems. However, when both of the suggested changes are made, there may be changes in the behavior of a number of other subsystems. Of course, not all proposed changes to a system will affect formal baselines. Within the DoD, changes to a system that do not affect functional baselines are generally under the purview of a Discrepancy Review Board (DRB). This board, where one exists, takes user identified performance discrepancies or defects and determines which system feature may require correcting. While proposed changes that might result from the efforts of a CCB require customer or client approval, those that result from the efforts of a DRB do not.

There are many systems management responsibilities. It may appear that the critical success factors affecting a systems acquisition effort, and its management and technical direction, need to be identified and resolved at the initial phase of system definition. This, to the extent possible, is correct. Effective systems management not only demands the generation of plans but also requires communicating them. There are many reasons for preparation of written plans. Generally, a good way to do this is through the systems engineering management plan and a configuration management plan, which would generally be a part of the SEMP.

Specific goals for a systems engineering management plan, and the written documentation concerning it, include sufficient details to indicate that the plan is satisfactory in the sense of enabling a cost effective and trustworthy system to be fielded. As a minimum, this must include evidence that the following are present:

There exists an understanding of the problem.

There exists an understanding of the proposed solution.

The system acquisition program is feasible from all perspectives, including costs, effectiveness, risk, quality, and timeliness.

The projects within the program each benefit the program.

The system acquisition risks are tolerable and explicable.

There exists an understanding of system integration and maintenance needs.

The fielded system is a quality system.

If the needed quality assurance cannot be provided, and if development risks are out of reasonable bounds, system acquisition should probably not proceed beyond the definition phase.

3.5 SUMMARY

There are a relatively large number of systems engineering tools and methods that are appropriate for risk and quality management efforts. There are also a number of operational mechanisms to use in risk management. One of the major ones is that of configuration management and configuration control. Figure 3.11 illustrates a summary of the central efforts in configuration management. Configuration management and risk management are each associated with and strongly related to many other systems management efforts, as we have indicated throughout our discussions here.

Efforts such as these are of particular need for areas like quality assurance and management, concurrent engineering, fast cycle time production, mass customization, and other efforts that have found special favor in risk management for software productivity [42–44], as have other approaches such as the use of lifecycle processes specifically tailored to risk management [45]. We illustrated some of these in Chapter 2 and will consider others in Chapter 8.

There has been a truly enormous amount of research in normative risk analysis. While less is available concerning descriptive and prescriptive decision making, the literature here is not at all inconsiderable. A number of approaches are described in [5]. Two edited works provide much discussion of the considerable variety of risk analysis approaches available [46,47]. Among efforts that discuss organizational risk management issues are a number of the references already cited in this chapter and [48] and [49]. Prospect theory, especially prescriptive versions of the theory, would appear to be a particularly suitable theory for many of these risk management investigations [50–54].

We now turn our attention to the subject of systematic measurement. We return to some of the conceptual themes in this chapter when we examine the strong interrelationships between systems management and strategic level quality assurance in Chapter 6, the implications of total quality management for organizational leadership and culture in Chapter 7, and systems reengineering in Chapter 8.

REFERENCES

[1] Slovic, P., and Lichtenstein, S., "Relative Importance of Probabilities and Payoffs in Risk Taking," *Journal of Experimental Psychology,* Vol. 78, Part 2, Nov. 1968, pp. 1–18.

[2] Rowe, W. D., *An Anatomy of Risk,* Robert E. Krieger Publishing Co., Malabar, IL, 1988.

[3] Libby, R., and Fishburn, P. C., "Behavioral Models of Risk Taking in Business Decisions: A Survey and Evaluation," *Journal of Accounting Research,* Vol. 14, 1977, pp. 272–292.

[4] Levy, H., "Stochastic Dominance and Expected Utility: Survey and Analysis," *Management Science,* Vol. 38, No. 4, Apr. 1992, pp. 555–593.

[5] Sage, A. P., *Systems Engineering,* John Wiley & Sons, New York, 1992.

[6] Fang, L., Hipel, K. W., and Kilgour, D. M., *Interactive Decision Making: The Graph Model for Conflict Resolution,* John Wiley & Sons, New York, 1993.

[7] Fishburn, P. C., *Nonlinear Preference and Utility Theory,* Johns Hopkins University Press, Baltimore, MD, 1988.

[8] Fishburn, P. C., "Generalization of Expected Utility Theories: A Survey of Recent Proposals," *Annals of Operations Research,* Vol. 19, No. 1, 1989, pp. 3–28.

[9] Morgan, M. G., and Henrion, M., *Uncertainty: A Guide to Dealing with Uncertainty in Quantitative Risk and Policy Analysis,* Cambridge University Press, New York, 1990.

[10] Yates, J. F. (Ed.), *Risk Taking Behavior,* John Wiley & Sons, Chichester, UK, 1990.

[11] Lowrence, W. W., *Of Acceptable Risk,* Kaufman, Los Altos, CA, 1976.

[12] Camerer, C. F., and Kunreuther, H., "Decision Processes for Low Probability Events: Policy Implications," *Journal of Policy Analysis and Management,* Vol. 8, No. 4, 1989, pp. 565–592.

[13] March, J. G., and Shapira, Z., "Managerial Perspectives on Risk and Risk Taking," *Management Science,* Vol. 33, No. 7, Nov. 1987, pp. 1404–1418.

[14] MacCrimmon, K. R., and Wehrung, D. A., *The Management of Uncertainty: Taking Risks,* Free Press, New York, 1986.

[15] Kahneman, D., and Lovallo, D., "Timid Choices and Bold Forecasts: A Cognitive Perspective on Risk Taking," *Management Science,* Vol. 39, No. 1, Jan. 1993, pp. 17–31.

[16] Air Force Systems Command Pamphlet 800–45, "Software Risk Abatement," Andrews Air Force Base, DC, Sept. 1988.

[17] Defense Systems Management College, "Risk Management: Concepts and Guidance," Ft. Belvoir, VA 22060-5426 March 1989.

[18] Armstrong, J. A., and Sage, A. P., *An Introduction to Systems Engineering,* John Wiley & Sons, New York, 1995.

[19] Meldrum, M. J., and Millman, A. F., "Ten Risks in Marketing High Technology Products," *Industrial Marketing Management,* Vol. 26, No. 1, Feb. 1991, pp. 42–54.

[20] Kouzes, J. M., and Posner, B. Z., *Credibility: How Leaders Gain and Loose It, Why People Demand it,* Jossey-Bass, San Francisco, CA, 1993.

[21] Rouse, W. B., *Strategies for Innovation: Creating Successful Products, Systems, and Organizations,* John Wiley & Sons, New York, 1992.

[22] Deutsch, M. S., "An Explanatory Analysis Relating the Software Project Management Process of Project Success," *IEEE Transactions on Engineering Management,* Vol. 38, No. 4, Nov. 1991, pp. 365–375.

[23] Singh, M. G. (Ed.), *Systems and Control Encyclopedia,* Pergamon Press, Oxford, UK, 1987.

[24] Covello, V. T., Menkes, J., and Mumpower, J. (Eds.), *Risk Evaluation and Management,* Plenum Press, New York, 1986.

[25] Merkhoffer, M. W., *Decision Science and Social Risk Management,* Reidel Publishers, Dordrecht, Holland, 1987.

[26] Porter, A., Rossini, F. A., Carpenter, S. R., and Roper, A. T., *A Guidebook for Technology Assessment and Impact Analysis,* North-Holland Publishers, New York, 1980.

[27] Porter, A. L., Roper, A. T., Mason, T. W., Rossini, F. A., and Banks, J., *Forecasting and Management of Technology,* John Wiley & Sons, New York, 1991.

[28] Rasmussen, J., Duncan, K., and Leplat, J. (Eds.), *New Technology and Human Error,* John Wiley & Sons, Chichester, UK, 1987.

[29] Reason, J., *Human Error,* Cambridge University Press, Cambridge, UK, 1990.

[30] Fischoff, B., "Informed Consent in Societal Risk–Benefit Decisions," *Technological Forecasting and Social Change,* Vol. 15, 1979, pp. 347–357.

[31] Sage, A. P., and White, E. W. "Methodologies for Risk and Hazard Assessment: A Survey and Status Report," *IEEE Transactions on Systems, Man, and Cybernetics,* Vol. 10, No. 8, Aug. 1980, pp. 425–446.

[32] Fischhoff, B., Lichtenstein, S., Slovic, P., Derby, S. L., and Keeney, R. L., *Acceptable Risk,* Cambridge University Press, New York, 1981.

[33] Covello, V. T., von Winterfeldt, D., and Slovic, P., "Risk Communication: A Review of the Literature," *Risk Abstracts,* Vol. 3, No. 4, Oct. 1986, pp. 171–182.

[34] Blanchard, B. S., *System Engineering Management,* John Wiley & Sons, New York, 1991.

[35] Buckley, F. J., *Implementing Configuration Management: Hardware, Software, and Firmware,* IEEE Computer Society Press, Los Alamitos, CA, 1993.

[36] Bersoff, Edward H., "Elements of Software Configuration Management," *IEEE Transactions on Software Engineering,* Vol. SE-10, No. 1, Jan. 1984, pp. 79–87.

[37] Babich, Wayne A., *Software Configuration Management: Coordination for Team Productivity,* Addison-Wesley, Reading, MA, 1986.

[38] Humphrey, Watts S., *Managing the Software Process,* Addison-Wesley, Reading, MA, 1989.

[39] Bersoff, E. H., and Davis, A. M., "Impacts of Life Cycle Models on Software Configuration Management," *Communications of the ACM,* Vol. 34, No. 8, Aug. 1991, pp. 105–118.

[40] U.S. Department of Defense Military Standard MIL-STD-483, *Configuration Management Practices for Systems, Equipments, Munitions, and Computer Programs,* U.S. Government Printing Office, Washington, DC, 1970.

[41] ANCI/IEEE Std 828-1983, "IEEE Standard for Software Configuration Management Plans," in *Software Engineering Standards,* IEEE, New York, 1987.

[42] Charette, R. N., *Software Engineering Risk Analysis and Management,* McGraw-Hill Book Co., New York, 1989.

[43] Chittister, C., and Haimes, Y. Y., "Risk Associated with Software Development: A Holistic Framework for Assessment and Management," *IEEE Transactions on Systems, Man, and Cybernetics,* Vol. 23, No. 3, May 1993, pp. 710–723.

[44] Chittister, C., and Haimes, Y. Y., "Assessment and Management of Software Technical Risk," *IEEE Transactions on Systems, Man, and Cybernetics,* Vol. 24, No. 2, Feb. 1994, pp. 187–202.

[45] Boehm, B. W. (Ed.), *Software Risk Management,* IEEE Computer Society Press, Los Altos, CA, 1989.

[46] Bell, D. E., Raiffa, H., and Tversky, A. (Eds.), *Decision Making: Descriptive, Normative, and Prescriptive Interactions,* Cambridge University Press, Cambridge, UK, 1988.

[47] Edwards, W. (Ed.), *Utility Theories: Measurements and Interactions,* Kluwer Academic Publishers, Norwell, MA, 1992.

[48] Singh, J. V., "Performance, Slack, and Risk Taking in Organizational Decision Making," *Academy of Management Journal,* Vol. 29, No. 3, Sept. 1986, pp. 562–585.

[49] Bromily, P., "Testing a Causal Model of Corporate Risk Taking and Performance," *Academy of Management Journal,* Vol. 34, No. 1, Mar. 1991, pp. 37–59.

[50] Fiegenbaum, A., and Thomas, H., "Attitudes Towards Risk and the Risk–Return Paradox: Prospect Theory Explanations," *Academy of Management Journal,* Vol. 31, No. 1, Mar. 1988, pp. 85–106.

[51] Fiegenbaum, A., and Thomas, H., "Prospect Theory and the Risk–Return Association: An Empirical Investigation in 85 Industries," *Journal of Economic Behavior and Organization,* Vol. 14, 1990, pp. 187–203.

[52] Kahneman, D., Knetsch, J. L., and Thaler, R. H., "The Endowment Effect, Loss Aversion, and Status Quo Bias," *Journal of Economic Perspectives,* Vol. 5, No. 1, Winter 1991, pp. 193–206.

[53] Tversky, A., and Kahneman, D., "Loss Aversion in Riskless Choice: A Reference-Dependent Model," *Quarterly Journal of Economics,* Vol. 102, Nov. 1991, pp. 1039–1061.

[54] Tversky, A., and Kahneman, D., "Advances in Prospect Theory: Cumulative Representation of Uncertainty," *Journal of Risk and Uncertainty,* Vol. 5, 1992, pp. 297–323.

Chapter **4**

Systematic Measurements

Success in implementation of systems management efforts is critically dependent on the availability of appropriate measurements. *Management and measurements are irretrievably interconnected.*

Organizational success is dependent on management quality.

Management quality depends on decision quality and organizational understanding.

Decision quality and organizational understanding depend on information quality.

Information quality depends on measurement quality and appropriateness.

These four sentences are clearly interrelated. If we believe each of them, it is hard to escape the conclusion that appropriate measurement is very important.

This chapter provides a number of foundations for instituting a program of systematic measurement that is supportive of enhanced organizational success. This success will occur because of the improved quality of delivered systems and products, improved quality of the processes used to develop these systems and products, improved predictability of product and system performance, improved schedule and cost accuracy and predictability, and maximized customer satisfaction that is thereby made possible.

This chapter should assist systems managers at all levels of the organization in obtaining measurements and information necessary to organize and direct individual programs associated with either RDT&E, systems acquisition and procurement, or systems planning and marketing. It provides frameworks for measurements at the level of product, process, and systems management of process and product.

In previous chapters and throughout this book, we have found it very helpful to think of systems engineering as a three-tiered process consisting of activities at three levels: (1) systems tools and methods, (2) systems methodology or processes, and (3) systems management. There is not an abrupt transition from activity at one level to activity at another, nor should there be. Measurements are needed at each of these levels.

At the level of systems methods and tools, the enabling elements are comprised of programming languages, control and communication theory, operations research, and so on. Metrics and measurements are needed to ensure that these have been used correctly. Systems methods and tools support product, process, and systems management.

At the level of systems engineering processes, we have a number of systems engineering lifecycles, including, for example, the evolutionary lifecycle. We can speak of an RDT&E lifecycle, and generally this is the lifecycle into which new concept and emerging technology development fits. Generally, this involves knowledge principles. We can also speak of a system acquisition or procurement lifecycle. Generally, this involves knowledge practices. Finally, we can speak of a marketing or planning lifecycle that involves primarily knowledge perspectives. Within each of these lifecycles, we have system definition, system development, and system deployment efforts. We also have configuration control, concurrent engineering methodologies, and the like that support these lifecycle efforts. There are a number of metrics that are associated with these, and with associated verification and validation (V&V) approaches, and these are generally the metrics that are associated with the functionality or the structure of the system. These metrics are made specific to the particular concurrent development that is followed and the particular configuration control approach selected.

At the level of systems management, we are concerned with strategic and process management-related issues. If we are to have effective systems management, there must be associated metrics. These are process related and purposeful metrics. In this context, the notion of a measurement maturity model is particularly important. This could also be associated with an organizational culture maturity model and a process maturity model, topics that are discussed in Chapter 7. The metrics needed at the level of systems management are primarily those that relate to purposeful attainments through systems management.

It is very important to always remember that metrics provide the medium through which the message of system management capability is measured and proactively enhanced. The metrics are strategic objectives measures at the level of systems management in that they are intended to reflect the degree to which purposeful attainment is realized. Metrics at the level of systems methodology, or process metrics, generally measure system functionality. At the level of systems tools and methods, metrics are associated with system structure and parameters within this structure. Thus metrics serve a very useful, in fact vital, supporting role in systems engineering.

While systematic measurements and associated metrics have a great many uses, there are abuses as well. There is a danger of allowing the medium of measurements to become the message itself. When the measurements or metrics become sublimated for the objective, all sorts of problems can result. When this happens, a quality software product is deemed to be one that scores high on some V&V test and the objective is not to produce a software product that satisfies the customer but one that will score highly on the inspection-oriented test. In an educational context, this amounts to associating high educational quality with obtaining a high score on the Scholastic Achievement Test (SAT). So doing well on the SAT becomes an objective, rather than the objectives measure that it should be.

This hopefully serves as a useful caution, and we believe that a caution is really needed. There are many instances that could be cited of entire institutions that sublimate the medium with the message, and we have cited only two instances here. We will see a number of unfortunate opportunities for this dangerous sublimation in Chapters 6, 7, and 8.

4.1 NEEDS FOR, AND APPROACHES TO, SYSTEMATIC MEASUREMENTS

One can approach systematic measurements from at least four perspectives.

1. *Inactive.* This denotes an organization that does not use metrics or does not measure at all except perhaps in an intuitive and qualitative manner.
2. *Reactive.* This denotes an organization that will perform an outcome assessment and after it has detected a problem or failure will diagnose the cause of the problem and often will get rid of the symptoms that produce the problem.
3. *Interactive.* This denotes an organization that will measure an evolving product as it moves through various phases of the lifecycle process in order to detect problems as soon as they occur, diagnose their causes, and correct the difficulty through recycling, feedback, and retrofit to and through that portion of the lifecycle process in which the problem occurred.
4. *Proactive.* These measurements are designed to predict the potential for errors and synthesis of an appropriate lifecycle process that is sufficiently mature such that the potential for errors is minimized.

All these perspectives on measurement purpose are needed. All but the first are appropriate, and there are perhaps very rare occasions when one might even justify an inactive approach that involves no measurements at all. Such might be the case, for example, in an environment dominated by opportunistic political considerations. We discuss some of these issues in Chapter 7.

Inactive and reactive measurements are associated with organizations that have a low level of process maturity, a topic we consider more fully in Chapter 6 and 7. As one moves to higher and higher levels of process maturity, the lower level forms of measurement purpose become less and less used. In part, this is so because a high level of process maturity results in such appropriate metrics for systems management that final product errors, which can be detected through a reactive measurement approach, tend to occur very infrequently. While reactive measurement approaches are also used at the higher levels of process maturity, they are not at all the dominant focus of measurement. In a very highly mature organization, they might be needed only on the rarest of occasions when some products will arise and be in need of correction.

In a very real sense, the metrics correspond to the three levels mentioned earlier—product, process, and systems management:

Product oriented, in terms of inspections and quality control of product (systems tools and methods metrics).

Process oriented, in terms of lifecycle evolution and configuration management of the product, such as to achieve operational level task quality assurance for the evolving product.

Systems management oriented, in terms of strategic level quality assurance and technical direction of the process.

Note also that these efforts at these three levels are generally also:

Reactive—product-oriented metrics that catch such defects as bugs in the code of programs and dysfunctional VLSI chips.

Interactive—process-oriented methods that attempt to assure real-time control of quality through operational level assurance at the process level, such as, for example, through verification at each lifecycle phase of the development process.

Proactive—in order to yield prospective and predictive control of quality such as to result in a process that can deliver a trustworthy and high quality operational product with high effectiveness, high product differentiation, and minimal development cost.

It is quite possible and desirable to connect this three-level view to notions of total quality management (TQM), a very important subject for our continuing efforts. We examine some of these issues in Chapter 6, in particular, and throughout the rest of our efforts in this text.

System or product quality is a major concern today on all fronts. Most of the approaches advocated in the past have been at the levels of operational and task management for product improvement. While necessary, these approaches will often not be sufficient. Also required will be efforts at the level of strategic systems management. Systems engineering and information technology based approaches can be used to address issues of quality at the strategic level. This will generally result in a set of strategic quality assurance and management plans and these, in turn, will enhance process quality at the level of systems management or management control. We argue that systems engineering provides a natural companion to strategic quality assurance and management or total quality management. The term total quality management (TQM) is generally understood to refer to the continuous improvement of processes and products through use of objectives and associated measures with which to determine objective satisfaction, an integrated systems management approach to a lifecycle process of product development through process-oriented organizational teamwork and associated process-related methods to achieve customer satisfaction.

Another essential feature of TQM is the notion of the *totality* of the approach. A second essential feature is that it is fundamentally related to process improvement, and through this to product and service improvement. It involves efforts at the level of strategic planning, management control, and operational and task control. It involves approaches to process and product and has a major focus on problems and issues addressed by the product. It is important to note that measurements or measures are an essential feature of TQM.

This advocacy of measurement might and should be contrasted with the often stated view of Deming [1] that management by current statistics and associated measurements is devastating to the goals of TQM. He further strengthens this with the admonition to eliminate numerical production quotas for the workforce and numerical financial goals for management. This seeming contradiction is not one at all, we believe. We believe that Deming is strongly cautioning against reactive and inspection-oriented metrics. Instead, proactive metrics at the level of systems management are encouraged. These metrics plan for quality, as contrasted with the reactive inspections that ultimately serve to eliminate the unfit. A further problem with the reactive measurement approaches, especially when used exclusively, is that they impose barriers that ultimately rob people of pride of work quality. Furthermore, they encourage the sublimation of objectives to objectives measures, and the seeking approaches to work that maximize objective measurement attainment and not necessarily objective attainment.

Thus we get to the nexus of many difficulties relative to innovation and productivity in general, and innovation and productivity relative to systems engineering products and processes in particular. These are strongly related to group and organizational issues and primarily concern very important and often neglected issues that relate to organizational culture and leadership. They relate to such important behavioral issues as how leaders create, imbed, and transmit organizational culture and thereby bring about process-related changes that lead to development of an intelligent enterprise that will enable successful coping with the challenge of organizational change for productivity enhancement. This relates strongly to organizational architectures that result from reengineering the organization. The resulting corporate culture and performance enable the reengineering of work through information technology to enable process innovation and profiting from innovation. Thus we should necessarily be very concerned with this subject of organizational culture and leadership for process-related improvements through systems management. It also relates well to managing complexity in high technology organizations through the strategic use of systems engineering and systems management based approaches. The enabler for much, if not all, of this is the development of systemic measurement approaches to enhance organizational development.

In many situations, there will exist potential conflict between the vision, which may well not be a shared vision, of organizational leadership and organizational culture. In reality, it is the organizational character or culture that is the essence of an organization's competitive advantage. Any attempt to impart a new vision on the organization may, unless very positively orchestrated, result in the organization losing the very substance of its success. Thus we need approaches:

To identify current competitive advantages.

To assess readiness for change to a new future that is better than the present.

To augment existing competitive advantages in such a manner as to move to new and better future perspectives while retaining the present strengths.

To develop appropriate proactive measurement strategies that may be used as trustworthy objectives measures of attainment.

Adaptation of these approaches to situations with multiple organizational cultures, such as is increasingly the case in many private and public sector organizational environments, is a potentially rewarding challenge for the development of sustainable approaches to improvement at that level of systems management, and then at the level of organizational processes, and then at the level of the result of these product lines, the final end user product itself.

Virtually all TQM efforts suggest several major interrelated efforts that comprise a systems approach to strategic quality enhancement. While we will discuss these in much greater depth in Chapters 6, 7, and 8, we might summarize them here as follows.

1. Know and understand customers, consumers, and clients and their motivations and needs.
2. Know and understand the internal and external environment of the organization.
3. Concentrate on continuously improving systems products and processes.
4. Identify appropriate process and product metrics for quality assurance measurements.
5. Do the right things right.
6. Then, and only then, do these things efficiently and effectively.
7. Exercise administration, management, leadership, and governance in a professional systems management setting that emphasizes equity and explicability and that is attuned to the cultural realities extant.
8. Develop and use appropriate proactive systems management and measurement approaches.
9. Empower people for maximum organizational achievement.

We will find much use for systematic measurement in our efforts to come.

One of the difficulties, we believe, with much past and present measurement practice is often that there is a separate measurement department that is in itself a closed system. In effect, these people become measurement czars. In addition, there is often a paucity of models supporting even the data obtained. So there is no meaningful way to provide the model-based management of data necessary to convert it into meaningful or actionable management information. This suggests five realities.

- Context-free data collection generally serves no purpose in that much of the data collected will be useless, and needed data will often not be obtained.
- This leads to great disrespect for the data collectors and their wasteful, context-free, efforts.
- Model-directed data collection is a real need, and model-based management of this data collection is needed as well.
- There is a major need for effective systems management of the organization to obtain relevant and useful information and economic collection of measurement data.
- There also needs to be appropriate dialogue generation and management such that management has available to it the sort of presentations that are supportive of high quality decisions.

This suggests ultimate development of a decision support system to aid management in the best use of systematic measurements [2] in the form of a *systematic measurement associate* (SMA). While we will not develop such a system here, there is a clear need for one.

There are a number of purposes for which measurements are critical: enhancing our understanding of the functional performance of the organization; identifying external threats and opportunities; identifying strengths and weaknesses of the organization; identifying the need for changes at the levels of systems management, processes, or product; improved quality of delivered systems and products; improved quality of the processes used to develop these systems and products; improved predictability of product and system performance; improved schedule and cost accuracy and predictability; and maximized customer satisfaction. There is a major need for models and model management of data to provide the actionable information for management decision and control, priority setting, and organizational steerage.

There are a number of objectives for systematic measurement. A rather incomplete set of these include the following: to identify potentially successful products, systems, and services and the associated needs for RDT&E and acquisition; to translate these needs into requirements for RDT&E; to translate these needs into requirements for systems acquisition and production; to transfer or transition successful emerging technologies from the technology base for RDT&E to the systems acquisition base; to establish a risk management program for strategic planning and systems management, as well as for process and product development; to determine the extent of customer and stakeholder satisfaction with these products; and to verify that the products of systems acquisition meet the requirements set forth in systems planning and marketing.

We believe strongly in the following two precepts that support quality and quality enhancements through systematic measurements:

- Quality should never be inspected in at the end through reactive-based testing only, except as a last resort when all else has failed, as this is a very expensive and ultimately debilitating approach.
- Quality is built in from the start through a program of proactive and interactive systematic measurements.

On the basis of these objectives and a preference for a balanced measurement approach that utilizes appropriate proactive, interactive, and reactive measurements; we know *why* we should measure. We are also in a position to discuss, *where, when,* and *what* should be measured and *who* should accomplish the measurements.

We may take ordinal or qualitative measurements, such as to observe that a software product functions with no errors, or we can make cardinal or quantitative measurements, such as measuring the average number of errors per thousand lines of code. Generally, and for most uses, cardinal measurements are preferred. We can measure efficiency facets of efforts, effectiveness facets of efforts, quality facets of efforts, and risk-related facets of efforts at the level of systems management, process, or product.

We measure because we wish to make continuous improvements. We measure all along the various organizational lifecycles and do so as soon as it becomes meaningfully possible to do so. We measure all aspects of systems management, process, and product-related activities. Systematic measurements are best made by the individuals who have major reasons to know the results of measurements and who can utilize them to enable continual improvements.

Systematic measurements are not cost free. Thus there is a need to select a systematic measurement program that is effective, efficient, and explicable, as well as one that yields results that are viewed as equitable by those whose products, processes, and systems management efforts are subject to measurement. These may be measured through reactive, interactive, and proactive approaches. In addition, we may have metrics that are associated with structure, function, and purpose. So we can imagine a three-dimensional representation for metrics, such as shown in Figure 4.1. This should be viewed as a conceptual picture only in that the boundaries between the 27 different measurement types shown in the figure are not at all sharp, as they appear to be in this figure.

We believe that there is a natural flow-through from improvements at the level of systems management to improvements at the levels of processes. There is also a natural flow-through from improvement efforts at the level of process to improvements at the level of product. Figure 4.2 attempts to illustrate this. It shows hypothetical improvements in cost–effectiveness that result from improvements at each of these three levels. There are major advantages to improvements at the level of product that result from proactive improvements at the level of systems management than there are from reactive efforts that are implemented directly at the product

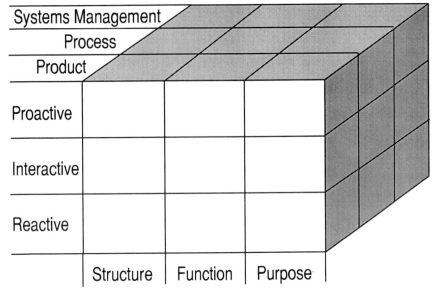

Figure 4.1   Conceptual illustration of 27 types of systematic measurements.

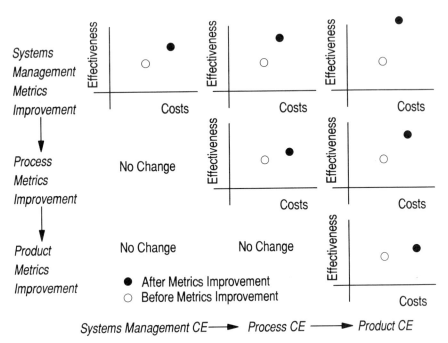

Figure 4.2   Hypothetical illustration of the payoff from investment in metrics at the levels of product, process, or systems management.

level. As represented in the illustration, enhancements to cost–effectiveness result from improvements at the level at which the metrics improvements are implemented and at lower levels.

There are a large number of competitive advantages that an organization may possess and a large number of associated competitive strategies that it may pursue. We will examine these in some detail in Chapter 8. Metrics need to be associated with relevant facets of both competitive structure and competitive strategy. It is the blend of competitive advantage with the chosen competitive scope that leads to a competitive strategy.

Fundamentally, an organization may possess competitive advantage because of being a low cost or high product differentiation producer. It may adopt a competitive scope, through market strategy, based on either a broad focus or narrow or niche focus. In most situations, an organization should select a single competitive advantage and a single competitive scope. If the organization is a low cost producer, it will be especially concerned with *maximum efficiency* or minimum production effort and scheduled production time. On the other hand, if it gains competitive advantage through high product differentiation, it will be concerned with *maximum product effectiveness and quality*. If an organization's competitive scope is in a broadly focused market arena, it will be very concerned with *minimum product defects*, since the large production volume would make it extraordinarily costly to accomplish broad scale repairs. If the organization is concerned with a narrow focused market, it should be very concerned with *maximum customer satisfaction* in the specialized niche market area in which the product competes.

Obviously, a mature organization is concerned with each of these approaches to success. Yet, it should be anticipated that one of the first two competitive advantage approaches, and one of the latter two competitive scope approaches will represent the competitive strategy adopted by a given organization. Even within this set of four possible strategy pairs, one of the approaches within each pair may dominate the other for any given organization. Thus we suggest that a given organization may focus on one of these product quality related measurement efforts as reflective and supportive of their prevalent approach to competitive strategy. This does not suggest that they neglect the other approaches but that the prevalent focus is on a single one of these four approaches. Nor does this suggest that they neglect attention to leadership, organizational processes, fast paced innovation, or the development of a high quality workforce.

These are similar to the observations of Robert Grady [3] in an excellent work concerned with software metrics at the levels of management and processes, and an earlier work concerned primarily with process and product metrics [4]. In the former work, Grady identifies three competitive strategies:

1. Maximize customer satisfaction.
2. Minimize engineering effort and schedule.
3. Minimize defects.

These are associated with user satisfaction, productivity in terms of labor efficiency, and quality in terms of defect minimization. We can also identify cost–effectiveness as an additional competitive strategy. This can be viewed as a composite and blend of the other three strategies. Neither of the set of three or four strategies is independent, and there are dangers in attempting to focus on one to the exclusion of the other.

The seven major characteristics of each of these strategies are identified by Grady as follows:

1. The major organizational factors driving each strategy.
2. The time in the overall product lifecycle when the strategy is most effective.
3. The essential characteristics and features of the strategy.
4. The most visible and useful metrics.
5. The organizational entity most likely to be responsible for the strategy.
6. The organizational entity most likely to be in contact with the customer.
7. The potential risks if the strategic focus is too restricted to only the selected strategy.

Associated with this should also be an identification of complimentary but secondary strategies to ensure that these risks do not materialize.

In this work, a goal–question–metric (GQM) paradigm initially due to Basili and Weiss [5], and which has been applied to develop software maintenance metrics [6], is suggested and used to develop metrics for the specific single competitive strategy that has been adopted. It is suggested that metrics from the ancillary competitive strategies be incorporated to avoid the risks associated with too narrow a focus. The GQM exemplar indicates who needs to know what and when, and why this knowledge is needed. The three principal steps involved in the GQM approach are suggested in Figure 4.3. The goals, questions, and metrics considered may be associated with the levels of systems management, process, or product. Three prototypical goal statements for each of these three levels might be:

To stay within budget

To maximize requirements stability and minimize requirements creep

To meet product performance objectives

While it might seem that these three goals are primarily associated with systems management, process, and product, we may attempt metrics at any level to improve on goal satisfaction. Thus we should determine the highest level at which we are concerned with improvements—management, process, or product. We then need to identify and to implement metrics that determine goal satisfaction at that level and at lower levels. The GQM approach would be implemented by associating these goals with an appropriate number of questions. Each of these questions would lead to a number of other questions. These may be posed at the level at which each goal statement is made and at lower levels. Finally, each of the identified questions are associated with a number of metrics or goal measures, such that it then becomes possible to measure the extent to which the goal statement is achieved.

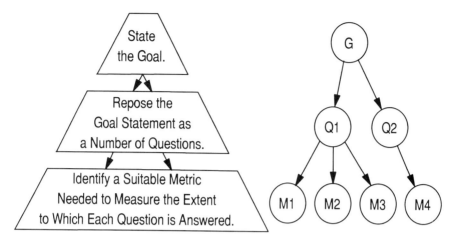

Figure 4.3 Representation of the goal–question–metric (GQM) approach.

The measurement-related concerns have been noted by others who often also indicate strategies for organizational excellence through measurement. In a truly seminal work, for example, Peters [7] suggests five major value-added strategies that ensure organizational excellence:

1. *Providing a top quality product* through mounting a quality improvement revolution and ensuring that quality is always defined in terms of customer perceptions.

2. *Providing superior, even fanatical, service* through emphasis on customer-related intangible elements, and measurement of the resulting customer satisfaction.

3. *Achieving extraordinary responsiveness* or total customer responsiveness (TCR) through bold new partnerships with customers, and aggressive creation of new markets.

4. *Becoming international* by selling, and perhaps producing, throughout the world.

5. *Creating uniqueness* of organization and purpose, and achieving an understanding of this uniqueness both inside and outside the organization.

To enable this development requires attention to five major prescriptive areas for organizational development:

1. *Customer responsiveness prescriptions,* which encourage organizational listening and quick responsiveness.

2. *Fast paced innovation prescriptions,* which encourage organizational flexibility and responsiveness in new competitive environments.

3. *Flexibility through empowered people prescriptions,* which suggest a rela-

tively small number of hierarchical layers in an organization and increased rewards to individuals for quality and productivity.

4. *Leadership prescriptions,* to promote adaptability among employees.

5. *Organizational processes prescriptions,* which address the need for appropriate systems management and systematic measurements and metrics to enable this.

We see major needs in this for attention to customers, efforts and schedule to assure low price and high quality as a competitive advantage, product differentiation, the organizational and leadership efforts that are concerned both with process and product, as well as with measurements to support the needed efforts. We examine the measurement implications of this in Section 4.5.1.

We now turn our attention to approaches for the determination of systematic measurements of customer satisfaction, effort and schedule, defects, and product differentiation in terms of product effectiveness and quality. We will be concerned with measurements at the level of product, process, and systems management, and approaches that are reactive, interactive, and proactive.

4.2 SYSTEMATIC MEASUREMENTS OF CUSTOMER SATISFACTION

Grady [3] suggests that the major organizational factor associated with customer satisfaction strategies is that of capturing market share through understanding of customer needs and beliefs and responding to these in an effective manner. While this is an effective strategy at any time, it is most effective when initially entering a market. It is often very difficult to establish when the initial customer satisfaction level is low. Thus the most effective implementation of a customer satisfaction strategy begins at the onset of product introduction. Customer communication and quick responses to concerns and inquiries are characteristic features of this strategic approach. As a consequence of this, surveys and interview data are important metrics, as are metrics associated with product performance and defects.

This strategy may be pursued at the level of the product only. Most of the direct metrics associated with customer satisfaction are at this level. Many have developed attribute trees for product quality that are based on customer satisfaction notions. Figure 4.4 presents an attribute tree used in [8] for product quality evaluation and that is based on efforts presented in [9] and [10], which also deal with product quality and related customer satisfaction issues.

Grady [3,4] also suggests use of a set of product attributes based on functionality, usability, reliability, performance, and supportability (FURPS). This approach, denoted by the Hewlett Packard Corporation as the FURPS+ model, where + denotes any of several extensions that have been considered, is represented in Figure 4.5 in terms of the three generic phases of the system acquisition lifecycle. This figure suggests that a number of objectives and objectives measures be identified for each FURPS attribute. The GQM methodology is a potential way to accomplish this.

Figure 4.6 represents these same FURPS attributes and associated evaluation of

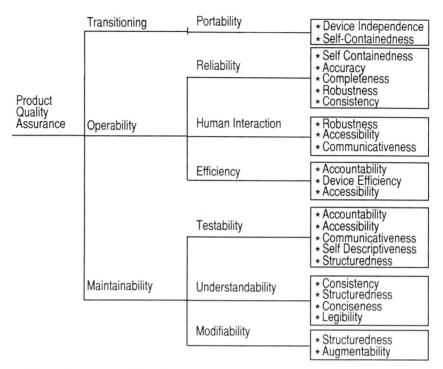

Figure 4.4   A possible attribute tree for software product quality assurance.

them by the customer. Each of the lowest level attributes is associated with an importance weight, as in standard multiple attribute utility assessment based approaches [2,11]. Rather than the generic FURPS attributes shown in the illustration, those importance weights associated with the specific FURPS attributes for the product in question should be included here. The customer evaluation of the current product and the new product being fielded may be scored and an overall evaluation of the performance of the current system and the new system obtained by multiplying the importance weights by the corresponding system or product scores and summing these. There are a number of normalization and anchoring issues involved [2,11] but the procedure is generally a very straightforward one and many are reported to have applied it with good results in a variety of application settings.

Grady suggests use of a quality function deployment-based approach to enable tracking of the various objectives, attributes, and metrics associated with determination of customer satisfaction. A quality function deployment matrix represents an actual or conceptual collection of interaction matrices that provides the means for transitional and functional planning and communication across groups. Basically, it is an approach suggested in the TQM literature that attempts to encourage an early identification of potential difficulties at an early stage in the lifecycle of a system. It encourages those responsible for fielding a large system to focus on customer requirements and to develop a customer orientation and customer motivated attitude

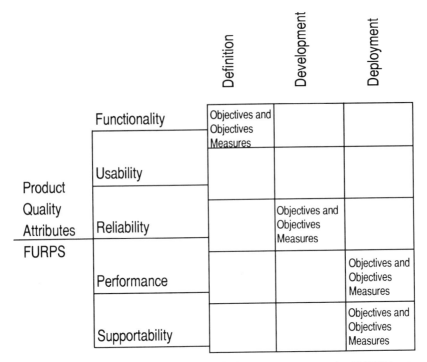

Figure 4.5   Identification of objectives and objectives measures for FURPS+ at each lifecycle phase.

toward everything. Thus the traditional focus on satisfying technical system specifications is sublimated to, but not replaced by, the notion of total satisfaction of customer requirements.

Quality function deployment (QFD) has been suggested as one successful approach to use in conjunction with implementation of TQM. A QFD interaction matrix is one approach for representation and communication of QFD results. The purpose of QFD is to promote integration of organizational functions to facilitate responsiveness to customer requirements. As described by Clausing [12], QFD is comprised of structured relationships and multifunctional teams. The members of the multifunctional teams attempt to ensure that (1) all information regarding customer requirements and how best to satisfy these requirements is identified and used; (2) there exists a common understanding of decisions; and (3) there is a consensual commitment to carry out all decisions. These are especially important for an organization that attempts customer satisfaction as the primary component of its competitive strategy.

Two applications to QFD are often suggested. One is a "house of quality" effort matrix, and the second is a "policy assessment" matrix. Generally, the associated interaction matrices might appear as illustrated conceptually in Figures 4.7, 4.8, and 4.9. Figure 4.7 illustrates some generic interactions among potential elements

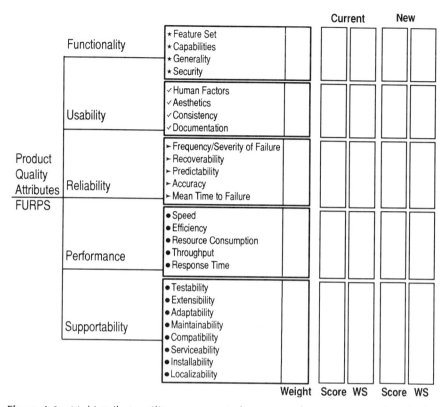

Figure 4.6 Multiattribute utility assessment of current and new systems using FURPS.

in the matrices. Figure 4.8 illustrates a more complete set of QFD matrices. Figure 4.9 presents an illustrative picture of these, as a house of quality and house of policy, that follows illustrative house of quality depiction of these interactions [13,14]. In this illustration, the system production output, which represents the product delivered to the customer, would be subject to the FURPS measurement represented in Figure 4.6 or through use of the attributes described in Figure 4.4.

The generic efforts involved in establishing the QFD deployment matrices would be as follows:

1. Identify customer requirements and needs. Establish these in the form of weighted requirements expressing their importance.
2. Determine the systems engineering architectural and functional design characteristics that correspond to these requirements.
3. Determine the manner and extent of influence among customer requirements and functional design characteristics and how potential changes in one functional design specification will affect other functional design specifications.

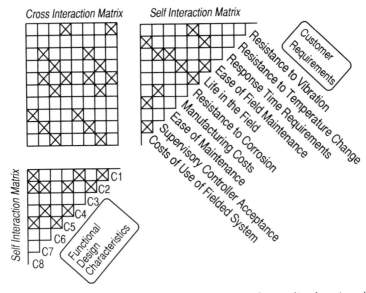

Figure 4.7 Typical self- and cross-interaction matrices for quality function development.

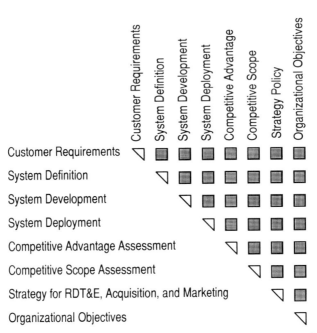

Figure 4.8 Interaction matrices for organizational policy assessment and quality function deployment.

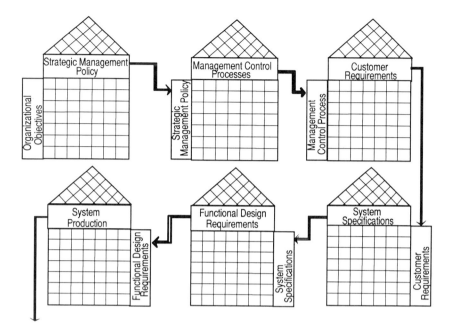

Figure 4.9 Interpretation of quality function deployment concepts.

As a related and more strategic matter, it would be necessary to determine the extent to which the specific systems acquisition effort, or RDT&E or marketing effort, under consideration is supportive of the long-term objectives of the organization, and the competitive position and advantage to be obtained through undertaking the development. We see that this QFD approach has uses in systems management to see if the management controls or systems management effort associated with the development of the system under consideration is supportive of the overall development strategies of the organization.

We see that the QFD approach is rather similar to approaches we discussed in Chapter 2. The various interaction matrix entries might well be completed with binary ones and zeros to indicate interaction and no interaction. Alternately, there would be major potential advantages in indicating the strength of interaction. Hypothetically at least, the QFD matrices provide a link between the semantic prose that often represents customer requirements, and the functional requirements that would be associated with technological system specifications. In a similar manner, an interaction matrix can be used to portray the transitioning from functional requirements to detailed design requirements. Thus they provide one mechanism for transitioning between these two phases of the systems lifecycle. One goal in this would be to maintain independence of the various functional requirements, to the extent possible. A measure of this independence can be obtained from the density and location of the interactions among the functional requirements.

As we have noted in the previous section, Peters [7] has identified customer

Create Total Customer	Create New Specialized Niche Markets
	Provide Top Quality Products
	Provide Superior Service
	Achieve Extraordinary Responsiveness
	Become International and Global
Responsiveness & Launch a Customer Revolution	Create Uniqueness of Product /Service
	Create Obsession with Listening
	Make Manufacturing a Marketing Weapon
	Make Heroes of Sales and Service Forces
	Pursue Fast Paced Innovation

Figure 4.10   Peters' prescriptions for customer representatives.

responsiveness prescriptions as a major driver for future organizational success. He associates ten important activities with attaining customer responsiveness and these are represented in Figure 4.10. Each of these ten activities can easily be written as goals or objectives and the GQM methodology used to obtain relevant metrics with which to measure customer responsiveness satisfaction.

Peters takes special care in identifying ten measures for customer satisfaction:

1. The frequency of measurements must be appropriate and should invariably include informal monthly surveys and more informal semiannual and annual surveys.
2. The survey format should include both informal customer focus groups and assessments made by the organization itself as well as third party or external surveys that are conducted by an independent organization.
3. The content of the surveys should include and call for important quantifiable and nonquantifiable responses. It should recognize that no single survey instrument will be best or sufficient by itself.
4. The design of the surveys should include both systematic approaches and less formal approaches and should emphasize both realities and perceptions.
5. Surveys should involve all stakeholders to the customer responsiveness issues being measured.
6. Surveys should measure the satisfaction of all stakeholders.
7. Combinations of measures should be employed to provide an index of performance and responsiveness.

8. The results of these systematic measurements should be used to affect compensation and other rewards.
9. The obtained customer satisfaction measures should be posted throughout the organization.
10. All job descriptions should include description of connectivity to the customer and performance evaluations should include assessments of customer orientation.

Peters is especially cogent in pointing out the need for subjective and objective, and systematic and informal, approaches to measurement.

Many, if not most, of the suggested metrics for customer satisfaction measures are at the level of product. Product quality and appeal to customers is, of course, very important. But attention to this *only* at the level of product is likely to yield disappointing results. The product line or process that resulted in the product represents a major opportunity for improvement in productivity, as does efforts at systems management.

4.3 SYSTEMATIC MEASUREMENTS OF EFFORT AND SCHEDULE

At first glance, it might appear that attempts to minimize effort and time required to produce a product or service are exclusively focused on the desire to become a low cost producer of a potentially mediocre product. While this may well be the case, it is not at all necessary that this be the focus of efforts in this direction. An organization desirous of high product differentiation, and perhaps such other features as rapid production cycle time, is necessarily concerned with knowing the cost and time required to produce a product or service.

Concerns with productivity at the level of processes naturally turn to the desire to maximize the benefit–cost ratio for a product. This allows an organization to cope with competitive pressures through the development of new and improved products, with simultaneous control on costs and schedule needed to produce a superior product in a minimal amount of time, that can be marketed at a lower price than might otherwise be the case. An exclusive focus on cost and schedule reduction can lead to poor results if other efforts are not also included. These include attention to product and process quality and defects, and attention to these effectiveness issues at the level of systems management as well.

In this section, we will comment on approaches for the minimization of effort, cost, and schedule. These process-related approaches are closely related to approaches to maximize quality and minimize defects. We will comment on these in our next section. Much of the discussion in the remainder of this text is related to these issues as well. We discuss total quality management in Chapter 6. We discuss organizational leadership and process-related issues in Chapter 7. Chapter 8 is concerned with reengineering efforts at the levels of product, process, and systems management. So we will find much related commentary in our subsequent efforts.

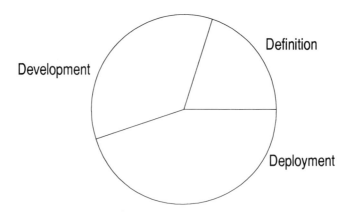

Figure 4.11   Hypothetical distribution of effort across acquisition lifecycle phases.

Our purpose here is to provide a measurement framework and perspective for these subsequent discussions.

In order to minimize effort, costs, and schedules necessary to produce a product or service, we need to know a good bit about the activities associated with production of a product or service. We interpret these activities in terms of effort, and then in terms of the associated costs and schedules. We might imagine that we could project the effort required for each of the lifecycle phases associated with a specific system acquisition effort, perhaps as a fraction of total required effort, such as illustrated in Figure 4.11.

Several pragmatic difficulties emerge. A three-phase lifecycle is hardly sufficient to describe the acquisition effort in sufficient detail for detailed costing. There are interactions across the various lifecycle phases. Thus process dynamics need to be considered. An increase in the effort associated with definition may well lead to a lowering of the effort required for system development. An increase in the development costs might well be associated with a reduced effort required at subsequent maintenance. Thus an increase in development costs might be associated with a reduction in the costs associated with deployment. The choice of a particular lifecycle is a very important matter also. Some acquisition programs or projects may well be more appropriate for a series of evolutionary or incremental builds than they are for a grand design lifecycle, for example. The use of prototyping, in any of several forms, and reusable software will doubtlessly influence acquisition effort considerably. It may be desirable to use new and emerging technologies as a part of a systems acquisition effort. Planning for all of this and associated marketing efforts need attention as well. Thus we have a number of lifecycles to consider and the representation in Figure 4.12 is, while more realistic than that shown in Figure 4.11, still simplistic because change in any one of the phases in either of these three lifecycles will have an impact on the efforts associated with the other phases. While the sort of representations shown in Figures 4.11 and 4.12 may well be a veridical representation of efforts expended on a major program, they will rarely be sufficient for selecting processes to use for a given program or for fine-tuning a specified set of processes such as to minimize program effort.

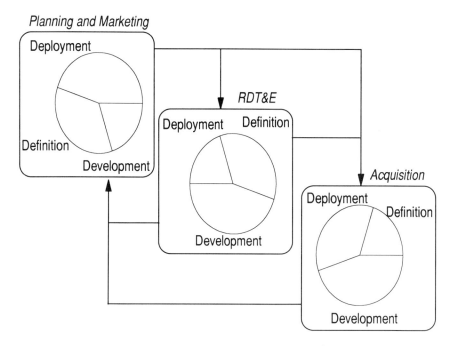

Figure 4.12 Hypothetical effort distribution across lifecycle processes.

Nevertheless, a historical knowledge of how costs and schedules are associated with efforts and activities is important in providing information that is of value for learning specific activities that minimize costs and schedules.

There are several approaches that we might use to estimate costs of an organizational activity program:

1. *Analogy* is an approach in which we identify a program with similar activities that has occurred in the past and use, perhaps with appropriate perturbations, the actual activity costs for that program.

2. A *bottom–up* approach to estimation would be based on a detailed analysis of the activities or work involved and the subsequent decomposition of these into a number of tasks, the cost for which is then estimated.

3. An *expert opinion* based approach would be based on soliciting the wholistic judgment of one or more individuals experientially familiar with the program under consideration or closely associated programs.

4. A *parametric model* based approach would be comprised of identification of a structural model for the program cost. Parameters within this structure would be adjusted to match the specific developments to be undertaken.

5. A *top–down* or *design to cost* approach would be based on beginning with a fixed cost for the program or set of activities under consideration. This cost would be allocated to various activities and phases of development.

6. A *price to win* approach to costing is not based on what it actually may cost to complete a set of activities but a price that is believed as the maximum price that will win a proposed competition for a contract.

These approaches are not mutually exclusive and may be used in combination with one another. Each is reasonable in particular circumstances. Each may be more appropriate for some phases of the lifecycle than are other approaches. The more analytically based approaches, for example, would generally be more useful for development than they would be for definition, for which analogy and expert opinion might be quite appropriate. There are a variety of other names used to denote these approaches. There are also a number of issues relating to support of the direct costs of labor, the accounting of these, and differences between direct costs and indirect costs. We will discuss some of these approaches here and in our next chapter.

4.3.1   Cost Estimation and Overhead

To estimate the cost of a set of activities, we need to know a number of direct cost rates for the individuals involved and a variety of nondirect costs. There are a number of approaches that may be used to estimate effort or cost rates. These include direct labor rate, labor overhead rate or burden, general and administrative rate, inflation rate, and profit. These are the direct costs associated with labor. Costs may also be associated with materials, parts, and supplies, including subsystems incorporated into a product but that are procured elsewhere.

As a very simple illustration of how we might cost a product, we consider an organization that manufactures or assembles personal computers. We assume that there is a single computer model being produced, a desktop machine perhaps. We assume that computers are manufactured on demand, perhaps through some just in time or fast cycle time process, such that there is no need for inventory. Also, we assume that there are no RDT&E or startup costs. The organization has an internal cost accounting system and can reliably state that the following costs are incurred to produce 1000 computers.

Cost Category	Cost
Materials and components	$ 400,000
Direct production labor (15,000 hours)	300,000
Fringe benefits on labor	60,000
Facility rental	45,000
Production and assembly equipment	35,000
Administration and support, including fringe benefits	70,000
Facility and other nondirect labor taxes	90,000
Total costs	$1,000,000

We denote the major items described above as total direct materials (*TM*), total direct labor (*TL*), total overhead (*TO*), and general and administrative (*G&A*). The total costs (*TC*) are clearly the sum of these items,

$$TC = TM + TL + TO + G\&A$$
$$= 760C + 240,000$$

and we note that this yields the correct total costs for 1000 computers. We should note that we have modeled total costs as a linear function of the number of computers produced. This should really be accepted as an approximation in the vicinity of 1000 computers being produced. Should the production drop dramatically, say, to 20, we would doubtlessly have to pay more per computer for the materials and components in each of the 20 computers produced. Also, we really should associate this production with some amount of time, such as a month.

The amount in the total cost equation that does not depend on the number of computers produced is the *fixed cost* and the cost that does vary is called the *variable cost*. The total revenue (*TR*) that we are going to obtain for sale of the computers is going to be

$$TR = P \times C$$

where *P* is the price of each computer and *C* is the number of computers sold. The total profit (*TP*) is then the difference between the total revenue and the production cost. We can obtain a greater profit by increasing the price of a computer, *P*, or by increasing the number of computers sold, *C*. Of course, there must be a consumer demand function for computers that suggests that the demand for computers will decrease as the price for them increases. There are many texts that discuss microeconomic analysis,* including supply–demand relations for issues such as this.

We may well be constrained to selling at a price that is determined by the market situation that results when there are a large number of other sellers who are selling the product at a given price. If there is no special product differentiation associated with our product, then any competitive advantage depends on an organization being a low cost producer and selling at, or perhaps somewhat below, the market price. Suppose here that the market price for the machine in \$1200. Then we have the total cost and total revenue relations depicted in Figure 4.13. If we can truly market 1000 computers, our profit is \$200,000 on the basis of the \$1,000,000 in total costs and the \$1,200,000 in total revenue. As sales decline, we continue to make a profit until the sales volume drops to 545 units. Below this level of production and sales, the profit is negative. At a production of 1000 units, the return on investment (*ROI*) is

$$ROI = (TR - TC)/TC = 0.20$$

or 20 percent.

*See Chapter 8 in [11] for a discussion of this topic and a selection of references.

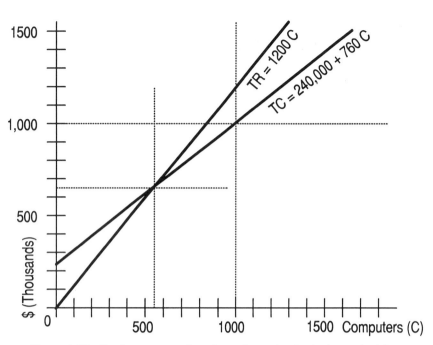

Figure 4.13 Total revenue and total cost for a simple single product firm.

There are a number of ways in which the fixed costs and variable costs may be defined in terms of how the total costs change as a function of production levels or activities associated with the cost allocation base. The usual way to think of this is in terms of the sort of relationship given by the foregoing total cost relationship. It is possible, however, to attempt to define indirect overhead (*IOH*) in terms of the direct labor costs only. Then we would need to consider an indirect general administration charge and apply it to the direct labor and materials costs. The fringe benefits associated with the direct labor would be included in the indirect overhead. If, for example, we wish to recover all indirect expenses through indirect overhead and have a zero *G&A* percentage charge, then we will require

$$TC = TL(1 + IOH) + TM$$

and, for a production of 1000 computers,

$$10^6 = 0.3 \times 10^6(1 + IOH) + 0.4 \times 10^6$$

and we see that the indirect overhead rate is then 1.00 or 100%. This overhead includes fringe benefits. The fringe benefits are 20% of direct labor charges and the direct overhead rate is 80%. The profit is 20% of the total cost, as before.

Other computations that yield this same price are possible. For example, we might wish to associate the cost of a computer as the cost of labor as escalated by an overhead amount. In this case, the relevant equation becomes

$$TC = TL(1 + FB + OB)$$

where FB represents the fringe benefit rate and OB represents the overhead burden. For the case assumed here, we have

$$10^6 = 0.3 \times 10^6(1 + 0.20 + OB)$$

and so we have a total burden rate of 233% and an overhead burden of 213%, a seemingly large amount. Thus if we wish to obtain the cost of production for a single computer, we use the amount of labor needed to produce a single computer, 15 hours, and the average wage for this labor, $20 per hour, to obtain a direct labor charge of $300. The total overhead burden is 233%, so we add $300 \times 2.33 = 700$ to the direct labor charge of $300 to obtain the cost for the computer as $1000. The 20% profit is added and the price for the computer, to be charged at the market, becomes $1200.

Alternately, we can assume that the labor burdened with fringe benefits and overhead is added to the material costs escalated by an overhead amount to obtain the total costs. This results in

$$TC = TL(1 + 0.2 + MTDCOH) + TM(1 + MTDCOH)$$

or

$$1 = 0.3(1.2) + 0.4 + 0.7MTDCOH$$

and so we obtain 34.2% as the modified total direct cost overhead ($MTDCOH$).

This indirect overhead rate of 80%, based on direct labor only, results in precisely the same situation as does the modified total direct cost overhead of 34.2% (indirect cost overhead associated with fringe benefits only and full overhead associated with materials and labor) and the total labor burden rate of 213%. The difference in the three stated overhead rates is considerable. The implications of using one approach to costing or the other may be quite different, especially when major changes in the production level are called for. Which approach is the most appropriate depends on the purposes at hand and whether or not direct materials are associated with an indirect cost. In general they are, and so the third approach, often called a modified total indirect cost, is a more trustworthy approach than the first one in which the overhead is assumed to be based, both in reality as well as in computation, on the direct labor only. It is a much better approach than the second one in which the costs of materials and components are assumed to be incorporated into the overhead rate.

However, we need to ask for what purposes is the approach better. From a strictly cost accounting perspective, there is not much real difference if we are just reporting data for producing 1000 computers. But if we wish to scale up production to 1500 units or scale it back to 500 units, the three approaches may result in considerably different recommendations. We will discuss this in greater detail in Section 4.3.3.

It is interesting to note that we answered a number of questions here without determining an explicit cost—an activity cost—for a computer. This cost per computer (CC) is actually a nonlinear function of the number of computers produced and is given by

$$CC = TC/C = 760 + 240,000/C$$

So we see that the cost of making a single computer, assuming that the linearity assumption underlying use of this model is correct, is very high. The cost per computer, if we make 545 of them, is \$1200. It becomes \$1000 if we make 1000 of them and decreases for greater production volumes.

We can expand this simple example further by assuming that our production firm now decides to also begin to make laptop computers. Suppose the fixed costs we described before for plant and administration are unchanged. Suppose that the total cost relationship becomes

$$TC = 240,000 + 760C + 1000L$$

where L denoted the number of laptop computers that are made. We see that there are greater material and labor costs associated with the production of the laptop computer than the desktop, at least in this example. Because of the fixed and unchanged capacity of the plant and administration, suppose that this production constraint is given by

$$C + 2L \leq 1000$$

Let us suppose that laptop computers sell for \$1800 each. If we make 0 desktop computers and 500 laptop computers, our total cost will be \$740,000. The revenue will be \$900,000 and our profit is \$160,000. This total revenue is less than the maximum revenue we could obtain if we are able to devote full production capacity to desktop computers, as this is \$200,000. But what is the cost of a desktop and what is the cost of a laptop? We do not have to specifically answer this in order to obtain the answers that we have obtained here. The marginal cost at full production capacity for each machine is \$760 for a desktop and \$1000 for a laptop. At prices of \$1200 and \$1800, the marginal profits are \$420 and \$800. This might make us believe that we are better off making laptop machines. But this is clearly not the case.

The results of even this simple example illustrate that overhead may be determined in different ways and that the concept of cost needs to be very carefully considered and explained. The answer to the question "*What is the cost?*" depends very much on the judgment and decision problem being considered and how that decision issue has been framed. Among the many types of costs that can be defined are the following:

Fixed costs and variable costs

Direct costs and indirect costs

Functional and nonfunctional costs

Recurring and nonrecurring costs

There are many others, such as incremental and marginal costs. So while there is doubtlessly an answer to the question, it is perhaps better to say that there may be many answers, and each of them may be correct. The extent to which a given approach to costing, or a cost, has value depends entirely on the purpose for which the information obtained is to be used.

There are a number of approaches to cost as pricing strategies. These include full cost pricing, investment pricing, and promotional pricing. Another approach to costs is determining the cost required to achieve functional worth, that is, to fulfill all functional requirements that have been established for the system. While this is easily stated, it is not so easily measured. A major difficulty is that there are essential and primary functions that a system must fulfill, and ancillary and secondary functions that, while desirable, are not absolutely necessary for proper system functioning.

After the functional worth of a system has been established in terms of operational effectiveness, it is necessary to estimate the costs of bringing a system to operational readiness. If this cost estimate is to be useful, it must be made before a system has been produced. It is easily possible to think conceptually of three different costs:

1. *Could cost*—the lowest reasonable cost estimate to bring all the essential functional features of a system to an operational condition.
2. *Should cost*—the most likely cost to bring a system into a condition of operational readiness.
3. *Would cost*—the highest cost estimated that might have to be paid for the operational system if significant difficulties and risks eventuate.

Each type of cost—minimum reasonable, expected, and maximum reasonable—should be estimated as this provides a valuable estimate not only of the anticipated program costs but also the amount of divergence from this cost that might possibly occur.

Quite obviously, it is very difficult to estimate each of these costs. The "should" cost estimate is the most likely cost that results from meeting all essential functional requirements in a timely manner. "Could" cost is the cost that would result if no potential risks materialize and all nonfunctional value-adding costs are avoided. "Would" cost is the cost that will result if risks of functional operationalization materialize. There is a strong notion of uncertainty in any discussion of costs such as these, and various probabilistic notions need to be used in obtaining useful cost estimates. Our discussions concerning risk management in Chapter 3 are useful to these ends.

4.3.2 Work Breakdown Structures and Cost Breakdown Structure

As we have often noted, there are three fundamental phases in the systems development lifecycle: system definition, system development, and system deployment. These phases may be used as the basis for a work breakdown structure (WBS) or cost breakdown structure (CBS) for depicting cost element structures. A WBS is mandated for proposals and contracts for work with the federal government in efforts that involve either, or both, of the first two phases of the systems lifecycle. Military Standard STD 881A governs this. In general, we would expect that the total acquisition cost for a system would represent the initial investment cost to the customer for the system. This would be the aggregate cost of designing, developing, manufacturing, or otherwise producing the system, and the costs of the support items that are necessary for it to be initially deployed. MIL-STD 881A does not cover extended deployment efforts, but the WBS approach could easily be extended to cover these. The extension is simple from a conceptual perspective. Actually doing it in practice may call for information that is difficult to obtain.

To initiate a WBS, the initial system concept should be displayed as a number of component development issues. Figure 4.14 illustrates a hypothetical structure for an aircraft systems engineering acquisition effort. The particular subsystem or system level for which a WBS is to be determined is selected. Three levels are defined in the DoD literature.

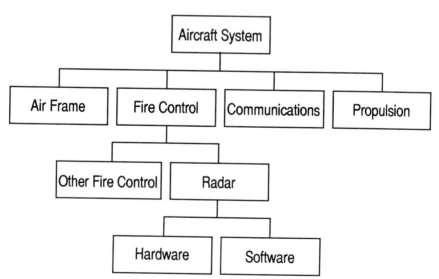

Figure 4.14   Subsystem elements in an aircraft system.

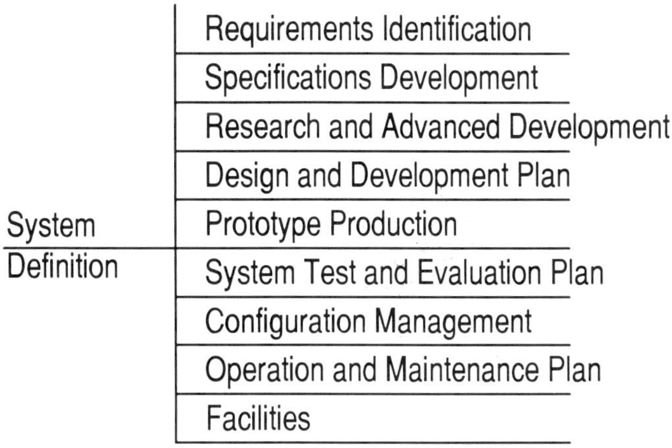

	Requirements Identification
	Specifications Development
	Research and Advanced Development
	Design and Development Plan
System	Prototype Production
Definition	System Test and Evaluation Plan
	Configuration Management
	Operation and Maintenance Plan
	Facilities

Figure 4.15 Work breakdown structure for system definition.

Level 1 represents the entire program scope of work for the system to be delivered to the customer. This level deals with overall system or program management. Program authorization occurs at this level.

Level 2 is associated with various projects and associated activities that must be completed to satisfy the program requirements. Program budgets are generally prepared at the project levels.

Level 3 represents those activities, functions, and subsystem components that are directly subordinate to the level 2 projects. Program schedules are usually prepared at this level. It is at this level that various detailed systems engineering efforts are described.

We may also identify a fourth level as the level for the various lifecycle phases associated with the overall acquisition effort. It is at this level that detailed WBS estimates are obtained.

Figures 4.15, 4.16, and 4.17 illustrate some of the many components that comprise a WBS or CBS for the three-phase systems engineering lifecycle. There are a number of related questions that, when answered, provide the basis for reliable cost estimation for the work breakdown structure suggested here. One DoD publication describes these in terms of organizational questions, planning and budgeting questions, accounting questions, analysis questions, and program and project revision questions. There a number of questions that can be posed, and the responses to these provide valuable input for estimating WBS and costs. Details of WBS and CBS type approaches may be found in [15–18].

In many cases, a WBS is provided as a part of a request for a proposal (RFP) and proposers are expected to provide this detailed costing information as a portion of their contract bidding information. It then becomes a part of the statement of work (SOW) for the contractor selected for the program effort. A completed WBS displays the complete system acquisition effort and the costs for major activities

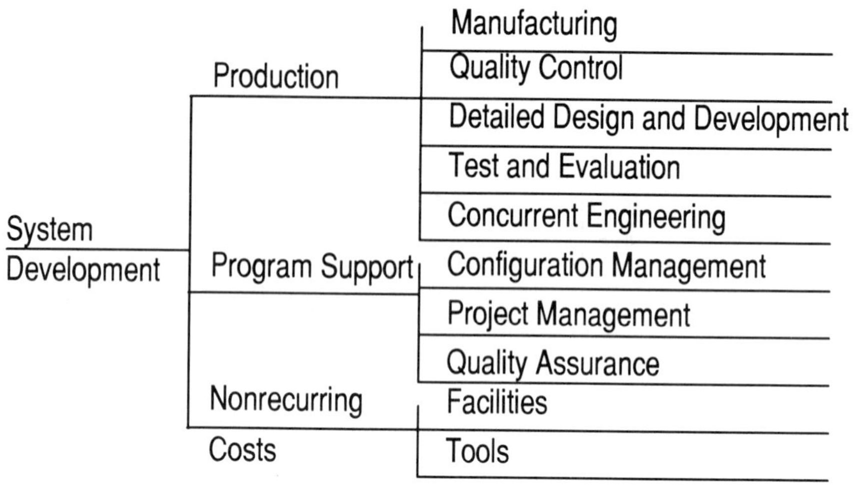

```
                              ┌ Manufacturing
              Production      ├────────────────────────────────
                             │  Quality Control
              ┌──────────────┼────────────────────────────────
              │               │  Detailed Design and Development
              │               ├────────────────────────────────
              │               │  Test and Evaluation
 System       │               ├────────────────────────────────
 Development──┤               │  Concurrent Engineering
              │ Program Support├───────────────────────────────
              │               │  Configuration Management
              ├───────────────┼───────────────────────────────
              │               │  Project Management
              │               ├────────────────────────────────
              │               │  Quality Assurance
              │ Nonrecurring  ├────────────────────────────────
              │               │  Facilities
                Costs         ├────────────────────────────────
                                 Tools
```

Figure 4.16 Work breakdown structure for system development.

associated with the effort in terms of schedule and costs, provides for subsequent performance measurement, and assists in the identification of risk issues. Our discussion of the 22 phase systems acquisition lifecycle in Chapter 2 (pages 58–62) includes this provision.

4.3.3 Cost Accounting Systems and Activity-Based Costing

There are a variety of possible cost measurement systems in use today. Many of these are described in an excellent work concerned with the rise and fall of various

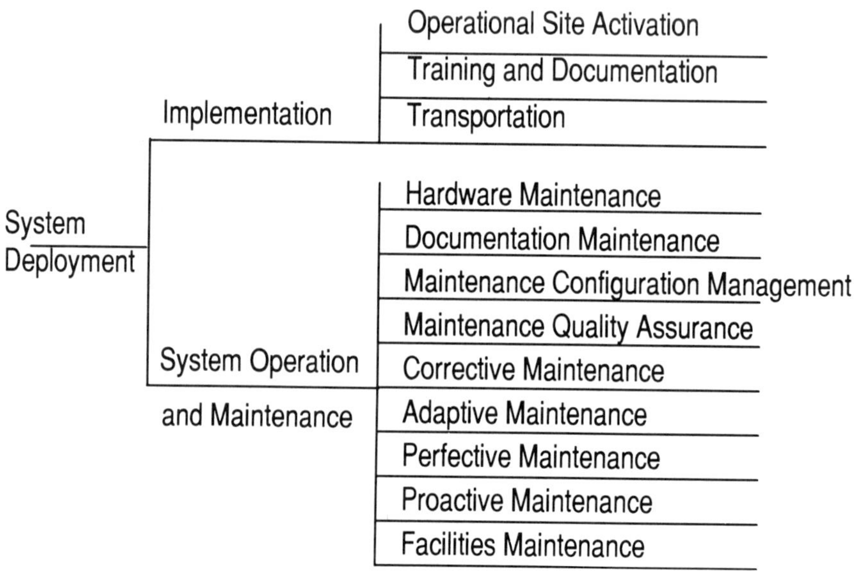

```
                               ┌ Operational Site Activation
                               ├────────────────────────────────
               Implementation  │  Training and Documentation
              ┌────────────────┼────────────────────────────────
              │                 │  Transportation
              │                ┌─────────────────────────────────
              │                 │  Hardware Maintenance
 System       │                ├─────────────────────────────────
 Deployment───┤                 │  Documentation Maintenance
              │                ├─────────────────────────────────
              │                 │  Maintenance Configuration Management
              │                ├─────────────────────────────────
              │                 │  Maintenance Quality Assurance
              │ System Operation├─────────────────────────────────
              │                 │  Corrective Maintenance
              │ and Maintenance ├─────────────────────────────────
              │                 │  Adaptive Maintenance
              │                ├─────────────────────────────────
              │                 │  Perfective Maintenance
              │                ├─────────────────────────────────
              │                 │  Proactive Maintenance
              │                ├─────────────────────────────────
                                 Facilities Maintenance
```

Figure 4.17 Work breakdown structure for system deployment.

management accounting systems [19]. Many consider that cost accounting, when applied to systems management related decisions that impact engineering efforts, is a major enemy of productivity today.

A major reason why this is said to occur is that cost accounting has shifted from being an engineering metric used to increase efficiency in development to a financial reporting tool only. Initially, the purposes of a cost accounting system were (1) to detect and diagnose opportunities within the organization for improvement through more cost-efficient use of resources, and (2) to control internal processes such that these improvements were realized. Sadly, the emphasis on the use of this engineering accounting information shifted from the provision of information for management decisions to providing a report of organizational profits.

This was replaced by a form of inventory costing in which all indirect costs, regardless of whether they were process or product based, are allocated to specific products. This is accomplished by allocating all costs other than direct labor as indirect costs calculated as a percentage of *only* the labor hours, or cost, required to produce the product. The resulting return on investment (ROI) calculations are said to be very misleading in many cases.

A number of illustrations of this are cited.

1. The allocation of indirect or overhead costs to direct labor only distorts the real cost of doing business. It may suggest that overall costs will be reduced through reduction in labor only, and not through reduction of equipment costs since overhead is not computed on them. When costs are distributed to products on such simplistic and arbitrary calculations, misguided decisions may easily result.

2. Attention may be focused on the short term through accounting systems that are focused only on the short term. When expenses of RDT&E, process improvements, and education and training "costs" are listed for accounting purposes as expenses for the period, regardless of whether these are considered as indirect or direct costs, then they become issues for improvement in the bottom line through reduction of these costs. The fact that they provide benefits over the long term may well be completely ignored. Short-term profit incentives can therefore lead to major decreases in long-term investments. While these costs are real, they can be capitalized over a long period of time, much as the expense of a building or a major piece of equipment, and this avoids the short-term drain on resources incurred by considering them as immediately occurring expenses.

3. Often, managerial accounting reports are concerned with issues that do not relate to economic and technological realities of the organization in that they do not provide timely and thorough information on process efficiency and effectiveness.

As a result of this, traditional financial management accounting systems are said to be often dysfunctional.

The usual approach implementing a cost system is comprised of a two-step procedure [20] for assignment of overhead costs to products:

In *stage 1*, indirect costs and support department costs are combined as the overhead cost and assigned to production cost centers.

In *stage 2*, the costs that are accumulated in the various production cost centers are assigned to the products of these centers, usually as a fraction of direct labor—either labor hours or direct labor costs.

This procedure is invariant with respect to the type of costing system that is being used. It is suggested that the efforts in stage 1 are usually performed very methodically. However, the efforts involved at stage 2 are often not handled very systematically. This is particularly the case in a unit-level-based cost system.

The unit-level-based cost system is the traditional accounting system that is generally found today. In a *unit-level-based* cost system, costs are assigned in strict proportion to production volume. Thus if the production volume increases by 25%, so will the number of labor hours or costs and the number of overhead hours. Unit-level-based costing systems are sometimes called volume-based costing. While this approach is said to be in use in about 75% of the cases in the United States today, a new system, which we now describe, is potentially much more accurate in terms of cost allocation.

The major objective of what has come to be known as *activity-based costing* (ABC) systems is to formulate and identify cost drivers and the activities that cause the costs to change, analyze the associated cost-driver relationships; and interpret these in an appropriate manner such that they can be implemented to reflect the true costs of various production activities. The costs at the various levels in an ABC system are assumed to be driven by a single activity or by a closely related set of activities such that changes in one activity produce strictly proportional changes in the other activities. Thus the activity drivers are said to be homogeneous. Furthermore, it is assumed that the costs are proportional to the activities.

One of the major objectives in an ABC system is to demonstrate how some costs that might otherwise be treated as indirect or overhead costs can be related in a direct manner to individual products. A traditional accounting system might allocate worker supervision costs to products as an indirect cost based on direct labor hours. An ABC system would interpret these, to the extent possible, as direct costs associated with the specific product in question. A number of illustrations of potential difficulties with existing systems and how ABC systems can potentially resolve these are provided in [21–24].

In an ABC system, it is assumed that not all of the overhead resources are consumed in direct proportion to the production volume. An ABC system allows for two more types of cost drivers than the traditional cost system. To design an ABC system, it is highly desirable to focus on the most expensive resources, whose consumption varies significantly across product and product type, and whose demand patterns are not well correlated with traditional unit-based allocation of direct labor, processing time, and materials [25]. The unit-based approaches almost invariably assign the largest, perhaps even all, of the indirect costs or overhead using a direct labor cost multiplier. Thus they are seriously flawed for a complex organization with many product lines.

To accommodate multiple product lines, two additional approaches may be defined.

A *batch-level-based* approach assumes that specific inputs only are consumed in direct proportion to the number of batches of each type of product that results from the production process.

A *product-level-based* approach assumes that specific inputs only are consumed in order to allow production of different products.

These three different bases for indirect cost accumulation are used in an ABC system. Since there are cost-based activities that are common to a variety of products, there is also a need for facility-level costs. Thus we have four different types of activities:

1. Unit-level activities that are performed each time a unit is produced.
2. Batch-level activities that are performed each time a batch of products results.
3. Product-level activities that support production of each different type of good.
4. Facility-level activities that support an organization's general processes.

The ABC approach is based on correct calculations of each type of activity.

It is suggested that two types of costs should be excluded from a system of ABC:

1. The costs of excess capacity should not be charged to individual products, but as a separate line item that represents a cost of the period to be allocated at the facility level and not at the individual product level.
2. RDT&E costs for new product lines should also be excluded from allocation to existing product lines and treated as an investment in the future.

It is necessary to split RDT&E costs into two categories: those associated with new products and those associated with existing products. RDT&E for new products can be capitalized and allocated as a facility-level cost. The RDT&E costs for emerging technologies for existing product lines should be associated with those products that potentially benefit from the new developments. The major thrust in this is to identify, accurately, the resource consumption flows that are a direct and indirect result of phased lifecycle efforts to define, develop, and deploy products and services that support customers. In this way, an accounting system becomes a decision support system rather than only a tool for use in making the annual report.

An ABC system is very much based on a lifecycle model for production activities. There is a lifecycle that encompasses definition, development, and deployment for marketing, acquisition, and RDT&E, as needed for the particular set of activities in question. The steps in implementing an ABC system may be described as follows:

1. The issue itself is formulated. A process flow map is identified that represents the flows of activities from product definition through development and ulti-

mately deployment. This will often be in the form of a very detailed CBS or WBS.

2. The various activities are analyzed and the functional costs are determined for the various activities associated with the lifecycle phases.
3. Interpret these costs by tracing them back to the appropriate levels—unit, batch, product, or facility—from which they came. The facility-level costs will doubtlessly be the most difficult ones with which to cope.

While the actual details and computations for a specific implementation can be quite extended, conceptually the approach is simple and appealing.

While there is much to support use of ABC systems over traditional unit-based or volume-based systems, there are some potential obstacles to overcome. Shank and Govindarajan [26] indicate three of these:

1. An ABC system may assign manufacturing costs to products without considering whether the costs are appropriate in a broader strategic sense. In other words, the approach may be very sound from an accounting perspective but this may not disclose deficiencies in technology or process. As a consequence, an activity may be performed inefficiently and it may not add value or effectiveness to the product. The ABC system will not necessarily suggest improvement. The authors denote this as taking a static, rather than a dynamic, view of cost.
2. The ABC system may make an improper distinction and associated allocation between short-term product costs and long-term costs that support the product development, such as RDT&E.
3. Even if the ABC system is such as to avoid obstacles 1 and 2, the activity chain obtained today will almost always be based only on today's strategy rather than on a possibly reengineered strategy for enhanced organizational productivity.

Shank and Govindarajan discuss a concept called *strategic cost management* [27] that is said to enhance the value of ABC systems, as a tool for strategic management. This strategic cost management concept is based on a *value chain analysis* approach, which links external value-creating activities throughout the organization's major lifecycles. This is combined with concepts of strategic positioning to enable a *cost driver analysis* for strategic repositioning and reengineering. This enables the inclusion of other than conventional economic cost drivers, such as quality and technology choices. We discuss salient facets of this approach, including the three main ingredients noted here, in Chapter 8.

H. Thomas Johnson [28,29] is also concerned with ABC systems and with expanding the horizon viewed by these systems to allow for other than purely economic factors to be included. He strongly encourages the inclusion of such nonfinancial information as competitive value, reliability and quality as relevant variables in the operating activity analysis efforts of organizations, as well as strategic cost information. Four steps are suggested to manage waste in operating activities.

1. Chart the flow of activities throughout the organization.
2. Identify the major sources of customer value in all activities and eliminate those activities that do not contribute customer value.
3. Identify and correct causes of low quality in every activity.
4. Measure and manage indicators of waste.

The major message here is to manage activities and not costs. The corollary to this must be that costs will take care of themselves through effective management of activities. This might well be called ABM—*activity based management.*

Johnson believes that relevance was lost primarily by the improper use of accounting information to control organizations in their engineering production decisions and not because of the use of improper accounting information. This improper use of accounting information allowed for control of the financial bottom line only, and generally over the short term, while failing to detect, diagnose, and correct problems that emanated from such areas as product quality and customer satisfaction. Bottom–up empowerment of everyone in the organization, in large part through use of new and emerging information technologies together with changes in organizational leadership and culture, is suggested as the needed replacement of the traditional top–down control through unit-based management accounting. In effect, this associates many of the total quality management concepts we discuss in Chapter 6, the leadership and process maturity issues we discuss in Chapter 7, and the reengineering concepts we discuss in Chapter 8 with those of an expanded activity-based costing system.

In many of our discussions to follow in subsequent chapters, we will examine notions relating to strategic quality assurance and management or total quality management. These notions carry over to cost considerations as well. While it is not unrealistic, and it is relatively standard practice, to attempt to place a cost on the production of high quality producers, it is potentially more meaningful to address the cost of poor quality (COPQ). This has been defined by Juran [30] as the sum of all costs that would disappear if there were no quality problems. There are other related definitions. Feigenbaum [31], for example, identifies quality costs as including both the cost of quality control to prevent defects from occurring and to appraise and correct those that do occur, and the costs of internal or external failure to bring about quality control.

The establishment of costs for a quality management and control program involves the formulation of quality costs and of the costs of poor quality. This involves the identification of both quality cost items and poor-quality cost items. These would include the direct costs of the operational level quality assurance items discussed in Chapter 4 of [11]. Importantly, it should also include the identification of the costs that are ultimately added to fielding a large system, such as rework and additional scrap, due to a low quality system development process. Identification of the costs of the strategic quality effort and the operational level costs of implementing this are also needed. This includes the costs of continuous improvement of quality of processes and products over time.

4.3.4   Model-Based Estimates of Cost and Schedule

The WBS, CBS, and ABC models of cost and schedule are microlevel models. Estimates of cost and schedule may be based on a structural model in which the parameters associated with the structure are appropriately matched to the specific program being undertaken. This is a potentially attractive macrolevel approach, especially when the activities to be undertaken are so new that a very detailed layout of a CBS or WBS is not feasible.

For example, a simple model for the cost of constructing a home might be that the cost is some function of the square footage

$$C = f(F)$$

In order to use a relation like this, we need to specify the function. We might specify this further as

$$C = a + F^b$$

A very crude model might use the same a and b parameters regardless of the type of construction. We might improve on the model by using different a and b parameters that depend on the type of construction: economy or luxury. There are surely other factors that determine the cost of a home, such as the number of bathrooms. We could attempt to expand on this model by adding successive factors such that it ultimately and ideally becomes a very useful model that we can use to predict the cost and schedule for activities yet to be undertaken. While such a model might yield a moderately good estimate of cost, we might well anticipate that it would not be as good a basis for cost determination as would a detailed set of architectural specifications from which the actual components that would go into the home might well be determined quite accurately.

The accuracy associated with a microlevel model of activity depends on the extent to which the various individual components of activity can be specified accurately. The accuracy associated with a macrolevel model is a function of the extent to which we can accurately specify the structure of the macrolevel model and the accuracy with which we can specify the parameters within this structure. We see that experiential familiarity with respect to specification of the various activities is a major factor, as is scope and scale of the effort itself, in determining the errors and risks that may be expected to be associated with use of an estimation model for time and schedule. For tasks that are reasonably small in scope and scale, and where we have accomplished the activities many times before, we should expect that we would be able to determine cost and schedule quite accurately. When one or both of these conditions are not satisfied, we might well expect that there might be signifi-

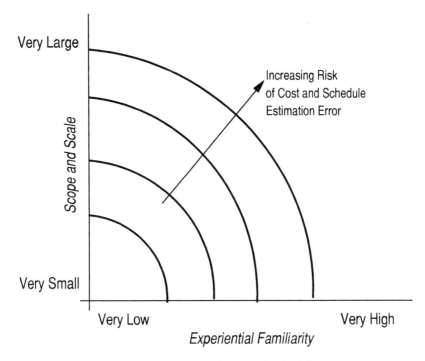

Figure 4.18 Contours of equal risk of cost and schedule estimation error.

cant errors associated with estimating the cost of a program, as represented in Figure 4.18.

For a large program, there will be activities associated with RDT&E, acquisition or production, and marketing. There will be costs associated with each of these lifecycles and, in turn, the phases that comprise them. As we have discussed in Chapter 2, the efforts in these three lifecycles need to be linked as their purposes are linked. This is true with respect to program cost analysis. Figure 4.19 illustrates some facets of this and the different fundamental drivers for these three lifecycles. While cost may seem to be the basic driver for only the acquisition or production phase, there are major acquisition cost implications to decisions made in the other two lifecycles.

A relatively simple macromodel for cost over a single lifecycle of effort might be expressed as the sum of the costs for each of the lifecycle phases:

$$C = CDEF + CDEV + CDEP$$

This really tends to assume that we are implementing a grand design lifecycle for development. If this is the cost of a single build for an evolutionary or incremental lifecycle, then we might write the cost for the *i*th build and the total cost as

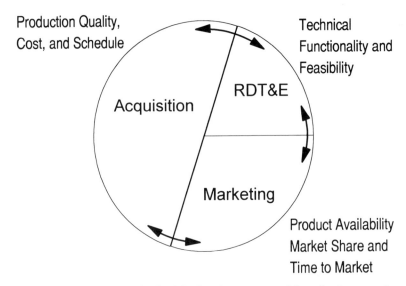

Figure 4.19 Potential cost and schedule distribution across lifecycle phases and major driver of each phase.

$$TC = \sum_{i=1}^{n} C_i$$

$$C_i = CDEF_i + CDEV_i + CDEP_i$$

This may well complicate things considerably in that there may well be a strong dependency relation of the cost at any given phase of the lifecycle on the efforts in the preceding lifecycle phases. We will address this issue, to some extent, in our next chapter and will not consider it further here.

To use a model of this sort, we need to develop more detailed expressions for the costs of the three lifecycle phases. Suppose we wish to develop a simple model for software acquisition. For definition, we might have

$$CDEF = aS^b + cF$$

where S represents the number of people who must be interviewed in order to obtain the user requirements and functional specifications for the system and F represents some assumed, and at this point hypothetical, "authority point" complexity of the specifications themselves. This would be expressed in such entries as the number of displays and data entry screens that must be implemented, the number of menus and command line features that must be implemented, the number of numerical and nonnumerical algorithms that must be developed, and the number of files that need be designed. a, b, and c are parameters that are perhaps determined on the basis of empirical and experimental observation of past development efforts.

For the development phase of effort, the costs might be expressed as

$$CDEV = \prod_{i=1}^{m} M_i^{d_i}$$

where the M_i represent development multipliers that depend on the number of authority points and such other development complexity points as the programming language that is being used, the proficiency of development personnel, and the availability of reusable software. The d_i represent power factors that are empirically determined on the basis of observed past development performance. For the development phase of effort, the costs might be expressed as

$$CDEP = \prod_{i=1}^{m} N_i^{g_i}$$

where the N_i represent deployment multipliers that depend on the complexity of the system that is being deployed and such other deployment complexity points as the need for integration of the new system with legacy systems, the proficiency of the deployment personnel, and the quality of the developed software and its needs for maintenance. The g_i represent power factors that are empirically determined on the basis of observed past deployment performance.

We will examine models like this in some detail in our next chapter for the specific case of software development. Although there is some controversy about particular approaches, these approaches are felt to yield generally useful results.

4.4 SYSTEMATIC MEASUREMENTS OF DEFECTS

Clearly, neither the customer nor the organization responsible for a product wishes to have defective products. Some organizations will place defect minimization as their most important objective. We will examine in this section some of the salient characteristics likely to be found in this type of organization.

Product defects may be omnipresent. Defects may be found in a product prior to its deployment and corrected at the development phase of the lifecycle. Defects may not be found until just after a product or system is initially delivered to the customer. There may remain defects long after a product has been released to a customer. Defects may fall into any of a large number of categories. Systematic measurements are needed to determine defects at each of these times in the lifecycle, and for a number of defect types. Defect removal involves detection, diagnosis, and corrective action. Generally, the measurements associated with defect removal are reactive and possibly interactive in nature. Defect prevention is also very important, in many ways more important than defect removal. Obviously, defects that do occur should be corrected.

Defect correction is very much a function of operational level quality control and quality assurance. Chapter 4 in [11] and Chapters 5 and 6 of [8] are devoted to a discussion of the many approaches for test and inspection, verification and valida- tion, and the many other approaches that may be taken to defect prevention and defect correction. Our discussion of systems lifecycles in Chapter 2 has covered some of the configuration management issues associated with this since configura- tion management is very needed as an interactive approach to defect prevention and removal. Important works that discuss a number of important approaches in this area, especially as applied to software, include [32–37]. Recent reprint books include [38] and [39]. A relatively extensive discussion of systems management use of defect metrics and the relationship between this approach as an organizational driver to other approaches are provided by Grady [3].

4.5 SYSTEMS MANAGEMENT AND SYSTEMATIC MEASUREMENT

Systems management is concerned with the approaches to measurement that we have described in our earlier sections, as well as approaches that maximize product differentiation. It needs necessarily to be concerned with the costs and effectiveness of product, process, and systems management efforts. Many have addressed these issues. Harrington [40], in a work we will examine in Chapter 8, indicates well the case for measurement at the level of systems management when he states that "to measure is to understand, to understand is to gain knowledge, to have knowledge is to have power." A six-phase process, called an opportunity cycle, is suggested to allow for corrective action through measurement. This involves the sort of assess- ment and detection of difficulties, analysis and diagnosis of the causes of the difficulty and potential corrective actions, implementation of a chosen corrective action, action to prevent recurrence, and measurement throughout.

4.5.1 The Case for Systematic Measurements at the Level of Systems Management

In his excellent management handbook, Peters [7] identified first-level prescriptions for excellence, which we illustrate in Figure 4.20. We have briefly discussed the customer responsiveness prescriptions in Section 4.2. They are represented in Fig- ure 4.10. Achieving fast paced innovation and creating a climate for innovation within the organization were viewed both as supportive of customer responsiveness and as a first-level prescription for excellence. Figure 4.21 illustrates the nine prescriptions that lead to fast paced innovation. While the meaning of each of these is reasonably evident from the figure, the cited work by Peters provides much additional discussion. Figure 4.22 illustrates the ten prescriptions that support em- powering people in the organization. Figure 4.23 illustrates the ten prescriptions for organizational leadership and Figure 4.24 illustrates the very important prescrip- tions for the development of excellent organizational processes.

Most of our discussions in Chapters 6, 7, and 8 relate to these prescriptions. They are very much associated with the principles of total quality, leadership and

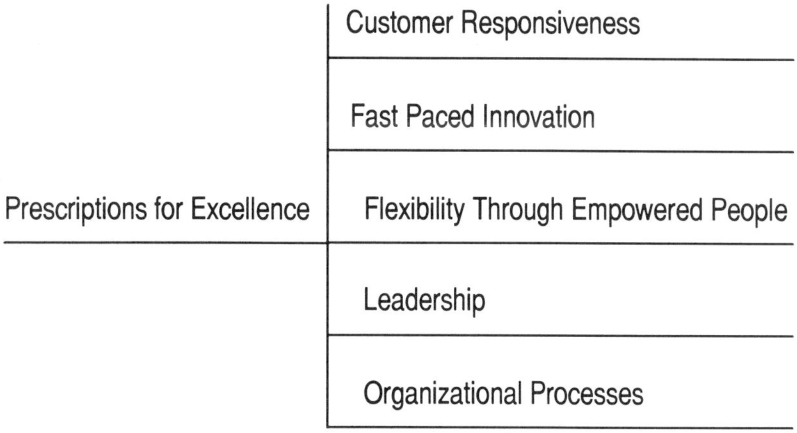

	Customer Responsiveness
	Fast Paced Innovation
Prescriptions for Excellence	Flexibility Through Empowered People
	Leadership
	Organizational Processes

Figure 4.20 Five first-level prescriptions for excellence.

processes, and reengineering, which we discuss in these chapters. Many appropriate measurements are associated with these various efforts. Peters suggests the importance of measurements in enabling each of these first-level prescriptions. There are a number of interactions across these 50 prescriptions as suggested by Figures 4.25 and 4.26. These need to be taken into account when considering deployment factors and measurements to allow for excellence.

Peters devotes an important chapter in this work to the need for measurements, and the need to measure what is important. He indicates that often the essential

	Invest in Application Oriented Small Starts
	Pursue Team Product and Service Delivery
	Encourage Prototypes of Everything
	Practice Creative Swiping
Pursue Fast Paced Innovation and Create an Organizational Capacity for Innovation	Encourage Systematic Verbal Marketing
	Support Committed Champions
	Be Innovative in Daily Affairs
	Support Fast Failures
	Set Quantitative Innovation Goals

Figure 4.21 Fast paced innovation prescriptions.

Prescriptions for Empowering People in the Organization	Involve Everyone in Everything
	Use Self-Managing Teams
	Listen, Reward, Recognize Performance
	Invest Time and Significant Effort in Recruiting
	Train and Retrain Present People
	Provide Incentive Pay for Everyone
	Provide Term Employment Guarantees
	Simplify/Reduce Organizational Structure
	Reconceive Role of Middle Management
	Eliminate Bureaucratic Rules/Conditions

Figure 4.22   Peters' prescriptions for empowering people.

Prescriptions for Creating Love of Change and a New Leadership View	Cope with Paradoxes and Conventional Wisdom
	Develop an Inspiring and Enabling Vision
	Manage and Lead by Example
	Manage Visibly - Reduce Information Distortion
	Pay Attention - Be a Compulsive Listener
	Emphasize Front Line People as Heroes
	Set the Context for and Delegate
	Pursue Horizontal Management - Bash Bureaucracy
	Evaluate Everyone on Love of Change
	Create a Sense of Urgency

Figure 4.23   The ten leadership prescriptions.

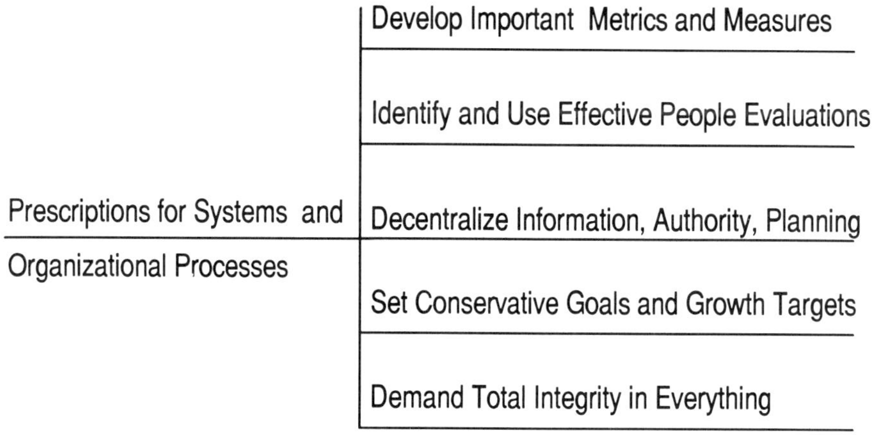

Prescriptions for Systems and Organizational Processes	Develop Important Metrics and Measures
	Identify and Use Effective People Evaluations
	Decentralize Information, Authority, Planning
	Set Conservative Goals and Growth Targets
	Demand Total Integrity in Everything

Figure 4.24 The five prescriptions for excellence of systems and organizational processes.

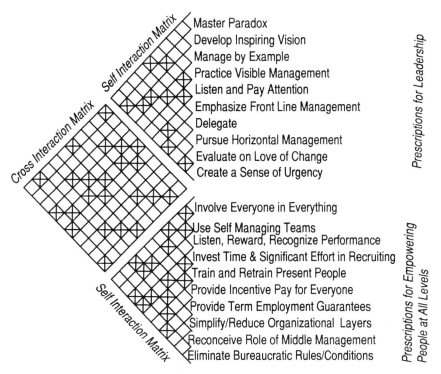

Figure 4.25 Hypothetical self- and cross-interaction matrices for prescriptions and for leadership and for empowering people.

Customer Responsiveness
Fast Paced Innovation
Empowering People
Enhancing Change
Organizational Processes
Customer Responsiveness
Fast Paced Innovation
Empowering People
Enhancing Change
Organizational Processes

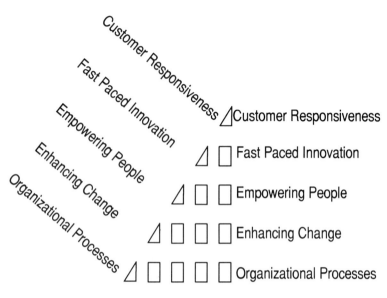

Figure 4.26 Interactions across the prescriptions for excellence.

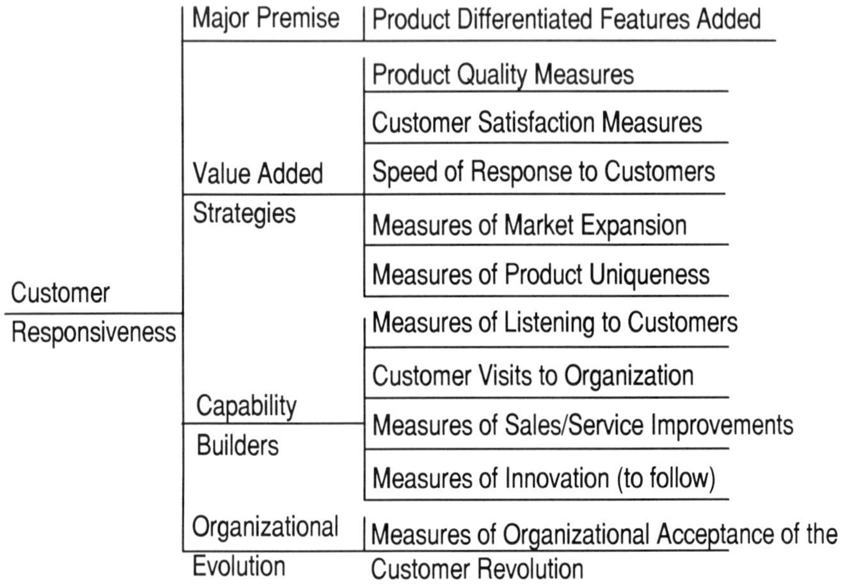

Customer Responsiveness
Major Premise
Product Differentiated Features Added
Value Added Strategies
Product Quality Measures
Customer Satisfaction Measures
Speed of Response to Customers
Measures of Market Expansion
Measures of Product Uniqueness
Capability Builders
Measures of Listening to Customers
Customer Visits to Organization
Measures of Sales/Service Improvements
Measures of Innovation (to follow)
Organizational Evolution
Measures of Organizational Acceptance of the Customer Revolution

Figure 4.27 Measures of customer responsiveness.

Fast Paced Innovation	Major Premise	Number of Innovative Small Starts
	Key Strategies	Measure of Service Innovations
		Number of Pilots and Prototypes
		Number of Benchmarked Ideas Adopted
		Measures of Word of Mouth Marketing
	Management Tactics	Number of Innovation Awards
		Number of Innovative Fast Failures Awards
		Measure of Revenues from New Products
		Measures for Quantitative Innovation Goals
	Organizational Evolution	Organizational Innovation Capacity Measures

Figure 4.28 Measures for organizational innovation.

Empowering People	Major Premise	Measures of Broadscope Involvement
	Empowerment Supports Added	Percentage of People in Teams
		Number of People Recognition Events
		Measure of Recruiting Time/Results
		Time and Effort for Skill Upgrading
		Measure of Compensation from Incentives
		Measures of Employment Stability
	Inhibitors Removed	Measures of Structural Simplification
		Measures of Boundaries Obliterated
		Measures of Bureaucracy Bashing

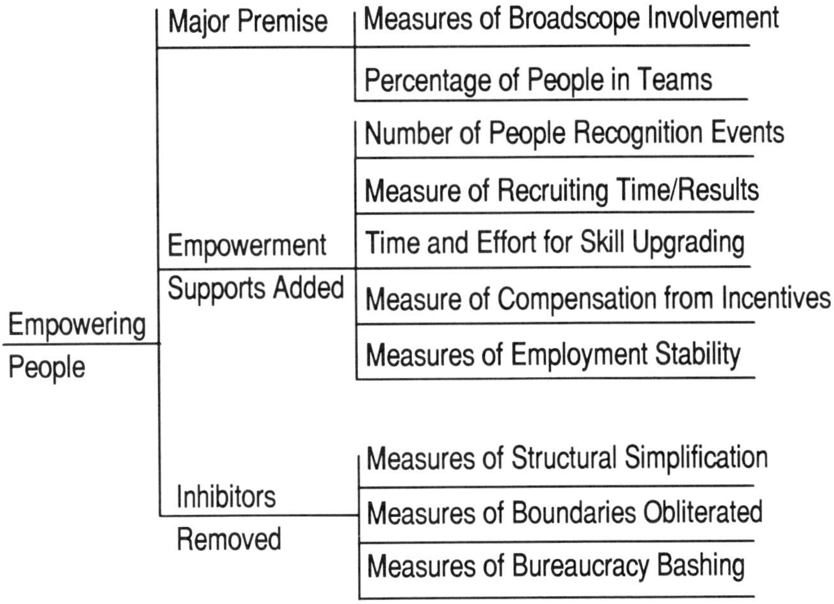

Figure 4.29 Measures for empowering people.

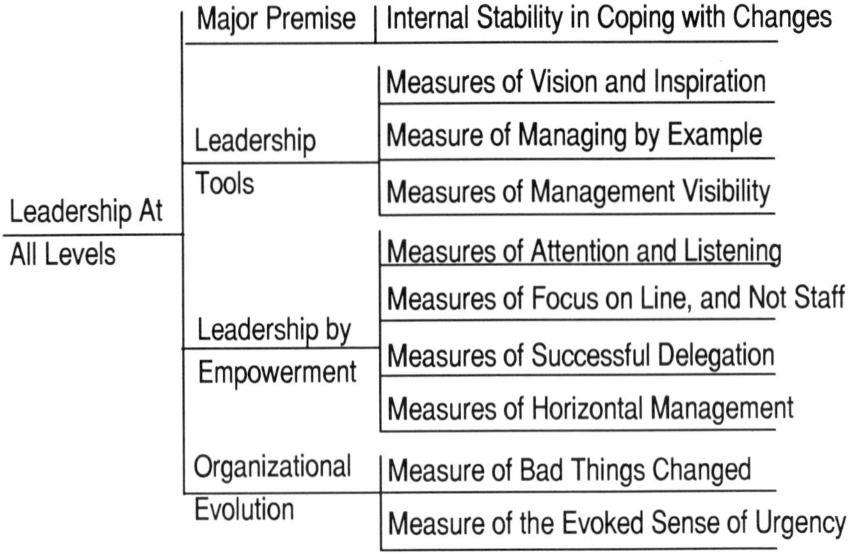

Major Premise	Internal Stability in Coping with Changes
Leadership Tools	Measures of Vision and Inspiration
	Measure of Managing by Example
	Measures of Management Visibility
Leadership by Empowerment	Measures of Attention and Listening
	Measures of Focus on Line, and Not Staff
	Measures of Successful Delegation
	Measures of Horizontal Management
Organizational Evolution	Measure of Bad Things Changed
	Measure of the Evoked Sense of Urgency

(leftmost column label: Leadership At All Levels)

Figure 4.30   Measures of satisfaction of leadership prescriptions.

variables are ignored even through they can be measured and he is especially concerned with inappropriate financial measurements that ignore such important variables, which are needed for organizational success, as product quality, customer satisfaction, time to market, and worker empowerment. He identifies metrics for many of the prescriptions for excellence associated with customer responsiveness, innovation, empowering people, and leadership. The others can be inferred. Figures 4.27 through 4.31 illustrate suggested measurements for the five first-level prescriptions for excellence shown previously as Figure 4.10 and Figures 4.21 through 4.24.

It is our strong belief that the many attributes and measurements suggested in this subsection, as well as earlier in this chapter, need to be used in determining the overall worth of proposed alternatives for organizational advancement. Cost–benefit and cost–effectiveness analyses have been traditional measures used to

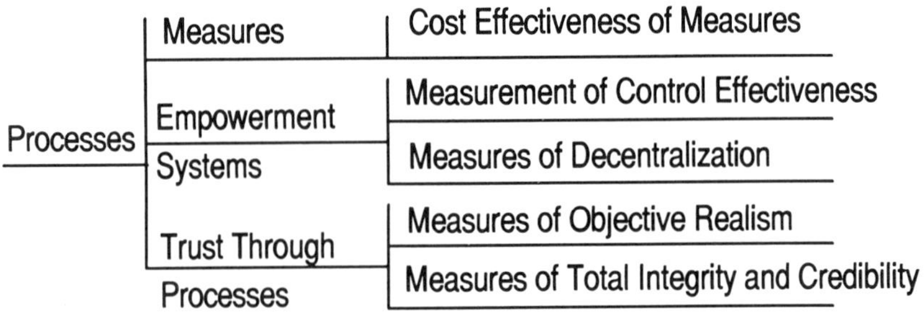

Measures	Cost Effectiveness of Measures
Empowerment Systems	Measurement of Control Effectiveness
	Measures of Decentralization
Trust Through Processes	Measures of Objective Realism
	Measures of Total Integrity and Credibility

(leftmost column label: Processes)

Figure 4.31   Measures associated with responsive systems and processes.

determine this worth and we now turn our attention to some summary comments on this important subject.

4.5.2 Cost–Benefit and Cost–Effectiveness Assessments

One of the standard approaches for evaluation of alternative courses of action is through use of cost–benefit analysis (CBA). In the terminology used here, the term "cost–benefit assessment" would be more appropriate because we do accomplish formulation, analysis, and interpretation of alternative courses of action through use of this approach. These alternative courses of action may represent alternative processes or product lines for development of a new or modified product. They may represent alternative marketing strategies or RDT&E efforts. Or they may well represent a combination of these.

The broad goals of cost–benefit analysis are to provide procedures for the esti-mation and evaluation of the benefits and costs associated with alternative courses of action. In many cases it will not be possible to obtain a completely economic evaluation of the benefits of proposed courses of action. This is surely the situation considered here. In this case, the word "benefit" is replaced by the term "effective-ness," and a multiattribute effectiveness evaluation is used. We may use cost–benefit analysis (CBA) and cost–effectiveness analysis (CEA) to help choose among potential new programs, to evaluate existing systems for various purposes, such as identifying potential process modification needs, or to identify possible new product development strategies. A set of phases for implementation of a CBA process is illustrated in Figure 4.32.

Identification and quantification of the benefits and costs of possible alternative courses of action are difficult tasks, although generally not quite as difficult as formulating meaningful alternatives themselves. Here we use the word benefits to mean the possible overall effects that result from implementation of a program. The program may well be a totally new and potentially innovative program, or it may well represent a series of possibly minor refinements to an existing program. The program under investigation is comprised of a number of alternative courses of action that must be decided upon. Regardless of which alternative program is adopted, there will be a set of benefits associated with that program. These include both positive and negative benefits, or disbenefits. We must first identify benefits and then assign quantitative values to them. Many benefits (and disbenefits) will be intangible and will accrue to differing groups or individuals in differing amounts, especially in public sector programs. Problems with intangibles are especially diffi-cult to deal with in the public sector, where agencies are designed primarily to deliver services or public goods, rather than products for individual consumption. A major goal of a classic private sector organization is profit maximization and it is relatively easy to measure profit as a benefit. The benefits of a public service, such as a school, or a public good, such as a subway system, are much more difficult to define because they are intangible or indivisible or both.

One valuation philosophy that we might adopt is based on two suppositions. The first of these is that the value of a program to an individual is equal to the fully

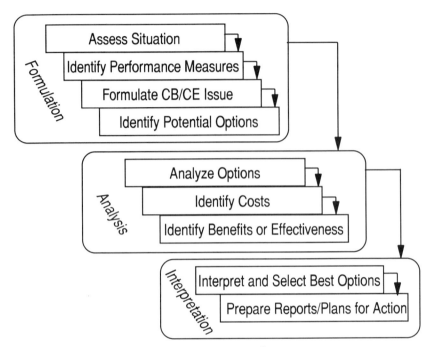

Figure 4.32   Generic cost–benefit and cost–effectiveness assessment process.

informed willingness of the individual to pay for the program. The second is that the social value of a program is the sum of the values of the program to the individual members of society.* The fundamental conclusion of microeconomics, under perfect competition conditions, confirms that these two suppositions or premises should, under very ideal conditions, serve as good guideposts for cost–benefit analysis.

Sadly, however, the "full information" called for in the first supposition is almost never available. Measurement problems also arise in determining the value of a complex program, such as a large sewage disposal system serving residential, commercial, and industrial users, or a wide-area computer network upgrade for a giant corporation. Usually, decomposition of the benefit of such a program into attributes and assigning of numerical values to these attributes will produce a more reliable indication of the value of a program than unaided intuitive judgment, especially when dealing with unfamiliar issues.

The implementation of any program will alter the supply of "inputs," consumed in the production process, and the supply of "outputs," resulting from the program. Such changes may, in turn, affect the ultimate value of the program. Another measurement problem with cost–benefit analysis arises in trying to foresee contin-

---

*For strictly private sector analysis, we could speak about the "organizational value" of a program as the potentially weighted sum of the values of the program to organizational stakeholders.

gencies. CBA may be a relatively simple technique when we are evaluating operational-level programs, such as the introduction of word-processing equipment in an office to replace electric typewriters. But many programs are predicated on substantial changes in external environments, such as population growth, business expansion, or changing consumer tastes. In situations such as these, the evaluation of alternative options must evolve over time. Useful descriptions of situations such as these often require very complex and very difficult judgments.

Usually, a financial accounting of the various alternative programs results in the information that is needed to identify and quantify economic benefits and costs, perhaps in a balance or spreadsheet format. However, adjustments to the financial accounting data are often needed. Sometimes we will find that the financial accounting will neglect some benefits and costs, particularly those of a secondary and/or intangible nature, that may be well necessary for a useful analysis of the economic benefits and costs of a program. Also, it will often be necessary to adjust financial information for those in which market prices either do not exist or, even if they do exist, do not reflect true economic value. As we have indicated in Section 4.3, there are potential problems in the usual unit-level costing approach used in many accounting systems. This has led to much interest in activity-based costing (ABC) systems, as we have discussed. It is also possible, of course, to speak of activity-based benefits (ABB) and activity-based effectiveness (ABE) approaches although this is much less common at this time.

Where competition is imperfect, such as with a monopoly, prices do not reflect value. Also, for products made for use internal to a given firm and not marketed, there is no market price. In all cases, investment decisions will likely be based on market prices, whether or not they reflect "true economic value," assuming the investor believes such prices are likely to be reasonably steady during the term of the investment.

While it is not difficult to state items of this sort, it is often quite difficult to fully account for them in practice. This makes it difficult to do a fully meaningful CBA and to read and understand those that have been conducted. When we consider the multiplicity of measures of effectiveness associated with the prescriptions for excellence that we have just discussed, we see that conversion of even a subset of these to purely economic measures is a very difficult, if not impossible, task.

Thus there will often be a variety of reasons why people will be uncomfortable with providing a strict economic measure for benefits. The word effectiveness is often used instead of benefit when a strictly economic valuation is not needed or is not possible. When "effectiveness" is substituted for "benefit" we obtain a cost–effectiveness analysis.

In cost–effectiveness analysis, we desire to rank programs, or one or more of the projects that comprise a program, in terms of effectiveness and costs, including in our consideration attributes measured according to different standards. Certainly we would wish to eliminate obviously inferior programs—that is, programs that are both more expensive and less effective—from consideration. Beyond this, a cost–effectiveness analysis does not specify which of the remaining programs is "best." This can be accomplished if one is willing to trade off cost for effectiveness, so as to obtain a scalar performance index. This can be done by considering cost as one of the attributes in the effectiveness evaluation.

The effectiveness of an alternative is the degree to which it satisfies identified objectives. The effectiveness assessment approach described here provides an explicit procedure for quantifying multiple attributes. This is accomplished by identifying and organizing the attributes into a tree-type hierarchy, attribute tree, or worth structure and then attaching measures of effectiveness to each such attribute tree. Effectiveness assessment is most appropriate when we want a single, consistent approach for measuring the impacts of proposed policies such as to enable ranking of these policies for selection of one or more of them for actual implementation or deployment.

Such an approach also results in an easily communicable picture of the effectiveness, value, or importance that individuals or groups place on different impacts of the proposed programs. Typically, there also results a significant amount of learning by decision makers concerning their own preferences, and the consistency of their evaluations and decisions regarding these preferences. Increased understanding of the decision process and of decision maker preferences for possible outcomes are other results of this approach. Generally, an effectiveness assessment study involves the following major steps.

1. *Formulation of the Issue.* The individual or group of people, whose preferences and values are to be used as standards of measure, is defined. The scope of the analysis to follow, including objectives or attributes to be studied, is determined. The attributes should be restricted to those of the highest degree of importance. No attribute should encompass any other attribute or objective. Each should be "independent," in the sense that the decision maker is willing to trade partial satisfaction of one objective for reduced satisfaction of another objective. Once the high-level effectiveness attributes have been established, they must be disaggregated into lower-level attributes. Each of these is further subdivided until the decision maker feels that program effectiveness can ultimately be measured. This dividing and subdividing process results in a tree-type hierarchical structure of effectiveness attributes.

2. *Selection of Appropriate Attributes of Effectiveness and Associated Performance Measures.* Some quantifiable characteristic of performance or effectiveness for an alternative is assigned to each lowest-level attribute.

3. *Definition of the Relationship Between Low-Level Attributes and Quantifiable Attribute Measures.* This relation is established by assigning an effectiveness score to all possible values of a given attribute measure. The score given a particular attribute can range from 0 to 1. Zero is the worst score, and one is the best score. In determining the score of each alternative on all lowest-level attributes, the following questions must be answered.

(a) Is the scale of attribute values continuous or discrete? Generally it can be discrete, such as a good or bad outcome.

(b) For a continuous scale, does the attribute measure possess either a logical upper bound or a logical lower bound, or both? If this is not the case, the particular attribute in question needs to be redefined.

(c) What values of each attribute measure are identified with alternative performance of 0 to 1?

(d) Does the rate of change of worth or effectiveness with respect to attribute measures stay fixed, or does it increase or decrease?

(e) If the rate of change of worth of the attribute varies, does it always decrease (or increase) or does it first decrease (or increase) and then increase (or decrease)?

4. *Establishment of Relative Importance Within Each Level of Attributes.* Some of the attributes within a given level are normally more important than others, and these differences need to be accounted for. The first step is to rank the subattributes of a particular attribute by relative importance. The most important subattribute is assigned a temporary value of 1.0. The second most important may be assigned a temporary value of $1.0 \times \frac{3}{5} = \frac{3}{5}$. If the third attribute is two-thirds as important as the second, it is assigned a temporary value of $\frac{3}{5} \times \frac{2}{3} = \frac{2}{5}$. This process is continued until all subattributes have been assigned temporary weights. Then those temporary weights are scaled so that the sum of attribute weights, for a particular attribute, is unity.

5. *Determination of the Equivalent Weights for Each Lowest-Level Attribute.* The relative weighting process is applied to all lowest-level attributes in the decision tree and the attribute weights are determined.

6. *Calculation of Effectiveness.* The effectiveness of each program is calculated by multiplying the equivalent weights of each attribute by its individual worth score and summing to yield an overall effectiveness score.

7. *Sensitivity Analysis.* In general, the sensitivity of the effectiveness scores to variation in parameters is determined by a sensitivity analysis, in which different values are assigned to the attribute worth scores, and the effectiveness scores are then recalculated.

8. *Presentation of Results.* The final results of the analysis are used for comparison, ranking, and prioritization of alternatives according to effectiveness.

The process involved is very much like that used for multiple attribute utility assessment (MAUT) in Chapter 7 of [11]. Any of the variants suggested for MAUT may be adapted for use here.

Any cost–effectiveness evaluation program must begin with a study of the goals of the program. In some cases, those planning the evaluation are given the goals. Some organizations have a very narrowly focused purpose. The goals may be focused on creation or development of a particular technology and may not allow the consideration of whether other technologies or approaches may address the same purpose more effectively.

Once the goals of the program or program to be evaluated have been fixed, it is necessary to determine how attainment of these goals will be measured. This is not difficult to do in some cases but impossible to do in others without considerable ambiguity. In many cases, the difficulty in assigning a measure of performance depends on how well the goals have been defined.

If there is a single objective goal to be served by a program and if it is very specific and readily quantifiable, then it is fairly simple to select a performance measure. If, however, there is a single goal that is very broad, there are likely no universally accepted measures. A goal such as this provides no direction to the research program and has no functional value other than as the first step toward more specific goals. In this case, step 1 cannot easily be completed.

If there are several different groups or individuals involved in the decision, it is unlikely that all will perceive the same trade-offs among measures. In very polarized cases, an increase in a measure may enhance perceived worth for one group while diminishing it for another; or one group may be insensitive to measures of great importance to another group.

Often, it will be necessary to employ sophisticated forecasting techniques to obtain answers to relevant questions. This will be particularly true for the costs of "long life" systems. Sadly, however, there is simply no way that forecasting could be described as a precise and exact science that always yields trustworthy and reliable results [41].

Costs are very important in forecasting. They arise from the many possible activities associated with purposeful effort. The two sources of innovation, demand pull and technology push, commonly influence such costs. Demand pull describes innovation arising from recognition of an unsatisfied demand. The innovator, noting a need, considers ways to address that need until one or more viable approaches are found. Technology push occurs when available or achievable technology makes it possible to do something that was not possible before, or to do something in a new and better way. The force behind technology push may be a new technology, or it may be a new material, process, or application of existing technology. Conceivably, a new view of an existing technology can be a source of inspiration for innovation and development.

Three kinds of forecasting will often be needed. The first is an economic forecast, which seeks to establish demand for new products, technologies, and services (both public and private) and the costs of providing these. Generally, the demand for new products is highest in expanding segments of the economy and lowest in those that are declining. Therefore patterns of economic growth are a principal topic for research.

A sociological forecast will also usually be needed. The objective here is to identify changes in the society, which affect the demand for new technologies and the environment for innovation. Specific areas that should be included in the forecast are as follows [42]:

Demographic structures, including location and makeup of future populations.

Spending priorities, including concerns relating to public versus private consumption, preference shifts within product groups, acceptability of new technologies, and emphasis on various areas of expenditure.

The role of government, including those activities of government that influence the demand for new technologies through both direct purchase and regulations that affect the use of existing technologies.

Public and legal attitudes toward business, including attitudes toward monopolies and oligopolies, patent issues, and public control of product, material, and service processes.

International affairs, including issues relating to foreign markets, foreign political shifts, tariff barriers, and international currency stability.

Labor conditions, including those conditions favorable to or adverse to the introduction of automation.

Education, including the number of trained scientists and engineers, level of consumer sophistication, and the propensity of university research to develop new products.

The need for inclusion of factors like these makes forecasting of future societal trends extraordinarily difficult.

A technological forecast assesses general developments in the specific technology area under consideration among competitors in that technological area. It is also necessary to consider emerging technology needs of customers. While it is difficult to identify opportunities for technology push, an appropriate forecast of technology pull or demand is also needed. This is even more difficult. Certainly, it is easier for a research organization to address known needs than to identify the potential for societal demand for new technologies. Normally, we will desire an economic forecast, a social forecast, and a technological forecast.

Cost–benefit and cost–effectiveness analyses are methods used by systems engineers to aid decision makers in the interpretation and comparison of proposed alternative plans or programs. They are based on the premise that a choice should be made by comparing the benefits or effectiveness of each alternative with its costs. Benefit is an economic term that is generally understood to be a monetary unit. Effectiveness is a multiattribute term used when the consequences of program implementation are not reduced to dollar terms. We will describe an approach for cost–benefit analysis (CBA) and then indicate modifications to adapt it to cost–effectiveness analysis (CEA).

First, objectives for the program must be identified and alternatives generated and defined carefully. Then the costs as well as the benefits of proposed programs are identified. These costs and benefits are next quantified and expressed in common economic units whenever this is possible. Discounting is used to compare costs and/or benefits at different times. Present worth is the usual discount criterion of choice. Overall performance measures, such as the total costs and benefits, are computed for each alternative. In addition to this quantitative analysis, an account is made of qualitative impacts, such as social aesthetic and environmental effects. Equity considerations regarding the distribution of costs and benefits across various societal groups may be considered. The cost–benefit analysis method is based on the principle that a proposed economic condition is superior to the present state if the total benefits of a proposed program exceed the total costs.

Among the results of a cost–benefit or cost–effectiveness analysis are the following:

Tables containing detailed explanations of the costs and benefits over time of each alternative program, and present value of costs or benefits of each alternative program.

Computation and comparison of overall performance measures, in terms of benefits and costs, for each of the alternative programs. Alternatively, effectiveness and costs may be used if a cost–effectiveness analysis is desired.

An accounting of intangible and secondary costs, such as social or environmental or even aesthetic, and the set of multiattributed benefits or effectiveness value that is associated with each alternative program.

Methods such as decision analysis and multiattribute utility theory can be used to evaluate effectiveness. We are able to use the resulting effectiveness indices in conjunction with cost analysis to assist in making the trade-offs between quantitative and qualitative attributes of the alternative programs. There are a number of studies available addressing this important subject, and references [43–50] are particularly recommended.

We will summarize many of our discussions in this section related to cost–effectiveness analysis to the problem of systems management of the research and development of emerging technologies. There are four major objectives in this:

1. To determine an appropriate specific process to use for the identification and evaluation of potential technologies for development and/or transfer.
2. To identify the groups that should be involved in this identification and evaluation process.
3. To identify the criteria that will be used to determine length and type of support.
4. To identify appropriate criteria to determine transferability of the technology to full scale operational deployment status or termination.

Our efforts are based, in large part, on previous research by Miller and Sage [51], Sage [52], and Benson and Sage [53].

One major product of research is information. Systems management of research and development must attach a value to this information, in terms of the final product that might be developed. This, unfortunately, is not easy. This is because the product is normally far downstream in the development process and because a single research effort normally contributes to a variety of technologies and products.

The large amount of uncertainty regarding the ultimate value of research often suggests that many parallel, generally low cost, research programs be initially funded. As a result, methodologies for early research cost–effectiveness studies must be able to deal with a large number of uncertain programs. Methodologies for later lifecycle cost–effectiveness analysis generally deal with a smaller number of less uncertain, but more costly, programs.

It might seem that the second task is easier than the first. But the large sums of money involved in the later stages of development make it critical to fund the best alternative for later development, test and evaluation efforts. The analysis of programs at the DT&E phases of the lifecycle may be easier, but the penalty for error is much greater than for errors at the stage of basic research. If we accept the view that the value of research may be measured by the value of the resulting products, the focus of program evaluation becomes the forecasting and estimation of the market performance of the innovations. Market penetration estimates and analysis of the expected return on investment are the principal measures of research worth. Conventional market methodologies may fail, however, when a technology is not explicitly marketed, or when it has no conventional competitor. This is one of the reasons why we considered the three lifecycles of RDT&E, acquisition or production, and planning and marketing in Chapter 2.

When an innovation does have a conventional competitor, the potential market for an emerging technology will be (1) that fraction of the conventional product's market in which the emerging technology enjoys an economic advantage; (2) minus some fraction of users of the conventional technology who are unable to convert to the new one for economic, environmental, institutional, technical, or other reasons; and (3) plus some additional market that was unable to use the conventional product but is now able to use the emerging technology. None of these three are particularly easy to estimate. When the emerging technology is mostly unlike anything else that exists at the time when the technology emerges, it is much more difficult to address issues associated with estimating the number of potential users of an emerging technology product, how rapidly they will adopt it, and much they are willing to pay for it. The second problem with assessing research programs by the market potential of final products is that, as we have noted, some products do not compete in a marketplace.

There are many other related concurrent variables and it is desirable to discuss some of these. Often there will be simultaneous development of two potentially competing technologies. When the products eventually compete, assuming that both are superior to existing products, the one with the lowest cost and the highest effectiveness will ultimately dominate the market.

If the technology that is marketed first is not the best but is still better than the conventional alternative by enough of a margin to justify the switch to it, then it will sell to those segments of the market that (1) are unaware of the forthcoming, superior technology; (2) are aware of the forthcoming technology but unwilling to wait for this better alternative; or (3) are willing to purchase the immediate alternative for use until the improved version is available. The market shares of the competing alternatives will therefore not reflect their relative economics because of the different time horizons associated with product introduction. The implication of this is that strategic management and management controls reflect timing when considering the effectiveness of emerging technology programs. The bottom line is that the value of a emerging technology development program completed some time in the future is usually not as great as the value of the same program completed now, except when market conditions related to supporting technologies prohibit immediate adoption of the emerging technology product under development.

Some products enhance the value of other products. The basic issue with augmenting one technology to support existing technologies is that of evaluating the conditional and independent worth of the individual technologies. The value of each technology must be evaluated assuming that none of the other new ones are successful, and then reevaluated for various possible outcomes of the other research programs. This is not an easy task. One very difficult complication is that the different technologies may compete in different markets. Market penetration for products is very difficult to estimate. In the special case where two or more emerging technologies are worthless without each other, but do have an estimable value when all technologies are adopted, the group of programs can be treated as one for management purposes. This may create a very significant problem in formulating or framing the emerging technology development issue. But the decision itself is simplified to a binary all-or-none comparison. This assumes a degree of centralization of authority over emerging technology developments, which may not always be achievable.

In the situation where there are several competing technologies that augment a third, effectiveness analysis becomes especially complicated. There must be careful study of the market, the decision makers and their preference structure, and the time horizon associated with product introductions.

When two programs share similar information, or software or hardware elements, the work on one technology can potentially be used to support efforts relative to the other. The associated information transfer can substantially complicate the cost–effectiveness evaluation process. If concurrent development of the two programs makes it possible to eliminate or reduce work in the common areas, the cost of doing both programs is not the sum of doing either without the other program. Thus it is not possible to use simple linear evaluation methods without modification to enable consideration of this dependence. Thus there can be some serious difficulties in modeling emerging technology program interactions. Clearly, this is the situation today with the very significant interest in such areas as computer integrated manufacturing, concurrent engineering, and reusable software development. It is for reasons such as these that activity-based and veridical determinations of costs, benefits, and effectiveness factors are so very important.

The appropriate approach to "augmenting technologies" will vary widely depending on the situation. As a consequence, it is neither feasible nor wise to try to develop a single, all embracing analytic approach that will fit all situations.

For example, imagine a small, highly specialized, not-well-capitalized firm developing a specific new product, say, a new kind of secure database management system. Say further that another research group in that firm's lab is working on programs that could "augment" the value of this system. Given these conditions, the firm is likely to allocate RDT&E funding for each program based solely on that program's clearly identified market potential for itself, without reference to synergism across the programs.

As another extreme, we might consider government investment in "big science" or other development programs. In such instances, it is generally agreed that no one can foresee all the possible uses to which such a program could be put, and that, in a sense, the sole purpose of such programs is to "augment" other technologies. To take a variation on this theme, advocates of a federal "technology" or "industrial" policy often like to talk about the need to fund "enabling technologies," the argument being that such technologies will be a catalyst for wide-ranging technological development.

Situations in-between these two extremes are also quite interesting. For example, consider a large, for-profit corporation conducting research in four interrelated areas: expert systems, reduced instruction chips, gallium arsenide substrates, and laptop computer design. Obviously, potential synergism exists among all four areas of research, and the corporation would surely like to identify these. But it would be very difficult to find a reasonably reliable methodology for identifying, quantifying, and ranking such synergism and, on the basis of these rankings, rationally apportioning research funds among them. In practice, a diverse kit of analytic tools to assess and prioritize such research appears very needed.

It is reasonable to begin cost–effectiveness assessment by evaluation of individual candidate programs. Analysis of a single program can be viewed as a two-step process. First, the technical outcome of each program is forecast. The objective of this is to characterize the technology that the program will ultimately produce. The second step is to relate the technical outcome of a program to its effectiveness. For example, in evaluating a program that is directed toward producing a commercial product, the relationship between various technical performance features and future sales volume should be forecast.

We recommend separating the technology forecast from the analysis of effectiveness, since the information and skills needed to forecast performance of an emerging technology are generally quite different from those needed to evaluate its long-term effectiveness. In the first case, technical specialty skills are most needed, while in the second case, a broad spectrum of information and accompanying interpretive skills are most needed. The value of an emerging technology is a complex function, including such factors as its performance relative to other technologies that have the same functional end and the resources and preferences of the consumers. Two excellent works by Alan Porter and his colleagues [45,54] describe a number of approaches for technology forecasting and evaluation.

After each emerging technology program is examined separately, it is necessary to consider combinations of programs, or portfolios, in order to determine which grouping maximizes the combined value of all programs under consideration. If the programs are independent, then the effectiveness of a portfolio is the sum of the individual effectiveness, and the cost of a portfolio is the sum of the individual costs. If the programs are not independent, then there must be a third analytical step in addition to the two discussed above. The third step is to characterize the relationship between the new technologies in their final market; that is, to develop a model of the impact of each program's technical success on the value of the other programs. The next and final step in the resource allocation methodology is to select the best portfolio.

An organization needs a general idea of how much revenue a new product will yield before it can make a wise decision concerning investments in that product.

Certainly, when demand is uncertain, various risk analysis approaches may be employed that might not be employed when demand is reasonably predictable. These lead to risk management strategies for the technology development in question. In the final analysis, however, it will still be the case in the future that

$$\text{Revenue} = \text{Price} \times \text{Quantity sold}$$

This is what management needs to know, and with some reasonable degree of precision. Profitability, as expressed in monetary terms, is the normal measure of market performance, although other measures are used in special circumstances, such as market share or profit-as-percent of sales. This, of course, is not all that management needs to know. There are many contemporary writers in this area, who suggest even that profit is not the major objective of the firm and that it is perhaps best regarded as an objectives measure that follows from more appropriate objectives as customer satisfaction.

Cost is not directly related to either the value of the technology or the number of units in use. Market price must first be determined. Assuming that it is possible to develop some relationship between number of units sold and market price in the form of a product demand curve, it is potentially a fairly simple effort to determine the market price that maximizes return of investment. If return on investment (ROI) is the measure of effectiveness to the technology developer or can be related to it in an appropriate manner, then a cost–effectiveness based formulation is quite appropriate.

As development of an emerging technology moves to the final stages, evaluation focuses on a smaller set of candidate programs, but with much more detailed and accurate cost and effectiveness measures. The value of a program to the developing organization can be a function of many attributes. Clearly, the best procedure for assessment depends on the measures of effectiveness applied. Any assessment of cost–effectiveness must include an estimate of how well the product will perform, which involves many performance attributes, and how much it will cost. The cost–effectiveness assessment may stop there, if the technology is being developed for internal use, or it may be carried through a forecast of market penetration, if the technology is intended for use outside the developing organization.

It is generally not possible to predict accurately how an emerging technology will perform in advance of its deployment. But forecasts do need to be made. Initially, it is appropriate to regard cost and effectiveness as uncertain parameters, with probability distributions, rather than as certain values. Given some measures of the effectiveness of an emerging technology under development, the next step in cost–effectiveness assessment is to estimate the number of units of the new technology that will come into use over time. Market penetration estimation is very important in many financial decisions. Consequently, market penetration models have been developed.

Market penetration potential may be defined as the number of units of the new technology, which could be adopted in a unit of time if every potential user preferred it to all other alternatives. Market share is the fraction of the potential market that is actually captured. If the technology addresses a totally new use such that there is no conventional alternative, the market share is necessarily 100%. The unit of time used in a penetration analysis should be chosen on the basis of expected rate of penetration and the market life of the product.

Implicit in the discussion that preceded this section is the assumption that the funding organization wishes to select a limited number of programs. The presence of such a resource constraint makes it necessary to consider not only the effectiveness of a program but also its cost in terms of money, people, equipment, and any other quantity that could be binding on the research program. Our earlier discussions of work breakdown structure and cost breakdown structure are quite relevant here. Relevant program costs include the following:

1. Sunk costs are costs already expended. In the idealized allocation problem, time begins when the allocation decision is made. Program history up to this point is not considered, except to the extent that it influences future effectiveness and cost. Of course, organizations normally have a stock of RDT&E programs in progress. The costs of the programs underway from initiation to the point in time used for the allocation analysis are defined as sunk costs.

2. The fixed costs of the organization are those that do not vary with the size of the organization or the size and makeup of the research program and cannot be directly associated with one or more specific programs.

3. The variable costs of the organization are similarly free of any association with individual programs, but they do vary with the size of the organization and the research program. The distinction between fixed and variable costs is often ambiguous. Some costs are fixed over ranges of organization and research program size but do vary when a major change in size occurs. Also, some costs are fixed for the short term but can be varied over the long term. The definition of which costs are fixed and which are variable must be made when the timing horizon and the size of a research program are determined.

4. The fixed costs of a program are those costs that are directly attributable to the program and do not vary with the level of effort. Equipment purchase would be a variable cost if equipment requirements were different in different configurations of the program.

5. The variable costs of a program are those costs that are directly attributable to one or more programs and that do vary with the level of effort in the associated programs. Equipment purchase would be a variable cost if equipment requirements were different in different configurations of the program.

In practice, the total cost of a large program is not easy either to define or to determine. The definition of total program cost is a function of the purpose for which detailed cost estimates are prepared. An evaluation of the overall effectiveness of the organization should include all cost elements. The fixed costs of the organization, which by definition are not attributable to an individual program, may or may not be used in the resource allocation analysis, depending on the objective of the cost accounting efforts. Even though fixed and variable costs of the organization do not enter into the comparison of alternative portfolios except in determining cost constraints, they play an important role in determining how large a research program the organization should undertake.

When the constituent programs in an emerging technology research portfolio are independent, in the sense that the effectiveness and costs of the portfolio equal the sum of the effectiveness and costs of the programs, evaluation is simple, and mathematical programming techniques can be used to isolate the optimal mix of programs quickly and inexpensively. When effectiveness and cost cannot be added in this fashion, evaluating a portfolio becomes substantially more difficult.

There are many reasons why the effectiveness of a group of programs may differ from the sum of the effectiveness of its members. The programs may produce technologies that enhance each other's effectiveness, so that the effectiveness of the group is greater than the effectiveness of the technologies alone. On the other hand, the programs may produce technologies that compete with each other, so that the effectiveness of the group is less than the effectiveness of the individual programs. It is rather difficult to define general classes of ways in which one product can enhance the effectiveness of another. There are numerous examples of how the development of one specific product has made another more valuable. Furthermore, the degree of the enhancement in effectiveness seems to cover a broad range depending on the specific products under consideration. In general, however, the steps illustrated in Figure 4.33 appear appropriate for a CEA of emerging technology RDT&E issues.

As we have noted, there is a danger in assuming that one or another technology is, in an absolute sense, "superior" to another or "cheaper" than another. Sound evaluation should start with a clear concept of the intended use or intended market of the technology if one hopes to be able to come up with reasonably meaningful

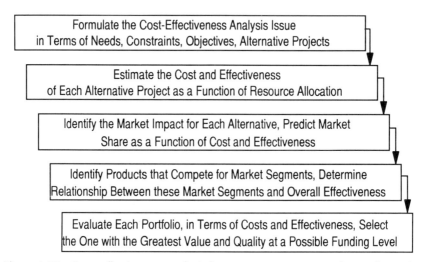

Figure 4.33   Cost–effectiveness analysis for systems management of emerging technology R&D.

quantitative evaluation. In brief, product RDT&E must have a market in mind! Basic scientific or engineering research is a completely different matter, as we have also discussed. There is an underlying notion of the quality of process and product in these issues also; and quality concerns should not be neglected—either the cost of quality or the cost of poor quality.

There are at least three ways to select the optimum portfolio from among a large number of alternatives:

1. Reduce the number of alternatives by some sort of elimination process. There are three very useful techniques for such a process: screening, ranking, and the use of stochastic dominance concepts.
2. Constrain the problem formulation such that the evaluation technique is compatible with optimization techniques such as mathematical programming.
3. Improve the numerical efficiency of the evaluation process so that a large number of alternatives can be considered.

These procedures are, of course, neither mutually exclusive nor exhaustive. Reference [11] provides additional details concerning their implementation, and a rather detailed example is considered in [55].

An excellent summary of the sort of evaluation criteria we have been discussing is provided in Dutton and Crowe [56]. There are three top level criteria and a number of attributes subordinate to these:

Technological merit
   Technological objectives and significance
   Breadth of interest of strategy
   Potential for new discoveries and understandings
   Uniqueness of proposed development strategy
Social benefits
   Contribution to improvement of the human condition
   Contribution to national pride and prestige
   Contribution to international understanding
Programmatic (management) issues
   Feasibility and readiness for development
   Technological logistics and infrastructure
   Technological community commitment and readiness
   Institutional infrastructure and implications
   International involvement
   Cost of the proposed strategy

These criteria form the basis for a multiple attribute evaluation and are associated with the gateways for RDT&E, acquisition or production, and marketing, as we have illustrated in Figure 1.18. Of course, the expanded set of effectiveness attributes we discussed earlier in this section could be used as well.

The theory surrounding the allocation of funds to research as a function of the costs and revenue requirements of the organization and the alternative options for investment is a large, complex, and heavily studied area and the interested reader will find it rewarding to consult recent studies in this area [57–59]. One particularly interesting study [60] develops a two-dimensional typography in which the degree of technological uncertainty is illustrated on one dimension and the scope of the system to be produced is on one dimension. As technological uncertainty increases, the probability of cost and schedule overruns increases. On the other hand, a high uncertainty associated with new technological developments may result in truly innovative products. Also, the scope of development may vary from very small systems or products, called arrays in the cited literature, to systems and supra-systems, called assemblies in the referenced work. Not only does the level of technology vary from low tech to super high tech in this development, the development work that is required changes considerably. Of much importance also, the managerial style and attitude and the appropriate organizational communications patterns vary considerably across these different types of development programs. In a real sense, this represents an extension of some of our discussions in Chapter 2, especially those leading to Figure 2.11. Figure 4.34 illustrates the two-dimensional

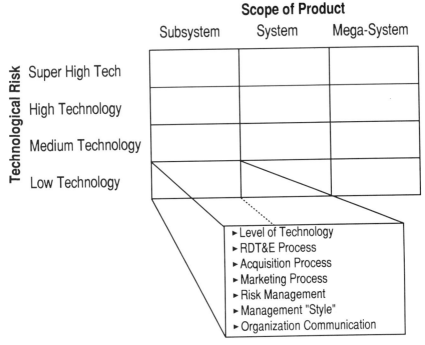

Figure 4.34   Conceptual illustration of the diversity of possible systems engineering programs.

typology suggested in this work and some of the major elements that need to be associated with each of the 12 cells of the resulting matrix, for use in the cost–effectiveness assessment studies suggested here.

While the subject of cost–effectiveness assessment is a very important measurement-related effort, we could only provide a very general overview of this important area of systems management here. There is still much that needs to be done to fully associate this with the newer approaches to systems engineering that we discuss in the last three chapters of this effort.

4.6 SUMMARY

We have described a number of perspectives from which we might view systematic measurements in this brief, but important, chapter. In particular, we discussed systematic measurements from the vantage point of an organization that wished to obtain competitive advantage through customer satisfaction, effort and schedule, defect minimization, or systems management, especially for product differentiation. Clearly, a combination of these perspectives is possible, and desirable as well. The first and third approach is mostly concerned with product. The second approach is mostly concerned with process. The last perspective is based on systems management use of metrics. All are related and, generally, all perspectives should be taken.

By including elements such as these, we could then discuss how a systematic measurement approach would differ across the various maturity levels. For example, we might have the following sort of descriptors across problem handling strategy:

Level 1. Problems are fought over when they are first diagnosed and usually with an improper and inadequate formulation of the problem. There is no measurement of anything. There is much screaming, accusations are made, and a confrontational atmosphere exists.

Level 2. Crisis management teams are set up to attack major problems as they occur through the development of short-range solutions. The reactive inspection of products creates the need for hypervigilance teams that create intra-organizational conflict. Long-term solutions are not sought and there is little organizational learning. This represents the beginning of measurement awareness, at the level of reactive measurements.

Level 3. Process measurements now occur, and there is a focus on measurement throughout the lifecycle. Problems are diagnosed early through the use of interactive measurements at the level of process. Problems are resolved in an orderly manner, generally due to internal V&V throughout the lifecycle. Learning is slow, however.

Level 4. Problems are identified at the planning stage and a high quality process is implemented that will result in doing the right things right the first time. This represents a high degree of interactivity and the beginnings of proactivity.

Level 5. Organizational learning has become very mature through experiential familiarity with proactive problem handling at level 4 and, as a result, problems are prevented from occurring through use of proactive and interactive measurements. Reactive measurements are used, but there is less reliance on them at this highest measurement maturity level.

It would be highly desirable to characterize an organization's measurement maturity according to a scale, such as provided by this description. Figure 4.35 represents a hypothetical mix of measurement costs and the resulting cost and effectiveness that might be associated with systematic measurements at each of these five levels. We will examine just this sort of effort when we consider process maturity and leadership models in Chapter 7. It could well be extended to cover measurement maturity.

We will examine a number of issues associated with strategic quality, or total quality, in Chapter 6. These are necessarily associated with a number of metrics and systematic measurements. There is much interest today in implementing approaches for organizational reinvigoration. This can occur at the level of systems management, process, or product. We will examine a number of reengineering approaches, the current name for reinventing and retrofitting, in Chapter 8.

One of the important need items in each of these is that of estimation of costs and schedule. While we examined some facets of this in Section 4.3, there is much more that can and should be said, and we do this in Chapter 5.

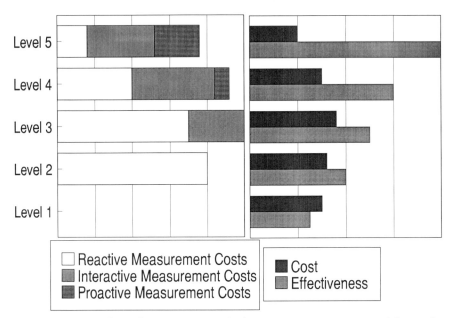

Figure 4.35 Hypothetical representation of relative measurement costs and the resulting organizational cost and effectiveness at each of five measurement maturity levels.

REFERENCES

[1] Deming, W. E., *Out of the Crisis,* MIT Press, Cambridge, MA, 1986.

[2] Sage, A. P. *Decision Support Systems Engineering,* John Wiley & Sons, New York, 1991.

[3] Grady, R. B., *Practical Software Metrics for Program Management and Process Improvement,* Prentice-Hall, Englewood Cliffs, NJ, 1992.

[4] Grady, R. B., and Caswell, D. L., *Software Metrics: Establishing a Company-Wide Program,* Prentice-Hall, Englewood Cliffs, NJ, 1987.

[5] Basili, V., and Weiss, D. M., "A Methodology for Collecting Valid Software Engineering Data," *IEEE Transactions on Software Engineering,* Vol. 10, No. 6, Nov. 1984, pp. 728–738.

[6] Rombach, H. D., and Ulery, B., "Improving Software Maintenance Through Measurement," *Proceedings of the IEEE,* Vol. 77, No. 4, Apr. 1989, pp. 581–595.

[7] Peters, T. J., *Thriving on Chaos: Handbook for a Management Revolution,* Alfred A. Knopf, New York, 1987.

[8] Sage, A. P., and Palmer, J. D., *Software Systems Engineering,* John Wiley & Sons, New York, 1990.

[9] Boehm, B. W., Brown, J. R., and Lipow, M., "Quantitative Evaluation of Software Quality," *Proceedings IEEE/ACM 2nd International Conference on Software Engineering,* Oct. 1976.

[10] Boehm, B. W., Brown, J. R., Kaspar, H., Lipow, M., McLeod, G. J., and Merritt, M. J., *Characteristics of Software Quality,* North-Holland, Amsterdam, 1978.

[11] Sage, A. P. *Systems Engineering,* John Wiley & Sons, New York, 1992.

[12] Clausing, D., "Quality Function Deployment: Applied Systems Engineering," *Proceedings 1989 Quality and Productivity Research Conference,* University of Waterloo, June 1989.

[13] Hauser, J. R., and Clausing, D., "The House of Quality," *Harvard Business Review,* Vol. 66, No. 3, May 1988, pp. 63–73.

[14] Clausing, D., and Pugh, S., "Enhanced Quality Function Deployment," *Proceedings of the Design and Productivity International Conference,* Honolulu, HA, Feb. 1991.

[15] Michaels, J. V., and Wood, W. P., *Design to Cost,* John Wiley & Sons, New York, 1989.

[16] Blanchard, B. S., *Systems Engineering Management,* Prentice-Hall, Englewood Cliffs, NJ, 1991.

[17] Fabrycky, W. J., and Blanchard, B. S., *Life-Cycle Cost and Economic Analysis,* Prentice-Hall, Englewood Cliffs, NJ, 1991.

[18] Kerzner, H., *Program Management: A Systems Approach to Planning, Scheduling, and Controlling,* 4th ed., Van Nostrand Reinhold, New York, 1992.

[19] Johnson, H. T., and Kaplan, R. S., *Relevance Lost: The Rise and Fall of Management Accounting,* Harvard Business School Press, Boston, MA, 1991.

[20] Cooper, R., "Cost Classification in Unit-Based and Activity-Based Manufacturing Cost Systems," *Journal of Cost Management,* Fall 1990, pp. 4–13.

[21] Cooper, R., and Kaplan, R. S., "How Cost Accounting Distorts Product Cost," *Management Accounting,* Apr. 1988, pp. 20–27.

[22] Kaplan, R. S., *Measures for Manufacturing Excellence,* Harvard Business School Press, Boston, MA, 1990.

[23] Kaplan, R. S., and Cooper, R., *Cost Management Systems,* Prentice-Hall, Englewood Cliffs, NJ, 1990.

[24] Anthony, R. N., Dearden, N. J., and Govindarajan, V., *Management Control Systems,* Richard D. Irwin, Homewood, IL, 1992.

[25] Cooper, R., and Kaplan, R. S., "Measure Costs Right: Making the Right Decisions," *Harvard Business Review,* Vol. 66, No. 5, Sept. 1988, pp. 96–103.

[26] Shank, J. K., and Govindarajan, V., *Strategic Cost Management,* Free Press, New York, 1993.

[27] Shank, J. K., and Govindarajan, V., "Strategic Cost Analysis of Technological Investments," *Sloan Management Review,* Vol. 34, No. 1, Fall 1992, pp. 39–51.

[28] Johnson, H. T., "Activity Based Information: A Blueprint for World-Class Management Accounting," *Management Accounting,* June 1988, pp. 23–30.

[29] Johnson, H. T., *Relevance Regained: From Top–Down Control to Bottom–Up Empowerment,* Free Press, New York, 1992.

[30] Juran, J. M., *Juran on Quality: An Executive Handbook,* Free Press, New York, 1989.

[31] Feigenbaum, A. V., *Total Quality Control,* 3rd ed., McGraw-Hill Book Co., New York, 1991.

[32] Conte, S. D., Dunsmore, H. E., and Shen, V. Y., *Software Engineering Metrics and Models,* Benjamin-Cummings Publishing Co., New York, 1986.

[33] Moller, K. H., and Paulish, D. J., *Software Metrics: A Practitioner's Guide to Improved Product Development,* IEEE Press, New York, 1993.

[34] Card, D. N., *Measuring Software Design Quality,* Prentice-Hall, Englewood Cliffs, NJ, 1990.

[35] Evans, M. W., and Marciniak, J. J., *Software Quality Assurance and Management,* John Wiley & Sons, New York, 1987.

[36] Vincent, J., Waters, A., and Sinclair, J., *Software Quality Assurance: Practice and Implementation,* Prentice-Hall, Englewood Cliffs, NJ, 1988.

[37] Fenton, N. E., *Software Metrics: A Rigorous Approach,* Chapman and Hall, London, 1991.

[38] Wheeler, D. A., Brykczynski, B., and Meeson, R. N. (Eds.), *The Software Inspection Process,* IEEE Computer Society Press, Los Altos, CA, 1994.

[39] Baumert, J. H., Fendrich, J. W., and Tripp, L. L., *Achieving Quality Software Through Standards, Measurements, and Process Improvements,* IEEE Computer Society Press, Los Altos, CA, 1994.

[40] Harrington, H. J., *Business Process Improvement: The Breakthrough Strategy for Total Quality, Productivity, and Competitiveness,* McGraw-Hill Book Co., New York, 1991.

[41] Makridakis, S. G., *Forecasting, Planning, and Strategy for the 21st Century,* Free Press, New York, 1990.

[42] Quinee, J. B., "Long Range Planning of Industrial Research," *Harvard Business Review,* Vol. 38, No. 4, July 1961, pp. 88–102.

[43] Bussey, L. E., *The Economic Analysis of Industrial Programs,* Prentice-Hall, Englewood Cliffs, NJ, 1978.

[44] Mishan, E. J., *Cost–Benefit Analysis,* Praeger, New York, 1976.

[45] Porter, A. L., Rossini, F. A., Carpenter, S. R., and Roper, A. T., *A Guidebook for Technology Assessment and Impact Analysis,* North-Holland, New York, 1980.

[46] Sassone, P. G., and Schaffer, W. A., *Cost–Benefit Analysis—A Handbook,* Academic Press, New York, 1978.

[47] Sugden, R., and Williams, A., *The Principles of Practical Cost–Benefit Analysis,* Oxford University Press, Oxford, UK, 1978.

[48] King, J. L., and Schrems, E. L., "Cost–Benefit Analysis in Information Systems Development and Operation," *Computing Surveys,* Vol. 10, No. 1, Mar. 1978, pp. 20–34.

[49] Ewusi-Mensah, K. K., "Evaluating Information Systems Programs: A Perspective on Cost–Benefit Analysis," *Information Systems,* Vol. 14, No. 3, 1989, pp. 205–217.

[50] Merkhofer, M. W., *Decision Science and Social Risk Management,* Reidel, Dordrecht, Holland, 1987.

[51] Miller, C., and Sage, A. P., "A Methodology for the Evaluation of Research and Development Programs and Associated Resource Allocation," *Computers and Electrical Engineering,* Vol. 8, No. 2, 1981, pp. 123–152.

[52] Sage, A. P., "Systems Management for Information Technology Development," in *Expanding Access to Science and Technology; The Role of Information Technologies,* Wesley-Tanaskovic, I., Tocatlian, J., and Roberts, K. H. (Eds.) United Nations University Press, Tokyo Japan, 1994, pp. 361–405.

[53] Benson, B., and Sage, A. P., "Case Studies of Systems Management for Emerging Technology Development," in Rouse, W. B. (Ed.), *Human Technology Interaction in Complex Systems,* JAI Press, Greenwich, CT, 1994.

[54] Porter, A. L., Roper, A. W., Mason, T. W., Rossini, F. A., and Banks, J., *Forecasting and Management of Technology,* John Wiley & Sons, New York, 1991.

[55] Miller, C., and Sage, A. P., "Application of a Methodology for Evaluation, Prioritization, and Resource Allocation to Energy Conservation Program Planning," *Computers and Electrical Engineering,* Vol. 8, No. 1, 1981, pp. 49–67.

[56] Dutton, J. A., and Crowe, L., "Setting Priorities Among Scientific Initiatives," *American Scientist,* Vol. 76, Nov. 1988, pp. 599–603.

[57] Roussel, P. A., Saad, K. N., and Erickson, T. J., *Third Generation R & D,* Harvard Business School Press, Cambridge, MA, 1991.

[58] Oral, M., Kettani, O., and Lang, P., "A Methodology for Collective Evaluation and Selection of Industrial R & D Programs," *Management Science,* Vol. 37, No. 7, July 1991, pp. 871–885.

[59] Liberatore, M. L., and Titus, G. J., "Managing Industrial R & D Programs: Current Practice and Future Directions," *Journal of the Society of Research Administrators,* Vol. 18, No. 1, 1986, pp. 5–12.

[60] Shenhar, A. J., "From Low to High Tech Project Management," *R&D Management,* Vol. 23, No. 3, July 1993, pp. 199–214.

Chapter 5

Systematic Assessments of Cost

The accurate prediction of the cost, including effort and schedule, of accomplishing activities associated with various lifecycles in an organization is a major need. In a similar manner, it is necessary to know the effectiveness that is likely to result from given expenditures of effort. When the costs of activities to be undertaken are underestimated, programs may encounter large cost overruns and this may lead to any of several possible embarrassments for the organization. Associated with these cost overruns are such issues as delivery delays and user dissatisfaction. When costs are overestimated, there may be much reluctance on the part of the organization or its potential customers to undertake activities that could provide many beneficial results. Thus cost is an important ingredient in risk management, as we have emphasized in Chapter 3. We have discussed a number of issues related to systematic costing in Chapter 4. Most of the discussions were relatively philosophical. In this chapter, we will examine costing for information technology and software development. Thus we will be able to provide somewhat greater specificity than was possible in the last chapter.

It is very important to note that a cost estimate is desired in order to predict or forecast the actual cost of developing a product. There are many variables that will affect cost. The product scope, size, structure, and complexity will obviously affect the costs to produce it. The newness of the product to the production team and to the development community, in general, will be another factor. The stability of the requirements for the product will be an issue as high requirements volatility over time may lead to continual changes in the specifications that the product must satisfy throughout the entire systems acquisition lifecycle.

The integration and maintenance efforts that will be needed near the end of the acquisition lifecycle are surely a factor influencing costs, as is the machine configuration and operating system on which software must run. Something about each of these factors must necessarily be known in order to obtain a cost estimate. The more detailed and specific the *definition* of the product is, the more accurate we should expect to be relative to the estimated costs for *development* and *deployment* of the product. One guideline we might espouse is to delay cost estimation until as late in the product definition phase as possible, and perhaps even postpone it until some development efforts have become known. If we wait until after deployment, we should have an error-free estimate of the costs incurred to produce a product or system. This approach is hardly feasible, as estimates need to be known early in the definition phase in order to determine whether it is realistic to undertake production.

We also see that there is merit in attempting to decompose an acquisition or production effort into a number of distinct components. A natural model for this is the lifecycle phases for production. We might, for example, consider the seven-phase software development lifecycle of Boehm [1], or any of the lifecycle models described in Chapter 2, and attempt to develop a work breakdown structure (WBS) of the activities to be accomplished at each of these phases. The work elements for each of these phases can be obtained from a description of the effort at each phase. We might have the following.

Phase 1: Systems Requirements Definition. The specification of systems require-
ments is the first phase of effort. In implementing this phase, it is assumed that the system user and the systems analyst are sufficiently informed about what the new (or modified) system is intended to achieve so as to be able to develop the system level requirements to an acceptable level such that they can be identified in sufficiently complete detail that preliminary design can be initiated. All this is to be done before detailed design and coding may be initiated.

Phase 2: Software Requirements and Software Specifications. The development of the software requirements phase focuses on the outcomes of the system or user level requirements identification carried out in phase 1 of this waterfall model of the software development lifecycle. It is concerned with the nature and style of the software to be developed, the data and information that will be required and the associated structural framework, the required functionality, performance, and various interfaces. Requirements for both the system and the software are re-viewed for consistency and then reviewed by the user to be certain that the software requirements faithfully interpret and produce the system requirements. A software requirements definition document is produced in this phase. It becomes a technol-ogy and a management guideline throughout all subsequent development phases, including validation and testing. These software requirements are then converted into a detailed software specifications, or requirements specifications, document.

Phase 3: Preliminary Design. The software specifications defined in phase 2 are converted into a preliminary software product design in this phase, which is primarily aimed at the further interpretation of the software specifications in terms of software system level architecture. The product of this phase is an identification and microlevel definition of the data structure, software architec-ture, and procedural activities that must be carried out in the next phase. Data items and structures are described in abstract or conceptual terms as a guide to the detailed design phase. For this reason, this phase is often called preliminary conceptual design. Instructions that describe the input, output, and processing that are to be executed within a particular module are developed. Preliminary software design involves representing the functions of each software system in a way that these may readily be converted to a detailed design in the next phase.

Phase 4: Detailed Design. The preliminary design phase resulted in insight as to how the system is intended to work at a structural level and satisfy the technological system specifications. Detailed design phase activities involve definition of the program modules and intermodular interfaces that are necessary in preparation for the writing of code. Specific reference is made to data formats. Detailed descriptions of algorithms are provided. All inputs to and outputs from detailed design modules must be traceable back to the system and software requirements that were generated in phases 1 and 2. During this phase, the software design is fine-tuned.

Phase 5: Code and Debug. In this phase, the detailed design is translated into machine-readable form. If the design has been accomplished in a sufficiently detailed manner, it may be possible to use automated code generators to perform all, or a major portion of, this task. After writing the software design requirements as a set of program units in the appropriate high level programming language, the resulting high level code is compiled and executed. Generally, "bugs" are discovered, and debugging and recoding take place to validate the integrity of the overall coding operations of this phase.

Phase 6: Integration, Testing, and Preoperation. At this phase, the individual units or programs are integrated and tested as a complete system to ensure that the requirements specifications drawn up in phases 1 and 2 are met. Testing procedures center on the logical functions of the software. They assure that all statements have been tested, and that all inputs and outputs operate properly. After system testing, the software is operated under controlled conditions to verify and validate the entire package in terms of satisfying the identified system requirements and software specifications.

Phase 7: Operations and Maintenance. This phase of the waterfall lifecycle is often the longest from the perspective of the entire useful life of the software product. The phases concerned with detailed design, coding, and testing are usually the most effort intensive. In phase 7, the system is installed at the user location and is tested, and then used, under actual operating conditions to the maximum extent possible. Maintenance commences immediately upon detection of any errors that were not found during the earlier phase. This detection, diagnosis, and correction of errors activity is usually not the intended purpose of maintenance, however. Maintenance is primarily the proactive process of improving the system to accommodate new or different requirements as defined by the user after the initial product has been operationally deployed.

The phases enumerated above normally take place in the sequential manner described. However, there is considerable iteration and interaction intended between the several phases. Each software development organization tailors the process to

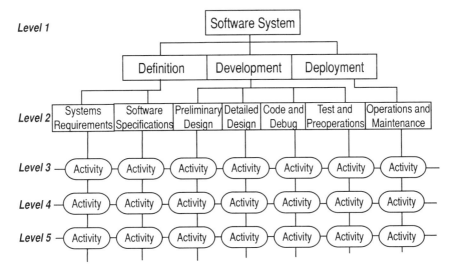

Figure 5.1 Work breakdown structure for the grand design waterfall software development lifecycle due to Boehm.

meet the particular characteristics of the personnel of the organization and, potentially and ideally, the needs of users of the software product as well.

Figure 5.1 illustrates a hypothetical WBS for this development lifecycle. We could attempt to base our estimates of cost on the detailed activities represented by this WBS, and a realistic WBS would be much more detailed than this, or we could attempt to develop a macrolevel model of development cost that is influenced by a number of primary and secondary drivers. The first approach was denoted as *activity-based costing* (ABC) in Chapter 4. The second approach might be called *model-based costing* (MBC) although this term is not at all standard. The unstated assumption in the development of Figure 5.1 is that we are going to undertake a grand design type approach for system production. This figure and the associated discussion need some modification for other than the grand design type approach.

We will examine MBC and ABC approaches in this chapter. We will first discuss some generic issues relating to system and software productivity. This will include the nature of the variables that are important for these measures. Then, we examine some early approaches that are now primarily of historical interest. Following that, we examine some MBC approaches. Next, we look at ABC approaches. Finally, we discuss some issues relative to model evaluation. Much of our discussion will concern production of information technology and software systems. Finally, we turn to a brief discussion of effectiveness—which is a principal subject for the remaining chapters in this text.

5.1 MODEL-BASED PARAMETERS FOR PRODUCTIVITY

There are a number of ways in which we could define system productivity. Relative to software in particular, we might be tempted to say that *software productivity is equivalent to the number of lines of source code that are delivered to the customer per person-month of effort.* Immediately, we sense that a real problem with this definition is that neither the complexity of the software, nor its intended use, enters into the definition. Also, there is an implied assumption that all that is important about software is programming. So we might be tempted to rework this definition in terms of programmer productivity rather than software productivity.

Even with this more restricted interpretation, we still may not have a very complete definition of programmer productivity. Our definition involves "lines of source code." But what is a line of source code? A line of source code might represent a high order language line of source code. Even here, we must be concerned with whether we should include only retainable lines of code in the resulting compiled code, or whether we should also include nonretainable lines of code, such as remark statements that may be extraordinarily helpful in providing clues to the software structure. Also, we should only include lines of source code that are delivered to the customer, and not all lines that were written and then perhaps discarded.

There are many concerns with approaches that suggest that the number of lines of code is an important and primary driver of software costs and schedule. Let us briefly examine some of these. An object line of code is a single machine language instruction either written as a machine language instruction or generated through some translation process from a different language. Immediately, we see a problem. Lines of code can only be meaningful at the end of a project after operational executable code is delivered and accepted by the client. Surely, delivered lines of code are not an unmeaningful measure of productivity. However, it does assume that *one line of code is equal to and has precisely the same value as any other line of code.* Clearly, there is no reason whatever to accept this assertion.

Yet, *source lines of code* (SLOC) are often used as the primary driver of software cost estimation models. Often, this is modified to *delivered SLOC* (DSLOC) through the simple artifice of multiplying the estimate of SLOC by some fraction, which would generally depend on programmer experience and other variables. Boehm [2] delineates some of the difficulties with this metric.

1. Complex instructions, and complex combinations of instructions, will receive the same weight as a similarly long sequence of very simple statements.

2. This is not a uniform metric in the sense that similar length lines of machine-oriented language statements, higher order language statements, and very high order language statements will be given the same weight.

3. It may be a demotivator of truly productive work if programming teams learn that their productivity is measured in terms of the number of lines of code they write per unit time and then seek to artificially increase this *productivity* through writing many simple and near useless lines of code.

4. It may encourage poor quality code by encouraging rapid production of many sloppily structured lines of code.

We could continue this listing by noting that maintenance costs may well increase through the implied encouragement to produce many lines of code if these are produced without regard to maintainability. Transitioning to a new environment is especially difficult when many lines of carelessly structured code are involved.

Even if we could agree that SLOC and DSLOC are worthwhile drivers of costs, there would still remain a major problem in effectively estimating either quantity prior to the start of a software acquisition effort.

Productivity could also be defined in terms of an importance weighted sum of delivered functional units. This would allow us to consider the obvious reality that different lines of code and different software functional units have different values. This is the basis for the "function points" measurement method of Allan Albrecht and others that we examine in Section 5.5. It leads, as we will see, to an approach where software costs are measured in terms of such quantities as input transactions, outputs, inquiries, files, and output reports. These are software product quantities that can be estimated when the requirements definition document is developed. Such an approach will enable us to estimate the cost and schedule required to develop software, and perhaps even the size of the computer code that is a part of the software, in terms of the following:

1. The *purpose to be accomplished,* in terms of such operational software characteristics as the operating system used and application for which the software was developed, and development and test requirements for support software.

2. The *function to be accomplished,* in terms of amount or size, complexity, clarity, and interrelation with other programs and computers.

3. *Use factors,* such as the number of users of code, sophistication of users, number of times code will execute, number of machines on which code will run, and hardware power.

4. *Development factors,* such as the operating system to be accommodated, development time available, development tools available, experiential familiarity of software development team, and the number of software modules.

Other taxonomies of factors for software acquisition are possible. For example, we might identify the six cost and schedule drivers illustrated in Figure 5.2. We could develop a model for costing that is based on these drivers. In general, the important factors will include the people, process, environment, product, and computer system to be used. The major requirement is that the factors be significant, general, measurable, observable, and independent. This poses major requirements, both for software costing and for software acquisition, as we shall soon see. We now turn our attention to some early models for software costing. Then we look at some contemporary efforts that are, to some extent, based on these early efforts.

5.2 EARLY MODELS FOR ESTIMATION OF COSTS, INCLUDING EFFORT AND SCHEDULE

Ideally, a software cost estimation model should describe the relationships among the characteristics of the overall software acquisition effort, so that we can determine the effort and schedule for software acquisition from these relevant charac-

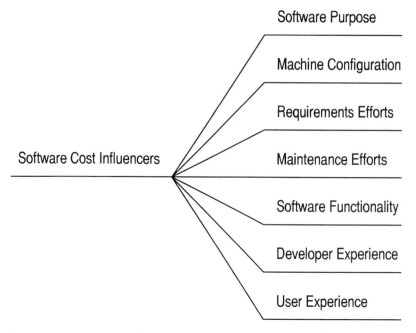

Figure 5.2   Some cost influences for software effort and schedule productivity.

teristics. The needed characteristics would usually exist at the level of the software specifications. It would be ideal if the estimation could be accomplished directly from user requirements, but this is generally not possible without many additional definitional efforts and assumptions.

Use of the software-level requirements specifications would be satisfactory also. If we had an automatic way of transitioning from system-level requirements to software requirements, and perhaps were able to solve the inverse problem as well, then knowledge of one would be equivalent to knowledge of the other.

The features useful as input to cost and schedule estimation models should include descriptions of not only the software to be developed but also the characteristics of the developing organization, such as personnel experience and capability levels, microlevel and macrolevel software development tools, and program management approaches.

This effectively assumes a deterministic software acquisition process, whereas there are a number of uncertain and imprecise matters associated with any large effort to acquire a new system. A deterministic approach to a stochastic acquisition process will not generally produce correct answers. The results generally obtained will be precise; in reality, the results should be stochastic and imprecise. Hopefully, however, the deterministic estimates will provide a reasonable approximation of the realized cost.

Software cost models usually involve at least two types of estimates. These are *effort* and *schedule*. These may be expressed according to the phases of the software lifecycle. Many existing software cost models estimate the number of weeks or months needed to produce a given software system. A time limit on system development is often identified by the client as one of the system-level requirements. This is generally assumed as a constraint in the transition of system-level requirements to software-level requirements and associated-effort requirements. For this reason, most cost models focus on effort requirements over a prescribed schedule horizon. As we will discuss, there is generally some virtually irreducible minimum time required to obtain a new system and increasing the acquisition costs for the system may well not be associated with a reduction in the associated acquisition schedule.

We will use effort estimates as input variables that result in the calculation of costs of development in terms of the human resources required to build the target system. Typically, this estimate is expressed in terms of the number of people needed integrated over the time to be spent, so that the measure of effort is labor-months or person-months or person-years. The actual cost in dollars can be generated from an effort estimate by multiplying the effort by the average cost of labor per unit time. More sophisticated models may be based on the fact that the cost per person-hour of effort depends on the type of labor involved. A development effort that involves much use of systems engineering talent for technical direction and rapid prototyping would thus be costed at a higher amount than an effort that involves little of this effort and a great deal of routine coding.

Many simple software cost models describe the size of the software development program only in terms of the size of the software product produced. This size is often measured in terms of *lines of code* delivered to the customer. Complexity figures, in terms of the number of programming operators and operands, and functionality measures are used in some models, as we have noted. For example, Walston and Felix [3] allow comment lines up to half of the delivered lines of code. Boehm [1] does not allow the inclusion of comment lines at all. Bailey and Basili [4] include the total number of lines of new code, including remarks, but only one-fifth of the total number of lines of reused code, including comments. There is no problem with any of these approaches, although it does make routine use of the same information on all models, as well as comparison of the various approaches, more difficult. The meaning of the expression "lines of code" must simply be interpreted for each model before use of the model.

An *experiential model* uses expert-wholistic-based judgment as the primary input to the cost estimation or forecasting process. The accuracy of the prediction is a function of the experience and perception of the estimator. In its simplest form, an estimate based on expert judgment involves one or more experts who make educated guesses about the effort that will be required for an entire software acquisition program or for a component project thereof. The estimate may be derived from either a top–down or bottom–up analysis of the proposed system. Often, experts are asked to make three predictions in a simple approach to forecasting: *optimistic, pessimistic,* and *most likely.*

If A represents the optimistic cost estimate, B the pessimistic one, and C the most likely cost estimate, then the final estimate of cost or effort is presumed to be given by

$$\text{Cost} = [A + 4C + B]/6 \qquad (5.2.1)$$

This is simply a weighted average in which it is assumed that the weight of the most likely estimate has a worth of four times that of either the most optimistic or most pessimistic estimate. Alternately, the resulting estimate can be said to follow what is called a beta probability distribution. The Delphi technique [5] can be used to generate A, B, and C as averages of many individual responses. Of course, there is no scientific basis to support use of this cost relation. Many people would, in a judgmental situation such as this, simply provide optimistic and pessimistic estimates that are equally spaced about the most likely estimate. In this case the most likely estimate is the average, which is halfway between the optimistic and pessimistic estimate.

A number of other more formal models add more structure to the expert judgment approach. Wolverton [6] developed a software cost matrix approach in which matrix elements represent the cost per line of code as calibrated from historical data. The multipliers in a vector product equation represent a phase–activity distribution as derived from the judgments of experts. The choice of element depends on expert judgment as to the type of software, novelty, and difficulty. Figure 5.3 represents a portion of the Wolverton model, which contains as many as 8 phases and 25 activities per lifecycle phase. Use of the model is generally predicated on breaking the software acquisition effort into phases and estimating their costs individually. A software effort may represent a *new* or *old* development effort depending on the

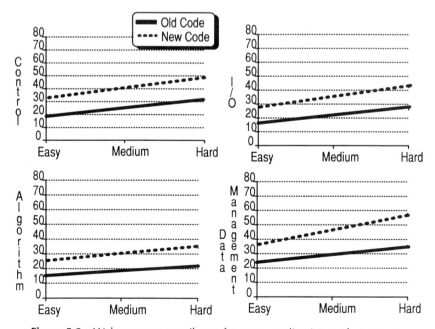

Figure 5.3 Wolverton cost attributes for some applications software types.

TABLE 5.1 Wolverton Dollar Cost Estimates for Old and New Code Development

Type	Difficulty					
	OE	OM	OH	NE	NM	NH
Control	21	27	30	33	40	49
I/O	17	24	27	28	35	43
Pre/postprocessor	16	23	26	28	34	42
Algorithm	15	20	22	25	30	35
Data management	24	31	35	37	46	57
Time critical	75	75	75	75	75	75

familiarity of the software developer. Here, for example, a 2000-object instruction module of old autopilot flight control algorithm software of medium difficulty would be priced at $36 per instruction, excluding remarks, for a total of $72,000.

Wolverton's software cost–effort model is based on subjective estimates of software complexity. These estimates are made by considering the different types of software to be developed and the development difficulty expected. A software cost matrix can also be used, as an alternate to the graphical approach of Figure 5.3. For example, we have the data shown in Table 5.1 for the six types of software considered in this early work. Clearly, the cost for developing time-critical software is large at $75 per line of code. Obviously, this includes all costs, not just the direct programming costs to write a line of code.

In using this table, the costs are based on the type of software, represented by the row name, and the difficulty of developing such software, as represented by the several columns. The difficulty is determined by two factors: whether the problem is old (O) or new (N), and whether it is easy (E), moderate (M), or hard (H). The matrix elements are the cost per line of code as calibrated from historical data. To use the matrix, the software system under development may be partitioned into modules i for $i = 1, 2, \ldots, n$. An estimate is made of the size S_i of each module, as measured in the number of lines of developed uncommented code, for each of the n modules. If the kth module is of type $t(k)$ and difficulty $d(k)$, then the cost of developing each of the various type components of the model is

$$C_t(k) = C_{t(k)d(k)} \tag{5.2.2}$$

where $C_{t(k)d(k)}$ represents the cost per line of code for that particular type or category of software. This is given by the tdth entry in the preceding matrix. To calculate the cost of the kth module, we multiply S_k by the appropriate $C_{t(k)d(k)}$ matrix entry in Table 5.2. We then sum this over all k modules to obtain the total cost of producing the system.

This estimate does not consider software process variables, except to the extent that they influence either Figure 5.3 or Table 5.1. Fundamentally, the software cost estimate is a function only of product characteristics unless one is to have a different graph or table for each change in process and management characteristics. It is not

TABLE 5.2   Doty Parameters for Effort Estimation

Application	Object Code		Source Code	
	a	γ	a	γ
All	4.790	0.991	5.258	1.057
Command and control	4.573	1.228	4.089	1.263
Scientific	4.495	1.068	7.054	1.019
Business	2.895	0.784	4.495	0.781
Utility	12.039	0.719	10.078	0.811

even clear, for example, how questions of acquisition management approach, software development organization experience, availability of CASE tools, and other process-related factors affect the resulting cost estimates.

The Doty model [7] relates effort to source lines of code as a function of application type according to the relation

$$E = aS^{\gamma} \tag{5.2.3}$$

where E is the effort in labor-months and where the a and γ parameters vary across application type as given in Table 5.2. The authors of this model realize that the use of lines of code will cause sizing error to have a very direct impact on the accuracy of obtained estimates. Guidelines for sizing estimates are provided in [7].

For better estimates, use of a number of environmental factors is recommended such that the estimate in Eq. (5.2.3) becomes

$$E = aS^{\gamma} \prod_{i=1}^{n} f_i \tag{5.2.4}$$

There are 14 of these environmental factors, f_i, in the Doty model. These include a number of realities relative to the development environment. The factors are different across the five different application types of Table 5.2.

The model also included an equation to estimate development time:

$$T = \frac{1}{99.25 + 2.33S^{0.067}} \tag{5.2.5}$$

where S represents the size of the object code program. While there appears to be little current interest in this particular model, it does serve as a historical predecessor of a number of similar models.

Almost all software cost and effort estimation models use program size as the dominant driving factor that influences needed effort. Other factors are often used to *tune* the results of a basic computation that uses primarily program size in estimating effort, as we see in the Doty model. The size of the program team is also a major component. A model that handles both program size and program team size factors must take into account not only the complexity of the software, in terms of the size estimate, but also the complexity of interactions among the project team members.

The *cooperative programming model* (COPMO) [8] incorporates both software size and software development staff size by expressing effort in terms of team interactions. Effort is defined as

$$E = E_1(S) + E_2(W) \tag{5.2.6}$$

where E is overall effort, $E_1(S)$ is the effort required by one or more people working independently on a size S module development who require no interaction with other modules, $E_2(W)$ is the effort required to coordinate the development process with other software development team members, and W is the average number of staff assigned to software program development.

Additional needed relations are

$$E_1(S) = a + bS \tag{5.2.7}$$

and

$$E_2(W) = cW^d \tag{5.2.8}$$

The parameters a, b, c, and d are determined using past development efforts. These equations are not especially different from the effort estimation equations used in the other models that we will soon study. The value of d can be inferred to represent the amount of coordination, management, and communication needed on a project. Similarly, c is a measure of the weakness of the communication paths among the individuals working on the software effort.

A *resource estimation model* has been proposed by Joe Fox [9]. He identifies a total of 27 contributors to software development costs. The eight major contributors to the cost of software development are identified in three major categories as:

Function

1. *Scale* (1 to 8), the amount of function to be developed.
2. *Clarity* (1 to 10), the degree to which functions developed are understood.
3. *Logical complexity* (1 to 10), the number of conditional branches per 100 instructions.
4. The need for *user interaction with system* (1 to 5) and the intensity of this interaction.

Use Time Environments

5. *Consequences of failure* (1 to 15), the effort required to meet reliability and recovery requirements.

6. *Real-time requirements* (1 to 5) in terms of how fast the various needed functions must be accomplished.

Development Time Factors

7. *Stability of the software support tools* (1 to 10).
8. *Stability of the use phase computer hardware* (1 to 20).

Each factor is assumed to contribute to costs per line of delivered code. The code costs can vary up to $83 per line, as this is the sum of the largest numbers for each of these factors. Fox encourages use of a circle-like diagram on which is sketched the relative difficulty for each factor. Figure 5.4 illustrates a sample estimation exercise for a hypothetical software development effort.

One of the very earliest of the software effort and schedule estimation studies was due to Nelson [10] at the System Development Corporation. In this study, 104 possible cost factors were identified in a study of 169 projects. Using the database of information for the 169 software projects, a least-squares curve fit was used to determine the coefficients of each attribute in the cost model. Ultimately, only the 14 most significant factors were retained in the final cost estimation model. Unfortunately, the errors in projecting costs are quite large, doubtlessly because the costs do not really increase linearly with the factors influencing costs. Nevertheless, this early model set a pattern for later efforts.

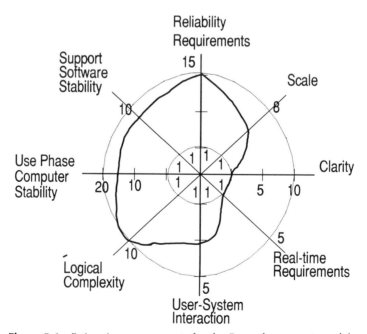

Figure 5.4   Estimation components for the Fox software cost model.

The Bailey-Basili [4] model was developed using data from a database of 18 large projects from the NASA Goddard Space Center. They make no claims that the model, based on empirical evidence from specific projects, applies to other than projects of the same general type. Most of the software in the NASA database used by Bailey and Basili was written in FORTRAN, and most of the applications they considered were scientific. Thus the database is very homogeneous. The total number of lines of code is defined to be the total amount of new code written plus 20% of the old code that is reused. Comment lines of code are included in each.

The basic estimator equation that they used expressed effort as

$$E = \alpha + \beta S^\gamma \qquad (5.2.9)$$

and the model parameters were identified such as to minimize the *standard error estimate* (*SEE*), where

$$SEE = \sum_{i=1}^{n} \left[1 - \frac{(\alpha + \beta S_i^\gamma)}{E_i} \right]^2 \qquad (5.2.10)$$

The sum is carried out over all the projects in the database. The parameters that minimize *SEE* were such that the estimation equation was

$$\hat{E} = 5.5 + 0.73 \, S^{1.16} \qquad (5.2.11)$$

and they obtain *SEE* = 1.25. If we assume that the error distribution is Gaussian, this says that we can multiply and divide the actual estimate obtained by 1.25 in order to obtain the upper and lower error bounds for one standard deviation of error.

It turns out that this fit is a very good one for the 18 software projects used to determine the parameters for the cost estimator. Bailey and Basili attempt to improve on the estimator by calculating bounds based on software complexity factors, rather than just using the 1.25 factor. The actual modification relation used takes into account 21 other variables that may affect the software production person-months of effort. These fit into three primary categories or factors:

- *Total method attributes*—METH—include nine attribute measures: chief programmer teams, code reading, design formulations, formal documentation, formal test plans, formal training, top–down design, tree charts, and unit development folders.
- *Cumulative complexity attributes*—CPLX—include seven attribute measures: application complexity, customer initiated design changes, customer interface complexity, database complexity, external communication complexity, internal communication complexity, and program flow complexity.
- *Cumulative past experience attributes*—EXP—include five attribute measures: overall team experience, programmer application experience, program-

mer language experience, programmer machine experience, and programmer qualifications.

A least-squares error regression is used to calculate coefficients $\hat{a}$, $\hat{b}$, $\hat{c}$, and $\hat{d}$ in the estimation error ratio relation

$$R_{adj} = \hat{a}\text{METH} + \hat{b}\text{CPLX} + \hat{c}\text{EXP} + \hat{d} \qquad (5.2.12)$$

and the adjustment factor is then used to modify the cost estimate up or down according to

$$E_{adj} = (1 + R_{adj})\hat{E} \qquad (5.2.13)$$

if it is believed that the complexity factors will increase the needed effort, or

$$E_{adj} = \hat{E}/(1 + R_{adj}) \qquad (5.2.14)$$

if it is believed that the complexity factors will decrease the required effort. The person-months of effort obtained in this approach are assumed to be that for the lifecycle development.

The Walston–Felix [3] model uses a size estimate adjusted by factors determined from the subjective answers to questions about 29 relevant software acquisition topics:

1. Customer interface complexity.
2. User participation in the definition of requirements.
3. Customer-originated program design changes.
4. Customer experience with the application area of the project.
5. Overall personnel experience and qualifications.
6. Percentage of development programmers who participated in design of functional specifications.
7. Previous experience with operational computer.
8. Previous experience with programming languages.
9. Previous experience with applications of similar or greater size and complexity.
10. Ratio of average staff size to project duration (people/month).
11. Hardware under concurrent development.
12. Access to development computer open under special request.
13. Access to development computer closed.
14. Classified security environment for computer and at least 25% of programs and data.
15. Use of structured programming.

16. Use of design and code inspections.
17. Use of top–down development.
18. Use of chief programmer team.
19. Overall complexity of code developed.
20. Complexity of application processing.
21. Complexity of program flow.
22. Overall constraints on program design.
23. Design constraints on program's main storage.
24. Design constraints on program's timing.
25. Code for real-time or interactive operation or executing under severe time constraint.
26. Percentage of code for delivery.
27. Code classified as nonmathematical application and input/output (I/O) formatting programs.
28. Number of classes of items in the database per 1000 lines of delivered code.
29. Number of pages of delivered documentation per 1000 lines of delivered code.

These process-related factors are quite specific. In the aggregate, they represent an attempt to measure understanding of the development environment, personnel qualifications, proposed hardware, and customer interface. Walston and Felix used these factors to supplement their basic equation with a productivity index. Using a large database of empirical values gathered from 60 projects in IBM's Federal Systems Division, they produced the foregoing list of 29 factors that can affect software acquisition productivity. The projects reviewed to determine parameters for the model varied from 4000 to 467,000 lines of code, were written in 28 different high level languages on 66 computers, and represented from 12 to 11,758 person-months of effort. For each mean productivity value x_i calculated from the database, a composite productivity factor P was computed from

$$P = \sum_{i=1}^{29} w_i x_i \qquad (5.2.15)$$

which is just a multiattribute utility theory (MAUT) type calculation [11]. The dimension associated with P is delivered source lines of code per programmer month of effort. Here, the weights were set to reflect enhancing, inhibiting, or neutral support to productivity. The variable x_i is set equal to 1 if the rating indicates increased productivity, 0 if the variable rating indicates nominal productivity, and -1 if the variable rating indicates decreased productivity. This productivity factor is used to modify the basic effort and schedule estimates. The weights, w_i, for the 29 attributes vary from 0.95 to 1.29 and are estimated by software development project managers. This leads to a computed expected productivity range, P, that varies from 115 to 340 delivered source lines of code per programmer month.

The Walston–Felix model of software production effort that results is fundamentally based on the basic effort equation

$$E = 5.25S^{0.91} \qquad (5.2.16)$$

where S is the number of thousands of source lines of code. Here, the lines of code variable S includes comments as long as they do not exceed 50% of the total lines in the program. At that point, no further lines of commentary are included in S. A similar equation is obtained for basic schedule, in terms of time to project completion,

$$T = 2.47E^{0.35} = 4.1S^{0.35} \qquad (5.2.17)$$

which is also obtained from a standard least-squares curve fit approach. The effort or cost, S, is estimated in person-months of effort and the schedule in months. We note that this implicitly specifies the project workforce. Many of the models that we consider assume that there is a reasonable minimum development time and that it is very unwise to compress this. Other equations of interest in this model are

$$L = 0.54E^{0.06} = 0.96S^{0.055}$$

and

$$Z = 7.8E^{1.11} = 49S^{1.01}$$

where L and Z represent the staffing requirements in people and the pages of documentation that will be needed, respectively. The result that essentially 49 pages of documentation are required for every thousand lines of code is interesting.

We note that the exponent for the term S in the Walston–Felix equation is less than 1. This implies economy of scale for software production and that the relative effort to produce a line of code will decrease as the number of lines of code increases. The notion of economies of scale for large projects is quite unsupported by available evidence, however. Just the opposite appears to be the case as large software projects increase the need for communication and interaction among the software team project members, and so effort and cost increase.

The commonalities and the differences among these approaches are interesting. Table 5.3 summarizes the central and basic features of many of the estimators we have obtained in this section, and provides the *constructive cost model* (COCOMO) results that we will discuss in our next section. These estimators show different economies of scale and multipliers. This is not unexpected since the data used to provide the estimators are different. The Boehm model equations are the most sophisticated of these, by far the most used, and allow for different environment assumptions. Each of these equations is necessarily associated with errors. According to DeMarco [12], uncontrollable factors in the development process will almost always result in 10% to 20% error in the accuracy of this type of estimate. Sadly, estimates using models of this sort are rarely this good, unless very careful attention

TABLE 5.3 Basic Estimate Relations for Various Software Cost Models

$E = 5.5 + 0.73S^{1.16}$	Bailey–Basili
$E = 2.4S^{1.05}$	Boehm—basic organic COCOMO
$E = 3.2S^{1.05}$	Boehm—intermediate organic COCOMO
$E = 3.0S^{1.12}$	Boehm—basic semidetached COCOMO
$E = 3.0S^{1.12}$	Boehm—intermediate semidetached COCOMO
$E = 3.6S^{1.20}$	Boehm—basic embedded COCOMO
$E = 2.8S^{1.20}$	Boehm—intermediate embedded COCOMO
$E = 5.29S^{1.047}$	Doty
$E = 5.25S^{0.91}$	Walston–Felix

is paid to the parameters that go into the estimates. We will now examine a number of model-based costing approaches, or effort and schedule models, to illustrate the similarities and differences among them. We begin with the COCOMO models of Boehm. After discussing this and other approaches, we will examine some concerns relative to modeling errors for model-based costing approaches. COCOMO is the only model in Table 5.3 that is of current interest.

5.3 CONSTRUCTIVE COST MODEL (COCOMO)

Barry Boehm has been intimately involved in almost all of software engineering, especially in developing and refining his *constructive cost model* (COCOMO) and associated database. His book on this subject [13] is generally regarded as a software engineering classic. There are a number of related papers as well [14]. COCOMO—actually there are three fundamental models involved—was derived from a database of 63 projects that were active during the period 1964 to 1979. The database included programs written in FORTRAN, COBOL, PL/1, Jovial, and assembly language. They range in length from 2000 to 1,000,000 lines of code, exclusive of comments. The COCOMO database is more heterogeneous than most that have been used for software cost projection, incorporating business, scientific, and supervisory control software. In addition to estimating effort, the COCOMO includes formulas for predicting development time and schedule and a breakdown of effort by phase and activity. This is a very extensive and thoroughly investigated model to which much serious thought has been applied. It is often used in practice. Also, there have been a number of extensions to the initial COCOMO developments. Thus it is appropriate for some detailed comments.

There are three COCOMO levels, depending on the detail included in, or desired in, the resulting cost estimate: *basic, intermediate,* and *detailed.* Each form of the COCOMO uses a development cost estimate of the form

$$E = aS^{\delta}M(\mathbf{x}) \tag{5.3.1}$$

where $M(\mathbf{x})$ represents an adjustment multiplier. The units of E are person-months or labor-months of effort. If we multiply the labor-months by the average cost of labor, we obtain the direct costs of the acquisition effort. Of interest also is the development schedule. The schedule time for development is given by

$$T = bE^\gamma \qquad (5.3.2)$$

where E is the cost estimate just obtained. The parameters δ, γ, a, and b are determined by the model and development mode, as we will soon discuss. In most representations of COCOMO, the units for S are thousands of lines of delivered instructions (KDSI), the units for E are person-months (PM) or labor-months (LM) of effort, and the units for T, the time for development (TDEV), are months. A person-month of effort is assumed to be comprised of 19 person-days of 8 hours each, or 152 person-hours. This figure allows for time off for sick leave, holidays, and vacations.

For the basic COCOMO, the adjustment multiplier is always 1.0. For the intermediate and detailed model, it is a composite function of 15 cost drivers x_1 through x_{15}. By setting these cost drivers to one in the intermediate model, we obtain an adjustment multiplier $M(\mathbf{x}) = 1$. Thus the form of intermediate COCOMO reduces to that of the basic model when the cost drivers are at their nominal value of 1.0.

The values a and δ *are not* obtained from least-squares regression, as with many other cost estimation models. Boehm incorporates his own experience, the subjective opinion of other software managers, the results from use of other cost estimation models, and trial and error, in order to identify the structural relations that lead to the cost model as well as the parameters within the structure of this cost model. His initial parameters were fine-tuned using the TRW database. Thus COCOMO is a composite model, basically combining experiential observations and wisdom together with statistical rule-based adjustments.

The parameters a and δ depend on what Boehm calls the *development mode* of a software acquisition project. He labels a project as belonging to an *organic, embedded,* or *semidetached* mode, depending on the project's independence from other systems. In the initial effort, these first three modes were described. Later effort extended this to Ada programming language development efforts [15]. The three modes may be described as follows.

1. The *organic mode* refers to the mode typically associated with relatively small acquisition programs that generally require relatively little innovation. They usually have rather relaxed software delivery time requirements and the effort is to be undertaken in a stable in-house development environment. The external environment is generally also stable. An organic software development program can often almost run by itself and will rarely require extraordinary systems management and technical direction efforts.

2. A *embedded mode* effort is relatively large and has substantial operating constraints. There is usually a high degree of complexity involved in the hardware to be used as well as in the customer interface needs. These result in system and user requirements, which need to be incorporated into the software acquisition effort. Often, the requirements for the to-be-delivered *em-*

TABLE 5.4 COCOMO Parameters for Basic and Intermediate Models

	Basic Model				Intermediate Model			
Mode	a	δ	b	γ	a	δ	b	γ
Organic	2.4	1.05	2.5	0.38	3.2	1.05	2.5	0.38
Semidetached	3.0	1.12	2.5	0.38	3.0	1.12	2.5	0.38
Embedded	3.6	1.20	2.5	0.38	2.8	1.20	2.5	0.38

bedded software are exacting, and there is generally a need for innovative design in typically one-of-a-kind development efforts that have not been accomplished before and which will likely not be repeated.

3. A *semidetached mode* program has requirements and development characteristics that lie somewhere between organic and embedded.

The a and δ parameters for basic and intermediate COCOMO are presented in Table 5.4. In the *basic* COCOMO, the cost driver or adjustment multiplier $M(\mathbf{x}) = 1$ for all x_i. If we are considering semidetached mode development, the a and δ parameters are the same for both the intermediate and basic COCOMO. For organic and embedded development, the a parameters are different. This suggests that semidetached development is the nominal development mode for which the intermediate COCOMO cost drivers are obtained. The fact that the a parameter is different in the basic model from that in the intermediate model, for other than semidetached developments, suggests that the meaning and interpretation of scaling of the cost drivers are different across these different development modes. In other words, the interpretation of the term "nominal" must be different in organic development efforts from that in embedded development efforts. Using the basic model a parameters and the scaling indicated results in cost and effort values that are too low for organic mode development and too high for embedded mode development. This indicates that the cost driver parameters are not independent of one another.

5.3.1 Basic COCOMO

A single cost estimate, in terms of development effort, is obtained in the basic model. This single effort measure is assumed to be distributed across the various phases of the software acquisition lifecycle. In Boehm's COCOMO effort, a four-phase lifecycle consisting of conceptual design, detailed design, programming and unit test, and integration and test is assumed.

For the basic model, no effort is assumed allocated to such deployment efforts as maintenance. The distribution of effort varies across phases as a function of the size of the developed product, in terms of lines of code, although the variation is not large. Figure 5.5 illustrates how this effort, in labor-months, is distributed across these four phases, for the three different development modes. As we would expect, the simpler organic mode of development results in a greater percentage of effort devoted to actual coding of a software product and less effort associated with the

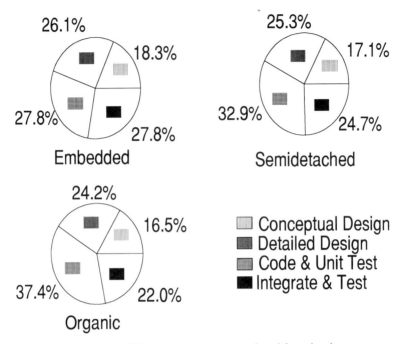

Figure 5.5 Effort distribution across four lifecycle phases.

conceptual architecture phase and detailed design phase. Of course, the simpler products also result in less effort being needed for integrate and test since there is less need for a large number of development modules. Even though the percentage effort for programming and unit test may be less with embedded software than it is for organic and semidetached software, the actual amount of development effort will generally be greater. Even if the number of lines of code is the same, the fact that the a multiplier is larger for embedded software will almost assure this. Figure 5.6 shows the companion results for the percentage distribution of schedule time across these four development phases. As we would expect, little effort needs to be devoted to conceptual design for organic software development. We can proceed almost directly to the detailed design and coding phases of development.

The very simple cost and schedule equations for the basic COCOMO are

$$E = aS^\delta \tag{5.3.3}$$

$$T = 2.5E^\gamma \tag{5.3.4}$$

where the parameters are as specified in Table 5.4. Figures 5.7 and 5.8 illustrate the development costs and schedule for the three modes of operation. Figure 5.7 illustrates how much more labor intensive development of embedded software is, as compared with organic software. For 1000 KDSI, which represents a very large software acquisition effort indeed, it takes approximately 4.23 times as much labor

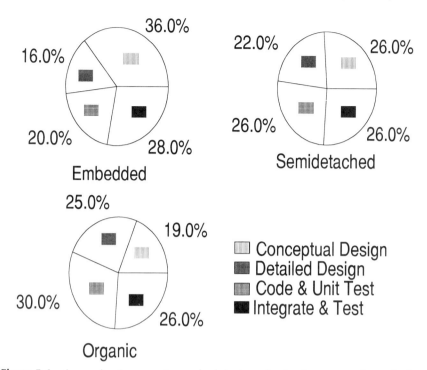

Figure 5.6 Approximate percentage schedule time distribution across phases for basic COCOMO.

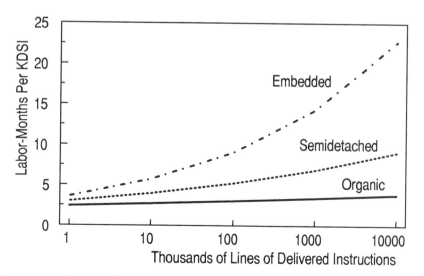

Figure 5.7 Labor-months required per thousand lines of delivered instructions for basic COCOMO.

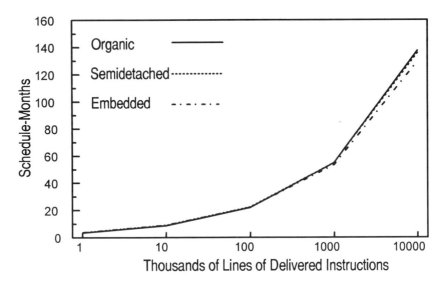

Figure 5.8   Schedule-months as a function of thousands of lines of delivered instructions.

(14.33 labor-months per KDSI) to produce a delivered line of source code in embedded software, as contrasted with the labor (3.39 labor-months per KDSI) required for organic software. As shown in Figure 5.5, the total development time that *should* be allocated to development is not appreciably different across the three development modes. For a 100-KDSI effort, the development time is approximately 54 months, or 4.5 years, regardless of the mode of development.* We can now use the effort and schedule distributions across phase results illustrated in Figures 5.5 and 5.6 in order to determine phasewise distributions of effort and schedule for the basic COCOMO. This results in a relatively complete set of effort and schedule plans for software development, as based on the assumptions inherent in the basic COCOMO.

We might wonder why there is an amount calculated for effort, in labor-months, and an amount calculated for schedule time, in months, through use of the basic COCOMO. It might seem that it should be possible to obtain virtually any schedule time desired simply through adjusting the number of people working on an effort. Sadly, this turns out to be the case only within relatively narrow limits. A very classic work illustrates this specifically for software development. We digress briefly to discuss this important result here.

Fred Brooks, in a truly seminal work [16], was perhaps the first to suggest a

*It should be remarked that it would be unreasonable to expect organic software development of as large a system as would be represented by 1 million lines of delivered source instructions (1000 KDSI). In a similar manner, it is probably also unrealistic that there could be an embedded software development as small as 1000 lines of delivered source instructions (1 KDSI). Thus the results shown in Figures 5.4 and 5.5 for these extreme cases would not be expected in practice as the cases themselves would rarely, if ever, occur.

power law relationship between lines of code, S, and software programming effort, E. The generic relationship is

$$E = dS^\beta \tag{5.3.5}$$

where the d and β parameters are dependent on the application being developed, programmer capability, and programming language used. In the work of Brooks, the parameter β was assumed to be 1.5, although few today would associate this large a diseconomy of scale. This is the structure of the basic COCOMO, where β ranges from 1.05 to 1.20.

Brooks attempted to increase the power of this model by such efforts as adding terms to represent communication difficulties among the N programmers assumed to be working together on the programming project. This might result in a relation such as

$$C = dS^\beta + c[N(N - 1)/2] \tag{5.3.6}$$

where c is a communication cost. The division of labor is such that programmer i produces code of size S_i. If each programmer has equal ability, we then have

$$E_i = dS_i^\beta \tag{5.3.7}$$

and since a total of S lines of code are produced,

$$S = \sum_{i=1}^{N} S_i = S_1 + S_2 + \ldots + S_N \tag{5.3.8}$$

where the summation extends over all N programmers. It is interesting to obtain the optimum allocation of effort among the programmers. To do this we use elementary variational calculus principles. We adjoin the constraint equation of Eq. (5.3.8) to the cost function of Eq. (5.3.6) by means of a Lagrange multiplier. We assume that each programmer has the same cost of communication. We also assume that each programmer produces the same amount of code such that $S = NS_i$. Then we minimize the effort relation

$$E = \sum_{i=1}^{N} dS_i^\beta + c[N(N - 1)/2] = NdS_i^\beta + C[N(N - 1)/2] \tag{5.3.9}$$

where we have automatically satisfied the equality constraint of Eq. (5.3.8). The Lagrange multiplier augmented cost function is

$$J(N) = \sum_{i=1}^{N} dS_i^\beta + \Gamma\left(S - \sum_{i=1}^{N} S_i\right) + c[N(N - 1)/2] \tag{5.3.10}$$

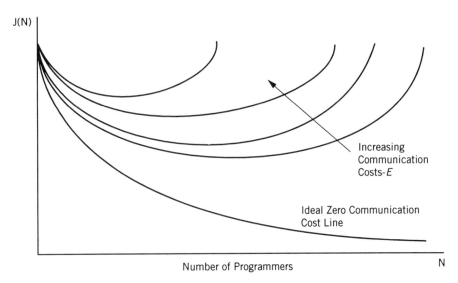

Figure 5.9 Effects of communication costs on the productivity of N programmers.

which now becomes

$$J(N) = Nd(S/N)^\beta + c[N(N-1)/2] \qquad (5.3.11)$$

Minimization with respect to N is a simple matter. We simple set $\partial J(N)/\partial N = 0$ and solve for the optimum number of programmers. In this particular case, it is perhaps more interesting to sketch the relationship

$$J(N)/d = N(S/N)^\beta + E[N(N-1)/2d] \qquad (5.3.12)$$

for several values of the economy of scale factor β and the communications effort ratio E/d.

The general results for negative economies of scale look like that shown in Figure 5.9. The very interesting observation that the amount of effort required does not continually decrease with an increase in the number of programmers is evident. Only for very small values of the communication effort ratio would this be the case. We would like to have the ideal result noted in the figure. But we will only get this if there is perfect communication, such that $E = 0$. In general, there is an optimum number of programmers for maximum code production. Increasing the number of programmers results in a decrease in the amount of code that they can produce in a given amount of time!

All this is potentially rather distressing. Not only do we have diseconomies of scale, but the addition of programmers to aid an already late software development project may well result in it being later! While there is nothing generic to software in this, software is perhaps more likely to suffer from diseconomies of scale than other production technology efforts.

What this sort of simple effort suggests is that we simply must bring about automated software production technologies—that is, those technologies that take advantages of the macroenhancement efforts of rapid prototyping, reusable software, and automatic code generation approaches to code production—if we are to be able to cope with truly large systems efforts. It seems highly doubtful that there are many major advances left to be obtained simply through only increases in programmer productivity. Of course, this is not an argument against programmer productivity, which is very necessary but not at all sufficient. Thus, we see that a cost and a schedule equation are each needed.

5.3.2 Intermediate COCOMO

The basic COCOMO is very simple and assumes a large number of nominal development parameters. The intermediate COCOMO allows for judgement relative to 15 important cost drivers. These cost drivers are sometimes called environmental factors.

For the *intermediate* COCOMO, the adjustment multiplier is calculated as the product of individual cost drivers, as given by

$$M(\mathbf{x}) = \prod_{j=1}^{15} m(x_j) \qquad (5.3.13)$$

The 15 cost drivers or environmental factors are grouped into four categories, as illustrated in Figure 5.10. Each of the 15 categories illustrated in Figure 5.10 is associated with an appropriate multiplier factor $m(x_i)$. In the basic COCOMO, each cost factor $m(x_i)$ is assumed to be equal to 1; and so each of the adjustment multipliers is equal to 1. In the intermediate COCOMO and detailed COCOMO, the cost factors $m(ix_i)$ vary as a function of the quantitative values of the various cost drivers. For each category, a scale of five or six values is used to represent the possible choices for each category. For many of the cost drivers, values were obtained for the COCOMO database using the classic Delphi technique to elicit expert opinion. Reliability cost, for example, can be rated from very low to very high, in accordance with the equivalence between verbal or semantic descriptors and a corresponding numerical driver shown in Table 5.5.

There is, in effect, a table like this for each of the 15 cost drivers in the database. It is assumed that one of the specific values called for in these tables will be used in that the model is validated only for these values. This should not preclude careful use of parameter values within the given ranges.

Appropriate descriptions for each of the 15 cost drivers in the intermediate COCOMO are as follows:

CPLX—Software Product Complexity. CPLX rates the complexity of the software
  to be developed on a scale varying from very low (0.70) to very high (1.65).
  CPLX is directly related to the type of processing required and the distance that
  the software is from the hardware, or compatibility between the software and
  hardware. It turns out that no metrics have proved universally acceptable in this

	CPLX	Complexity of the system
Product	DATA	Size of the databases
	RELY	Required software reliability

	STOR	Storage constraints
	TIME	Execution time constraints
Computer	TURN	Computer turnaround (response) time
	VIRT	Virtual machine volatility

	ACAP	Capability of the analysts
	AEXP	Applications experience
Personnel	LEXP	Programming language experience
	PCAP	Programmer capability
	VEXP	Virtual machine experience

	MODP	Use of modern programming practices
Project	SCED	Existence of required development schedule
	TOOL	Use of software development tools

Figure 5.10   Intermediate level COCOMO cost drivers or multipliers.

area, so the rating is often done by analogy. A recommended input value for CPLX of HI would mean that the software development needs involve hardware input/output interfaces, advanced data routines, and the use of such tools as third-generation compilers. A CPLX rating of HI translates into a value of 1.15 as an environmental factor or multiplier.

DATA—Database Size. DATA rates the extra effort that is required to create software that involves manipulation and maintenance of a sizable database. This factor is evaluated by considering the ratio of the database size (in bytes) to the number of deliverable source instructions (DSI). DATA varies from low (0.94) to very high (1.16).

RELY—Required Software Reliability. RELY rates the criticality of the software to be acquired in performing its intended function in an accurate and timely manner. RELY may vary from very low (0.75) to very high (1.40).

TABLE 5.5   Reliability Categories and Multipliers (RELY)

Rating	Effort of Lack of Factor	Multiplier
Very low	Slight inconvenience if there is a problem	0.75
Low	Losses due to problems easily recovered	0.88
Nominal	Moderate difficulty in recovery	1.00
High	Major financial loss if problems develop	1.15
Very high	Risk to human life	1.40

STOR—Storage Constraints. STOR measures the additional work for software development that results from constraints on memory availability in the target computer. Memory is defined as the random access storage or read only memory (ROM) that is directly accessible to the central processing unit (CPU) or I/O processor. STOR may vary from nominal (1.00) to extra high (1.56).

TIME—Execution Time Constraints. TIME relates to measures of the approximate percentage of the available CPU execution time that will be used by the software. It may vary from nominal (1.00) to extra high (1.6). A nominal recommended input value for TIME, NM, is associated with a multiplier of 1.00 and reflects that there are no constraints on the CPU execution time.

TURN—Computer Turnaround. TURN rates the average time spent waiting for the host or developmental computer to complete an action, such as compile a section of code or print a listing. TURN may vary from low (0.87) to very high (1.15).

VIRT—Virtual Machine Volatility. VIRT rates the degree of change that the host and target machines are projected to undergo during the development phases of the software acquisition effort. Machine here refers to the hardware and software that the project calls on to complete its task. VIRT may vary from low (0.87) to very high (1.30). A low (LO) value of VIRT would result when no changes are expected across the development phases.

ACAP—Analyst Team Capability. ACAP measures the capability of the analyst team doing the following: definition and validation of the system requirements and specifications, preliminary design specifications, software inspection and test plans, consulting efforts during detail design and code and unit test phases, and participation during the integration and test phase. ACAP may vary from very low (1.46) to very high (0.71). A recommended input value for ACAP of very high (VH) might be based on a rating of high for previous program performance, a rating of extra high for analyst team educational background, and a rating of good for analyst team communication.

AEXP—Project Application Experience. AEXP rates the project development team with respect to their level of experience in working on other development projects of similar scope and difficulty. AEXP may vary, in the COCOMO, from very low (VL = 1.29) to very high (VH = 0.82). A recommended input value for AEXP of high (HI) might be based on the fact that the development team has much experience on projects of similar complexity that varies from 5 to 12 years for team members.

LEXP—Language Experience. LEXP measures the design analyst and programmer teams experience with the programming language that will be used to design the software. It may vary from very low (VL = 1.14) to high (HI = 0.95).

PCAP—Programming Team Capacity. PCAP measures the capability of the programmers performing the detailed software module design during the critical design phase and during the writing and testing of the physical code during the coding and integration testing phases. It may vary from very low (VL = 1.42) to very high (VH = 0.70). A recommended nominal input value for PCAP (NM = 1.0) might be based on a rating of nominal for previous program performance, a rating of average for programming team educational background, and a rating of average for programming team communication.

VEXP—Virtual Machine Experience. VEXP measures design analyst and programmer experience with the hardware and software of the host and target computers. Software refers to both the operating system and application software. It may vary from very low (VL = 1.21) to high (HI = 0.90). A recommended input value for VEXP of HI might be based on the fact that the acquisition contractor is not using a high order language (HOL) in a machine-independent fashion and is experienced with the host and target machines.

MODP—Modern Programming Practice. MODP quantifies a contractor's use of and commitment to modern programming practices. MODP includes top–down requirements analysis and design, structured design notation, design and code walkthroughs, and structured code. It may vary from very low (VL = 1.24) to very high (VH = 0.82). A recommended value for MODP of VH might be based on the fact that modern programming practices are prescribed by company policy and an education and training program is in effect.

SCED—Existence of Required Development Schedule. SCED reflects the extent to which there exists a required acquisition schedule that is realistic. SCED measures schedule compression and stretchout. Attempting to develop software when the time required for development is too short results in a high rating for this multiplier. While it might seem that a very relaxed time schedule would result in a low rating, the value is actually increased above the nominal value of 1.0 because of inefficiencies that may be introduced when the amount of slack in development is very high. The value of SCED varies from very low (VL = 1.23), which relates to too short a development time, to nominal (NO = 1.0), to very high (VL = 1.10), which relates to too slack a development schedule.

TOOL—Use of Software Development Tools. TOOL relates to the contractor's use of automated software tools and the extent to which these tools are integrated throughout the software development process. TOOL may vary from very low (VL = 1.24) to very high (VH = 0.83). A value of VH might be associated with a contractor's use of automated software tools in a moderately integrated development environment consisting of UNIX or a Minimum Ada Programming Support Environment (MAPSE), configuration management (CM), extended design tools, automated verification systems, cross-compilers, display formatters, and data entry control tools.

Table 5.6 illustrates the values for the intermediate COCOMO effort multipliers as initially presented by Boehm. The overall or aggregate effects of these cost driver multipliers may be large if they are set close to the extreme positions. If each driver is set at the lowest possible value given in this table, the product of the cost drivers is 0.0886. The largest possible product of the cost drivers is 72.379. It is, of course, unreasonable to expect this sort of range in practice. The lowest possible value would be associated with a truly excellent development team attacking an extraordinarily simple acquisition effort. The largest value would be associated with a virtually incompetent team attacking an extraordinarily difficult effort.

TABLE 5.6   Cost Drivers for COCOMO Function Multipliers

	Multiplier Values $M(x_i)$					
Cost Driver	Very Low	Low	Nominal	High	Very High	Extra High
Product						
CPLX	0.70	0.85	1.00	1.15	1.30	1.65
DATA		0.94	1.00	1.08	1.16	
RELY	0.75	0.88	1.00	1.15	1.40	
Computer						
STOR			1.00	1.06	1.21	1.56
TIME			1.00	1.11	1.30	1.66
TURN		0.87	1.00	1.07	1.15	
VIRT		0.87	1.00	1.15	1.30	
Personnel						
ACAP	1.46	1.19	1.00	0.86	0.71	
AEXP	1.29	1.13	1.00	0.91	0.82	
LEXP	1.14	1.07	1.00	0.95		
PCAP	1.42	1.17	1.00	0.86	0.70	
VEXP	1.21	1.10	1.00	0.90		
Project						
MODP	1.24	1.10	1.00	0.91	0.82	
SCED	1.23	1.08	1.00	1.04	1.10	
TOOL	1.24	1.10	1.00	0.91	0.83	

At these extremes, there would be little reason to suspect that the COCOMO would have great validity. It is more reasonable that there would be correlation between product, project and computer complexity, and development team capability. If this is the case, then the multiplier products vary from 2.601 for a very low capability team working on a simple problem to 2.706 for a high capability team working on a most difficult acquisition effort.

Intermediate level COCOMO uses the same approach as basic COCOMO to allocate costs and schedules across a four-phase development lifecycle.

Let us describe the use of the intermediate COCOMO in some detail. The steps given here can be shortened such that they are applicable to the basic COCOMO. The intermediate COCOMO estimates the effort and cost of a proposed software development in the following manner.

1. A *nominal development effort* is estimated as a function of software product size, *S*, in thousands of delivered source lines of instructions. To make this

calculation, we use the basic COCOMO effort determination equation $E = aS^\delta$, where a and δ are as given in Table 5.4.

2. A set of effort multipliers, or environmental factors or cost drivers, is determined from the rating of the software product on the set of 15 cost driver attributes that we have described in Table 5.7. Each of the 15 cost drivers have a rating scale and a set of effort multipliers that indicate the amount by which the nominal estimate needs to be multiplied to accommodate the additional or reduced demands associated with these cost drivers.

3. The actual estimated development effort is determined by multiplying the nominal development effort estimate, using the a and γ parameters for intermediate COCOMO, by all the software product effort multipliers. For a specific software development project, we compute the product of all the effort multipliers for the 15 cost driver attributes. The resulting estimated effort for the entire project is the product of all these terms times the nominal effort determined in step 1.

4. Additional factors are then used to obtain more disaggregate elements of interest from the development effort estimate, such as dollar costs, development schedule, phase and activity distribution, and annual maintenance costs. In addition to calculating the development effort E, in terms of person-months of effort, it is often desired to obtain the development schedule in months in terms of either the number of lines of code or the total person-months of effort. This turns out to be given by $T = bE^\gamma$, where b and γ are also given numerical values, for the three software modes, as indicated in Table 5.4.

Figure 5.11 illustrates the general set of steps to be followed in obtaining a cost and schedule estimate using COCOMO. It suggests the initial use of basic COCOMO and then a switch to intermediate COCOMO to accommodate environmental factors that differ from the nominal.

The amount of variability of the 15 drivers about the nominal value of 1 varies considerably, as we see in Figure 5.12. Here, the order of the drivers is arranged such that those associated with greater variability are to the right of the figure. These tend to be drivers associated with human capabilities and problem complexity, not the ones associated with the availability of automated tools.

There are a number of possible cost drivers that are not included in the intermediate COCOMO. Among these are such factors as requirements volatility, management quality, customer (interface) quality, amount of documentation, hardware configuration, and privacy and security facets. Boehm discusses these and other factors. He suggests that parsimony is among the major reasons why other factors are not included and that inclusion of many of these factors would unnecessarily complicate the analysis while not providing for greatly enhanced fidelity of cost and schedule predictions. This does not mean that these factors are necessarily neglected; they are assumed to be at some nominal values and that changes in them will not materially affect results.

It is not difficult, in principle, to incorporate other parameters. For example, we

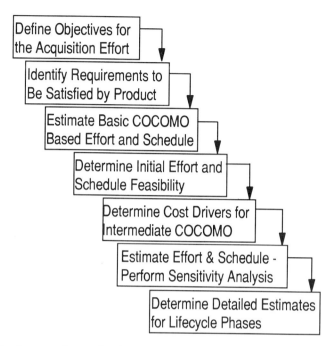

Figure 5.11 Suggested steps for determination of effort and schedule using intermediate COCOMO.

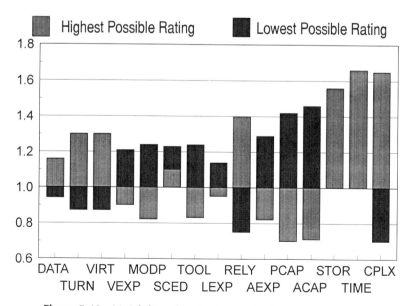

Figure 5.12 Variability of cost driver multipliers across ratings.

TABLE 5.7 Effort Multipliers for Requirements Volatility (RVOL)

Rating	Effect	Multiplier
Low	Essentially no requirements volatility	0.91
Nominal	Infrequent, noncritical redirection efforts needed	1.00
High	Occasional, moderate redirection efforts needed	1.19
Very high	Frequent, moderate redirection efforts needed	1.38
Extra high	Frequent major redirection efforts needed	1.62

might wish to modify intermediate COCOMO to a two-level version such that it becomes possible to consider *requirements volatility,* or requirements creep, which is interpreted to mean the tendency for requirements to change after they have been initially identified and where software development has proceeded beyond the requirements phase.

The first intermediate COCOMO 1 level is restricted to the cost drivers identified in Figure 5.10. Our new intermediate COCOMO 2 would include an additional driver for requirements volatility, with values ranging from a low of 0.91 to a high of 1.62. This assumes that these multipliers are experientially, or experimentally, determined to be correct for given amounts of "volatility." Table 5.7 presents the effort multipliers for requirements volatility. This is then assumed to be a 16th cost driver in the COCOMO equations obtained earlier. We can describe this 16th cost driver as follows.

RVOL—Requirements Volatility. RVOL measures the amount of redesign and redevelopment that is the result of changes in custumer-specified requirements. The nominal value for this parameter is 1.0, which indicates no volatility or creep in requirements. This assumes that there will be only small and noncritical redirections.

An interesting question arises concerning whether or not the other drivers in the intermediate COCOMO need to be changed in order to accommodate this new driver. If we can assume that the drivers are independent, the answer is no. While there is no strong reason to assume independence, it is reasonable to assume near independence for small enough changes in the driver parameters.

There are a number of similar extensions of the COCOMO. A very useful one has led to what is known as *REVIC,* a revised COCOMO. REVIC,* actually revised intermediate COCOMO, predicts the development of lifecycle costs for software acquisition across the three basic phases of definition, development, and

---

*In the area of public domain software, there have been many attempts to implement COCOMO. The WICOMO effort at the former Wang Institute is one example of this. REVIC is a relatively complete and very user friendly package. It is available from the Air Force Cost Center, 1111 Jefferson Davis Highway, Suite 403, Arlington, VA 22202. The telephone number is (703) 746-5840. A bulletin board, from which the software may be potentially downloaded, is located at (703) 746-5875.

deployment. It encompasses costs and schedule from requirements analysis through completion of the software acceptance testing and later through maintenance. As with COCOMO, the number of delivered source lines of code is the basic cost driver.

There are two major extensions to the development lifecycle assumed in intermediate COCOMO that enables REVIC to include many aspects of the definition and deployment phases of the acquisition lifecycle.

1. The lifecycle for COCOMO does not include the software requirements engineering phase. The amount of effort expended in this phase can vary dramatically. REVIC predicts the effort and schedule in the software requirements engineering phase by taking a percentage of the development phases. REVIC utilizes a default value, 12% for effort and 30% for schedule, for the percentage to be used for nominal software acquisition programs and allows the user to change this percentage if desired. Of course, the very initial portions of the definition phase, perhaps accomplished during proposal preparation or specified as part of the request for proposals (RFP), must contain some user requirements. REVIC estimates the cost of transitioning from a set of user requirements and system specifications to software specifications.

2. The COCOMO lifecycle really ends at the end of the software development phase, that is, when successfully completing the integration and test phase. This phase is characterized by successful integration of computer software components (CSCs) into computer software configuration items (CSCIs) and associated testing of the CSCIs against the test criteria developed during the software acquisition program. This does not include the system level integration of CSCIs and associated system level testing to ensure that the system level requirements have been met. This is generally accomplished as part of the operational test and evaluation (OT&E) phase, as this is sometimes called. REVIC predicts effort and schedule for this phase similarly to the requirements specification phase, by taking a percentage of the development phase estimates. REVIC provides a default percentage, 22% for effort and 26% for schedule for this phase as nominal amounts, and allows a user to change this percentage if desired.

3. REVIC provides an estimate for the maintenance of software over a 15-year period by implementing the equation

$$M = aS^\delta A\eta \tag{5.3.14}$$

where M is the maintenance effort in labor-months, A is an annual percentage code change factor (expressed as a fraction) or annual change traffic, and η represents a set of maintenance environmental factors. REVIC provides a default percentage for the annual change traffic and allows this to be varied, if desired. REVIC assumes the presence of a transition period after the initial deployment of the software, during which time residual errors are found. After this, there exists a close to steady-state condition, which allows a positive fraction—declining over time—to be used for the annual change traffic during the first 3 years of deployment. Beginning with the fourth year, REVIC assumes that the maintenance activity consists of both error corrections and new software enhancements.

4. The essential difference between REVIC and intermediate COCOMO is the set of environmental factors used as cost drivers in the equations for *C* and *T*. An enhanced set of drivers is used, as we will soon describe. REVIC was calibrated using more recent data than available for COCOMO and this results in different quantities for some of the environmental factors. On the average, the parameter values used by the basic effort and schedule equations are slightly higher in REVIC than they are in COCOMO.

5. One of the additional cost drivers relates to the use of reusable code. When reusable code is present, an adjustment factor needs to be calculated and used to determine the size of a number of modules that are developed. A separate estimate for cost and schedule is determined through use of REVIC or COCOMO for each of these modules. The overall effort or cost is the sum of these. We describe this adjustment factor in more detail in our treatment of the detailed COCOMO, as it is the same factor that is used there.

6. Other differences occur in obtaining distribution of effort and schedule for the various phases of the development lifecycle and in an automatic calculation feature for the standard deviation associated with risk assessment efforts. COCOMO provides a table for distributing effort and schedule over the development phases, based on the size of the code being developed and the mode of development, as we illustrated in Figures 5.5 and 5.6. REVIC provides a single weighted "average" distribution for the overall effort and schedule and has the ability to allow a user to change the distribution of effort allocated to the specifications and OT&E phases. Thus the value of the SCED parameter is set equal to nominal or 1.0. The software user can set the actual development schedule through forcing it below that which results from the nominal calculation. This will always increase both labor-months of effort and associated costs.

There are 19 environmental factors in REVIC. Those four not included in the intermediate COCOMO are:

RVOL	Requirements volatility
RUSE	Required reusability
SECU	DoD security classification
RISK	Risk associated with platform

We have already described requirements volatility. Appropriate descriptors of the other three are as follows:

RUSE—Required Reusability. RUSE measures the extra effort that is needed to generalize software modules when they must be developed specifically for reuse in other software packages. The nominal value for reuse, NM, is 1.0, which means that there is no contractually required reuse of the software.

SECU—Classified Security Application. SECU measures the extra effort required to develop software in a classified area or for a classified security application. We note that this factor does not relate to the certification of security processing levels by the National Security Agency.

RISK—Management Reserve for Risk. RISK is the REVIC parameter that provides for adding a percentage factor to account for varying levels of program risk. If it is determined that the software development has a very low program risk, we use very low for the risk factor and this translates into a numerical value of 1.00 for the cost driver or environmental factor.

Thus REVIC is essentially intermediate level COCOMO with the addition of four additional environmental factors, an updated database, and considerable ability for "what if" type analysis and sensitivity studies.

A standard set of two-letter descriptors associated with each of the seven cost multipliers, one more (extra extra high) than generally described in intermediate COCOMO, is used to describe the extent to which each environmental factor differs from the nominal amount:

VL	Very low
LO	Low
NM	Nominal
HI	High
VH	Very high
XH	Extra high
XX	Extra extra high

Some anchoring of the scoring for the factors is employed to calibrate the use of the REVIC algorithms. This anchoring is particularly necessary because many of the environmental factor terms need specific definition across the people responsible for providing estimates, if these estimates are to be compatible and consistent. The environmental factors and calibration presented in Table 5.8 were used in version 9 of the REVIC software. Many of the parameters are precisely the same as those used in the intermediate COCOMO.

What results from this is a somewhat enhanced version of intermediate COCOMO and a software package especially suited for systems management prediction of the effort and schedule needed for software development. The possibility of performing various sensitivity analysis studies for changing parameters is especially attractive. We can also reuse the software to develop the several estimates needed for incremental and evolutionary development of software.

Of course, it is easily possible to implement intermediate COCOMO on any of the currently available microcomputer spreadsheet programs. One of the objectives in any of these implementations is to be able to predict costs and schedules for the various lifecycle phases, such as to obtain the sort of results identified in Figures 5.13 and 5.14.

TABLE 5.8   REVIC Environmental Factor Calibration and Scoring

Product Attributes

Software Product Complexity—CPLX

VL	Simple	0.70
LO	Data processing	0.85
NM	Math routines	1.00
HI	Advanced data structures	1.15
VH	Real-time and advanced math	1.30
XH	Complex scientific math	1.65

Database Size—DATA

LO	DB bytes/program SLOC, D/P < 10	0.94
NM	$10 \leq D/P < 100$	1.00
HI	$100 \leq D/P < 1000$	1.08
VH	$D/P \geq 1000$	1.16

Required Software Reliability—RELY

VL	Slight	0.75
LO	Easy	0.88
NM	Moderate	1.00
HI	MIL-STD/high finance	1.15
VH	Loss of life	1.40

Computer Attributes

Main Storage Constraints—STOR

VL	None	1.00
LO	None	1.00
NM	None	1.00
HI	70% Utilization	1.06
VH	85% Utilization	1.21
XH	>95% Utilization	1.56

Execution Time Constraints—TIME

VL	None	1.00
LO	None	1.00
NM	60% Utilization	1.00
HI	70% Utilization	1.11
VH	85% Utilization	1.30
XH	>95% Utilization	1.66

Computer Turnaround (Response) Time—TURN

VL	<6minutes	0.79
LO	<30 minutes	0.87
NM	<4 hours	1.00
HI	>4 hours	1.07
VH	>12 hours	1.15

Virtual Machine Volatility—VIRT

VL	No changes	0.87
LO	One change in 6 months	0.87
NM	One change in 3 months	1.00

TABLE 5.8 (*Continued*)

Computer Attributes

HI	One change every month	1.15
VH	Several changes every month	1.30
XH	Constant changes	1.49

Personnel Attributes

Analyst Capability—ACAP

VL	15th Percentile	1.46
LO	35th Percentile	1.19
NM	55th Percentile	1.00
HI	75th Percentile	0.86
VH	90th Percentile	0.71

Project Application Experience—AEXP

VL	Less than 4 months	1.29
LO	1 year	1.13
NM	3 years	1.00
HI	6 years	0.91
VH	Greater than 12 years	0.82

Language Experience—LEXP

VL	None	1.14
LO	Less than 1 year	1.07
NM	From 1 to 2 years	1.00
HI	2 years	0.95
VH	Greater than 2 years	0.95

Programming Team Capability—PCAP

VL	15th Percentile	1.42
LO	35th Percentile	1.17
NM	55th Percentile	1.00
HI	75th Percentile	0.86
VH	90th Percentile	0.70

Virtual Machine Experience—VEXP

VL	None	1.21
LO	Less than 6 months	1.10
NM	Less than 1 year	1.00
HI	From 1 to 2 years	0.90
VH	Greater than 2 years	0.90

Project Attributes

Modern Programming Practices—MODP

VL	None	1.24
LO	Beginners	1.10
NM	Some	1.00
HI	In general use	0.91
VH	Routine	0.82

TABLE 5.8   (*Continued*)

Project Attributes

Existence of Required Development Schedule—SCED

NM		1.00

Use of Software Development Tools—TOOL

VL	Very few primitive	1.24
LO	Basic microcomputer tools	1.10
NM	Basic minicomputer tools	1.00
HI	Basic mainframe tools	0.91
VH	Extensive, but little tool integration	0.83
XH	Moderate, in an integrated environment	0.73
XX	Full use, in an integrated environment	0.62

Additional Drivers in REVIC

Requirements Volatility—RVOL

VL	None	0.91
LO	Essentially none	0.91
NM	Small, noncritical redirection	1.00
HI	Occasional, moderate redirection	1.19
VH	Frequent moderate, occasional major redirection	1.38
XH	Frequent major redirection	1.62

Required Reusability—RUSE

NM	No reuse	1.00
HI	Reuse of single mission products	1.10
VH	Reuse across single mission products	1.30
XH	Reuse for any and all applications	1.50

Classified Security Application—SECU

NM	Unclassified	1.00
HI	Classified (secret or top secret)	1.10

Management Reserve for Risk—RISK

VL	Ground systems	1.00
LO	MIL-SPEC ground systems	1.20
NM	Unmanned airborne	1.40
HI	Manned airborne	1.60
VH	Unmanned space	1.80
XH	Manned space	2.00
XX	Manned space	2.50

There have been a considerable number of efforts to evaluate the accuracy of COCOMO. In one of the more detailed studies [17], based on evaluation of seven new software development efforts, it was found that COCOMO was able to predict costs and schedule for all seven projects with less than 20% relative error. To make predictions of this quality requires detailed familiarity with past organizational practices and careful calibration of the COCOMO to reflect these characteristics.

30
25
20
15
10
5
0
0 1 2 3 4 5 6 7 8
Integrate and Test
Code and Unit Test
Detailed Design
Conceptual Design
Requirements

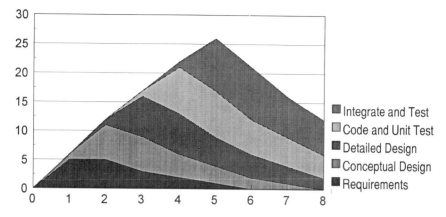

Figure 5.13 Generic distribution of labor-months over time.

5.3.3 Detailed COCOMO

The detailed COCOMO adds refinements not included in the basic COCOMO and intermediate COCOMO. Detailed COCOMO introduces two more components to the model. Phase-sensitive effort multipliers are included, as a set of tables, in order to reflect the fact that some phases of the software development lifecycle are more affected than others by the cost driver factors. This phasewise distribution of effort augmentation is the primary change over intermediate COCOMO. It provides a basis for detailed project planning in order to complete the software development program across all lifecycle phases.

In addition, a three-level product hierarchy is employed, so that generally different cost driver ratings are supplied for the assumed four phases of effort for four cost drivers that primarily affect software modules (CPLX, LEXP, PCAP, and VEXP) and for the 11 drivers that primarily affect subsystems (ACAP, AEXP, DATA, MODP, RELY, SCED, STOR, TIME, TOOL, TURN, and VIRT). These drivers are presumably used at the level at which each attribute is most susceptible to

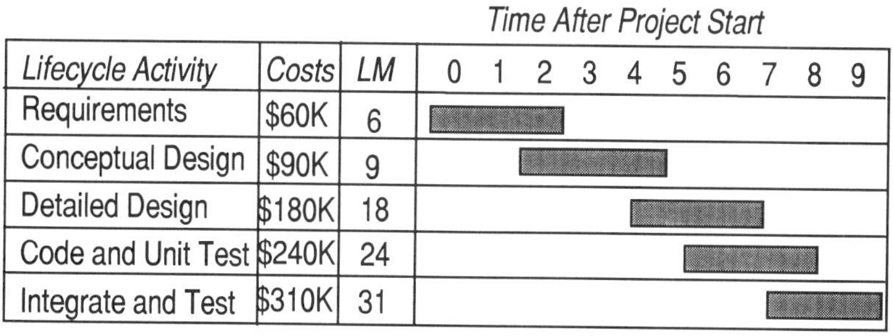

Time After Project Start
Lifecycle Activity
Costs
LM
0 1 2 3 4 5 6 7 8 9
Requirements $60K 6
Conceptual Design $90K 9
Detailed Design $180K 18
Code and Unit Test $240K 24
Integrate and Test $310K 31

Figure 5.14 Gantt chart of schedule and phasewise estimates of costs and effort.

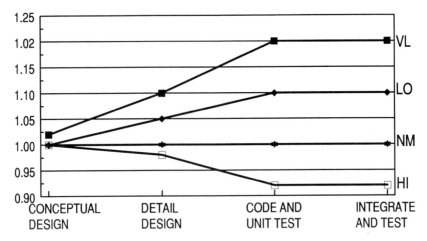

Figure 5.15   Distribution of multiplier weights across phases for language experience (LEXP) factor in detailed COCOMO.

variation. As in the basic COCOMO and intermediate COCOMO, all nominal cost drivers have a value of unity. Multipliers have been developed for detailed COCOMO that can be applied to the total project effort and total project schedule completion time in order to allocate effort and schedule components to each phase in the lifecycle of a software development program. There are assumed to be four distinct lifecycle phases. The effort and schedule for each phase are assumed to be given in terms of the overall effort and schedule by the same general equations as for intermediate COCOMO, but with the use of phase-sensitive effort multipliers. Figures 5.15 and 5.16 illustrate the way in which two of these multipliers vary across

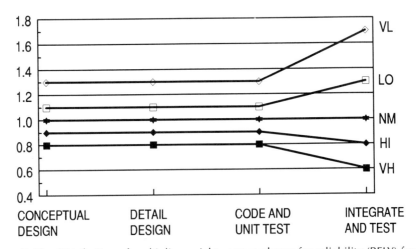

Figure 5.16   Distribution of multiplier weights across phases for reliability (RELY) factory in detailed COCOMO.

the four assumed lifecycle phases. In general, there is usually not much difference in the multipliers for the detailed design phase and those for the code and unit test phase between detailed COCOMO and intermediate COCOMO.

For some of the cost drivers, such as the two illustrated in Figures 5.15 and 5.16, there is not much difference at the conceptual design phase (denoted as the requirements and product design phase by Boehm) between intermediate COCOMO and detailed COCOMO. There is a major difference, however, at the integrate and test phase. We would expect this with respect to such factors as programmer capability, modern programming practice, use of software tools, and needed system reliability. For others, such as analyst team capability and project application experience, we would expect a considerable difference at the conceptual design phase because this is the phase at which these experiences are most critical. Figures 5.17 and 5.18 illustrate the variations in these multipliers over the four development phases. In each case, the multiplier associated with the intermediate COCOMO is a composite of these multipliers across the four phases shown. Much more detail concerning implementation of the detailed COCOMO is available in [13].

5.3.4 Reuse and the COCOMO

The COCOMO also has provisions for adjusting estimates of software costing when the software is developed, in part, from existing code. The adjustment is made at the module level, and each module is evaluated to determine how much code will be used without modification and how much will be modified. *DM* is the percentage of the design features of the reused product that have been modified, *CM* is the

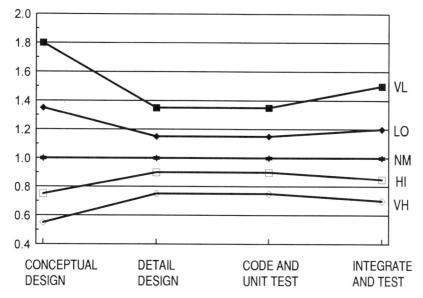

Figure 5.17 Distribution of multiplier weights across phases for capability of the analysts (ACAP) in detailed COCOMO.

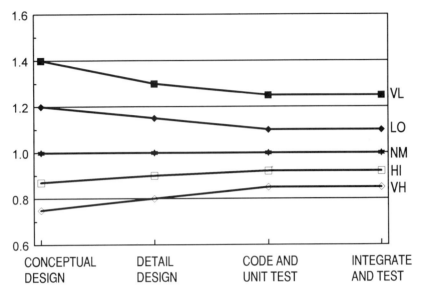

Figure 5.18 Distribution of multiplier weights across phases for applications experience (AEXP) in detailed COCOMO.

percentage of the code in the product to be reused that needs to be modified, and *CI* is the percentage of effort that has been required to integrate the reused code into the overall software product and to test the resulting product as compared with that for non-reused software of comparable size. There is no reason why any of these percentages cannot be greater than 100, although this suggests that it might be better not to employ the reused code. It is assumed that 40% of the effort in developing a software product is expended in the design phase, 30% in the coding phase, and 30% in the integrate and test phase. Thus an adjustment factor *AF* is calculated to be

$$AF = 0.4DM + 0.3CM + 0.3CI \qquad (5.3.15)$$

This says that, for example, if 100% of the product design is modified from the original design ($DM = 1.0$), if 100% of the code in the final product is new code ($CM = 1.0$), and if the effort required to integrate the reused software into the final product and test is 100% of the nominal effort for all new software ($CI = 1.0$), then the adjustment factor is 1.0. There is, in this case, no benefit to using the reused software in terms of cost. If each of these factors is zero, then the final software module is an unmodified version of the initial software and the adjustment factor is 0.0.

The size of each module is adjusted according to the formula

$$S_i^a = S_i \times AF \qquad (5.3.16)$$

where the S_i represent the number (in thousands) of source lines of code in the software product represented by the *i*th module. This adjusted code size represents the weighted size of the combination of new and reused code. The adjusted code size, S_i^a, is used in the detailed COCOMO calculations. These relations can also be used in the basic and intermediate COCOMO calculations. In this case, there is no need for the module concept, as only single software products are considered.

One potential difficulty with these relations is that only one category of reuse is considered. Balda and Gustafson [18] have proposed a variant of this in which the final software product consists of new and unique code, S_N; code that is adapted for reuse, S_A; and code that is reused without any modification whatever, S_R. The suggested model for effort is given by

$$E = a[S_N^\delta + \sigma(20S_A^\delta + S_R^\delta)] \qquad (5.3.17)$$

$$T = 2.5E^\gamma \qquad (5.3.18)$$

where the a, δ, and γ parameters are those for basic COCOMO. To obtain the relation for intermediate COCOMO, we would use the appropriate values for these parameters and a separate environmental multiplier for each of the three types of code. It would be necessary to calibrate and validate such a model, using related and relevant past development efforts, for it to be most useful.

5.3.5 Ada COCOMO

A recent variation of COCOMO is called Ada COCOMO [15,19]. It is very similar to the original COCOMO with only a few differences to allow for explicit incorporation of rapid prototyping, the spiral lifecycle, risk management, and requirements volatility. In Ada COCOMO, the nominal initial effort estimate is obtained from

$$E_n = 2.8S^{1.04 + \sum\limits_{i=4}^{4} w_i} \qquad (5.3.19)$$

where the weights w_i, depend on characterization of the development process:

w_1	Experience with Ada process model
w_2	Design thoroughness at project conceptual design level
w_3	Risks eliminated at project design review level
w_4	Requirements volatility during development

Each weight is assigned a value ranging from 0.00 to 0.05. Table 5.9 illustrates possible scoring practice for these weights. We note that the effect of these multipliers is different from the other cost drivers in intermediate COCOMO. There, they act as multipliers of the exponentially weighted KDSI. Here, they are a part of the exponent itself.

There are other changes to form the intermediate Ada COCOMO. One of the original cost drivers VIRT (volatility of the virtual machine) is eliminated and replaced by two others: VMVH (volatility of the host system) and VMVT (volatility of the target system). Two additional cost drivers—SECU (development of a classi-

TABLE 5.9 Weights and Ratings for Ada COCOMO

Rating and Weight w_i	Experience with Ada Practices	Conceptual Design Thoroughness	Risk Eliminated by Conceptual Design	Requirements Volatility
XH 0.00	Successful on many mission-critical programs	Extra high (100%)	Complete (100%)	None at all
VH 0.01	Successful on one mission-critical program	Very high (90%)	Almost all (90%)	Small and noncritical changes
HI 0.02	General familiarity	High (75%)	Many (75%)	Frequent but noncritical changes
NM 0.03	Modest familiarity	Nominal (60%)	Some (60%)	Occasional moderately critical changes
LO 0.04	Little familiarity	Low (40%)	Slight (40%)	Frequent moderately critical changes
LO 0.05	None	Very low (20%)	Few (20%)	Many major critical changes

fied security application) and RUSE (a measurement of required reusability) are included. Thus we now have a total of 18 cost drivers. Table 5.10 illustrates suggested ratings and weights for these drivers. It shows very slight modification from Table 5.6, which illustrated the initial version of the intermediate cost drivers.

The various versions of COCOMO have probably been subject to more use, critical study, and evaluation that any other cost and schedule estimation model. While the model has generally been determined to be valid and valuable when used with care, the use of lines of delivered instructions (KDSI) as the major determinant of cost and schedule has often been subject to criticism. We will address this criticism later.

5.3.6 COCOMO for Non-Grand Design Lifecycles

In general, the COCOMO appears most appropriate for the grand design waterfall lifecycle in which software is built right and completely in a single pass through the lifecycle. It is easily modified to allow for other modes of development. We simply calculate an effort for each of the successive, iterative, or evolutionary builds. This has been suggested in [18] and by a number of other researchers. Conceptually, the relation to use, for intermediate COCOMO, is given by the effort and schedule required for the ith acquisition cycle

TABLE 5.10   Cost Drivers, or Multipliers, and Weights for Intermediate Ada COCOMO

Multiplier	VL	LO	NM	HI	VH	XH	XX
CPLX	0.73	0.85	0.97	1.08	1.22	1.43	
DATA		0.94	1	1.08	1.16		
RELY	0.75	0.88	0.96	1.07	1.24		
STOR			1	1.06	1.21	1.56	
TIME			1	1.11	1.3	1.66	
TURN	0.79	0.87	1	1.07	1.15		
VMVH		0.92	1	1.09	1.17		
VMVT		0.93	1	1.07	1.16		
ACAP	1.57	1.29	1	0.8	0.61		
AEXP	1.29	1.13	1	0.91	0.82		
LEXP	1.26	1.14	1.04	0.95	0.86		
PCAP	1.3	1.12	1	0.89	0.8		
VEXP	1.21	1.1	1	0.9			
MODP	1.24	1.1	0.98	0.86	0.78		
SCED	1.23	1.08	1	1	1		
TOOL	1.24	1.1	1	0.91	0.83	0.73	0.62
RUSE			1	1.1	1.3	1.5	
SECU			1	1.1			

$$E_i = aS_i^\delta \prod_{j=1}^{15} m_i(x_j) \tag{5.3.20}$$

$$T_i = bE_i^\gamma \tag{5.3.21}$$

and the summation of these, which gives the total acquisition cost, in terms of effort and schedule. We obtain

$$E = \sum_{i=1}^{m} E_i \tag{5.3.22}$$

$$T = \sum_{j=1}^{m} T_i \tag{5.3.23}$$

where we assume that there are m builds. A potential difficulty here is that the builds are not at all independent of one another. If we are only interested in replicating what actually happened in a development situation, we can use the various values for S_i that resulted historically, together with the appropriate multipliers. In a real design situation, however, we wish to identify the amount of code to develop at each successive lifecycle, such that the overall cost of acquisition is low and the overall quality is high. The values of the S_i that are needed in a realistic situation are not at all independent. Thus costing would need to be accomplished through some potentially exhaustive, iterative analysis effort that examined a number of possible build scenarios. From these, an appropriate acquisition scenario would be chosen that resulted in cost–effectiveness competitive advantages for the effort and the resulting product.

5.4   RESOURCE ALLOCATION MODELS FOR SOFTWARE DEVELOPMENT

The previous model developments were macrolevel models based on the assumption of a given structure for the model and then determining parameters within this structure to match observed data. An alternate approach is possible in which we attempt to postulate a theoretically based model for resource expenditures in developing software. The Rayleigh equation provides one such basis.

5.4.1   Putnam Resource Allocation Model—SLIM

It is not unreasonable to postulate that development time will influence overall project effort and cost. Norden [20] was perhaps the first to suggest a time sequencing of typical project effort. In investigating projects at IBM, he observed that the staffing of these software development projects resembled a Rayleigh distribution, shown in Figure 5.19. This sort of distribution is what might be empirically observed in practice or obtained as a result of the sort of modeling effort that might have led to Figure 5.13. Norden's observations were entirely empirical and it was only the shape of the Rayleigh curve that was of interest rather than any of its underlying theoretical and probabilistic constructs.

The curves in Figure 5.19 are obtained from a Rayleigh differential equation for software project *effort rate*

$$dy/dt = 2Kat \exp(-at^2) \tag{5.4.1}$$

This is solved with the initial condition $y(0) = 0$ to obtain

$$y(t) = K[1 - \exp(-at^2)] \tag{5.4.2}$$

Here, it is presumed that $y(t)$ represents total person-months of effort. It is interesting to note that $y(\infty) = K$. Thus the total lifecycle effort will ultimately become K, presumably due to continued maintenance. The peak effort rate on the project occurs at $t = T = (2a)^{-0.50}$, where T is the peak project effort rate. So if we use this normalization, the effort equation (5.4.2) may be written as

$$E(t) = y(t) = K\{1 - \exp[-0.5(t/T)^2]\} \tag{5.4.3}$$

At the time when the peak project effort rate occurs, $t = T$, we have for the total effort expended, $E(T) = 0.3945K$.

We now imagine that we have a number of curves like that shown in Eqs. (5.4.2)

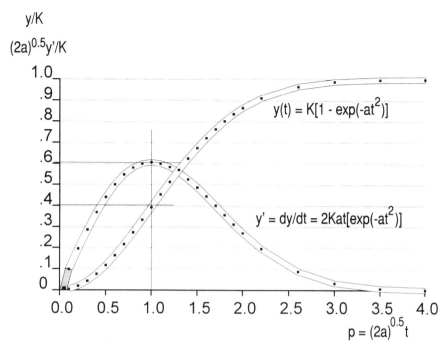

Figure 5.19 Normalized Rayleigh Equation Solutions.

and (5.4.3). Each of these represents the effort and effort rate for a particular lifecycle. These are given by

$$\frac{dE_i(t)}{dt} = 1.414K\{\exp[-0.5(t/T_i)^2]\}/T_i^2 \qquad (5.4.4)$$

$$E_i(t) = K\{1 - \exp[-0.5(t/t_i)^2]\} \qquad (5.4.5)$$

Now we can attempt to find individual effort rate and effort curves for individual phases that comprise the lifecycle. We can add these to obtain the total effort rate. We can integrate this sum, or sum the time integrals of the individual effort rates, to obtain the total effort at any time *t*.

Putnam [21–23] uses Norden's observations for project effort expenditures to develop a model of software costing. Putnam initially studied 50 projects from the Army Computer Systems Command and 150 other projects, thus developing one of the largest databases to support cost estimation. This *resource allocation* model, which has been developed under the name **software lifecycle management** (SLIM), includes several effort factors:

Volume of work

A difficulty gradient that measures complexity

A project technology factor that measures staff experience

Delivery time constraints

Putnam constructed a model for staffing that is based on total cumulative staff, a project acceleration factor that measures how quickly the project can absorb new staff members, and the number of 8-hour workdays in a project month.

To derive the Putnam model, we use the Rayleigh differential equation and integrate it to yield $y(t)$ as the cumulative staff needed up to time t. If we set $dy^2(t)/dt^2 = 0$ and solve the resulting equation, we obtain values at which maximum effort rate occurs. In so doing, we easily obtain $a = 0.5t^{-2}$. At this value of time, which we may denote by $T = (2a)^{-0.5}$, the Raleigh equation solution is the time where maximum project effort rate occurs. At this value, we obtain y_{max} $(t = T) = 0.3945K$. Each phase of development is assumed to have the same general type of curve with K differing from phase to phase but with T representing the total project duration time, as we have just indicated.

Putnam is especially concerned with what is termed a *difficulty metric*, defined by

$$D = K/T^2 = 2aK \qquad (5.4.6)$$

that plays a major role in software development effort and cost. When we use the defined value of a, we obtain for the original Rayleigh equation

$$dy/dt = (K/T^2)t \exp[-0.5(t/T)^2] = Dt \exp[-0.5(t/T^2] \qquad (5.4.7)$$

and when we time scale by letting $p = t/T$, we obtain

$$dy/dp = Kp \exp(-0.5p^2) = DT^2p \exp(-0.5p^2) \qquad (5.4.8)$$

$$y(p) = K[1 - \exp(-0.5p^2)] = DT^2[1 - \exp(-0.5p^2)] \qquad (5.4.9)$$

From these relations, we see that we may now scale the amplitude by letting $Y = Ky$. Then, the scaled time and amplitude functions expressing the proposed effort evolution over time,

$$dY/dp = p \exp(-0.5p^2) \qquad (5.4.10)$$

$$Y(p) = 1 - \exp(-0.5p^2) \qquad (5.4.11)$$

are immutable over the many alterables that must surely be present in the milieu of activities associated with software development. We have illustrated these normalized values in Figure 5.19. We note that $Y_{max}(p) = 0.3945$ and $[dY(p)/dp]_{max} = 0.6065$, and that these occur at normalized time $p = 1$. There is, of course, some minor flexibility within the normalization of this in the sense that $y_{max}(t) = y(t = T) = KY(p = 1) = 0.3935DT^2$ and $[dy(t)/dt]_{max} = 0.6065DT$.

Rather than associating overall scope of a project with the value of $y(t)$ for very large time values, which is $y(p) = DT^2$, it is not unreasonable to associate it with the ratio of the maximum effort rate to the time for peak effort rate. In a *simple scope* project, the peak effort rate is small and the time to peak can be large. For a *complex* or *large scope* project, the peak effort rate is large and the time allowed before the peak buildup occurs is small. However, $[dy(t)/dt]_{max} = 0.6065DT$ and thus we see that project complexity is directly proportional to D.

Putnam appears to use a rationale such as this and postulates that D is small for easy to develop systems. Likewise, for systems that are hard to develop, D is large. There are other fundamentally useful relations. It is often stated, for example, that *the average software project productivity is defined to be the number of source lines of code per peak person-month of overall effort for the entire project or*

$$P = S/E \tag{5.4.12}$$

and it is further postulated by Putnam that productivity is proportional to the difficulty metric

$$P = \phi D^{\mu} = \frac{S}{E} \tag{5.4.13}$$

Using nonlinear regression, Putnam determined from the aforementioned analysis of 50 army projects that

$$P = \phi D^{-2/3} \tag{5.4.14}$$

where P is a measure of productivity. In general, this relationship may be written as

$$S = \phi K^{1/3} T^{4/3} \tag{5.4.15}$$

where S is measured in thousands of lines of code and ϕ is a factor reflecting hardware constraints, program complexity, personnel experience levels, and the programming environment extant.

Putnam calls ϕ a *technology factor* or *productivity factor*. He proposes use of 20 discrete values for this factor, which vary from 610 to 57,314. These are quite analogous to the environmental factors we discussed for the intermediate COCOMO. In the Putnam model, K is expressed in programmer-years and T in years. Alternatively, the technology factor can be identified on the basis of historical data for a particular organization. The term K/T^2 is called a *manpower buildup index* (MBI). The MBI affects the slope of the initial part of the Rayleigh buildup curve. The larger a number we choose for this, the faster will be the buildup of the project staff. This is assumed to be a value that is specified by the user of the Putnam algorithms or, alternately, determined from specification of the 22 productivity parameters, which includes the 20 needed to determine ϕ. The MBI also determines when the time T will be reached.

Putnam assumes that there is a constant ratio, for a given software acquisition project, which is given by

$$\beta = \frac{K}{T^3} \tag{5.4.16}$$

and that the constant β is fixed by the difficulty of the system under acquisition. For a very new and complex system, this value might be as low as 7.3, whereas for a simple system we might have a value as large as 89.0.

Equation (5.4.16) is much the same as that of Walston and Felix, who obtained $T = 2.4E^{0.33}$, and the similar relationship of Boehm. For specified values of ϕ and β, we can solve these latter two equations for the acquisition effort K and the acquisition time T.

SLIM, like the other models studied here, is basically a macrolevel model that is based on a combination of expertise and statistical computations. The theoretical basis for this is the Rayleigh effort relationship. This model like the other models, is fundamentally a static model. The use of a differential equation for project life does allow computation of project life in terms of other variables, however, and in this very restricted sense it is a dynamic model.

SLIM could be used effectively for predictive purposes if we had a suitable algorithm that we might use to predict the value of ϕ for a software project. Unfortunately, such a relationship does not exist at this time. In addition, there appears no truly formal theory that suggests use of the Rayleigh differential equation as a model for project buildup and diminution over time. As we have noted, there is very little freedom associated with the evolution over time of this relation. It seemingly does not allow, for example, much increased attention to be devoted during the requirements phase of a project in the hope that this would result in much lower costs during the operational implementation and maintenance phases of the project.

If we solve Eq. (5.4.15) for cumulative project effort, we obtain

$$K = \left(\frac{S}{\phi} \right)^3 T^{-4} \tag{5.4.17}$$

which indicates that *cumulative project effort varies inversely as the fourth power of time to peak project development* if we can somehow believe that the technology factor, ϕ, varies linearly with the number of source lines of code. It is, of course, very reasonable to believe that significant compression of project schedules will bring about major problems.

A potential advantage to the Putnam model is that there is an explicit trade-off, in the form of the foregoing equation, between total development effort K and total development time T.

A number of potentially useful user-specified functions are provided in the SLIM model:

Calibration, to enable productivity measurements

Build, to define a new software development effort

Estimate, to identify minimal development time and costs for a development effort

What if, to specify development parameters for a fixed cost for development effort

Management constraints, to enable trade-offs among costs and parameter changes

Implementation functions, to define requirements and lifecycle staffing

Development program management parameters

Documentation

To accomplish all this, the SLIM model necessarily requires much input information. This is classified in three sections:

Section 1: Calibration

Development effort (worker-months)

Development time (months)

System name

System size (source statements)

Section 2: New System Information

Fully burdened labor rate ($/worker-year)

Function name for each module

Inflation rate (decimal fraction)

Largest possible number of source statements for each module

Level of system

Most likely number of source statements for each module

Overall personnel skills

Personnel experience with programming language(s)

personnel experience with system of similar size and application

Primary development language

Project start date

Proportion of development computer capacity used for other production work

Proportion of development computer dedicated to effort

Proportion of development in on-line, interactive mode

Proportion of memory of target machine utilized by the software system

Proportion of real-time code

Proportion of system coded in a higher order language

Smallest possible number of source statements for each module

Standard deviation of the labor rate

System name

Technology factor

Type of system

Use of chief programmer teams (yes or no)

Use of design and code inspection (yes or no)

Use of structured programming (yes or no)

Use of top–down development (yes or no)

Section 3: Constraints and Options

Criteria for optimization (e.g., design to cost)

Desired mean time to failure

Level of acceptable risk

Maximum allowable development cost (dollars)

Maximum development time (months)

Minimum and maximum number of people at peak staffing time

Output request (e.g., for graphic displays or Gantt charts)

Request for trade-off analysis

There are corresponding outputs. The model provides the calibration used, in terms of the technology factor, and the *minimum time* solution, resulting from some use of linear programming algorithms. Associated with this is an estimate of the standard deviation of each computer variable. There are a large number of output options, including Gantt charts, displays of major milestones, graphical displays of some aspects of the linear programming solutions, estimated code production per month, and outputs for other optimization criteria.

An investigation of the accuracy of SLIM by the Purdue Software Metrics Research Group [24] indicates that the model exaggerates the effect of schedule compression on development. Another potential problem evolves from such heavy reliance on the project lines of code and development time characteristics. The value of the environmental factor ϕ should also reflect a great many other factors. To use the model, the software systems engineer must be able to supply or otherwise obtain each of the 22 components of the technology factor. The cumulative effort estimate is very sensitive to the choice of ϕ, or the value that is obtained for this from elicitation of the characteristics of the software development organization and issue being attacked, especially since this term is cubed in the foregoing equation. A 25% error in ϕ will produce a 100% error in the estimate of K. This extreme sensitivity would seem quite bothersome. Kemerer [25] has also performed an evaluation of the SLIM model, as well as COCOMO and several other software packages.

To initiate use of the SLIM model, we need the following

- An estimate of the number of thousands of delivered source lines of code
- The technology available for the software acquisition effort
- The maximum permitted difficulty gradient

On the basis of these inputs, SLIM will yield the following outputs:

- The complete acquisition lifecycle costs, in labor-years or person-years, including such deployment efforts as operations and maintenance
- Development costs, in person-years or labor-years

- Acquisition schedule length, in years
- Staffing level over time

There are many useful graphical outputs that can be obtained, and sensitivity studies for changing input assumptions are easily accommodated.

Parr [26] has suggested a variation of the SLIM model. It is based on the observation that, on many projects, the staff is already familiar with the project's tools, requirements, and methods and is ready to work. Thus the work rate can begin at some positive point on the work axis, rather than at the origin as required through use of the Rayleigh equation. Both the Parr and Putnam models include maintenance and other effort-consuming activities over the development lifecycle. In other words, they reflect staffing needs over the entire development lifecycle.

A potential need in Putnam's model is the ability to accommodate reusable code. Londeix [27] proposes a modification to SLIM that will adjust for software reuse. He considers two cases: (1) reuse without any change to the existing reused source code and (2) reuse involving change of this code. This model is quite new, and there is no empirical evidence at this time to judge its validity, although there is every reason to expect that its performance should be similar to that of the basic Putnam model.

While the theoretical bases for the Putnam model and the other models we consider in this chapter are different, each results in an equation of the form

$$S = \mu K^\kappa T^\sigma \tag{5.4.18}$$

where S is the software size (KDSI); K is the total development effort in labor-years; T is the development time in years; and μ, κ, and σ are parameters that represent sophistication of the development environment and the complexity of the software to be developed.

In an interesting conceptual result, Tausworthe [28] defines the unproductivity ratio

$$\rho = \frac{K}{\sigma} \tag{5.4.19}$$

and indicates that the amount of augmented effort required to shorten the schedule increases as this unproductivity ratio increases. Thus a software organization should strive for a low value of this ratio. It is interesting to note that, from Eq. (5.4.15), the ratio is 4 for the Putnam model—a rather high number. We now turn to a model with a much lower value, $p = \frac{1}{2}$, for this unproductivity factor.

5.4.2   Jensen Resource Allocation Model—SEER

Jensen [29] has proposed a variation to Putnam's SLIM model. Because the Putnam model is so sensitive to performance schedule compression, Jensen suggested a modification that uses an equation with an effective technology constant that is calculated differently from Putnam's original one. The suggested modification involves use of the equation

$$S = \xi T K^{0.5} \qquad (5.4.20)$$

rather than Eq. (5.4.15). Here, the multiplier ξ is an effective technology factor that is similar to but calculated differently from the Putnam technology factor ϕ. We may easily solve this equation for K, which is the total project lifecycle effort. We obtain

$$K = \frac{S^2}{\xi^2 T^2} \qquad (5.4.21)$$

In his work, Jensen described a basic technology factor, ξ_0, and a total of 13 environmental adjustment multiplier factors, ϵ_i, that modify the basic technology factor according to

$$\xi = \xi_0 \prod_{i=1}^{13} \epsilon_i \qquad (5.4.22)$$

These environmental adjustment factors are very similar to those defined by Boehm for use in the COCOMO that we have just discussed. The adjustment factors include aspects of the project involving project personnel, computer systems used, and the nature of the user organization. These, which are much like the inputs to the COCOMO algorithms, which do not include the Rayleigh-based staffing distribution over the software lifecycle, are the inputs to the Jensen algorithms. These input factors include the following:

Number of delivered source lines of code, including various adjustment factors to reflect preexisting concurrent ADP hardware development
Complexity of software to be developed
Personnel capabilities and experiences
Development support environment
Product development requirements, including quality assurance and requirements volatility
Product reusability requirements
Development environment complexity
Target environment
Schedule, including constraints on this
Staffing, including staffing level constraints
Software requirements formality and completeness
Needed software to software integration

Needed software to hardware integration

Software maintenance needs and characteristics

Average personnel costs

Extension of the basic Jensen model have been implemented in a software product known as *system evaluation and estimation of resources* (SEER). When provided with these inputs, the software will determine software cost and schedule estimates.

5.5   FUNCTION POINT MODELS OF SOFTWARE SIZING

Another important example of an expert judgment-based approach for software sizing is the Albrecht [30] *function point model* for software sizing. This model attempts to develop an evaluation of several important functional measures that describe the basic inputs and outputs of the system. Subjective assessments of the complexity of the software system are based on these functions, as generally provided by expert judgment and incorporated into the parameters of the model. As we have noted in our earlier discussions, there are a number of difficulties associated with counting lines of code. These difficulties become even more of a problem when we realize that we need to predict lines of code, and then use this prediction as the major driver of costs in a yet to be completed software acquisition effort. The function point approach, which represents an alternative approach to software sizing that is not inherently based on lines of code [31], has been the subject of much recent study. The initial function point developments were intended for information systems applications, and, for the most part, this is still the case.

One of the major advantages of the function point concept is that the number of function points in a to-be-acquired software product depends on the complexity of the product, but not on the specific programming language used for development. They can be estimated from system or software level requirements, and it thus becomes possible to estimate effort and schedule earlier than through use of lines of source code [32]. It should be possible to directly trace a change in requirements through to the corresponding change in function points. Thus reestimation of costs and schedule should be more reliably accomplished than through use of lines of code as the basic effort and schedule driver. In general, function points appear to be a more reliable cost driver than lines of code [33]. Unfortunately, there are few cost and schedule models that use function points directly. Most accomplish the equivalent of obtaining lines of code from function points and then using the resulting lines of code to drive the cost and schedule estimate.

In the initial function point developments, four elements were assumed to be representative of the functionality of a software product:

1. ***External inputs*** (*EI*) *to the application.*
2. ***External outputs*** (*EO*) *from the application.*
3. ***Number of external inquiries*** (*EQ*) *by users* of the software as combinations of input requests and output retrievals.

4. **Number of master internal logical files** (*ILF*) that would be maintained and updated by the application.

It was soon recognized that an additional element was needed:

5. **Number of external interface files** (*EIF*) of other applications.

The first three of these five function types represent transactional functions. The last two represent data.

Each of the five function types is rated on a scale of complexity ranging across low, average, and high. Table 5.11 represents the function point weight associated with each of the five function point types and three complexity ranges.

The function count is determined from multiplying the number of function points at each complexity level by the appropriate weight, as given in Table 5.11, and summing this weighted number of function points. Mathematically, this results in

$$FC = \sum_{i=1}^{5} \sum_{j=1}^{3} w_{ij} x_{ij} \qquad (5.5.1)$$

Here, x_{ij} represents the number of function points, fp_i of type j and weight level i. w_{ij} represents the weight associated with function point type j at complexity level i. These function counts are also called the number of unadjusted function points.

The weight entries in Table 5.11 are generated by expert opinion and are therefore based on informed but subjective judgments. The addition called for by Eq. (5.5.1) can easily be obtained. The final number of function points, *FP*, is obtained by multiplying the function count, *FC*, by a complexity factor, *C*, obtained from

$$C = 0.65 + 0.01 \sum_{k=1}^{14} z_k \qquad (5.5.2)$$

where the z_k are the scores obtained on the responses to 14 complexity questions that reflext general system characteristics (GSC). These questions, based on [34] and as modified somewhat in [35] are as follows.

TABLE 5.11 Function Point Computation Chart

	Weight		
Description of Function Point	Low	Average	High
EI—number of distinct input external data items	3	4	6
EO—number of distinct output screens or reports	4	5	7
EQ—number of external inquiries	3	4	6
ILF—number of internal logical files	7	10	15
EIF—external interface files	5	7	10

1. Are data communications required?
2. Are there distributed processing functions?
3. Is the system performance critical?
4. Will the system configuration run in an existing, heavily utilized operational environment?
5. Does the system require rapid transaction rates?
6. Does the system require on-line data entry?
7. Does the on-line data entry require the input transaction to be built over multiple screens or operations such that the system is designed for end-user efficiency?
8. Are the master files, or internal logical files, updated on-line?
9. Are the inputs, outputs, files, inquiries, and internal processing complex?
10. Is the code designed to be reusable?
11. Are conversion and installation requirements included in the design process such that installation of the software is facilitated?
12. Is ease of use of the operational software critical?
13. Is the system designed for multiple installations in one or more different organizations?
14. Is the application designed to facilitate change over time and ease of use by the user?

A simple "yes" or "no" answer is insufficient here. What is desired is a set of complexity adjustments that go into the function point calculation. Each of the 14 complexity adjustment factors is rated on a scale from 0 to 5 in accordance with subjective feelings about the *degrees of influence* (DI) of these on the software complexity. The unanchored scale used is:

0—no influence or not present
1—incidental influence
2—moderate influence
3—average influence
4—significant influence
5—strong or essential influence throughout

To complete calculations using this model, the sum of the 14 complexity adjustment values as weighted by the degrees of influence is obtained. This sum will clearly range from a low of 0.00, in which case the software acquisition is very trivial, to 14 times 5 or 70, in which case the value adjustment factor (VAF) is 1.35.

There exists an International Function Point Users Group (IFPUG) that is very concerned with improvements in and promulgation of function point based software sizing estimates. In recent publications [36,37], three types of function point counts are described.

1. The *development project function point count* is the count associated with initial installation of new software and measures the function provided to the end users by the acquisition project.

2. The *enhancement project function point count* is that associated with the enhancement of existing software.

3. The *application function point count* is that total count associated with an installed application. This represents a running total of the current functionality, as measured by function points, provided to the end user of the software. It does not include functionality provided by conversion activities.

When software is upgraded, the old value of the application point count is augmented by new functionality in the enhancement project. When old software is replaced by new software, the application point count becomes the development project function point count minus the functionality associated with any conversion activities to transition data from the old software format to the new. This leads to an enhanced equation for the adjusted function point count of an application (*AFP*) of the form

$$AFP = [(UFPB + ADD + CHGA) - (CHGB + DEL)]VAFA \quad (5.5.3)$$

where *UFPB* is the unadjusted function point count of the application before the enhancement, *ADD* is the unadjusted function point count of those functions added by the enhancement project, *CHGA* is the unadjusted function point count of those functions that were modified by the enhancement and after the modification, *CHGB* is the unadjusted function point count of those functions that were modified by the enhancement and before the modification, *DEL* is the unadjusted function point count of functions deleted by the enhancement project, and *VAFA* is the value adjustment factor of the application after the enhancement project. If *UFPB* is initially unavailable, it may be calculated from

$$UFPB = AFPB/VAFB$$

where *AFPB* is the adjusted function point count before the enhancement project and *VAFB* is the value adjustment factor before the enhancement project is integrated in with the existing application. This equation simplifies to

$$AFP = (ADD)(VAFA)$$

when functionality is only being added.

In a similar way, we can calculate the development function point count, *DFP* (which includes data conversion requirements), from

$$DFP = (UFP)(VAF) \quad (5.5.4)$$

where *UFP* is the unadjusted function point of the application, *VAF* is the value adjustment factor, and *DFP* is the development project function point count. Finally, the enhancement project function point count (*EFP*) is obtained from

$$EFP = (ADD + CHGA)VAFA + (DEL)VAFB \qquad (5.5.5)$$

where all of the terms in this expression have already been defined.

Each of these three types of functionality is associated with a boundary, as represented in Figure 5.20. These establish the processing relationships that are needed to accommodate accurate function point counts. It is highly desirable that each of the distinct business information technology functions be associated with a separate boundary. We may, of course, disaggregate a complete software acquisition project into a number of smaller projects. We could then use the function point approach to estimate the sizing for each of the smaller projects. The extent to which this approach will have merit is dependent on our ability to disaggregate the projects according to some meaningful set of smaller-size projects, such that it is then meaningful to obtain estimates for each of the individual projects. The resulting function point estimates may be added to obtain the total function point estimate for the entire project.

Several variations on the function point exist. In one of these, Symons [38] has developed an approach, called *Mark II*, in which a software system is viewed as consisting primarily of logical transaction types. Any object, real or abstract, about which the system provides information is a logical transaction type, according to this model. Rather than having the function points reflect functionality values of the

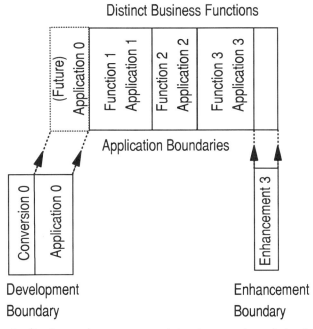

Figure 5.20 Application, enhancement, and development boundaries for use in detailed COCOMO.

system as delivered to the user, which is the general intent of software cost models as well as that of Albrecht in this particular case, Symons relates software system size to the effort that is required to analyze, design, and develop the system.

Symons also appends six questions to the 14 technical complexity adjustment questions noted before:

15. Is there a need to interface with other applications?
16. Is there a need for special computer software security features?
17. Is there a need for direct access for third parties?
18. Are there (extraordinary) documentation requirements?
19. Is there a requirement for special user training facilities, such as a training subsystem?
20. Is there a need to define, select, and install special hardware or software unique to this application?

Symons, in using these 20 factors for calibrating technical complexity adjustment, found that the coefficient of 0.01 in Albrecht's formula would be more accurate if readjusted to a value of 0.005 for some of the factors. A clear connotation from this suggestion is that function points, here or in Albrecht's model, are not at all independent of the structure of the model or the technology used for system development and implementation. This is very unlike the claim by Albrecht, who seems to suggest this independence. The seeming lack of anchoring of the scales used would also suggest a lack of independence, as well as indicating potential difficulties in interpretation of the results obtained. It is important to note that the detailed questions posed in the IFPUG manual [36,37] provide sufficient detail for anchoring.

The function point approach is certainly based on the software requirements and specifications, as translated from the client's system level requirements. Given this, an estimate of costs can be made early in the software lifecycle. Much of the cost estimation is, however, based on very subjective data. The empirical constants used are said to have been identified "by debate and trial" [31] in the business information system applications for which the function point approach has been used.

There needs to be either a direct contextual meaning or interpretation for the function point concept or at least some knowledge of how function points relate to software production efforts. One way of approaching this, although not necessarily any sort of best way, is to attempt to obtain a relationship between function points and lines of code. Albrecht and Gaffney [31], for example, made an effort to relate the computed function points to the number of lines of code. They experimented with COBOL, PL/1, and a fourth-generation data manipulation language and found that 110, 65, and 25 lines of code in these languages corresponded to one function point. Given this sort of information, we could use a model like COCOMO, or the Putnam or Jensen model, to estimate cost and schedule [39].

The extent to which the basic function point model may be fully appropriate for such diverse applications as real-time concurrent flight control systems or embedded command and control systems is an open question at present. Another potential problem with function points relates to calculating the unadjusted function points that are needed in the first step of model usage. Many of the calculated function points will arise from the external processing requirements associated with inputs, outputs, interfaces, and queries. For programs involving highly complex algorithms, often occurring in autopilot and other physical system areas, neither program size nor complexity may be adequately captured by this model. Another more general complication may result from the three-level classification of all system modules as low, average, or high complexity. It appears that this could lead to a computation in which one component having a very large number of data elements cannot be assigned any more than twice the number of points that must be assigned to a component that contains only one data item. Oversimplifications like this, of course, need to be avoided.

Another modification of the function point model is intended to enable it to address other than business information system applications [35,40]. A sixth function point category is introduced, that denoted by the number of algorithms. The empirical weights are simplified somewhat by only utilizing a single weight for each function point category. This results in a modification and minor extension of the function point approach to software sizing that is called *feature points*. Table 5.12 suggests a relatively simple way to calculate the total number of feature points.

The computation proceeds in a relatively straightforward way. The complexity adjustment factor is computed just as in the related function point approach. One of the potential limitations to this approach is that algorithms come in all sorts of shapes and complexities. To weight each algorithm, regardless of complexity, with the same weight, 3, is doubtlessly not realistic. In more recent work [35], the weights associated with an individual algorithm are allowed to vary from one to ten. The weight to be used depends on the number of rules in the algorithm and the total number of data values, or variables, that are contained in the algorithm in question.

While this approach is still developing, the progress that has been made to date indicates one useful way in which the function point concept can be extended to a

TABLE 5.12 Feature Point Calculations

Feature Point Parameter	Number of Function Points	Empirical Weight	Totals
External inputs—EI	_____	×4	= _____
External outputs—EO	_____	×5	= _____
External inquiries—EQ	_____	×4	= _____
Internal logical files—ILF	_____	×7	= _____
External interface files—EIF	_____	×7	= _____
Number of algorithms—A	_____	×3	= _____
Unadjusted total			_____
Complexity adjustment factor			× _____
Adjusted total feature points			= _____

broader class of application areas than was possible with the initial developments. A recent paper [41] provides a definitive evaluation of the basic function point approach for software sizing.

5.6 ACTIVITY-BASED COSTING APPROACHES TO SOFTWARE ACQUISITION

In Section 4.3.3, we discussed the advent of a new form of accounting system called *activity-based costing* (ABC) [42–47]. As we noted there, it is the activities required to produce a product that consume resources and that have value (or lack thereof) for customers. One of the major objectives of an ABC system is that of associating costs with the activities that lead to products.

This is accomplished by first assigning all resources to either products or customers. The resources of an organization include direct labor, materials, supplies, depreciation, and fringe benefits. The organizational support units are separated into major functional units. Each of these functional units should have a significant cost associated with it and each should be driven by different activities. The support unit or department costs are separated into a number of functional cost pools. These department costs should be fully burdened and all costs should be associated with the set of departments. The costs for each department are assigned to the various functional units such that each function has its own cost pool. The functional unit cost pools are next assigned, using first-stage cost drivers, to each of the activity centers. Measures of activity, such as customer orders, are very important first-stage cost drivers in that they are also measures of productivity. The organizational support costs are assigned to products or customers through these activity centers. An activity center is a functional economic grouping that contains similar or homogeneous sets of processes. The product-driven activity centers are those to which costs associated with the product lines or processes are assigned. The customer-driven activity centers are those driven by customers, such as sales and order department costs, which represent the costs of supporting customers and markets. Figure 5.21 illustrates the flows we have just described.

The substance of an ABC system is associated with the set of second-stage cost drivers. As we noted, the total cost of every activity center is separated into a number of cost driver pools. The costs associated with each cost driver pool are assigned to products using a second-stage cost driver. As activity measures, these second-stage cost drivers lead to resource consumption.

As we noted in Section 4.3.3, there are a number of levels for product cost drivers. These include unit cost drivers, batch cost drivers, product cost drivers, and facility cost drivers. In a traditional accounting system, only unit cost drivers are considered. They model cost behavior as if there were no product line costs and assume that all costs are proportional to production volume. There are also four levels for customer cost drivers: order cost drivers, customer cost drivers, market cost drivers, and enterprise cost drivers. Figure 5.22 represents this hierarchy of costs and cost drivers. We need to implement the equivalent of a spreadsheet

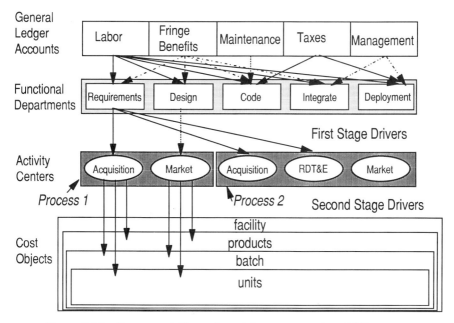

Figure 5.21   Conceptual illustration of the structure of an ABC system.

representation of each of these elements in order to determine an ABC analysis of an organization's efforts. In order to provide somewhat greater specificity to this notion, we examine some particular efforts concerning costing for software acquisition.

We develop an ABC approach assuming that MIL-STD-2167A is used to pre-

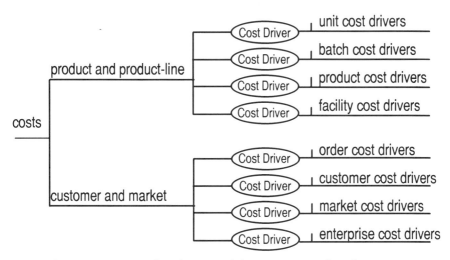

Figure 5.22   Hierarchy of costs and drivers in activity-based costing.

scribe a basic phasewise activity descriptor. The major phases that are prescribed include:

System requirements analysis/design
Software requirements analysis
Preliminary design
Detailed design
Coding and CSU testing
CSC integration and testing
CSCI testing
System integration and testing

These could be used as the basis for a work breakdown structure that would enable ABC. Alternatively, we could use the generally comparable set of phases identified in the new draft standards MIL-STD-SDD, which is destined to become MIL-STD-498.

Figure 5.23 illustrates these major phases. We then identify an effort estimate for each of these phases per unit of output. For convenience, and really for lack of a better single indicator at this time, we use KDSI as the normalization variable. Clearly, the effort required to produce 1 KDSI is going to be a function of the maturity of the organization relative to each of these phasewise efforts. In Chapter

Activity	Build #1 New Code	Build #1 Reused Code	Build #2 New Code	Build #3 Reused Code
Project Planning	0.500	0.300	0.600	0.400
Establish Software Development Environment	0.200	0.200	0.250	0.250
System Requirements Analysis	0.460	0.125	0.600	0.180
System Design	0.500	0.300	0.500	0.300
Software Requirements Analysis	1.160	0.095	1.430	0.110
Software Architectural Design	0.500	0.062	0.600	0.094
Software Detail Design	0.600	0.074	0.600	0.090
Coding and Unit Testing	2.500	0.150	2.700	0.175
Unit Integration and Testing	1.000	0.105	1.200	0.190
Computer Software Configuration Item Testing	0.800	0.160	1.100	0.220
CSCI Integration and Subsequent Testing	0.400	0.080	0.550	0.240
Software System Testing	0.400	0.100	0.600	0.200
Preparation for Software Use and Support	0.200	0.050	0.250	0.080
Preparation for Software Delivery	0.100	0.020	0.200	0.060
Software Product Evaluations	0.200	0.100	0.200	0.200
Software Configuration Management	0.156	0.050	0.178	0.180
Process Evaluation and Correction	0.368	0.250	0.400	0.260
Joint Technical and Management Reviews	0.200	0.100	0.200	0.100
Other Management Activities	0.150	0.080	0.150	0.080
Totals	**10.394**	**2.401**	**12.30**	**3.409**

Figure 5.23 Hypothetical effort in labor-months per KDSI for various project phases in software acquisition.

7, we discuss process maturity as a major indicator of the effort that will likely be required to produce a given 1000 lines of delivered source instructions of a given quality. As we note, quality is another important ingredient and we discuss a number of quality relevant issues in Chapter 6 and also throughout the remainder of the text.

This figure assumes two incremental or evolutionary builds. The productivity numbers shown are realistic but are not obtained for any particular project. Each software development would have to estimate these normalized effort parameters on the basis of past experience. At the very early lifecycle efforts, the size of the product to be developed may well not be known. This may have to be estimated with little prior information initially and then refined as additional information is obtained.

Suppose that there is to be a single build. There may also be considerable requirements volatility. This may well require that much of the initial effort in the early phases of the single build lifecycle be repeated until the requirements volatility diminishes toward the end of the acquisition effort. Suppose further that we have 800 KDSI of new code and 500 KDSI of reused code. The reused code is to be used with very minor modification. Thus we might use the sort of multipliers shown in Figures 5.24 and 5.25.

It might well be the case that it is not easily possible to provide these phasewise estimates of effort per KDSI. In this case, each of the phases in the acquisition lifecycle may be described in terms of a number of component phases and estimates

Activity	Build #1 New Code E/KDSI	Multiplier	Estimated Unit Effort E/KDSI	Estimated Total Effort (Labor Months)
Project Planning	0.500	1.400	0.700	560
Establish Software Development Environment	0.200	1.400	0.280	224
System Requirements Analysis	0.460	1.350	0.621	497
System Design	0.500	1.300	0.650	520
Software Requirements Analysis	1.160	1.300	1.508	1206
Software Architectural Design	0.500	1.250	0.625	500
Software Detail Design	0.600	1.200	0.720	576
Coding and Unit Testing	2.500	1.100	2.750	2200
Unit Integration and Testing	1.000	1.000	1.000	800
Computer Software Configuration Item Testing	0.800	1.000	0.800	640
CSCI Integration and Subsequent Testing	0.400	1.000	0.400	320
Software System Testing	0.400	1.000	0.400	320
Preparation for Software Use and Support	0.200	1.000	0.200	160
Preparation for Software Delivery	0.100	1.000	0.100	80
Software Product Evaluations	0.200	1.000	0.200	160
Software Configuration Management	0.156	1.100	0.156	125
Process Evaluation and Correction	0.368	1.050	0.384	307
Joint Technical and Management Reviews	0.200	1.200	0.240	192
Other Management Activities	0.150	1.100	0.165	132
Totals	**10.394**		**11.899**	**9519**

Figure 5.24   Spreadsheet effort calculation for ABC Model, 800 KDSI of new code.

Activity	Build #1 Reused Code	Multiplier	Estimated Unit Costs	Total Effort in Labor Months
Project Planning	0.300	1.200		
Establish Software Development Environment	0.200	1.200		
System Requirements Analysis	0.125	1.100		
System Design	0.300	1.000		
Software Requirements Analysis	0.095	1.000		
Software Architectural Design	0.062	1.000		
Software Detail Design	0.074	0.700		
Coding and Unit Testing	0.150	0.000		
Unit Integration and Testing	0.105	1.000		
Computer Software Configuration Item Testing	0.160	1.000		
CSCI Integration and Subsequent Testing	0.080	1.000		
Software System Testing	0.100	1.000		
Preparation for Software Use and Support	0.050	1.000		
Preparation for Software Delivery	0.020	1.000		
Software Product Evaluations	0.100	1.000		
Software Configuration Management	0.050	1.000		
Process Evaluation and Correction	0.250	1.000		
Joint Technical and Management Reviews	0.100	1.050		
Other Management Activities	0.080	1.050		
Totals	**2.401**			

Figure 5.25 ABC spreadsheet for reused code, partially completed.

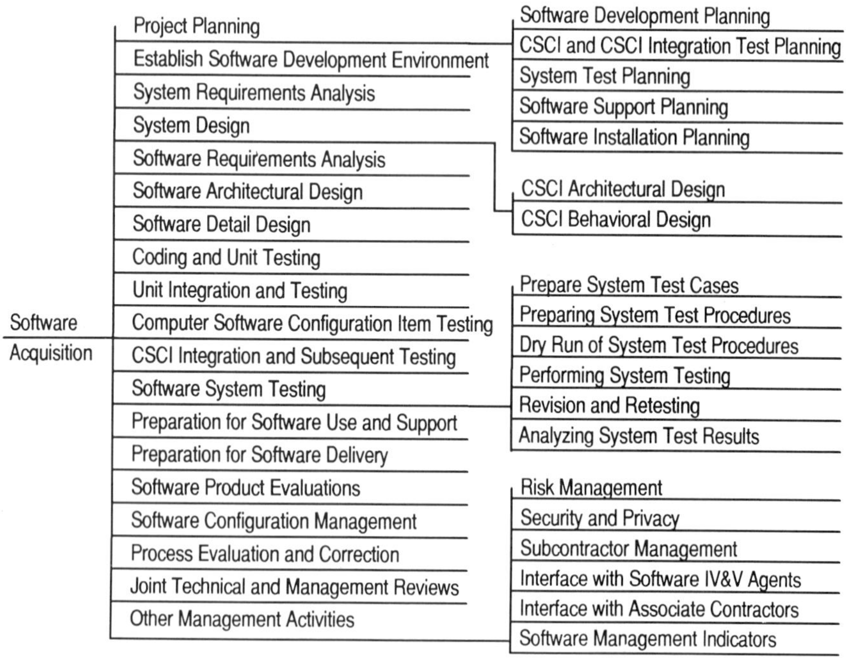

Figure 5.26 Partially expanded activity tree for MIL-STD-SDD.

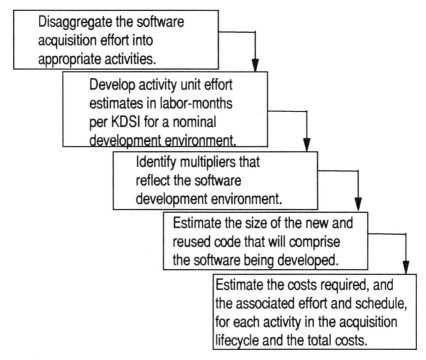

Figure 5.27 General steps in establishing ABC for software development.

provided for each of these more microlevel estimates. In this case, we might discuss the MIL-SDD lifecycle in terms of as many of the more detailed activities as needed to establish effort estimation relations. Figure 5.26 illustrates some of these more detailed components. Figure 5.27 suggests steps in implementing this ABC procedure for the case of an individual product line in a software development organization.

While much more than this could be said, and we have by no means developed a full ABC tree, this does point toward the general principles that are involved. We need to be especially careful in costing the reuse components, for example, such that there is some potential charge associated with projects that will make future use of reused code when it is developed for the first time. If this is not done, the cost of initially developing very easy to reuse code may appear unjustified. So what we have shown here is really only a part of an overall ABC approach for an entire organization. While the spreadsheets of Figures 5.23, 5.24, and 5.25, as well as the associated analysis, are of much value, they will be even more valuable when this sort of approach is extended to cover virtually all of an organization's efforts.

There are many ingredients that go into a systems acquisition project other than cost, and associated effort and schedule, estimates. Some of these include the overall organizational structure, function, and purpose and how these combine to suggest the systems management, systemic product lines or processes, and organi-

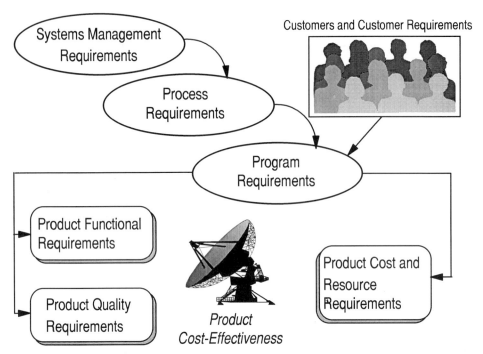

Figure 5.28 The role of systematic costing in a bigger scheme of activities.

zational products. These ingredients and the organizational leadership characteristics influence the maturity of an organization and its inherent cultural values. They all combine to result in various degrees of effectiveness of an organization. At the bottom line relative to this are the products of the organization and how the organization's competitive strategy, in terms of what it senses as its competitive advantage and competitive scope, drives the products that an organization will produce in terms of costs or resources allocated to production, functional characteristics of the product, and the quality requirements that will be attained by the product.

We can describe each of these in terms of a number of constituent elements. Cost estimates are often based primarily on functional requirements. The combination of the functional requirements and the quality requirements leads to effectiveness requirements for the product. While such estimates as KDSI and function points may be made on only functional requirements, there are a number of intangible requirements that affect system or product quality and that will strongly influence customer acceptance of a product. So while we can easily express a view of cost–effectiveness as in Figure 5.28, it is in no way a trivial matter to relate these three major requirements in order to come up with systems that satisfy the real needs of real customers and that are cost competitive. The functional requirements are often set by system users. At least indirectly, this is the case also for quality requirements. A wise organization surely attempts to produce a product that meets functional requirements, that has as high a quality satisfaction figure of merit as possible, and that is cost competitive. We can approach achieving a high quality product at the level of the product itself. Or we can approach the achievement of a high quality product through adoption of efficacious processes and systems management strategies, as we shall soon see.

5.7 VALIDATION OF SOFTWARE EFFORT AND SCHEDULE MODELS

The accuracy of the estimators generated by the various software effort and schedule models can be considered a test of how well a particular model reflects the actual relationships among those factors that affect development. We should be able to demonstrate that a proposed model of the software acquisition process is valid, that is, that it accurately portrays the interactions among the components of the process. One way of doing this, perhaps the only scientific way, is to demonstrate that the metrics and the predicted results stemming from the model are valid. In particular, we validate an effort or schedule model by comparing the estimated values that are predicted to occur with the actually obtained values and then attempt to examine and explain the differences.

Validation of models is necessarily an empirical effort since a model is generally a hypothetical description of what is believed to be a real-world process. The creator of a process model usually begins with a theory of how the functional elements in the process relate to one another. This theoretical framework is used to express the relationships among the process elements in a formal way, usually as an equation, an algorithm, or a diagram of some kind. A verbal or semantic framework is acceptable for a model also. We may express ideas in terms of words, mathematics, and graphics; and a model is just a conceptualization of an *idea.*

A model is generally based on both theory and data. Emphasis is placed an specification of structural relations, based on software production theory, and the identification of unknown parameters, using available data, in the behavioral equations. Sadly, the state of the development of a theory of software productivity is not well advanced. The postulation of a model should always be followed by a collection of empirical evidence that might be used to demonstrate that the model is correct. Once the model is completely defined, additional statistics are generated from the database and used to compare predicted values with actual results.

If the statistics compare the *model-generating database* (i.e., the database used to develop the model initially) with the model, then the model is said to be undergoing *internal validation.* If the model is tested with data other than those from which the model was derived, we say that the model is undergoing *external validation.* In either case, the database used to test a model is called a *validating database.*

To model software systems program development cost, effort is the usual dependent variable. A determination of program cost is then obtained by the simple act of multiplying the predicted effort by the value of a unit of effort. For example, if effort is measured in person-months, then cost is the product of the number of person-months and the monthly salary of the average employee. In our discussion to follow, predicted effort will be denoted by $\hat{E}$, while actual effort will be denoted by E. The validating database may include historical data about n projects. Each project will have a predicted value of effort, $\hat{E}_i$, and an actual value of E_i, where i ranges from 1 to N.

Often, we want to test the degree to which the estimate and actual values are linearly related. The coefficient of multiple determination, which is also the square of the correlation coefficient, provides this and is defined by

$$R^2 = 1 - \frac{\displaystyle\sum_{i=1}^{N} (E_i - \hat{E}_i)^2}{\displaystyle\sum_{i=1}^{N} (E_i - \bar{E})^2}$$

where $\bar{E}$ is the mean of the values of E_i across the software projects of the particular type being considered, or

$$\bar{E} = \frac{1}{N} \sum_{i=1}^{N} E_i$$

The coefficient of multiple determination must always be less than or equal to 1. If the estimated values are close to the actual values, the term resulting from the sum in the numerator will be small. For a perfect estimate, this term would be zero. When this term is very small, the estimator is quite accurate, and the value of R^2 is close to 1. When multiple regression analysis is used to determine the parameters, it is possible to associate this coefficient of multiple determination with the percentage of the variance that is accounted for by the independent variables used for the analysis. A large value suggests that inclusion of additional structural parameters is unlikely to provide much improvement in model accuracy.

Another way to determine the validity of a model is to examine the *relative error* (*RE*) defined as

$$RE = \frac{E - \hat{E}}{E}$$

For a set of N projects, the *average relative error* $\overline{(RE)}$ is obtained in terms of the relative error for individual estimates as

$$\overline{RE} = \frac{1}{N} \sum_{i=1}^{N} \overline{RE}_i$$

If a model is a relatively good predictor of actual effort, the values of E and $\hat{E}$ for the specific software program undergoing analysis should be essentially the same. This will lead to a small relative error for the particular program in question, and a small average relative error for like programs or projects when we average over an ensemble of them. However, the converse is not always true. A small average relative error may be the result of the canceling of large individual relative errors that are of different sign.

To make these measures more useful, we might consider the absolute value of the relative error, called the *magnitude of relative error* (MRE_i) for the ith project. This expression is

$$MRE_j = |RE_j| = \left| 1 - \frac{\hat{E}_i}{E_i} \right|$$

The magnitude of relative error is an indicator of the quality of the prediction. A small *MRE* means the effort or cost prediction is good, while a large value of *MRE* means that the prediction is bad.

We can continue on with this. For example, we can calculate the *mean magnitude of relative error* (*MMRE*) for a set of N data points through use of the expression

$$MMRE = \overline{MRE} = \frac{1}{N} \sum_{i=1}^{N} MRE_i$$

A small *MMRE* indicates that, on the average, the model is a good predictor of the actual effort that resulted. In much work in this area, a model is considered to be acceptable if it has an *MMRE* of 0.25 or less.

Another figure of merit often calculated for software costing models is an indicator of how many of the predicted values fall within a given range of the actual value. Suppose that the values of E_i and $\hat{E}_i$ are compared for each of N projects. If K of the N projects have a magnitude of relative error (*MRE*) of $j/100$ or less, then we write $PRED(j) = K/N$. This means that K/N of the predicted effort values fall within $j\%$ of their actual value. Often a software cost and effort model is considered to be acceptable if $PRED(0.25) \geq 0.75$. In other words, we say that an estimate is reasonable if 75% of the predictions are within 25% of the actual value. COCOMO has often been evaluated within this range but obtaining this accuracy depends on good model calibration.

The validation of software cost models is difficult because the amount of data to be collected for a validating database is generally very large. To confirm that a model is applicable to a wide variety of situations, such a database must include measures from a large number of development environments. Even here, validation may overlook a fundamental difficulty. The usual situation is that we take an already completed project, determine the number of lines of delivered source code, and then apply regression analysis using the model, the number of lines of code, and other factors needed by the model. The major problem here is that we do not really know how many lines of code are needed in a to-be-developed project in order to complete the development. In using data from previous projects, we do know the number of lines of code that were needed to deliver the software product.

We believe that costing models hold potentially great promise, not only in providing accurate estimates of effort and schedule but also in assisting us in identifying and understanding those factors that have the largest potential for improving systems engineering productivity, including software. The fact that some existing models may yield disappointingly inaccurate predictions of effort and cost is only an indication of the need for higher quality analytical, behavioral, and empirical research in this area. These models, to be of maximum utility, need to be interactive with the models for quality, leadership, and process maturity to which we will now turn.

5.8 SUMMARY

In this chapter, we have examined a number of issues surrounding the costing of software. While most of our efforts concerned costing, we did provide some comments concerning valuation, effectiveness, and other important issues.

Modeling and estimation of software effort and schedule are relatively new endeavors. Most models are validated from databases of cost factors that reflect a particular user and developer organization's characteristics. Such models are useful when developer organizations are stable and continue to produce systems similar to those developed in the past for users who have similarly stable environments and needs. However, models have little utility if the mixture of personnel experience or expertise changes or if the development organization attempts to develop a new type of system or a user organization specifies a new system type.

It would be desirable to build models that are independent of either user or developer organization, so that the models can be transported to other development teams and user situations. This is clearly foolish, however, as it assumes context-free solutions to problems, and this is very unrealistic. The *major conclusion from this is that it is absolutely necessary to consider developer and user organization characteristics in the software cost estimation models that we build.*

A second problem is the use of cost-influencing factors and the relationship expressed among them. It is not clear that the appropriate factors are identified; nor is it clear that they have been related correctly mathematically. Many of the cost models use adjustment multipliers in which the cost factors are summed or multiplied together.

A third issue involves changes in technology, tools, and methods. The contribution made to cost by these three aspects of project development is not as well understood as it should be for high quality valuation purposes. Consequently, the appropriate change required in the cost equation is not known when technology, tools, and methods differ from those in place when the supporting database for a model was generated. Many of the databases used for contemporary cost and effort models use decades old information, which is surely not reflective of current practices. Very few of the cost estimating models are able to incorporate the potential benefits (or disbenefits) brought out by the use (misuse) of CASE tools. Nor do they consider the macroenhancement approaches of reusability, prototyping, and knowledge-based systems for software development.

The development process itself presents a fourth set of needs. Some models examine the *software product* rather than the *software development process* to obtain information about cost- and effort-influencing factors. An examination of only product-related variables will generally never provide sufficient information to allow us to estimate effort and cost. More work needs to be done to determine what aspects of the development process contribute most to software cost. The major improvements in software productivity will come about through better software development processes, and not at all through only implementing methods that ensure higher programmer productivity.

Most of the available methods select a single important deliverable—source lines of code—and use this variable as the core variable for estimation purposes. Various multipliers of this variable are proposed that presume to represent realities of conditions extant as contrasted with the nominal conditions under which the effort relationship to source lines of code was determined. While this is not necessarily an inappropriate way to go, it might be more meaningful to develop a software program development plan in terms of client needs and then cost each of the phased or distributed efforts of the plan.

It is vitally important to develop cost (including effort and schedule) estimation models that can be used very early in the software development process. The purposes of these models are to predict software development lifecycle costs and efforts as soon as possible and to provide information about the costs and effectiveness of various approaches to the software acquisition process and its management. This will allow one to develop accurate information about software development programs that clients might wish to fund and to allocate the appropriate resources to these developments. It will also result in feedback of important software development information that will predict how changes in user requirements, software specifications, design, maintenance, and other factors will affect cost, effort, performance, and reliability. This would seem to require a model with the salient ABC based features of COCOMO and function points.

A recent study of cost estimation [48] provides nine guidelines for cost estimation.

1. Assign the initial cost estimation task to the final system developers.
2. Delay finalizing the initial cost estimates until the end of a thorough study of the conceptual system design.
3. Anticipate and control user changes to the system functionality and purpose.
4. Carefully monitor the progress of the project under development.
5. Evaluate progress on the project under development through use of independent auditors.
6. Use cost estimates to evaluate project personnel on their performance.
7. Management should carefully study and appraise cost estimates.

8. Rely on documented facts, standards, and simple arithmetic formulas rather than guessing, intuition, personal memory, and complex formulas.
9. Do not rely on cost estimation software for an accurate estimate.

While these guidelines were established specifically for information system software, there is every reason to believe that they have more general applicability. This study identifies the use of cost estimates as selecting projects for implementation, staffing projects, controlling and monitoring project implementations, scheduling projects, auditing project progress and success, and evaluating project developers and estimators. Associated with this, we suggest, is evaluating the costs of quality, or the benefits of quality, and the costs of poor quality. In a recent work, Jones [35] has identified six characteristics of successful software organizations. We augment this list with an additional two characteristics and say that successful systems engineering and software systems engineering organizations may be characterized as follows:

1. They measure productivity and quality of the product and the process accurately. This is a necessary criterion as well as an important one and without this, none of the other criteria will help produce high quality or productivity.
2. They plan and estimate software projects accurately.
3. They have capable management and technical staffs.
4. They have excellent organizational structures.
5. They have effective software methods and tools.
6. They have adequate staff office environments, including physical environment, cultural environment, and social environment.
7. They have excellent organizational leadership and, in particular, a major learning capacity.
8. They have a *total quality culture*.

With this said, we turn to an examination of these latter two subjects.

REFERENCES

[1] Boehm, B. W., "Software Engineering," *IEEE Transactions on Computers,* Vol. 25, No. 12, Dec. 1976, pp. 1226–1241.

[2] Boehm, B. W., "Improving Software Productivity," *IEEE Computers,* Vol. 20, No. 9, Sept. 1976, pp. 43–57.

[3] Walston, C., and Felix, C., "A Method of Programming Measurement and Estimation," *IBM Systems Journal,* Vol. 10, No. 1, Jan. 1977, pp. 54–73.

[4] Bailey, J. W., and Basili, V. R., "A Meta-model for Software Development Resource Expenditures," *Proceedings of the Fifth International Conference on Software Engineering,* 1981, pp. 107–116.

[5] Porter, A. L., Roper, A. T., Mason, T. W., Rossini, F. A., and Banks, J., *Forecasting and Management of Technology,* John Wiley & Sons, New York, 1991.

[6] Wolverton, R. W., "The Cost of Developing Large-Scale Software," *IEEE Transactions on Computers*, Vol. 23, No. 6, 1974, pp. 615–636.

[7] Doty Associates Inc., "Software Cost Estimation Study: Study Results" and "Software Cost Estimation Study: Guidelines for Improving Software Cost Estimating," in Herd, J. R., Postak, J. N., Russell, W. E., and Stewart, K. R. (Eds.), *Software Cost Estimation Study—Study Results—Final Technical Report*, RADC-TR-77-220, Doty Associates, Inc., Rockville, MD, June 1977.

[8] Thebaut, S. M., and Shen, V. Y., "An Analytic Resource Model for Large-Scale Software Development," *Information Processing and Management*, Vol. 20, No. 1-2, 1984, pp. 293–315.

[9] Fox, J. M., *Software and Its Development*, Prentice-Hall, Englewood Cliffs, NJ, 1985.

[10] Nelson, E. A., *Management Handbook for the Estimation of Computer Programming Costs*, AD-A648750, System Development Corporation, Santa Monica, CA, Oct. 31, 1966.

[11] Sage, A. P., *Systems Engineering*, John Wiley & Sons, New York, 1992.

[12] DeMarco, T., *Controlling Software Projects*, Yourdon Press, New York, 1981.

[13] Boehm, B. W., *Software Engineering Economics*, Prentice-Hall, Englewood Cliffs, NJ, 1981.

[14] Boehm, B. W., "Software Engineering Economics," *IEEE Transactions on Software Engineering*, Vol. 10, No. 1, Jan. 1984, pp. 10–21.

[15] Boehm, B. W., "Rapid Prototyping, Risk Management, 2167, and the Ada Process Model," *Proceedings of the Electronic Industries Association Workshop*, Washington, DC, 1987, pp. G33–G34.

[16] Brooks, F. P., *The Mythical Man-Month*, Addison-Wesley, Reading, MA, 1975.

[17] Helm, J. E., "The Viability of Using COCOMO in the Special Application Software Bidding and Estimating Process," *IEEE Transactions on Engineering Management*, Vol. 39, No. 1, Feb. 1992, pp. 42–58.

[18] Balda, D. M., and Gustafson, D. A., "Cost Estimation Models for the Reuse and Prototype Software Development Life-Cycles," *ACM SIGSOFT Software Engineering Notes*, Vol. 15, No. 3, July 1990, pp. 1-18.

[19] Boehm, B. W., and Royce, W., "Ada COCOMO: TRW IOC Version," *Processing, Third COCOMO Users Group Meeting*, Carnegie-Mellon University, Software Engineering Institute, Nov. 1987.

[20] Norden, P. V. "Useful Tools for Project Management," *Operations Research in Research and Development*, John Wiley & Sons, New York, 1963.

[21] Putnam, L., "A General Empirical Solution to the Macro Software Sizing and Estimating Project," *IEEE Transactions on Software Engineering*, Vol. 4, No. 4, July 1978, pp. 345–361.

[22] Putnam, L. H., *Software Cost Estimating and Life-Cycle Control, Getting the Software Numbers*, IEEE Tutorial Catalog Number EHO-165-1, 1980.

[23] Putnam, L. H., and Myers, W., *Measures for Excellence: Reliable Software on Time, Within Budget*, Pergamon Press, Tarrytown, NY, 1992.

[24] Conte, S. D., Dunsmore, H. E., and Shen, V. Y., *Software Engineering Metrics and Models*, Benjamin-Cummings Publishing Co., New York, 1986.

[25] Kemerer, C. F., "An Empirical Validation of Software Cost Estimation Models," *Communications of the ACM*, Vol. 30, No. 5, May 1987, pp. 416–429.

[26] Parr, F. N., "An Alternative to the Rayleigh Curve Model for Software Development," *IEEE Transactions on Software Engineering,* Vol. SE-6, No. 3 , May 1980, pp. 291–296.

[27] Londeix, B., *Cost Estimation for Software Development,* Addison-Wesley, Reading, MA, 1987.

[28] Tausworthe, R. C., "Staffing Implications of Software Productivity Models," Jet Propulsion Laboratory, Report 42-72, 1982.

[29] Jensen, R. W., "A Comparison of the Jensen and COCOMO Schedule and Cost Estimation Models," *Proceedings of the International Society of Parametric Analysis,* 1984, pp. 96–106.

[30] Albrecht, A. J. "Measuring Application Development Productivity," *Proceedings of the IBM Application Development Symposium,* Monterey, CA, Oct. 1979, pp. 83–92.

[31] Albrecht, A., and Gaffney, J., "Software Function, Source Lines of Code, and Development Effort Prediction: A Software Science Validation," *IEEE Transactions on Software Engineering,* Vol. SE 9, No. 6, Nov. 1983, pp. 639–648.

[32] Low, G. C., and Jeffery, D. R., "Function Points in the Estimation and Evaluation of the Software Process," *IEEE Transactions on Software Engineering,* Vol. 16, No. 1, Jan. 1990, pp. 64–71.

[33] Kemerer, C. F., "Reliability of Function Point Measurements: A Field Experiment," *Communications of the Association for Computing Machinery,* Vol. 36, No. 2, Feb. 1993, pp. 85–97.

[34] Arthur, L. J., *Measuring Programmer Productivity and Software Quality,* John Wiley & Sons, New York, 1985.

[35] Jones, C., *Applied Software Measurement: Assuring Productivity and Quality,* McGraw-Hill Book Co., New York, 1991.

[36] *IFPUG: Function Point Counting Practices Manual,* Revision 3.4, International Function Point Users Group, Blendon Office Park, 5008-28 Pine Creek Drive, Westerville, OH 43081-4899, 1992.

[37] Deveaux, P., "Counting Function Points," in Keys, J. (Ed), *Software Engineering Productivity Handbook,* McGraw-Hill Book Co., New York, 1993, pp. 191–227.

[38] Symons, C. R., "Function Point Analysis, Difficulties and Improvements," *IEEE Transactions on Software Engineering,* Vol. SE-14, No. 1, Jan. 1988, pp. 2–10; also in DeMarco, T., and Lister, T., *Software State of the Art: Selected Papers,* Dorset House, New York, 1990, pp. 161–177.

[39] Itakura, M., and Takayanagi, A., "A Model for Estimating Program Size and Its Evaluation," in DeMarco, T., and Lister, T., *Software State of the Art: Selected Papers,* Dorset House, New York, 1990, pp. 179–1188.

[40] Jones, C., *Programmer Productivity,* McGraw-Hill Book Co., New York, 1986.

[41] Matson, J. E., Barrett, B. E., and Mellichamp, J. M., "Software Development Cost Estimation Using Function Points," *IEEE Transactions on Software Engineering,* Vol. 20, No. 4, Apr. 1994, pp. 275–287.

[42] Johnson, H. T., and Kaplan, R. S., *Relevance Lost: The Rise and Fall of Management Accounting,* Harvard Business School Press, Boston, MA, 1991.

[43] Kaplan, R. S., *Measures for Manufacturing Excellence,* Harvard Business School Press, Boston, MA, 1990.

[44] Kaplan, R. S., and Cooper, R., *Cost Management Systems,* Prentice-Hall, Englewood Cliffs, NJ, 1990.

[45] Anthony, R. N., Dearden, N. J., and Govindarajan, V., *Management Control Systems,* Richard D. Irwin, Homewood, IL, 1992.

[46] Cooper, R., and Kaplan, R. S., "Measure Costs Right: Making the Right Decisions," *Harvard Business Review,* Vol. 66, No. 5, Sept. 1988, pp. 96–103.

[47] O'Guin, M. O., *The Complete Guide to Activity Based Costing,* Prentice-Hall, Englewood Cliffs, NJ, 1991.

[48] Lederer, A. L., and Prasad, J., "Nine Management Guidelines for Better Cost Estimating," *Communications of the Association for Computing Machinery,* Vol. 35, No. 2, Feb. 1992, pp. 51–59.

Chapter 6

Strategic Quality Assurance and Management

There are numerous contemporary works that address needed improvements in vital U.S. industries, such as electronics [1,2]. A number of blueprints have been suggested to enable continued developments in world class manufacturing [3,4], for example. Suggestions now abound for integrating innovation and technology management [5], such as to develop a pattern for excellence in managing manufacturing processes [6]. A major thrust in this is the development of market-driven strategies and processes for creating value [7]. Most of the suggested approaches involve adaptive and proactive planning for quality through a sequence of lifecycle process phases that involve, in effect, the three lifecycles for RDT&E, acquisition or production, and systems planning and marketing, which were emphasized in Chapter 2.

Most of the suggested strategies involve major attention to what we denote as systems engineering and systems management concerns, including such concerns as enhancing strategic level quality assurance and management. Enhanced quality of products and systems results primarily through process improvements. It has been suggested that profiting from the innovations made possible through emerging technology developments and subsequent technology transfer will require success relative to several systems management challenges that include the following [8]:

Encouraging intelligent risk taking and risk management

Nurturing emerging technology champions

Developing useful technological information systems

Organization and management of joint development efforts

Supporting technology push and technological pull through a phased lifecycle that is tuned to technology transfer

Hopefully, accepting these challenges and others will enable industry, government, and education to obtain much enhanced productivity through learning organizations of people that mold new process-driven strategies for product development [9] and services [10], that will enable timely competition in global markets [11], and that will ensure competitive advantage [12,13] for enhanced life quality.

Three major strategies are generally suggested as dominant in achieving these objectives. Much greater attention must be paid to notions of:

1. Planning strategies that work [14] in shaping future business design through information technology [15] and the "revolution in real time" [16] needed for the remainder of this century and the initial portion of the next.

2. Better systems management, through the strategic use of information technology [17] and its integration in organizations [18,19] to enable enhanced sources of innovation and entrepreneurship.

3. Customer-driven total quality of process and product that will result in the development of strategies for excellence [20] and a passion for excellence [21] that will support thriving on chaos [22], in order to deliver us from the present predicament.

Figure 6.1 illustrates a needed integration of systems planning and systems management to result in process quality and then product quality. In this way, responsive organizational systems lead to the desired end result of enhanced productivity and innovation. We make the representation that it is systems management that potentially enables a bridging of the gap between organizational systems and

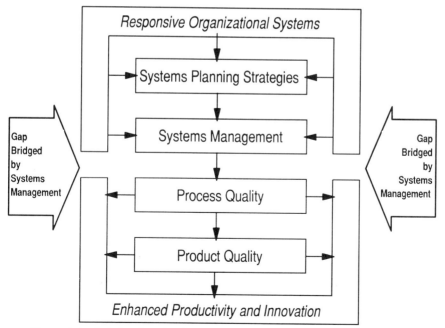

Figure 6.1 Relationships leading to enhanced productivity and innovation.

enhanced productivity. Thus the figure is suggestive of truly broad scope strategic planning for enhanced quality and productivity of processes and products. Of course, many other ingredients could be shown as playing a role in this effort.

We wish to address each of these points in our subsequent sections, especially as they relate to strategic level quality assurance and management. Our primary focus is on information technology—both as a support for enhanced quality and as a benefactor of enhanced quality—and software engineering. Our arguments have much to do with the real world of industry and organizations, as there is an inexorable linkage between technology and organizations [23]. This is especially the case for information technology, which provides necessary hardware and software architectures to support organizational intelligence.

Thus we continue with a discussion of the enhancement of technology and organizations through systems management. In Section 6.2, we discuss some notions regarding systems management for the unsurpassed quality of products that results from extraordinary attention to the processes that produce products and services. Section 6.3 continues this discussion of total quality related concepts with specific application to information technology and software engineering processes.

6.1   SYSTEMS MANAGEMENT FOR TOTAL QUALITY

In a truly seminal work [21], Peters argues forcefully that there are four major contemporary realities that can create crisis situations:

1. *Generic uncertainty* throughout the world, due to a variety of factors.
2. *Technology revolution,* due to a number of newly emerging technologies.
3. *New competitors* for established organizations.
4. *Changing tastes* and values.

Earlier, Peters and Waterman [13] had developed eight strategies for excellence:

1. *Bias for Action.* While formal analytical approaches are needed, one must avoid the "paralysis of analysis." Successful organizations know who they are and where they are going. With this vision, a bias for action and the associated results can thrive.
2. *Close to the Customer.* A successful organization is very customer oriented, with understanding of its customers and their desires and needs.
3. *Autonomy and Entrepreneurship.* A successful enterprise allows its employees to assume responsibility and act in an enterprising manner, even though they "generate a reasonable number of mistakes" in the process.
4. *Productivity Through People.* A successful organization realizes that people are its most important attribute and helps its employees to enhance their abilities and overcome their limitations.
5. *Hands-on, Value Driven.* Successful organizations excel at clarifying and

communicating their values and objectives, and thereby avoid vacuous plans and slogans that generate cynicism. Organizational words and deeds are congruent.

6. *Stick to the Knitting.* A successful organization will define its "knitting," or activities that support objectives, and will remain steadfast in pursuit of these activities. It does not subordinate strategic planning and objectives to momentarily attractive new market niches that are not part of its knitting.

7. *Simple Form, Lean Staff.* The successful organization is a dynamic organism that adjusts its structure to serve evolving needs, ideally employing simple form and lean support staff. Structure is necessarily subordinate to purpose.

8. *Balancing Controls with Autonomy.* The successful organization promotes *autonomy and entrepreneurship* while remaining *hands-on and value driven.* Vision and values are clearly guided by management, while employees are given a relatively free hand to pursue this vision.

They validated each of these eight strategies as continuing useful strategies for turbulent times in a later work [20] in which some of the initially selected organizations had fallen from the grail of excellence.

The important lesson in these latter two studies is that a major and central role for organizational management is the wise harnessing of the social forces in the organization in order to shape and guide organizational values.* All three of these excellent works [13,20,21] encourage: (1) a broadly shared culture that motivates employees to search for appropriate solutions to organizational goals and (2) a sense of purpose emanating from love of product, provision of top quality service, acknowledging the innovations and contributions of fellow employees, and the realization that it is peer pressure rather than orders from the boss that is the main motivator. This sense of shared purpose enables simultaneous "loose-tight" organizational management structures, which are highly desirable. This is especially so in environments where there are a large number of professional workers because it permits a concurrent balancing of firm management guidance and considerable operating autonomy. It strongly supports management for total quality and professionalism. Thus it is particularly suited for implementation in university and high technology corporate environments and cultures, and other industries comprised of many highly educated and skilled professional workers. To do this well will require that the three major defining terms for an organization—structure, function, and purpose—be properly integrated. In Peters' work, the purposeful efforts of an organization are identified with strategy and the functional efforts are associated with five human-based endeavors as illustrated in Figure 6.2.

Peters' more recent management revolution handbook [21] disaggregates the principles for excellence into a total of 50 prescriptions for excellence. There are five major prescriptive areas.

---

*This relates very closely to the subjects of organizational culture and organizational leadership. These are the central theses for our discussions in Chapter 7.

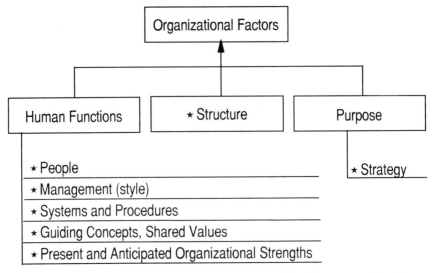

Figure 6.2 Major organizational factors supporting quality (the seven critical factors identified by Peters are indicated with an asterisk).

1. *Customer responsiveness prescriptions* encourage organizational listening and quick responsiveness.
2. *Fast-paced innovation prescriptions* encourage organizational flexibility and responsiveness in new competitive environments.
3. *Flexibility through empowered people prescriptions* suggests a relatively small number of hierarchical layers in an organization and increased rewards to individuals for quality and productivity.
4. *Leadership prescriptions* promote adaptability among employees.
5. *Organizational processes prescriptions* address the need for appropriate systems management and metrics.

These top level prescriptions, illustrated in Figure 6.3, can help achieve the following five value-added strategies.

1. *Provide a top quality product* through mounting a quality improvement revolution and ensuring that quality is always defined in terms of customer perceptions.
2. *Provide superior, even fanatical, service* through emphasis on customer-related intangible elements and measurement of the resulting customer satisfaction.
3. *Achieve extraordinary responsiveness* or total customer responsiveness (TCR) through bold new partnerships with customers and aggressive creation of new markets.

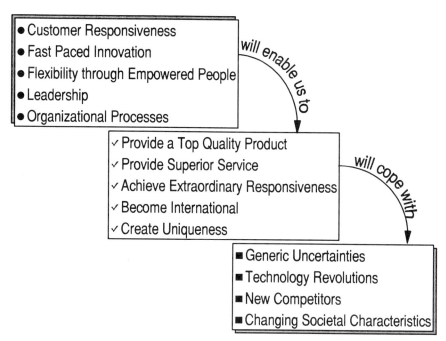

Figure 6.3 Five generic prescriptions to achieve five value-added strategies that cope with contemporary realities.

4. *Become international* by selling, and perhaps producing, throughout the world.

5. *Create uniqueness* of organization and purpose and promulgate understanding of this uniqueness both inside and outside the organization.

Achieving these will, in turn, lead to the ability to cope with the four contemporary realities illustrated in Figure 6.3.

Those prescriptions relating to quality are of particular significance here. Peters envisions 12 primary attributes of a successful quality revolution:

1. Management is obsessed with quality.

2. There is a guiding system or ideology that provides both a passion for and a systematic process to support quality.

3. Quality is measured by the work team or department itself, in order to avoid bureaucratization, and not exclusively by quality control inspectors. Quality measurement begins at the start of a project, extends throughout the process, and must be visible and reportable.

4. Quality is rewarded.

5. Everyone is trained in techniques for quality assessment.

6. The quality of every major function in the organization is measured in a cooperative and nonadversarial manner.

7. There is no such thing as an insignificant improvement.

8. There is constant stimulation of quality enhancement efforts.

9. While there may be a parallel organizational structure devoted to quality improvement, there is also the recognition that this parallel structure must be carefully controlled such that it does not deteriorate into a new, apathy-creating, layer of bureaucracy that negates attribute 3.

10. Everyone is a player in the organization's quality assessment and management process.

11. Quality improvement is the primary source of cost reduction, through simplification of the production process.

12. Quality improvement is a never-ending objective.

The customer must be viewed as the final judge of quality. This is a very consistent theme throughout virtually all contemporary quality management literature.

It is necessary to note that the *customer* for some goods (or bads), such as public goods (or bads), is sometimes difficult to definitively identify. This will create additional, but by no means insurmountable, difficulties in defining quality assurance and management strategies in many public sector efforts and in many "third-sector" efforts [24], such as universities and consortia. Nevertheless, it is important to create total customer empathy and demand through *product quality and responsiveness* and associated *innovation* in developing trail-blazing products and services. In his management revolution handbook, Peters has identified three central guidelines as exceptionally vital in order to achieve excellence.

1. *The needed flexibility is achieved through empowering people.*

2. *Leadership must be developed to ensure needed change at all organizational levels.*

3. *Responsive organizational systems must be set up.*

These themes are ubiquitous throughout the quality management literature.

The term *total quality management* (TQM) is generally understood to refer to the continuous improvement of processes and products through use of an integrated systems management approach to a lifecycle process. This leads to product development through organizational teamwork and the methods of statistical quality control to achieve indomitable customer satisfaction. An essential feature of this is the notion of the *totality* of the approach. It involves efforts at the level of strategic planning, management control, and operational and task control. It involves approaches to process and product and major focus on problems and issues addressed by the product.

In his recent book on process quality, Deming [25] describes a number of obstacles to quality management, including the following.

1. *Lack of Constancy of Purpose.* Organizations may not stick close to the knitting in a continuous manner over time.

2. *Focus on Profit over the Short Term Only.* Deming espouses the view that current American management is often obsessed with short-term profit [26], to the exclusion of developing processes, products, and services that support success over the longer term. This leads to a lack of interest in research, education, training, and other efforts that reflect a constancy of purpose. This neglect has created many contemporary problems, including, as some would say, an age of diminished expectations. It leads to disinterest in developing the technologies and manufacturing the products and systems that will ensure increasing market share and the associated long-term accomplishments and subsequent and affiliated affluence of a productive America.

3. *Emphasis on Performance Ratings and Annual Reviews.* Deming sees this as management by fear. It promotes a short-run, reactive inspection and evaluation of what has occurred, rather than a long-term proactive effort to promote achievement orientation. Besides, these views tend to be more focused on the shortcomings of people rather than the management system, which is more often than not, in Deming's view, the real culprit.

4. *Mobility of Management.* Rapid management turnover encourages a short-term view, rather than long-term commitments to quality and productivity.

5. *Management by Current Statistics.* There are a number of important factors—such as customer satisfaction, quality, and productivity improvements—that may not easily be measurable over the short run, but which have important long-run consequences for profitability. It can be devastating to ignore these long-run indicators, as has often been done.

Unfortunately, these obstacles to success are neither mutually exclusive nor collectively exhaustive. The effect of a combination of these is potentially deadly. It is easily possible to take exception to some of these due to the specific way in which they are worded. For example, item 2 appears as a unique criticism of management. To the degree that the statement is true, it reflects a Wall Street mentality that reflects interests in the short-term profits often made possible by manipulative efforts. The real culprit may be all of us who want quick, risk-free, investment performance. If management is obsessed, it is perhaps us who collectively enable and encourage the obsession.

Many others have made not dissimilar observations. In an insightful work, Krugman [27] examines three possible scenarios for America in the 1990s: a happy-ending scenario associated with a rebirth of American productivity, a hard-landing scenario associated with a major American debt crisis that is brought about by the mammoth trade and budget deficits now extant, and a drift scenario associated with slow erosion in American living standards and accompanying diminished expectations to rationalize this gradual decline. The probabilities associated with the scenarios are 0.20, 0.25, and 0.55. The most likely scenario, one of drift and slow erosion, is called the "age of diminished expectations." Galbraith [28] uses the term "culture of contentment" to describe essentially the same set of current short-run policies. He envisions severe economic crises, international military misadventures, and insurrection of an angry underclass that has been denied opportunities for advancement, as the major threats to this evolving state of contentment. There is little optimism in this work for emergence of any redemptive alternative scenarios to the present culture of contentment, other than one of the three even less desirable situations that are identified as likely to eventuate from a most likely continuation scenario that represents the present culture of contentment.

Deming thinks American management is currently in a crisis situation, due to the five obstacles to quality management just identified, and he proposes 14 strategies to lead us *out of the crisis.*

1. Create constancy of purpose for improvement of product and service.
2. Adopt the new philosophy.
3. Cease dependence on inspection to achieve quality.
4. End the practice of awarding business on the basis of price alone. Instead, minimize total cost by working with a single quality-conscious supplier.
5. Continually improve planning, production, and service.
6. Institute on-the-job training efforts.
7. Adopt and institute leadership.
8. Drive out fear from the workplace.
9. Break down communications and other barriers between staff areas.
10. Eliminate slogans, exhortations, and targets for the workforce to use in enhancing production.
11. Eliminate numerical production quotas for the workforce and numerical financial goals for management.
12. Remove barriers that rob people of pride of workmanship. Eliminate the annual rating or merit system.
13. Institute a vigorous program of education and self-improvement for everyone.
14. Involve everybody in the company in this transformation.

These quality desiderata are highly focused on quality through process improvements. The work of Deming, to some extent, has its roots in the very early quality control theories of Shewhart [29]. In particular, Shewhart was concerned with the following:

Special or peculiar causes that relate to the performance of specific individuals and called assignable causes.

Systems management difficulties, called *system causes,* which are only resolvable by top management.

Cooperation and communication among all elements of the enterprise (marketing, design, engineering, production, sales, accounting, etc.).

Statistical quality control, including a number of new charting approaches.

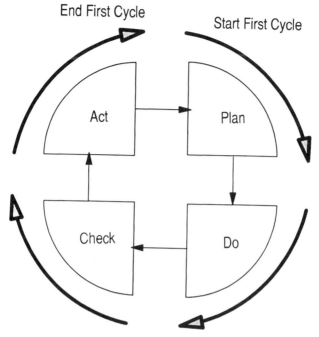

Figure 6.4 The PDCA cycle of Shewhart and Deming.

He identified a four-phase approach to quality management that involves a continuous set of activities involving planning, doing, checking, and acting. This is often called a PDCA cycle and/or a Shewhart–Deming cycle. It is illustrated in Figure 6.4.

1. We *plan* (P) for an improvement in quality and identify potentially appropriate metrics.
2. We *do* (D) a trial or prototype implementation of the plan and the metrics on a small scale.
3. We *check* (C) on the effects of the implementation on the trial plan.
4. We *act* (A) on the information that was just learned.

We repeat the process in an iterative manner. The suggested effort is generally one of continuous incremental and evolutionary improvements for increasing quality.

Operational improvements in product and system functionality and quality result primarily from process quality improvements. Given this process or product line focus, as contrasted with a direct product focus, the PDCA cycle is very appealing. This suggests that we achieve improvements in product through improvements in process. It suggests major use of interactive and proactive approaches to management and metrics, and the use of reactive approaches only to the extent necessary to complement the interactive and proactive. Figure 6.5 shows an interpretation of the 14 TQM strategies of Deming as imbedded into the three central guidelines for

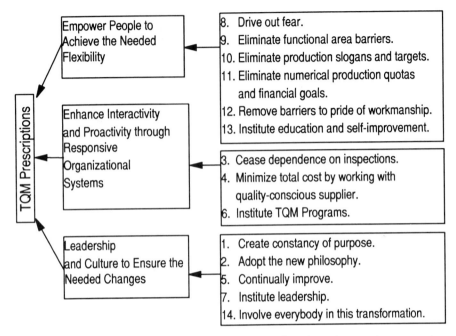

Figure 6.5 Clustering of 14 Deming TQM prescriptions into three major categories.

excellence of Peters. In all of these thoughts, we see that quality achievement and continued improvements in quality can be viewed as a major causal factor supporting organizational success. The reason why this occurs is that enhanced quality leads to many other improvements as well, including increased and sustained customer satisfaction with the resulting product, and this directly supports organizational success.

Before continuing with our discussions of contemporary views of strategic or total quality management, let us examine the history of quality evolution and how it has led, somewhat naturally, to a focus on strategic level quality. Then we return to a more detailed examination of strategic level quality.

6.2   BRIEF HISTORY OF QUALITY

Actually, quality concepts have been around for quite a long time. In the very earliest times, quality was a function of the individual artisan or craftsperson. With the industrial revolution came production of goods not primarily made by an individual, but by teams. Historically, the first modern notions of quality were reactive and inspection oriented. This approach evolved into the use of statistical quality control techniques. More recently, notions of quality assurance and management for quality have emerged. A recent book by Garvin [30] provides a very readable and comprehensive account of the historical emergence and present developments concerning various notions of quality. A brief summary of the development of quality-related notions is given in [31].

In these historical discussions, we can see the emergence of quality consciousness at four levels, following an initial level at which no attention is paid to quality:

1. *Inspections* to identify, and cull out, defective products.
2. *Statistical quality control* to provide cost-effective metrics on performance through efficient and effective sampling inspections of products, initially of the products of manufacturing technology.
3. *Operational task level quality assurance and management* through quality measurements throughout the lifecycle of production to provide for operational controls that will ensure quality.
4. *Strategic quality assurance and management* to ensure market competitiveness through the involvement of all organizational elements of the process and product under consideration.

Paying no attention at all to quality can be viewed as inactive quality. Inspections can be viewed as a reactive approach to quality, as can most of statistical quality control through product inspections. Operational level quality assurance is generally interactive in that efforts are attempted throughout the entire lifecycle. Finally, strategic quality assurance and management is, or at least should be, proactive. While statistical quality control was doubtlessly inspection and reactively oriented initially, we can also use statistical approaches for interactive and proactive measurements and associated quality improvements. Figure 6.6 illustrates this natural evolution of quality consciousness.

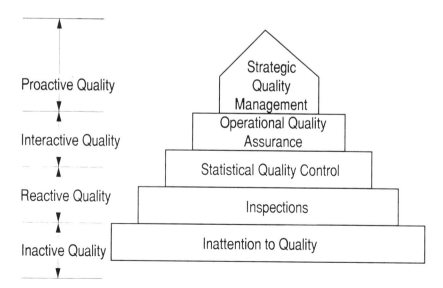

Figure 6.6 Five evolutionary approaches to quality.

Clearly, these quality concerns are not mutually exclusive. Inspections and reactive measurements, for example, will surely be a part of strategic quality assurance and management. However, strategic management for quality assurance will not *depend* on inspections and other reactive approaches. In brief, we might state that these four levels correspond to the following:

- Inspected quality or reactive quality
- Statistically controlled quality, generally by sampled inspections or sampled reactive measurements
- Built-in or manufactured quality by interactive effort throughout the production lifecycle
- Proactively managed quality

While each is important, it is the latter two that will result in maximum competitiveness of processes and products. Together, these comprise what has been called *total quality management* (TQM).

While there are a number of definitions, Stuelpnagel [32] suggests that TQM involves customer satisfaction, continuous improvement, robust design, variability reduction, statistical thinking, management responsibility, supplier integration, quality control, education and worker training, teamwork, cultural change, and stakeholder interfaces. These ingredients involve each of the levels of quality we noted previously.

The many perspectives and definitions of quality doubtlessly reflect the great range of philosophers, economists, operations researchers, managers, artists, and engineers who have addressed the topic. Philosophers tend to be concerned with axiological and definitional issues. Those in product marketing are more likely to be concerned with customer appeal and satisfaction, and those in engineering with design and manufacturing for quality. It is often not clear whether quality is conceived objectively or subjectively, and whether it may be measured absolutely or only relatively.

There are, we believe, specific quantitative metrics that may be used to address quality issues. Some of these have been addressed in our last two chapters. We will discuss some others here. Some of the more easily identified attributes of quality include purposes served or performance objectives; operational functions performed; structural features; and reliability, availability, and maintainability. Doubtlessly, there are other dimensions, such as beauty or aesthetic appeal, and we can disaggregate each of these dimensions. Quality is also influenced by such factors as cost to produce, selling price, demand or market share, advertising strategy, marketing strategy, and profit.

Many quality discussions in [30], including most of those in Chapter 4, were concerned primarily with operational level quality considerations. In this systems management work, we are especially concerned with strategic quality assurance and management. Basically, strategic quality assurance involves systems management of processes, thereby aiming to secure product quality. Quality assurance practices below the level of systems management will generally produce operational level quality control and inspections for product quality only.

David Garvin [33] has identified five perspectives on quality.

1. *Transcendental Perspective.* From this perspective, quality is synonymous with *inherent excellence* and is recognizable by all. In this view, quality cannot be precisely defined, but *you know it when you see it.* A popular book appeared two decades ago that took this perspective [34], which we might call a *wholistic* or gestalt viewpoint.

2. *Product-Based Perspective.* From this perspective, quality is a descriptive, measurable attribute, made up of microlevel attributes. This approach provides a *holistic* definition, one in which we attempt to see the whole through the sum of its parts. From this perspective, quality differences among products are due to the different components that comprise the products.

3. *User or Customer Perspective.* Each user has a view of quality so this perspective is necessarily subjective. It is the approach taken, at least in principle, by advocates of the subjective utility theory of decision analysis that we will examine in our next chapter. A challenge it presents to product planners is combining these individual preferences to gain meaningful insights into aggregated market preferences. The user perspective on quality reflects the demand side of market equilibrium. Juran is a major proponent of this view of quality and has stated that *quality is fitness for use.* Quality therefore consists of meeting or exceeding the customer requirements and expectations.

4. *Manufacturing Perspective.* The manufacturing or production perspective on quality focuses on standardization in system design and production. From this perspective, a quality product is designed, produced, and fielded correctly to specifications, *the first time.* Product reliability, availability, and maintainability are critical attributes; and statistical quality control is used to detect and correct defects in the production system. Cost reduction and on-time fielding of products are important aspects of this perspective. In summary, quality means conformance to requirements and specifications, including those relating to cost and schedule. Philip Crosby is a major proponent of this view of quality and has stated that *quality means conformance to requirements.*

5. *Value Perspective.* From this perspective, a quality product is one that provides sufficient performance at an acceptable price. This approach blends quality as a measure of goodness with quality as a measure of utility. Quality, then, can be maximized only for *certain* customers, unless the product has very universal appeal. Armand Feigenbaum is a major proponent of this view of quality as the best product for the customers in terms of the selling price and its fitness for the use contemplated for the product.

Each of these perspectives has its uses, but in the final analysis, it is the end user who ultimately sets the standards for quality. Of course, there are numerous steps involved in moving an emerging technology to an acquired system, and those attributes that account for end user quality perceptions need attention at all these steps. But all the fundamental determinants of quality relate to final use.

Garvin [30,33] has suggested eight dimensions or attributes of quality that relate to these five perspectives:

1. *Performance* of the end use system or product.
2. *Features* of the end use system or product.
3. *Reliability* of the end use system or product.
4. *Conformance* of the end use system or product to internal and external, quality and performance standards.
5. *Durability* or maintainability of the end use system or product.
6. Character of the human aspects of *serviceability* of the end use system or product.
7. *Aesthetic* aspects of the end use system or product.
8. *Perceived overall quality* of the end use system or product.

Figure 6.7 illustrates our view of these eight quality attributes. It seems possible to speak of planned quality, realized quality, and perceived quality and to have each of the first seven of these eight quality attributes supporting these higher level attributes. In any case, quality involves the following:

- Planning for the right product or planning to do the right thing
- Acquiring or producing it the right way
- Acquiring it right the first time
- Acquiring it on time
- Satisfying the customer needs and expectations
- Being responsive to customer needs for maintenance and product upgrades
- Treating each and every customer with courtesy and respect

We can, of course, identify many other attributes of quality. Let us now turn our attention to an examination of several different approaches to achieving quality and assuring quality through strategic management.

The principles of total quality control perhaps first emerged in the 1950s with the publication of a definitive handbook on the topic by Joseph Juran [35]. Juran was to become revered in Japan for introducing a number of quality control technologies. To this day, he continues as one of the major figures in the quality movement [36–38]. The generic phases in Juran's quality improvement effort are based on a detection, diagnosis, and correction set of 12 activities that will lead to total quality management, explicitly through statistical quality control approaches.

1. Assign priority to production projects.
2. Conduct a Pareto analysis of symptoms of quality control problems.
3. Identify hypotheses concerning cause of symptoms.

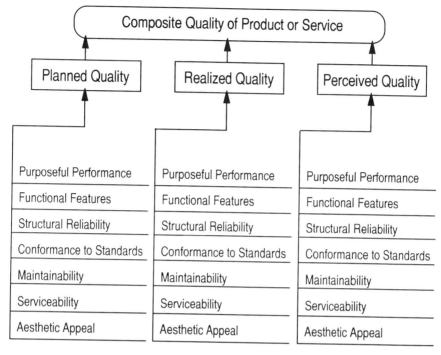

Figure 6.7   A three-perspective view of quality facets.

4. Test hypotheses through collection and analysis of data.
5. Select appropriate hypotheses.
6. Design experiments for particular quality diagnostic efforts.
7. Obtain management approval for experimental designs.
8. Conduct specific experiments to determine product defects and diagnose their cause.
9. Propose corrective strategies or remedies.
10. Test corrective strategies or remedies.
11. Apply corrective action to effect remedy.
12. Proceed to establish quality control at a higher standard.

The first five of these efforts involve planning for statistical quality control. Steps 6 to 8 involve diagnosis and detection of specific product quality deficiencies. Steps 9 to 12 involve providing corrective action to processes to greatly reduce defects in the resulting product.

Juran [39] identifies three major efforts as a quality control trilogy: quality *planning,* quality *control,* and quality *improvement.* He compares them with the analogous steps in financial control processes: budgeting, cost control, and cost reduction. Figure 6.8 illustrates these generic efforts.

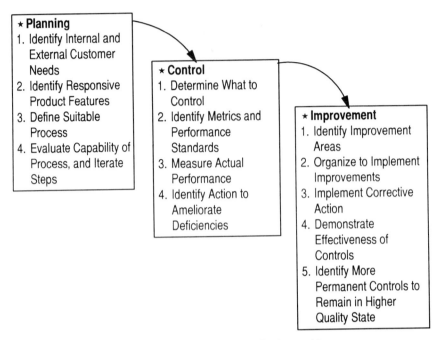

Figure 6.8   The quality control trilogy of Juran.

In the quality planning effort, internal and external customers and their needs are identified. Generic product features that are responsive to customer needs are identified, as well as associated quality goals. A dependable and trustworthy process is then designed to meet or exceed product specifications, including product quality specifications. The capability of the process to produce the intended result is then established and this leads to the desired quality improvement. In general, the overall quality and production effort moves, in sequence, from customer needs to product features, from product features to process features, and finally from process features to process development and actual production. We could now take each of the steps needed to implement this three-stage process and illustrate three quality lifecycles, one each for planning, control, and improvement. Systematic measurements are, of course, necessarily applied throughout the entire effort.

One of Juran's many contributions is the notion that we should address not only the cost of quality (COQ) but also the cost of poor quality. He defines the cost of poor quality (COPQ) as the sum of all costs that would disappear if there were no quality problems.

Juran expresses the view that management, and not labor, must assume a majority of the blame for poor quality. The nexus of this argument is that it is the process that is at fault and not the direct effort on the product. Not only is management often the source of the process-related problems, but there is also a lack of recognition of the major gains that can be realized through quality improvements. These views are relatively ubiquitous throughout much of the quality management literature.

Feigenbaum [40] is also one of the early, seminal, and prolific professionals in this area. Quality control is disaggregated into three parts, with each providing a needed form of insurance, in this effort.

1. *New design quality control* is needed to ensure that the design of the product permits proper manufacturing.
2. *Incoming materials quality control* is needed to ensure that the materials of production meet quality standards.
3. *Product quality control on the shop floor* is needed to ensure that the manufacturing process does not introduce faults.

Cost analysis, product specifications, and the use of careful measurements to determine product reliability and quality were the major tools of these efforts at securing quality. Management, planning, and control were from this point forward integrated into the process of statistical quality assurance, first at the operational level and later at the strategic management level.

Feigenbaum [40] has identified the following time periods in the evolution of quality management approaches.

1. The period of time up to 1890 was the *operator control period*. During this time, entire products were normally manufactured by one person only, or at most a small group of people working closely together. The pride of the individual worker was directly reflected in the quality of the finished product.
2. The period from 1900 to 1920 was the *foreman quality control period*. This was when the concept of mass production blossomed. Labor became specialized and the quality of an entire product was no longer principally due to the efforts of one person. Supervisors now became responsible for quality.
3. The *inspection quality control period* existed from the 1920s until the 1940s. Products and processes became more complex and production volume per worker was increasing, as was the number of workers per supervisor. It was during this era that notions of standards and statistical quality control first emanated.
4. The period from 1940 through 1960 is called the *statistical quality control period*. Sampling, rather than inspection of the entire output of a production line, became commonplace.
5. The period from 1960 to 1970 is termed the *total quality control period*. This generally involved operational level quality assurance.
6. The period after 1970 is termed the *total quality control organization-wide period*. Concepts such as "zero defects" and "quality control circles" were introduced. Organizations, in this period, have become very quality conscious and the customer has become regarded as the definer of quality.

These correspond to, and represent a slight expansion of, the four quality periods that we identified earlier.

Feigenbaum is also much concerned with identification of the cost of quality. This is broadly interpreted to include both the cost of quality and the cost of poor quality.

The *cost of conformance* with quality standards can be thought of as the *cost of quality control* to prevent defects from occurring and the *cost of detection* or appraisal of those quality problems that do occur.

The *cost of nonconformance* is due to internal failures and external failures. The *cost of internal failure* is that associated with defects that are discovered before a product reaches the final end user and includes the costs of diagnosis and correction efforts, including rework, and scrap or nonreworkable products, in attempts to make the product right the second or later time this is attempted. The *cost of external failure* is the cost incurred when an end user or customer receives a defective product. This could include extensive maintenance costs and possibly legal costs as well. Ultimately, feelings of low quality become pervasive and this impacts on the willingness of customers to continue to purchase the product.

Feigenbaum, like Deming and Juran, has been and is a major force in the development of contemporary strategic quality thought.

Crosby [41,42], also a seminal worker in this area and who was the originator of the concept of *zero defects planning,* identified 14 imperatives for strategic quality assurance and management.

1. Establish management commitment to quality.
2. Form quality improvement team.
3. Accomplish quality measurement.
4. Identify the cost of quality evaluation efforts.
5. Become aware of quality issues.
6. Implement corrective action.
7. Accomplish zero defects planning.
8. Implement quality education.
9. Obtain a zero defects day.
10. Accomplish goal setting.
11. Identify and remove the cause of errors.
12. Implement recognition efforts to reward quality achievements.
13. Establish quality councils.
14. Do it over again through repeated iterations of the first 13 steps.

Crosby [43] has identified five symptoms that suggest a major need for strategic level quality efforts.

1. The product or service produced generally contains deviations from customer requirements and/or agreed upon standards.

2. The organization has an extensive maintenance network skilled in rework and other corrective actions on delivered products in order to retain some semblance of customer satisfaction.

3. Management has failed to provide quality leadership, standards, or even definitions, and, as a result of this neglect, individuals in the organization develop their own.

4. Management is unaware of the real costs of nonconformance to quality, or conformance to standards and user requirements. As a consequence, much is spent on doing things wrong and the necessary rework such that they are then made better.

5. Management denies that it is the major cause of the quality-related problems.

According to Crosby, quality is conformance to requirements. The lack of conformance to requirements results in a lack of quality. Conformance to standards and specifications is necessary, or course. But this will not guarantee conformance to requirements unless the technical specifications are a correct representation of requirements.

In related recent efforts, he has developed a set of completedness principles [44]. These are intended to cause employees, suppliers, and customers to be successful through the efforts of organizational leadership. Crosby has also developed four quality management philosophies that are persistent throughout most of his writings:

- Quality is defined as conformance to customer requirements, not goodness.
- Quality is achieved through defect prevention, not through product appraisals.
- The quality performance standard is zero defects and not minimally accepted quality levels.
- Quality is measured not by indices but by the price of nonconformance to requirements.

The major theme appears to be the insistence on interactive and proactive approaches and not on reactive approaches for quality assurance and control. Also, there is a strong message not to sublimate the objective for the objective measure. Thus satisfaction of user requirements is the objective, not simply meeting the technical performance specification, which may well not fully represent the customer needs and requirements. Crosby is also the originator of a management maturity framework that is of much value. We will discuss this in our next chapter.

Earlier, we noted Deming's truly major contributions to the quality management effort. Each of his 14 prescriptions is important and deserves additional commentary. To this end, we will provide a brief commentary and interpretation of the 14 prescriptions in Deming's studies.

1. *Create Constancy of Purpose.* The organization's objectives should be very clear and should address the organization both as it exists today and as it is meant to exist in the future. Innovation and faith in the future are both called for. Continual

incremental improvements, even of a very small nature, will eventually produce substantial improvements. These result from the elimination of such *quality-destroying characteristics* as delays and defects in purchased products and adverse human behaviors and attitudes. They also result from long-range planning, continuous education and training, elimination of unsafe and degrading working conditions, and improved communications up and down the organization.

2. *Adopt the New Philosophy.* The philosophy embodied in the other 13 prescriptions should be explicitly adopted. Adoption requires more than endorsement; it requires action. Endorsing and espousing anything without manifestation of change will almost always lead to cynicism regarding the organization's sincerity.

3. *Cease Dependence on Inspection.* One of Deming's major arguments is that lasting quality is not created by screening out defective products through massive inspection at the output stages of production. Instead, quality comes by improving the production process. This requires major efforts at the strategic management and planning level. Deming proposes methods of statistical process control to achieve such improvements, but not at all through reactive inspections of product. These methods are explained in his book, *Out of the Crisis,* and its predecessor, and some of the statistical quality control literature that is specifically concerned with TQM.

4. *End the Practice of Choosing Suppliers Based Solely on Price.* The lowest-price components will often not be the least expensive ones, especially over the long term. If the lowest-price components are not of good quality, and especially if the vendor of these does not provide appropriate maintenance services, it is likely that these components will create quality problems, and long-run costs will be increased. Deming advocates working with a single supplier when its quality and service meet the needs of the organization. Above all, we should buy for quality and not for price alone. Relationships with suppliers, who are also very much like customers, are very important.

5. *Continually Improve Processes.* Improving productivity should be a never-ending task. The objective should not be to "fix" problems, once and forever, but to commit to continued improvement through process improvement. This approach should be implemented across all aspects of an organization's activities.

6. *Institute Training Programs for Quality Improvement.* While education and training cost money, lack of education and training may cost more over the long run. Productivity improvements are largely achieved by people, so these people should be educated or trained for the tasks they need to perform. Unfortunately, investments in education and training often do not appear on the financial records of an organization as assets. These appear as costs! An a result, they are often not looked on as investments or benefits, but merely as costs to be avoided whenever possible in the search for short-term profit.

7. *Adopt and Institute Leadership.* The most fundamental role of management is to provide leadership, and this leadership should focus on continual quality improvement. Management must take a leadership role in implementing the TQM philosophy, particularly when introducing contemporary approaches to systems management and management control.

8. *Drive Out Fear.* Employees may avoid expressing ideas and admitting mistakes for fear of losing status, position, or even their jobs. However, the process of organizational improvement is enhanced if every lesson that is learned is also communicated. Thus management must assure that people feel sufficiently secure to proactively communicate lessons learned from their mistakes. Mistakes may provide very valuable learning opportunities.

9. *Break Down Barriers Between Organizational Units.* Quality is best achieved by having people in each functional area of the organization understand the other functional areas and communicate regularly with people in these areas. For example, people in design and manufacturing need to work with those in marketing to introduce new high quality products and systems that are market oriented. This prescription has found much recent favor and supports much of the reengineering efforts we study in Chapter 8.

10. *Eliminate Slogans.* Slogans such as "quality counts" are useless; indeed, they are counterproductive without appropriate methods, controls, and management commitment. Continual identification and correction of problems with processes and products will lead to quality improvements; slogans alone will not.

11. *Eliminate Numerical Quotas and Goals.* The mandate to pursue specific quantitative targets holds back the best people and frustrates below-average people who cannot achieve them. While it is important to be able to predict production rates and sales, these metrics themselves should not become the primary objectives of either the organization or its management. Again, we should not sublimate objectives to objectives measures. The proper role for systematic measurements is very important in this context, as discussed in some detail in Chapters 4 and 5.

12. *Remove Barriers to Pride of Workmanship.* Job performance should be evaluated and rewarded in terms of the work quality and productivity of the individual, not through an organizationally mandated, inspection-oriented, rating form. People will take pride in and be motivated by individual judgments of their workmanship. Similar results do not occur through use of rating forms. Deming's view is that performance appraisal, particularly when accompanied by inflexibility and inappropriate metrics, is the number one problem facing American management today. Essentially, it is a reactive inspection-oriented approach to people.

13. *Institute Education and Self-improvement.* Broadly based, not just specifically job-related, education and other self-improvement efforts are important for everyone in the organization. The organization can encourage education with reimbursement incentives. Much more important, however, is top management's personal commitment to and establishment of educational objectives.

14. *Put Everybody to Work.* The quest to achieve each of Deming's 14 prescriptions is likely to require a major transformation of the organization. This effort will be substantially facilitated by obtaining a consensus throughout the organization and involving everyone in the effort.

Deming's 14 points seem quite simple and straightforward, but they are not necessarily easy to implement. It would be easy to create chaos through the inept application of these principles. Generally, all of them must be implemented and it is a mistake to believe that one can select a favorite one, implement only it, and hope to obtain significant improvement. Thus the approach to implementation of TQM— or any related approach to strategic quality assurance and management—is a critical issue.

Figure 6.5 illustrated these 14 points, clustered about the three major need ingredients in strategic quality management for operational product quality:

- Developing organizational leadership, *management*, and culture
- Empowering *people*
- Developing responsive organizational systems and *processes*

It is interesting to note that only prescriptions 3, 4, and 5 relate specifically to quality improvement and explicitly include statistical quality control. The others are much less operationally and product focused. They relate more to the philosophy of management, the organizational systems, and developing human resources. This same sort of identification follows for the prescriptions of other leaders in TQM.

6.3 MAJOR PERSPECTIVES ON TOTAL OR STRATEGIC QUALITY

There has been a major focus on quality in the United States and throughout the world in recent times. Doubtlessly, much of this has been due to the Japanese success in fielding very high quality products and systems. It appears that the major quality award in Japan is the Deming Prize, established by the Japanese Union of Scientists and Engineers (JUSE) in 1951.

There are three award categories for the Deming Prize.

The *Deming Prize for an Individual Person* is awarded to one who has excellent accomplishments in the theory, application, or dissemination of statistical quality control.

The *Deming Application Prize* is given to individuals in public or private sector enterprises who achieve distinctive improvements in organizational performance based on statistical quality control.

The *Deming Application Prize to Overseas Companies* is much the same as the application prize, which is restricted to Japanese companies.

There are ten attribute areas for evaluation, based on excellence in quality, as defined by this prize.

1. Planning and policy for management quality.
2. Organizational management for quality.
3. Quality control education and dissemination.
4. Collection and utilization of information on quality.

5. Analysis of critical quality issues.
6. Establishment and use of appropriate standards.
7. Control, as determined by establishment, review, and revision of standards.
8. Quality assurance and reliability.
9. Effects of the implementation of quality controls.
10. Future plans for continual quality improvement.

Each attribute places considerable emphasis on results achieved in application of quality approaches. Companies who succeed at winning a Deming Application Prize are eligible to compete for the Nippon Prize.

Within the United States, the Malcolm Baldrige National Quality Award was established by act of Congress in 1987. The purposes of the award are to promote quality awareness and to recognize quality achievements. Some ancillary purposes are to help elevate quality standards and expectations, to facilitate wide scope communication of key quality requirements, and to serve as a working tool for planning and assessment. Manufacturing companies, service companies, and small businesses may apply in one of the three corresponding categories in which up to two awards are given each year. The seven major categories for the Malcolm Baldrige National Quality Award and their point values are:

Leadership (100)

Information and analysis (80)

Strategic quality planning (60)

Human resource utilization (150)

Management of process quality (140)

Quality results (180)

Customer satisfaction (300)

These attributes are each further described in terms of a relatively large number of attributes that, taken together, more fully describe these seven higher level attributes. Figure 6.9 illustrates the causal relations among these seven attributes. Figure 6.10 illustrates the 32 detailed attributes that comprise the Malcolm Baldrige Award criteria. Although seven top level criteria have been used since the award first originated, the weights of these attributes have changed slightly. The number, names, and weights of the lower level attributes have also changed somewhat, generally to reflect an increased focus on process and appropriate information and analysis.

The award criteria, or attributes, are based on ten precepts:

1. *Customer-driven quality,* in which the customer is the final judge of quality, is a strategic concept that must be addressed in all quality processes.
2. *Leadership* in achieving excellence, including substantial personal commitment and involvement, must be an essential part of a quality strategy.

Figure 6.9 Some causal influences among the Malcolm Baldrige National Quality Award attributes.

1.0 Leadership	100
1.1 Senior Executive Leadership	45
1.2 Quality Values	10
1.3 Management for Quality	25
1.4 Public Responsibility	20
2.0 Information and Analysis	**80**
2.1 Scope and Management of Quality Data and Information	15
2.2 Competitive Comparisons and Benchmarks	25
2.3 Analysis of Quality Data and Information	40
3.0 Strategic Quality Planning	**60**
3.1 Strategic Quality Planning Process	35
3.2 Quality and Performance Plans	25
4.0 Human Resource Utilization	**150**
4.1 Human Resource Management	20
4.2 Employee Involvement	40
4.3 Quality Education and Training	40
4.4 Employee Recognition and Performance Measurement	25
4.5 Employee Well-Being and Morale	25

5.0 Management of Process Quality	140
5.1 Design and Introduction of Quality Products and Services	40
5.2 Process Management - Product Production and Delivery	35
5.3 Process Management - Support Services	30
5.4 Supplier Quality	20
5.5 Quality Assessment	15
6.0 Quality Results	**180**
6.1 Product and Service Quality	75
6.2 Business Operational Results	45
6.3 Business Process Results	25
6.3 Supplier Quality Results	35
7.0 Customer Satisfaction	**300**
7.1 Customer Relationship Management	65
7.2 Commitment to Customers	15
7.3 Determining Customer Satisfaction	35
7.4 Customer Satisfaction Results	75
7.5 Customer Satisfaction Comparison	75
7.6 Determination of Future Requirements and Expectations	35

Figure 6.10 One breakdown of the Malcolm Baldrige National Quality Award performance attribute weights.

3. *Continuous improvement* in quality is the way to achieve the highest quality levels. This includes value enhancement for the customer, reducing errors and waste, improving product delivery responsiveness, and improving effectiveness in everything. Systematic measurements are viewed as the basis for assessing progress and obtaining information to enable future improvement.

4. The workforce must be completely committed and this must result in *full participation* in quality efforts. This requires education and training and attention to health and safety on the job.

5. Market success is dependent on *fast response*. Response time, quality, and productive objectives simultaneously support one another.

6. *Design quality and problem prevention,* and other efforts during the early lifecycle phases, must be major objectives.

7. A *long-range perspective* is needed, including regular reviews and assessment of progress, as progress relates to long-range plans and perspectives.

8. *Management by fact* and reliable information, generally obtained through systematic measurements and performance indicators, used to support analysis and decision making, should provide a basis for action and customer satisfaction.

9. *Partnership development,* on both a long- and short-term basis as well as the development of internal and external partnerships, should serve organizational interests in efficiency and effectiveness.

10. *Public responsibility,* including ethics and safety, is also an area for continuous improvement.

The scoring guidelines for the award include *approach* to each critical factor or success attribute, *deployment strategy* utilized in order to obtain high performance on each attribute, and *results* obtained.

Occasionally, the Malcolm Baldrige Award is criticized for being more oriented to activities than it is to results. On the other hand, it has been criticized for being too results focused. Inspection of Figures 6.9 and 6.10 does indicate that there is a focus both on process and product and on organizational leadership and people empowerment in the award criteria. Thus the criteria appear to have an appropriate focus on all four of these major ingredients necessary for quality. A sometimes stated ancillary view is that the award criteria are more appropriate for organizations at lower levels of quality process maturity, a subject we discuss in some depth in Chapters 7 and 8. To the extent that these criticisms are correct, the difficulty would appear to lie not with the objectives of the award but with the measures or metrics used to determine the extent to which the objectives are satisfied. Garvin [45] provides an excellent and extended discussion of the workings of this award, in theory and in practice.*

---

*Some of the later issues of this reference contain a number of interesting commentaries on the awards, as well as Garvin's paper. Further information concerning this award may be obtained from the National Institute of Standards and Technology, Gaithersburg, MD 20899.

In addition to these quality awards, there are now a European Quality Award (EQA), sponsored by the European Foundation for Quality Management and first presented in 1992, and an Australian Prize. Each of these attest to the contemporary importance of strategic quality management. The EQA, for example, is comprised of two major and equally weighted criteria and nine subcriteria. There are a total of 100 points in scoring performance of a given organization.

Enablers
    Leadership (10)
    People management (9)
    Policy and strategy (8)
    Resources (9)
    Processes (14)
Results
    Employee satisfaction (9)
    Customer satisfaction (20)
    Societal impact (6)
    Business results (15)

It would be of much interest to contrast and compare the Baldrige Award and the Deming Prize with one another, and perhaps with the Deming 14 point plan, the Juran prescriptions, and the Crosby prescriptions, as well as the strategies and prescriptions for excellence given by Peters. An appropriate framework for this comparison is the people–process–leadership taxonomy and the results that follow.

This suggests that a position such as *Chief Quality Officer (CQO)* might well become important in organizations that adopt the new quality management philosophy. This would be so *only* if the CQO works in such a manner that quality remains everyone's objective. Such a CQO would necessarily need a perspective that encompassed much more than classical mathematical statistics, however. The CQO would also be involved in strategic management and systems management efforts that include *detection* of problems with process and/or products, *diagnosis* of the root causes of the difficulties, and generation of alternative courses of control effort to effect a *correction* of the difficulties through improved quality and productivity. Important also is the *planning* effort necessary to evolve meaningful operational quality tactics. With the notion of quality remaining everyone's objective, each member of the organization is a quality-responsible person. In that sense, the office of the CQO would be a support office for organizational members. This CQO would be concerned with quality at the level of planned quality, realized quality, and perceived quality; as we have indicated in Figure 6.7. Above all, the CQO cannot be a quality czar. If there is a CQO and if the CQO is a czar, then it is very unlikely that quality will be everyone's business. Rather, it will be the business of the czar. We made similar comments about systematic measurement czars in Chapters 4 and 5.

Although our discussions here have been relatively extensive, there is no way that they could possibly discuss the wealth of approaches to quality that have been suggested. Most of these are variations on the several themes discussed here. Among the many recent works that discuss contemporary quality issues are those by Greene [46], Hunt [47,48], Ernst & Young [49], Barry [50], Weaver [51], Talley [52], Rosander [53], Dobyns and Crawford-Mason [54], Ross [55], Bogue and Saunders [56], Zeithaml, Parasuraman, and Berry [57], Kinlaw [58], Hoffherr, Moran, and Nadler [59], Rogers and Sergesketter [60], and Walton [61,62]. Of these, the works of Hunt and Walton are especially readable. The book by Green is, by some considerable measure, the largest of this set and perhaps the most provocative. While much of the early efforts in TQM relate to quality improvements in production industries, there has been much recent interest in quality improvements in services and in such third-sector efforts as higher education. There has also been considerable recent work concerning software quality. We address this in a forthcoming section.

6.4 GUIDELINES FOR IMPLEMENTATION OF A STRATEGIC QUALITY PROGRAM

Today, it is recognized that operational task level quality assurance programs are necessary, but not sufficient, to assure appropriate quality of products. The earlier approach of statistical inspections to discover product defects has evolved to systems management controls at the strategic level to assure quality throughout the lifecycle of a product. As we have noted, quality consciousness has now emerged at four levels:

1. *Inspections* to identify, and cull out, defective products (inspected quality).
2. *Statistical quality control* to provide cost-effective metrics on the performance of manufacturing technology (controlled quality).
3. *Operational task level quality assurance and management* through quality measurements and planning and design, to provide for operational controls that will ensure quality (built-in or manufactured product quality).
4. *Strategic quality assurance and management* to ensure market competitiveness through the involvement of all organizational elements involved in the process and product under consideration (proactively managed process quality).

Clearly, these concerns are not mutually exclusive. Inspections, for example, will surely be a part of strategic quality assurance and management. However, strategic management for quality assurance will not depend exclusively on inspections. Together, these four quality levels comprise what is now often called total quality management (TQM). The major improvements made possible through TQM come about because of attention at level 4, the process level. In our next chapter, we will describe process maturity and systems management models that incorporate these notions. Figure 6.11 presents a conceptual view of the role of organizational leader-

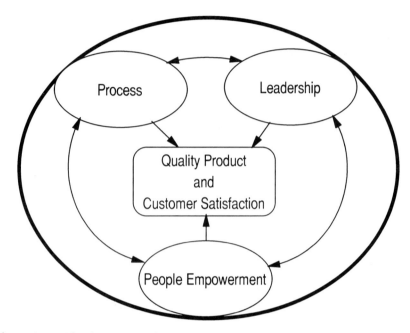

Figure 6.11   The three major drivers of product quality and customer satisfaction.

ship and culture, systems process management, and people empowerment as the dominant proactive influencers of quality products that lead to customer satisfaction. A natural and needed role exists for interactive and reactive quality controls but these, especially reactive inspections, are not the major drivers of total quality.

In the final analysis, it is the end user or customer or client who ultimately, even if indirectly, sets the standards for quality. This is especially so as the fundamental determinants of quality relate to final use. Thus it is very important to understand customer requirements. We also express strongly that results are what are desired. Activities are only the means to the end and not the end in themselves. Thus the focus on quality should necessarily be on results [63] as, without results, plans and activities are more show than substance. In effect, they sublimate the desire for rain to a desire for a rain dance that may not even be associated with producing rain. In more precise systems engineering terminology, they confuse objectives with objectives measures and promote attainment of the latter as if they guarantee the former. When the objectives measures are additionally not fully characteristic of the objectives, and when achievement of them is promoted, truly significant difficulties may ensue. But it must continually be remembered that the drivers for the results are leadership, process, and people empowerment. To only and exclusively focus on results, while ignoring the three major drivers of quality, is very likely to be quite counterproductive. This exclusive focus on results is, in effect, a reactive approach.

A primary means of pursuing strategic quality assurance and management is through TQM, which we may define as *a total and integrated management control*

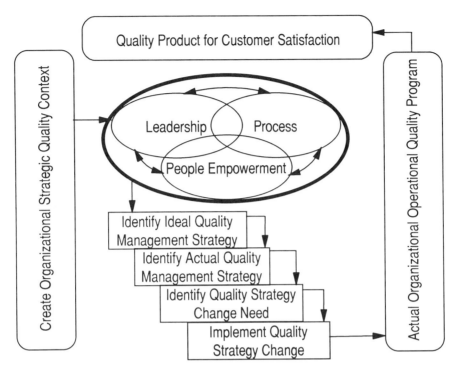

Figure 6.12 Influencers on operational quality.

process that specifically addresses all aspects of system and product quality during all phases of the lifecycle. Thus TQM is focused on both technological and management system design. It is concerned with the lifecycles of research, development, test and evaluation (RDT&E); system manufacturing, production, or acquisition; and systems planning and marketing. It is very concerned with the functional capability, quality, and trustworthiness of the products of these efforts in meeting customer needs. It is much concerned also with an extended lifecycle that encompasses maintenance to ensure that the product or service is continually useful. Total customer satisfaction is a major objective of TQM, as compared with the often-used approach of fielding the least expensive design that conforms to minimum customer requirements.

Figure 6.12 provides an overall picture of the implementation of a TQM concept. There are, of course, a number of variations on the specific steps shown in this illustration that might be incorporated into the general TQM picture. We see a number of common features among many of the strategic quality assurances and management approaches. The critical focus is invariably on improvements through management processes and through such affiliated notions as understanding customer requirements and empowering all in the search for continued improvement in quality through leadership, process, and people empowerment.

Virtually all strategic quality efforts suggest several major interrelated efforts that comprise a systems approach to quality enhancement. These might be posed as follows:

- Exercise administration, management, leadership, and governance in a professional setting that emphasizes equity and explicability.
- Empower people.
- Know and understand customers, consumers, and clients for the organization.
- Know and understand the internal and external environment of the organization, including the capabilities and likely strategy of competitors.
- Concentrate on continuously improving processes or product lines.
- Identify appropriate process and product metrics for quality assurance measurements.
- Identify the right things to do.
- Then, and only then, do the right things right.
- Then, and only then, do these things efficiently and effectively.

There are many challenges here, of course. It is necessary for the organization to adopt a strategic quality management focus itself with respect to all of its efforts, from the top down as well as from the bottom up. This organizational leadership will result in high quality products that customers sincerely want to have in preference to all others. Figure 6.13 illustrates, conceptually, a somewhat more complete process model of the steps that might be used to implement strategic management for total quality. The net result of these is risk management and delivery of a high quality product that the customer or end user recognizes as a functionally remarkable and trustworthy item.

Many have suggested implementation strategies such as these. For example, Barry [50] suggests a set of 14 phased activities for a process to support implementation of a TQM strategy.

1. Identify the present management and measurement system, including the extent to which it is customer driven and supplier driven.
2. Assess the structural and cultural facets of the organization, including its quality culture.
3. Identify the top management commitment to TQM.
4. Create a strategic organizational vision and philosophy that is supportive of TQM.
5. Identify an appropriate TQM strategy for the organization under consideration.
6. Identify a management control structure to implement the TQM strategy.
7. Identify education and training needs to accomplish the implementation.
8. Identify resource needs for implementation of the TQM strategy.
9. Select suppliers of this education and training program.

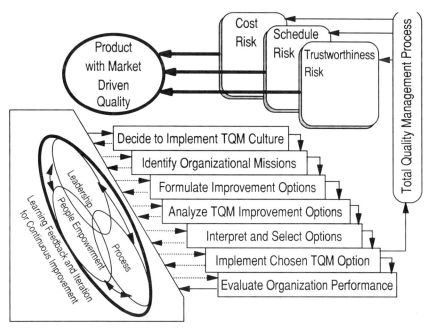

Figure 6.13 A more complete representation of TQM process implementation.

10. Identify quality standards and metrics, in order to ensure continuous quality improvement and efficiency and effectiveness of the process-driven adaptation to TQM.
11. Institutionalize TQM such that it becomes a part of the organization's culture and normal mode of doing business.
12. Monitor and evaluate the results of the TQM implementation.
13. Proactively adapt the specific TQM process to the organization in question on the basis of actual operating experience with TQM.
14. Continue the improvement through TQM.

These might represent specific activity steps to be incorporated into the appropriate portions of Figure 6.13 in order to provide an overall picture of the implementation of a TQM concept. There are, of course, a number of variations on these specific steps that might be described and a number of case stories of its implementation [62].

We note that these descriptions involve all the systems engineering efforts discussed here and in our previous works [31,64,65]. What is not shown fully in Figures 6.12 and 6.13, however, is the very significant impact of cultural variables that need to be strongly considered in efforts of this sort. We will discuss this subject in much of the remainder of this book, especially in Chapters 7 and 8. Of particular interest will be a possible lifecycle model of organizational growth, maturity, decay,

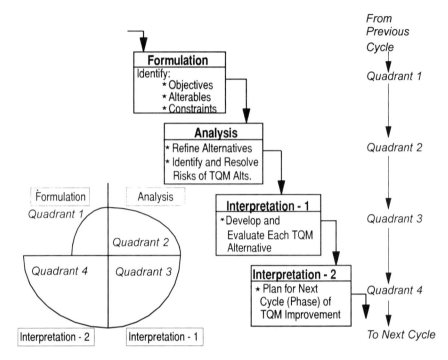

Figure 6.14 Generic spiral for selection of TQM process.

and rebirth that can be materially influenced in large part through the organization's quality culture. Not only is this a dynamic evolutionary process, but the state of the organization in each of the resulting phases of evolution can be very significantly altered by the nature of the controls that are applied to the system.

There are many ways in which we could illustrate a generic TQM implementation process. In addition to that illustrated in Figures 6.12 and 6.13, we could accomplish an evolutionary or spiral-like lifecycle to identify the most appropriate TQM process for a given organization. Figure 6.14 illustrates the generic concept. It is based on our discussions in Chapter 2 and is a synopsis of Figures 2.37 through 2.40. We see here that we can speak about the process of generating, evaluating, and selecting process options in much the same way as we can the process of producing a product itself. The formulation, analysis, and interpretation steps are seen at each of the cycles of the spiral. One of the major uses of the spiral, or evolutionary, lifecycle is to allow for more explicit consideration of risk and the development of an appropriate risk management strategy. There are, of course, risks that need to be managed in implementation of a TQM process. In the first cycle of the spiral process we would accomplish the following:

1. We formulate the TQM issue in terms of the organizational mission and environment and identify needs, constraints, and alterables. Then we would generate a number of possible TQM implementation alternatives.

2. We refine and analyze each of these alternative TQM plans. This includes identifying the impacts and risks of each of these plans on the needs and objectives of the organization.

3. In the third step or third quadrant of the cycle, we accomplish the first part of the interpretation effort. This involves the evaluation of each TQM option and interpretation of these in terms of organizational values, including costs and benefits, such as to enable selection of TQM implementation tactics.

4. In the fourth quadrant, we evaluate the actual functional efficacy of the selected option and plan for the next stage of continuous improvement.

As part of the interpretation-2 effort, illustrated in Figure 6.14, we obtain a commitment to proceed with continuous improvement. Of course, a commitment to initiate the first cycle was necessary also. Generally, it would be anticipated that this would be easier to obtain for the second cycle, especially if the results from the first cycle were beneficial. As suggested by Figures 6.12 and 6.13, there should be organizational learning that occurs as the process evolves. The effort required to obtain commitment varies across organizations. Generally, however, there are several stages of commitment that are possible, and we might imagine a hypothetical commitment thermometer such as illustrated in Figure 6.15. One of the major ingredients in this notion of commitment is that personal commitment and involve-

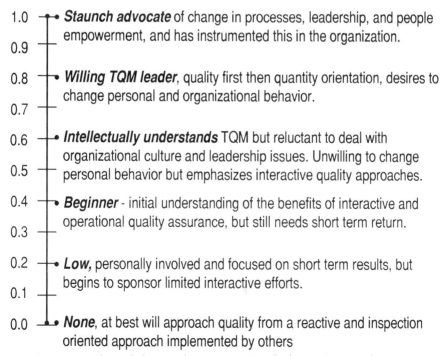

Figure 6.15 Hypothetical degree of commitment scale for strategic quality management.

Figure 6.16 Baldrige Award scores for no quality commitment.

ment are needed. This is rarely accomplished by delegating full authority and responsibility to another person or group, such as a TQM group. Personal leadership and commitment are very needed if the effort is to be a sustaining one. This ideally improves over time as strategic quality efforts become endogenous to the organization. We might imagine that scoring on each of the seven Baldrige Award criteria might proceed as indicated in Figures 6.16 through 6.18 as commitment increases over time together with associated efforts at leadership and the development of people resources and processes. The progress to be made is uneven but continuous over time. It should endure with continued attention to strategic quality. Of course, the productivity, cost–effectiveness, and profitability of the organization should increase as well.

The organizational context has now become somewhat modified as a result of the first cycle of TQM implementation efforts. The relevant TQM issue formulation variables are, in effect, updated and we proceed through a second cycle. The process continues. As a by-product of this effort, the TQM process maturity of the organization increases. We devote much of our next two chapters to a discussion of this topic.

We can interpret risk and risk management in a number of ways. Risk is inherently related to quality, broadly defined. Risk is also associated with organizational transgressions, and it is of value to discuss risk and quality from this perspective. In a recent and thought-provoking article, seven deadly corporate sins are recited by Pearson [66]. These might be expressed as follows:

1. Product quality is inconsistent.
2. There is a slow response to marketplace needs for change.

Figure 6.17   Baldrige Award scores for beginning quality commitment.

3. There is a lack of innovative and responsive organizational programs and the leadership to assure these.
4. There is a high cost structure that is beyond society's willingness to support.
5. There is inadequate employment involvement and participation in relevant facets of the organization.

Figure 6.18   Baldrige Award scores for advanced beginner relative to quality commitment.

6. There is unresponsive service to the customers of the organization.
7. There is inefficient and ineffective resource allocation, often due to allocations made from opportunistic-political, rather than professional and innovation-oriented, perspectives.

Many of these difficulties may easily be believed to be management induced. But it must also be recalled that there are major external influences that frame the organizational culture and leadership patterns in an organization, including government policy.

Pearson also describes six concepts that are claimed to be capable of transforming the corporate work environment into a productive one, primarily by eliminating a highly bureaucratic and politicized work environment. These may be described as follows:

1. Recognize what the organization and the specific units that comprise it stand for and what its purposes are that are distinguished and competitively significant.
2. Establish high aspirations and performance standards, at both a personal and an organizational level, enforce them, and elevate them continuously over time.
3. Adopt and subscribe to organizing concepts that stimulate continuous improvement and demonstrable results in productivity and quality. This is especially to be contrasted with efforts that reward promised activity rather than demonstrated results, efforts that do not focus on lifecycle processes but only on products and results, efforts that confuse objectives measures with objectives, and efforts that accept advertising and promotion as equivalent to and potentially more important than marketing and planning.
4. Enable organizational management to become personally involved in all substantive areas of effort in the organization and not just in the administrative function alone, such that managers are able to approach management functions as knowledgeable professionals *and* as managers.
5. Secure and encourage the appropriate talent for a progressive, productive, and high quality organization.
6. Establish and adhere to a culture and a reward system, and associated processes and beliefs, that emphasize quality performance and integration of all facets of the organization.

These do indeed appear to be reasonable leadership and management objectives. They appear to also provide much support for related TQM objectives, especially management quality.

We will conclude here with a discussion of the implications of strategic level process management and total quality management on the cost and operational effectiveness of the resulting operational products. The following process efforts are suggested as positive influencers of quality and effective products. These are based on Deming's 14 points.

1. The current preoccupation with product and current outcome must be abandoned and replaced by process improvement objectives, and objectives that relate to leadership and people empowerment.

2. The notion of reactive inspections to identify defective products should be sublimated to efforts that involve defect deterrent strategies, in an interactive manner, throughout the lifecycle to enable timely correction to potential difficulties, before they materialize, and proactive process improvements that enhance product quality and trustworthiness.

3. Employees, and human resources in general, are an organization's most valuable resource. When they perform poorly, much if not most of the blame must be shared by management for failure to provide the leadership, people empowerment, and processes that ward against errant individual behavior.

4. Quality of product is the major product consideration. It leads directly to market share, sales volume, and profits. Quality of product results from quality of process.

5. Continuous process improvement for the purpose of maximum customer satisfaction is the most important process consideration.

6. Flexible relative standards that call for proactive and interactive improvements are invaluable in supporting excellence in all critical processes and the resultant products.

7. Management must lead through example, through education, through long-range strategic planning, through understanding the essential statistical variability of key processes, and through the pursuit of venturesome and well thought out breakthroughs that lead to major increases in quality, competitive advantage, market share, and profitability.

8. Employees must be motivated to improve work processes and work product as if they were partners in the enterprise.

9. Organizational plans should be theories of action in practice documents that enable everyone in the enterprise to understand what they must do in order to support the organization in pursuit of strategic objectives.

10. Education is a long-term investment leading to increased market share and profitability of the enterprise. It is an investment and not an expense. All employees should receive generous directed educational support to enhance quality and productivity.

11. Selection of product suppliers based on initial price alone must be abandoned and replaced with selection based on total lifecycle cost–effectiveness maximization and long-term organizational success.

12. Reward systems that strongly encourage teamwork and group effort must be encouraged and traditional reward systems must be reoriented to reflect

individual contributions that are within the framework and supportive of overall unit performance.

13. Organizational structures must be redesigned to support cross-functionality and to enhance rapid communications and decision making through efficient and effective reporting structures. All managers are employees. All employees are managers.

14. Organizational processes, policies, and procedures are not only words; they are a strategy for thinking, culture, and people appraisal.

There are many more relations, at a variety of levels, that can be stated. Organizational quality maturity is important and is discussed in our next chapter. We could bring in notions of concurrent engineering, enterprise integration, benchmarks, breakpoints, reverse engineering, just-in-time manufacturing, integrated product teams, integrated product development, fast-cycle time, risk management, horizontal management, and other approaches that are discussed in Chapter 8 on systems reengineering.

We will now turn our attention to the new International Organization for Standardization (ISO) standard for quality, ISO 9000. Then we conclude our discussion in this chapter with an overview of some of the specific applications of TQM-like concepts to software systems engineering that have recently appeared.

6.5 INTERNATIONAL QUALITY STANDARDS

Standards are potentially very important for both strategic and operational level quality. In this section, we provide a brief introduction to standards. We focus, in particular, on recent international quality standards promulgated by the International Organization for Standardization (ISO). Before we formally discuss these standards, it is desirable to briefly comment on the organization of the ISO and related bodies.

6.5.1 Very Brief History of Standards

There are many types of standards. In the most general sense, standards embody the behavioral norms and mores of a particular social group. Standards are metrics, often quantifiable, that a group agrees to adhere to in order to influence behavior. Standards may be of a process or of a product nature. Most standards are product standards. Standards may be of an implementation nature or they can be of a conceptual nature. A conceptual standard would influence all products of a generic class. When a standard is realized in a specific product, this represents an implementation standard.

Standards may be of a voluntary type on the part of the group espousing the standards, or they may be of a regulatory type, which are generally imposed. With voluntary standards, there may be no effective enforcement vehicle to ensure compliance. Regulatory standards that require adherence to a rigid standard may reduce vigor in dealing with changing conditions. There are, of course, trade-offs in choosing standards and, indeed, questions whether standards should be used at all in some instances.

We may also have personal or organizational internal standards, which are unique to a given individual or organization, and external standards, which are promulgated by industry or national or international organizations and which are intended to be adhered to by many, ideally all, organizations. In general, internal standards and voluntary standards are equivalent. Regulatory standards are normally equivalent to external standards.

An enlightened standard should have certain essential properties.

- A standard should be approved by relevant stakeholder groups and should express a consensus view of these stakeholders.
- A standard should be documented and widely available to relevant stakeholder groups.
- Standards should relate to processes as well as to product, thereby providing regulations for human action and intent, as well as providing minimum acceptable specifications for product or system attributes.
- There should be reasons supporting every standard, or component of it, and these should be explicated in such a fashion as to be understood and appreciated by those who are obligated to follow the standard.
- Illustrations of the benefits associated with following a standard, and the problems associated with not following it, should be provided.
- Standards should be kept up-to-date and abreast of contemporary technological and societal needs for them.
- Standards should be introduced to increase the common good and to encourage competition in the marketplace and should never be capable of being used as an instrument to bar potential competition from entering a market with an otherwise useful product or service.
- Standards should be applicable, complete, consistent, enforceable, modifiable, traceable, usable, unambiguous, and verifiable.
- Product standards should also support operations and maintenance of the product.
- Process standards should support the efficient and effective production of trustworthy and high quality systems and products.
- Standards that are unenforceable, and in particular those that represent an imposition of a solution as contrasted with resolving a potentially impending problem, should not be established.

A standard expresses a minimum acceptable requirement. Although most standards express minimum acceptable scores for a process or product on each of a number of attributes, standards may also allow for trade-offs among attribute scores. Closely related to the concept of a standard is that of a guideline. While standards are requirements, guidelines are simply suggestions for products and processes. The major difference between a guideline and a standard is that a guideline offers considerably greater flexibility and room for judgment.

There are a large number of systems engineering-related standards and guidelines that have been promulgated by the many groups having interests in this area. An excellent and very readable discussion of standards, from both a general technology and information technology perspective, is available in [67].

There are two primary types of standards organizations—formal and informal. The formal standardization bodies are responsible for the definition and promulgation of defined public standards. They are comprised of national and international standardization groups, professional organizations, and trade associations. These public standards are generally called formal or accredited standards.

Informal or industry standards are created by the informal standards bodies. The purpose of these is to assist in the implementation of formal standards. As initially formulated, these informal standards are perhaps better called specifications. An informal standard or specification is generally intended for submission to a formal standards group for subsequent approval, perhaps after modification, as a recognized formal standard.

Most countries in the world have their own standards organizations. In the United States, standards, including systems engineering standards, are established by the American National Standards Institute (ANSI), the Institute of Electrical and Electronics Engineers (IEEE), the American Society of Mechanical Engineers (ASME), the National Institute for Measurements and Standards (NIMS), the Electric Industries Association (EIA), the Human Factors Society (HFS), the American Society for Quality Control (ASQC), the Department of Defense (DoD), and others.

The National Institute of Standards and Technology (NIST), formerly known as the National Bureau of Standards (NBS), is the major U.S. government organization involved in standardization. The NIST provides a national standards laboratory and is also specifically charged to assist university, government, and private sector industry in technology transfer and in maintaining technological competitiveness. One of the functions of NIST is that of providing oversight and administration of the Malcolm Baldrige National Quality Award.

The ANSI is a coordinating body for standards activities in the United States. Five U.S. engineering societies have joined to create the American Engineering Standards Committee (AESC) and to support ANSI. ANSI does not create standards. Rather, it manages and coordinates private sector standards activities. Under the leadership of ANSI, three types of organization can create a standard. These are the Accredited Sponsor, the Accredited Organization, and the Accredited Standards Committee. Each attempts, in somewhat different ways, to obtain openness, equity, and effectiveness in the standards it promotes and the way it promotes those standards.

Under the Accredited Sponsor (AS) approach, an approved or accredited organization may invite comments on a proposed standard. When deliberations have been concluded with due process, the resulting standard is submitted to ANSI for publication as a standard. In this approach, a group of stakeholders reach consensus on a standard to which they will adhere. The programming language standard Ada was developed in this manner. When there is substantial stakeholder disagreement, this approach will often have difficulties.

Under the Accredited Organization (AO) approach, a standard is established by a group of experts in the subject area. Usually, professional societies and trade groups take this approach to the creation of a standard. They notify ANSI of their intent and agree to abide by the consensus decision. The resulting standards are known as American National Standards (ANS). Challenges to this approach usually concern whether the group possesses the necessary expertise or whether the group is truly representative of the various stakeholder groups.

Under the American Standards Committee (ASC) approach, an ad hoc committee is formed to develop a standard. A secretariat is formed to provide legal, management, and economic support for the undertaking and to maintain administrative contact with ANSI. The ASC controls its own agenda and usually operates through a number of subcommittees, publishing iterative versions of a standard until a consensus is finally accepted. This approach is most often used when the issues are highly contentious.

ANSI encourages these groups to formulate standards and to submit them to ANSI for approval as ANS. While standards other than ANS may appear, the lack of endorsement by the ANSI will generally preclude widespread acceptance in the United States.

In order to have the highest stature, a standard should be agreed to and accepted by international standards bodies. There are a number of international standards groups. These include the International Organization for Standardization (ISO), the International Electrotechnical Commission (IEC), and the International Telecommunication Union (ITU). The ISO is a federation of standards groups of participating nations and is concerned with standards in all technological areas except electrical and electronics engineering and telecommunication systems. It does, however, include software. The purposes of ISO are to facilitate international exchanges of products and services and to encourage cooperation in economic, technical, scientific, and other endeavors. It is the foremost standards body in the world today and is comprised of 73 countries as members. ANSI and other national standards groups have membership in the ISO. The membership of international standards bodies is generally comprised of countries, professional organizations, and trade associations.

The ISO was established in 1947 and is comprised of about 2400 groups, including 200 technical committees, each of which represents some industry sector or product. Committee 176 is specifically concerned with quality management and quality assurance. The American Society for Quality Control (ASQC) is the U.S. professional society responsible for U.S. representation, through its administration of the U.S. Technical Advisory Group (TAG). The ISO Standard 9000 series, relating to quality assurance and management and to be discussed here, is a product of one of these committees. Many of the ISO standards have historical antecedents in a number of military standards. One of the ultimate hopes of some is that military standards will ultimately be replaced by ISO standards.

There are a plethora of regional standards groups such as the European Computer

Manufacturers Association (ECMA). Under the CCITT (Comité Consultatif International de Télégraphique et Téléphonique—International Telegraph and Telephone Consultative Committee) approach, the CCITT functions as a committee of the ITU. The CCITT is typically considered a peer with ISO. The CCITT, as a committee of the UN chartered ITU with treaty-status government representatives, typified perhaps by the United States when represented by the State Department, is the formal peer of the ISO, which is not governmental at all. It is a strictly voluntary and nongovernmental membership effort.

Most developed nations have national standards groups that function in a similar manner to those in the United States. These include the Association Francaise de Normalization (AFNOR), which is a French national standards body. The secretariat of many of the ISO committees is, by design, from the AFNOR. The British Standards Institute (BSI) has similar responsibilities for the United Kingdom. Deutsches Institut für Normung (DIN) is the German national standards body. The Japanese Industrial Standards Committee (JISC) develops and promulgates Japanese standards and also represents Japan on the ISO and IEC.

We can classify standards and pseudo-standards in several categories.

1. *Codes of practice and guidelines* indicate desirable good professional practice for which precise conformance is not mandated. *Standard specifications* are precise and conformance evaluation may be conducted using appropriate metrics.

2. *Product standards* are specifications that must be adhered to by each individual item produced, regardless of the way in which it was produced. *Process standards* are specifications that must be adhered to in determining conformance of a given product line. While the end user may only be concerned with product standards, a producing organization must be concerned with process standards as the approach to fielding effective and efficient products.

3. *Retrospective standards* are standards established after a technology has matured, at least to some considerable extent. This may require much retrofit, on behalf of early producers of a technology, to conform to a retrospective standard.

4. *Prospective standards* are established in advance of a technology's full emergence. The potential difficulty here is that early standards establishment may result in immature standards that need to be changed dramatically as experience with the technology accumulates. The open systems architecture and open systems integration (OSI) standards are one example of prospective standards [68–70].

5. *Functional standards* are generally groups of related standards that, together, are intended to serve some user need for a given functionality. The standards in OSI are also functional standards.

6. *Structural standards* specify the physical layout or detailed architecture of a product. A simple example of such standards are the Underwriters Laboratory (UL) standards for electrical wiring and interconnections.

It is possible to distinguish other types. We have previously referred to formal and informal standards, for example. We could also speak of reference model or framework standards, which indicate the process by which other related standards will be formulated. This would need to be contrasted with actual standards. Just as a process represents a framework or product line for producing a product, so does a model reference standard serve as a meta-standard for the construction of a standard.

Although there are certainly other standards that relate to quality, the ISO 9000 series standards are the most comprehensive quality assurance and management standards that have emerged to date. These are both process and product standards. We now turn to a description of these very important international standards.

6.5.2 ISO Quality Standards

The ISO has developed, and is in the process of developing, a number of 9000 series standards that represent a series of quality management and assurance standards. These are intended to enable quality management systems, both internal and external, for products and services. The standards are intended to be industry independent and require interpretation for specific industries. There are, in many cases, specific standards that accomplish this tailoring. For example, ISO 9000-3 are quality management and quality assurance standards for software. They provide guidelines and standards for the application of standard ISO 9001 to development, deployment, and maintenance of software.

The numbering convention used in the ISO series is such that a higher numbered standard is generally included in that of a lower numbered standard in the same series. Figure 6.19 illustrates the central features of this numbering convention for the ISO 9000 series standards. There is also a ISO 8402 document that is devoted to quality management and quality assurance vocabulary. This document, for example, says that "quality is the totality of features and characteristics of a product or service that bears on its ability to satisfy stated or implied needs. A Quality Management System (QMS) is comprised of the organizational structure, responsibilities, procedures, activities, and resources that ensure quality." It also states that "TQM is a management approach to an organization which is centered on quality and based on participation of all the members who aim for long term success through the customer satisfaction and benefits to the members of the organization and all of society."

The purpose of each of the ISO 9000 standards is suggested in Figure 6.19 and is as follows:

- ISO 9004 is really more of a document of guidelines than standards. The term "should" is used rather than the word "shall," which is used in the other ISO 9000 series standards. It relates specifically to system elements rather than lifecycle process elements. There will be a migration of some of the guidelines in ISO 9004 into one of the ISO standards. For example, a quality plan is not specified as part of the specifications but is included as part of the ISO 9004 guidelines. In all likelihood, this will become a part of the standards in future versions.

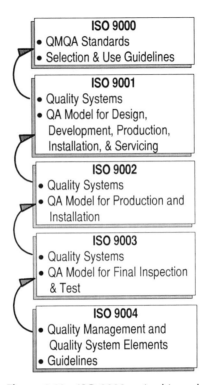

Figure 6.19 ISO 9000 series hierarchy.

- ISO 9003 represents the standards for final inspection and test. These standards might only be sufficient for an organization whose effort does not involve RDT&E or production but only the supply of already available products. The vendor of software products represents an example of a commodity supplier that might need to become familiar with this standard.
- ISO 9002 deals explicitly with production and installation of products and systems. The focus here is on system acquisition type efforts for products that are not new and that do not involve RDT&E.
- ISO 9001 is for use by organizations that need to be engaged in RDT&E, new product planning and marketing, and any other efforts needed for a new and emerging technology to achieve actual functional use in a quality conscious manner. While it encompasses system definition through deployment (and disposal), it does not appear to encompass all of the definitional activities needed in the first generic phase of systems engineering lifecycles to identify user requirements and translate these over to technological specifications.
- ISO 9000 is an overview document that provides suggestions and guidelines for implementing the more detailed standards: ISO 9001, ISO 9002, and ISO 9003. A principal focus is on documentation standards.

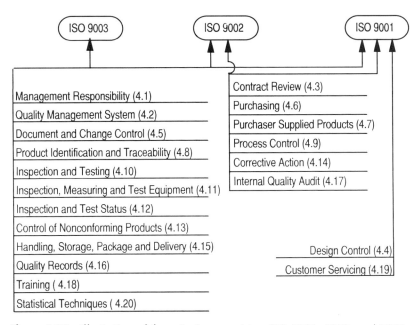

Figure 6.20 Illustration of the criteria comprising ISO 9001, 9002, and 9003.

Many of the major industrialized nations have translated and published, or republished, ISO standards in terminology and language more appropriate for internal use. These include a European version, a United Kingdom version, a United States version, a Japanese version, and a version for The Netherlands. In the United States, the ISO Standards 9000, 1, 2, 3, 4 have been published by ANSI and ASQC efforts and bear the numbers Q91, Q92, Q93, and Q94.

There are 12 quality system requirements in ISO 9003, 18 in ISO 9002, and 20 in ISO 9001. Figure 6.20 illustrates these requirements and their hierarchical relationships within the various standards. Also shown in this figure is the section number in which discussion of the standards and efforts at their compliance is to appear in a quality manual (QM), which is prepared by individual organizations. For organizations not seeking approval at the highest level, ISO 9001, certain sections of the quality manual may be omitted. In the most general case, where ISO 9001 is used, these 20 sections also define the 20 major requirements for a quality management system (QMS).

1. *Management responsibility* is a need. The organization is required to define and document management policy, objectives, and processes that indicate a commitment to quality. It must ensure that these policies are understood and implemented at all organizational levels, from the top down, and especially by those who verify and maintain quality assurance practices.

2. A *documented quality management system* must be established. This system

must address all quality facets and must document these in the form of a quality manual (QM) that identifies the QMS in force in the organization. Ideally, the QMS is accredited by an appropriate body recognized by the ISO, as we will discuss in Section 6.5.3.

3. A *contract review* procedure must be established to ensure that all contracts begin with a mutually agreed upon set of customer requirements for a system that will satisfy the system user. The procedure must also ensure that the system developer, or contractor, is capable of delivery of an acceptable product to the end user.

4. *Design control* must be established in order to ensure that the system developer utilizes the procedures identified in the contract review in order to verify and control the design quality of the system to be produced such as to ensure that it meets stated system requirements. These quality control procedures should cover the following: the requirements that are input to the design process; design outputs, to ensure customer satisfaction with the intended final product; design verification in terms of reviews that ensure compliance with customer requirements and government and industry standards; and design changes and modifications to accommodate potentially changing customer needs and requirements.

5. *Document control* and change control procedures must be established in order to ensure that configuration management information is made available to all appropriate people and at all appropriate organizational locations.

6. *Purchasing* plans must be addressed whenever it is desired to incorporate products of others as subunits in the final product. This must include assessment of potential subcontractor ability to meet quality and other performance standards. This must include assessment approaches to ensure that items procured from subcontractors satisfy stated requirements. It must also include proper records management for subcontractor-supplied items. This is especially important when third-party items are incorporated into a product.

7. Procedures must be established to specify, identify, verify, store, and maintain third-party products, or *purchaser supplied products,* when they are appropriate for inclusion in an organization's final product.

8. *Product identification and tractability* needs must be addressed in order to ensure proper configuration management of an evolving system throughout the system acquisition lifecycle.

9. *Process control* procedures must be established in order to ensure a well planned and executed product line. This necessarily includes monitoring in terms of interactive systematic measurements throughout the lifecycle.

10. *Inspection and testing* are required throughout the lifecycle, from initially received materials and products, to in-production efforts, to efforts on the final product at the time of deployment. This includes appropriate record keeping.

11. *Inspection, measuring, and test equipment* must also be properly controlled

in terms of appropriateness to the tasks for which they are used and in terms of quality as well.

12. The *inspection and test status* of the evolving product or system must be identified throughout the lifecycle. For example, design specifications should indicate whether they have been subject to final review and approval, or whether they are initial draft specifications for the design. Conforming products that have been approved and released for the next phase of effort should be identified by the appropriate release authority.

13. *Control of nonconforming products* must be established to ensure that products which do not meet standards are identified such that they cannot be inadvertently used. An appropriate detection, diagnosis, and correction procedure is needed such that nonconforming products may be scrapped, reworked into conforming products, returned to their supplier, or otherwise disposed of appropriately.

14. *Corrective action* procedures must be established. It must be possible to do this at the reactive level of the product and at the interactive level of the process. In other words, faults must be removed from products, or they must be otherwise disposed of, and the process must be examined and potentially modified in order to prevent recurrence of the nonconformity. This may well require a considerable amount of formulation, analysis, and interpretation of the process itself in order to prioritize remediation efforts in order to make the most cost-effective improvements in the process.

15. *Handling, storage, packaging, and delivery* procedures must be established such that there is an audit trail of the evolving product from its initial conception through deployment.

16. *Quality records* must be prepared, kept, and maintained. These must be able to demonstrate that the requisite quality has been achieved and also that the QMS and associated processes are appropriate and that the QMS is used in practice.

17. *Internal quality audits* must be established, including independent party evaluations of products, processes, and the QMS. The findings of these audits must be reported to organizational management for corrective actions.

18. *Training,* including the identification of training needs, must be such as to enable people to perform their work with the highest standards of quality.

19. *Servicing of customers,* both internal and external, must be addressed. This must include identification of customer service responsibilities and record keeping.

20. *Statistical techniques,* where appropriate, must be established in order to verify the appropriateness and reliability of products, processes, and the QMS.

It is very clear that the ISO 9001 standards, or the ISO 9002 or ISO 9003 subsets thereof, are exhaustive. Following them will require much effort, but the effort should result in considerable productivity and quality dividends for an organization and its members.

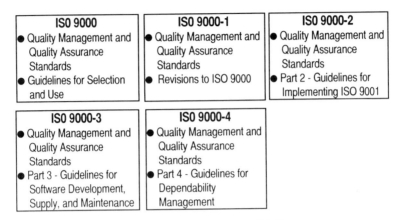

Figure 6.21 New ISO 9000 guidelines.

The ISO 9000 series of standards and guidelines is a living document. Figures 6.21 and 6.22 indicate some of the new standards and works in progress as modifications or extensions to ISO 9000 and 9004. We recall that ISO 9004 represents a set of guidelines that promulgate through all the other (ISO 9003, 9002, 9001, 9000) documents as suggested by Figures 6.18 and 6.19. First issued in 1987, the standards are subject to continued revision and refinement, by ISO Technical Committee 176 for which the ASQC is the U.S. national representative. The information here represents efforts current in December 1993, as the standards are reviewed and revised every 5 years and the latest revision was in 1992. The next revisions are due in 1997. An ultimate goal for the ISO 9000 series is stated in Vision 2000 [71]:

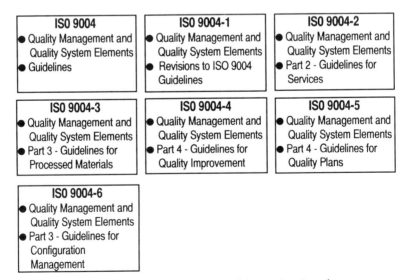

Figure 6.22 New ISO 9004 guidelines (*Continued*).

Universal acceptance, such that the standards will continue to meet wise scope customer needs in a useful and easy to use manner.

Current compatibility, such that all future documentation is consistent with and supportive of present documentation.

Forward compatibility, such that the necessary evolutionary revisions will not constraint efforts through the imposition of inappropriate requirements.

Forward flexibility, such that the revisions are broadly applicable and continually supportive of quality progress.

The ISO standards are formally voluntary and compliance with them is formally optional. But development may be such that they, in effect, become mandatory options for one who wishes to be competitive in an increasingly competitive world.

The significant level of interest in the ISO 9000 series standards is due primarily to marketplace considerations and, to a somewhat lesser extent, by government regulations. European purchasers often desire ISO registration of suppliers. Product safety and liability laws, especially in Europe, often place a burden on producers to furnish a documented set of quality assurance procedures. An ISO 9000 registered supplier will be better able to demonstrate that its products have no defects. We will examine issues of registration and audits in our next subsection.

There has also been a considerable move, primarily by government agencies, in the United States to utilize ISO 9000 standards. This includes efforts by the Food and Drug Administration (FDA), the Federal Aviation Administration (FAA), and the National Aeronautics and Space Administration (NASA). The Department of Defense plans to replace several military (MIL) quality system standards by ISO 9000, and contemplated changes in the Defense Federal Acquisition Regulations would allow use of ISO 9000 by contractors.

It is, we feel, important to issue a cautionary note here. Most of the ISO 9000 standards can be interpreted as objectives measures and not as objectives. If this is done, then it is entirely possible that a given organization may configure itself such as to achieve a "high score" on a formal evaluation of the QMS. This does not immediately guarantee that the ultimate product produced will be of high quality. This potential problem, of sublimating objectives with objectives measures, is ubiquitous across many areas of effort and not uniquely related to quality management. Of course, a goal should be to establish a sufficiently broad scope and scale for objectives measures or attributes, such that it becomes increasingly difficult for a high score on an evaluation or audit to be unindicative of high performance in achieving objectives. With this said, we turn to the subject of quality audits.

6.5.3 Assessments, Audits, and Conformance in ISO 9000

There are four actors involved in auditing efforts: the *auditee* or the organization being audited, the *auditor* or group that does the auditing, the *customers* of the organization or supplier, and the *client* for the audit. There may be overlap among these groups. When the client for the audit is the auditee, we have a first-party audit.

This is true regardless of whether the audit team consists of employees of the auditee, or whether they are contracted for this purpose by the auditee. When the auditor is hired by the customers of the organization, we have an external audit. When they are hired by another client group, such as a government or regulatory group, we have a third-party audit.

There are three types of assessment, audit, or verification that may be used to indicate conformance with standards in general and ISO 9000 in particular.

1. *First-party assessment* or *internal assessment* is comprised of an audit by the supplier or producer organization, conducted against the appropriate standard. This self-appraisal may result in a standard conformance certificate.

2. *Second-party assessment* or *external assessment* is an audit performed by the end user or customer as the client for an audit of the supplier organization.

3. *Third-party assessment* or *extrinsic assessment* is generally performed by an auditor who may be certified or otherwise formally qualified for this purpose, and who is not contracted for by either the organization (auditee) or its customers. Thus the auditor is independent of the auditee and its customers.

These assessments may lead to certification of a producer. Those who meet and surpass minimum standards are issued a certificate of registration or conformance. In some cases, this registration is associated with an indication of the score, or maturity level, of the supplier or producer. The third, extrinsic assessment, approach may also lead to registration if the audit is performed under controlled conditions and by an "accredited" auditor.

We have at least four types of verification and these can result in either certification or registration or both. There are two types of certification and they may be described as follows:

- A producer or other supplier organization may personally attest to and ensure the quality of the product. This is *self-certification*. Generally, it would be associated with internal or first-party assessment.
- The product may be inspected at the time of deployment to the customer. Usually, this validation is by the external customer as a second-party assessment or by an external third-party auditor who is independent of the supplier but who is contracted by the customers. This is *product certification*.

There are also two types of registration.

- *Product registration* is the purpose of the third form of verification. This results from an extrinsic product-only audit by an accredited inspector. Since only a single product, or potentially a group of products, is inspected, only that individual or group of products should be associated with registration. For this reason, product registration is generally neither feasible nor appropriate for many situations.

- *Quality system registration* or *process registration* is the purpose of the fourth form of verification. This is generally by means of a quality audit of the quality system of product line by an independent and accredited third party. Some sample of the products that result from the process are, almost invariable, also inspected. Quality system or process registration also implies product registration. Usually, this audit is repeated periodically in order to maintain registration or accreditation.

Accordingly, it has become common to speak of two levels for certification and the pertinent level for registration.

The ISO standards relate to extrinsic third-party audits and assessments. As we might imagine, third-party assessments or third-party verifications are becoming important in the provision of objective evidence that nonconformance to standards does not occur. First-party and second-party assessments may be unreliable and are very often based on reactive inspections of products. While an individual product may be of high quality, this may not represent an unbiased sample from the product line. This product certification is in no way an assurance of product line quality or of quality for a representative unbiased sample of products from the product line.

ISO 9003 calls for an accredited quality management system (QMS) and this promulgates through the other ISO standards, 9002 and 9001. In some way, this could be considered the most important of the 20 ISO criteria, with the management

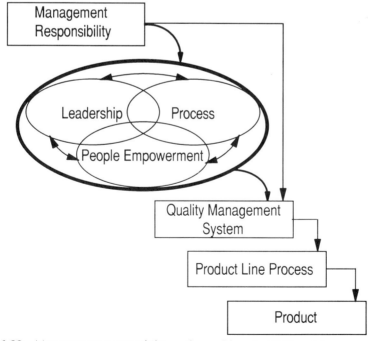

Figure 6.23 Management responsibility as the enabler of a QMS and the scope of ISO 9000.

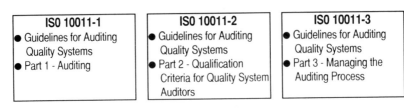

ISO 10011-1	ISO 10011-2	ISO 10011-3
• Guidelines for Auditing Quality Systems • Part 1 - Auditing	• Guidelines for Auditing Quality Systems • Part 2 - Qualification Criteria for Quality System Auditors	• Guidelines for Auditing Quality Systems • Part 3 - Managing the Auditing Process

Figure 6.24 Three new auditing guidelines.

responsibility criteria acting as drivers of an excellent QMS. Figure 6.23 illustrates this and shows the anticipated role of ISO 9000 at the several levels of the organization's quality effort as one mechanism for recognition, accreditation, and conformance of an organization and its products. Thus we see that the scope of ISO 9000 is indeed very broad.

Three guidelines currently exist, as suggested by Figure 6.24, that suggest desirable characteristics of ISO quality audits:

- ISO 10011-1 describes some fundamental auditing principles as they affect planning, conducting, and reporting the results of quality system audits. This general guideline can be applied to any process or product, after proper interpretation for a specific organizational product type.
- ISO 10011-2 suggests general guidelines for the efficient, effective, and equitable conduct of audits. It also describes qualifications for auditors in terms of education and experience.
- ISO 10011-3 suggests guidelines for the auditing process and management of an actual audit, including reporting and ethical conduct.

The purpose of an ISO quality audit is to evaluate the extent to which quality plans, processes, activities, and results are commensurate with those planned and whether these are implemented such as to achieve quality objectives. There are several objectives served by such a quality audit:

1. To evaluate the efficiency and effectiveness of an organization's quality system.
2. To identify quality documentation difficulties.
3. To detect, diagnose, and determine corrective actions for identified defects in the quality system.
4. To increase organizational understanding of quality issues.
5. To allow an organization to become registered as being in compliance with ISO 9000.
6. To meet regulatory agency requirements.
7. To determine conformance or nonconformance to a specific set of customer requirements such as to lead to appropriate certification levels for suppliers.

The last five of these relate to ultimate goals for auditing and the ISO 9000 series standards. Objectives 4 and 5 serve the organization itself. Objective 6 serves the public good. Objective 7 serves specific customers of the firm. But each of these latter four also serve to aid the organization in understanding quality issues, making continual improvements, and becoming registered as being in full and satisfactory compliance with ISO 9000.

We recognize, in these objectives, that there are three distinct groups served by an audit: (1) the *client* requesting, authorizing, or commissioning the audit; (2) the *customers* of the organization; and (3) the *auditee,* which is the organization that is being audited. In some cases, the client may also be the auditee. A fourth group is also involved, the *auditor,* as we have noted. Often, there will be an auditing group and one of these will be selected to be the lead auditor. In an extrinsic audit, the auditor is an independent party from the auditee and the client. In an internal audit, the auditor will be the auditee. In an external audit, the auditor is the client. There are many potential benefits to and objectives served by a quality audit. Those seven just identified are only the top level objectives. Hutchins [72] identifies many others in a recent work on quality auditing.

There are three phases associated with performance of an ISO audit and with auditing in general.

1. *Audit planning is accomplished in a pre-audit.* The audit must be planned such that the time of no one is wasted and such that normal operations of the organization are not disordered. The reason for efficiency is obvious. If the auditee's normal way of doing business is altered for the audit, what is measured may well not be reflective of the organization's normal quality effectiveness. The client for the audit normally defines the quality systems that are to be audited, but this will generally require support from the auditee. Both the auditee and the client should, at least ideally, have the same objectives in mind relative to this definition of scope of the audit. This definition of scope of the audit should lead to the development of plans for the audit. The auditee and the client must provide information about the organization and purpose for the audit in order that plans can be developed for an actual audit. These plans include the identification of desirable characteristics for the auditor(s), the duration of the audit, and the specific quality facets to be audited. A set of checklists outlining specific tasks to be accomplished during the actual audit should be prepared by the lead auditor.

2. *Audit implementation is the actual conduct of the audit.* The first task here is to determine the extent to which quality documentation, the quality manual for ISO audits, satisfies the important 20 auditee requirements for ISO 9001 audits, the 18 for ISO 9002, or the 12 for ISO 9003. After this, the audit team obtains and evaluates information to determine the extent to which these requirements are actually fulfilled in practice—as contrasted with the in-principle satisfaction that may be contained in the quality manual. One of the major objectives in evaluation of the QMS is to determine the extent to which there are internal, and perhaps external as well, auditing approaches that allow the organization to self-correct possible quality faults. This portion of the examination specifically relates to requirements 14 (cor-

rective action) and 17 (internal quality audits) of the ISO 9001 and ISO 9002 standards, and the several inspection and test standards of all three ISO standards. Of course, each of the 12, 18, or 20 requirements are examined to determine the extent to which they are satisfied. Usually, the audit begins with an initial startup meeting. The auditee provides overview information that indicates enthusiasm for the audit. Final arrangements and responsibilities are agreed to and audit responsibilities are established, including the responsibilities of the auditee and the auditor. After the actual audit, a closing meeting is generally held. At this meeting, the lead auditor presents a summary of the findings, including a tentative identification of potential deficiencies in meeting the standard. For first-party audits, recommendations for corrective action are generally presented at the conclusion of this closing meeting.

3. *A post-audit report is sent from the auditor to the client for the audit.* If the ISO requirements have not been met, the audit report provides a diagnosis of them. This is formally called a Corrective Action Report (CAR). This CAR identifies and discusses the defects in meeting the standard that were detected. It diagnoses them but does not prescribe how they may be corrected. The actual request for corrective action should come as a result of this phase. It comes to the auditee from the client for the audit or from the auditor depending on the purpose of the audit and whether a second-party or third-party audit has occurred. If the client is an external customer organization, the auditor informs the client of the diagnosis, and the client suggests corrective action to the auditee. If the client is a regulatory group, such that the audit is an extrinsic audit, the auditor generally informs the auditee of the diagnosis and suggestive corrective action.

A critical nonconformance with standards is said to exist when there are health or product safety failures. A major nonconformance exists when there are functional discrepancies with the ISO standards. Minor nonconformances are also reported to the auditee. Registration is withheld until a correction action plan is submitted and complied with. This may require a post-audit visit to the auditee or an entirely new audit. There are three stages to the registration effort: preregistration, registration, and postregistration. Preregistration efforts may lead to registration. After an organization is registered, it enters a postregistration phase, where it is necessary to maintain registration through renewed efforts that are not dissimilar to those described for registration.

There are many unresolved, and therefore extant, issues surrounding ISO registration. Concerns have been expressed that the ISO standards themselves are open to much subjective interpretation. Furthermore, the quality of the audit teams is sometimes open to suspicion. In general, the auditors cannot be experts relative to a specific organization and its environment, and corrective action suggested by auditors may be open to any of a number of questions. Nevertheless, despite the newness of the ISO process, there is evidence that it is gaining in acceptance, and rapidly. The advantages are relatively self-evident. It can serve as a TQM paradigm for an organization and can improve the competitiveness, especially in international markets, of the registered organization. Most importantly, it can assist the organization in the continued improvement over time so that the organization will be sought after for its products or services.

Within the United States, the Registrar Accreditation Board (RAB) [73,74] is a private accreditation and certification agency. The RAB is an affiliate of the American Society for Quality Control (ASQC). Together with the American National Standards Institute (ANSI), the RAB formed a joint accrediting venture in 1992. They have developed criteria that relate to certification of quality auditors for ISO standards compliance. RAB and ANSI have developed procedures that lead to certification of auditors for ISO 9000 quality system appraisals. They also approve registrars through their accreditation efforts. These registrars offer auditor training courses. It is also possible for a U.S. based firm to become a registrar by establishing a memorandum of understanding to this effect from an approved certification body in other countries. Much further information concerning ISO registration is available in [75] and [76]. Further information may be obtained directly from the various organizations involved in ISO standards.*

Product certification or registration generally involves inspection and test of products, often by an auditor that is responsible to a user or consumer group. The steps involved in process registration are generally more encompassing and almost invariably involve some form of product inspection as well. The auditing steps we have described here, which are applicable both for ISO registration and for such efforts as military certification, may be summarized as follows.

Preregistration

   (a) The organization develops an understanding of its environment and competition and determines that a quality product and formal registration of this are needed.

   (b) The organization becomes familiar with the relevant ISO or other standards to which conformance is desired.

   (c) The organization establishes a quality system that is intended to conform.

   (d) The organization prepares a quality manual that documents the quality management system.

   (e) The organization selects a team and develops plans for the accreditation visit.

   (f) The organization conducts a self-assessment, potentially with assistance from external consultants.

   (g) The organization revises the quality manual and management system on the basis of this self-assessment.

   (h) The organization requests a formal accreditation visit and selects a registrar.

Registration

   (a) The accreditation team visits the organization, generally for several days.

   (b) The accreditation team reviews the quality manual and the QMS.

   (c) The accreditation team evaluates appropriateness of the quality manual

*These include: ANSI, 11 West 42nd Street, New York, NY 10036; ASQC or RAB, 611 East Wisconsin Avenue, Milwaukee, WI 53201; and ISO, Rue de Varembe 1, CH-1211 Geneva 20, Switzerland.

and the extent to which the QMS, in practice, conforms with statements in the quality manual.

(d) The lead accreditor presents findings to the organization in a closing meeting.

(e) The corrective action request (CAR) is issued for nonconformances of a recurring, critical, or major nature relative to the standards.

(f) The organization or auditee identifies and takes corrective action.

(g) Registration occurs.

Postregistration

(a) Continuous improvements are maintained by the organization.

(b) Registration is maintained by this continuous attention to quality systems.

(c) The organization is reaudited to determine this continued conformance. This maintenance surveillance may occur as frequently as every 6 months for ISO 9000 accreditation.

When administered by proactive and future-oriented registrars and when standards are continually kept abreast of contemporary needs, the accreditation, registration, and certification process can be a very beneficial effort for an organization. Our discussions in the remainder of this text support this postulate.

6.6   QUALITY AND STANDARDS IN INFORMATION TECHNOLOGY AND SOFTWARE ENGINEERING

Quality is an interesting word. Everyone is for it and wants everything that they do, or have, to possess quality at a very high level. So it would be hard to get major disagreement with the thought that *quality* should necessarily be a primary driver of all information technology and software design and development processes. But quality is a very evasive expression. In practice, we note that it is often missing. Many of us might say that we know it when we see it, even though we cannot define it. There are many problems with this sort of attitude, especially when we cannot act entirely as individuals but must function as part of a group or team. If we cannot define quality, then we will doubtlessly have difficulties in communicating it or in assisting others to recognize it. In this section, we will explore some interpretations of quality in systems engineering, information technology, and software engineering.

Quality is a subjective term and a multiattributed one as well. DoD Standard 2168 on software quality [77] provides a very simple definition of quality: "Software quality is the degree to which the attributes of the software enable it to perform its specified end-item use." The IEEE Standard for Software Quality Assurance Plans [78] uses a similar definition for quality assurance: "Quality Assurance is a planned and systematic pattern of all actions necessary to provide adequate confidence that the item or product conforms to established technical requirements." For the most part, these are very reasonable definitions, but they are very definitely definitions of product quality and operational quality assurance to measure quality. Each contains the notion of a metric to indicate the *degree of quality* or degree of conformance to the requirements of the user or client. Neither, however, is as specific as might be desired relative to the need for quality assurance of the software requirements specifications themselves. The actual implementation of these standards, however, does require attention to lifecycle quality at the level of processes. We need appropriate metrics or indicators of software quality to be able to obtain an early warning indicator of potential difficulties and make appropriate design changes early in the software development lifecycle. Neither of them are directed, in any major way, to strategic systems management issues that affect quality. Thus reactive inspections and interactive lifecycle-based quality concerns are addressed, if not proactive, concerns.

Of course, quality assurance indicators should lead to the detection of errors, if any, and the diagnosis of errors, such as to identify them as coding errors or logic errors in programming and software development. Correction of coding, or logic, or specification errors is, however, an activity that should be performed by a very different group of people than those responsible for quality assurance. This is the major reason for not including code debugging as a part of quality assurance. It is simply a part of the coding and unit test phase in the system lifecycle.

Product level quality assurance can be conducted from either a structural, a functional, or a purposeful perspective. From a structural perspective, software would be tested in terms of microlevel details that involve programming language style, control, and coding particulars. From a functional perspective, software quality assurance and testing involve treating the software as a black box and determining whether the software performance conforms to the software technical requirements specifications. From a purposeful perspective, software must be tested to determine whether it does what the client really wishes it to do in terms of user requirements. This is generally known as *validation* testing.

These perspectives are surely not mutually exclusive, and each needs to be employed in a typical quality assurance effort, as shown in Figure 6.25, at the levels of systems management, process, and product. There are problems in implementing each of these, of course. At the level of systems management, we are concerned with strategic quality assurance and management. We are concerned with proactive establishment of systems management structure, function, and purpose such that the system evolvement process has minimal likelihood of bringing about quality problems. At the level of process, we are concerned with interactive lifecycle appropriateness in terms of correcting potential difficulties before they become real ones. At the level of product, we are concerned with inspection and test to enable detection, diagnosis, and correction of those faults that do occur.

It is generally not possible to accomplish complete structural, functional, or purposeful evaluation and test at either of these three levels. At the level of software product, complete functional testing will often, perhaps almost always, be impossible in practice because this would require subjecting the software to all possible inputs and verifying that the appropriate output is obtained from each of them. There will generally be insufficient time to allow this, and there will often be other

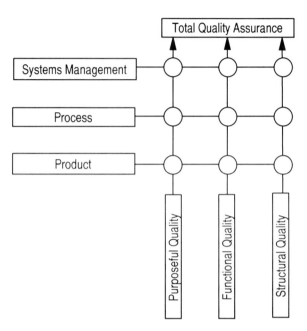

Figure 6.25   Needs for quality assurance at systems management, process, and product levels of systems engineering.

difficulties also. For instance, we will generally not have sufficient ability and experiential familiarity with a particular application to identify all possible inputs. Complete structural testing would involve identifying a number of tests such that each possible path through the code is exercised or is processed at least once. There will usually be a very large number of possible paths through any large program, and so complete structural testing is impractical. Generally, clients are not able to express perfect knowledge about their needs, and so complete purposeful testing is not feasible either. Of course, all this says is that we must recognize that we live in a real world.

Generally, a client or user group will initially be concerned only with the *quality* of the software delivered to it in terms of usability of the *software product* for an assumed set of purposes, which are often difficult to specify in advance. But the quality of the end product is a direct function of the quality of the *process* that produced the end product. We therefore see that *software processes may be the most important software product from the point of view of evolving a quality product.* Of course, there are drivers that influence process quality, and these have been illustrated in Figure 6.11 and elsewhere in this book.

As time progresses, the interest of the user group may expand to also include not only software product operation but also software revision to meet evolving needs, and transitioning of the software product to meet new needs in an efficient and effective way. This introduction of time as an important dimension in software utilization leads to the hierarchically structured notion of quality assurance attributes, as we have indicated in Figure 6.23.

Useful rudimentary efforts toward quality infusion into systems engineering efforts involve three steps associated with the nine intersections shown in Figure 6.25:

1. Identification of quality attributes important for a specific situation, such as an ISO 9000 quality audit.
2. Determining importance weights for these attributes.
3. Defining and instrumenting operational methods of determining the attribute scores for specific evaluation and assessment of quality.

When only a single software development approach is being considered, we obtain an evaluation of this approach. Corrective strategies may then be identified to remove quality deficiencies. When assessment of an entire organization is being considered—for ISO 9000 registration purposes, for example—this information would be used to determine the Corrective Action Report. The multiattribute utility theory approaches of decision assessment [31] may be quite useful for this.

Software quality assurance is the name often associated with efforts that lead to the equivalent of a *guarantee* for a software product. Generally, this guarantee is with respect to the software quality attribute measures exceeding minimum performance standards on all quality attributes. But there are other approaches that allow compensatory trade-offs. *Quality control* is the act of inspecting an established product—that is, the result of a specific software development process—to make sure that it meets some minimum defined set of standards. Here we are much more concerned, as engineers, with the more general term "quality assurance," which also implies design for quality and not just inspections to eliminate the unworthy. We examined a number of metrics that are potentially useful for these purposes in Chapters 4 and 5.

Verification is the activity of comparing the product produced at the output of each phase of the lifecycle with the product produced at the output of the preceding phase. It is this latter output that serves both as the input to the next phase and as a specification for it. *Validation* compares the output product at each stage of the lifecycle, occasionally only the final product phase, to the initial system requirements. Often these activities are performed by people outside the systems engineering development organization and the prefix "independent" is sometimes used in these cases.

Verification and validation generally do not address the appropriateness of the system requirements and may not, as a consequence, determine whether a system really satisfies user needs. While verification seeks to determine whether the system product is being built correctly, validation seeks to determine whether the right product has been produced form an assumed set of correct specifications. So verification and validation are quality control techniques and a part of quality assurance.

The formal process of determining that a system product is suitable for an intended application is often termed *system certification*. While products are, or may be, certified, an organization will be registered. These two different concepts are important. An individual product is certified, usually by inspection, for quality assurance purposes. An organization or individual is registered as a mark of quality.

Certification is a warranty or representation that a product will perform in accordance with agreed-on requirements. Registration is a warranty or representation that an organization or product line is capable of producing high quality products. Obtaining a high degree of organizational productivity, and productivity for the products of the organization, requires a number of related product, process, and quality management system assurance approaches.

There are many perspectives that can be taken relative to software quality indicators. It is possible to speak of the metrics that should be used at the different phases in the system development lifecycle. We realize that this would represent an internal assessment of quality. An external assessment of the developed and implemented software would generally need to be made also to ensure that concerns of product revision and product transition are addressed, as well as that of operational functionality. This reflects the fact that, throughout its lifecycle, a system or product will typically undergo the following:

Identification of need and specification of requirements

Initial design and development

Controlled introduction to a customer market

Release to customers

Use in the operational time until the need for the system changes

Modification to meet evolving needs

Transition to a new environment

Attributes and attribute measures or metrics are needed that serve project management needs during initial design and controlled introduction of the system to the client group. There are also needs at the corporate level of management to ensure that a product should be released, modified, and transitioned to a new environment and perhaps a new customer base as well.

This chapter continues with our discussions of methodological and management issues for quality as they impact information technology and software engineering. Our focus, however, is shifted slightly from concerns that more directly affect the lifecycles of RDT&E, acquisition, marketing, and associated systems management, to concerns that relate to quality assurance (QA) or system quality assurance (SQA) as a part of systems management. There are a number of other related issues, such as strategic level quality assurance and management or total quality management (TQM), that we have examined earlier in this chapter and that are also of importance here.

There are a number of critical events and activities, often called milestones, that should be planned to occur at designated points in the system's lifecycle. This suggests that the lifecycle models of Chapters 1 and 2 might be expanded to include evaluation and reviews and associated feedback to ensure production and delivery of an operational system that is of high quality and that satisfies user needs or requirements. These quality assurance efforts should be ubiquitous throughout all phases of the systems engineering lifecycle. There will generally be a number of opportunities for efforts such as reviews and audits to verify and validate system baselines for configuration management and to assure system quality. In general, baselines are designated points in the system's lifecycle, where some important features of the system configuration are defined in detail and which serve as reference points for further efforts in the system's lifecycle. There are a number of baselines that can be identified:

User requirements baseline
System specifications baseline
Functional baseline
Allocated baseline
Product baseline

A baseline is much like a "benchmark" and seems to establish important configuration information. We will have considerably more to say about benchmarks, except that we will be speaking about organizational benchmarks rather than product development benchmarks, in Chapter 8.

Configuration management (CM) is appropriate as a quality assurance effort. The purpose of CM is to manage change throughout a systems development process. Some of the many causes of change in the lifecycle process of systems engineering are as follows.

1. During system development it is discovered that the system specifications have not been properly identified and that a system designed to satisfy the initially identified requirements will not actually satisfy user requirements.
2. At some phase in the systems acquisition lifecycle, it is determined that the user requirements have changed and that system specifications need to be changed to reflect this.
3. During system evaluation, or perhaps at other phases in the lifecycle, a fault in the evolving system is detected and the subsequent correction of this fault requires a change in the system design concept.

In each case, there is a need to know that a change is necessary, what kind of change is needed, that all stakeholders to the systems acquisition process agree with the change and are informed of pending changes, and that careful records are kept of changes to be made. These records should include the following:

The rationale supporting the changes
The people who made the changes
What the changes were
When the changes were made

All these are CM functions and support the primary quality assurance purpose of CM. This purpose is provision of system acquisition stability in producing a trust-

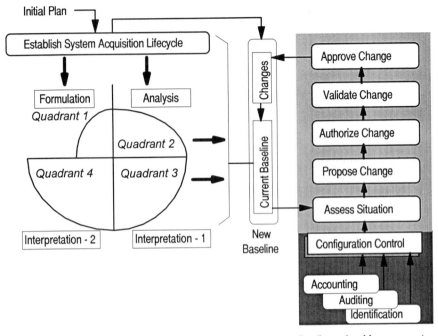

Figure 6.26   Conceptual illustration of configuration management efforts.

worthy system. Figure 6.26 illustrates some CM activities that occur throughout the systems eningeering lifecycle. Configuration management generally is a necessary ingredient to assure operational or product level quality.

CM is the systems management process that identifies needed functional characteristics of systems early in the lifecycle, controls changes to those characteristics in a planned manner, and documents system changes and implementation status. Determination and documentation of who made what changes, why the changes were made, and when the changes were made are the functional products of CM. CM is a subject of considerable interest in systems engineering management [79] and particularly in software systems engineering [80–84]. These are four essential functions or "baseline" efforts:

Configuration identification
Configuration control
Configuration status accounting
Configuration audits and reviews

These comprise CM in the initial DoD configuration management standards [85] that have served to foster most subsequent developments in this area. They are illustrated in Figure 6.26. These and many other CM issues are also discussed in [31] and will not be repeated here.

There are a rather large number of acronyms in use today to describe various systems engineering quality assurance indicators. Many of these have originated in information and software systems engineering [86–95], which has been very concerned with quality assurance, especially at an operational level. In many cases, the terms have been transferred to software engineering from more generic systems engineering efforts, especially those involving defense efforts. These acronyms are generally employed at various phases in the systems engineering lifecycle as part of the quality assurance effort through internal auditing. Figure 6.27 illustrates one systems engineering lifecycle, for system acquisition, and a number of audit and review indicators. The acronyms used in this figure are defined as follows:

SRR   *System requirements review* is a review to evaluate and determine the adequacy of the requirements that are stated in the system requirements specifications (SRS). Planning for system testing is accomplished here. The SRS should clearly and precisely describe each of the essential requirements for the system as well as the external interface. Each of these specifications should be defined so that it is possible to develop an objective metric to verify and validate achievement level by a prescribed method.

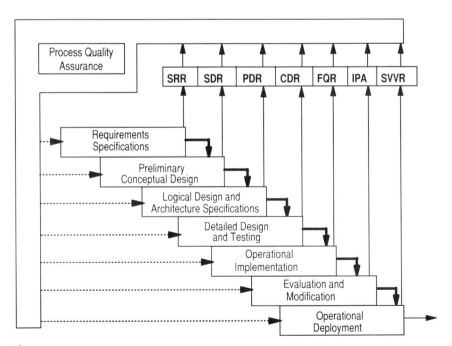

Figure 6.27   Role of quality assurance metrics in the lifecycle for systems acquisition.

SDR   *System design review* occurs after configuration management has been accomplished and the system design document (SDD) has been written. The SDR should describe each of the major subsystems that comprise the overall design specifications, such as databases and internal interfaces. Tools required for verification are also identified as a by-product of this effort. The SDD is prepared to indicate the design specifications for the system that is to be developed. A SDD defines the system architecture, modules, and interfaces for a system that (presumably) satisfies the specified system requirements. It also contains the computer code that describes or specifies the system capabilities.

PDR   A *preliminary design review* has the purpose of enabling an evaluation of the extent of acceptability of the preliminary system design, as specified by a preliminary version of the SDD. It represents a technical review of the basic design approach for each major system subsystem. System development and verification tools are identified. If changes are recommended, particular care is used to determine their propagation throughout the system development lifecycle in a consistent manner.

CDR   The object of a *critical design review* is to examine the SDD to determine the extent to which it satisfies the requirements of the SRS. Special concern is associated with determining that all design specification change requests have been accommodated.

FQR   The *formal qualification review* or formal qualifications test (FQT) is an acceptance testing procedure designed to determine whether a final system or subsystem, one that is ready for integration and implementation, conforms with the final system technical specifications and requirements.

IPA   At various times in the system development process, *in-process audits* may be conducted to evaluate consistency of the system design at that phase of the lifecycle, including system performance versus conceptual design requirements, hardware and system interface specifications, functional requirements and design implementations, and functional requirements and review-audit prescriptions. It should be noted that an IPA may include both a functional configuration audit (FCA) as well as a physical configuration audit (PCA). A FCA, sometimes called a functional audit or FA, is an audit held just prior to final system delivery in order to verify that all the requirements of the SRS have been met by each of the subsystems and associated documentation. The FCA is sometimes replaced or augmented by a final development review (FDR).

SVVR   The results of execution of the system verification and validation plan (SVVP) and the results of all reviews, audits, and tests of the software quality assurance (SQA) plan are contained in the *system verification and validation report*. The SVVP describes the inspection, analysis, demonstration, or test methods that are used to verify that the specifications in the SRS are implemented in the design expressed in the SDD, to verify that the design expressed by the SDD is indeed implemented by the resulting system of hardware and software, and to validate that the operational specifications are in compliance with the requirements that are contained in the SRS.

We immediately see that these audits and reviews are often defined in terms of other reviews and audits. Figure 6.27 illustrates how many of these reviews and audits flow from one to another, and how they are matched to the various phases in the systems engineering lifecycle. A major objective in development of a system quality assurance plan (SQAP) is to enable these efforts. There are, of course, a large number of other reviews and audits that could be identified.

This concludes a very brief discussion of the various plans, reviews, and audits associated with configuration management and associated system quality and system product quality assurance. Some of these may be implemented as metrics on a continuous scale and some as metrics on a binary scale. Some of these are performed in a static fashion, through the examination of code, system hardware, documentation, and a prototype constructed to emulate customer requirements. Others may be performed through functional operation of subsystems or execution of the programming code or of the system hardware product itself.

Operational level product or system quality assurance can be enhanced through walkthroughs and inspections, formal verification and validation efforts, and other approaches that provide confidence that a systems engineering product conforms to established technical specifications and to the user requirements. These are expensive and time-consuming activities. They must provide benefits that justify their cost, or their use may be counterproductive. This is especially the case when they result in system development delays without a corresponding increase in system functionality. It is very important that we keep the normative component of quality assurance in mind. While it is important that we detect and ultimately correct errors, it is much better to establish systems engineering lifecycle design and development procedures such that error occurrence is minimized and the operational system is trustworthy and produced in a cost-effective manner. As we have noted, this requires efforts involving strategic quality assurance and management.

Less emphasis has been placed on strategic level quality assurance and management in the information technology and software engineering areas, until recent times. The situation is changing rapidly. Weinberg [96,97] has published a recent two-volume work that demonstrates well the influence of strategic level thought on software development. The edited book by Keyes [98] contains a number of strategic management-related discussions supporting software quality and productivity. Schulmeyer and McManus [99,100] have edited two recent works that are specifically concerned with software quality assurance through total quality management and other strategic approaches to software quality. Ould [101] and Arthur [102] have authored texts that specifically concentrate on strategic and operational quality assurance and management for software acquisition. Although not specifically focused on quality, the recent open systems efforts [68–70] are very concerned with ISO 9000 and quality-related organizational issues. A recent effort by Schmauch

[103] does focus both on quality and ISO 9000 and contains some discussion of the various TQM approaches within the context of ISO 9000. There is also some discussion of the ISO 9000 standards for software developers.

These are very important issues in the minds of many. Yourdan [104], for example, identifies quality and quality-related concerns as among the many necessary efforts to avoid the decline and fall of the U.S. software industry. There are many related efforts and similar sugestions of strategies and techniques proven at today's most successful companies [105], and works that illustrate how the trilogy of the Deming Award, the Baldrige Prize, and ISO 9000 [106] enhance systems for quality management. Not unexpectedly, there are many struggles involved in the ensuing quality wars [107] and these will surely continue.

6.7   SUMMARY

In this chapter, we have examined a number of approaches to strategic quality assurance and management, or total quality management. There are a number of essential steps in this and there are a number of related developments, many of which we will examine in Chapters 7 and 8. A fitting penultimate summary to our efforts here is given in Figure 6.28. This is an illustration of the Shewhart–Deming PDCA cycle for quality improvement in information technology and software engineering.

There are also a number of themes that are relatively ubiquitous throughout recent quality related efforts.

- Poor quality costs a great deal more than is often realized by many, including organizational management.
- Many organizations approach quality only from a reactive perspective of fixing things after it is discovered that they do not work. This focusing of effort in the wrong place wastes organizational resources.
- There is much more to be gained from interactive and proactive approaches to quality in that prevention of quality defects and doing it right the first time will reduce the need for, and expense of, reactive inspections as well as eliminate many of the costs of failure since things will then be unlikely to fail.
- The provision of high quality and trustworthy products through interactive and proactive approaches provides major cost savings and results in higher product quality and the differentiation among competing products that comes with this quality.
- All in the organization, especially top management, must be fully committed to quality.
- It is possible to develop organizational leadership and culture such that a very high quality maturity level results.
- It is possible to reengineer organizations for greater efficiency and effectiveness through appropriate competitive strategies.

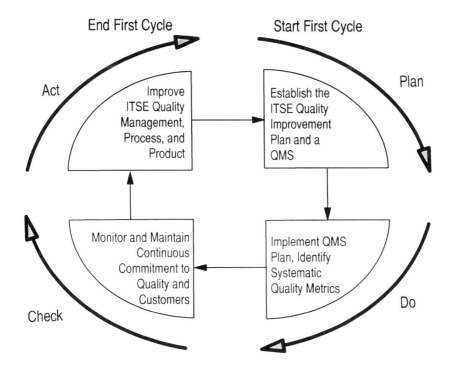

Figure 6.28   The PDCA cycle of Shewhart and Deming applied to information technology and software engineering.

Many of these statements defy the conventional wisdom of the immediate past. Generally, it has been assumed that there is a cost of quality that increases as we increase quality. It has been assumed that there is a cost of poor quality that increases as we decrease quality. The sum of these two is the cost of quality. It has a minimum somewhere, as suggested in Figure 6.29. It is the job of the operations analysis department to find the minimum cost of quality and that is the quality level at which we should produce. This is the conventional view.

This statement is claimed to be absolutely wrong by those who follow the precepts of total quality through interactive and proactive approaches. The minimum obtained in Figure 6.29 only results through reactive-oriented inspection approaches. When we approach quality through interactive and proactive means— and this requires change in organizations and in processes in most cases—we continue to reduce the cost per unit product as we continue to improve quality. The thought that the cost of quality necessarily increases as we increase quality beyond some optimum level is simply not correct, if we are taking a wise approach to quality management.

We will provide evidence to support this, and approaches to enable total quality implementations in our next two chapters. These are very concerned with the last two themes in the above listing of themes.

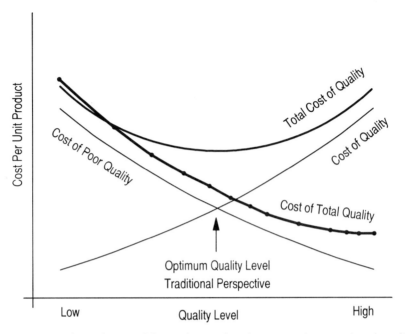

Figure 6.29   Traditional view of the total cost of quality versus the cost of total quality.

REFERENCES

[1] Fasser, Y., and Brettner, D., *Process Improvements in the Electronics Industry,* John Wiley & Sons, New York, 1992.

[2] Shina, S. G., *Concurrent Engineering and Design for Manufacture of Electronic Products,* Van Nostrand Reinhold, New York, 1991.

[3] Schonberger, R. L., *World Class Manufacturing: The Lessons of Simplicity Applied,* Free Press, New York, 1986.

[4] Schonberger, R. L., *World Class Manufacturing Casebook: Implementing JIT and TQC,* Free Press, New York, 1987.

[5] Edosomawan, J. A., *Integrating Innovation and Technology Management,* John Wiley & Sons, New York, 1989.

[6] Woodgate, R. W., *Managing the Manufacturing Process: A Pattern for Excellence,* John Wiley & Sons, New York, 1991.

[7] Day, G. S., *Market Driven Strategy: Processes for Creating Value,* Free Press, New York, 1990.

[8] Howard, W. G. Jr., and Guile, B. R. (Eds.), *Profiting from Innovation: The Report of a Three-Year Study from the National Academy of Engineering,* Free Press, New York, 1992.

[9] Hayes, R. H., Wheelwright, S. B., and Clark, K. B., *Dynamic Manufacturing: Creating the Learning Organization,* Free Press, New York, 1988.

[10] Zeithaml, V. A., Parasuraman, A., and Berry, L. L., *Delivering Quality Service: Balancing Customer Perceptions and Expectations,* Free Press, New York, 1990.

[11] Porter, M. E., *Competitive Advantage: Creating and Sustaining Superior Performance,* Free Press, New York, 1985.

[12] Porter, M. E., *The Competitive Advantage of Nations,* Free Press, New York, 1990.

[13] Peters, T. J., and Waterman, R. H. Jr., *In Search of Excellence,* Harper & Row, New York, 1982.

[14] Roberts, R. B. (Ed.), *Generating Technological Innovation,* Oxford University Press, New York, 1987.

[15] Drucker, P. F., *Innovation and Entrepreneurship,* Harper & Row, New York, 1985.

[16] Goodman, P. S., Sproull, L. S., and Associates, *Technology and Organizations,* Jossey-Bass, San Francisco, 1990.

[17] Walton, R. E., *Up and Running: Integrating Information Technology and the Organization,* Harvard Business School Press, Boston, MA, 1989.

[18] Zuboff, S., *In the Age of the Smart Machine: The Future of Work and Power,* Basic Books, New York, 1988.

[19] von Hippel, E., The *Sources of Innovation,* Oxford University Press, New York, 1988.

[20] Peters, T. J., and Austin, N. K., *A Passion for Excellence,* Random House, New York, 1985.

[21] Peters, T. J., *Thriving on Chaos: Handbook for a Management Revolution,* Alfred A. Knopf, New York, 1987.

[22] Madnick, S. E. (Ed.), *The Strategic Use of Information Technology,* Oxford University Press, New York, 1987.

[23] Jain, R. K., and Triandis, H. C., *Management of R&D Organizations: Managing the Unmanageable,* John Wiley & Sons, New York, 1990.

[24] Nutt, P. C., and Backoff, R. W., *Strategic Management of Public and Third Sector Organizations,* Jossey-Bass, San Francisco, 1992.

[25] Deming, W. E., *Out of the Crisis,* MIT Press, Cambridge, MA, 1986.

[26] Jacobs, M. T., *Short Term America: The Causes and Cures of Our Business Myopia,* Harvard Business School Press, Cambridge, MA, 1990.

[27] Krugman, P., *The Age of Diminished Expectations: U.S. Economic Policy in the 1990s,* MIT Press, Cambridge, MA, 1990.

[28] Galbraith, J. K., *The Culture of Contentment,* Houghton Mifflin, Boston, MA, 1992.

[29] Shewhart, W. A., *Economic Control of Quality of Manufactured Products,* Van Nostrand, New York, 1931.

[30] Garvin, D. A., *Managing Quality: The Strategic and Competitive Edge,* Free Press, New York, 1988.

[31] Sage, A. P., *Systems Engineering,* John Wiley & Sons, New York, 1992.

[32] Stuelpnagel, T. R., "Total Quality Management," *National Defense,* American Defense Preparedness Associations, 1988, pp. 57–62.

[33] Garvin, D. A., "What Does 'Product Quality' Really Mean?," *Sloan Management Review,* Vol. 26, No. 1, Fall 1984. Reprinted in Hax, A. C., *Planning Strategies that Work,* Oxford University Press, New York, 1987, pp. 152–174.

[34] Pirsig, R. M., *Zen and the Art of Motorcycle Maintenance,* Bantam Books, New York, 1974.

[35] Juran, J. M. (Ed.), *Quality Control Handbook,* McGraw-Hill Book Co., New York, 1951 (4th edition, 1988).

[36] Juran, J. M., *Juran on Planning for Quality,* Free Press, New York, 1988.

[37] Juran, J. M., *Juran on Leadership for Quality: An Executive Handbook,* Free Press, New York, 1989.

[38] Juran, J. M., *Juran on Quality by Design: The New Steps for Planning Quality into Goods and Services,* Free Press, New York, 1992.

[39] Juran, J. M., "The Quality Trilogy: A Universal Approach to Managing for Quality," *Quality Progress,* Aug. 1988, pp. 19–24.

[40] Feigenbaum, A. V., *Total Quality Control,* 3rd ed., McGraw-Hill Book Co., New York, 1991.

[41] Crosby, P. B., *Quality is Free: The Art of Making Quality Certain,* McGraw-Hill Book Co., New York, 1979.

[42] Crosby, P. B., *The Eternally Successful Organization,* McGraw-Hill Book Co., New York, 1988.

[43] Crosby, P. B., *Quality without Tears: The Art of Hassle Free Management,* McGraw-Hill Book Co., New York, 1984.

[44] Crosby, P. B., *Completedness: Quality for the 21th Century,* Dutton Division of Penguin Books, New York, 1992.

[45] Garvin, D. A., "How the Baldrige Award Really Works," *Harvard Business Review,* Vol. 69, No. 6, Nov. 1991, pp. 80–91.

[46] Greene, R. T., *Global Quality: A Synthesis of the World's Best Management Methods,* ASQC Quality Press, Milwaukee, WI, 1993.

[47] Hunt, V. D., *Quality in America: How to Implement a Competitive Quality Program,* Business One Irwin, Homewood, IL, 1992.

[48] Hunt, V. D., *Managing for Quality in America: Integrating Quality and Business Strategy,* Business One Irwin, Homewood, IL, 1993.

[49] The Ernst & Young Quality Improvement Consulting Group, *Total Quality: An Executive's Guide for the 1990s,* Business One Irwin, Homewood, IL, 1990.

[50] Barry, T. J., *Management Excellence through Quality,* ASQC Quality Press, Milwaukee, WI, 1991.

[51] Weaver, C. N., *TQM: A Step-by-Step Guide to Implementation,* ASQC Quality Press, Milwaukee, WI, 1991.

[52] Talley, D. J., *Total Quality Management Performance and Cost Measures: The Strategy for Economic Survival,* ASQC Quality Press, Milwaukee, WI, 1991.

[53] Rosander, A. C., *Deming's 14 Points Applied to Services,* Marcel Dekker, New York, 1991.

[54] Dobyns, L., and Crawford-Mason, C., *Quality or Else: The Revolution in World Business,* Houghton Mifflin, New York, 1991.

[55] Ross, J. E., *Total Quality Management: Text, Cases and Readings,* St. Lucie Press, Delray Beach, FL, 1993.

[56] Bogue, E. G., and Saunders, R. L., *The Evidence for Quality: Strengthening the Tests of Academic and Administrative Effectiveness,* Jossey-Bass, San Francisco, 1992.

[57] Zeithaml, V. A., Parasuraman, A., and Berry, L. L., *Delivering Quality Service: Balancing Customer Perceptions and Expectations,* Free Press, New York, 1990.

[58] Kinlaw, D. C., *Continuous Improvement and Measurement for Total Quality: A Team Based Approach,* Business One Irwin, Homewood, IL, 1992.

[59] Hoffherr, G. D., Moran, J.W., and Nadler, G., *Breakthrough Thinking in Total Quality Management,* Prentice-Hall, Englewood Cliffs, NJ, 1993.

[60] Rogers, H. V., and Sergesketter, B. F., *Quality is Personal: A Foundation for Total Quality Management,* Free Press, New York, 1993.

[61] Walton, M., *The Deming Management Method,* Putnam, New York, 1986.

[62] Walton, M., *Deming Management at Work,* Putnam, New York, 1990.

[63] Schaffer, R. H., and Thomson, H. A., "Successful Change Programs Begin with Results," *Harvard Business Review,* Vol. 70, No. 1, Jan. 1992, pp. 80–91.

[64] Sage, A. P., and Palmer, J. D., *Software Systems Engineering,* John Wiley & Sons, New York, 1990.

[65] Armstrong, J. E., and Sage, A. P., *An Introduction to Systems Engineering.* John Wiley & Sons, New York, 1995.

[66] Pearson, A. E., "Corporate Redemption and the Seven Deadly Sins," *Harvard Business Review,* Vol. 70, No. 3, May 1992, pp. 65–75.

[67] Cargill, C. F., *Information Technology Standardization: Theory, Process, and Organizations,* Digital Press, Bedford, MA, 1989.

[68] Judge, P., *Open Systems: The Guide to OSI and Its Implementation,* QED Information Sciences, Wellesley, MA, 1988.

[69] Simon, A. R., *Enterprise Computing,* Bantam Books, New York, 1992.

[70] Wheeler, T., *Open Systems Handbook,* Bantam Books, New York, 1992.

[71] Marquadt, D., Chove, J., Jensen, K., Pyle, J., and Strahle, D., "Vision 2000: The Strategy for ISO Series Standards in the 1990s," *Quality Progress,* Vol. 3, No. 3, May 1991, pp. 25–31.

[72] Hutchins, G., *Quality Auditing,* Prentice-Hall, Englewood Cliffs, NJ, 1992.

[73] Stratton, J., "What Is the Registrar Accreditation Board?" *Quality Progress,* Vol. 4, No. 1, Jan. 1992, pp. 67–69.

[74] Registrar Accreditation Board, *Guide to Software Quality System Construction and Registration,* RAB Issue 0.1, Milwaukee, WI, 1993.

[75] Hutchins, G., *ISO 9000: A Comprehensive Guide to Registration, Audit Guidelines, and Successful Certification,* Oliver Wright Publications, Essex Junction, VT, 1993.

[76] Lamprecht, J. L., *ISO 9000: Preparing for Registration,* ASQC Quality Press, Milwaukee, WI, 1993.

[77] U.S. Department of Defense, *Defense Systems Software Quality Program—DoD-STD-2168,* Apr. 1967.

[78] IEEE Software Engineering Standards, *ANSI/IEEE STD 730-1984, Software Quality Assurance Plans,* IEEE Press, New York, 1987.

[79] Blanchard, B. S., *System Engineering Management,* John Wiley & Sons, New York, 1991.

[80] Bersoff, E. H., "Elements of Software configuration Management," *IEEE Transactions on Software Engineering,* Vol. SE-10, No. 1, Jan. 1984, pp. 79–87.

[81] Babich, W. A., *Software Configuration Management: Coordination for Team Productivity,* Addison-Wesley, Reading, MA, 1986.

[82] Humphrey, W. S., *Managing the Software Process,* Addison-Wesley, Reading, MA, 1989.

[83] Bersoff, E. H., and Davis, A. M., "Impacts of Life Cycle Models on Software Configuration Management," *Communications of the ACM,* Vol. 34, No. 8, Aug. 1991, pp. 105–118.

[84] Berlack, H. R., *Software Configuration Management,* John Wiley & Sons, New York, 1992.

[85] U.S. Department of Defense Military Standard MIL-STD-483A, *Configuration Management Practices for Systems, Equipments, Munitions, and Computer Programs,* U.S. Government Printing Office, Washington, DC, 1970.

[86] Card, D. N., *Measuring Software Design Quality,* Prentice-Hall, Englewood Cliffs, NJ, 1990.

[87] Evans, M. W., and Marciniak, J. J., *Software Quality Assurance and Management,* John Wiley & Sons, New York, 1987.

[88] Perry, W. E., *Quality Assurance for Information Systems: Methods, Tools and Techniques,* QED Information Sciences, Wellesley, MA, 1991.

[89] Bryan, W. B., and Siegel, S. G., *Software Product Assurance: Techniques for Reducing Software Risk,* Elsevier Science Publishers, New York, 1988.

[90] Vincent, J., Waters, A., and Sinclair, J., *Software Quality Assurance: Volume I—Practice and Implementation; Volume II—A Program Guide,* Prentice-Hall, Englewood Cliffs, NJ, 1988.

[91] Freedman, D., and Weinberg, G., *Handbook of Walkthroughs, Inspections and Technical Reviews,* Dorset House Publishing, New York, 1990.

[92] Whitten, N., *Managing Software Development Projects: Formula for Success,* John Wiley & Sons, New York, 1990.

[93] Hollocker, C. P., *Software Reviews and Audits Handbook,* John Wiley & Sons, New York, 1990.

[94] Dunn, R. H., *Software Quality: Concepts and Plans,* Prentice-Hall, Englewood Cliffs, NJ, 1990.

[95] Glass, R. L., *Building Quality Software,* Prentice-Hall, Englewood Cliffs, NJ, 1992.

[96] Weinberg, G. M., *Quality Software Management: Volume 1—Systems Thinking,* Dorset House Publishing, New York, 1992.

[97] Weinberg, G. M., *Quality Software Management: Volume 2—First Order measurement,* Dorset House Publishing, New York, 1993.

[98] Keyes, J. (Ed.), *Software Engineering Productivity Handbook,* McGraw-Hill Book Co., New York, 1993.

[99] Schulmeyer, G. Go., and McManus, J. I. (Eds.), *Handbook of Software Quality Assurance,* 2nd ed., Van Nostrand, New York, 1992.

[100] Schulmeyer, G. Go., and McManus, J. I. (Eds.), *Total Quality Management for Software,* Van Nostrand, New York, 1992.

[101] Ould, M. A., *Strategies for Software Engineering: The Management of Risk and Quality,* John Wiley & Sons, New York, 1990.

[102] Arthur, L. J., *Improving Software Quality: An Insider's Guide to TQM,* John Wiley & Sons, New York, 1993.

[103] Schmauch, C. H., *ISO 9000 for Software Developers,* ASQC Quality Press, Milwaukee, WI, 1994.

[104] Yourdan, E., *Decline and Fall of the American Programmer,* Yourdan Press, New York, 1992.

[105] George, S., and Weimerskirch, A., *Total Quality Management: Strategies and Techniques Proven at Today's Most Successful Companies,* John Wiley & Sons, New York, 1994.

[106] Mahoney, F. X., and Thor, C. G., *The TQM Trilogy: Using ISO 9000, the Deming Prize, and the Baldrige Award to Establish a System for Total Quality Management,* AMACOM, American Management Association, New York, 1994.

[107] Main, J., *Quality Wars: The Triumphs and Defeats of American Business,* Free Press, New York, 1994.

Chapter 7

Organizational Leadership, Cultures, and Process Maturity

Success in implementation of a set of TQM philosophies and practices in an organization will be very dependent on organizational leadership. This was a focal point of many of our discussions in Chapter 6. Here, we wish to expand on these discussions by considering the major roles that organizational leadership and culture play in bringing about the organizational changes necessary to implement strategic and operational level improvements.

First, we examine some of the many works concerning organizations. Our goal in this will be to identify salient characteristics of importance for organizational leadership. In doing this, we find that organizational learning is also an essential characteristic and driver of needed change. Both organizational leadership and learning are related to the culture that has been established in an organization. So we turn our attention to organizational cultures. In some of our overviews in this area, a distinction is made between the executive functions of leadership, management, administration, and governance. We examine this and related organizational efforts in planning. In the penultimate portion of the chapter, we explore a number of approaches to planning. In part, this will cause us to relearn and, in some cases, unlearn some of the viewpoints that may have been adopted from reading the portion of Chapter 2 that deals with planning and some generally held perceptions about planning. One of the major results of change adoption is evolutionary and incremental changes in various lifecycle processes or an organization. We conclude our discussions with an overview of recent efforts of the Software Engineering Institute to establish a capability maturity model for organizations that is intended to lead to evaluation, assessment, and improvements in software development related processes.

7.1   CLASSIC VIEWS OF ORGANIZATIONS

There have been a plethora of studies of organizational leadership, organizational design, and planning and human performance in organizations. Among these are such very classic and excellent works as the organizational studies of March and Simon [1], the organizational design studies of Galbraith [2], the strategic planning studies of Ansoff [3] and Andrews [4], the organizational psychology studies of Leavitt [5] and Schein [6], and the public sector efforts of Lindblom [7] and Wildavsky [8]. Discussions of the wealth of theory and research in these closely related areas are provided in definitive handbooks on leadership [9], organizational design [10], and human performance technology [11]. A recent work [12] reprints many of the seminal works of March and his colleagues on decisions and organizations, including many of the papers referenced in this chapter. A special issue on organizational learning in *Organization Science* [13] documents a number of other contributions.

Organizations can be viewed from a closed system perspective, which views an organization as an instrument designed to enable pursuit of well-defined specified objectives. In this view an organization will be concerned primarily with four objectives [14]:

Efficiency
Effectiveness
Flexibility or adaptability to external environmental influences
Job satisfaction

Four organizational activities typically follow from this:

Complexity and specialization of tasks
Centralization or hierarchy of authority
Formalization or standardization of jobs
Stratification of employment levels

In this view, everything is functional and tuned such that all resource inputs are optimum and the associated responses fit into a well-defined master plan. This has led to the development of Theory X of management and revisions to accommodate various perceived limitations such as to result in Theories Y, Z, and W. These are discussed in [15] and in many other references.

March and Simon [1] discuss the inherent shortcomings that are associated with the theory X based, closed system model of humans as machines. Not only is the *human as machine* view inappropriate, there are pitfalls associated with viewing environmental influences as only *noise*. Cyert and Simon [16] describe *behavioral rules* as modes of deportment that an individual or an organization develop as guidelines for decision making in complex environments characterized by uncertainty and incomplete information. These rules incorporate the decision maker's assumptions about both the nature of the internal environment of the organization and the external environment of the world surrounding the organization. In this model, judgment is capable of being decomposed into a set of behavioral rules that change and move closer to those described by simple known situations as uncertainties give way to certainty and as knowledge increases.

In the open system view of an organization, concern is not only with objectives but with appropriate responses to a number of internal and external influences. Weick [17,18] describes organizational activities of *enactment, selection,* and *retention,* which assist in the processing of ambiguous information that results from an organization's interactions with ecological changes in the environment. The overall result of this process is the minimization of information equivocality such that the organization is able to (1) *understand its environment,* (2) *recognize problems,* (3) *diagnose their causes,* (4) *identify policies to potentially resolve problems,* (5) *evaluate efficacy of these policies,* and (6) *select a priority order for problem resolution.* These are the primary steps in the systems engineering formulation, analysis, and interpretation efforts we have discussed throughout this text and elsewhere.

The result of the enactment activities of the organization is the enacted environment of the organization. This enacted environment contains an external part, which represents the activities of the organization in product markets, and an internal part, which is the result of organizing people into a structure to achieve organizational goals. Each of these environments is subject to uncontrollable economic, social, and other influences. Selection activities allow perception framing and editing and interpretation of the effects of the organization's actions on the external and internal environments, such as to enable selection of a set of relationships believed of importance. Retention activities allow admission, rejection, and modification of the set of selected knowledge in accordance with existing knowledge and integration of previously acquired organizational knowledge with new knowledge. There are potentially a large number of cycles that may be associated with enactment, selection, and retention. These cycles generally minimize informational equivocality and allow for organizational learning, such that the organization is able to cope with complex and changing environments.

Daft and Weick [19] suggest an organizational learning model that is comprised of three major components.

1. *Scanning* is concerned with monitoring and situation assessment of the environment such as to obtain information of value relative to some issue.

2. *Interpretation* represents the effort of translating observed events such as to develop meaning in terms of concepts that are consistent with our prior beliefs concerning the world and the environment. There are four basic interpretation types that result from whether the environment is capable of being analyzed or not, and whether the organizational intrusiveness or willingness to look outside its own boundaries is active or passive. These lead to undirected and

conditioned viewing, for passive organizational intrusiveness, and enacting and discovering, for active organizational intrusiveness.

3. *Learning* represents the knowledge about the relationships that exist between organizational state and the environment of the organization, and the actions that are taken.

It is not immediately obvious how to extend individual learning results to organizational learning. Clearly, organizations are not simply collections of individuals. Yet, organizations are collections of individuals.

Much of individual learning occurs in group and organizational situations, as well as in individual information processing and judgment situations. Individuals often join "groups" to enhance survival possibilities and to enable pursuit of career and other objectives. These coalitions of like-minded people pursue interests that result in emotional and intellectual fulfillment and pleasure. The activities that are perceived to result in need fulfillment become objectives for the group. Group cohesion, conformity, and reinforcing beliefs often lead to what has been called "groupthink" [20,21]. This is an information acquisition and analysis structure that enables information to be processed only in accordance with the belief structure of the group. The resulting selective perceptions and neglect of potentially disconfirming information preclude change of beliefs.

Vroom and Yetton [22] have researched leadership and decision making. Their primary concern is with effective decision behaviors. They develop a number of clearly articulated normative models of leadership style for individual and group decisions. These should be of use to those attempting to structure normative or prescriptive models of the leadership style portion of decision situations, which are capable of operational implementation. It is the apparent goal of Vroom and Yetton to come to grips with, and use explicitly, leadership behavior and situational variables to enhance organizational effectiveness. This is, of course, a primary purpose of a leadership model.

Keen [23] acknowledges four causes of inertia relative to organizational information systems.

1. Information is only a small component task.
2. Human information processing is experiential and relies on simplification.
3. Organizational change is incremental and evolutionary, with large changes being avoided.
4. Data are a political resource to particular groups as well as an intellectual commodity.

Each of these factors suggests problems in determining how information is processed by organizations. Thus we see that information is a major concern relative to organizational efforts that also involve leadership, learning, and culture.

Tushman and Nadler [24] have developed a number of propositions, based on their own and others' research that reflects various aspects of information processing in organizations. The general conclusion of these studies is that, in an effort to enhance efficiency, organizational information processing typically requires selective routing of messages and summarization of messages. In the classic normative theory of decision making, it is easily shown that information about the consequences of alternative courses of action should be "purchased" only if the benefits of the information—in terms of precision, relevance, reliability, and other qualities— exceed the cost.

Feldman and March [25] present an alternate point of view in their description of information use in organizations. Their discussions of information incentives indicate systematic bias in estimating the benefits and costs of information due to the fact that the costs and benefits do not occur at the same place and at the same time, such that one group has responsibility for information use whereas another has responsibility for information availability. Also, people are prone to obtain more information than is needed since, under uncertainty conditions, the post-outcome probabilities of events that do occur will be judged higher than the prior probabilities of these events. This will suggest that less information was obtained than should have been obtained and will typically lead to incentives to obtain too much information.

Feldman and March also indicate that much of the information that is obtained is obtained for surveillance purposes to uncover potential surprises rather than to directly clarify uncertainties for decision making. Strategic misrepresentation of information, due to interpersonal conflicts and power struggles, is a third factor suggested as decoupling information gathering from decision making. In this case, information must be suspected of bias. Finally, information is a symbol that indicates a commitment to rationality. There are many incentives to displaying the symbol even if it is not used.

These ideas have been utilized by many concerned with executive functions. While most of this has been with respect to private sector enterprise, academic enterprises have also been considered. Keller [26], in a seminal work concerned with university perspectives, indicates that strengthened management and strategies are major needs of universities today. He indicates that there are four generic roles for university executives.

1. *Administration* provides services to faculty and students, somewhat in the form of a "conclerge." This is a needed caretaking role in an organization. Administration is concerned with efficiency.

2. *Management* is concerned with seeing that the right things are done, as contrasted with the strictly administrative function of seeing that things are done right. Management is concerned with effectiveness.

3. *Leadership* is concerned with setting forth a vision and ensuring that people act diligently in acceptance of the vision and in support of it.

4. *Governance** is concerned with ensuring that all relevant stakeholders in the

---

*A commonly accepted definition of governance is that it is the act of governing. In turn, one definition

enterprise are aware and supportive of management policies. University governance, in which faculty play a major role, is typically concerned with equity and explicability of judgments and actions and generally seeks a consensus on these by senior faculty, university managers, and potentially others that have a stake in issues under consideration.

Keller indicates that strategic planning, as a vitally needed executive effort, is active and not passive and that it is concerned primarily with looking outward to keep the organization tuned to the environment. It is encouraging of competition and development of competitive advantage. It focuses on decisions and the resultant outcomes. The suggested strategy recognizes the four enterprise control or jurisdiction roles: administration, management, leadership, and governance. This distinction among the executive roles in an organization is important, as we will soon discuss.

Keller indicates that six factors need to be considered in the development of a strategic plan for a university. These appear equally applicable for an enterprise of any type.

1. *Traditions, values, and aspirations* of the community, as broadly defined.
2. *Competitive and fiscal strengths and weaknesses.*
3. *Priorities and capabilities of organizational leadership.*
4. *Contemporary environmental trends, threats, and opportunities.*
5. *Preferences, impressions, and directions of the market for university products and services.*
6. *The competitive situation, including both opportunities and threats.*

Many of these characteristics take on the roles of needs, constraints, alterables, and objectives for strategic planning. In essence, these encompass the strengths and weaknesses of the organization, the threats and opportunities it faces, the culture of the organization, and the environment in which it exists.

As we have noted in Chapter 2, these need to be associated with activities and activities measures to comprise a complete set of program planning linkages. These would then be subject to analysis and interpretation in order to complete the standard systems engineering planning trilogy of formulation, analysis, and interpretation. This needs to be preceded by an effort at situation assessment and followed by action implementation, response determination, and iterative adaptation to continually refine the strategic plan. The result of this is a set of interaction matrices

---

of govern is to *exercise continuous sovereign authority such as to control and direct the making and administration of policy.* A second preferred definition is that *to govern is to rule without having sovereign power and usually without the authority to determine basic policy (Webster's Collegiate Dictionary).* While the first definition is appropriate in a public sector effort, the second is generally appropriate in such third-sector enterprises as higher education. Surely, this is the definition intended by Keller.

representing various program planning linkages for *quality function deployment*, a subject we briefly considered in Chapter 5.

An organization is normatively concerned with enhancing efficiency, effectiveness, and explicability relative to administrative, governance, leadership, and managerial functions. There are four generic approaches that can be taken in response to coping with organizational exigencies in pursuit of these attributes. These correspond to organizational typographies as follows.

- An *inactive* organization will attempt to avoid problems in the belief, or hope, that they will go away in a natural manner. If accorded sufficient protection from the external environment, such as guaranteed entitlements, survival is indeed possible in an inactive organization.

- A *reactive* organization is one that will respond to difficulties after they develop, generally using approaches that have worked well in the past. This may well be a proper response if the situation is one with which the decision maker is experientially familiar, *and* if the situation has been identified correctly. A reactive organization will be very conservative and risk averse and will not typically anticipate crises or chaotic situations. These are organizations primarily concerned with their own internal environment and with its maintenance. An inactive or reactive organization will not be able to attend to crises, at least until after they eventuate, and will have a persistence and survival as its highest aspiration.

- An *interactive* organization is one that is concerned with its external environment. Such an organization will adapt to external change, at least at the level of symptoms. It will attempt to cope with crisis situations through the development of better responses to the external environment. The interactive organization may, however, fail to learn through an inability to anticipate future perspectives and thereby will also fail to fully align theories in practice to espoused theories, as we will discuss in Section 7.2.1. Thus, although an interactive organization might be able to respond well to crisis situations that impinge from the outside, it will not necessarily become better in responding to a new crisis that is of a fundamentally different type than previously experienced.

- The organization that accomplishes "double-loop" learning, such that it learns how to learn better, is a *proactive* organization. It is able to apply knowledge principles and future perspectives that enable it to thrive in the face of continual change, including change of a chaotic nature, through adaptive behavior to enable it to adjust its structure, function, and purpose as appropriate for continued productivity through organizational learning how better to learn.

These four generic response types have been used, in part, as cultural characteristics that influence the design of higher education decision support and executive support systems in [27].

7.2 ORGANIZATIONAL LEARNING

In this section, we discuss a number of recent views of organizational learning. A very important feature and need in organizations is that of *organizational learning*. Mistakes will occur. Hopefully, individuals and organizations learn from mistakes such that things are done better next time. Almost all our discussions in the previous chapter concerned enhanced quality through continuous improvement. It is difficult to imagine continuous improvement without learning. In our next chapter, we examine organizational improvements in systems management, processes, and product through various reengineering efforts. If an organization is to reengineer, there must be some forms of learning or there is no reason to believe that the same mistakes that were made before will not be made again. So we all need to learn—continuously and throughout a lifetime. "We" is a generic term here and refers to us, me, you, and organizations.

Learning involves the use of observations of the relationships between activities and outcomes, often obtained in an experiential manner, to improve behavior through the incorporation of appropriate changes in processes and products. Thus learning represents acquired wisdom in the form of skill-based knowledge, rule-based knowledge, or formal reasoning-based knowledge [15,28,29]. Thus it may involve know-how, in the form of skills or rules, or know-why, in the form of formal reasoning-based knowledge.

Learning involves situation assessment, detection of a problem, synthesis of a potential solution to the problem, implementation of the solution, evaluation of the outcome, and the resulting discovery that eventuates from this. This is a formal description of the learning process. It is also the problem-solving process and involves the basic steps of systems engineering.

While learning, as we have defined it, appears highly desirable, much of the individual and organizational learning that occurs in practice is not necessarily beneficial or appropriate in either a descriptive or a normative sense. For example, there is much literature showing that organizations and individuals use improperly simplified and often distorted models of causal and diagnostic inferences, and improperly simplified and distorted models of the contingency structure of the environment and task in which these realities are embedded. Let us look at some of the learning models that have been proposed.

7.2.1 Organizational Theory of Reasoning, Learning, and Action

Organizational learning results when members of the organization react to changes in the internal or external environment of the organization by detection and correction of errors. Argyris and his colleagues [30–33] have developed a theory of reasoning, learning, and action-based model for individual and organizational learning. In this model, learning is fundamentally associated with detection, diagnosis, and correction of errors.

The notion of error is singularly important in this theory. An error is a feature of knowledge that makes action ineffective; detection and correction of error results, ideally, in learning. Individuals in an organization are agents of organizational action and learning. In the studies just referred to, Argyris cites two information-related factors that inhibit organizational learning: (1) the degree to which information is distorted such that its value in influencing quality decisions is lessened, and (2) lack of receptivity to corrective feedback. Two types of organizational learning are defined. Each is appropriate in different circumstances and for different reasons.

Single-loop learning, illustrated in Figure 7.1, is learning that does not question the fundamental objectives or actions of an organization. It is essential to the quick action that is often needed. This would often be supported by rule-based or skill-based knowledge. Errors may occur. Members of the organization may discover sources of error and identify new strategic activities, which might correct the error. These activities may be identified either through use of a different rule or experientially based skill or through the application of formal reasoning-based knowledge to the situation at hand. The activities are then analyzed and evaluated, and one or more are selected for implementation. In an organization, single-loop learning allows for the use of present policies to achieve present objectives. The organization may well "improve" but this will be with respect to the current way of doing things. Organizational purpose and even process are seldom questioned.

In simple cases, this approach may be quite valid. It can often, however, be inappropriate. For example, environmental control and self-protection through control over others, primarily by imposition of power, are typical strategies. The consequences of this approach may include defensive group dynamics and low production of valid information.

This lack of information does not result in disturbances to prevailing values. The resulting inefficiencies in decision making encourage frustration and an increase in secrecy and loyalty demands from decision makers. All this is mutually self-reinforcing. It results in a stable autocratic state and a self-fulfilling prophecy with

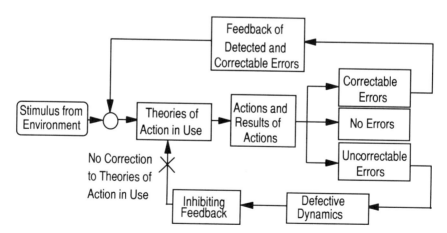

Figure 7.1   Single-loop learning and associated error detection, diagnosis, and correction.

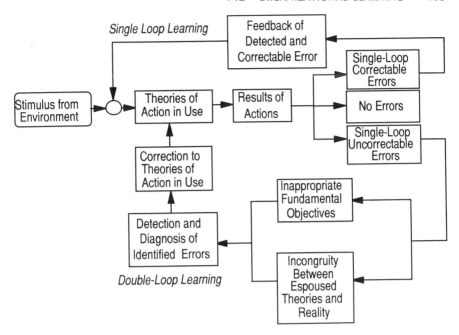

Figure 7.2 Interpretation of double-loop learning or metalevel learning for improved theories of action in use and conformance to espoused theories.

respect to the need for organizational control. So while there are many desirable features associated with single-loop learning, there are a number of potentially debilitating aspects as well. These are quite closely related to notions of organizational culture. We discuss some of these in Section 7.3.

Double-loop learning, shown in Figure 7.2, involves identification of potential changes in organizational goals and of the particular approach to inquiry that allows confrontation with and resolution of conflict, rather than continued pursuit of incompatible objectives as this generally leads to intergroup conflict. Not all conflict resolution is the result of double-loop learning, however. Good examples of this are conflicts that are settled through imposition of power rather than through inquiry. Double-loop learning is the result of organizational inquiry, which resolves incompatible organizational objectives through the setting of new priorities and objectives. New understandings are developed, which result in updated cognitive maps and scripts of organizational behavior. Studies show that poor performance organizations learn primarily on the basis of single-loop learning and rarely engage in double-loop learning. Thus the underlying organizational purpose and objectives are questioned in double-loop learning.

Double-loop learning is particularly useful in the case when people's *espoused theories of action,* which are the "official" theories that people claim as a basis for action, conflict with their *theories in use,* which are the descriptive theories of action that may be inferred from actual behavior. While people are often adept at identifying discrepancies in other people between espoused theories of action and theories in use, they are not equally capable of self-diagnosis. The dictates of tactfulness normally prevent us from calling to the attention of others the observed inconsistencies between their espoused and actual theories of action. The result of this failure is inhibition of double-loop learning.

Two other major inhibitions to learning are also noted. *Distancing* is the art of not accepting responsibility for either problems or solutions. *Disconnectedness* occurs when individuals are not fully aware of their theories in use and the relationships between these theories and associated actions.

There are several potential dilemmas associated with this theory of action building. Among these nonmutually exclusive dilemmas, which aggregate together to result in conflicting and intolerable pressures, five are particularly important:

1. *Incongruity* between espoused theory and theory in use, which is recognized but not corrected.

2. *Inconsistency* between theories in use.

3. *Ineffectiveness* as objectives associated with theories in use become less and less achievable over time.

4. *Disutility* as theories in use become less valued over time.

5. *Unobservability* as theories in use result in suppression of information by others such that evaluation of effectiveness becomes impossible.

Detection and correction of inappropriate espoused theories of action and theories in use are suggested as potentially leading to a reduction in those factors that inhibit double-loop learning.

Of course, single-loop learning often will be appropriate and is encouraged. The result of double-loop learning, which includes single-loop learning, is a *new* set of goals and standard operating policies that become part of the organization's knowledge base. It is when the environment, or more generally the contingency task structure, changes that double-loop learning is appropriate. Inability to accommodate double-loop learning is a flaw. Ability to successfully integrate and utilize the appropriate blend of single- and double-loop learning is called deutero, or dialectic, learning.

Learning is said to take place when new knowledge is somehow translated into a form that is capable of replication. This is much like the Piaget model for translation of formal thought into concrete thought as discussed in [15] and illustrated in Figure 7.3. A model much like the four-phase Shewhart–Deming PDCA model, discussed in Chapter 6, could also be used for this representation. This would involve what is sometimes called a "discovery–invention–production–generalization" cycle of learning. It can be illustrated in much the same way as Figure 7.3. Through use of this lifecycle, an organization can move beyond adaptive leading, which will enable it to cope with changing conditions, to generative learning, which will enable it to expand capabilities through double-loop learning. One of the major exemplars of this form of learning is Peter Senge. We now examine this work.

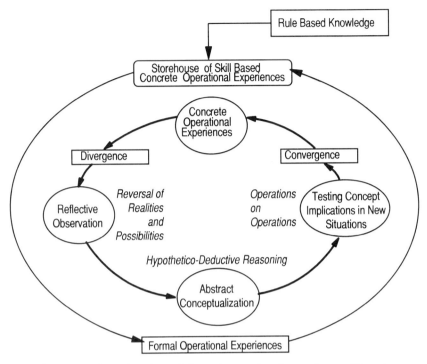

Figure 7.3   Learning through formal operational experiences (Piaget).

7.2.2   Learning Organizations

Peter Senge [34,35] has devoted much attention to the design of *learning organizations*. According to Senge, learning organizations are "organizations where people continually expand their capacity to create the results they truly desire, where new and expansive patterns of thinking are nurtured, where collective aspiration is set free, and where people are continually learning how to learn together." Five component technologies, or disciplines, are suggested as now converging to enable this learning:

1. Systems thinking.
2. Personal mastery through proficiency and commitment to lifelong learning.
3. Shared mental models of the organization markets and competitors.
4. Shared vision for the future of the organization.
5. Team learning.

Systems thinking is denoted as the *fifth discipline* and is the catalyst and cornerstone of the learning organization that enables success through the other four dimensions. Lack of organizational capacity in one of these disciplines is called a learning disability. One of the major disabilities is associated with people having deeply rooted mental models without being aware of the cause–effect consequences that result from use of these models. Another is the tendency of people to envision themselves in terms of their position in an organization rather than in terms of their aptitudes and abilities. This often results in people becoming dislocated when organizational changes are necessary and this leads to disconcertment.

Each of the five learning disciplines can exist at three levels. These are termed principles, the guiding ideas and insights that suggest practices; practices, the existing theories of action in practice; and essences, the wholistic and future-oriented understandings associated with each particular discipline. These correspond very closely with the principles, practices, and perspectives we have used to describe approaches to knowledge and systems engineering.

Based primarily on works in system dynamics, an approach for the study and modeling of systems of large scale and scope, and on efforts by Argyris and others, 11 laws of the fifth dimension are stated:

1. Contemporary and future problems often come about because of what were presumed to be past solutions.
2. For every action, there is a reaction.
3. Short-term improvements often lead to long-term difficulties.
4. The easy solution may be no solution at all.
5. The solution may be worse than the problem.
6. Quick solutions, especially at the level of symptoms, often lead to more problems than existed initially. Thus quick solutions may be counterproductive solutions.
7. Cause and effect are not necessarily related closely, either in time or in space. Sometimes actions implemented here and now will have impacts far away at a much later time.
8. The actions that will produce the most effective results are not necessarily obvious at first glance.
9. Low cost and high effectiveness do not have to be subject to compensatory trade-offs over all time.
10. The entirety of an issue is often more than the simple aggregation of the components of the issue.
11. The entire system, comprised of the organization and its environment, must be considered together.

Neglect of these laws can lead to any number of problems. Most of these are relatively evident from Senge's description and our interpretation of the 11 laws of the fifth dimension. For example, failure to understand law 11 leads to the fundamental attribution error in which we credit ourselves for our successes and blame others for our failures.

On the basis of these laws, several leadership facets are suggested. Leaders become designers, stewards, and teachers. These are especially important for learning organizations. Each of these leadership characteristics enables everyone in the organization to improve on their understanding and use of the five important dimensions of organizational learning. This is said to result in creative tension throughout the organization. Planning is one of the major activities of the learning organization and it is through planning that much learning occurs.

Others have expanded on these notions. In an excellent work, Garvin [36] indicates three pragmatic needs to bring about a learning organization in practice. He cites these in the form of three Ms.

1. *Meaning* for the concept must be provided, in terms of an actionable, easy to apply, and well-grounded definition of organizational learning.
2. *Management* guidelines for practice must be supplied to enable operational activities as well as high aspirations.
3. *Measurement* tools must be provided to enable outcome assessment of learning activities.

These will enable the potential for improvement to be associated with the reality of improvement.

Five "building blocks" are suggested by Garvin:

A systematic problem-solving process

Experimentation

Learning from past experiences

Learning from others

Transferring the resulting knowledge throughout the organization

The systematic problem-solving process is particularly important here. Figure 7.4 illustrates a representation of the suggested process, which is apparently based on efforts at the Xerox Corporation. Associated with each of the six steps of this problem-solving process are a set of questions to be answered through the efforts associated with each step, illustrations of what to look for at each step, and an indication of what is needed to proceed to the next step of the problem-solving process.

Associated with these five building blocks are collateral efforts associated with fostering an environment conductive to learning and opening up boundaries and stimulating the exchange of ideas. It is claimed that these two efforts, when associated with the five building blocks and the three Ms, provide a solid foundation for any learning organization with a commitment to learning in order to enable continuous improvement.

In an interesting work, Kim [37] addresses the link between individual and organizational learning. As in the previous work, he is also concerned with the meaning of organizational learning. Learning is simply defined as "increasing one's capacity to take effective action." He associates individual mental models, strongly

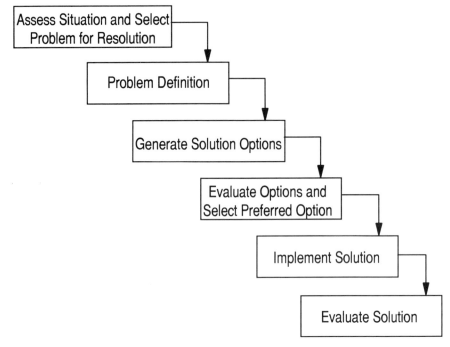

Figure 7.4   Problem-solving process.

held mental images of how the world works, with an adaptation of the Piaget formal and concrete operational thought model of Figure 7.3. Two modes of individual learning are identified. Conceptual learning is based on formal knowledge processes associated with the divergence portions that comprise formal learning. Concrete operational learning is the result of conceptual learning. These learning modes are supported by the framework, or formal belief system, and routine, or skill- and rule-based models of action, portions of mental models, respectively.

Organizational learning is defined here as "increasing an organization's capacity to take effective action." Kim devises a model of organizational learning that incorporates linkages to individual learning. It is basically a combination of the double-loop learning model of Argyris, a Piaget-like model of learning, individual mental models, and shared mental models. The ways in which these shared mental models are formed appears to be critical to this model. Improper formation can lead to the following:

Situational learning, in which an individual learns something in a single-loop learning fashion only and there is no long-term impact on the organization.

Fragmented learning, in which there is no linkage between individual mental models and the organizationally shared mental model.

Opportunistic learning, in which a segment of the organization takes actions that are not based on any widely shared mental model for the organization.

Much of the complexity of this model, as in Senge's model, is associated with the system dynamics and the interactions among the five dimensions and disciplines associated with organizational learning.

As we have seen, leadership is much associated with culture. We now examine a variety of organizational culture issues.

7.3   ORGANIZATIONAL CULTURES

The subject of organizational culture is very closely related to that of organizational learning. Culture is related to a number of other factors, such as religious beliefs and ethnicity. A not uncommon definition of culture is that it is the totality of societally transmitted behavior patterns. This would include all the thought characteristics of a given community, as influenced by needs, belief, institutions, values, and all other products of human thought and effort. We qualify culture here by the adjective organizational. Even so, it is still quite a broad construct. Rouse [38] is among those who explore some of this breadth.

Much of our discussion in Chapter 6 is really associated with organizational culture, and much of that in Chapter 8 will also be. We will be concerned specifically with organizational culture in this section, although much of the entire chapter could really be denoted as a study in organizational culture. Still, we can only scratch the surface of this important subject.

The culture in organizations with a large contingent of professionals in the workforce is of particular importance for our efforts here. Six functional characteristics of professionals have been identified [39]:

Expertise
Autonomy
Commitment
Identification
Ethics
Standards

Expertise refers to the wisdom obtained from lengthy education and experience associated with application of a body of abstract or theoretical knowledge. Autonomy refers to the ability to choose the method of approach used to resolve situations. Commitment refers to dedicated advocacy and interest in pursuit of those knowledge practices that are associated with the profession. Identification refers to formal professional structures or associations that recognize the profession. Ethics refers to the delivery of services without becoming emotionally involved with the client receiving the services or otherwise attempting to create a conflict of interest situation. Standards refers to organizing such as to be able to regulate and safeguard the profession and its members through efforts originating from within the profession itself. Professionals generally adhere to these guidelines for professional conduct.

Usually, they expect that others will deal with them in a similar way, especially in matters concerning their own professional employment. Some of these characteristics become desiderata for professional development. For example, autonomy needs are undoubtedly present in a professional environment. As appropriate modification to the Maslow needs hierarchy, illustrated in a portion of Figure 1.18 and Figure 2.8, can potentially be made to accommodate these additional needs of professional workers.

Culture is closely related to character. Wilkins [40] suggests three major success ingredients, or critical success factors, associated with organizational character:

1. *Shared vision* is important in that it results in a common understanding of organizational purpose. Function and structure, if they do not follow from and support purpose, will often be inappropriate.
2. *Motivational faith* and *credibility* are needed, especially with respect to ability of organizational and individual leadership and fairness of the judgments of individuals and the organization.
3. *Distinctive skills,* in terms of technologies and networks of excellence, are needed in order to ensure organizational competence.

Often, culture change in an organization is such as to promote loss of one of these critical success factors. This produces demotivation and can lead to once excellent organizations becoming mediocre. Thus, while culture change is often needed, it is also necessary to avoid the culture shock that may potentially result from change.

Wilkins identified four ways in which organizations may fail through cultural revolutions:

1. There may be no commonly shared vision of an impending crisis. Thus people in the organization may persist in traditional ways in the belief that they are fully acceptable and that currently perceived difficulties are not real.
2. There may be no commonly shared vision of a way out of the impending crisis. People do not understand or are unable to implement newly suggested approaches.
3. The suggested culture change does not produce the intended result. In some cases, change may be for the worse and not the better.
4. People learn, but they learn inappropriately. Often they learn how to resist change while giving every appearance of being fully in support of change.

It is necessary to avoid these failure pitfalls while attempting to change organizational culture and also maintaining and obtaining, through retention or refurbishment, those critical success ingredients or factors that are associated with organizational character and the basic competence, communication, and commitment characteristics of individuals.

Wilkins recognizes that resistance to change often comes about despite the recognition that some sort of change is needed. Often, people do not know either how or in what direction to change. Resistance to change often comes about because of poor abilities at double-loop learning that emanate from (1) the assumption that past competence provides a guaranteed path to future success, (2) thinking in stereotypical terms and developing superstitious commitments to past practices, and (3) the resulting fall into ideological routines.

He suggests a multiphase approach for successfully changing organizational culture:

1. Access corporate character.
2. Identify approaches to changing organizational culture without loss of organizational character. This involves appropriate honoring of the past while simultaneously growing in new and better ways.
3. Negotiate a shared vision and identify future perceptions that are appropriate for obtaining competitive advantage. This involves developing a clear statement of organizational purpose. It also involves more than this in that it is much easier to write visionary statements and purposeful plans than it is to implement them in a successful and meaningful manner.
4. Deploy the shared vision, and associated culture, throughout the organization.

Figure 7.5 illustrates an interpretation of this suggested model for organizational culture and character change.

There are, of course, many other studies of how to change organizational culture.

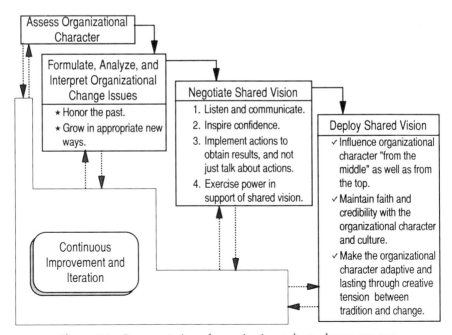

Figure 7.5   Representation of organization culture change process.

For example, a recent work [41] is devoted in large part to preventing individual and organizational tragedies associated with culture change. We now turn our attention to several models of organizational culture.

7.3.1 Culture Clash

Raelin [42] identifies three distinct cultures associated with conflict issues between professionals and managers. While industrial environments are studied in this enquiry, there is no reason to expect a very different set of cultures in a university, government, or other environment.

1. The *corporate culture* is one that stresses allegiance, first and foremost, to the company or organization.

2. The *professional culture* is one in which a given knowledge area is emphasized strongly, and loyalty to the profession is felt much more strongly than is loyalty to the organization, which may be comprised of a number of professional cultures.

3. The *social culture* represents the basic social values of the individuals within the organization and ways in which these values coalesce across individuals.

In general, it is the social culture of the organization that determines how resolution of potential clashes between managers and salaried professionals will occur.

Raelin cites the following fundamental clash areas.

- Managers prefer salaried professionals to become very specialized in the specific product area of the firm. Professionals may wish to become and remain expert in a particular professional specialty regardless of the extent to which this supports organizational goals. In a university environment, for example, faculty may feel untoward, externally exerted pressure toward great efficiency in the classroom at the expense of keeping abreast of a changing knowledge base in their specialty area. Clearly, the equivalent may occur in any professional organization.

- Managers may overspecify the means through which professional practice will attempt to achieve an end but may underspecify the end itself. A professional, however, may desire not only autonomy over means but almost total autonomy over ends as well. The university for example, may wish almost lesson plan-like control over a classroom syllabus. However, little if any thought may have been devoted to the purposeful objectives served by the course itself. On the other hand, some faculty members may see only academic freedom involved in their decision to teach subject X in a course that has been developed for the purpose of teaching subject Y.

- Managers may wish to employ microlevel supervisory control over salaried professionals. Professionals may wish professional standards of evaluation over outcomes only and may resist close supervision. The university, for example, may insist on almost total presence of a faculty member on campus during the work week. A faculty member may feel that it is teaching and research results only that count and that should be evaluated, as contrasted with mere presence on the campus for 40 hours per week. This illustrates the need of professionals for autonomy.

- Managers generally show respect for authority and may wish to formalize their control of the professional practice of others, as an authority mechanism. Professionals may defy both authority and organizational processes. This illustrates the need for professional responsibility and accountability as a necessary adjunct to autonomy.

- Professionals may be more interested in knowledge principles than in knowledge practices. Some managers, especially those tuned to short-term profit goals, may devalue knowledge principles considerably and endorse the performance of tasks that require routine knowledge practices only and that are quite mediocre in intellectual challenges for their professional workers.

- Managers may be interested primarily in organizational efficiency and effectiveness and the resulting short-term profits. Professionals may be more interested in ethical responsibilities.

Suggestions are given by Raelin to ameliorate the organizational decay and demise effects of these potential conflict situations, generally through more attention to the social culture in the organization. Other major suggestions concern efforts to encourage compatibility between professional and organizational goals. It is suggested that, generally, the managers of professionals should themselves be professionals. This enables much better management understanding of issues at hand and supports trust in their managers on the part of professionals in the organization.

In many situations such as these, there will exist potential conflict between the vision, which may well not be a shared vision, of organizational leadership and organizational culture. In his insightful work, Wilkins [40] indicates the reality that it is the organizational character or culture that is the essence of an organization's competitive advantage. Any attempt to impart a new vision on the organization, unless very positively orchestrated, may result in the organization losing the very substance of its success. The approaches suggested by Wilkins should allow an organization desirous of meaningful culture change to identify current competitive advantages, to assess readiness for change to a new future that is better than the present, and to augment existing competitive advantages in such a manner as to move to new and better future perspectives while retaining the present strengths. Adaptation and use of these approaches to situations with multiple cultures, such that compatibility between professional goals and organizational goals is a reality, are a potentially rewarding challenge to ensure competitive advantage and to ameliorate potential culture clashes.

7.3.2 Cultural Value Model

Birnbaum [43] has identified four general types of universities, each with a distinctive mix of cultural values relative to the nature of organizational life and change:

collegial, bureaucratic, political, and anarchical. Although this study was specifically for university cultures, there is no reason to suspect that the general principles are not applicable to other than university organizations.

1. The *collegial institution* depends primarily on tradition and associated precedents as the primary determinant of informal power. Formally rational administrative processes are not generally used. The organizational structure is quite heterarchical: all members have equal voice, and the resulting thoroughness and deliberation typically result in long decision-making processes that generally reflect consensus judgments. The system is a closed one, and there is a virtually impenetrable barrier that separates the institution from the environment and the external world surrounding it.

2. The *bureaucratic institution* has an organizational chart and everyone fits into a well-defined box that exists on the chart. The chart itself is typically very hierarchical but is so complex for other than very small institutions that understanding of responsibilities, and occasionally even where authority is truly vested, is quite vague. On the surface, formal rationality guides choice making and the same criteria, in principle, are applied to all in order to ensure equity. Under these conditions, rational planning is a goal, and not a reality, because of organizational complexity, and sociopolitical rationality overtakes formal rationality. In such an institution, the willingness of a person to accept a bureaucratic directive is more a determinant of the perceived success of the directive than it is a reflection of the power of the person issuing the directive. The propensity of acceptance of directives, and their effectiveness, is an inherent function of the authority culture of those receiving them. University staff and administrators will, for example, be more likely than professors to accept directives without challenge.

3. The *political institution* is one in which subgroups or subcultures form and vie with one another, often through the formation of temporary coalitions, for judgments that support their cause. We will have more to say about political institutions, and opportunistic organizational politics later.

4. The *anarchical institution* is comprised of a diverse and loosely organized faculty and student body with incommensurate and generally conflicting objectives. In such an institution, thinking does not precede action, actions are not based on choices that necessarily serve rationally determined purposes, and even the purposes that exist are not necessarily related to consistent objectives. Furthermore, judgment and choice are not generally based on understood or assumed relations between alternative courses of action and the impacts of these. This is probably just as well in this shoot–ready–aim–assess situation type of ordering of decision actions. A challenge for management in a situation such as this is to develop organizing approaches that encourage more responsible behavior.

Birnbaum provides a number of illustrations of institutions whose actions embody these models of institutional functioning. He indicates that the anarchical institution is becoming functionally dominant in American education today.

7.3.3 Cultural Framework Model

Bolman and Deal [44] describe four university frameworks: structural, human relations, political, and symbolic. These frameworks are descriptive of ways of organizing and each is associated with a culture. Although the particular cases considered here are all university environments, the results of the study appear to be more generally applicable.

1. The *structural framework* is one in which formal rationality and associated analytical approaches are the preferred method of organizing. Problems and issues are often seen as a result of a poor structure, and a new structure is generally proposed as a hoped for cure of perceived problems.

2. The purpose of an organization, from a *human relations framework,* is centered on support for the people in the organization. Furthermore, any divergence in goals between people and organization will generally result in situations in which some individuals exploit others and perhaps even attempt to exploit the organization as a result. Alternatively, a good match will lead to humans finding meaningful and gratifying work, and organizations that easily find the human genius and enthusiasm they need for success.

3. The *political framework* is one in which an organization is viewed as a coalition of diverse interests, most of which are based on and express very different values and perceptions of reality. The coalitions of subcultures are not fixed but change from issue to issue. Conflict and a confrontational environment are common features of this framework and the objectives and decisions of the organization can only be viewed from the perspective of the resulting negotiations of highly fluid coalitions in their allocation of scarce resources.

4. The *symbolic framework* is one in which it is realized that the meaning or interpretation of the same event across subcultures will generally be very different. There is generally a great deal of organizational ambiguity due to information imperfections, uncertainties, and other factors. Formal rational analysis becomes very difficult to use. In an effort to minimize the resulting equivocality, humans create symbols that, in and of themselves, become surrogates for more fundamental and meaningful events. The resulting delusions and mores help people find meaning in their experiences.

These frameworks are closely related to other models of organizational culture that we describe here.

7.3.4 Another Cultural Framework Model of a University

Four cultures exist in a university environment, according to Bergquist [45].

1. The *collegial culture* is founded on notions of diversity of perspective and autonomy of effort. This is the culture that supports academic governance. It is generally associated with committee and deliberative group activities of an autono-

mous nature. It strongly supports disciplinary scholarship and research. It supports eccentricity, individualism, diffusion of powers, and a charisma and value system that will be more political in nature than found in a profit-oriented business. The academic rank and tenure structure are natural products of a collegial culture. Organization and coherence are not natural by-products of this culture.

2. The *managerial culture* is closely associated with junior colleges and military academies and some developing colleges and universities. In general, it should be associated with any academic unit in which there is very strong top–down leadership. While acceptance of a detailed lesson plan to use in classes would be abhorrent to a person in the collegial culture, it might be expected in the management culture. Efficiency and effectiveness of operations would be major goals of a managerial culture unit. Control is a key word.

3. The *developmental culture* is one in which organizations and their processes are designed to effectively accommodate the needs of the university in efforts to fulfill the university mission. Institutional research may be a major focus in supporting strategic planning. Teaching and learning are generally held in higher esteem than research and scholarship. Leadership generally occurs in nontraditional ways through staff–management oriented persuasion roles, as contrasted with the direct leadership of the management culture.

4. The *negotiating culture* is very concerned with the personal and financial needs of the faculty and staff of the university. It is believed that change takes place through confrontational efforts and the effective use of scarce resources to obtain conformance, often through collective bargaining efforts. Equity and egalitarianism, leading to absolute equality of return for all, are major values in a negotiating culture.

These organizational and management frameworks or perspectives are neither mutually exclusive nor collectively exhaustive.* Cultural mixtures may easily occur.

7.3.5   Cultural Dynamics Model of Organizational Forms

A very sophisticated and excellent model of organizational culture may be found in the works of Henry Mintzberg, who has become very well known and widely acclaimed for his studies of management and managerial tasks. Two recent works are devoted, in large part, to designing effective organizations [46,47]. He indicates that there are six basic mechanisms that describe work coordination approaches in industrial organizations.

---

*It is interesting that there is no explicit mention of the different roles that students may play in these various frameworks, how various alumni and legislative groups influence culture, or how the role of such governing bodies as Boards of Visitors may be influenced by, and may influence, a particular prevalent culture or framework. Clearly, these do have an impact, potentially a vigorous and strong one, for good or not for the good of the organization.

1. *Mutual adjustment* results in coordination through informal communications among employees.

2. *Direct supervision* results in coordination through the delivery of orders from one person to others, who execute the orders.

3. *Standardization of work processes* results in the explication of work tasks and standards that enable coordination among workers.

4. *Standardization of outputs* results in coordination through specification of the results to be achieved.

5. *Standardization of skills and knowledge* results in coordination through the provision of established training and education.

6. *Standardization of norms* results in the entire organization holding the same beliefs and functioning according to these beliefs.

These coordination media are neither mutually exclusive nor collectively exhaustive. Several coordination media may be found in any given organization, and some are preferred to others in any given organization. For the most part, the desirable coordination medium depends on the prevailing systems of organizational influence and culture.

According to Mintzberg, there are four basically different systems of influence in an organization.

1. *Authority* results from some legally approved power.

2. *Expertise* is a result of officially certified wisdom and power.

3. *Ideology* results from accepted values and beliefs.

4. A *political system of organizational influence* is one that is neither formally authorized nor officially certified.

The political system of organizational influence is especially interesting. It results from a power base that is not formally legitimate, in that the means used are not sanctioned even if the ends promoted are worthwhile. He describes 13 very interesting games of organizational political influence and indicates that they are best characterized in terms of the processes used to exercise power, rather than in terms of the structure of the organization. There are, of course, other forms of influence. Persuasion and coercion are two potential types. Power, influence, and authority are very closely related concepts. There are a number of works that deal with such issues as influence without authority [48] and politics and influence in organizations [49].

Mintzberg identifies four forms of political organization, or organizational politics, and the types of conflicts likely to result in such organizations:

1. *Confrontational,* which is characterized by strong, restricted, brief, and unstable conflicts.

2. *Shaky alliance,* which is characterized by moderate, confined, and potentially enduring conflict of a relatively stable nature.

3. *Politicized,* which is characterized by conflicts that are moderate and pervasive and relatively enduring and stable.

4. *Complete,* which is characterized by intensive, pervasive, and brief but stable conflicts.

In most instances, the functional role of politics in organizations* is indicated to be very debilitating because it generally encourages resource expenditures, including human resources, for nonproductive purposes. However, organizational politics is indicated to be beneficial in a few situations, such as when it enhances the decline and fall of a dysfunctional organization and results in replacement of it by a functional and purposeful one.

In the first cited Mintzberg work [46], five different forms or structures of organizing are identified. These five and two new ones are identified in the latter work [47]. They are described in terms of structure, context, preferred strategy, and characteristics of the particular organizing form. All are very important for organizational systems analysis and management.

1. An *entrepreneurial organization* has a very simple structure with little staff. It operates with strong leadership in a simple and dynamic environment. It is led by a visionary who exercises personal and informal control. It is generally a responsive organization with a sense of mission. It coordinates through direct supervision and authority is the major source of influence, particularly since there is one single source of power.

2. The *machine organization* has a centralized bureaucratic structure, formalized procedures, and standardized work. It is usually a large mature organization and may function well in simple and stable environments. Its strategy is basically that of strategic programming and it is resistant to change. It may be efficient, reliable, and effective in a stable environment. Obsession with control may lead to human resource problems, including coordination difficulties.

3. The *professional organization* has a bureaucratic but decentralized structure in which the skills of its worker-professionals are standardized such that they can function autonomously within clusters, or "pigeonholes" or departments, and subject to the controls of the profession. It is usually a service sector organization and has a complex but stable environment. There are many fragmented strategies that occur primarily by administrative decree, by professional judgment, and by collective choice or in a collegial manner. While it has advantages of democracy, there are problems of coordination across clusters, opposition to innovation, and abuses due to misuse of professional privileges. Managers often spend much time handling

---

*This refers to organizational political power and opportunistic politics, as contrasted with governmental political power, which is both authorized and legitimate. One inherent quandary associated with our discussions here is that many English language terms often have rather different contextual interpretations.

structural disturbances within and across the various clusters. Expertise, also and generally associated with a weak system of authority, is the major source of influence. The generally weak administrative structure is supportive of transition to a political organization.

4. The *diversified organization* contains a number of divisions that are market centered, potentially autonomously operated, and subject to management controls. These divisions are loosely coupled and have a centralized administration. Larger and more mature organizations, both in the public and private sectors, often have this structure. The centralized administration manages corporate strategy and each individual division manages the individual business strategies. Often there are a number of evolutionary stages as an organization transitions itself to a diversified one. Lack of innovation and coordination across divisions can represent potential problems and diversified organizations have many features in common with machine organizations. Authority is the major source of influence, but the often distributed nature of this may lead to a political organization.

5. The *innovative organization* or *adhocracy* is often a high technology organization that involves much creativity. It vigorously avoids any form of bureaucratization. Often it involves a multidisciplinary team, a matrix organizational structure, and coordination through collective agreements. Often the effectiveness in innovation is obtained at the price of inefficiency. It is difficult to maintain an innovative spirit over a long term and the organization may transition itself to some other form. Either operating adhocracies or administrative adhocracies may exist, and both may exist simultaneously. Strategy formation is an especially interesting challenge here. Expertise, as contrasted with authority, is the major source of influence; this may lead to transition to a political organization if corrective strategies are not available to preclude this.

6. The *missionary organization* is one based on ideology and has a very strongly held system of beliefs and values. It has a strong sense of mission. Coordination exists through standardization of expectations and is reinforced by socialization and indoctrination of organizational members. Often it is highly decentralized and has powerful normative controls over behavior. Many Japanese companies are missionary or ideological organizations, so are monasteries and religious orders, and missionary organizations may be cloistered organizations.

7. The *political organization* results from the desire of some group to change the basic system of organizational influence. Confrontations often result. The three legitimate forms of influence—authority, expertise, and ideology—may be used to cause an end that is not legitimate or proper. In this sense, the illegitimate means of political influence might be used to achieve a legitimate and desirable end. Thus a political organization may, but by no means always will, correct bad situations.

Mintzberg indicates that these forms of organizing are not at all mutually exclusive. For example, a university organization is a typical professional organization. As such, it might be expected to employ a formal, rational decision-making framework. There have been a number of studies, however, in which universities and organizations are represented by garbage-can [50–53] or temporal-sorting models of organizational choice. We will discuss this representation shortly.

Mintzberg indicates four lifecycle phases in organizational evolution: *formation, development, maturity,* and *decline.* Obviously, finer grained disaggregations are possible and would result in a larger number of states. These four are surely the dominant stages of growth.

Many organizations begin life as entrepreneurial organizations. Depending on circumstances, they may develop and mature as machine, diversified, missionary, innovative, or professional organizations. They often decline and suffer demise after becoming political organizations. Diversified and professional organizations are very prone, especially in the absence of external controls, to eventually become political organizations. In the absence of organizational renewal efforts, or sufficient artificial resource support to enable continuation, a political organization ultimately self-destructs or enters a demise phase from which there is little hope of recovery.

We show an enhanced lifecycle model of *organizational culture* in Figure 7.6. In this figure, an organization is portrayed in terms of the seven describing characteristics of Mintzberg, the four executive functions of Keller, and the four executive engagement support styles (inactive, reactive, interactive, and proactive) discussed earlier in this chapter and illustrated in Figure 1.21 in our introductory discussion. A given organization is presumed to be capable of being characterized as comprised of some mixture of the 112 cells of each three-dimensional matrix in Figure 7.6. A particularly interesting challenge is to determine the ensconced powers needed to

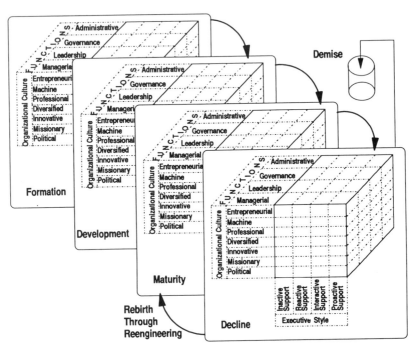

Figure 7.6   Dynamics of organizational growth, maturity, decline, and rebirth.

enable or inhibit transitions from one of the seven characteristic organizational configuration modes to the other, and which powers enable an organization to enter and remain in a healthy state of maturity and to recover to this state from a state of decline. Mintzberg, in his compelling treatment of organizations, provides some information on drivers of these transformations.

Much more needs to be done relative to models of this sort, such that proactive change occurs and the conclusion of Mintzberg that "society is unmanageable as a result of management" is then escapable. This clearly has major implications for all types of organizations and their management.

One of the many potential issues that influence management in information technology and software engineering related areas, and this encompasses a growing portion of the world's population, is that there are many who perceive of themselves as professionals. In fact, a given individual may have allegiance to more than one profession, such as electrical engineering and higher education. This, in itself, can provide some dissonance. It is only natural that professionals expect professional management of professionals. Immediately, this brings about an additional potential clash of cultures. We have examined some aspects of this important matter in our earlier discussions.

7.3.6 International Perspectives on Culture

In two interesting works, Hofstede [54,55] indicates five dominant and virtually independent dimensions associated with cultural values.

1. *Power distance* represents the degree of inequality among people that is considered normal by the population in that country.
2. *Uncertainty avoidance* represents the extent to which the people in a given country prefer structured situations over unstructured ones.
3. *Individualism* contrasts with collectivism. It represents the extent to which people prefer to act as individuals rather than as members of a group.
4. *Masculinity,* as contrasted with femininity, refers to the extent to which such values as performance, competition, assertiveness, and success are preferred to quality of life, maintaining warm personal relationships, tenderness, and concern for the weak.
5. *Long-term orientation,* as contrasted with short-term orientation, refers to the extent to which a given culture is synthesis and virtue oriented or analytical and truth oriented.

These five factors influence leadership and behavior differently across countries.

Power distance and uncertainty avoidance are identified as the major influencers of the way people in different countries organize. Power distance determines how decisions will be made, whether by a small elite group or by a larger collective body. Uncertainty avoidance determines the extent to which a country will be highly structured and rule oriented. In the particular study cited here, the United States is less power oriented and less attuned to uncertainty avoidance than most countries of the world. The Arab countries, Mexico, and West Africa were much more power

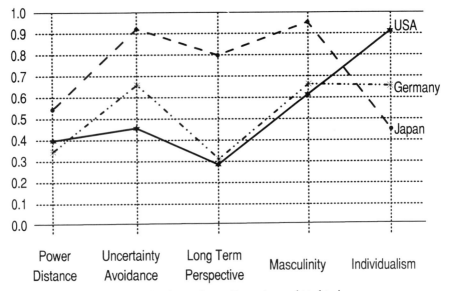

Figure 7.7 The five culture dimensions of Hofstede.

distance oriented than the United States. Uncertainty avoidance and power distance are also said to influence the way in which various authors approach organizational issues.

Long-term orientation is also of importance. This is the fifth dimension and it was not included in Hofstede's initial study. It is included in the second. Oriental nations tend to be very long-term oriented whereas most Western nations tend to be short-term oriented. That this dimension was neglected in some of the earlier studies is said to indicate that organizational writers may be products of their own culture. This leads to not asking potentially important questions in empirical studies. Figure 7.7 present a chart that illustrates these five cultural dimensions and some of the scores obtained by Hofstede in his studies. Although it might appear that a "neutral" score of 0.5 on all dimensions might be a "best" culture, this is nowhere stated. Best is a subjective term and we really need to ask: Best for what purpose?

7.3.7 Competing Perspectives on Culture

In a recent and notable effort, Joanne Martin [56] identifies three competing and incommensurate perspectives that are used to model organizational cultures:

Integration
Differentiation
Fragmentation

It is suggested that one of these perspectives is typically adopted as representative of a given organization at a given moment of time. Then evolution over time may produce changes from one of these three cultural perspectives to another.

From an integration perspective, all externalizations of culture are interpreted as saying the same thing, all members of the organization share a consensus view, and there is no ambiguity or equivocality in the environment. This is a leader-centered organization. Top–down control and seeking for a culture-strategy fit are essential characteristics.

From a differentiation perspective, cultural substantiations may well be quite inconsistent, consensus will not necessarily occur across different subcultures, and ambiguity may exist across subcultures but never within the same subculture. The management control approach of leaders may have a strong influence, individuals will generally be submerged in subcultures, and little direct action advice is available to managers of subordinate groups.

From a fragmentation perspective, ambiguity is the central theme and essence or organizational culture. Organizational power is very interspersed throughout the organization. Constant flux results at an organizational level and at the level of subcultures. A stable organizational consensus does not exist and consensus within subcultures will also be rare. Individuals believe they are powerless in influencing behavior across the organization.

In this work, a mythical company named OZCO is described from each of these three perspectives. From an integration perspective, the organization is described as participative, innovative, and with much concern for employee welfare. From a differentiation perspective, the participative nature of the organization is questioned, impediments to innovation are identified, and instances of lack of concern for employee welfare are cited. Contradiction, conflict, and lack of management commitment to employees are suggested. For the most part, the differences in observations from those with an integration perspective come about from identification and examination of different subcultures in the organization, with one each being primarily associated with engineering, marketing, and production. When studied from a fragmentation perspective, the organization is seen as confused about the values of participative efforts, such as innovative efforts as reengineering, and also disconcerted relative to its consideration of employee welfare. Ambiguity, multiplicity, and flux are seen as the dominant characteristics of the organization.

A description of six aspects likely to be observed from the integration, differentiation, and fragmentation perspectives are provided. These include role of the leader, role of the external environment, organizational level impact, subcultural level impact, individual level impact, and action implications. The primary gist of the work is that it is not appropriate to view an organization from one of these perspectives only, and that a multiperspective approach should be taken in order to identify the salient characteristics of the cultural facets present in an organization as it evolves over time.

7.3.8 Culture and Leadership I

A number of contemporary writings discuss the interaction of culture and leadership and the role of these in creating excellence. Hickman and Silva [57] suggest that there are two dominant foundations for excellence—strategy and culture—and these must be mutually coordinated to achieve excellence. This enables not only the creation of a vision for excellence, through strategy, but an appropriate framework through which to implement the vision, through culture. Strategy and strategic thinking are associated with satisfying customer needs, sustaining competitive advantage, and capitalizing on organizational strengths. This needs to be associated with knowledge of potential threats and opportunities that exist externally. Cultural awareness is associated with the ability to obtain *commitment* to a common purpose, the *competence* to deliver superior performance, and organizational *consistency* in perpetuating commitment and competence. Each of these three Cs are important in building a strong successful culture.

They identify six "new age skills" deemed to be necessary for future productivity and competitiveness. These can be aggregated under three more generic categories such that the three need categories and six skills can be described as follows:

1. The need to *forge a strong foundation* for excellence through:
   (a) *creative insight,* which involves the ability to ask appropriate questions and to form strategies; and
   (b) *sensitivity,* such as to recognize and act on the reality that people are an organization's greatest asset.
2. The need to *integrate organizational and individual skills* through:
   (a) *vision,* which will enable the organization to anticipate and forecast the need for change; and
   (b) *patience,* such as to enable the organization to exist for the long haul and not just for short-term profit.
3. The need for *adaptation* through:
   (a) *versatility,* such as to enable the organization to be multidimensional in its search for opportunities; and
   (b) *focus,* which will enable the organization to concentrate on relevant activities that produce results.

Numerous suggestions are provided in the cited work that assist in obtaining these skills. All are associated with culture, especially the first two skills, and each is also associated with organization leadership.

Kotter and Heskett [58] identify shared values and group behavior norms as the two major ingredients of organizational culture. Values are virtually invisible and are difficult to change. Norms, which result from values, are easier to identify and to change. Any attempt to change norms, without an accommodating change in values, is likely to produce very unsatisfactory results.

They suggest a multistage development approach that illustrates how organizational cultures often emerge.

1. The top management in a new organization attempts to implement a strategic vision to support organizational strategy.
2. The deployment is successful and organizational personnel are guided by the new vision and strategy.
3. The successful deployment leads to organizational success that continues over a number of years.

4. A culture results that reflects the vision, strategy, and experiences of organizational leadership.

Many have noted the fact that cultures develop when people interact over a sustained period of time and when they are successful in producing desired results. The longer the initial solution works, the deeper the particular culture becomes imbedded in the organization. Any number of external threats and opportunities may challenge the then prevalent organizational culture. The extent to which it can adapt to future needs determines the extent to which the organization will survive as an excellent organization. Figure 7.6 has illustrated the typical evolutionary pattern. The studies of these authors indicate several important cultural realities.

- Organizational culture will often have a very significant impact on the long-term performance of an organization.
- The importance of culture will increase in the future.
- Organizational cultures that are debilitating to long-term performance are not uncommon, even in firms with accountable and clever people.
- Organizational cultures can, if the need exists, be changed to allow enhanced performance even though the change is not an easy one.

This effort is primarily concerned with identification of the characteristics of cultures that will be most supportive of excellent performance. Immediately, we sense a question. Is strong culture enhancing of strong performance, or is strong performance enhancing of strong culture? The answer, of course, is yes to both questions. There are dynamic feedback loops involved. Two major desiderata are associated with both strong culture and strong performance.

- We should treat all people, both internal to and external to, the organization with dignity and respect and as if they were customers.
- We should perform all tasks such as to accomplish them in a high quality and trustworthy fashion.

Again, this is associated both with culture and leadership. In particular, it is associated with the need for everyone in the organization to believe in its fundamental prescriptions and carry out the associated mandates in a high quality manner.

There is an implied assumption here that strong culture is strongly appropriate culture. It is, of course, also possible to have strongly inappropriate culture. That would be associated with strongly inappropriate, or poor, performance. The difficulty is that there are dynamics involved and what is a strongly appropriate specific culture at one time may not be appropriate at some other time. Clearly, the two generic principles just indicated are always appropriate. A difficulty, however, is that what are appropriate tasks at one time may not be appropriate tasks at another time. For example, an organization that focuses heavily on becoming a low cost producer but ignores market realities may become a low cost producer of an outmoded product.

Kotter and Heskett denote the strong culture/strong performance hypothesis as Theory I. They identify the essential incompleteness of this theory, or perspective, as outlined above. They then propose a Theory II hypothesis that organizational cultures must motivate and align people in an appropriate manner to enhance organizational performance. This suggests that common values and behavior are at least as important as the notion of strength. Fit is an important ingredient here and what is a good fit for one organization may well not be a good fit for another organization. Three linked elements are of major importance:

Culture

Key organizational strategies in terms of formal structures and processes, and leadership efforts associated with shared vision and strategy,

External competitive environments for the organization that are comprised primarily of financial markets, product or service markets, and labor markets

When there is a good to excellent fit between these elements, excellent performance is said to result. When there is a poor fit between one of these elements and presumably the other two elements (although this is not explicitly claimed) poor performance results. Figure 7.8 illustrates the general context for Theory II, the appropriate fit hypothesis. Generally, this hypothesis was supported by empirical evaluation. To make this assertion, it is necessary to allow for dynamic evolution of the three ellipses illustrated in Figure 7.8. Just because there is an excellent fit at one point in time does not necessarily mean that an organization can adapt itself,

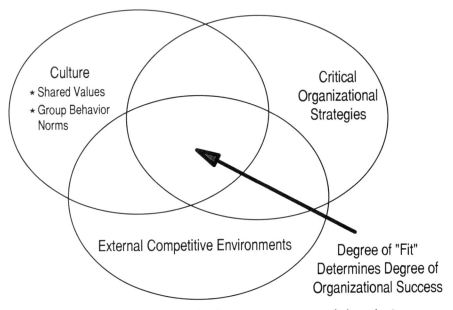

Figure 7.8   Representation of culture–strategy–context fit hypothesis.

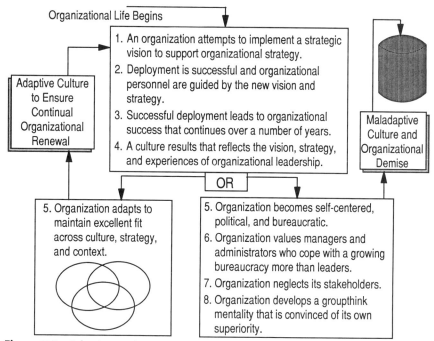

Figure 7.9 Adaptive and maladaptive behavior following initial organizational success.

including its culture and associated strategies, such that the fit still exists under changed external competitive environments.

This leads Kotter and Heskett to suggest a Theory III perspective, which is based on adaptive cultures. The Theory II culture ideal is when organizational leadership initiates appropriate change to satisfy all decorous interests of all stakeholders (employees, stockholders, customers, suppliers, etc.) of the organization. Thus adaptive organizational cultures are those that value all organizational stakeholders and select appropriate strategic processes to create beneficial and innovative changes over time. Maladaptive organizations are those that are self-centered and value orderly and low risk strategies that generally conform to existing practices much more than appropriately adaptive leadership aspirations that support appropriate "fit" despite changes in external competitive environments.

While the empirical evidence cited does not fully support Theory III, it is supported to a greater extent than Theory II, which is in turn supported to a greater extent than Theory I. Figure 7.9 indicates an extension of Theory III to accommodate both adaptive and maladaptive behaviors.

Three characteristics are deemed essential for leadership to bring about appropriate culture adaptation over time: an effective leader, with an "outsider's" perspective on the organization, but with an "insider's" resources, both knowledge resources and financial resources. It is stressed that an appropriate person for this role must be a leader, in addition to being a good manager or administrator. The essential characteristics of the two are not at all the same. The essential abilities of the manager are associated with operational planning and budgeting, organizing and staffing, controlling and problem solving, and producing a high degree of predictability and order. These are essentially the classic POSDCORB activities of management (Planning, Organizing, Staffing, Directing, COordinating, Reporting, Budgeting) that are described in most enterprise management texts. In contrast, a leader is more concerned with establishing strategic directions, aligning people in support of strategy, motivating and inspiring people to overcome organizational politics and bureaucratic barriers, and changing production to provide dramatic increases in stakeholder value.

7.3.9   Culture and Leadership II

In a landmark work, Edgar Schein [59] identifies ten phenomena that exist in a culture. On the basis of these and additional stability and integration requirements, he poses a comprehensive definition of group or organizational culture.

> Group culture is "a pattern of shared basic assumptions that the group learned as it solved its problems of external adaptation and internal integration, that has worked well enough to be considered valid and, therefore, to be taught to new members as the correct way to perceive, think, and feel in relation to those problems."

There are three major elements in this definition: (1) socialization issues, including the process of how one learns; (2) behavior issues; and (3) issues of subcultures and the extent to which they will develop. From this perspective there are causal dynamics involved in culture and leadership. Leaders initially create cultures when creating groups and organizations. Once a culture exists, it will determine the criteria for leadership. A leader in a dysfunctional culture must either change it, such that the group survives, or the culture will ultimately govern the leader.

Schein suggests three levels at which culture may be studied.

1. At the unconscious level of basic underlying assumptions, there are often unarticulated beliefs, thoughts, and feelings that represent the ultimate top level source for the resulting values and organizational structures and processes.
2. At the level of espoused values, formal statements of organizational objectives, purposes, and philosophies may be found.
3. At the level of artifacts, which are comprised of organizational structures and processes or functions, the organization attempts to implement its espoused values.

We can represent this lowest level of artifacts as two levels, one corresponding to process or function and the other corresponding to organizational structure or the product of the culture. Figure 7.10 presents our representation of these, now four, levels of culture.

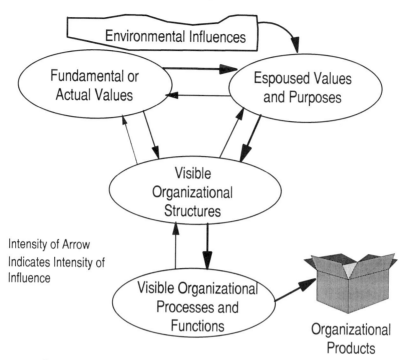

Figure 7.10   Illustration of four levels of organizational culture.

We can most easily observe the cultural product that is embedded in an organization's structure. With potentially a little more difficulty, we can observe organizational artifacts as represented by processes or organizational functions. It is more difficult to examine the espoused value for the organization, and even more difficult to determine the actual values from the espoused values. These actual values represent the basic and foundational assumptions that drive organizational culture. Figure 7.10 illustrates our interpretation of four levels of organizational culture impacts. While it is more difficult to measure cultural facets at the level of espoused purpose and inherent values, it is important that this be done since measurements at the levels of process and structure will allow for good inferences about espoused values but will not easily lead to information about actual values. Actual values may be identified through observations of espoused values and the processes and structure implied by these, and the products of the actual value system in terms of processes, structure, and organizational products.

Schein identifies a five-phase lifecycle of culture formation for the purposes of survival in, and adaptation to, an organization's external environment. The ultimate accomplishment in this is internal integration of organizational processes and structural artifacts in an effort to ensure the ability of the organization to continue to survive.

1. The organization develops a set of shared assumptions and understandings of the organizational mission and strategy that is appropriate for achieving fundamental objectives.

2. The organization develops a set of shared assumptions about operational goals that will accomplish its mission and achieve its strategic objectives.

3. The organization develops a set of shared assumptions about operational means that will accomplish its operational goals. Generally, this is reflected by organizational structures and the operational task control system.

4. The organization develops a set of shared assumptions about the measurement criteria and the information systems that will be used as indicators of success in goal achievement, or lack thereof.

5. The organization develops a set of shared assumptions relative to the corrective efforts that will be used when it turns out that the detection and diagnostic efforts in the previous phase indicate that goals are not being achieved.

Figure 7.11 indicates this lifecycle of culture formation. Clearly, any of these phases could be described in terms of a larger number of related phases. Not shown in this illustration are the external or internal environmental influences on culture formation. Culture has an impact on leadership, and leadership impacts culture. Each influences the actual functioning of the organization. The actual organizational purpose, function, and structure are clearly functions of the espoused purpose

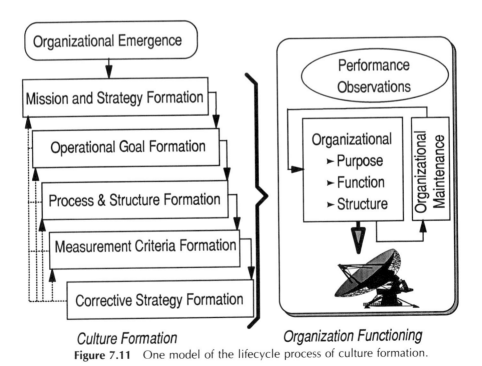

Figure 7.11 One model of the lifecycle process of culture formation.

function and structure. Furthermore, the culture formation process occurs at each of the several levels identified in Figure 7.10. Whether or not the actual culture that results from this lifecycle process is functional or dysfunctional depends on a number of issues. In Figure 7.11, we use the word "formation" rather than "formulation." This usage is portentous of some very recent and seminal work of Mintzberg that we will soon discuss.

One of the major ingredients also not depicted in Figure 7.11 is that of the internal integration process that leads to a set of shared, or not shared, assumptions. There are many issues and needs that affect this integration. Schein identifies six of these:

1. The need for communication and a common language and set of concepts to enable this.
2. The need for group definition and identity and for boundaries and criteria to determine group membership.
3. The need for determination of power distribution protocols.
4. The need for development of peer relationship protocols within the group.
5. The need for determination of the approach used to define and allocate rewards for success and penalties for failure.
6. The need to determine how to cope with risks that materialize and unexplainable and uncontrollable events.

These represent a number of very philosophical and pragmatic issues that, as a consequence, have both moralistic and realistic overtones. They involve such fundamental issues as the definition of what comprises truth, acceptable and unacceptable human activities and relationships, and how authority is used. Generally, these are described well in the works of Hofstede [54,55].

Two basic ways of studying organizational culture are identified by Schein. The first of these is comprised of an internal culture study by members of the organization. The second involves a study conducted by someone from outside the organization. In either case, cooperation from individuals within the organization is needed. There are risks associated with either approach. The analysis of the culture might well not be correct. Regardless of whether or not correct conclusions are obtained, the organization may not be prepared to accept feedback of any type regarding its culture. When an external analysis is contemplated, there are additional risks associated with having an organization's culture displayed to others. The associated ethical issues are discussed.

Six observables are identified as primary means to embed culture in an organization. Each measures, to some extent, the underlying assumptions, beliefs, and value system of the organization's leaders and represents a strong drive of an organization's culture. These observables are as follows:

1. The critical factors that leaders measure and control.
2. The approaches taken in response to crises and critical incidents.

3. The observed criteria for resource allocation.
4. The activities of leaders as role models, teachers, and coaches.
5. The observed criteria, used in practice, to allocate organizational rewards and status.
6. The observed criteria, used in practice, for recruitment of new organizational members and for outplacement of existing organizational members.

There are a number of supportive mechanisms that relate to organizational structure and processes, symbols and rituals, and formal statements of organizational purpose and philosophy. The formation of subcultures is an important aspect of organizational leadership. Subgroup and subculture formation is an inherent likelihood that results from the differentiation process that invariably occurs as an organization expands and grows. Differentiation may be functional, geographical, divisional, and hierarchical or may result across products or markets. Subcultures are, in no sense, always harmful. They may be supportive or harmful to an organization's mission depending on how they are grown and how they mature.

In the concluding portions of this work, Schein devotes much effort to organizational growth, maturity, decline, and rebirth; the role of information technology in organizations; and development of a learning culture.

Our discussion of efforts by Mintzberg covers organizational growth dynamics. We will discuss some information technology culture issues in our next chapter when we consider the very interesting work of Davenport concerning information technology cultures [60]. This very much supports the notion that we should first focus on how people use information and then focus on how machines should process information [61] to enhance organizational learning. We examined aspects of the learning organization earlier in this chapter.

One of the major issues associated with organizational culture development is how to bring it about successfully. This is especially critical for a new leader in an organization who does not have major experiential familiarity with the prevalent culture. It is particularly necessary in situations like this to obtain a relatively complete understanding of the existing culture before attempting to assess and alter it. A learning process is needed. While people may be capable of being taught, and while they may learn, they cannot be learned. That is, one cannot impose learning on people. One reason for this is that people need to be actively involved in the learning process if they are to learn. Schein suggests leadership by example as one major way to being this about. All this is very supportive of the notion of developing a broadly shared culture that motivates everyone in the organization to search for appropriate solutions that enhance success in obtaining organizational goals. It supports the notions of treating everyone with respect and dignity and performing all tasks in a high quality conscious manner. A great many suggestions are provided in this work and in two earlier works devoted to the role of external consultants in organizational process development and improvement [62,63].

In another effort, Schein [64] identifies critical psychological realities that enhance or inhibit organizational learning and change such as to become perpetual learning organizations. He identifies three contexts for organizational learning.

1. A *knowledge acquisition and insight* context is one in which the learner has the ability and willingness to learn something new. The learner or learning organization proceeds to acquire new formal knowledge, new rules, or new skills. This occurs through a process in which the learner assesses the situation, recognizes a problem, and proceeds to solve the problem in a manner that is appropriate for the particular contingency task structure at hand.

2. A *habit and skill learning* context is one in which there are incentives placed to perform certain tasks in terms of rewards for successful performance. Errors are not punished, but they are not rewarded either. Thus the learner focuses on improvement through adoption of behavior patterns that earn the reward for successful task performance. This sort of learning is slow, but it is a reliable form of learning, in that it generally involves trial and error until success is obtained. Overcoming old bad practices and cultural impediments to learning that are dysfunctional will require "unlearning" and this may pose a considerable problem. A potentially valuable attribute of this context for learning is that learning through errors is, in principle, possible. A potential problem with this mode of learning is that the learner may well become extraordinarily risk prone.

3. An *emotional conditioning and learned anxiety* context is one in which the learner is penalized for errors committed. Schein cites the Pavlovian dog illustration in which a dog is placed in a green room in which a loud bell rings and the dog receives a painful electric shock. The dog soon "learns" to avoid green rooms, even when the act of entering a green room is not necessarily associated with the penalty. A potential problem with this context for learning is that the learner may well become very risk averse.

Clearly, learning context 1 is the most appropriate in most situations, learning context 2 is acceptable, and learning context 3 is associated with a number of unpleasantries, especially if we are the ones receiving the equivalent of the electric shock.

Schein indicates that a common anxiety, for both individuals and organizations, is that of inability or unwillingness to learn something new, often because it appears too difficult or too disruptive to present practices to which one is accustomed. This is a natural anxiety and it is called Anxiety 1. To overcome this anxiety, Schein suggests the creation of Anxiety 2. This fosters feelings of fear, shame, or guilt as a fine for failure in learning something new. Anxiety 2 must be greater than Anxiety 1 in order for willful positive change to occur.

As we have also noted before, change requires some amount of receptivity to change, or "unfreezing." Schein suggests three motivators that encourage unfreezing:

1. *Disconfirmation* of present practices must occur as organizational members recognize that present practices are dysfunctional. This may bring about Anxiety 1 and this alone will result in acts to prevent change and can only lead to frustration if this occurs.

2. *Guilt or anxiety feelings* must occur because individuals and organizations are

able to connect information about present bad practices to some result with which they are concerned. Thus Anxiety 2 should also occur and it should be greater in its impact than the impact of Anxiety 1. Even together, these two anxieties will not bring about successful change.

3. *Psychological safety* must also be created such that individuals and organizations, through reduction of the impacts of natural Anxiety 1 and the severe shame aspects of Anxiety 2, are motivated to accomplish successful change. This requires training and practice opportunities, support and encouragement to overcome error phobias, norms that tolerate errors, and norms that reward innovative thinking and experimentation and successful performance.

Parallel learning systems and support groups are identified as major ways to enable these motivators. The critical facet of this paper [64] is that successful management of Anxiety 2 is a major motivator of organization and individual learning.

7.4   LEADERSHIP AND MANAGEMENT

As with the previous subjects considered in this chapter, much has been written on the subject of leadership. Some of this has been discussed in previous sections of this chapter as leadership relates strongly to such needs as quality, learning, and organizational culture. In this section, we wish to provide some specific commentary on organizational leadership.

We have previously indicated four facets of organizational oversight, as identified by Keller: administration, management, leadership, and governance. Unfortunately, the literature often uses each of these terms somewhat interchangeably. They are, of course, closely related; generally all are needed.

There are many studies of individual and organizational leadership. In a very popular work, Covey [65] cites seven habits of highly effective people and devotes a chapter to discussion of each. These "habits" of effectiveness relate to formally cultivated knowledge (what and why issues), skill- and training-based knowledge (how issues), and human desire properties (want issues). We state the seven "habits" in the form of objectives:

1. To be proactive.
2. To initiate activities with the end results supported by the activities in mind.
3. To put first things first, in the sense of developing an orderly problem-solving process.
4. To always think in a "win/win" fashion, such that Pareto optimality across people is achieved whenever possible.
5. To understand critical facets of problems and the views and values of others, as well as to communicate such that others understand our views and values.
6. To develop and encourage teamwork and synergy.
7. To develop principles of balanced self-renewal and self-learning in all relevant areas that support effectiveness.

The first three of these effectiveness objectives relate to individual concerns, the following three relate to group and organizational issues, and the last objective concerns individual and group learning and renewal. A major focus in this effort is the counterbalancing of independence and dependence relations such that an effective form of interdependence results.

In a more recent work [66], these seven interpersonal principles of effectiveness are extended to managerial and organizational leadership situations. They are also related to the 14 points of Deming that we discussed in Chapter 6. Eight characteristics of "principle-centered leaders" are identified. These leaders are said to be (1) continually learning, (2) service oriented, (3) satiated with positive energy, (4) believers in other people, (5) leaders of balanced lives, (6) participants in life as an adventure, (7) synergistic, and (8) strongly motivated for learning and self-renewal.

Clearly, these are closely related to the seven "habits" or characteristics of effective people.

Covey identifies three primary traits of effective leaders: integrity, maturity, and abundant mentality. Three generic inhibitors to leadership effectiveness are noted as appetite and passion, pride and pretension, and blind aspiration and ambition.

Seven deadly sins are identified:

1. Wealth without work, generally obtained through fraud.
2. Pleasure without conscience.
3. Knowledge without character.
4. Business and commerce without ethics and morality.
5. Science without humanity.
6. Religion without sacrifice.
7. Politics without principles.

These are, of course, to be avoided in the quest for leadership.

Three types of power or influence are identified.

1. *Principle-centered power* is based on honor or the eight characteristics of principle-centered leaders.
2. *Utility power* based on fairness, as represented by the useful exchange of products and services or the equivalent in terms of money.
3. *Coercive power* is based on fear, generally of adverse consequences, and adverse reactive control.

These are each related to various contexts for learning, as generally identified by Schein and as we discussed earlier. Covey suggests *management empowerment* and *organizational alignment* as two master principles supporting principle-centered leadership. He identifies four paradigms that might be used as a basis for leadership.

1. The *scientific management* paradigm is basically authoritarian and based on a Theory X type of approach to management. It addresses needs at the level of technoeconomic rationality and is based on fairness.

2. The *human relations* paradigm is based on social benevolence and kindness.
3. The *human resources* paradigm is based on cognitive science studies and the best psychological approaches to development.
4. The *principle-centered leadership* paradigm is said to be based on spiritual concepts associated with the whole person and meaning for all human beings.

The principle-centered leadership paradigm is suggested as better and more appropriate than the other three. Comparisons of this sort, however, need to be made very carefully because there is little to suggest that these four paradigms are necessarily mutually exclusive. Nor is there any reason to believe that these four are collectively exhaustive. There are other forms of leadership and culture, as we have noted earlier, that may exert major influences on organizations at various lifecycle phases of development. The conclusion that principle-centered leadership is a major facet of successful leadership is undeniable.

Six needs and conditions to enable management empowerment for principle-centered leadership are defined:

Character
Skills
Win/win negotiations and agreements
Self-supervision as contrasted with organization control
Supportive organizational processes and structures
Accountability through personal self-evaluation

This involves people in the organization and thereby enables organizational alignment. Establishing organizational mission statements that reflect these principle-centered leadership characteristics and creation of principle-centered learning environments are suggested as major ways to implement this paradigm. We see from this listing that the characteristics of principle-centered leadership do indeed encompass and include major facets of other forms of leadership.

Badaracco and Ellsworth [67] identify three leadership philosophies. Each of these is based on a set of fundamental assumptions about human nature and the resulting behavior patterns of people in organizations.

1. *Political leadership* is a result of trade-offs between the dividing forces that act to diffuse the efforts of an organization and bureaucratic forces that create inertia and reluctance to change. Out of a melting pot of feudal and bureaucratic organizations is likely to emerge opportunistic political leadership. In this situation, the most effective strategy for leadership is said to be that of moving forward, or muddling forward, in small incremental steps. Generally, the leader orchestrates this improvement from behind the scene, rather than in an up-front position. Political leadership is based on the assumed belief that people are inherently selfish and motivated primarily, if not exclusively, by self-interests. To serve these self-interests, people search for power and associated wealth and position and obtain this at the expense of others.

2. *Directive leadership* is a formal approach that is associated with the importance of information and the substance of organizational decisions. Generally, it is associated with personal involvement of organizational leadership in aiming the organization toward a strategically competitive position. Objective assessments of internal strengths and weaknesses, and external threats and opportunities, form the basis for action, as contrasted with internally and opportunistically political supports for decisions. There is a strong preference for substantive results over stylistic actions. Directive leadership also believes that humans are driven to achieve in competition and strive to higher levels of attainment on the human hierarchy of needs. This is accomplished by organizational cohesion and blending self-interests with organizational interests.

3. *Values-driven leadership* is strongly associated with shaping the organization such that the values and ideals of the organization have the strongest appeal possible for all members of the organization. Values-driven leadership is not suggested to replace opportunistic political leadership or directive leadership, but to transcend these forms of leadership. Thus a values-driven leader extends the directive leadership efforts to enable people to find meaning in life through their work and dedication to quality. It is based strongly on treating everyone with respect and dignity and striving for high quality performance.

Approaches are suggested that will achieve the three essential needs of setting and communicating goals and strategy, managing formal processes and structures, and resolving conflict. Suggestions for operational management and task control are also provided for each of these three leadership modes. While each of these three may be viewed as a complete management philosophy, organizations may not always be able to eliminate all forms of opportunistically political behavior.

The second major part of this first-class work is concerned with integrity and leadership dilemmas. The authors recognize that integrity is a major need to bring about values-driven leadership. In the way used here, integrity means wholeness and coherence, and rightness and ethical soundness. While a formal definition of integrity is not provided, uncompromising adherence to a code of sound values can be viewed as the inferred definition.

Several potential leadership dilemmas are suggested. These involve the need for trade-offs among competing concerns.

1. The desire for clarity and precision may conflict with the need for flexibility. The authors associate clarity and precision with integrity and generally prefer this over flexibility when conflicts among these desirable facets of leadership arise.

2. There are benefits to be obtained from top–down influence and from bottom–up influence. The three identified forms of leadership provide different guiding philosophies concerning this. Political leadership depends on opportunistic influences from lower organizational levels and thus tends to emphasize bottom–up organizational influences. Directive leadership emphasizes top–down influences. Values-driven leadership emphasizes both top–down and bottom–up influences as appropriate for specific situations. It is important to maintain an appropriate balance among these two forms of organizational influence. The authors suggest that inter-

vention and top–down leadership are more associated with integrity than bottom–up leadership.

3. It is generally very important to determine whether it is more appropriate to attack a problem by working on the problem itself or working on the problem-solving process. We have seen this concern before, and we will see it again in our subsequent efforts in Chapter 8 as the trade-off between product engineering and process engineering. Badaracco and Ellsworth term this the conflict between substance and process. Emphasizing either to the detriment of the other is inappropriate. These authors suggest that "substance is foremost . . . yet process does matter." Certainly, integrity will be lost if there is no substance associated with efforts. On the other hand, an inefficient process may well not lead to high quality results, regardless of the amount of substantive effort involved.

4. Confrontation versus compromise is identified as the fourth dilemma. They represent the two extreme approaches to dealing with disagreement and conflict. The authors suggest that the honesty and fairness values associated with integrity will generally not encourage leaders to hide their real feelings and beliefs. This may sometimes be associated with negotiation. This, plus leadership vision and commitment, suggests that integrity is more associated with a preference for respectful confrontation and communication rather than it is with compromise.

5. Conflicts between tangibles and intangibles represent the fifth dilemma faced by each of the three identified forms of leadership. These concerns also involve short-term issues, which are often very tangible, and long-term issues, which are often rather intangible. They involve possible conflicts between organizational performance and ethical standards, between organizational values and competitive pressures, and between social obligations and financial performance. Directive and values-driven leadership is generally concerned with intangible issues, whereas organizational political leadership is usually amoral and will desire to maintain flexibility and compromise in order to achieve short-term tangible objectives. These authors strongly advocate confronting the "tyranny of the tangibles," making intangibles tangible to the extent possible, and building commitment to long-term intangibles. This maintains integrity much more than alternative approaches.

In each of these dilemmas, we see a strong preference for values-driven leadership, and directive leadership, and a blend of these two in many cases. These are generally much more associated with leadership integrity than approaches based on opportunistic politics.

Rothschild [68] indicates that leaders share a number of common characteristics. Good leaders are said to be:

Committed to long-term survival, prosperity, and growth for themselves and the organization.

Focused on making organizations unique.

Endowed with a rare blend of insight, intuition, and analytic capabilities.

Capable of attracting, motivating, and maintaining an appropriate workforce.

Able to demonstrate consistency and predictability.

Able to determine where they want the organization to move and when it is time to migrate in favor of more appropriate leadership.

If there is a deficiency in any of these, there is a leadership deficiency. Achievement of objectives associated with these characteristics requires courage and dedication, passion and devotion, credibility, unique talents, ability to implement results-driven action, ability to organize and maintain teams, an excellent sense of timing, and the flexibility and willingness to relinquish power when this is needed for the good of the organization.

To achieve these ends, Rothschild identifies four major leadership roles:

Risk-takers, often the creators of an organization who have the dedication and talent to implement a strategic vision.

Care-takers, who nurture an organization beyond its growth stage into a healthy maturity.

Surgeons, who examine diseased portions of an organization and correct or remove those portions of the organization with diagnosed illness.

Undertakers, who harvest and/or merge the organization in order to mercifully lay to rest an unsalvageable organization and rescue those portion of the organization that are capable and in need of rebirth in a new form.

Clearly, these roles have a very natural association with the organizational lifecycle dynamics we identified in Figure 7.6. Rothschild examines each of these roles in product-oriented leadership, problem-solving leadership, marketing leadership, and systems and infrastructure creation leadership. He then examines efforts to support the leadership's transition from the present decade into the next.

The proper roles for leadership are identified as a function of the following:

The phase of the organizational lifecycle in which the organization finds itself.

The types of customers for the organizations's products.

The needs of the organization stakeholders.

The dynamics of the technologies associated with the organization.

Not only can the four leadership roles be directly associated with the organizational lifecycle dynamics, they can also be associated with customers, stakeholders, and technologies. Rothschild describes each of these associations in such a facile and direct manner that they appear almost self-evident.

The major part of the book is comprised of a lucid description of leadership tasks, for each of the four leadership roles, in product leadership, problem-solving leadership, marketing leadership, and systems and infrastructure leadership. Figures 7.12 through 7.15 describe some of the salient characteristics of these four leadership roles for different organizational functions.

Six critical characteristics of leadership, associated with each of the four leader-

Product Leadership	Problem-Solving Leadership
1. Recognize product needs first. 2. Protect the innovation against marauders. 3. Educate others about the product's value. 4. Organize for high quality and success; obtain needed money and human resources. 5. Maintain quality, regardless of cost. 6. Maintain demand through pricing that reinforces product uniqueness. 7. Prepare for the next needed innovation.	1. Assess situations to understand real problems. 2. Organize for long-term commitment/ sponsorship. 3. Create and meet realistic expectations. 4. Be flexible in adapting to client needs, admitting mistakes, and trying again. 5. Prepare for solution resistance and bad side effects. 6. Leverage results, enhance problem-solving ability, and prepare for the next problem.
Marketing Leadership	**Systems and Infrastructure Leadership**
1. Identify innovative way to market. 2. Protect marketing innovation by rapid deployment. 3. Select appropriate marketing setting for deployment of efforts. 4. Focus on a specific product and customer segment. 5. Match the approach to the product and service lifecycle.	1. Acquire the best system possible prior to the demand for the system. 2. Retain control of all long-term financial resources. 3. Be prepared for both success and the reaction of adversary groups. 4. Invest in interactive and proactive maintenance to retain competitive position. 5. Prepare for the future, including the next system; find a caretaker successor for the present system.

Figure 7.12 Characteristics of risk-taking leadership.

Product Leadership	Problem-Solving Leadership	Marketing Leadership
1. Assess the organization's threats and opportunities. 2. Diagnose organization's strengths and weaknesses. 3. Evaluate rationale for past failures and successes. 4. Build confidence of customers, suppliers, and stakeholders. 5. Use responsive pricing to cope with both long-term and short-term needs. Maintain market position and long-term cost advantage. 6. Know where and how the organization secures profit. 7. Prepare for the next product acquisition. 8. Continue to meet customer expectations.	1. Select clients who want long-term relations, know they have problems, and will pay for a solution. 2. Organize for long term commitment/ sponsorship. 3. Use "relationship pricing" based on results. 4. Listen and learn. 5. Offer complete problem-solving services. 6. Meet or surpass customer expectations. 7. Standardize problem-solving approaches. 8. Know when the effort is over. 9. Always make the best recommendations.	1. Optimize inventory for customer demand response. 2. Recognize that customers may have short memories. 3. Practice flexible and innovative pricing. 4. Create and meet customer expectations. 5. Develop partnerships with vendors. 6. Experiment with variations in the current approach.

Figure 7.13 Characteristics of care-taking leadership.

```
┌─────────────────────────────────────────────────┐
│               Product Leadership                  │
│ 1. Assess situation objectively and make a quick diagnosis │
│    of strengths and weaknesses.                   │
│ 2. Detect rationale for past successes and failures. │
│ 3. Assess the competitive situation.              │
│ 4. Establish customer, supplier, and stakeholder  │
│    confidence.                                    │
│ 5. Formulate strategic sourcing decisions.        │
│ 6. Utilize "responsive pricing" for short-term survival and │
│    long-term growth.                              │
│ 7. Establish and maintain ability to meet long-term │
│    demands.                                       │
└─────────────────────────────────────────────────┘
```

```
┌─────────────────────────────────────────────────┐
│              Marketing Leadership                 │
│ 1. Optimize inventory for customer demand response. │
│ 2. Recognize that customers may have short memories. │
│ 3. Practice flexible and innovative pricing.      │
│ 4. Create and meet customer expectations.         │
│ 5. Develop partnerships with vendors.             │
│ 6. Experiment with variations in the current approach. │
└─────────────────────────────────────────────────┘
```

Figure 7.14 Leadership characteristics of the organization surgeon.

ship roles and with each of the four organizational functions, are identified in the closing sections of Rothschild's work.

1. Never confuse asset stripping with leadership.
2. Never be greedy and self-serving.
3. Always plan for leadership succession.
4. Cultivate a tolerance for a reasonable number of failures.
5. Do not avoid change, but never change only for the sake of change.
6. Always lead through strategic drivers.

```
┌─────────────────────────────────────────────────┐
│               Product Leadership                  │
│ 1. Communicate realistic organizational difficulties early │
│    and well and with honesty and trustworthiness. │
│ 2. Assume personal responsibility for guiding people │
│    through mergers and/or downsizing.             │
│ 3. Reward outstanding performance and solicit stakeholder │
│    ideas for organizational improvement.          │
│ 4. Demand continued productivity improvements in order to │
│    improve organizational effectiveness and enhance │
│    marketability of workers.                      │
│ 5. Maintain all organizational facilities.        │
└─────────────────────────────────────────────────┘
```

Figure 7.15 Organizational undertaker characteristics.

Each of these characteristics is concerned with organizational lifecycle phases, customers, stakeholders, and technology usage in the organization. Whether or not there exists a single leader or leadership pattern that is appropriate for all lifecycle phases and all leadership functions is an interesting question. Very clearly, as suggested by the last four illustrations, the needed leadership patterns change across the various functions of product, problem-solving, marketing, and system and infrastructure leadership roles suggested in this study. Whether a single individual can fit all these various roles is a related question. Rothschild argues strongly that this is generally not possible.

Kotter [69] is among those who have taken care to distinguish between leadership and management. He indicates that leadership involves moving people from one state to a better state without transgressing on the rights of others in the process. To do this, leadership involves three principal activities that roughly correspond to the definition, development, and deployment—or formulation, analysis, and interpretation— efforts in systems engineering.

1. *Agenda Creation.* Direction setting is needed to establish a future vision and strategies for the needed changes to enable realization of the vision.
2. *Developing Human Networks.* Communication of the strategic vision and developing a set of shared assumptions and understandings of the vision are needed to achieve and alignment of people who are committed to organizational progress.
3. *Action Implementation or Execution.* Motivating and inspiring people to move in directions appropriate to achieve the strategic vision despite competing short-term opportunistic political challenges and bureaucratic barriers.

These are contrasted with generally comparable management efforts involved in operational planning and budgeting, organizing and staffing, and controlling and coordinating (problem-solving). While management produces a considerable degree of predictability and order that supports organizational productivity, leadership produces dramatic and useful change. Both are needed. Leadership provides focus and management provides a verification and validation of this focus in terms of more operational realities. Of course, there is a continuum between these two, and there are roles for administration and governance as well. Within each of these two, or four, roles for organizational oversight there is a range of focus, which might simply be described as strong at one extreme and weak at the other. In reality, performance in one of these executive functions is a multiattributed concept.

Kotter devotes major attention to describing the differences in approach for each of these three major roles and the outcomes from each that may be anticipated. Figure 7.16 provides an interpretation of this perspective on management and leadership. There are a number of potential feedback loops not shown here. Clearly, there is no sharp line of demarcation between leadership and management that we might seem to suggest in the figure.

Coordination of management and leadership roles is also discussed by Kotter, including the different patterns of growth that may be experienced for one individual

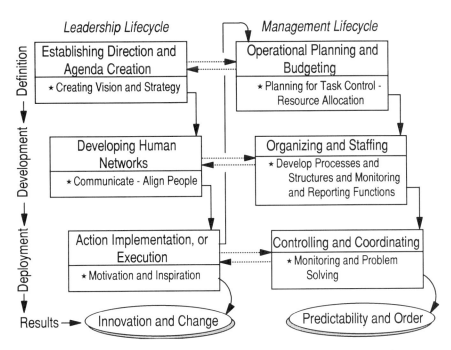

Figure 7.16 Interpretation of management and leadership lifecycle.

in a two-dimensional space comprised of strong and weak management on one axis and strong and weak leadership on the other.

Jaques [70] discusses what is denoted as "requisite organization" in a work on organization and leadership. In this eclectic work, a requisite organization is defined as one that performs with efficiency and competitiveness through the release of human imagination. Such an organization is concerned both with executive effort in assuring effective operation and improvement in existing organizational structures and with entrepreneurial effort in growing the organization through such work as restructuring, mergers, and acquisitions.

A *stratified systems theory* (SST) is identified to enable realization of a requisite organization. This is based on identification of the values and culture of the organization. From this, organizational purpose and functions may be determined. From organizational purpose and functions follows organizational structure. Jaques' main concern is that the organizational structure is that of a requisite organization. From this structure for a requisite organization follow any number of information and control subsystems that enable the organization to function efficiently and effectively. Six phases to developing sound organization and leadership are identified.

1. An organizational mission is articulated in terms of the purpose and primary functions to be carried out by the organization. This presumes some strategic leadership vision to enable the organizational mission to be established.

2. Functional alignment is achieved in terms of allocating these functions across various levels of a to-be-designed organizational architecture or structure.

3. An appropriate organizational structure or architecture is defined and developed in order to support these identified functions. This includes assignment of humans and tasks to the organizational structure.

4. Information, operational planning, and control subsystems are then established.

5. Human resources subsystems are then established. These are more or less operational efforts associated with personnel and training, but such efforts as the compensation and reward system are also established here.

6. Managerial leadership is established throughout all organizational strata. This is associated with power, in the form of authority, and persuasion, in the form of inducement to follow guidance willfully.

Individual chapters in this work address each of these development phases.

It is particularly interesting here that information and control subsystems are established prior to the establishment of human resource subsystems. It would appear that this might well be appropriate for an entirely new organization; it may be very difficult to achieve in an existing organization, which finds obsolete technologies in need of product reengineering. There are a number of implications in this for reengineering, and we discuss many of these in our next chapter.

The concept of a stratified systems theory has to do with implementation of this organizational planning and leadership model across a hierarchy such as identified in Figure 7.17. Clearly, what is pictured here amounts to a steep hierarchy. Such hierarchies have come under major criticism recently, and we examine some of this in our next chapter. Jacques envisions four different types of organizational structure.

1. The *manifest organization* is represented by the official or espoused organizational structure.

2. The *assumed organization,* or perceived organization, is the organizational structure as envisioned by each person viewing actual organizational functioning.

3. The *extant organization* is that represented by the organizational structure in practice or how the organization actually works.

4. The *requisite organization* is the organization and organizational structure as they should exist according to the prescriptions set forth in this work.

In some ways, Jacques work provides a challenge to much of the contemporary wisdom associated with empowered teams and group efforts. In a related work [71], Jacques praises hierarchy and suggests that managerial hierarchy is often neither well described nor adequately used and that a major problem with group and team effort is the difficulty of holding a group accountable for its work products.

There are a number of other works that relate organizational and leadership issues to organizational structure and architecture. In a recent and definitive work

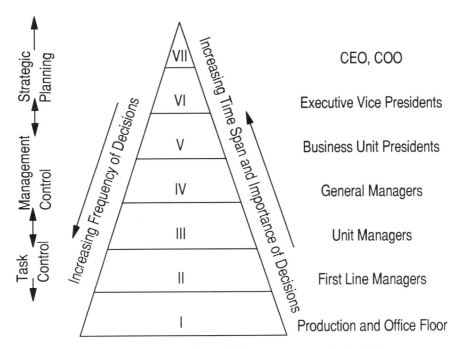

Figure 7.17   Steep hierarchy and decisions at organizational layers.

[72], a number of new and innovative approaches for the structuring and architectural design of organizations are discussed. Organizational change and redesign issues are discussed by a number of authors in [73], primarily from a behavioral and organizational science perspective. The journal *Organization Science* regularly publishes definitive papers in this area. An editorial in a recent issue [74] provides a succinct discussion of the need for sound empirical research in this area to provide needed perspectives on both theory and practice.

7.5   A NECESSARY CAVEAT

In this chapter, and in both the preceding and subsequent chapter, we provide overviews of a number of suggested approaches to organizationally related constructs. While these have generally clear implications to systems management, it is only natural to ask how much of this is hype, and how much of it is meaningful dialogue. We need to be able to separate the two. In an insightful work, Eccles, Norhia, and Berkley [75] seek to discover the essence of management and to separate this from much of the speechcraft describing management actions. In their work, no clear distinction is made between management and leadership.*

*It would be unusual indeed to enter into a public or private sector establishment, of any type, and expect to find individuals designated as "leaders" and who have such a title. It would not, of course, be unusual to find people designated as "managers" or "administrators." In a similar way, the term "governor" is uncommon in the way that it is used here.

They suggest seven underlying principles of management-initiated action.

1. Managers often act under conditions of uncertainty. Full, complete, and perfect information will generally never be obtained. Thus risk management is an important facet of management.

2. Management constantly allows for and provides flexibility. Often, situations will change and what comprises appropriate action at one time may well have to be changed in order to adapt to changing conditions.

3. Management is politically astute. It is recognized that organizational and opportunistic politics will generally arise, despite the potential harm that may be done to the organization in the long run. Skillful managers become knowledgeable about the potentially hidden agendas and actions of others and attempt either to thwart these or to reorganize them as appropriate to best achieve organizational objectives.

4. Management has a critical sense of time. Managers know when to hold the cards and when to fold the cards. They know when to act and when to hide or run. They know that what is an appropriate action today may well not be an appropriate action tomorrow.

5. Management is necessarily associated with good abilities at judgment and decision making.

6. Management is able to use rhetoric and oratory effectively.

7. Management must necessarily deal with many agendas in a simultaneous or current fashion.

Many of these observations, especially the last one, relate very strongly to the comparable and earlier studies of Mintzberg on the nature of managerial work [76]. They also relate to the observations of Winograd and Flores [77], who indicate that mangers cannot avoid acting, cannot retreat to contemplate on potential actions, cannot predict the outcome of actions with certainty, do not have a stable assessment or representation of the situation, cannot provide unequivocal truth but instead only representations of actions and outcomes, and must realize that their language must have action interpretations by others. In short, management is necessarily down-to-earth and pragmatic. And so is leadership, at least to a point.

These authors [75] suggest four language needs in strategic statements that are intended to define organizational purpose and to serve as guides for organizational action.

1. The core concepts of the language most provide fresh and powerful insights.

2. The language must be such as to allow clear guidelines for action to be defined.

3. The language must enhance the ability to communicate strategy and clarify the implications of actions in terms of accomplishing purposes of the organization.

4. It should be possible to use the language for multiple organizational purposes.

In this chapter, to some extent, and particularly in our next chapter, we examine a considerable number of approaches for improvements in organizational productivity. It would be especially interesting to evaluate the extent to which the "new languages" offered by these approaches comply with these guidelines.

Strategy and strategic plans should lead to action. The organization has a number of past and present strengths and weaknesses. At present and in the future, there will be a number of threats and opportunities. Strategy is intended to traverse these internal characteristics, generally associated with the past and the present, such as to enable the organization to cope with present and future threats and opportunities. From the perspective of actions to follow, effective strategies are said to have the following desirable qualities:

They act as a bridge that traverses the past, the present, and the future.

They are both consciously planned and opportunistic.

They involve a very wide range of alternative courses of action.

It is necessary that organizational processes and structure be tuned to strategy and results, and that systematic measurements, which are generally at the level of process and product, provide useful guidelines for strategy. These observations lead to a number of useful suggestions to put new ideas into a useful perspective and focus on the action, results, and pragmatism that is management. We have identified some of these needs in our earlier efforts, such as the discussion in Chapter 5 of the role of systematic measurements and activity-based costing in systems management approaches. Others also discuss them [78,79].

7.6 PLANNING, CULTURE, AND LEADERSHIP

As with the other topics we have discussed, many have written about planning. Here, we wish to provide an overview of planning as it relates to organizational culture and leadership. We have discussed a number of aspects of planning in Chapter 2. Our discussions here compliment these earlier discussions, generally from somewhat different rationality perspectives [80–82]. In particular, we will examine planning and leadership from the perspective of technoeconomic rationality and from a composite perspective that does not totally rely on technoeconomic rationality.

7.6.1 Technoeconomic Rationality in Planning

A recent and exceptional work by Boar [83] takes a contemporary and generally conventional view of strategic planning. There are three major guidelines concerning purpose, function, and structure.

   1. The purposes of strategic planning include direction setting, obtaining consistency of purpose and concentration of effort, and obtaining flexibility as well in order to enable an organization to improve its competitive position.

2. The functions of strategic planning include identification of organizational objectives in response to observed or perceived threats and opportunities and the selection of activities and allocation of resources to fulfill these objectives. This functional definition established a framework for important organizational processes associated with strategic planning. These include the formulation of objectives, the identification of a set of alternative courses of action to fulfill these, the analysis of these alternatives, and interpretation of this analysis such as to lead to decision making and resource allocation.

3. The structure of the strategic planning process is comprised of three phases.

(a) *Situation assessment* is concerned with detecting issues that are of vital importance and those of little importance, the causal factors driving important issues, and the interrelationships between issues and issue formulation variables. In addition to these conclusions concerning opportunities, threats, and potential problems, situation assessment is also concerned with identification of evidence, in terms of warrants and backings, and generation of courses of action that are potentially responsive to problem resolution needs. Essentially, it is concerned with examining present and future scenarios relative to the organization's competitive position, in addition to the detection and diagnosis of external threats and opportunities, and internal strengths and weaknesses, that exist. On the basis of these, potential alternative courses of action are identified.

(b) *Strategy analysis* involves both definition of what should be accomplished by the analysis effort and the development, through analysis, of the means to accomplish this. It involves more explicit formulation of strategic actions than is accomplished in the situation assessment effort. The consequences, including risks, of alternative courses of action need to be identified. Boar suggests six approaches to formulate these strategic actions for analysis: rule-based *formula methods* as identified from past, successful, and codified experiences; *formal analytical methods* based on strategic thrust and market opportunity analysis; *strategy coherence* analysis to force alignment of each set of potential strategic actions with objectives, generic *principles,* or exemplars associated with wise and prudent behavior; use of *key findings* from the situation assessment effort; and skill-based *art.*

(c) *Execution* involves interpretation of the strategic plans and deployment of the selected plan as action. This requires a commitment plan, a change management plan, selection of owners or champions for various parts of the strategy, human resource architectures, wide-scope and large-scale participation, and support for and training in project management. At a more philosophical level, successful deployment depends on having a planning process that earns respect and having a credible strategic plan that is worthy of effort and that captures the imagination. At a very pragmatic level, it requires a reward system that provides incentives for adoption of desired behavior patterns, and a measurement system to evaluate customer satisfaction and organizational performance.

These efforts may be viewed as either phases that correspond very closely to the definition, development, and deployment phases described so often here, or as steps that correspond to the formulation, analysis, and interpretation efforts that comprise a given phase of effort. If strategic planning is viewed as a process, our terminology would associate phases with these efforts. If strategic planning is viewed as a phase in an overall organizational effort, then the term step is more appropriate and in keeping with our terminology.

The approach taken by Boar is decidedly that of technoeconomic rationality in which planning is a formal process of producing a plan in the form of an integrated set of decisions that assist in achieving organizational long-term objectives.

He is well aware that organizational politics present a difficult barrier to overcome and that it is natural for organizational politics to emerge through the hierarchical stratification into functional units that occur in most organizations. "Heritage" is also identified as another barrier in which people, through being conditioned by a bureaucratic risk avoidance culture, believe that there is little to be gained and much to lose through entrepreneurship and seek minimax risk avoidance strategies that minimize the maximum possible loss. Of course, there are benefits that are associated with heritages and legacies, as well as potentially unacceptable behavior constraints.

Boar recommends a management *commitment plan* as a set of actions taken to modify organizational behaviors such that the organization willingly and enthusiastically repositions itself in accordance with strategic plans. Commitment is said to provide tangible illustrations of courage, and courage is needed to establish commitment. Establishing credibility is a major need as a prerequisite to obtaining commitment.

Thus credibility is identified as a major facet of planning leadership. A recent work by Kouzes and Posner [84] provides an excellent discourse on four major leadership traits that support, and are prerequisites to, credibility: honesty, forward looking, inspiring, and competency.

Credibility is associated primarily with belief in the consistency between the words and the actions of others. Kouzes and Posner identify three major supports for credibility: (1) *clarity* of statements, (2) statements that support *unity* in building an organization with shared values and shared vision, and (3) *intensity* of beliefs and feelings about the worth of the espoused values and vision.

They suggest six practices, called "disciplines," that need to be practiced for a person to become or remain credible as a leader:

1. A discovery of self, in terms of beliefs, values, and standards.
2. An appreciation for colleagues, in terms of dignity and respect.
3. A developed and affirmed set of shared values to build a strong sense of community while still allowing for diversity.
4. A developing capacity for learning and action, both on an individual basis and for the organization as a whole.

5. The establishment of personal behavior and judgmental actions that are associated with serving a purpose.

6. Sustaining hope, through support and compassionate behavior to others that also demonstrates dignity and respect for them.

A major chapter is devoted to each of these disciplines and their support for credibility.

Boar [83] devotes major chapters to quality assurance in strategic planning, administration, and management of the strategic planning process, and a major concluding chapter on understanding and improving contemporary information movement and management (IM&M) technology and management efforts. The major thrust of this definitive work and an earlier work [85] concerns strategic perspectives for information technology.

Boar recognizes, as does Mintzberg [86] in a work that discusses rationalist and other approaches as well, that the strategy realized will seldom be the formally intended strategy or the strategy as initially formulated. There will be unrealized portions of intended strategy that are not realized either because they are incapable of realization or because there is some form of "noise" in the realization process. What is left after the unrealized strategy is removed from the intended strategy is the deliberate strategy. This deliberate strategy represents that portion of the intended strategy that is realized in practice. To this is augmented an emergent strategy which is not at all intended, but which comes about because of the exigencies of the particular situation extant. The result of this implementation is the realized strategy, that is, those portions of the intended strategy as augmented by the emergent strategy. Figure 7.18 illustrates this view of technoeconomic rational planning. Because of the presence of unrealized and emergent strategies, Mintzberg calls this process the strategy formation process, as contrasted with formulation process.

Boar suggests that the strategic planning or strategy formulation process be analytically and quantitatively based, participatory across relevant stakeholders, and quality focused, both with respect to the process itself and the results of the process strategic plans. These are highly desirable across all perspectives on rationality. For other than technoeconomic rationality perspectives, the focus on analytical and qualitatively based assessment of the technical and economic worth of alternative planning approaches, while possibly a factor and perhaps even a strong one, is not the dominant driver of the planning process.

7.6.2 Strategic Planning as Strategic Programming

There are many who have written about strategic planning failures. In recent and excellent efforts, Mintzberg [86,87] discusses the technoeconomic rationality approach to planning. He indicates three basic premises to the "planning school" of technoeconomic rationality.

1. Strategic planning and strategy formulation are controlled and formalized processes comprised of a finite number of phases, each of which is supported by a number of analytical approaches.

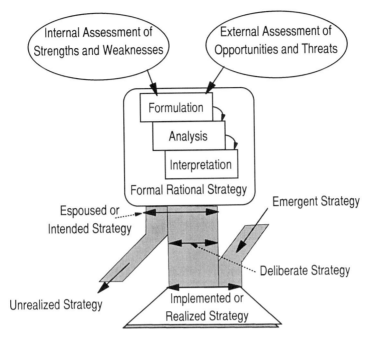

Figure 7.18 Technoeconomic rationality and the resulting realized strategy.

2. In principle, responsibility for strategic planning processes lies with the chief executive officer (CEO). In practice, the definition, development, and deployment of strategies are handled by a staff planning office that reports to the CEO.
3. The strategies that result from the planning process are implemented as organizational structures, operational controls such as budgets, programs, and operating plans.

The sort of plans that evolve are assumed to have the structure illustrated in Figure 7.19. Our discussions of planning in Chapter 2 are based, more or less, on this analysis-based model of the planning process.

Scheduling the planning process and reviews and evaluation of the results of planning are inherent parts of this process. Each of the functional or operating units in an organization may have a plan. Thus we might have plans for systems acquisition, RDT&E, marketing, finance and administration, and even plans for the planning unit. These individual organizational units may also have plans. We may have, for example, a basic research plan, an applied research plan, a development plan, an RDT&E marketing plan, and an RDT&E management plan. These might be tactical plans in support of the RDT&E strategic plan. The tactical plans would then be disaggregated into various operational plans. The major ingredients contained in a strategic planning document are objectives, strategies, programs, and budgets. These ingredients are contained in each of the more detailed tactical and operational plans, with generic name changes to elements like goals, controls, and projects.

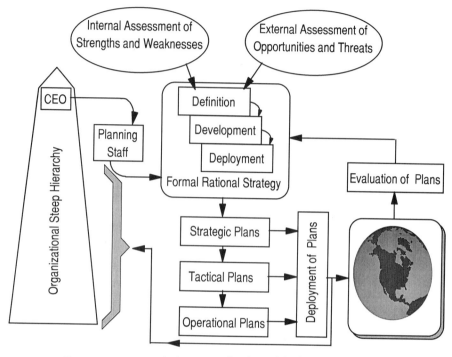

Figure 7.19   Formal planning school model of strategic planning.

While the term budget is ubiquitous throughout the plans, there is a (generally steep) hierarchy of budgets. Of course, there are also hierarchies of objectives, strategies, and programs.

The strategies and programs portions of these hierarchies at lower hierarchical levels of planning comprise the *action planning* part of a planning effort. The objectives, or goals, and budgets elements comprise more routine performance *command and control* activities at these lower levels. In technoeconomic rationality-based approaches to planning, objectives influence strategies and these, in turn, influence programs. Programs lead to budgets and these lead to actions at the highest levels of the hierarchy. The budget is something responsive to objectives, strategies, and programs, which is an enabler of actions. At the lower levels in the organization, however, budgets are "handed down" and these actually drive what is done. When we attempt to align the steep hierarchies of objectives, strategies, budgets, and programs and show their influence on actions, we find that there is indeed much opportunity for obfuscation, as very well indicated by Mintzberg. Figures 7.20 and 7.21 illustrate some of the potential difficulties. In particular, Figure 7.21 illustrates the difference in these two approaches to action—planning at the top of the hierarchy and planning near the bottom. It is, of course, hopelessly incomplete but does illustrate the complexity dilemma that is present. Mintzberg also considers a third form of strategic planning that is based on capital budgeting as an organizational control mechanism.

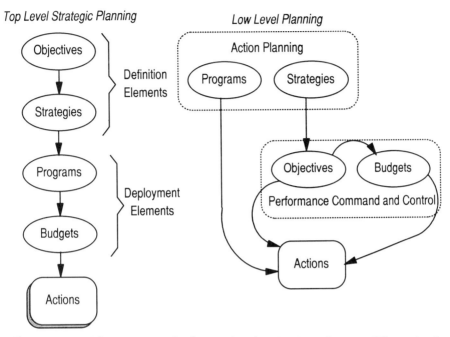

Figure 7.20 Linkages among the four major planning ingredients at different levels.

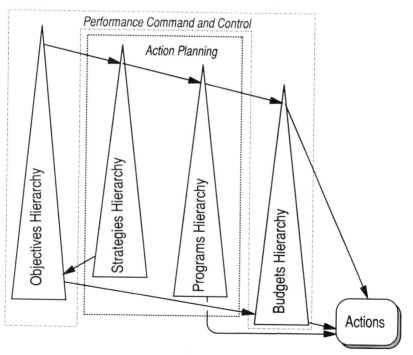

Figure 7.21 Another view of linkages among the four major planning ingredients at different hierarchical levels.

He provides major evidence to show that this planning school or technoeconomic rationality-based approach to planning seldom, if ever, works. Two major pitfall levels of the planning school or formal technoeconomic planning rationality are identified. The first of these generic levels represent more-or-less common explanations concerning why strategic planning often fails. The second level is the level of greatest concern here. A number of pitfalls are identified within each of these two levels.

The generic characteristics required for successful planning are difficult to achieve because of several barriers.

1. *Commitment*. Planning is a very centralized process, which, as a by-product of this centralization, is likely to annihilate precisely that commitment required for success. This annihilation may occur at the top of the organizational hierarchy, lower down, or throughout. Even when central staff planners are facilitators, there are issues associated with freedom and concerns with whether planning may be little more than routine calculation.

2. *Change*. A climate that is congenial to planning may not be congenial to strategy making and a hostile climate for planning may be more attractive to the making of successful strategy. Successful strategy requires flexibility to accommodate the needed changes and planning often supports incrementalism and inflexibility rather than change. Planning may be more directed at today than the future.

3. *Organizational Politics*. Planning represents a method of political influence. The trappings of efficiency, effectiveness, consistency, and systematic planning may well be desired as symbols, rather than because of the inherent value of the plans themselves. Thus organizational planning politics may well develop. As noted earlier in this chapter, organizational politics may not necessarily be inherently bad. Nevertheless, it is generally a threat to the legitimacy of plans.

4. *Planning and Control Conflicts*. Planning may be based more on public relations and efforts to gain an illusion of control than upon substance.

There are several fundamental fallacies of formalized strategic planning.

1. Formal planning assumes, in many ways, that the future can be predetermined at the time the plans are made. Forecasting, especially in areas where discontinuities are likely, is notoriously inaccurate. Planning may assume an illusion of control that is only realistic if humans have control over the environment and the behavior of others. The use of alternative future scenarios, each associated with a probability of occurrence, is also associated with difficulties. It leads to contingency planning and this may result in a lack of commitment to any plan. While this may result for a number of scenarios that are different only in incremental ways and have small probabilities of occurring, there are challenges in accommodating very different scenarios where each has a relatively probability of occurrence.

2. The assumed desirability of detachment of strategy from operations is quite erroneous. It is not desirable and cannot be brought about without potentially great

harm to the organization. Detachment is a desirable attribute because attention to an excessive number of nitty-gritty operational details may be so all time consuming that there is little time left for thinking about the future and appropriate strategy for that future. The advocated detachment of strategy from operations, and the provision of what is presumed to be operational knowledge and wisdom to support strategic analysis and planning, is based on several assumed qualities of quantitative information that are often not justified. Quantified information is often very limited in scope and fails to properly represent noneconomic information and information that is not easily quantifiable but which may be of much value. Quantified operational information may often be too highly aggregated for effective use. Alternately, it may be aggregated in a manner specifically chosen to disguise important trends. For this reason, and for other reasons, it may be unreliable. Much aggregated quantified information is presented too late to be of value for use in strategy formation. Neither planners who formulate strategic plans nor those who rely on strategic plans should be separated from strategy making. Yet, this is assumed by the planning school. It is a foolish assumption that formulation can be separated from implementation, that thinking can be separated from action, or that we can have two entirely different groups of people involved in definitional, developmental, and deployment phases of effort in planning. These efforts need to be fastened together and integrated and a failure of deployment has to be generally regarded as a failure in definition as well. Also, it is necessary to associate words, actions, and results; not doing so advocates the notion that *continuous hype is the most important product.*

3. Formalization (only) leads to failure. It assumes that a formal analysis process is equivalent to a synthesis process. While analysis may support design and synthesis, it is not and cannot be used as a substitute for it.

Because of these difficulties, and in particular because of the difficulty associated with the formalization dilemma, Mintzberg states that *"strategic planning is not strategy formation."* His basic concern is, of course, with strategy formation.

To this end, he is much concerned with coupling analysis with intuition. He identifies the major role of (classic) strategic planning as actually that of *strategic programming.* From this perspective, formal planning is useful in an effective organization in programming the strategies already in existence in the organization and to formally elaborate and operationalize them as organizational processes. Thus formal planning, as described in the foregoing, is more concerned with effective tactics and operations than it is strategy. In other words, the essential recommendation is that formal planning is not used to create or synthesize strategies. Rather, it should be used to analyze strategies and interpret strategies for tactical and operational planning.

A three-phase effort is suggested to enable this strategic programming.

1. Provide greater and more explicit *definition* of the strategy in terms of codifying it. By codifying, Mintzberg means clarifying and expressing it in a form

that is sufficiently operational that it can be analyzed and interpreted, and communicated to others in the organization.

2. Elaborate the strategy through *development* and decomposition of the strategy into hierarchical structures that begin with substrategies and end with specific action plans for the four hierarchies shown in figure 7.21. Mintzberg calls the result of this effort the elaborated strategy.

3. Accomplish *deployment* of the strategy in terms of converting the developed strategy or elaborated strategy into specific and implemented changes in action. Mintzberg indicates that this involves crossing the divide from action planning to performance command and control. It involves reconsidering the budgets and objectives of the performance command and control portion of implementation action in response to and to reflect the restated programs and strategies that are associated with action planning.

The major accomplishment in this is that of repositioning strategic planning and associating it more with the process of implementation and not as much with the process of high level strategy formation. He recognizes, of course, the inherent dangers of disassociating formulation and interpretation, or definition and deployment, and does not, in any sense, suggest this. The major point is that the conventional planning school model is not so much wrong as misdirected in terms of the suggested area of application.

Plans as the result of strategic programming are viewed therefore as tools for communications and control. Two very vital roles for planning as strategic programming are identified.

- Planning, as strategic programming, serves as a most valuable communications medium.
- Planning, as strategic programming, serves as a most valuable management control apparatus.

Thus planning as strategic programming provides a very suitable vehicle for strategic control, management control, or systems management. It is therefore an inherent part of systems engineering and, for this reason, we emphasize it in this text.

Strategic control requires the tracking of realized or actually implemented strategies. It also requires the tracking of envisioned or intended strategies. In this manner, there is some degree of knowledge obtained concerning the nature of unrealized strategies and emergent strategies. This is of value in determining the extent to success, or lack thereof, of the realized strategies, and the extent to which the intended strategy has been realized. Planners may be of great use in this management control role. For example, if an intended strategy is realized in practice, failure of the realized strategy is indicative of an ineffective technoeconomic rational planning process. Success of the realized strategy represents a success for formal plans. If an intended strategy is not realized in practice and if the realized strategy is successful, this represents success for the emergent strategy and a need for learning about the ingredients that led to success. If the intended strategy is not realized and if the realized strategy is not successful, then there are major failures and everything needs to be redone.

On the basis of planning discoveries such as these, Mintzberg identifies three major roles and one potential support role for planners.

1. Planners are strategy finders. They aid in the discovery of realized patterns in actual operations, assessment of these patterns, and interpreters of actions as policy. This pattern recognition function is a potentially very important one.

2. Planners are strategy analysts. The result of this strategy analysis is information that may provide valuable pragmatic inputs, of a surveillance nature, to the policy formation process. Planners may assist in internal efforts associated with benchmarking and legitimation. As analysts, planners are also strategy evaluators. They may assist greatly in the investigation and careful scrutiny of strategies that are made as part of the strategy-making process.

3. Planners are catalysts who encourage planning, both at a formal and informal level, and future thinking. They can be testers of organizational vision.

4. Planners may be strategists with insight and creativity who can also contribute to the strategy formation process.

The latter of these potential roles is, while desirable, not absolutely necessary. In the concluding portions of this work, some suggestions are given for the role of planning as strategic programming in the seven different organizational forms we discussed in Section 7.3.5.

7.6.3 Temporal Sorting Model for Planning

In an important recent work concerned primarily with public sector institutions, March and Olsen [88] indicate that there are two generic types of models of organizational behavior and politics. One of these is termed the *rational competition model* and is familiar to those involved in quantitative systems analysis and systems engineering. As we have noted, we would prefer to call this technoeconomic rationality as there are other forms of rationality [15]. The formal decision-making process involves activities of situation assessment and action implementation. Most of the illustrations of process models that we provide in this text are of this formal rational competition model.

In a group situation, we necessarily must consider how alliances of people are formed and broken. This raises a number of issues related to using self-interested individuals as agents for other self-interested individuals. This can lead to a number of political models and to political rationality.

The second generic model identified by March and Olsen is a *temporal sorting model,* which attempts to embrace the many complicated happenings that involve the empirical or experiential observation of collective decision making. Rules, routines, and standard operating policies reduce the potential for chaos in situations that are governed by a temporal sorting model. The authors identify a set of six propositions that indicate how one comes to believe what one believes.

1. People trust others who are perceived as enabling relevant events that they like and inhibiting events that they dislike.
2. People will ultimately believe that those they trust enable events that they like. In a similar way, people will ultimately believe that those they distrust enable events that they dislike.
3. People will ultimately believe that events are relevant if they agree with people they trust relative to the event and disagree with those they distrust relative to these same events.
4. People may be considered active relative to the extent to which their perceptions and actions relative to an event are unambiguous.
5. People will, to the extent allowed by their activity level and the political system, seek out those they trust and avoid contact with those they distrust.
6. People will feel integrated into a political system to the extent that they like the relevant events that result from and through their participation in the system.

There are many virtues assumed to be present in order for people to believe in others, such as integrity and credibility.

This temporal sorting model view challenges the conventional one that life is organized around choices that are made only from a technoeconomic perspective. From this perspective, life not only involves choice but also interpretation. Symbols and ritual are very important in this interpretation effort. The interactions of rationalist and temporal sorting models are thus of major importance in providing the ability to realistically describe organizations and organizational processes of judgment and choice. These two very different models of organizational systems provide a theoretical basis for analysis of judgment and choice issues, and for establishing any number of rationality perspectives that fit on a continuum between these two extremes.

These propositions stress the organization of belief as essential to the substance of belief. The predictions that can be made with such a temporal sorting model depend on the way in which the organization is able to orchestrate contact and experience. For example, when meaning develops, there is a tendency for a population to partition itself into groups that share interpretations and preferences within, but not across, groups. If there is sufficient slack time, subcultures may develop. This view challenges the conventional one that life is organized around choices and replaces it with the view that life involves choice and interpretation.

Major portions of this effort are devoted to organizational transformation, including and emphasizing the transformation of political organizations. Rules and standard operating procedures bring about stability and reduce the potential for organizational chaos that might occur through use of a technoeconomic rationality-based model. Institutional reform is considered both as an ad hoc activity and as deliberate public policy. Much of the decision-based guidance supports the organizational ambiguity models that have led to the garbage can models of organizational choice.

When the realities of organized ambiguity are associated with organizational problem-solving and decision making, the result is what is termed a *garbage can model* of organizational choice [50–53]. In this model, which has generated much recent interest, there are five fundamental elements:

Issues or problems

Organizational structure

Participants, actors, or agents

Choice opportunities and actions

Solutions or products of the choice process

These problems, solutions, and choice opportunities are assumed to be quasi-independent, exogenous *"streams"* that are *linked* in a fashion that is determined by organizational structure constraints. There are several of these. The most important are *access structure,* or the access of problems to choice opportunities, *decision structure,* or the access of choice opportunities to solutions, and *energy structure,* which evolves in a dynamic fashion in terms of the number of problems or solutions that are linked to choice opportunities at a particular time.

The participants in the process can also be regarded as variables since they "come and go" over time and devote varying amounts of time and energy to problems, solutions, and choice opportunities due to other competing demands on their time. This relatively new organizational decision model views organizational decision making as resulting from four variables: problems, solutions, choice opportunities, and people.

Decisions result from the interaction of four factors:

Solutions looking for problems

Problems looking for solutions

Decision opportunities

Participants in the problem-solving process

The garbage can model allows for these variables being selected more or less at random from a garbage can. The interaction of these variables provides the opportunity for decision making. Generally these interactions are not controlled. Rather, they occur in an almost random fashion due to the vexing equivocality associated with problematic preferences, unclear procedures, and fluid participants. The major reason for the garbage can approach is the chronic ambiguity and considerable equivocality that is present in the environment.

This mixture of decision factors is not necessarily associated with poor management. Doubtlessly, this is often the case, but it is not necessarily the case that garbage can decisions are poor decisions, or that garbage can environments are poor environments. They may simply be unavoidable from the perspective of a given human in a given situation. We can easily envision numerous instances of well-run organizations in which these four factors would come together to drive the decision-making process. For example, many of the high tech defense contractors trying to expand into commercial markets find their decision making driven by these four factors. The existing environment may well suggest this approach to decision making.

In a garbage can environment, decisions generally occur through rational problem solving, through ignoring the problem until it goes away or resolves itself, or through the oversight of having the problem solved inadvertently by having another related problem solved. Doubtlessly, this is a realistic descriptive model. It has been used to analyze a number of existing decision situations, especially in a university decision context [52]. Examination of garbage can decision environments has led to conclusions concerning normative strategies to maximize decision effectiveness [89].

Three areas of equivocality are generally present in a garbage can environment:

1. *Problematic preferences,* in that different decision-making units have different objectives, and these generally evolve over time in an imprecise and unpredictable manner.
2. *Unclear procedures for making decisions,* in that responsibility and authority are usually separated and fragmented.
3. *Fluid decision participation,* in that the members of the decision-making units change over time, in an often unpredictable manner.

In the garbage can model, the problems, solutions, and choice opportunities are mixed together in *garbage cans.* The division of human effort among problems, solutions, and choices is fuzzy and not fixed in any highly organized way. Problems, solutions, and choice opportunities may not coalesce in the right way at the right time such as to lead to a formal rational solution to a problem.

There are many unanswered questions relative to descriptive and normative use of this interesting model, and there is much study in progress at this time concerning extensions of this model. One of the most potentially useful facets of the garbage can model, or garbage can rationality, is that it is a definitive approach for relating social structure to cognitive structure. Not only does it have this descriptive appeal, but it is a potentially useful organizational model that can explain behavior and provide suggestions for improvement in such potential crisis situations that result from a breakdown in organizational communications [90] or other stress-related causes [91]. Figure 7.22 illustrates some central features of the garbage can model of organizational choice.

Distributed decision making often occurs in garbage can modeling situations [92]. Fundamentally, distributed decision making is the process of organizational decision making that occurs when the information and responsibility for the decision are distributed across time, space, and the various decision-making entities. A decision-making unit can be a single human, a group of humans, a machine, or collection of humans and machines—each of which is responsible for some part of an overall decision. From this perspective, organizational decisions are a product of

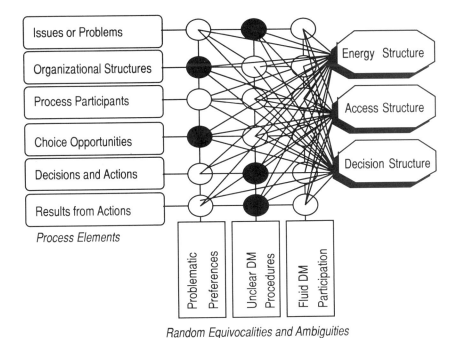

Issues or Problems

Organizational Structures

Process Participants

Choice Opportunities

Decisions and Actions

Results from Actions

Process Elements

Energy Structure

Access Structure

Decision Structure

Problematic Preferences

Unclear DM Procedures

Fluid DM Participation

Random Equivocalities and Ambiguities

Figure 7.22   Linkages among the major elements in a garbage can model.

the human information processing and associated decision making in organizational units.

Coordination takes place across the various information-processing and decision-making units. Each unit generally take parts in this coordination process. Each unit will have access to somewhat different information. It will have somewhat different standards for acquiring, processing, and evaluating information. The information-processing factors affecting decision making in an organization will depend on the structure of the organization, the environment, and the information processing and decision making capabilities of the organizational units. In a recent effort, this is extended to issues of organizational learning and personnel turnover [93]. Thus this is an environment for organizational decision making. Nevertheless, the model is sufficiently robust that economic, legal, social, political, legal, and other rationality perspectives fit within the model.

Improved decision-making efficiency and effectiveness, and support and training aids to this end, can only be accomplished if we understand human and organizational decision making as it is as well as how it might be and allow for incorporation of this understanding in the design of systems. One of the requirements imposed will be relevance to the individual and organizational decision-making structure. Another requirement is relevance to the information requirements of the decision-maker. Especially important also is accommodation of organizational learning, a topic that we have also addressed here. These lead to a model of the elements for

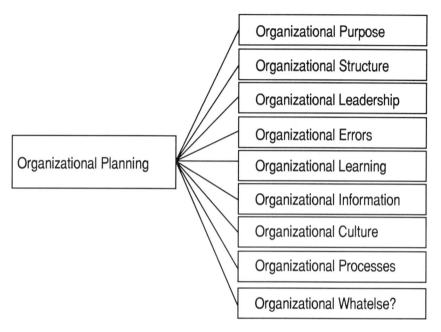

Figure 7.23 The many elements affecting organizational planning.

planning large scale problem solving and decision making, a model that has relevance for systems management activities associated with all these functions. A conceptual model of this is illustrated in Figure 7.23. Each element actually influences the others and there are a number of feedback loops not shown in this figure. One of the major ingredients in this figure, and in many of our discussions, is that of organizational processes. There have been a number of efforts to develop models for organizational process maturity. We close our discussions in this chapter with a section that comments on these efforts.

7.7 PROCESS MODELS AND PROCESS MATURITY

The notions of organizational culture and evolution over time that we have discussed here are, of course, not unrelated to quality issues. In the "quality is free" effort, for example, Crosby [94] identifies five stages of development of quality maturity.

1. The *uncertainty* stage is one of confusion and lack of commitment. Management has no knowledge of quality at the strategic process level and, at best, views operational level quality control inspections of finished products as the only way to achieve quality.
2. The *awakening* stage is one in which management recognizes that quality is needed. Statistical quality control teams will conduct inspections whenever problems develop.

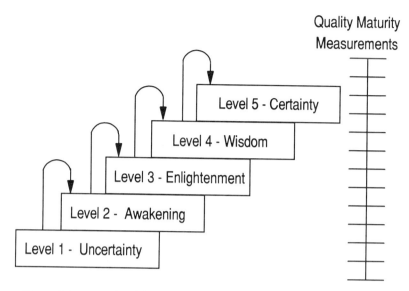

Figure 7.24 Levels of the quality maturity model identified by Crosby.

3. At the stage of *enlightenment,* decisions are made to adopt a formal quality improvement process. The cost of quality is first identified at this stage of development, which is the beginning of operational level quality assurance.

4. At the *wisdom* stage, identification of quality costs become systematized, and quality-related issues are generally handled satisfactorily in what is emerging as strategic and process-oriented quality assurance and management.

5. Finally, those organizations who enter the *certainty* stage know why they do not have problems with quality. Very few quality-related problems occur at this ultimate process maturity level.

Figure 7.24 illustrates these stages of quality maturity growth. This model relates to process and organizational quality. It has apparently not been instrumented in any detailed way for actual use and we are unable, without this additional effort, to associate needed measurement scales with this model. It has, however, inspired other maturity models for which appropriate systematic measurement scales have been devised.

Some organizations have very mature lifecycle organizational processes. In others, these processes are less mature. In an immature organization, lifecycle processes may be improvised in an ad hoc manner by systems management for each individual acquisition, RDT&E, or marketing program. Even if a lifecycle process is specified, it may not be followed or enforced in a systematic manner, either for the particular product being fielded or for subsequent products. Rather than taking an interactive or proactive approach, the immature organization is reactionary, and systems managers focus on solving immediate crises. Planned time schedules and budgets are generally overrun; often, this is because estimates of time and cost are not based on realistic factors. In some cases, there may not even be an attempt to make realistic estimates or to use systematic measurements at all.

In some cases, there is no basis for predicting product quality or for solving product or process problems that are quality related. When it is necessary to impose a fixed delivery date or fixed budget, product quality and functionality are then sacrificed in order to meet the delivery date or budget. Activities intended to enhance quality, such as verification and validation efforts, and other configuration management practices, may be forgotten or performed in a perfunctory manner when program costs exceed the planned costs or when programs fall behind schedule. In a great many cases, this only makes matters worse, not better.

A mature systems engineering organization possesses the capability to manage all appropriate lifecycle processes well. Salient information about these organizational processes is communicated to all who need to know, and all activities are completed according to an agreed upon configuration management plan and systems engineering management plan. These defined processes are revised when and as needed, and improvements are developed through appropriate reengineering approaches and buttressed by systematic measurements. Responsibilities for efforts are clear to program management, as well as throughout the entire organization. Managers provide oversight on the quality of processes, products, and customer satisfaction with products. There is a systematic basis for judging product and process quality and for detection, diagnosis, and correction of problems with either product or process. Time schedules and budgets are not based on idealistic or unrealistic performance information. They are generally based on past practices and are invariably realistic. The specified and predicted cost, time schedule, functionality, and quality of the product are routinely, and with rare exception, achieved.

A "process mature" organization exists because a disciplined process is established and consistently followed, and because the members of the organization function as self-empowered teams who have a common shared set of values and who understand the value of doing everything with the highest level of quality. Also there is a systems management infrastructure and a leadership that has strategic vision, supports development and use of appropriate lifecycle processes, and treats all internal and external stakeholders with respect and dignity.

It would be highly desirable to be able to characterize organizations on a maturity framework scale. This would allow us to evaluate organizations in terms of their capability to produce a functionally trustworthy and high quality product. More importantly, it would also suggest guidelines to assist organizations in improving their process maturity in order to achieve the highest possible product quality and trustworthiness, and the resulting customer satisfaction. Thus there is much motivation for construction of a systems engineering process maturity framework. This framework might describe organizational processes that vary from ad hoc and chaotic to mature and highly disciplined. It provides a needed foundation for supporting improvements in process maturity. As an organization matures, the various organizational lifecycle processes become of higher quality, better defined, and more consistently implemented.

From these perspectives, organizational lifecycle process maturity represents the extent to which specific processes are explicitly defined, managed, measured, controlled, and effective in achieving their intended purpose. The term maturity is used to imply the potential for growth in capability and indicates the quality of an organizations' processes and the consistency with which they are applied to programs throughout the organization. Organizational lifecycle processes are well understood in a mature organization. This comes about through appropriate leadership, and also because of the resulting education and training. Mature processes are continually being monitored and improved by systems management. Process maturity suggests that the productivity and quality of everything in the organization that results from an organization's processes, and everything and everyone that contribute to organizational processes, are improved over time through consistent gains in quality and productivity.

As an organization gains in process maturity, it generally institutionalizes its lifecycle processes through policies, controls, and standards. This does not suggest that these processes and the associated organizational structures and architectures are rigid, inflexible and incapable of change. They are capable of change. The change is planned, with the interpretation of planning we have used in our previous section. This involves building an organizational infrastructure and an organizational culture that support the shared vision of the organization and the resulting strategy and strategic programming that result in methods, practices, and procedures. Thus we see that a process maturity model for systems engineering organizations must necessarily consider the many issues we have described in our efforts up to this point, and the approaches to reengineering we describe in our next chapter as well.

It is reasonable to question why a capability maturity model (CMM) or process maturity model (PMM) is needed. After all, experienced systems managers generally know about the problems they face. But they may well disagree on which improvements are most important, and whether these should be improvements in process or in product. If we do not have an organized and orchestrated strategy for process and/or product improvement, it is very difficult to obtain general organizational agreement on which improvement activities are important, which are relatively unimportant, and how these can be prioritized such as to develop a plan for organizational improvement.

To achieve long-term results from organizational process improvement, it is desirable to develop strategies and the strategic capabilities for increasing an organization's process maturity in stages. Improvements at each stage then provide a foundation on which improvements undertaken at the next stage may be based. Thus a process maturity framework provides support for continuous process improvement.

We will first describe some of the extensive efforts that have been devoted to creating a PMM for software development. Then we briefly turn our attention to the need for a more general and more extensive systems engineering PMM.

The CMM for software, developed by the Software Engineering Institute (SEI) at Carnegie-Mellon University, provides software organizations with guidance on processes for developing and maintaining software. It also enables evolution toward an organizational culture for software engineering management excellence. The CMM is based on Crosby's five stages of quality maturity. It initially evolved as a PMM but the term CMM is more commonly used at this time.

The CMM is designed to guide software organizations in selecting process improvement strategies that lead to product improvement. It accomplishes this by first determining the current process maturity of an organization. Then those issues most critical to software product quality improvement through process improvement are detected and diagnosed. Through use of the CMM, and by organizational process improvement approaches based on it, an organization is able to improve its software processes, in terms of continuous and lasting improvements in software process capability. These process improvements lead to product quality and trustworthiness improvements.

The structure of the CMM is based on principles of strategic quality assurance and management that we discussed in Chapter 6. These principles have been adapted by the SEI into a process maturity framework that establishes systems management and systems engineering foundations for the process improvement for definition, development, and deployment efforts involving software intensive systems. As noted earlier, the process maturity framework into which these quality principles have been adapted is that of Crosby [94]. We have just described this quality management maturity grid in terms of five evolutionary stages for adopting quality practices. This maturity framework was adapted to the software process by Watts Humphrey and his colleagues and described [95] in terms of five levels of process maturity.

1. At the *initial level,* the process is not under statistical measurement control at even the operational level. No systematic process improvement is possible. The process is undisciplined and ad hoc. Success is very much a function of individual efforts and those who achieve success under these circumstances are organizational heroes. When the hero leaves, the organization suffers greatly. Product quality and trustworthiness are unpredictable. There is little or no effort at risk management. Process management is, at best, reactive in nature.

2. At the *repeatable level,* a measure of thorough operational level product control is achieved through metrics associated with cost, schedule, and product configuration changes. Thus basic program management processes are established. Earlier successes may be repeated for very similar applications. The beginnings of an interactive approach to process management have been established.

3. At the *defined level,* the process has been adequately understood and specified such that operational quality control is able to yield products of specified trustworthiness with predictable costs and performance schedules. The organization has a set of standardized, consistent, and repeatable processes. Process management is interactive. These standardized processes are well integrated across the organization.

4. When a *managed maturity* level is reached, comprehensive process-related measurements are possible and significant improvements in product quality

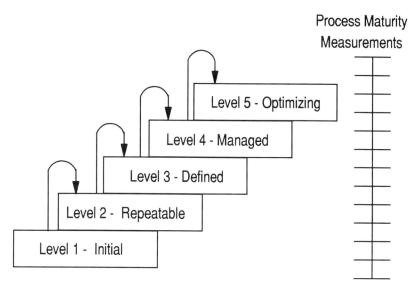

Figure 7.25 Levels of process maturity model identified by the Software Engineering Institute.

are possible through the understanding and control thereby made possible. Interactive process management processes are well in place, and some proactive approaches are in evidence.

5. When the *optimizing level,* the zenith of maturity, is reached, the organization is then able to make continuous improvements in products and services through continuous process improvements. Innovative ideas and leadership abound. There is much double-loop learning and this further supports this highest level of process maturity. Process management is highly proactive; also, there are interactive and reactive controls and measurements.

Figure 7.25 illustrates growth in maturity as indicated by the PMM. It also shows a scale for measurement. Clearly, we can easily imagine organizations below and above these five stages in process maturity. The positive features of each maturity level are retained in each higher maturity level. Thus Figure 7.26 is a more accurate, but somewhat cumbersome, representation of the partial nestedness across the maturity levels.

As process maturity improves, the software process becomes more visible. The probability density function of realized cost and schedule becomes narrower and more centered about forecast values, as suggested in Figure 7.27. The difference between the forecast and averaged actual values of the cost and scheduled completion approaches zero. Furthermore, and of great significance, there would be a smaller variance associated with the initial cost and schedule estimates,* as sug-

*There does not appear to be any empirical or experimental data that confirm these hoped for results at this time.

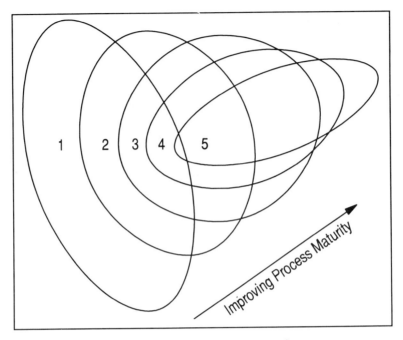

Figure 7.26   Process maturity levels.

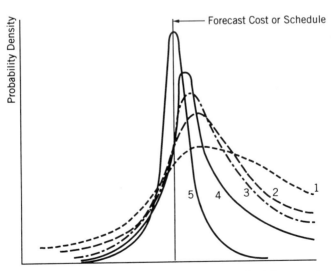

Figure 7.27   Hypothetical probability versus costs or schedule at various maturity levels.

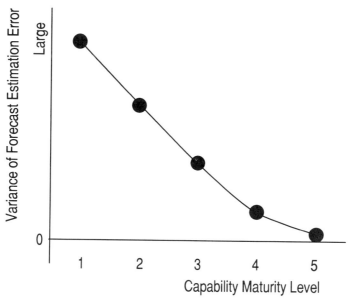

Figure 7.28 Variance of error in forecast cost or schedule versus actual cost and schedule.

gested by Figure 7.28. This suggests, indeed, that the optimized level of process maturity is that described as the certain level of performance in Crosby's work.

While it might be viewed as desirable to complete efforts at a lower cost and in a shorter time than initially predicted and budgeted, an organization that consistently does this is clearly not estimating costs and schedules accurately. This will clearly result in a competitive disadvantage, regardless of the type of contract that is negotiated. Thus there is every reason to want to be able to accurately estimate activity-based costs and schedules.

There have been many pragmatic efforts to more fully develop this model and we describe some of these here. In particular, these efforts will allow us to associate measurement scales with the levels shown in Figure 7.25 and to take systematic measurements that enable evaluation of an organization's process maturity for software acquisition and, more importantly, to suggest strategies for organizational improvement in process maturity.

It is assumed that continuous process improvement is based on many small, evolutionary steps rather than on revolutionary or radical permutations. We will have a great deal more to say about improvement through revolutionary and radical change in our next chapter.

The CMM represents a framework. It is comprised of the identified five maturity levels that provide a foundation for evolutionary and incremental improvements of a continuing nature in process maturity. These five maturity levels may be viewed as a scale that enables measurement of the maturity of an organization's software processes, and for evaluation of their capabilities in producing a high quality and trustworthy product.

In general, the SEI cautions against attempting to skip maturity levels in an organization's efforts to achieve even higher performance. This is due to the need to establish a foundation for the next higher level before attempting to attain a higher level. If we attempt to move from level 1 to level 5, for example, the changes required may be so massive that any quick effort to make such a revolutionary and radical move may being about chaos. In part, the simplified illustration of Figure 7.26 illustrates this.

It is of interest here to describe the efforts of the SEI in developing an assessment tool that determines the process maturity level of a software development organization [96,97]. There are a number of key process areas, each of which has a set of specific objectives. There are no key process areas associated with level 1, the initial, ad hoc, undisciplined level. These key process areas, the levels at which they occur, and the accomplishments associated with them include the following:

- *Requirements management* (level 2—repeatable) requires establishing a common understanding between the customer and organization with respect to the customer's requirements that will be addressed by the software project or program under development. This requires an effective change control process, as generally implemented through configuration management, to cope with and manage such difficulties as requirements creep and volatility.

- *Software project planning* (level 2—repeatable) requires the establishment of appropriate plans for the software acquisition program, including managing the program. Without a set of realistic plans, effective program management is an accident and generally will not occur.

- *Software project tracking and oversight* (level 2—repeatable) requires adequate visibility into the actual program progress so that systems management can take effective actions to detect, diagnose, and correct performance that is significantly different from that in the systems engineering management plan (SEMP) and other plans.

- *Software subcontract management* (level 2—repeatable) requires selection of qualified software subcontractors and an operational plan to manage them effectively. This requires such technical direction efforts over subcontractors as requirements management; software program planning, tracking and oversight; quality assurance; and configuration management.

- *Software quality assurance* (level 2—repeatable) provides systems management with appropriate high level visibility into the processes being used for systems acquisition and the evolving details of the software product itself.

- *Software configuration management* (level 2—repeatable) establishes and maintains integrity of all products of the software acquisition lifecycle and is an integral part of most systems engineering and systems management processes for software intensive systems.

- *Organizational process focus* (level 3—defined) establishes organizational responsibilities for all software process lifecycle activities. This results in the set of software process assets described in organizational process definition and used in integrated software management.

- *Organizational process definition* (level 3—defined) results in a usable set of software process assets to improve process performance across a variety of acquisition efforts. It provides a basis for long-term organizational benefits that can be institutionalized through such efforts as education and training.

- *Training programs* (level 3—defined) develop the skills needed for people to perform assigned work in an effective and efficient manner.

- *Integrated software management* (level 3—defined) results in integration of the software systems engineering and management activities into a coherent and defined acquisition process. This may be evolved from an organization's standard software process and related process assets. Integrated software management evolves from and is an extension of the related efforts at level 2.

- *Software product engineering* (level 3—defined) describes such technical activities as requirements and specifications analysis, design, code, and test. It results from the execution of a well-defined systems engineering process that integrates all software development efforts to produce a high quality software product in an effective and efficient manner.

- *Intergroup coordination* (level 3—defined) establishes procedures to enable the software acquisition team to participate actively with the other engineering groups so a large software intensive system product is better able to satisfy customer needs. This extends beyond software systems engineering itself to include integration, coordination, and interaction efforts with other groups in the organization.

- *Peer reviews* (level 3—defined) result in the removal of defects from software products as early in the lifecycle, and as efficiently and effectively, as possible.

- *Quantitative process management* (level 4—managed) controls process performance and represents the result achieved from following a mature software process. This adds a systematic measurement program to the various other key process areas at this level.

- *Software quality management* (level 4—managed) results in the development of quantitative understandings of software product quality. It results from application of a comprehensive systematic measurement program to software products as they evolve during the lifecycle.

- *Defect prevention* (level 5—optimized) results in detection, diagnosis, and correction of defects and the implementation of management controls to prevent them from recurring.

- *Technology change management* (level 5—optimized) is needed to identify beneficial new technologies and processes and to transfer them into the organization in a suitable manner to enable continuous innovation.

- *Process change management* (level 5—optimized) takes incremental and evolutionary improvements discovered in the other key process areas for level 5 and makes them available throughout the organization.

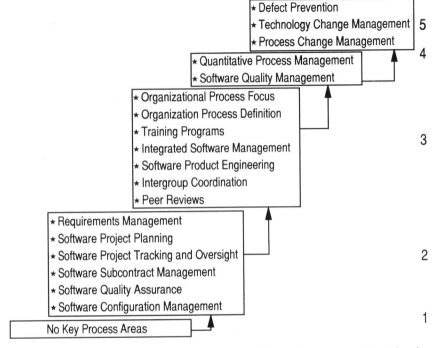

Figure 7.29   Key process areas as incorporated at each process maturity level.

The key process areas at each lower level are contained in all higher levels. That an organization has achieved a given level, such as level 2, and mastered the key processes at that level, such as software configuration management, does not suggest at all that there are no further improvements to be obtained in this key process area at higher organizational levels.

Figure 7.29 associates these key process areas with the several process maturity levels. At level 2, each of the six key process areas is associated with software program management. At level 3, the key processes are associated with software engineering efforts, software systems management efforts, and organizational management efforts at the highest level. Level 4 requires efforts for both software engineering and software systems management, and level 5 requires efforts for all three of these groups.

Each of the five, or upper four at least, levels and the key process areas at each level are associated with appropriate systematic measurements. All key process areas have a set of six common features associated with them:

1. *Goals* specify purposes to be served through implementation of the associated key process areas.
2. *Commitment to perform* describes those actions that an organization must implement in order to be sure that the key process area in question is established and that it will endure, and continually improve, over time.

3. *Ability to perform* describes the capacity and capability of organizational structures and resources that must exist if the organization is to successfully implement the key process area.

4. *Activities performed* represents roles, tactics, and procedures required to implement the goals associated with a specific key process area.

5. *Systematic measurement and analysis efforts* result in measures of effectiveness of activities performed and are comprised of metrics needed to accomplish process diagnosis, detection, and correction.

6. *Implementation verification* represents efforts to ensure that activities performed are in compliance with and supportive of the key process area.

Each of these is a systems management function.

Figure 7.30 indicates the general structure of the CMM and Figure 7.31 represents one view of this for a single key process area—requirements management. Needless to say, the complete CMM is a rather intricate model. It is well described in [96] and [97].

There are a number of key practices associated with each key process area as well. As indicated in Figure 7.29, some of the key process areas are associated only with higher levels of process maturity. It is especially important that we relate these notions to that of organizational cultures and environments. These are presently unmet development needs, relative to the present CMM, at this time.

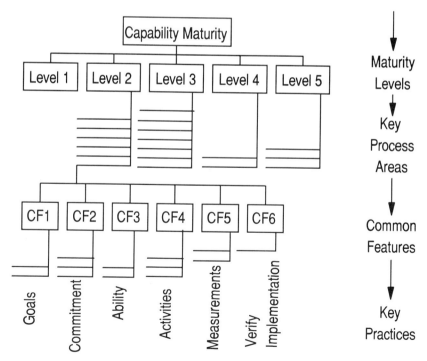

Figure 7.30 Generic structure of the capability maturity model.

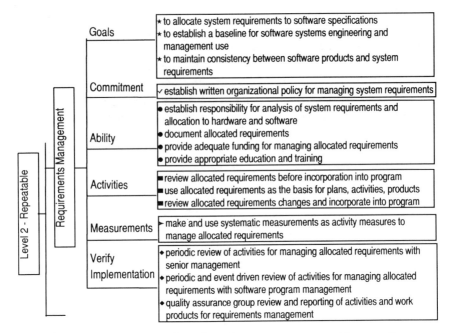

Figure 7.31   Representation of requirements management key practices.

The SEI provides detailed guidelines for use of the CMM. These are comprised of two efforts:

- *Software process assessments* are used internal to an organization in order to assess its current software processes and, on the basis of this, to detect and diagnose process-related issues and to obtain organizational commitment for corrective efforts that will result in process improvement.
- *Software capability evaluations* are used to identify organizations that are qualified to perform particular software efforts, and to monitor the software process actually in use on a given software acquisition effort.

The CMM provides a foundation for both of these. There are a number of common steps in software process assessments and software capability evaluations even though the purposes of the two are different. Each is comprised of a preinspection report and analysis, an on-site inspection, and a post-visit analysis, report, and follow-up. As is apparent, there is much in common between the CMM and associated assessment and evaluation efforts, and the ISO 9000 efforts we discussed in our last chapter. An interesting recent work provides a partial contrast and comparison of these [98].

The majority of organizations in practice today are at levels 1 and 2, with very few at levels 3, 4, and 5. The indicated references and a recent focused issue of *IEEE Software* [99] contain a number of interesting articles on the CMM and related quality improvement efforts.

In related developments, Curtis [100] has identified a software human resource model comprised of five levels: herded, managed, tailored, institutionalized, and optimized. Weinberg [101] has identified a six-stage model of organizational congruence. This is intended to reflect potential discrepancies between the espoused theories of action and actual organizational practice. The patterns identified are oblivious, variable, routine, steering, anticipating, and congruent. Clearly, these relate strongly to the management activity levels of inactive, reactive, interactive, and proactive already noted. A very interesting challenge is to relate these several maturity notions to the organizational lifecycle dynamics illustrated in Figure 7.6. In part, this may be accomplished by refinement of the executive management style levels—inactive, reactive, interactive, and proactive—to include the more general maturity levels and their inherent process quality levels that we have just discussed. The really major challenge is to identify those systems management strategies that enable an organization to alter its process maturity level such as to ascend to higher and higher standards of quality and, if necessary, to enter a rebirth phase that will reverse the direction of movement of declining organizations.

Thus there is much motivation to extend the excellent and detailed CMM for software to include more generic systems engineering efforts. At a conceptual level, the extension is relatively straightforward and we can easily recast the discussions in this section to include systems engineering efforts in a more generic sense. To evolve such a model to encompass the detailed measurement guidelines suggested by the CMM is another matter. There are ongoing efforts at the SEI and elsewhere to obtain a systems engineering CMM.

While the CMM represents an excellent framework for assessment and improvement at levels 1, 2, and 3, it is reasonable to question the extent to which it is truly able to cope with the very highest levels of organizational process maturity. As many of our discussions in this chapter have indicated, there are major relations between process maturity and the leadership style and culture in an organization. The CMM does not focus in any major way on issues associated with this. To date, there has been a very limited amount of experience with programs, and none at all with organizations, at levels 4 and 5, as very few programs are at that level now. It will be extraordinarily interesting to observe evolution of the CMM as greater experience is gained with efforts at the higher maturity levels.

7.8 SUMMARY

In almost all contemporary discussions of quality, a clear distinction is made between strategic level quality assurance and management, or TQM, and operational level measures of quality. Much of our commentary has related to the former topic, although the latter is clearly needed in order to provide necessary instrumental measures of the former. Virtually all TQM efforts suggest several major interrelated efforts that comprise a systems approach to quality enhancement. These might be summed up as follows.

1. Know and understand all stakeholders, including customers and clients, and treat all of them with dignity and respect.

2. Know and understand the internal and external environments of the organization.

3. Concentrate on continuously improving the quality and responsiveness of systems and processes.

4. Identify appropriate process and product metrics for quality assurance measurements.

5. Do the right things right.

6. Then, and only then, do these things efficiently and effectively.

7. Exercise administration, management, leadership, and governance in a professional setting that emphasizes equity and explicability.

8. Empower people.

There are several TQM challenges here. What is not particularly evident in our summary thus far is the very significant impact of cultural variables that need to be strongly considered in efforts of this sort. Of particular interest is the lifecycle model of growth, maturity, decay, and rebirth. Not only is this a dynamic evolutionary process, the state of the organization in each of the resulting phases of evolution can be very significantly altered by the nature of the controls that are applied to the system.

In any TQM implementation, it is quite important to note that evaluation and outcome assessment are of particular interest and value. Outcome assessment can be approached from a structural, functional, or purposeful perspective. Product quality is more easily assessed than process quality. Purposeful outcomes are also difficult to assess. We can surely read statements of program objectives and attempt to determine whether the structural realization of the purposeful programmatic objectives is likely to lead to successful accomplishment of the stated purposes of an organization or program within it. While this has value, it is somewhat hypothetical. To achieve a more pragmatic assessment represents a major challenge in many cases, especially in situations like education where the real quality of the product may not be known until quite some time after production.

In a recent and thought-provoking article, seven deadly corporate sins are recited by Pearson [102]:

1. Product quality is inconsistent.

2. There is a slow response to marketplace needs for change.

3. There is a lack of innovative and responsive products and the leadership to assure these.

4. There is a high cost structure that is beyond customer willingness to support.

5. There is inadequate worker involvement and participation in relevant facets of the organization.

6. There is unresponsive service to the customers of the organization.

7. There is inefficient and ineffective resource allocation within the organization, often due to allocations made from political rather than professional and innovation-oriented perspectives.

Many of these difficulties may easily be believed to be management induced. But it must be recalled that the prevalent organizational culture is a major factor also. There are internal and external influences that frame this culture, including leadership.

Pearson describes six concepts that are claimed to be capable of transforming the organizational work environment into a productive one, primarily by eliminating a highly bureaucratic and politicized work environment. The following management guidelines are suggested:

1. Recognize what the organization and its specific units stand for and what its purposes are that are distinguished and competitively significant.

2. Establish high aspirations and performance standards, at a personal and an organizational level, enforce them, and elevate them continuously over time.

3. Adopt and subscribe to organizing concepts that stimulate continuous improvement and demonstrable results in productivity and quality. This is especially to be contrasted with efforts that reward promised activity rather than demonstrated results; that confuse objectives measures with objectives, especially those that also identify objectives measures for some purposes that are unobtainable as objectives; and that accept advertising and promotion as equivalent to and potentially more important than marketing.

4. Organizational management should become personally involved in all substantiative areas of the organization and not just in the administrative function alone, if true leadership and management are to be established. Thus managers are able to approach management functions as knowledgeable professionals *and* as managers.

5. Secure and encourage the appropriate talent for a progressive, productive, and high quality organization.

6. Establish and adhere to a culture and reward system, and associated processes and beliefs, that emphasizes quality performance and integration of all facets of the organization.

In addition to these being most reasonable leadership and management objectives, they appear to also provide much support for related TQM objectives, especially management quality.

This suggests, and strongly, that a subject such as process maturity cannot be addressed independently of the organizational context in which organizational processes are to be found. This context involves the specific competitive strategy adopted by an organization and its leadership and culture. These need to be examined from both a descriptive and prescriptive perspective in order to accomplish process engineering. Figure 7.32 provides a summary of these ingredients, as well as a fitting summary graphic for this chapter.

We have set forth a large number of issues associated with systems management as catalysts for innovation and quality through leadership and process maturity. There have been a number of important concerns that, primarily for lack of space, we have not discussed. For example, we indicated the need for self-empowered

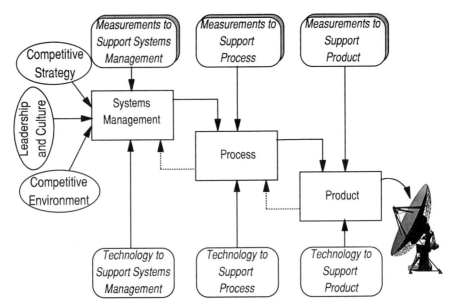

Figure 7.32   Some of the many ingredients influencing product quality and trustworthiness.

work teams at several points in our discussions. Some of the given references discuss this important topic. There are others that are specifically concerned with this [103–107]. We will also provide much discussion relevant to various parts of this chapter in our last chapter, from both a philosophic and a pragmatic perspective. We believe both are needed. The belief that one can be successfully pragmatic without a guiding philosophy and the belief that sound philosophic guidance can be provided without pragmatic implementation are both misleading. They are as misleading as the assumption that one can well understand the parts of a system without understanding the whole system, or that one can understand the whole system without any knowledge of the parts. Perhaps this is the major systems engineering and systems management fallacy, although it is clearly not restricted to this area of endeavor only.

REFERENCES

[1] March, J. G., and Simon, H., *Organizations,* John Wiley & Sons, New York, 1958.

[2] Galbraith, J. R., *Organizational Design,* Addison-Wesley, Reading, MA, 1977.

[3] Ansoff, H. J., *Corporate Strategy,* McGraw-Hill Book Co., New York, 1965.

[4] Andrews, K. R., *The Concept of Corporate Strategy,* Richard D. Irwin, Homewood, IL, 1971.

[5] Leavitt, H. J., and Bahrami, H., *Managerial Psychology: Managing Behavior in Organizations,* 5th ed., University of Chicago Press, Chicago, 1978. (The original

edition is Leavitt, H. J., *Managerial Psychology,* University of Chicago Press, Chicago, 1958).

[6] Schein, E. H., *Organizational Psychology,* 3rd ed., Prentice-Hall, Englewood Cliffs, NJ, 1980 (1st edition, 1965).

[7] Lindblom, C. E., *The Policy Making Process,* Prentice-Hall, Englewood Cliffs, NJ, 1968.

[8] Wildavsky, A., *Speaking Truth to Power: The Art and Craft of Policy Analysis,* Little Brown, Toronto, 1979.

[9] Bass, B. M., *Stogdill's Handbook of Leadership: A Survey of Theory and Research,* Free Press, New York, 1981.

[10] Nystrom, P. C., and Starbuck, W. H. (Eds.), *Handbook of Organizational Design— Volume 1: Adapting Organizations to Their Environments; Volume 2: Remodeling Organizations and Their Environments,* Oxford University Press, Oxford, UK, 1981.

[11] Stolovitch, H. D., and Keeps, E. J., *Handbook of Human Performance Technology: A Comprehensive Guide for Analyzing and Solving Performance Problems in Organizations,* Jossey-Bass, San Francisco, 1992.

[12] March, J. G. (Ed.), *Decisions and Organizations,* Basil Blackwell, Cambridge, MA, 1988.

[13] Cohen, M. D., and Sproull, L. S. (Eds.), Special Issue on Organizational Learning: Papers in Honor of (and by) James G. March, *Organization Science,* Vol. 2, No. 1, 1991, pp. 1–147.

[14] Haye, J., "An Axiomatic Theory of Organizations," *Administrative Science Quarterly,* Vol. 10, No. 3, Dec. 1965, pp. 289–320.

[15] Sage, A. P., *Systems Engineering,* John Wiley & Sons, New York, 1992.

[16] Cyert, R. M., and Simon, H. A., "The Behavioral Approach: With Emphasis on Economics," *Behavioral Science,* Vol. 28, 1983, pp. 95–108.

[17] Weick, K. E., *The Social Psychology of Organizing,* Addison-Wesley, Reading, MA, 1979.

[18] Weick, K. E., "Cosmos Versus Chaos: Sense and Nonsense in Electronic Contexts," *Organizational Dynamics,* Vol. 14, No. 3, 1985, pp. 50–64.

[19] Daft, R. L., and Weick, K. E., "Towards a Model of Organization Interpretation Systems," *Academy of Management Review,* Vol. 9, No. 2, 1984, pp. 284–295.

[20] Janis, I. L., *Groupthink,* Free Press, New York, 1982.

[21] Janis, I. L., *Crucial Decisions: Leadership in Policymaking and Crisis Management,* Free Press, New York, 1989.

[22] Vroom, V. H., and Yetton, P. W., *Leadership and Decision Making,* University of Pittsburgh, Pittsburgh, 1973.

[23] Keen, P. G. W., "Information Systems and Organizational Change," *Communications of the Association for Computing Machinery,* Vol. 24, No. 1, Jan. 1981, pp. 24–33.

[24] Tushman, M. L., and Nadler, D. A., "Information Processing as an Integrating Concept in Organizational Design," *Academy of Management Review,* Vol. 3, No. 3, July 1978, pp. 613–624.

[25] Feldman, M. S., and March, J. G., "Information in Organizations as Signal and Symbol," *Administrative Science Quarterly,* Vol. 26, 1981, pp. 171–186.

[26] Keller, G., *Academic Strategy: The Management Revolution in American Higher Education,* Johns Hopkins University Press, Baltimore, MD, 1983.

[27] Palmer, J. D., and Sage, A. P., "Information Technology Management of University Education," *International Journal of Technology Management* (Part I: An Overview of University Executive Functions) Vol. 2, No. 3, 1987, pp. 391–404; (Part II: Case Histories of Information Management) Vol. 4, No. 1, 1989, pp. 77–94; (Part III: A Methodology for Information System Design and Development) Vol. 5, No. 2, 1990, pp. 217–239.

[28] Rasmussen, J., *On Information Processing and Human–Machine Interaction: An Approach to Cognitive Engineering,* North-Holland, New York, 1986.

[29] Rasmussen, J., Pejtersen, A., and Goodstein, L. G., *Cognitive Systems Engineering,* John Wiley & Sons, New York, 1994.

[30] Argyris, C., and Schon, D. A., *Organizational Learning: A Theory of Action Perspective,* Addison-Wesley, Reading, MA, 1978.

[31] Argyris, C., and Schon, D. A., *Theory in Practice: Increasing Professional Effectiveness,* Jossey-Bass, San Francisco, 1974.

[32] Argyris, C., *Reasoning, Learning, and Action: Individual and Organizational,* Jossey-Bass, San Francisco, 1982.

[33] Argyris, C., *Overcoming Organizational Defenses,* Prentice-Hall, Englewood Cliffs, NJ, 1990.

[34] Senge, P. M., *The Fifth Discipline: The Art and Practice of the Learning Organization,* Doubleday, New York, 1990.

[35] Senge, P. M., Roberts, C., Ross, R. B., Smith, B. J., and Kleiner, A., *The Fifth Dimension Fieldbook,* Doubleday, New York, 1994.

[36] Garvin, D. A., "Building a Learning Organization," *Harvard Business Review,* Vol. 71, No. 4, July 1993, pp. 78–91.

[37] Kim, D. H., "The Link Between Individual and Organizational Learning," *Sloan Management Review,* Vol. 35, No. 1, Fall 1993, pp. 37–50.

[38] Rouse, W. B., *Catalysts for Change: Concepts and Principles for Enabling Innovation,* John Wiley & Sons, New York, 1993.

[39] Kerr, S., Von Glinow, M. A., and Schriesheim, J., "Issues in the Study of Professionals in Organizations: The Case of Scientists and Engineers," *Organizational Behavior and Human Performance,* Vol. 18, 1977, pp. 329–345.

[40] Wilkins, A. L., *How to Successfully Change an Organization Without Destroying It,* Jossey-Bass, San Francisco, 1989.

[41] Pauchant, T. C., and Mitroff, I. I., *Transforming the Crisis-Prone Organization: Preventing Individual, Organizational, and Environmental Tragedies,* Jossey-Bass, San Francisco, 1992.

[42] Raelin, J. A., *The Clash of Cultures: Managers Managing Professionals,* Harvard Business School Press, Boston, MA, 1991.

[43] Birnbaum, R., *How Colleges Work: The Cybernetics of Academic Organization and Leadership,* Jossey-Bass, San Francisco, 1988.

[44] Bolman, L. G., and Deal, T. E., *Reframing Organizations: Artistry, Choice and Leadership,* Jossey-Bass, San Francisco, 1991.

[45] Bergquist, W. H., *The Four Cultures of the Academy: Insights and Strategies for Improving Leadership in Collegiate Organizations,* Jossey-Bass, San Francisco, 1992.

[46] Mintzberg, H., *Structure in Fives: Designing Effective Organizations,* Prentice-Hall, Englewood Cliffs, NJ, 1983.

[47] Mintzberg, H., *Mintzberg on Management: Inside Our Strange World of Organizations,* Free Press, New York, 1989.

[48] Cohen, A. R., and Bradford, D. L., *Influence Without Authority,* John Wiley & Sons, New York, 1990.

[49] Pfeffer, J., *Managing with Power: Politics and Influence in Organizations,* Harvard Business School Press, Boston, MA, 1992.

[50] Cohen, M. D., March, J. G., and Olsen, J. P., "A Garbage Can Model of Organizational Choice," *Administrative Science Quarterly,* Vol. 17, No. 1, 1972, pp. 1–25.

[51] March, J. G., and Olsen, J. P., *Ambiguity and Choice in Organizations,* Universitetsforlaget, Bergen, Norway, 1979.

[52] Cohen, M. D., and March, J. G., *Leadership and Ambiguity: The American College President,* The Carnegie Commission on Higher Education, McGraw-Hill Book Co., New York, 1974.

[53] March, J. G., and Wessinger-Baylon, T. (Eds.), *Ambiguity and Command: Organizational Perspectives on Military Decision Making,* Pitman, Boston, MA, 1986.

[54] Hofstede, G., *Culture's Consequences: International Differences in Work Related Values,* Sage Publications, Beverly Hills, CA, 1980.

[55] Hofstede, G., *Culture and Organization: Software of the Mind,* McGraw-Hill Book Co., London, 1991.

[56] Martin, J., *Cultures in Organizations: Three Perspectives,* Oxford University Press, New York, 1992.

[57] Hickman, C. R., and Silva, M. A., *Creating Excellence: Managing Corporate Culture, Strategy and Change in the New Age,* Penguin, New York, 1984.

[58] Kotter, J. P., and Heskett, J. L., *Corporate Culture and Performance,* Free Press, New York, 1992.

[59] Schein, E. H., *Organizational Culture and Leadership,* 2nd ed., Jossey-Bass, San Francisco, 1992.

[60] Davenport, T. H., Eccles, R. G., and Prusak, L., "Information Politics," *Sloan Management Review,* Vol. 34, No. 1, Fall 1992, pp. 53–65.

[61] Davenport, T. H., "Saving Its Soul: Human Centered Information Management," *Harvard Business Review,* Vol. 72, No. 2, Mar. 1994, pp. 119–133.

[62] Schein, E. H., *Process Consultation: Volume I—Its Role in Organizational Development,* Addison-Wesley, Reading, MA, 1988.

[63] Schein, E. H., *Process Consultation: Volume II—Lessons for Managers and Consultants,* Addison-Wesley, Reading, MA, 1987.

[64] Schein, E. H., "How Can Organizations Learn Faster: The Challenge of Entering the Green Room," *Sloan Management Review,* Vol. 34, No. 2, Winter 1993, pp. 85–92.

[65] Covey, S. R., *The Seven Habits of Highly Effective People: Restoring the Character Ethic,* Simon & Schuster, New York, 1989.

[66] Covey, S. R., *Principle Centered Leadership,* Simon & Schuster, New York, 1992.

[67] Badaracco, J. L. Jr., and Ellsworth, R. R., *Leadership and the Quest for Integrity,* Harvard Business School Press, Boston, MA, 1989.

[68] Rothschild, W. E., *Risktaker, Caretaker, Surgeon, Undertaker: The Four Faces of Strategic Leadership,* John Wiley & Sons, New York, 1993.

[69] Kotter, J. P., *A Force for Change: How Leadership Differs from Management,* Free Press, New York, 1990.

[70] Jaques, E., *Requisite Organization: The CEO's Guide to Creative Structure and Leadership*, Cason Hall, Arlington, VA, 1989.

[71] Jaques, E., "In Praise of Hierarchy," *Harvard Business Review*, Vol. 68, No. 1, Jan. 1990, pp. 127–133.

[72] Nadler, D. A., Gerstein, M. S., Shaw, R. B., and Associates, *Organizational Architectures: Designs for Changing Organizations*, Jossey-Bass, San Francisco, 1992.

[73] Huber, G. P., and Glick, W. H. (Eds.), *Organizational Change and Redesign: Ideas and Insights for Improving Performance*, Oxford University Press, New York, 1993.

[74] Daft, R. L., and Lewin, A. Y., "Where Are the Theories of the 'New' Organizational Forms?" *Organization Science*, Vol. 4, No. 4, Nov. 1993, pp. i–vi.

[75] Eccles, R. G., Norhia, N., and Berkley, J. D., *Beyond the Hype: Rediscovering the Essence of Management*, Harvard Business School Press, Boston, MA, 1992.

[76] Mintzberg, H., *The Nature of Managerial Work*, Harper & Row, New York, 1973.

[77] Winograd, T., and Flores, F., *Understanding Computers and Cognition*, Addison-Wesley, Reading, MA, 1986.

[78] Kochan, T. A., and Useem, M. (Eds.), *Transforming Organizations*, Oxford University Press, New York, 1992.

[79] Beyer, J. M., and Trice, H. M., *The Culture of Work Organizations*, Prentice-Hall, Englewood Cliffs, NJ, 1993.

[80] Sage, A. P. (Ed.), *Information Processing in Systems and Organizations*, Oxford University Press, Oxford, UK, 1990.

[81] Sage, A. P., *Decision Support Systems Engineering*, John Wiley & Sons, New York, 1991.

[82] Sage, A. P., and Palmer, J. D., *Software Systems Engineering*, John Wiley & Sons, New York, 1990.

[83] Boar, B. H., *The Art of Strategic Planning for Information Technology*, John Wiley & Sons, New York, 1993.

[84] Kouzes, J. M., and Posner, B. Z., *Credibility: How Leaders Gain and Loose It, Why People Demand It*, Jossey-Bass, San Francisco, 1993.

[85] Boar, B. H., *Implementing Client Server Computing: A Strategic Perspective*, McGraw-Hill Book Co., New York, 1993.

[86] Mintzberg, H., *The Rise and Fall of Strategic Planning*, Free Press, New York, 1994.

[87] Mintzberg, H., "The Fall and Rise of Strategic Planning," *Harvard Business Review*, Vol. 72, No. 1, Jan. 1994, pp. 107–116.

[88] March, J. G., and Olsen, J. P., *Rediscovering Institutions: The Organizational Basis of Politics*, Free Press, New York, 1989.

[89] Padgett, J., "Managing Garbage Can Hierarchies," *Administrative Science Quarterly*, Vol. 25, No. 4, 1980, pp. 583–604.

[90] Carley, K., "An Approach for Relating Social Structure to Cognitive Structure," *Journal of Mathematical Sociology*, Vol. 12, No. 2, 1986, pp. 137–189.

[91] Carley, K., "Organizational Designs Suited to High Performance Under Stress," *IEEE Transactions on Systems, Man, and Cybernetics*, Vol. 25, No. 1, Jan. 1995.

[92] Carley, K., "Distributed Information and Organizational Decision Making Models," In Sage, A. P. (Ed.), *Concise Encyclopedia of Information Processing in Systems and Organizations*, Pergamon Press, Oxford, UK, 1990, pp. 137–144.

[93] Carley, K., "Organizational Learning and Personnel Turnover," *Organizational Science,* Vol. 3, No. 1, Feb. 1992, pp. 20–46.

[94] Crosby, P. B., *Quality is Free,* McGraw-Hill Book Co., New York, 1979.

[95] Humphrey, W. S., *Managing the Software Process,* Addison-Wesley, Reading, MA, 1989.

[96] Paulk, M. C., Curtis, W., Chrissis, M. B., and Weber, C. V., "Capability maturity Model for Software, Version 1.1," Software Engineering Institute Report CMU/SEI-93-TR-24, Feb. 1993.

[97] Paulk, M. C., Weber, C. V., Garcia, S. M., Chrissis, M. B., and Bush, M., "Key Practices of the Capability Maturity Model, Version 1.1," Software Engineering Institute Report CMU/SEI-93-TR-25, Feb. 1993.

[98] Bamford, R. C., Deibler, W. J. II, "Comparing, Contrasting ISO 9001 and the SEI Capability Maturity Model," *IEEE Computer,* Vol. 26, No. 10, Oct. 1993, pp. 68–71. (Also see comments on this article in *IEEE Computer,* Vol. 27, No. 2, Feb. 1994, pp. 81–82.)

[99] Theme Articles on the Maturity Movement, *IEEE Software,* Vol. 10, No. 4, July 1993, pp. 12–64.

[100] Curtis, B., "The Human Element in Software Quality," *Proceedings, Monterey Conference on Software Quality,* Software Productivity Research, Cambridge, MA, 1990.

[101] Weinberg, G. M., *Quality Software Management: Vol. 1, Systems Thinking,* Dorset House, New York, 1992.

[102] Pearson, A. E., "Corporate Redemption and the Seven Deadly Sins," *Harvard Business Review,* Vol. 70, No. 3, May 1992, pp. 65–75.

[103] Katzenbach, J. R., and Smith, D. K., *The Wisdom of Teams: Creating the High Performance Organization,* Harvard Business School Press, Boston, MA, 1993.

[104] Katzenbach, J. R., and Smith, D. K., "The Discipline of Teams," *Harvard Business Review,* Vol. 71, No. 2, Mar. 1993, pp. 111–124.

[105] Ryan, K. D., and Oestreich, D. K., *Driving Fear Out of the Workplace: How to Overcome Invisible Barriers to Quality, Production, and Innovation,* Jossey-Base, San Francisco, 1991.

[106] Manz, C. C., and Sims, H. P. Jr., *Business Without Bosses: How Self Managing Teams Are Building High Performance Companies,* John Wiley & Sons, New York, 1993.

[107] Pfeffer, J., *Competitive Advantage Through People: Unleashing the Power of the Work Force,* Harvard Business School Press, Boston, MA, 1994.

Chapter **8**

Reengineering

We conclude our discussion of systems management with a relatively wide scope discourse of reengineering and related approaches toward organizational and technology revitalization.

Responsiveness is very clearly a critical need today. By this, we mean organizational responsiveness in providing products and services of demonstrable value to customers, and thereby in the provision of value-added capabilities to organizational stakeholders. This must be accomplished by efficiently and effectively employing leadership and empowered people such that systems management strategies, organizational processes, human resources, and appropriate technologies are brought to bear on the production of high quality and trustworthy goods and services. Figure 8.1 illustrates these ingredients and some of their linkages in the production of products and services. It is a composite of several representations we have used in our discussions of the systems management process and indicates the many ingredients responsible for trustworthy and high quality products.

At first glance, these two paragraphs may not seem necessarily related. Much of our discussion in the last two chapters has, however, indicated the need for continual revitalization in the way in which we do things, such that they are always done better. This is the case even if the external environment is static and unchanging. However, when we are in a period of high velocity environments, then continual organizational change and associated change in processes and product must be considered as a fundamental rule of the game for progress.

In many ways, past progress can act to impede future progress. This is especially the case when we become very accustomed to a particular way of doing things and have allowed a very large overhead situation to accumulate around what were once highly successful efforts at the production of quality products and services. It is especially difficult to change when what we are doing now is done very well. Yet, it

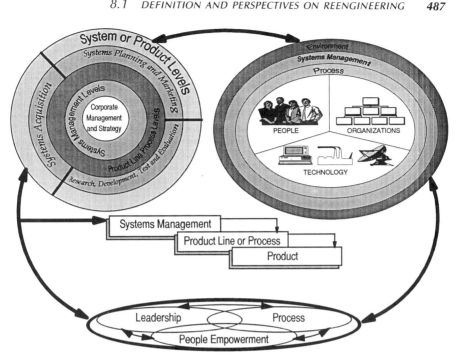

Figure 8.1 All organizational ingredients as candidates for top–down reengineering.

is entirely possible that a competitor may be able to do it better, in any number of ways or soon will be. Thus, what we do well now may well not be what we will need to be doing in the future.

This does not suggest, in any sense, that either management or labor is primarily at fault because of inattention to the tasks they perform. Rather, and more often than not, it suggests that the tasks themselves are in need of restudy and renovation. These tasks may be strategic in nature, or tactical, or purely operational. Most often, however, attempts at improvement through attention at *only* operational levels will yield very modest improvements for the effort invested. As many have indicated, *it is the strategic and tactical system that is at fault* and these faults lead to deficient products. We wish to continue further with these discussions and also to indicate a number of potential improvement approaches, through reengineering, that may be taken. Figure 8.2 indicates some of these improvement approaches. They are interrelated and our listing is not complete. One objective in this chapter is to provide a perspective on, and organization for, the many reengineering approaches and methodologies that have been suggested.

Figure 8.3 represents a generic view of reengineering. The entity to be reengineered can be either systems management, process, product, or some appropriate combination of these. We will expand on this illustration and its interpretation in our discussions to follow.

We can approach a discussion of reengineering from several perspectives: structural, functional, and purposeful. Alternately, or in addition, we can examine reen-

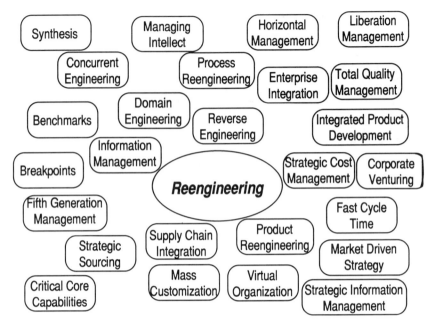

Figure 8.2   Some activities associated with reengineering.

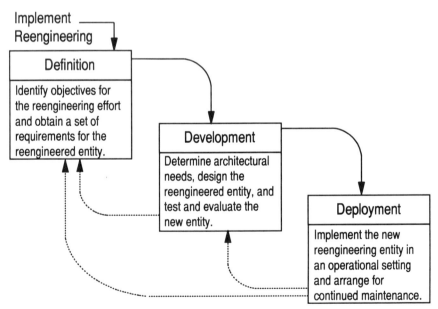

Figure 8.3   Generic implementation of reengineering at the level of product, process, or systems management.

gineering at the level of systems management, process, or product. We may examine reengineering issues at any or all of the three fundamental systems engineering lifecycles: research, development, test, and evaluation (RDT&E); systems acquisition, procurement or production; or systems planning and marketing. Within each of these lifecycles, we could consider reengineering at any or all of the three generic phases of definition, development, or deployment. At the level of systems management, we potentially reengineer each of these phases and potentially all other processes within the company for integrated improvement. At the level of process reengineering only, as we define it, only a single process is redesigned, with no fundamental changes in the structure or purpose of the organization as a whole. Changes, when they occur, may be radical and revolutionary or incremental and evolutionary. These may occur at the levels of systems management, processes, products, or any combination of these.

One fundamental notion of reengineering, however, is the reality that it must be top–down directed if it is to achieve the significant and long-lasting effects that are possible. Thus there should be a strong, purposeful, and systems management orientation to reengineering, even though it may have major implications for such lower level concerns as structural facets of a particular product.

Our chapter is organized as follows. We first provide some definitions of reengineering. Then we indicate some of the many perspectives that have been taken relative to reengineering. Finally, we indicate a number of techniques, such as illustrated in Figure 8.2, that need to be associated with reengineering to bring this endeavor to productive fruition.

8.1   DEFINITION AND PERSPECTIVES ON REENGINEERING

In this section, we provide definitions and perspectives on what we consider to be three related but different types of systems reengineering efforts: reengineering at the levels of (1) product, (2) process or product line, and (3) systems management. There have been a number of formal and informal definitions of reengineering. The word is occasionally spelled as re-engineering. We choose the former spelling here; both are correct.

8.1.1   Product Reengineering

The term reengineering could mean some sort of reworking or retrofit of an already engineered product. This could well be interpreted as maintenance or refurbishment. As we have noted previously [1], maintenance can be viewed from reactive or corrective, interactive or adaptive, and proactive or perfective perspectives. In addition, reengineering could be interpreted as reverse engineering, in which the characteristics of an already engineered product are identified, such that the original product can be subsequently modified and reused or so that a new product with the same purpose and functionality may be obtained through a forward engineering process. Inherent in these notions are two major facets of reengineering.

1. Reengineering improves the product or system delivered to the user for enhanced reliability, maintainability, or an evolving user need.
2. Reengineering increases understanding of the system or product itself.

We see that this interpretation of reengineering is almost totally product focused. We will call it product reengineering and define it as follows:

Product reengineering is the examination, study, capture, and modification of the internal mechanisms or functionality of an existing system or product in order to reconstitute it in a new form and with some new functional and nonfunctional features, often to take advantage of newly emerged technologies, but without major change to the inherent purpose and functionality of the system.

This definition indicates that product reengineering is basically structural reengineering with, at most, minor changes in purpose and functionality of the product that is reengineered. This reengineered product could be integrated with other products having rather different functionality than was the case in the initial deployment. Thus reengineered products could be used, together with this augmentation, to provide new functionality and serve new purposes. A number of synonyms for product reengineering easily come to mind. Among these are renewal, refurbishing, rework, repair, maintenance, modernization, reuse, redevelopment, and retrofit.

A specific example of a product reengineering effort might be that of taking a legacy system written in COBOL or FORTRAN, reverse engineering it to determine the system definition, and then reengineering it in C^{++} or Ada. Depending on whether or not any modified user requirements are to be incorporated into the reengineered product, we would either "forward engineer" the product just after reverse engineering had determined the initial development (technical) system specifications or "reverse engineer" far enough to determine, and then update, existing user requirements. This reverse engineering concept [2], in which user requirements or technological specifications are recovered from examination of characteristics of the product, predates the term product reengineering and occurs before the "forward engineering" that comprised the latter portions of product reengineering.

Figure 8.4 illustrates product reengineering conceptually. An IEEE software standards reference [3] states that "reengineering is a complete process that encompasses an analysis of existing applications, restructuring, reverse, and forward engineering." The IEEE standard for software maintenance [4] suggests that reengineering is a subset of software engineering that is comprised of reverse engineering and forward engineering. We have no disagreement with the definition at all; but we prefer to call it product reengineering for the reasons just stated. It is also necessary to consider reengineering at the levels of processes and systems management if we are to take full advantages of the major opportunities offered by generic reengineering concepts. Thus the qualifier "product" appears appropriate and desirable in the context used here.

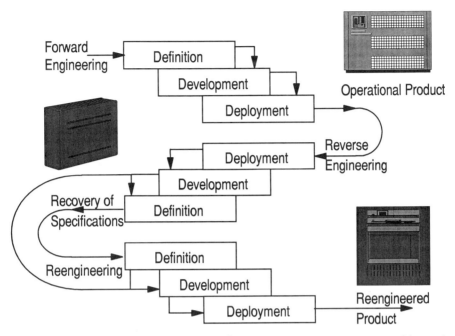

Figure 8.4 Basic notions concerning product reengineering as a sequence of forward, reverse, forward engineering.

8.1.2 Process Reengineering

Reengineering can also be considered at the levels of processes and systems management. At the level of processes only, the effort would be almost totally internal. It would consist of modifications to whatever standard lifecycle processes are in use in a given organization in order to better accommodate new and emerging technologies or new customer requirements for a system. For example, an explicit risk management capability might be incorporated at several different phases of a given lifecycle and accommodated by a revised configuration management process. This could be implemented into the processes for RDT&E, acquisition, and systems planning and marketing. Basically, reengineering at the level of processes would consist of the determination, or synthesis, of an efficacious process for ultimately fielding a product on the basis of a knowledge of generic customer requirements, and the objectives and critical capabilities of the systems engineering organization. Figure 8.5 illustrates, conceptually, some of the facets of process reengineering. Process reengineering may be accomplished because of the desire to obtain better products, or it can be accomplished as support for efforts to obtain a "better" organization.

In accordance with this discussion and by analogy to our definition of product reengineering, we offer the following definition:

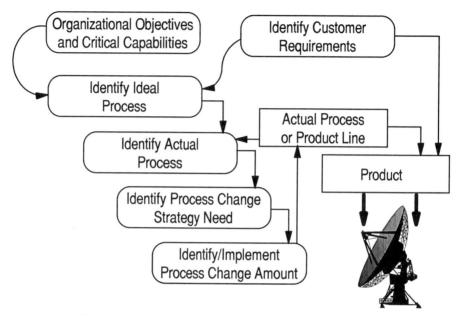

Figure 8.5   Conceptual illustration of process reengineering.

Process reengineering is the examination, study, capture, and modification of the
internal mechanisms of functionality of an existing process, or systems engineer-
ing lifecycle, in order to reconstitute it in a new form and with new functional
and nonfunctional features, often to take advantage of newly emerged or desired
organizational and/or technological capabilities, but without changing the in-
herent purpose of the process itself that is being reengineered.

We could reengineer either the process for RDT&E, system acquisition or production, or systems planning and marketing. One of the first discussions of this sort of
effort at business process reengineering, although the word redesign was used rather
than reengineering, is in a contemporary paper by Davenport and Short [5]. This
was greatly expanded on in a recent and seminal text by Davenport [6], which does
make use of the term reengineering. We will provide an overview of this major work
in a later section.

These and other authors recognize that redesign of processes only and without
attention to reengineering at a higher level than processes only may, in many
instances, represent an incomplete and not fully satisfactory way to improve organizational capabilities. Thus the processes considered as candidates for reengineering
in [5] and [6] are high level managerial as well as operational processes. Information technology is considered to be a major enabling catalyst for process reengineering. Continuous process improvement and institutionalization are advocated.

Reengineering at the process level, and the resulting improvement in product that
results from improvement in the product line, is essentially what AT&T Bell Labo-

ratories have used to identify a common tailorable systems acquisition process for federal systems advanced technology (FSAT) use as a deployment methodology for all process management teams (PMTs) at this organization [7]. The indicated benefits to using a common and understood lifecycle include:

Shorter development cycles
Fewer engineering change orders
Products that fulfill customer expectations
Reduced program and product development costs throughout the lifecycle

Thus the process improvement results ultimately in an increase in effectiveness of product for the same cost, or a reduction in cost for the same effectiveness, or some blend of these two.

Essentially what we call process reengineering here is termed "domain engineering" by the Software Productivity Consortium (SPC) [8]. The combination of domain engineering with the "application engineering" or lifecycle effort needed to produce the actual product is termed "synthesis." It is intended for use in the systems acquisition, procurement, or production lifecycle. Figure 8.6 illustrates the synthesis concept, which is intended, in part, to facilitate the incorporation of reusable software products into new software systems. The synthesis process proceeds as follows.

1. A set of six domain engineering phases is used to develop the product line. In the first phase, process or product line planning is accomplished. This is presumably based on knowledge of the organization and its critical core capabilities and customer needs, as in Figure 8.5.

2. This is followed by a process definitional phase, called product line analysis by the SPC, in which the requirements for the process or product line are specified.

3. This leads to product line or lifecycle process development.

4. A modeling and simulation environment is next constructed such that it will be possible to accomplish prototyping in the actual lifecycle for production of the product.

5. A product library is next constructed. This is comprised of reusable software modules and code generators, which can produce executable code from a set of input technical specifications. A code generator can be viewed as a special type of reusable software product.

6. A process or product line test and evaluation facility is constructed next. This has the capacity for test and evaluation of products from the product line. Following this phase, the applications engineering lifecycle begins. This involves actual definition, development, and deployment on the basis of the just engineered product line or process lifecycle.

7. Product definition is the first phase in actual production of the software

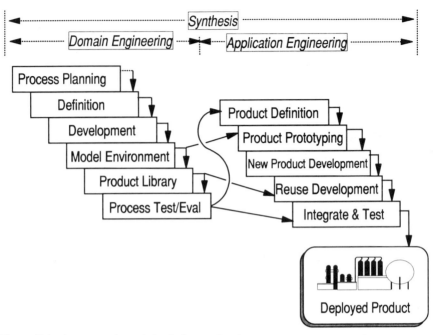

Figure 8.6 Interpretation of the Software Productivity Consortium synthesis process.

product. This is achieved by identifying the user requirements for a software product and translating them into a set of specifications.

8. Product prototyping occurs in the second phase of the applications engineering lifecycle. Here, a prototype is built and, with user interaction presumably, is used to refine the technical specifications for the software product. The modeling and simulation environment, built earlier in domain engineering, is used for this purpose.

9. New product development occurs next. In this particular instance, this refers to the production of custom-built executable code for those portions of the software product that are not to be comprised of reusable code.

10. Reuse development occurs next. In this phase the reengineered code that has become reusable code, and code produced by applications generators in phase 5 of domain engineering, is integrated in with the customized code to result in a complete functioning product.

11. In the final phase, integration and test of this functional software occur. This phase generally involves use of the test suites produced by the product line test and evaluation facility.

12. The product to be deployed results from this effort.

As indicated in Figure 8.6, there are several entry points from domain engineering to application engineering as several of the results of intermediate phases of domain engineering are used in the actual lifecycle that is developed as a result of domain engineering.

8.1.3   Reengineering at the Level of Systems Management

At the level of systems management, reengineering is directed at potential change in all business or organizational processes and thereby the various organizational lifecycle processes as well. Many authors have discussed reengineering the corporation. Arguably, the earliest use of the term *business reengineering* was by Hammer [9], in 1990, and more fully documented in a more recent work on *Reengineering the Corporation* [10]. There are a small plethora of related works, as we will soon discuss.

Hammer gives the following definition of reengineering: "Reengineering is the fundamental rethinking and radical redesign of business processes to achieve dramatic improvements in critical, contemporary measures of performance, such as cost, quality, service and speed." This is a definition of what we will call reengineering at the level of systems management. There are four major terms in this definition.

Fundamental refers to a large scale and broad scope examination of virtually everything about an organization and how it operates. The purpose is to identify potential weakness that is in need of diagnosis and correction.

Radical redesign suggests disregarding existing organizational processes and structures and inventing totally new ways of accomplishing work.

Dramatic improvements suggest that, in Hammer's view, reengineering is not about making marginal and incremental improvements in the status quo. It is about making "quantum" leaps in organizational performance.

Processes represent the collection of activities that are used to take input materials, including intellectual inputs, and transform them into outputs and services that have value to the customer.

Hammer suggests that reengineering and revolution are almost synonymous terms. He identifies three types of firms that attempt reengineering—those in trouble, those who see trouble coming, and those who are ambitious and seek to avoid impending troubles. Clearly, it is better to be proactive and be in this latter category, rather than to be reactive and seek to emerge from a realized crisis situation.

He indicates that one major catalyst for reengineering is the creative use of information technology. Reengineering is not just automation, however; it is the ambitious and rule-breaking study of everything about the organization to enable more effective and efficient organizational processes to be designed.

We essentially share this view of reengineering at the level of systems management. Our definition is similar.

Systems management reengineering is the examination, study, capture, and modification of the internal mechanisms or functionality of existing system manage-

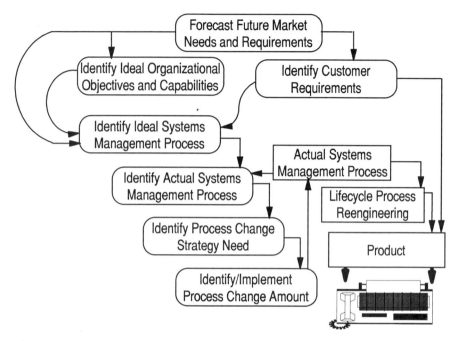

Figure 8.7   Conceptual illustration of reengineering at the level of systems management.

ment processes and practices in an organization in order to reconstitute them in a new form and with new features, often to take advantage of newly emerged organizational competitiveness requirements, and often through use of new and emerging technologies.

We make no representation that this definition, or the other two for that matter, of reengineering is at all the same across the many works that we discuss. Figure 8.7 represents this concept of reengineering at the level of systems management. Lifecycle process reengineering occurs as a natural by-product of reengineering at the level of systems management. This may or may not result in the reengineering of already existing products. Generally it will; new products and new competitive strategies are each a major underlying objective of reengineering at the level of systems management, or organizational reengineering as it is more commonly called.

8.1.4   Perspectives on Reengineering

This very brief discussion of reengineering suggests that we can consider reengineering at three levels: systems management, lifecycle processes, and product. The major purpose of reengineering, regardless of whether it is at the product level or the process level or the level of systems management, is to enable us to produce a better product for the same cost, or a lower cost product that performs in a manner comparable to initial product performance. Thus reengineering improves competitiveness of the organization in coping with changing external situations and environments. We may approach reengineering, at any or all of these levels, from either of three perspectives: (1) *reactive,* because we realize that we are in trouble and perhaps in a crisis situation, and reengineering is one way to bring about needed change; (2) *interactive,* because we wish to stay abreast of current changes as they evolve; or (3) *proactive,* because we wish to position our organization now for changes that we believe will occur in the future, and to emerge in the changed situation as a market leader.

In our next section, we examine some of the many contemporary ideas that have been expressed about the subject of reengineering.

8.2 OVERVIEW OF REENGINEERING APPROACHES

It is possible to consider reengineering at the levels of strategy and systems management, process or product line, or product. In this section, we provide an expanded overview of each of these forms of reengineering by means of an overview of contemporary literature on reengineering.

Without question, more has been written about reengineering at the levels of strategy or systems management than at the other levels. This is not unreasonable since reengineering efforts at the level of organizational strategy have direct implications for management at the levels of management control (and thence at the level of process to implement management controls) and product.

It is difficult to trace the origins of reengineering in any unique manner. The notions of reengineering are very interrelated with those of systems engineering, information technology, strategic planning, and many other subjects. It seems most appropriate here to provide a summary of many perspectives on systems reengineering. This potentially uncommon term, systems reengineering, can be interpreted to mean reengineering at the level of system or product, reengineering at the level of lifecycle process, and reengineering of the structure and functionality of the organization or any combination of these.

8.2.1 Business Process Improvement

In 1991, Harrington published a seminal work on business process improvement [11]. The major thesis of the work is that it is business and manufacturing processes that are the keys to error-free performance. His view, that the process is the problem and not the employees, is essentially that of Deming and others in the TQM areas. Harrington defines a process as a group of activities that take inputs, add value to them, and produce an output that is in support of an organization's objectives. Two generic types of processes are identified. Production processes are directly concerned with yielding the output product or service. Business processes support production processes. These include design of production processes, payroll processes, and engineering change processes.

Initiate Business Process Improvement

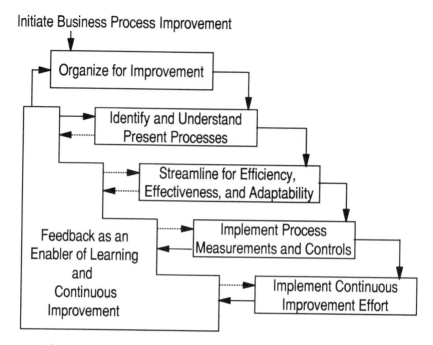

Figure 8.8   Interpretation of business process improvement process.

Many works on reengineering recognize a dichotomy between organizational processes and organizational functionality. Most organizations are structured into vertically functioning groups or hierarchies, and most processes are organized into horizontal phases for work flow. The many waterfall lifecycle models we have illustrated in our effort surely demonstrate this. Three desirable attributes of *business process improvement* (BPI) are *efficiency,* in terms of minimizing the cost of the resources used; *effectiveness,* in terms of producing desired results; and *adaptability,* in terms of flexibility in accommodating changing customer and organizational needs. To achieve these attributes requires processes with the following well-defined characteristics: ownership and accountability, boundaries and scope, interfaces and responsibilities, work tasks and training requirements, measurement and feedback controls, customer-related measurements and targets, cycle times, and formalized change procedures.

Harrington suggests five phases for BPI (Figure 8.8):

1. *Organize for improvement.* This phase involves several steps. First, it is necessary to establish an executive improvement team (EIT). Then a BPI champion is appointed and executive training is provided. A normative improvement model is identified and BPI objectives are communicated to employees. Next, it is necessary to review business strategy and anticipated customer requirements. This enables the organization to identify and select critical processes for improvement and to appoint process owners. Finally, *performance improvement team* (PIT) members are selected.

2. *Develop an understanding of the various processes currently in use.* This phase includes defining the scope and objectives of current processes and the boundaries within which they are functional. This includes a variety of analysis functions, such as structuring current processes and detection and diagnosis of defects in areas that need potential improvement.

3. *Streamline organizational processes for enhanced efficiency, effectiveness, and adaptability.* Current processes are corrected through various streamlining approaches that are responsive to the diagnosis performed in the last phase. This includes eliminating bureaucracy, reducing the opportunity for errors, reducing non-value-added activities, and otherwise simplifying processes such as to reduce cost and increase effectiveness.

4. *Implement a program of systematic measurement and controls.* In this phase, a program of systematic measurements is used as a quality control and monitoring system in order to both maintain the new process productivity and keep from regressing into poorer process implementations only because they have been used in the past. An extensive program of measurements, feedback, and action is suggested. This includes audits of what are denoted as *poor quality cost* (PQC) facets.

5. *Continue the evolutionary improvement.* Periodic reviews of the effort are used to enable detection, diagnosis, and correction of difficulties as improvement continues. A formal program of business process qualification is suggested through use of a six-level PBI scale for process maturity status. The levels are unknown, understood, effective, efficient, error-free, and world class.

Harrington has had much experience in efforts of this sort, and this is much in evidence in his high caliber writing. These efforts have much in common with those we studied in Chapter 6. The work also has relevance to benchmarking, a topic we will soon discuss, and to the systematic measurement subjects considered in Chapters 4 and 5.

8.2.2 Intelligent Enterprise

The efforts of James Brian Quinn are focused on knowledge-based services as a necessary complement to manufacturing efforts. His view of an organization is basically that of a collection of service activities and that service- and product-oriented organizations alike will obtain their major competitive advantages not from superior physical facilities and materials alone, but from knowledge- and service-based capabilities. In three recent works [12–14] concerning technologies in services, the claim is set forth that it is services and not manufacturing activities that provide the major sources of value to consumers. This does not suggest that services replace manufacturing, but rather that if it were not for the value added by the services that are associated with a manufactured product, there would be a diminished value to the product itself. Several characteristics of new organizations are cited:

"Infinitely flat" or horizontal

"Spider web" like or nonhierarchical and with highly networked interconnections

"Hollow corporations" in which outsourcing of both products and services becomes an increasing reality

Demolished bureaucracies and vertical integration

"Intellectual holding companies" in which intellectual technologies are critical

It is represented that this will lead to precise and swift strategy execution, the leveraging and retention of key people, and "creative management for profits."

A 1992 text by Quinn [15] represents a definitive integration and synthesis of earlier efforts on this subject. It is concerned with concentrating organizational strategy on core intellectual competencies and core service competencies. He suggests four key rules to follow in order to generate success in this regard.

1. Focus internal organizational resources on those relatively few basic sources of intellectual strength and service strength that will create and sustain a real and meaningful distinctiveness to the customer over the long term.

2. Approach the remaining capabilities as a noncritical set of service activities that may be supplied internally or outsourced from external suppliers who compete well in functional activities related to these capabilities.

3. Sustain success by building entry barriers around those selected critical core capabilities to prevent a competitor from assuming a substantial market position.

4. Plan and control outsourcing such as never to become either dependent on or dominated by external suppliers.

Strategic sourcing, including outsourcing, is a major ingredient in these maxims; we discuss it later. Appropriate interfaces between production efforts and service efforts are also stressed as is the management of knowledge-based intellect and professional intellect.

Seven types of innovative organizations are identified in this work.

1. *Basic research organizations* support large RDT&E units. They select products for development on the basis of careful and conservative trade-offs among risk and potential profit.

2. *Large system producers* develop large scale systems that generally cost a great deal and must perform in a reliable manner for a very long time.

3. *Dominant market share oriented companies* are often not the first to introduce an emerging technology into the marketplace. They often support large research units and plan market entry and product evolution to obtain maximum penetration, decreased risk, great product reliability, and lower overall costs.

4. *State of the art technology development companies* are preeminent in their knowledge of a specific technology. Often they operate in markets in which

technical performance criteria are the major drivers of demand and are therefore able to self-define the characteristics of next-generation technology.

5. *Discrete freestanding product line companies* form strong research divisions
and act as entrepreneurial units. They depend more on technology push for
their initiatives than demand pull. They will often introduce new products on
a small scale and obtain real-time market test of these, rather than pay for
very expensive marketing studies that may not be as effective as small scale
product introduction and subsequent interactive modification of the product to
meet consumer needs.

6. *Limited volume* or *fashion companies* provide small scale and limited quantity
products to a specialized market niche.

7. *Job shop* or *custom design* companies provide one-of-a-kind products that
meet an individual customer's requirements. These may often involve flexible
manufacturing or mass customization approaches to enable highly specialized
design to met an individual customer's requirements.

Clearly, this is not a mutually exclusive listing. Nor is the listing collectively
exhaustive. Each of the industry types may be associated with an organizational
strategy and a configuration that are tuned to providing maximum success opportunities. Each type will have a different propensity for organizational growth, maturity, decline, and rebirth as we discussed in our last chapter. In his effort, Quinn
discusses the typical product lifecycle for each organizational characteristic, the mix
of attributes that describe typical innovations, and recommended organizational
structures for RDT&E, acquisition or production, planning and marketing, and
interfaces between marketing and customers. Approaches for managing the intelligent enterprise are also suggested. These involve efforts that also encompass core
capabilities, outsourcing, total quality management, and benchmarking, as well as
some of the other ingredients illustrated in Figure 8.2.

8.2.3 Process Innovation

In the aforenoted text by Davenport [6], a careful distinction is made between
process improvement and process innovation. The fundamental distinctions are that
improvement is continuous and incremental in nature, deals with the existing process, can be accomplished in a relatively short time, is a bottom–up activity, and is
a narrow scope effort with relatively moderate attendant risks. On the other hand,
innovation is generally a discrete phenomenon that is revolutionary and radical in
nature. It starts with a zero base as contrasted with the existing process, can only be
accomplished over a long time, is a top–down activity, is a broad scope effort that
cuts across all the functional areas and processes in the organization, and is usually
characterized by high associated risks.

Of course, there may exist questions of whether an innovation is a major improvement and whether a set of incremental improvements does not add up to an
innovation. Rather than a binary scale to separate these two, perhaps it would be

best to consider a continuous scale. This would enable us to consider incremental improvement at one end and radical innovation at the other. Obviously, either can be appropriate or inappropriate in specific situations. Change increments may be so small that centuries would be required to accomplish any change with appreciable value added. On the other hand, radical innovation may be so dramatic that the organization is culturally and otherwise unable to adapt. Culture shock and customer revolt are often the results.

Information technology is suggested as a major enabler of process innovation, together with the organizational and human enabler, and an enabler based on measurements associated with process information and management of the information environment. Essentially these three were suggested as enablers in Figure 8.1. The process innovation effort itself is comprised of five phases, and a number of activity steps within each phase, as connoted by Figure 8.9. We note that there are opportunities both for traditional incremental improvement and the more extreme innovative improvement. Presumably, the overall process is iterative and this leads to continual innovation, as suggested by the feedback from phase V to phase I in the illustration of Figure 8.9.

Not explicitly shown in this figure are the organizational communications that occur at each phase of the effort and the commitment building that is also needed. Davenport examines a number of enablers of specific processes including planning, research, development, design, production, marketing, and sales.

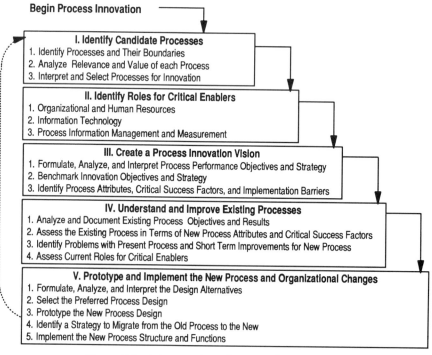

Figure 8.9 Interpretation of process innovation.

Also considered briefly are the role of organizational culture in shaping desirable innovation strategies. In a related work [16], this is considered in greater detail. Five models of information culture, denoted as information politics, are defined.

1. *Technocratic utopianism* is a formal analytical approach to information management. It stresses highly quantitative approaches, major reliance on emerging technologies, and full information assets. There is an underlying assumption that technology will resolve all problems. Organizational and political issues are generally ignored, perhaps because they are considered unmanageable. In reality, the major focus may be on the technologies used to process data rather than on the information content in the data. The major objectives are modeling and use of organizational data. Data engineering and some aspects of information engineering are considered kings. All that is really needed for organizational paradise is the selection of the best hardware and software and use of the most appropriate CASE tools to assist in constructing the most appropriate entity relationship diagrams and data flow models.

2. *Feudalism* was the model of information politics most often encountered in this study. In this model, a number of people in several distinct feudal departments individually control information acquisition, representation, storage, analysis, transmission, and use. The language used for information representation is often different across the various departments. Critical information that affects the organization as a whole is often not collected. When a subset of this is collected by an individual department, it may not be passed on outside the boundaries of the department. Making organizationally informed decisions for the common good is often very difficult, as a result of the information-poor environment. Sometimes, however, strategic alliances across feudal departments are possible and innovation within these units may be possible.

3. *Monarchy* is a pragmatic solution to the difficulties inherent in the feudal model. Information management is centralized and there is little autonomy concerning information policies. A benign monarch who is enlightened concerning information technology and organizational needs for information may set up, potentially through a Chief Information Officer (CIO), a very effective and efficient system. A constitutional monarchy may well accomplish this; a despotic monarchy seldom will perform satisfactorily. An executive information system (EIS) or executive support system (ESS) [17] may well be a beneficial product of a constitutional monarchy. One problem with a constitutional information monarchy, however, is the problem of succession when the monarch dies, retires, or is overthrown. This can lead to information anarchy.

4. *Anarchy* is the result of complete absence of any information policy. Usually this is not a willfully imposed model but a result of a breakdown of one of the centralized approaches, such as a monarchy. This results in individuals and units in an organization managing their own information resources and developing information reports that serve their own needs rather than the needs of the organization as a whole. The major shortcoming of an information anarchy is not the wasted effort involved in the redundant information processing and storage effort across units, but

the Tower of Babel effect that results in terms of providing information that is useful for the entire organization. There will seldom exist any interoperability across units, at the level of either data or information. As a consequence of this, the various units may well present entirely different results from using the same data on the generally very different alternative model management systems, including intuitive model management systems, that will be in use.

5. *Federalism* involves the use of negotiations [18–20] to bring competing and noncooperative individuals and units into consensus on information-related issues. Strong central leadership and an organizational culture that encourages learning, cooperation, and consensus are required in order for this model to work. Understanding by top organizational management of both information technologies and the value of information is a need if a shared information vision is to be created.

It seems quite clear that these models are neither mutually exclusive nor collectively exhaustive. A given organization may well function with a hybrid model, and the model that is in use at a given time may evolve from one form to the other with changes in organizational dynamics. Some of the models of organizational cultures we discussed in Chapter 7 seem very plausible as information cultures as well.

In a study of the information culture at 25 companies, Davenport and his colleagues found that the feudal model was the most common model in 12 companies. Federalist, monarchist, and technocratic utopianist models were found with approximately equal frequency in that eight, seven, and nine companies were found predominantly following the prescriptions of these models. Only four organizations followed the anarchist model. They also ranked these five alternative models of information cultures according to their scoring on four attributes of information value:

Commonality of vocabulary
Access to information
Information quality
Information management efficiency

Each of the four attributes had equal weight in this study. Their conclusion, that the federalist and monarchist models are most appropriate in most situations, seems inescapable. The feudalist and anarchist models, which actually seem to have a lot in common, were the poorest performers.

In order to determine a "best" model for a given organization, we need to know the current model that is in use and the evolutionary or revolutionary model for the information culture to which the organization should be moving. Four suggestions are given; our interpretation of these is as follows:

1. Match information management strategies to the organizational culture that is extant and the organizational culture that the organization is desirous of adopting.

2. Practice technological realism, both in terms of information technologies themselves, interoperability across potentially different platforms, and the value of information that is not always easily captured in electronic form.

3. Select appropriate information managers, both from the standpoint of technical skills and broad scope organizational understanding skills.

4. Avoid building information empires, such as through creation of despotic monarchies and information czars.

Explicit recognition of information management cultures and managing them constructively are suggested as the bottom line. In conformance to our discussions in the previous chapter, we would call these information management styles and information cultures or information management cultures, rather than "information politics," a term used by Davenport and colleagues. As we have noted before, there are semantic differences in use by the many workers in these areas. In terms of the vocabulary we use here, the organizational political cultures identified by the authors are the anarchist and the feudalist models. These are not to be encouraged. On this, of course, we agree strongly with the authors of this excellent work.

8.2.4   Corporate Reengineering

In the work by Hammer and Champy [10], the forces of three Cs—*customers* who demand customized products and services that are of high quality and trustworthy, *competition* that has intensified on a global scale in almost all niches, and *change* that now becomes continuous—are suggested as combining together to require massive, discrete-level, transformations in the way organizations do business. Radical and dramatic reengineering of fundamental organizational strategy and of all organizational processes is suggested as *the* path to change.

The authors are much concerned with organizational processes that have a number of common characteristics. Our interpretation of these is as follows:

1. The steps and phases in the process are sequenced in a logical order in terms of earlier phase results being needed for later activities. The phases are not necessarily in a linear order. They are sequenced in a concurrent fashion whenever possible such as to generally enable obtaining results from the effort in minimum time.

2. The various business processes are integrated throughout the organization, and often a number of formerly distinct efforts are combined to produce savings in costs and increased effectiveness as well.

3. There are multiple versions of many processes such that mass customization is thereby made possible.

4. Work is shifted across organizational boundaries to include potential outsourcing and is performed in the most appropriate setting.

5. Decision-making efforts become a part of the normal work environment and work is compressed both horizontally and vertically.

6. Reactive checks, controls, and measurements are reduced in frequency and importance in favor of greater use of interactive and proactive approaches.

7. There is always a point of contact or "case manager" who is empowered to provide service to each individual customer and a customer need never go beyond this point of contact.

8. Organizational operations are a hybrid of centralized and decentralized structures, as best suited to the particular task at hand.

Several, generally beneficial, changes are claimed to result from this. Work units change from functional departments to multifunctional, process-oriented teams. Performers of simple tasks now are able to accomplish multidimensional work. People become empowered rather than controlled. The major needed job preparation changes; it becomes education rather than training. The focus of measures and performance shifts to results rather than activities. Promotion or transfer to a new organizational assignment is based on ability for the new assignment and not performance in a former assignment. Values change from reactive and protective to productive and proactive. Managers become coaches as well as supervisors, executives become leaders and not just scorekeepers, and organizational structures shift away from the hierarchical to the flat. And, as we have noted, information technology is represented to be a major enabler of all this.

8.2.5   Business Process Reengineering

Another view of process reengineering is provided by a team of authors from Coopers & Lybrand [21]. They view a given organization as being driven by market forces and production forces. Organizations are viewed as having a balance of process-oriented horizontal operations and bureaucratic hierarchical operations. The more successful contemporary organizations will be market driven and will have a process orientation. A metric called value, based on four facets of value, is defined as

$$Value = \frac{(Quality)\ (Service)}{(Cost)\ (Cycle\ Time)}$$

where these four facets are, in turn, defined in terms of a number of lower level attributes.

Process reengineering is indicated to be one of a family of three related and process-oriented methodologies:

Total quality management (TQM)

Just-in-time (JIT) manufacturing

Breakpoint business process reengineering

There is much in common in these three efforts. According to Johanson et al. [21]: "a breakpoint is the achievement of excellence in one or more value metrics where the marketplace clearly recognizes the advantage, and where the ensuing result is a disproportionate and sustained increase in the supplier's market share." Thus a breakpoint is defined as the achievement of excellence in one or more value metrics.

Breakpoints are indicated to be necessary as metrics to support process reengineering. The two notions, breakpoints and business process reengineering, are viewed as virtually inseparable. Business process reengineering (BPR) is the means by which an organization achieves radical change in performance on those value-added facets of organizational products and services that are measured by cost, cycle time, service, and quality. This results from the application of tools and techniques that focus on an organization as a set of integrated customer-oriented core processes, rather than a set of functions. A breakpoint represents the achievement of excellence in one of the facets of value. The combination of the breakpoint construct and the process reengineering construct is termed *breakpoint business process reengineering*.

There are three essential phases suggested for BPR. These, which appear totally equivalent to the generic lifecycle phases of definition, development, and deployment that we have suggested here and illustrated in Figure 8.3, may be described as follows:

1. *Discovery* is the phase in which the organization identifies and defines a strategic vision and needs to achieve that vision.
2. *Redesign* or development involves detailed planning and engineering of the strategic vision in terms of business processes.
3. *Realization* or deployment of the developed strategic plan is needed in order to operationalize the strategic vision.

Each of these phases is described in terms of a number of supporting steps. As with the other approaches to process reengineering noted earlier, the major focus is on redefinition, redevelopment, and redeployment of all major organizational processes for greater organizational responsiveness and productivity as measured by customer satisfaction.

Defining a strategic vision for an organization is a key part of this effort. In a very insightful pair of articles, Schoemaker [22,23] discusses scenario planning and the identification of strategic vision and core capabilities for an organization and their linkages. The framework for defining a strategic vision is as follows:

1. Generate broad scope scenarios of possible futures for the organization.
2. Conduct a competitive analysis of the fields of interest of the organization.
3. Analyze the core capabilities of the organization and its competitors.
4. Define and develop a strategic vision and identify possible strategic options.

Figure 8.3 can easily be tailored to represent the BPR perspective described here.

In the process of defining a strategic vision, an organization must necessarily consider a number of related facets, such as organizational leadership and culture, and forecasted future scenarios for these. This leads to selection of strategic options that implement the strategic vision. This approach of Schoemaker appears most useful for completing the effort at BPR suggested here.

Another key characteristic of this approach is the identification of breakpoints and the identification of core business processes in which appropriate breakpoints may exist. Critical processes, where appropriate breakpoints may exist, are said to include those processes (1) that require very radical process redevelopment due to large discrepancies between theoretical and realized process capabilities, (2) that have major potential improvements in customer receptivity, (3) that could become the source of critical competitive products, and (4) that are responsive to either external competitive pressures or regulatory requirements. Process mapping is an approach to understanding existing processes well and that may suggest potential breakpoints for exploitation. Essentially, this involves structural modeling and simulation of processes such as to enable determination of a vision for new processes.

8.2.6 Breakpoints

In our last subsection, and in others in this chapter, we have referred to the notion of a breakpoint, which represents the achievement of excellence in one of the facets of value. This is a more or less internal definition. In a recent work concerning breakpoints, Paul Strebel [24] provides more of an external perspective on a breakpoint with the suggestion that it is a sudden radical change in the rules of the business game, in particular, of market conditions, that will shape the future course of an industry or organization. A given organization, however, may create a breakpoint by proactive creation of competitive barriers, in the form of performance gaps, that others must then attempt to overcome. These two interpretations of the concept are very similar, although the inherent discontinuity notion does not seem to be necessarily associated with the first interpretation. In reality, a breakpoint is an internal concept that is intended to drive organizational activities to produce results that represent continuous improvement. It is also externally focused in that external reference points are needed to establish a breakpoint in a meaningful way.

We see that an organization may approach breakpoints from an inactive, reactive, interactive, or proactive perspective.

1. An inactive approach is one in which an organization simply does not concern itself with the market, and the status of the products and/or services of the organization relative to the market, at all.

2. A reactive approach to breakpoints is associated with marshaling organizational forces to a crisis situation, relative to the status of the organization's products and the market for these, after a crisis has eventuated. Ultimately, the organization attempts to exploit the breakpoints that are found to exist after diagnosing the damage that has been done and determining an appropriate correction and implementing it.

3. An interactive or anticipatory approach to breakpoints would be associated with attempting to keep abreast of changing market situations as they occur, rather than after they have eventuated and caused damage.

4. A proactive approach to breakpoints would involve forecasting conditions such that the organization can prepare itself to create change and then position itself to take maximum advantage of the resulting competitive breakpoint.

An inactive approach, which is actually not discussed, is a path to disaster. Similarly, a reactive approach should be avoided, as it is generally preferred to avoid difficulties rather than to emerge from them after they have materialized. Sometimes, it will not be possible to anticipate crisis situations. Thus reactive strategies are always needed. An anticipatory and interactive approach works generally better than a reactive approach. To reach a high degree of excellence, a proactive approach is needed.

We see that there is much in common between the breakpoint concept and that of systematic measurements. We can view a breakpoint as a metric, or we can view it as a process. Actually, there are three processes involved, one each for reactive, interactive, and proactive breakpoint management. We can use the results of the breakpoint management process to affect the products of an organization or the product line of the organization, or we can attempt systems management strategy shifts that will change the essential characteristics of both processes and products. Figure 8.10 illustrates the three generic phases for breakpoint process management and suggests the use of breakpoints to alter systems management, product line processes, or products. As we have also noted, we may implement benchmark

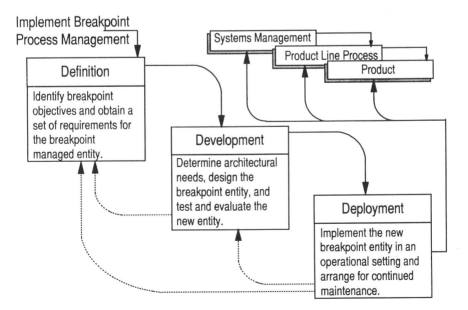

Figure 8.10 Breakpoint process management for systems management, product line, or product enhancement.

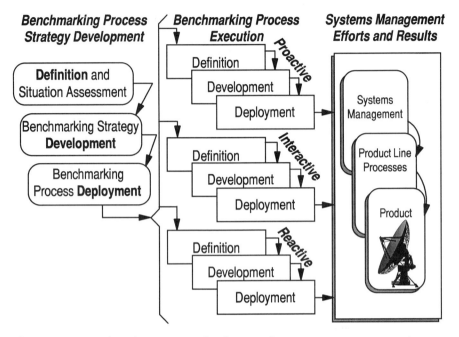

Figure 8.11 Benchmarking strategy development for reactive, interactive, and proactive benchmarking.

process management from either a reactive, interactive, or proactive perspective, or ideally a combination of these perspectives. Figure 8.11 illustrates this. It shows breakpoint strategy formulation and deployment in terms of reactive, interactive, and proactive benchmarking efforts.

In his effort, Strebel describes what we would call here the three lifecycles for proactive, interactive, and reactive breakpoint management processes. The terminologies of creating, anticipating, and exploiting breakthroughs are used. Our interpretation of these lifecycles is illustrated in Figures 8.12 through 8.14. Each of the phases illustrated, for each lifecycle, is described in a number of formulation, analysis, and interpretation-like steps. The discussion by Strebel [24] of these lifecycles is extensive.

8.2.7   Benchmarking

A benchmark is much like a breakpoint. Actually, the concept of a benchmark predates that of a breakpoint. Much further discussion of benchmarking is available in [25–27]. A recent and definitive work by Watson [28] provides an excellent overview of many current efforts concerning benchmarking. He identifies four types of benchmarking efforts.

1. *Internal benchmarking* involves observations taken entirely within the same organization, generally of the best practices that have resulted in one segment

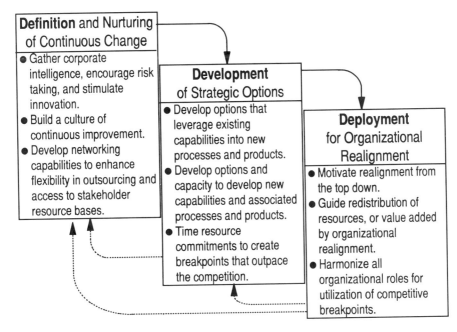

Figure 8.12   Interpretation of proactive breakpoint management process.

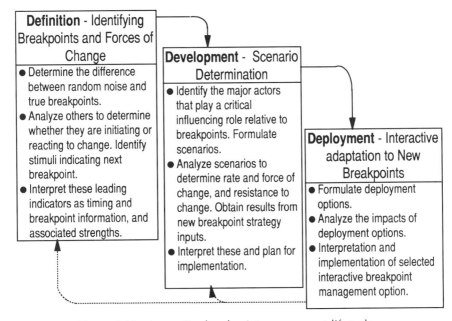

Figure 8.13   Interactive breakpoint management lifecycle.

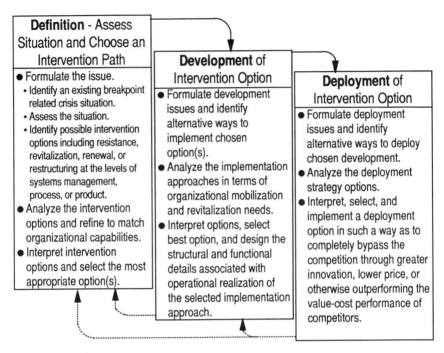

Definition - Assess Situation and Choose an Intervention Path
- Formulate the issue.
  - Identify an existing breakpoint related crisis situation.
  - Assess the situation.
  - Identify possible intervention options including resistance, revitalization, renewal, or restructuring at the levels of systems management, process, or product.
- Analyze the intervention options and refine to match organizational capabilities.
- Interpret intervention options and select the most appropriate option(s).

Development of Intervention Option
- Formulate development issues and identify alternative ways to implement chosen option(s).
- Analyze the implementation approaches in terms of organizational mobilization and revitalization needs.
- Interpret options, select best option, and design the structural and functional details associated with operational realization of the selected implementation approach.

Deployment of Intervention Option
- Formulate deployment issues and identify alternative ways to deploy chosen development.
- Analyze the deployment strategy options.
- Interpret, select, and implement a deployment option in such a way as to completely bypass the competition through greater innovation, lower price, or otherwise outperforming the value-cost performance of competitors.

Figure 8.14   Reactive breakpoint management process.

of the organization that are desired to be transferred into another segment of the organization. Internal benchmarking efforts at Hewlett-Packard are described.

2. *Competitive benchmarking* involves targeted best practices in an external organization. These can be at the level of systems management, processes, or product. Often, much secondary research is used for competitive benchmarking. The competitive benchmarking studies of the Ford Motor Company, and their use of these in developing Ford Taurus, are described.

3. *Functional benchmarking** is concerned with performance investigation within a specific functional area for an industry-wide function. The results of functional benchmarking are especially suited to identifying process improve-

*The terminology used is that of Watson. In our terminology, we would use the term functional product benchmarking to refer to benchmarking of the directly measurable aspects of a product. These serve to describe the operational capabilities that are supplied to the user of the product or service. The nonfunctional attributes of a product are those constraints, alterables, or limitations that relate to the structural or purposeful properties of the product that are not a part of the functional properties. The nonfunctional attributes of a product relate to such important characteristics of a product as reliability, maintainability, quality, and availability. Thus what was accomplished here would not be described, using our terminology, as functional product benchmarking. It is really nonfunctional product benchmarking in our terminology. The study conducted by GM was not restricted to automotive products. It was a study of quality processes at 11 cooperating organizations in a variety of product areas. They had established ten hypotheses for empirical evaluation and these relate very closely to quality processes. It would therefore be very appropriate to denote this type of benchmarking as *functional process benchmarking*.

ment related benchmarks. The efforts of the General Motors Corporation in September 1994, which led to major GM strides to enhance product quality and reliability, are described.

4. *Generic benchmarking* is concerned with studying the best processes in actual use in practice in a given organization such as to enable analogous development of enhanced processes by the organization(s) sponsoring the benchmarking study. A generic benchmarking study by Xerox, which ultimately led to understanding and analogous modification and adoption of facets of the shipping processes activities of the catalog causal-clothing sales organization L. L. Bean, are described. This effort was so successful that it led to establishment of a *benchmarking effectiveness strategy team* (BEST) network to transfer lessons learned throughout the Xerox Corporation.

Like a breakpoint, a benchmark involves a baseline comparison of existing practices of an organization with those best practices as used by one organization or perhaps many other organizations. These practices may be at the level of product, process, or systems management. Breakpoints and benchmarks have the same ultimate purpose, that of enabling and enhancing organizational improvements for customer satisfaction. The use of a benchmark can be reactive, in which case we desire to emulate the best practices of others that have already been established and perhaps excel in these. In can be interactive or anticipative, in which case, we desire to foresee efforts that are now occurring and adjust organizational practices, more or less in real time, to keep abreast of the competition. We can use benchmarks for forecasting purposes such that we evolve entirely new forms of organizational results in the form of system management strategies, processes, and products that are each world class in quality and trustworthiness. In all cases, benchmarks are based on systematic measurements, both internal and external measurements, and serve as a catalyst for action and results. In this regard, benchmarks are also very much related to critical success factors (CSF) [29,30]. The two terms are almost synonymous.

We see that a benchmark is a standard of excellence or achievement or CSF that provides a baseline against which to measure or evaluate similar entities. While the benchmarking notion may seem quite simple at first, there are really a number of benchmarking features that need to be examined. There are at least seven important and interrelated questions that need to be asked before we benchmark.

Why do we benchmark?

What do we benchmark?

Which benchmark measures do we need?

Who do we benchmark?

Where do we benchmark?

When do we benchmark?

How do we benchmark?

We can and should ask these questions of our organization and, to the extent possible, we can and should ask these questions of those organizations that represent competitors. We can and should ask these questions in the search for structural, functional, and purposeful answers. A similar set needs to be asked after we benchmark. Benchmarking efforts can be conducted relative to issues at the level of systems management, process, or product. Answers to these questions need to be obtained in terms of implications for each of these levels.

There can be some obvious ethical, moral, and legal concerns relative to benchmarking. Some aspects of benchmarking may seem to amount to spying or espionage. Clearly, successful benchmarking should not, and cannot, involve behavior that is either immoral, unethical, or illegal. One of the major activities of the International Benchmarking Clearinghouse Committee of the American Productivity and Quality Center (APQC) has resulted in a set of guidelines, known as a Code of Conduct, for benchmarking that have been subscribed to by a considerable number of companies and that are generally felt to be above reproach [31]. There are nine principles in the Benchmarking Code of Conduct. They may be summarized as follows:

1. *Legality.* The acquisition of trade secrets is proscribed, as is doing benchmarking without first requesting approval by the benchmarkee. All actions and intents should be legal ones.

2. *Exchange.* The same type and level of information should be provided both by the benchmarked organization and the organization doing the benchmarking in an openly communicated exchange.

3. *Confidentiality.* Benchmarking communications should be considered as confidential to the organizations involved and obtained information concerning benchmarking should not be divulged outside the concerned organizations without prior consent of all parties.

4. *Use.* Benchmarking information should only be used for formulation of improvement options for processes or products within organizations participating in the study. Attribution of benchmarking partner names requires prior permission, and benchmarking information must not be used for marketing or sales purposes.

5. *First-Party Contact.* Benchmarking information contacts with a partner organization should be made through the point of contact established by the benchmarking partner. Mutual agreement must be reached for delegation of responsibility in this regard to other parties.

6. *Third-Party Contact.* Prior permission must be obtained before divulging the name of the benchmarking point of contact to a third party or in an open forum.

7. *Preparation.* A benchmarking contact with the point of contact at another organization should only be made after proper planning and preparation of an interview guide, in order to make the encounter efficient and effective.

8. *Completion.* Each benchmarking study must be completed to the satisfaction of all benchmarking partners in a timely manner, as agreed to prior to the study.

9. *Understanding and Action.* All partners should be treated with mutual respect and understanding, and information should be used as mutually agreed.

It seems quite clear that these conduct codes are also applicable as ethical codes of conduct, as well as being very useful standards for benchmarking practice.

The APQC has recently established three awards for benchmarking: a research prize, a benchmarking study prize, and an award for excellence in benchmarking. There are five achievement categories for benchmarking and these are further disaggregated into a number of subcategories. Figure 8.15 illustrates an attribute tree and provides attribute weights for the benchmarking excellence awards. The total weight of 1000 points is distributed such that results and measured improvements from the benchmarking process are the most important attribute with 300 points or a normalized weight of 0.30. In this category, specific benchmarks that have been adopted over the past three years are examined to determine results obtained in terms of customer satisfaction, quality and productivity, cycle time, employee well-being and morale, and environmental impact. Also examined are the measures used to evaluate and improve the benchmarking process within the organization, and how the objectivity and validity of the benchmarking study results are established. Linkages of the benchmarking process to improvement activities, resource allocation, and employee improvement effort deployment are measured by a benchmarking linkages attribute, which is assigned a normalized weight of 0.25. The integration of benchmarking with the strategic planning initiative in the organization, and how this is supported by the information structure for use of benchmarking in the organi-

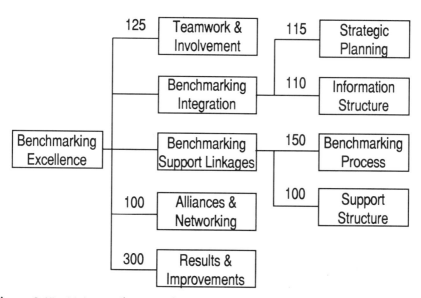

Figure 8.15 Major attributes and attribute weights for benchmarking recognition award criteria.

zation, is the third most important attribute and is assigned a weight of 0.225. Teamwork and stakeholder involvement in the benchmarking process and organizational alliances and networking for benchmarking are considered relatively less important and are assigned weights of 0.125 and 0.10. Each lowest level identified for attribute measures is scored on an absolute scoring basis by a set of evaluators in terms of the approach taken, deployment of the approach, and results obtained.*

There are several ways in which a benchmarking study may be conducted. In each case, there needs to be formulation, analysis, and interpretation at each of the phases in a benchmarking study. We generally need to define what it is we wish to benchmark. We need to develop an appropriate benchmarking process in terms of determining how to go about benchmarking. Then we need a deployment strategy in terms of an effort that puts the development tactics into operational implementation. The questions we asked earlier in this subsection each need answers in order to develop the actual benchmarking plans and implementation effort. The references cited earlier provide a number of relatively specific implementation discussions and case studies of benchmarking. Watson, for example, illustrates how Hewlett-Packard, Ford, General Motors, and Xerox each performed benchmarking studies. Often, it is suggested that organizations follow the plan–do–check–act cycle of Schewhart and Deming, which we discussed in Chapter 6. This would involve (1) planning for the benchmarking process, (2) implementing the plan and obtaining benchmarking information, (3) checking and analysis of the benchmarking information, and (4) acting by improving the organization on the basis of the analyzed information.

Benchmarking is not altogether dissimilar from the other related improvement approaches we describe in this chapter on reengineering. It is very closely related to the strategic quality management approaches we discussed in Chapter 6 and the organizational culture, leadership, and process maturity approaches we discussed in Chapter 7. The metrics and systematic measurements associated with benchmarking are, for the most part, the metrics we discussed in Chapters 4 and 5.

8.2.8 Competitive Advantage and Competitive Strategy

Michael Porter has been much concerned with competitive advantage and competitive strategy and has written three seminal texts in this area [32–34]. He identifies four forces that determine and intensify organizational competition:

Threats from potential new competitors

Bargaining power of suppliers

Bargaining power of potential customers

Threats due to substitutable products

Together with threats from existing competitors, the net result is rivalry and competition in the marketplace.

---

*Further information on these awards is available from: The American Productivity and Quality Center, Benchmarking Award Administrator, 123 Post Oak Lane, Houston, TX 77024-7797.

Figure 8.16   Five major factors influencing marketplace competition.

These are external factors. Figure 8.16 represents our interpretation of these five factors and their influence on marketplace rivalry. The extent to which each of these factors is a dominant influence in the marketplace is said to depend on industry structure. The internal structure within an individual organization is a major factor also, for that organization. Structural change in a given industry sector may change the way in which these potential factors influence actual competition. Changes in an individual organization may have a constructive or destructive effect on a given industry. A given organization may have little or much ability to cause structural change in the industry in which it operates.

Seven major barriers may act to prohibit an organization from entering a given market area.

1. *Economies of scale* may make it very difficult for a firm, especially one without very deep pockets, from entering a new market area in which it cannot obtain a competitive cost advantage until it has captured a significant share of the market.

2. *Product differentiation* may pose another barrier to entry, especially when the marketing efforts for presently competing products have been very successful and they are perceived as highly differentiated products with superior functional features and performance characteristics.

3. *Capital requirements* to enter a given market may be very high.

4. *Experiential familiarity barriers to entry* may exist whenever there is major experiential familiarity based expertise associated with competitors, and where

this is not available to organizations potentially desirous of entering the market with a new product. This generally leads to cost disadvantages that will exist even for organizations with a large available financial resource base that could be used to sustain themselves to obtain economies of scale if they could obtain the needed, but unavailable to them, experiential base needed for success.

5. *Access to product distribution channels* may be difficult to obtain for an organization with a new product.

6. *Government policy and controls* may, through licenses and regulations, make it very difficult if not impossible for an organization to enter a product market that is new to them.

7. *Fear of retaliation* from a larger competitor now in the market, particularly if the smaller firm is also a supplier to the larger competitor, may provide a significant barrier to entry.

There are, of course, other barriers to entry. Supports and barriers for the external factors influencing marketplace entry, illustrated in Figure 8.16, are generally provided by Porter. The conditions under which customer and supplier groups are powerful and the threats of new entrants and substitute products are major influencers on competitive advantage of an organization and combine with market conditions to support or deny competitive advantage for a given organization.

Two basic facets of *competitive advantage* are identified.

- *Cost* is a major influencer of competitive advantage. If the functional and nonfunctional characteristics of a product or service are presumed to be the same, positive competitive advantage will accrue to a lower cost product, or one that can be produced, delivered to customers, and supported more efficiently. It can be sold at a lower price than a higher cost product of comparable value and this results in greater profits per unit product delivered than would be the case if production costs were higher.

- *Differentiation* is a second major influencer of competitive advantage. Among products or services that cost the same to produce, there will be a positive competitive advantage to those products that have greater perceived differentiated value, as the weighted sum of functional and nonfunctional features of the product is greater.

We see that lowering production costs, through greater production efficiency, will enable competitive advantage. In a similar way, increasing product effectiveness or differentiated value will increase competitive advantage. Competitive advantage is one major ingredient of competitive strategy. The competitive advantage for an organization's products will be very dependent on how the organization manages all of the organizational processes (RDT&E, acquisition or production, marketing, and such related subprocesses as warehousing, supplier relations, and distribution) that relate to the final product or service. Porter uses the terms "value chain" and "value system" to refer to the linkages created by these various processes and the entire system.

Competitive focus or *competitive scope* of products and services is a third major generic ingredient of competitive strategy. There are two market foci or competitive scope targets:

- A *broad target* general market exists for some products and services.
- A *narrow target* or highly focused, segmented, or niche market exists for other products and services.

Together, these comprise competitive scope. An organization can target its products broadly or narrowly. It can do this with low cost products that are undifferentiated in their features, or with higher cost products that are differentiated in their features from the products of competitors.

At first glance, it appears that there are two other types of competitive advantage strategies that are possible. One could attempt to offer high cost products that are undifferentiated in their features. Clearly, this would only result in major competitive disadvantage as a special, but rather undesirable, form of competitive advantage. Only some form of sales and marketing camouflage could make this succeed, but the success would generally endure only over the short term. Alternately, an organization could conceivably have a product that is differentiated in features from its competitors and that also has lower cost. In this highly desirable situation, there would exist a major competitive advantage due both to lower cost and greater differentiation. So we see that these two types of competitive advantage are not necessarily mutually exclusive.

Porter identifies four generic competitive strategies. These involve a mix of the two identified types of competitive advantage and the two types of competitive focus.

1. *Differentiation strategies* involve offering a large number of highly competitive and specialized products that appeal to a wide segment of the market, often at premium prices.
2. *Focused differentiation strategies* involve targeting narrow market segments with highly specialized products offered at very premium prices.
3. *Cost focused strategies* involve offering relatively simple basic and generally undifferentiated products to a narrowly targeted market at low prices.
4. *Cost leadership strategies* involve offering many types of products to a broadly targeted market that are of good but generally not superior quality and that are offered at very low prices.

Since there are a variety of ways in which a given organization may focus its product(s) and differentiate among competing products in order to appeal to different market segments, there are a potentially large number of variations of a given strategy. No one of these four strategies can be called universally "best" or most appropriate. Industry and organizational structure will strongly influence the range of competitive strategy options that will be available and which may be successful if adopted.

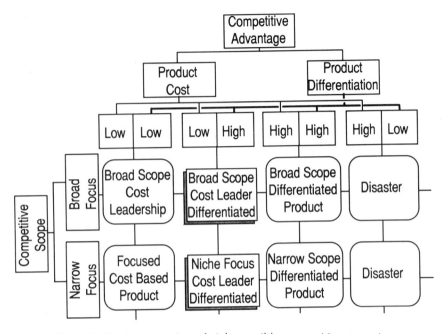

Figure 8.17   Interpretation of eight possible competitive strategies.

Figure 8.17 illustrates the three generic competitive strategy dimensions—product cost, product differentiation, and market scope—and our interpretation of the eight possible strategies that may be implemented. Two of these are disaster strategies, that of entering any of the two generic markets with a product with no competitive advantage whatever. While it might appear highly desirable to attempt to implement several of the strategies simultaneously, that is, to enter both a broad scope and a narrow scope market simultaneously, this will generally be a foolish move and a strategic recipe for poor performance. Thus there are some combination situations or strategies in this figure that may be bad.

Generally, only one strategy should be adopted for a given specific organizational product. Of course, there can be strategy migration over time. For example, an organization might initially have a product that is a low cost, highly differentiated product and attempt to enter a broadly targeted market. This is what we have called a broad scope, cost leadership, highly differentiated product. It may well occur that the initial cost leadership opportunities vanish over time for any of a number of reasons, such as a new technology that makes low cost production opportunities that are available to many organizations. The organization may then wish to reposition itself as a producer of a broad scope, highly differentiated product and forego the initially held competitive advantage position of cost leadership. This might well lead, however, to image difficulties due to the changed marketing strategy that is needed. In such a situation, it might have been better for the organization to have established its competitive advantage on the basis of product differentiation only. It could have converted the initial cost leadership position into increased profits, while the cost leadership existed, and marketed the product as a broad target, highly differentiated product only. It is for reasons like this that Porter does not suggest the two competitive strategies associated with low cost, high differentiation competitive advantage but does encourage use of only one of the four generic strategies we described earlier.

He suggests three conditions under which a firm can concurrently market a low cost product and have high product differentiation competitive advantage.

1. The other competitors are "stuck in the middle" in the sense that they have tried to concurrently implement several generic strategies but are not successful in implementing any one of them. Thus they are not powerful enough to force a situation where low cost and high product differentiation become inconsistent. Eventually, however, one or more competitors will satisfactorily implement one of the four generic strategies suggested by Porter. They will place enormous pressure on either the low cost or the product differentiation advantage held by the organization that once excelled in both and will ultimately cause it to yield on one of these, unless it wishes to also become stuck in the middle.

2. The cost leadership position is more strongly determined by the large market share that is associated with a specific product, rather than by process and technology or service factors. A cost leadership position will often develop when an organization is the first to market a specific product. It can also occur when an organization has sufficiently deep pockets to market a product at a price lower than the development and deployment cost for small quantity production would otherwise justify, and the organization is then able to sustain and endure the loss situation until the product has captured sufficient market share that economies of scale result in lower production cost to the organization and result in a profit for each product sold.

3. An organization has the benefit of a major new innovation and is the only organization that can benefit from this innovation.

This does not say, however, that an organization should not attempt efforts aimed at both low cost and high product differentiation. Clearly, an organization should pursue low cost when it does not sacrifice product differentiation. It should also pursue high product differentiation through measures that are not very expensive. In this sense, it needs to strive for Pareto optimality [35] such that there will be no allocation of effort or reallocation of the resources of the organization that will increase differentiation without increasing costs, and no reallocation that will decrease costs and that will also not decrease differentiation. Figure 8.18 suggests the notion of Pareto optimality and a desirable Pareto frontier relative to the trade-off between low cost and product differentiation. An organization should select a single competitive advantage perspective, of either being a high differentiation or a low cost producer, and adopt a competitive strategy that is supportive of this.

Five causal factors that may result in innovations and new ways of competing are identified:

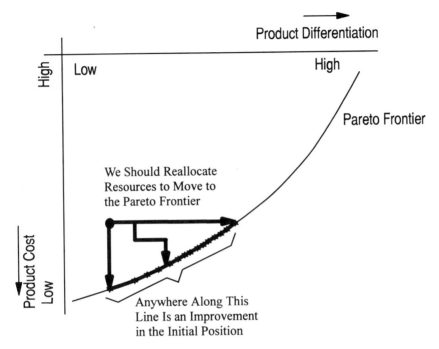

Figure 8.18   Pareto optimality and improvement in cost leadership and differentiation.

New technologies
New or changing customer needs
Emergence of new industry segments
Changing cost or availability of the input factors to production
Changes in government regulation

These factors will, of course, influence organizational competition. We discussed innovation in Chapter 2 and will not specifically comment on this important topic further here.

It is not only necessary to establish competitive advantage, it is necessary to sustain it. Porter indicates three approaches to accomplish this.

1. The *source* of competitive advantage may be sustained. Some sources of competitive advantage are relatively easy to reproduce or emulate. This is particularly the case for lower cost advantages, such as those due to lower labor costs and cheap raw materials. Product differentiation advantages will be much more difficult to replicate. These advantages are generally and primarily due to innovative RDT&E products or innovative and specialized marketing, customer relations and service, or product reliability and quality. This reality strongly supports the strategic quality management efforts described in Chapter 6. Often, lower cost advantages

can be offset quite dramatically by the greater product differentiation that results from careful and sustained investments in people, processes, technologies, and organizational facilities.

2. The *number of distinct sources of competitive advantage* is as important for sustaining advantage as it is for initially establishing it. If an organization obtains competitive advantage due only to one source, this may easily be overcome. A low labor cost producer may be upset because of technological improvements that increase the productivity of highly educated, motivated, and well paid empowered workers.

3. *Constant improvement and upgrading* are cited as the most important sustainers of competitive advantage.

An organization can approach competitive advantage and its sustenance in a reactive, interactive, or proactive fashion. If the approach is reactive, then there will likely be a constant challenge of continuing to react to competitors after their new and superior products have emerged. Change is costly, and it is difficult to establish the motivation and momentum required when the existing products and services have initial competitive advantage. Thus sustaining competitive advantage may be more difficult for a given organization than was the effort in initially establishing it.

There are risks associated with choice of either, or both, of the competitive advantage strategies. Either cost leadership is not sustained, or high product differentiation is not sustained, or both. With no doubt at all, we can state that the risks associated with not sustaining both cost and differentiation leadership are greater than the risks associated with not sustaining either one of these. It is not immediately clear that the risk of losing either the advantage due to cost leadership or the advantage due to high differentiation standard is greater than either the risk of losing cost leadership when only that is established or the risk associated with losing product differentiation when only that is initially established. Porter provides compelling verbal arguments that suggest that this will almost always be the case, however. There are also risks associated with choice of a narrow target or niche market. Essentially, the selected competitive advantage may successfully be imitated or the targeted niche becomes unattractive because either the structure of that segment of the market changes greatly or the product demand vanishes in that specialized niche. Our risk management approaches in Chapter 3 should be of value in suggesting appropriate risk management controls.

Four interacting causes of national competitive advantage in international markets are cited in the work on competitive advantage of nations [34].

1. *Factor conditions* are needed in order to enable an industry to compete satisfactorily in a given market. These conditions include human resources, educated professionals, information technology and knowledge resources, raw materials and physical resources, physical infrastructure, capital resources, and other factors of production. Today, the advanced information and knowledge-based factors may be more important than traditional basic factors, such as raw materials. The factor proportions that are needed to be deployed efficiently and effectively in various industries, however, differ widely.

2. *Demand conditions* for a given product or service must generally exist in the home nation. Porter found that quality is more important than quantity in this regard and that it is very advantageous if home-based customers are anticipatory of international demand for a product in terms of their own present demands. It is generally difficult to sustain competitive advantage when the only demand for a product is far away geographically.

3. *Related and supporting industries,* which are internationally competitive, are generally needed. This provides for competitiveness conditions in supplier industries through continuous patterns of innovation and process improvement. It is rare that a given nation can maintain competitive advantage if it must import high quality items, or significant quantities of well educated labor, necessary to establish a high quality supplier base.

4. *Firm strategy, structure, and rivalry* are important factors. Organizational culture and leadership, and the resultant process maturity, are clearly of vital importance. Of major importance also are individual objectives and motivations and the influence that national leadership provides to enhance human resources. Rivalry among competitive organizations is needed to motivate the needed development of appropriate organizational strategy and purpose. It acts as a major catalyst for needed change for enhanced national competitive advantage. National or governmental leadership and chance play roles as influencers also. A major caution is given that attempts to preserve everything will most likely result in lowering national standards, and not raising them. On the other hand, attempts to create a single national industry leader will fail as any success significantly impedes the development of a very needed national rivalry in that industry sector.

Porter makes a major argument that productivity is the single most useful measure of national economic strength. National productivity depends less on the traditional macroeconomic management of money supply, and other macroeconomic controls, than it does on successful government programs that encourage continuous improvement on all fronts, especially human related fronts. It is argued that balancing the money supply may lead to short-term advantage and not the long-term competitive advantage that is needed. Similar arguments are made by those who advocate total quality management for high productivity and customer satisfaction.

That each of the four factors of national competitive advantage is mutually supportive and causal to each of the other three factors is very significant. It suggests that one of the four factors might well be absent, and that this will delay and reduce the amount of competitive advantage ultimately possible. But it will not prevent it. As with the cost and product differentiation facets that led to competitive advantage for a given organization, we need to associate these national competitive advantage strategies with a suitable market focus or scope, which now becomes international, and therefore establish a very broad and distributed geographic scope in order to obtain an international competitive strategy.

It would not be possible in a few brief pages to capture other than the highlights of these very seminal and important works. They are true pacesetters and set forth many prescriptions for reengineering, especially at the level of systems management and processes, that involve government and organizational policies and strategy for enhanced advantage. Much additional information is available in the three cited references and in [36] and [37]. There are, of course, many other works that discuss related approaches concerning managing and forecasting for strategic success [38], managing to cope with dual strategies for ensuring success today *and* success tomorrow [39], and other important strategy needs for competitive positioning [40].

8.2.9 Time and Reengineering

Time is of much concern in virtually all systems engineering and systems reengineering efforts. In this subsection, we discuss recent efforts to manage time-related facets for enhanced productivity and trustworthiness.

Many have commented on the relationship between time and productivity [41,42]. Schmenner [43], for example, has documented the results of several studies of productivity improvement and concluded that the only approaches that were demonstrably successful were those that focus on time as the single most important determinant of overall productivity. This "productivity" included not only delivery of products faster but also improved quality and process effectiveness.

George Stalk [44] has noted that "as a strategic weapon, time is the equivalent of money, productivity, quality, even innovation." Time-based competition is therefore a potential source of competitive advantage. In this work, flexible manufacturing, just-in-time manufacturing, and other modes of time-based competition are viewed as generally superior strategies than more traditional ones that rely on low wages, which, it is claimed, reduce responsiveness as well as cost. Time-based management also reduces costs but it accomplishes this through greater efficiency and effectiveness of organizational processes and thereby enhanced responsiveness.

In a more recent work, Stalk and Hout [45] expand on the just cited earlier work. They indicate several tasks that must be satisfactorily performed in order to bring about time-based competition as a critical parameter for strategic management.

1. The value-delivery system of the organization must become much faster and much more flexible than that of competitors.
2. The organization must identify the ways in which their customers relate to value and responsiveness issues, and then focus on those customers with the greatest sensitivity to value and responsiveness.
3. This responsiveness must be used to stay close to customers such that, in effect, customers become dependent on the organization and competitors then have to deal with "less attractive" customers.
4. The organization must identify and implement strategies that "surprise" competitors with the resulting innovative and time-based competitive advantage.

Four very beneficial results of implementing time-based competition arc identified.

1. Organizational productivity is increased.

2. Product prices may be increased.
3. Organizational risks are reduced.
4. Market share is increased.

We should not believe that time-based competition is simply equivalent to having everyone work faster and harder. It does not at all advocate a shortening of time horizons and concentration on short-term profits so often obtained by disabling the organization. It is much more concerned with working smarter, and primarily through process improvements and the resulting lifecycle time compression. In addition, competing with time as a competitive advantage recognizes and supports the basic competitive advantages of low price and high product differentiation and such supports for differentiation as *quality, consistency,* and *conformity* in satisfying customer requirements and in fulfilling customer needs; and *adaptability, innovativeness,* and *perceptiveness* in coping with many organizational environments and in being able to respond to changes in organizational environments and customer needs. These linkages suggest, again, the major role of processes in determining successful products and markets for those products. They provide further evidence of the role of competitive strategy in determining the paths to success.

A recent work by Meyer [46] is concerned with implementing a fast cycle time (FCT) strategy. It is concerned with a systemic organizational strategy and the associated tools and measurements to bring this about. Establishing leadership, multifunctional teams, people empowerment, and reengineering of core organizational processes are the primary activities associated with this effort. Organizational systems and organizational learning are the critical foundations on which FCT results are constructed. The fundamental premise of FCT is that "the competitor who consistently, reliably, and profitably provides the greatest value to the customer first wins." According to Meyer, "fast cycle time is the ongoing ability to identify, satisfy, and be paid for meeting customer needs faster than anyone else."

It is continually emphasized that FCT results are obtained by fundamental change in organizational processes to achieve reduced costs and increased product quality. Again, it is not simply working faster. Nor is it only associated with the introduction of new tools. While new tools may be introduced, this introduction follows from needs established by the process reengineering effort. On some occasions, a new tool or method may well be the driver of process change. But the major improvements in organizational responsiveness occur from process change for effectiveness. These changes are generally top–down directed from the level of systems management, rather than bottom–up directed for efficiency improvement from tools and methods for production.

Four basic principles support the FCT strategy.

1. Organizations and their strategies should be driven by the source of value-added revenue: that is, paying customers.
2. FCT organizations should strive for continuous improvements in processes to produce results and should consider results that fail to meet expectations as symptomatic of process errors.

3. FCT organizational units are interdependent systems that are managed using cycle time measures.

4. FCT organizations deploy their quick learning and rapid change abilities for competitive advantage.

FCT organizations are not structured in the traditional line and staff like steep-horizontal structure. Nor is the structure that of a matrix, although the structure does resemble a matrix structure more than the traditional functional line organization. The major elements of the FCT organization include multifunctional* teams that are networked both to each other and to centers of excellence. The organizational structure is focused on support for processes that result in high value delivery to the customer. Organizational learning and unlearning are major by-products of the FCT organization. We could now suggest a hypothetical structure for an FCT organization. As we would then see from our later discussions, there are major similarities between an FCT organization and an integrated product development (IPD) organization, a horizontal management organization, and the TQM and learning organizations we discussed in Chapters 6 and 7.

Considerable time and attention are devoted to identifying a lifecycle process for FCT reengineering. This is comprised of four phases, as illustrated in Figure 8.19:

Recognition and definition of the problem

Development of FCT strategy

Deployment of FCT strategy as a set of organizational tactics

Ongoing change management and learning as the process changes are implemented, as experience with FCT is obtained, and as the FCT reengineering process is continued for improvement in subsequent efforts

A number of steps within this lifecycle are also identified.

One of the major issues in any sort of organizational change effort is that of obtaining the needed momentum and commitment of energy for successful implementation. Meyer makes a number of suggestions to this end.

These studies are concerned with reducing the overall cycle time for a product or service. This is comprised of the cycle time for RDT&E, product acquisition or manufacturing, and planning and marketing. Some works have seen specifically concerned, at least in part, with lead time reduction for RDT&E efforts [47–49]. There have also been efforts specifically directed at reduction of acquisition or production lead time [50,51].

In a recent study, Robertson [52] is specifically concerned with reducing market penetration cycle times. First, concerns relative to product development time, in-

---

*The terms crossfunctional and multifunctional, and rarely hyperfunctional, are virtually synonymous. It is just as well that we consider them this way. With respect to a team, we might question whether either term means that it is each individual who has the capability to function across departments, or whether it is the group of individuals and the leadership that comprise the team who need to be functionally very dexterous.

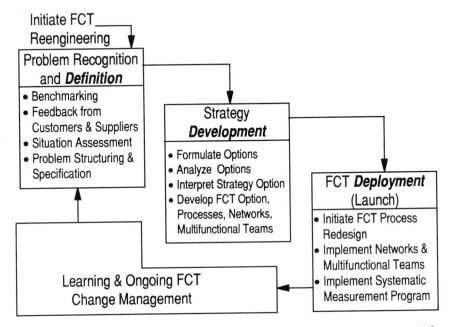

Figure 8.19 Four fundamental phases and learning for continuous improvement in fast cycle time reengineering.

cluding RDT&E time as needed, are separated out from the overall cycle time. He suggests five guidelines to enable fast market penetration time.

1. Get the organization's product or service on the market first.
2. Announce forthcoming availability of the product or service before it actually reaches the market.
3. Innovate continually, both with respect to product and marketing.
4. Saturate the marketplace with multiple products to occupy the entire range of product differentiation and positioning foci, and develop wide scope alliances to establish the equivalent of a defacto standard for the product or service in question.
5. Evaluate and monitor market penetration in accordance with several customer decision stages: awareness, attitude formation toward product, initial product purchase and test, and repeat purchase by the same customer.

Necessary caveats, which must be associated with each of these suggestions, are discussed. It must also be recognized that, to some considerable extent in many cases, there is necessarily time overlap and concurrency in efforts devoted to the RDT&E, production, and marketing lifecycles. This strongly suggests approaches that consider the interdependence of these lifecycles, or alternate awareness of the associated concurrency that may exist. Time issues are also addressed by concurrent engineering and integrated product development efforts. We will soon examine these approaches to reengineering.

8.2.10 Strategic Cost Management

The purpose of a management accounting system is the provision of timely and useful information to enable management of the affairs of an organization, including management control of the various organizational lifecycle processes. Many volumes have been written on the subject of management accounting systems. No one seriously questions whether finance and accounting systems are a very necessary part of an organization. On the other hand, there is concern that many management accounting systems are neither sufficient nor adequate to cope with contemporary technological, organizational, and societal change.

We can view the major purposes of organizational management and leadership as follows:

- *Definition* of appropriate strategies, including the formulation, analysis, and interpretation of a variety of strategy options to enable selection and communication throughout the organization of the selected strategies.
- *Development* of tactics that implement the strategies, including the formulation, analysis, and interpretation of a variety of tactical options and selection and design of appropriate tactics for implementation as management controls.
- *Deployment* of these as operational task controls, obtained through another formulation, analysis, and interpretation cycle to result in implementation of task controls to ensure efficient and effective performance of operational tasks.

There is organizational learning, hopefully at least, and iteration of the process for continued improvement. We may view this as a sequence of three lifecycle phases for the overall organization, much as we have viewed the other lifecycles we examine here, or as a three-level hierarchy of strategic planning, management control or systems management, and task control as in the seminal work of Anthony [53]. Figure 8.20 illustrates each of these views of the organizational management lifecycle. Obviously, there are many opportunities for systematic measurement, including accounting information, at all of the phases, including the learning phase, and for all processes in this lifecycle.

In a definitive work, Shank and Govindarajan [54] indicate that management accounting is not an end in itself but a means to help achieve organizational success. Furthermore, specific accounting systems must be evaluated in terms of the extent to which they support this end. They recognize that particular management accounting information constructs and information may not necessarily have, nor are they intended to have, knowledge that is of value for everyone. Nevertheless, each accounting system must serve some purposeful need in supporting humans in fulfilling some organizational role. Accounting systems need to be evaluated with respect to the ends they serve. A system appropriate for an organization attempting compet-

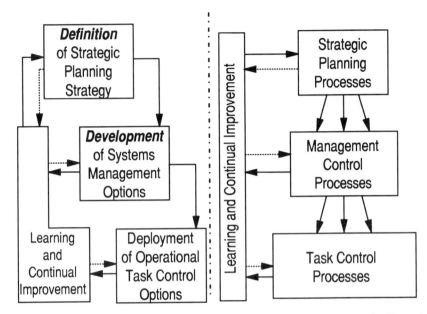

Figure 8.20 Two alternative views of organizational management, each illustrating that systematic measurement needs exist at all phases and for all processes.

itive advantage through being a low cost producer may not be at all appropriate for one desirous of obtaining highly differentiated product status. Entirely analogous statements apply to systematic measurements in general.

Shank and Govindarajan pose three questions about accounting systems, which we rephrase about systematic measurements in general.

- Does the systematic measurement program serve organizational objectives and purposes?
- In terms of the specific purposes that each measurement serves, does the relevant systematic measurement process enhance possibilities of obtaining the supported objective?
- Does the objective whose attainment is facilitated fit strategically within the overall organizational plan?

The queries suggest the relationship between cost ideas and cost information, the organizational hierarchy and the processes illustrated in Figure 8.20.

The authors approach what they term strategic cost management (SCM) from three perspectives: *value chain analysis, strategic positioning analysis,* and *cost driver analysis.* We discuss each of these related concepts here.

Porter [32–34] has identified the value chain of an organization as the linked set of value-creating activities that exist throughout the organization. The links of this value chain begin with material and subsystem acquisition from suppliers and include such other linkages as RDT&E, production, marketing, and delivery of a product to the customer and associated maintenance. The value chain concept is intended to be a broad externally based concept that also includes the value chain of the other units that interface and interact with the organization. It is not just an internal concept based only on value-added notions. It involves much use of lifecycle costing throughout the various organizational processes, and consideration of the effects of possible changes of these on other processes. The approach suggested by Shank and Govindarajan for construction and use of value chains is interpreted as follows:

1. Formulate the organization's value chain, detect costs and revenues that are associated with the various value chain activities, and identify potential competitive advantage options.
2. Analyze the value chain to diagnose the cost drivers that cause the various costs and revenues associated with value chain activities.
3. Interpret the results of the analysis in order to select an appropriate and sustainable competitive advantage option for implementation. Accomplish this through implementation and control of cost drivers that are better than those of competitors, or through restructuring of the value chain itself if no appropriate cost drivers result from the initial formulation.

We see that the value chain concept is not at all independent of either the strategic positioning or the cost driver concept.

There are three basic strategic positioning strategies: *building,* for increased market share; *holding,* to retain an organization's present market position; and *harvesting,* to maximize short-term earnings often at the expense of market share over the longer term. The most appropriate strategy in any given market depends on whether the organization obtains competitive advantage through low cost or high differentiation of the product in question. These three market strategies may be disaggregated into a number of others. In particular, we can split each of them up into broadly focused or selectively (narrowly) focused strategies. This enables us to concurrently adopt more than one strategy. For example, we can simultaneously pursue a selective harvesting in one market area while building or holding in a different market segment.

Generally, strategic planning is more important for a building strategy than it is for a harvesting strategy. On the other hand, more formal financial analysis and decisions are needed for harvesting than for building. The criteria for capital expenditures depend on information that is not strongly financial, such as that relating to market share and efficient use of RDT&E expenditures. For harvesting, there is much more interest on cost–benefit and other strictly financial information. Holding strategies are in the middle relative to these considerations. In a similar way, the compensation system of a building market strategy organization depends on mostly non-cost-related criteria and subjective judgments associated with success through a building strategy. For a harvesting organization, compensation based on financial formulas is recommended.

Generally, a high product differentiation focus is associated with greater risk than a low cost differentiation due to three factors: (1) technological innovation is needed for differentiation, (2) broader mass-customization type product lines are often needed for differentiation, and (3) higher prices associated with highly differentiated products may be difficult to sustain. Changing environmental conditions, internal and external, also influence strategy choice or mission. Finally, the market scope or focus of the organization needs to be considered. Thus we need to devote simultaneous attention to mission and competitive advantage needs, as suggested by Shank and Govindarajan.

We could also consider the interaction of strategic mission, competitive advantage, and competitive scope or focus on strategic costs and competitive advantage for each of these three market positioning strategies. It seems apparent that a building strategy is difficult to accomplish for an organization with a low cost product-focused competitive advantage. This would seem to be even more the case where the product is focused on a broad and potentially large market. In a similar way, a harvesting strategy is difficult and risky to bring about for an organization whose competitive advantage is based on product differentiation. This becomes even more difficult when the market scope is narrow. Figure 8.21 suggests the 12 cells that exist, many of which need to be considered in determining organizational controls and cost and revenue management systems for implementation of one of the

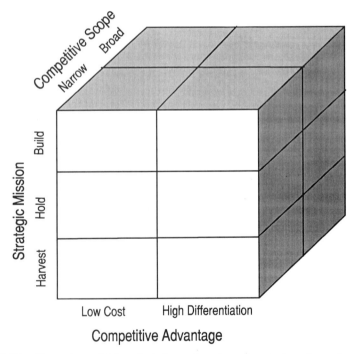

Figure 8.21   Illustration of 12 cells influencing strategic mission determination and associated organizational controls.

three possible strategic missions. Each cell needs to be analyzed in order to determine cost and other competitive strategy facets, such as risk.

The strategic competitive advantage position of the organization determines the appropriate ways to use strategic cost and management accounting information. As we recall from our discussion of Porter's competitive advantage concept, this may range from cost leadership to product differentiation. If, for example, the organization's competitive advantage for a given product is associated with high product differentiation, then the role of marketing is crucial since the product must be targeted and represented very correctly. On the other hand, if the organization is attempting competitive advantage through cost leadership, then the most important management issues are those that directly affect product cost, such as manufacturing and engineering costs and competitive product pricing. There are, of course, a number of noncost or nonfinancial performance measures that need to be considered as well as financial ones in determining an appropriate strategic mission in any given situation.

Cost drivers are the third important ingredient in strategic cost management. Among the suggested strategic cost drivers or factors are the following:

Scale of the investments needed in the lifecycle processes for RDT&E, acquisition or production, and planning and marketing

Scope of these processes in terms of vertical integration

Technological leadership and the extent to which new and emerging technologies are used throughout the organization's value chain

Experiential familiarity of the organization with use of these processes for this product

Complexity and breadth of the products and services to be offered to customers

Capacity utilization needed to produce at a given output level

Plant layout efficiency

Workforce empowerment and effectiveness

Process and product quality

Product effectiveness in terms of function and purpose

The generally accepted way to determine cost is to assume that it is some multiplicative function of the various cost-driver factors, as weighted by importance. Just as in Chapter 5 for the cost of software production, we obtain

$$COST = C_0(F_1)^{m_1}(F_2)^{m_2}(F_3)^{m_3}(F_4)^{m_4}(F_5)^{m_5}(F_6)^{m_6}\cdots$$

where C_0 represents the nominal cost of some basic product. This can be written in the product form, where there are N cost factors

$$COST = C_0 \prod_{i=1}^{N} F_j^{m_i}$$

and the cost driver analysis proceeds much as we have indicated in Chapter 4. Product line and product complexity are each major sources of the factors that determine product cost. Shank and Govindarajan suggest activity-based costing (ABC) as an adjunct to this approach for cost driver analysis. The ABC approach is very similar to our ABC and work breakdown structure (WBS) approaches in Chapter 4. In either approach, such factors as the cost of low quality and the cost of technological innovation can be included in the results of the strategic cost analysis.

8.2.11 Strategic Sourcing: Outsourcing and Insourcing

Several of our commentaries have mentioned the notion of outsourcing to obtain component products and services by the organization responsible for a product or service. Outsourcing may be mandated when the component product or subsystem needed simply cannot be produced by the organization needing it. In most cases, however, outsourcing is a matter of choice. Thus the choice should be based on the myriad of issues that are involved in strategic policy and planning determination. The basic issue is that of determining the extent to which a necessary part of a product or service could be obtained more efficiently and effectively from inside or outside the organization itself. An issue of equal, and perhaps greater, importance in some cases is whether insourcing or outsourcing supports or inhibits the organization relative to related efforts that are also of importance. The strategic sourcing question is therefore an extrapolation of the make-or-buy decision to include strategic systems management and process-related considerations that need to be examined for almost all make-or-buy decisions.

The principles supporting strategic sourcing decisions are conceptually simple and nicely stated by Venkatesan [55].

1. The organization should focus on those components and subsystems that are crucial to the product itself and where the organization has critical core capabilities [56–58] that support the efforts required and that the organization desires to sustain. This enables an organization to exercise judgment concerning subsystems that are strategic and those that are nonstrategic. It potentially eliminates difficulties that result from conflicting priorities and sourcing decisions.

2. Components and subsystems should be outsourced where there exist potential suppliers with a distinct competitive advantage at producing these. These competitive advantages could be either those of lower cost producers or higher subsystem differentiation.

3. Outsourcing should always be used in such a manner that it supports continuing employee commitment and empowerment. It is necessary to outsource this in such a manner that there is minimum opportunity for exploitation and hollowing of the organization, including its people, by the external supplier.

These principles lead to a process for strategic sourcing.

Venkatesan suggests a multistage process for strategic sourcing. Figure 8.22 presents our interpretation of this.

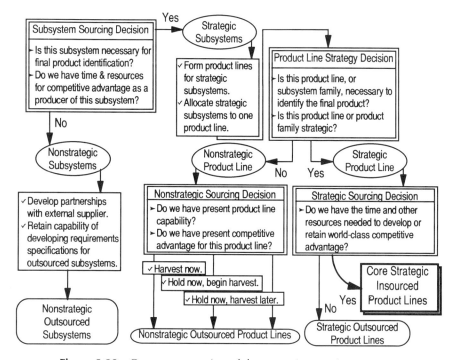

Figure 8.22 One representation of the strategic sourcing process.

1. The first phase of the strategic sourcing process is actually concerned with subsystem sourcing decisions. The organization distinguishes possible options for strategic sourcing at the subsystem level and distinguishes strategic subsystems from nonstrategic subsystems through a formulation, analysis, and interpretation process. A major architectural issue in doing this is that of determining the proper architectural level of abstraction for the various options that will be subject to analysis. This architecture can be comprised of individual components or entire large subsystems. In exceptional circumstances, an entire product or system might be outsourced and the parent organization may act as a marketing agent only. The nonstrategic subsystems are generally comprised of mature technologies for which there exists an external supplier with outstanding competitive advantage relative to their production. The strategic subsystems are generally comprised of those subsystems which the organization has significant reason for retaining or developing the capabilities needed to produce them.

2. In the second major phase of the strategic sourcing process, the strategic subsystems identified in the first phase are grouped into a number of families, each having common product line requirements. Each product line or process is able to produce the entire family assigned to it. The major decision made at this phase is whether each product line is strategically important to the organization. If the answer is no, then this product line is an appropriate candidate for either a hold or a harvest decision relative to retaining the existing capability at this product line in the firm.

3. The final phase in our interpretation of this strategic sourcing process results from the need to deploy the strategic product line decision outcomes and the nonstrategic product line outcomes reached by the decision at the previous phase. Thus this phase can be described in two parts or subphases, depending on whether we are dealing with strategic or nonstrategic product lines.

(a) We need a subphase that represents deployment for nonstrategic product lines. If we have present capabilities and competitive advantage, we deploy a holding strategy for the present and identify plans for gradual harvesting, potentially over a sustained time period. If we have present capabilities but are not competitive, we adopt a holding strategy for a very short period and then harvest. On the other hand, if our present product line capabilities are incapable of coping with present needs, we immediately outsource this entire product line.

(b) If the product line is of strategic importance to the firm, we should deploy necessary resources and time if feasible in order to either hold or build the requisite capabilities. If either the time or the resources are unavailable, we outsource the associated product line for which this is the case. If the resources and time are available, we insource and hold or build the requisite capability to retain or obtain world class competitive advantage. Thus this subphase is concerned with sourcing decisions for strategically important product lines.

These three phases are associated with four significant questions and answers. The first two are obtained relative to strategic subsystems and nonstrategic subsystems. The strategic subsystems are aggregated into a, generally smaller, number of product lines. These product lines are then partitioned into nonstrategic product lines, which are outsourced over time, and strategic product lines. This leads to two additional questions and answers. The strategic product lines are insourced wherever possible and outsourced only when there is insufficient time and other needed resources to bring about world class competitive advantage.

As a result of this, we have nonstrategic outsourced subsystems, nonstrategic outsourced product lines, and strategic outsourced product lines. These sourcing strategies and decisions will need to be reexamined over time. In particular, it will often be desired to convert an initial decision to outsource strategic product lines to an insourcing decision when and if resources and timing become supportive of such a decision. This may occur because of technological or other changes. Indeed, we see that sourcing questions are fundamentally reengineering questions as well.

In a fine work concerned primarily with information system (IS) outsourcing, Lacity and Hirschheim [59,60] identify three generic types of outsourcing.

Body shop outsourcing is a way to meet short-term demands that cannot be met by people internal to the organization even through the decision would otherwise be favorable to insourcing.

Project management outsourcing involves the use of external suppliers to furnish a subsystem or service activity, such as training. This would seem closely equivalent to product line or subsystem outsourcing.

Total outsourcing exists whenever an external supplier is responsible for all, or a very major portion, of a complete turnkey-like information system function.

Each of these outsourcing options needs to be considered.

Lacity and Hirschheim identify several theoretical underpinnings of outsourcing. There are two major issues to be considered.

Transactions costs for outsourcing are composed primarily of direct production costs and indirect coordination or support costs. Transactions, as exchanges of resources, may be described in terms of frequency and degree of specificity or customization.

Organizational systems of influence and culture are composed primarily of ingredients that may support or inhibit IS influences on the organization. We have said much about these issues in our last chapter and in Section 8.2.3 on process innovation.

They indicate six primary reasons for considering outsourcing possibilities.

1. We desire to improve operational efficiency. This improvement may be obtained by determining whether the IS service can be externally supplied in a more effective manner than it can be internally supplied.
2. We need to acquire resource capabilities, such as hardware or expertise, not available internally to the organization and perhaps to support a new startup organization or an organization in a crisis situation relative to unfilled IS needs.
3. We desire to replicate the success stories of others who have outsourced their IS functions.
4. We wish to reduce uncertainties and risks associated with unpredictable demand for products and services.
5. We wish to eliminate a potentially troublesome function or process and let others cope with it.
6. We wish to enhance credibility for an organization, unit, or individual.

These reasons were obtained from a survey of senior management in some 13 organizations and were specifically concerned with information systems outsourcing. This behavior would appear to be much more descriptive than either normative or prescriptive. It may also be reflective of the fact that information systems may be regarded as very necessary but either as nonstrategic subsystems or nonstrategic processes in many organizations.

The major conclusions from this study were as follows:

1. Commonly available sources may paint an overly optimistic picture of IS outsourcing benefits.

2. IS outsourcing may be symptomatic of inherent difficulties in demonstrating the value of IS capabilities to non-IS top managers.

3. Cost efficiency improvement may well not be a dominant reason for implementation of IS outsourcing.

4. The internal IS department may not be inherently more efficient than an external supplier.

5. An internal IS department may achieve results of comparable or greater efficiency and effectiveness than an external vendor by internal reengineering of the IS structure and function.

6. The contract with an outsourcing IS supplier is the only mechanism, as contrasted with partnership considerations, that may ensure accountability and satisfaction of outsourcing expectations. Outsourcing suppliers will only become partners when and if the profit motive is shared.

7. The belief that IS is a nonstrategic utility, commodity, or process is erroneous.

The bottom line summary message of Lacity and Hirschheim is that one really cannot successfully outsource the management of information systems. There seems to be much agreement with this, especially as concerns information support for the highest level managerial decisions [61,62]. Particularly when there is considerable outsourcing to external suppliers, there will be a major mandate for very careful integration of all aspects of the supply chain and an understanding of the relationships between the supply chain and the value chain.

8.2.12   Mass Customization

Mass customization is also concerned with quick responsiveness. It calls for flexibility in turbulent and changing environments by continuing to adapt to changing customer needs and in being able to supply these needs with high quality and trustworthy products and services. The focus is highly customized goods and services that fill these needs. Thus it is an approach for a line of adaptable, highly differentiated products.

A recent text by Pine [63] and an associated companion work [64] provide much insight into this process. The text begins with a discussion of the mass production process and its assumption of long product development lifecycles and the resulting low cost, consistent quality, low differentiation product that results from this. It indicates that this may be an acceptable approach in a homogeneous market with stable demand. In the mass production system, a producer enters the marketplace with a low cost, consistent quality, nondifferentiated product, and a homogeneous mass market with stable demand is said to result from this. As long as there is no alternative product available, these dynamic influences will continue and will result in the long product development lifecycle that is necessary to support the mass production and low product cost.

Pine indicates that this mass production system ran into trouble in the decade of the 1960s. The difficulties exacerbated in the 1970s, but with management becoming very able to detect this only in the 1980s. While the difficulties were detected, the attachment to mass production was so great and so culturally ingrained that the causes of the difficulties were not then diagnosed. Corrective attempts began in the 1990s and this has resulted.in efforts to change to a new set of guiding principles and rules. While it is indicated that this has led to "continuous improvement" schools of thought and such emphasis areas as total quality management, it is stated that these continuous improvement approaches do not generally allow for questioning the basic design tenants of the products being built and the hidden assumption that the design specifications are really indicative of what the customer wants. Instead, they tacitly assume markets that are relatively stable and predictable.

It is suggested that mass customization goes one step further by allowing for high velocity markets and environments, rapidly changing technologies, and associated changing of customer requirements and needs. Continuous improvement, through processes like TQM, are viewed as generally necessary for mass customization. The change is presumed to require augmenting, and perhaps even disbanding or replacing, cross-functional teams with teams obtained through the formation of dynamic networks. Whereas the mass production system encouraged vertical integration of teams, with each performing an isolated incremental task, continuous improvement generally replaces vertical integration needs with horizontal integration needs. In horizontal integration, individual teams have responsibility and authority over task control areas.

This trend continues with the advent of mass customization and is associated with the organizational structure becoming more horizontal. Processes or product lines become flexible modules that are coordinated and potentially linked together in a dynamic network-like structure. This is said to reverse the causal dynamics of the system such that it becomes possible to respond to turbulence in demand changes and heterogeneous markets. This leads to recognition of the need for high quality customized products and mass customized processes that are responsive to this need.

While many, if not most, economic and competitive structure paradigms would associate high price with high quality, rapidly changing and highly differentiated products; the mass customization approach is said to accommodate these differentiated product attributes at a low product cost. In mass production, a product is designed first and the processes that will eventuate in the product are developed. In mass customization, this flow is revesed; processes are generally created first and support the rapidly changing characteristics of the products that follow. This enables a low price, highly differentiated, set of products that appeal to a variety of niche markets.

In [65], the potential conflict between customization and rapid response is noted. This results because rapid product acquisition is generally dependent on much standardization of the production processes and products. Customization requires much innovation and flexibility. Anticipatory use of knowledge perspectives and forecasting of demand can potentially result in production of highly differentiated and customized products before there is an actual demand for them. While this will reduce the response time, there are obvious risks involved if the anticipated market does not materialize.

These authors note that customization and product differentiation can be infused into a product early or late in the acquisition lifecycle. If differentiation occurs early in the production process, it is more difficult for an organization to be responsive than if the differentiation occurred at a later stage in the lifecycle. If differentiation must occur early in the lifecycle and if customers demand quick delivery and especially if there is a high degree of customization required for sales, then a *build-to-forecast* (BTF) approach is appropriate but necessarily associated with risk. Otherwise, make-to-stock (MTS), make-to-order (MTO), or assemble-to-order (ATO) approaches, which are inherently less risky, are more appropriate.

A three-phase process of analyzing customer expectations, assessing the organization's capabilities, and selecting and implementing appropriate tactics is suggested. This can lead to one of six possible options to cope with the customization responsiveness squeeze.

1. Change the design of the production process through use of concurrent approaches, cellular manufacturing, and other flexible process technologies.

2. Change the product design through use of such approaches as computer-aided design and standardized subsystems that may be integrated together to produce a variety of customized products.

3. Demand management may be improved through better forecasting approaches such as to reduce the very significant inventory and other difficulties that occur when demand is forecast incorrectly.

4. Supply management can be improved: internally, through development of insource capabilities to manufacture long production time subsystems and through development of a production management approach that is tuned to customer demand; and externally, through altering arrangements with suppliers to provide for rapid delivery of outsourced subsystems.

5. Slack resources, when they occur, can be used in an optimum manner.

6. BTF strategies may be based on production orders that are forecasts of periodic demand; incoming customer orders that can be adapted to nearly finished products that can be finished completely; and retrofitting approaches, which may be used to make late lifecycle phase modifications to products in order to accommodate customer demand in a rapid manner.

These options are not at all mutually exclusive, and they may be blended with other existing practices. Fundamentally, the judgment relative to the degree of customization that will be accommodated for any given product line and product is a very strategic one. Thus we see that the seemingly oxymoronic term "mass customization" is both appropriate and descriptive of a concept well worth detailed exploration for specific applications.

8.2.13   Market-Driven Strategy

In a somewhat earlier work on market strategy, Day [66] notes that new specialty niche market opportunities appear as the era of mass marketing reaches its final days. This suggests that conventional understandings of organizations and their strategies for competitive advantage necessarily must be augmented, if not replaced, by a market-driven approach to competitive strategy. The new competitive strategies should result in a choice of the following:

Markets to be served and customer segments to be targeted

Product differentiation for competitive advantage

Communication and distribution channels to realize market potential

Scale and scope for support activities to convert competitive strategies into competitive success stories

Future growth areas and strategies for continued success

These choices are driven by three contemporary realities:

1. Information technologies enable major changes in the way organizations operate. They may, and generally will, accelerate the pace of decision making and the results of this may often blur boundaries between organizations and markets.

2. Rapid technological change and innovation reduce the time during which a product may be successfully deployed. This occurs because of customer demand for increasingly higher levels of product functionality and quality. Technological change potentially enables shortening of the development life-cycle time as well as a resulting improvement in responsiveness.

3. Former mass markets are becoming fragmented into narrow speciality, or niche, markets that may be global in scope.

Day emphasizes the major role for a shared strategic vision, which is driven by the need to be responsive to customer requirements and market needs, in realizing successful strategy.

According to Day, *strategy is a set of integrated actions implemented for the pursuit of competitive advantage.* He is very concerned with planning processes that yield adaptable and effective strategy. A successful strategy is comprised of the following:

1. *Definition* of the organization and strategic strengths that comprise the basis of competitive advantage.

2. *Development* of an associated set of organizational objectives and investment strategies that specify both resource sources and uses.

3. *Deployment* of these strategies in terms of functional programs that support the strategies.

Several measures of effectiveness, stated in the form of test questions, are suggested to determine soundness of identified strategy options.

Are the assumptions used to formulate and analyze the strategy option valid?

Is implementation of the option feasible, supportable, and consistent with other organizational strategies?

Will the strategy option create and maintain competitive advantage, through either low cost or product differentiation?

Do potential returns from implementing the option justify the risks of failure, is the strategy option associated with unacceptable internal or external risks, and have appropriate risk management strategies been identified?

These very useful questions and the associated measures of effectiveness, which are not independent, relate well to the meaningfulness of the inputs used to generate the potential benefits, the amount of competitive advantage created by implementation of the option and the associated risks, and whether the option itself is consistent with other aspects of organizational mission.

Day suggests benefits and disbenefits to both bottom–up incremental planning and top–down strategic planning and indicates that a balanced or adaptive blend of these two is generally superior to either one when taken alone and implemented on an exclusive basis. Mintzberg [67,68] expresses similar conclusions in his recent works on strategic planning. He indicates that strategic planning, as often practiced, is not strategic thinking but rather the analysis and programming of already existing strategies. He suggests that strategic thinking and the resulting strategy change require the synthesis of new approaches and not the incremental rearrangement of old ones. He rejects detachment from real problems and overformalization of approaches and suggests that strategic planners should be strategy finders and not just analysts and forecasters. This "finding" is associated with "learning by walking around" and other bottom–up approaches to understanding organizational realities and customer needs. This sort of adaptive planning enhances the ability to learn from experience and was discussed in Chapters 6 and 7.

There are four essential phases in Day's adaptive planning strategy.

1. Situation assessment involves identification of current strategies and their strengths and weaknesses in terms of the market and general environment, present and potential competitors, and organizational resources and objectives. It also involves examination of the present and potential future market and identification of potential threats and opportunities.

2. Strategic thinking involves the generation or definition of optional courses of action or strategies. It also includes analysis and choice of options for further development.

3. Negotiation and decision making are associated with the efforts involved in the development of the selected options in terms of resource allocations for specific tactical efforts.

4. Implementation represents the activities undertaken to deploy the developed tactics.

The first two of these phases appear equivalent to the generic definitional phase of a planning lifecycle. The other two phases are directly analogous to definition and deployment. Adaptive learning occurs in that the various phases are exercised both in a top–down and in a bottom–up fashion.

Following this come efforts to understand the competitive situation and the nature of competitive advantage. An organization may place different degrees of emphasis on customers and competitors. If it emphasizes neither, it is self-centered. If it places a major emphasis on customers and minor emphasis on competitors, it is customer oriented. If it places major emphasis on competitors and only minor emphasis on customers, it is competitor oriented. The more appropriate realization of an organization's competitive advantage is obtained when it places major emphasis on both customers and competitors. These are denoted as market-driven organizations.

Customer-oriented assessments and competitor-oriented assessments are each important. Included in this are customer perceptions of the competitive position of our organization versus that of competitor organizations. Value chains, including supplier value chains and customer value chains as well as organizational value chains, are also important. Market considerations, related to customers and competitors, are the driver and integrator of these value chains and assessments alike. This results in something like the 12 competitive strategy cells we illustrated in Figure 8.21 and the suggestions for development of a competitive strategy option. All of this results in the decision concerning how to compete; deciding where to compete and gaining access to the selected markets are discussed as well. The bottom line message of this work is that understanding and implementing strategy for developing an appropriate market leadership position, continually seeking new approaches and methods that result in competitive advantage, and measuring progress against achievement and using this information to guide future efforts will assure market-driven success.

8.2.14 Horizontal Management

There have been an abundance of recent studies associated with strategies to regain the productive edge, such as [69]. This excellent MIT Commission on Industrial Productivity study identified four presently existing adverse facets that detract from American productivity in a changing world economy:

1. *Technological weaknesses in development and production,* especially in terms of design for manufacturability and quality.

2. *Neglect of human resources* in terms of formal education and training, and neglect also of on-the-job reeducation and retraining.

3. *Failures of cooperation* within individual organizations, in an interorganizational sense, and with respect to labor–management relations.

4. *Government and industry at cross-purposes,* especially with respect to regulatory policies, technological infrastructure issues, and the lack of technology

transfer mechanisms to capture direct and indirect benefits of military research and development.

This discerning work suggests a number of strategies for industry, labor, government, and education that will potentially lead to a more productive America. These authors identified critical attributes among what are called *best-practice firms:*

- Concurrent improvement in quality, delivery, and cost
- Closer interaction with customers and suppliers alike
- Effective use of technology for strategic advantage
- More flexible organizations that are less hierarchical and compartmentalized in order to give employees greater responsibilities
- Continuous learning, teamwork, participation, and flexibility through enlightened human resource policies

These identified critical success factors are of particular interest here as they relate most strongly to TQM and reengineering efforts.

Other authors reach similar conclusions. In a very thought-provoking work, Thurow [70] provides suggestions for a game plan to "reengineer" the United States:

- Develop abilities to cooperate effectively with direct competitors.
- Focus on process innovation as contrasted with product innovation.
- Encourage intense development of seven key technologies.*
- Provide a major focus on redeveloping a highly skilled and educated work force.
- Emphasize both individual and team achievements.

Most of these are centered on the rediscovery of quality in process and product, and enhancement of manufacturing processes through effective systems management and through advantageous use of information technologies. These findings indicate that we need to rediscover the importance of manufacturing. They suggest that it is a counterproductive myth that there can be a successful postindustrial economy that is not based to a very large extent on the manufacturing of high quality technological products and systems [71]. While the information and/or knowledge technologies can be expected to play a truly major role in augmenting support for advanced and appropriate manufacturing, they will in no way replace manufacturing.

Various other contemporary investigations have suggested strategies for reinventing the factory [72] such as to enhance American participation in the ongoing quest for world markets. Competitiveness through increased advancement of emerging information technologies is a major thrust of many of these works. In [73], for

---

*These seven key technologies are microelectronics, biotechnology, new materials, civilian aviation, telecommunications, robots and machine tools, and computers and software.

example, it is argued strongly that information technology studies and developments extend much beyond the neoclassic engineering of data processing to incorporate intellectual property laws, public and private sector policy considerations, and economic and systems management considerations. Two of the major strategies suggested in this effort relate to redefining the technology base to include information as an essential ingredient and leading in the development and application, often through technology transfer, of new and emerging technologies. While there are a number of important suggestions in these efforts—particularly as related to the importance of quality, human resources, and processes—our emphasis in this subsection is on the need for flatter organizations and the use of these flatter organizational hierarchies or structures to enhance organizational productivity though information technology, the abolition of the steep organizational hierarchy, and the teamwork of ad hoc, cross-functional teams.

In an inspiring work, Savage [74] illustrates five recognitional stages, denoted as "days," in the life of many contemporary organizations. These findings may be described as follows:

1. The organization is arranged into a set of hierarchically related personnel and applications functional units. These carry such titles as R&D, engineering, manufacturing, sales, service, and accounting. They report in a traditional line structure and the various functional units do not interact.

2. In order to cope with the need for interaction, various application groups are set up. This creates a necessary linkage or network between one functional unit in the organization and the others that are needed for a particular application, such as product development or product marketing. Since the people in the various functional units cannot communicate well, or even at all, with one another because they speak different "languages" than those in other functional units, a "translator" or "expediter" is needed. Since there are many applications in a given organization, the network linkages become numerous, as does the need for expediters and translators.

3. The difficulties of working in parallel across functional units become apparent and ways are sought to cope with the resulting complexity. Someone suggests having customer expectations as the thematic drivers of considerations that relate to such nonfunctional efforts as process, quality, market, and service.

4. Concerns arise with respect to how the various cross-functional teams are to be managed. Organizational vision is suggested as the monitor and controller of the cross-functional teams through the resultant strategic plans, organizational mission statements and objectives, and realistic management controls. Knowledge is recognized as a valuable resource in this regard in terms of various "knows." This knowledge is responsive to the same sort of questions used in benchmarking, except that it relates to a common knowledge base and capability for describing the various elements needed for each of the applications for which a cross-functional team is responsible. Thus a knowledge base is needed in terms of the following

Know why

Know what

Know which
Know who
Know where
Know when
Know how

This represents the organizational knowledge base. It is what the various cross-functional teams bring to bear on various applications, such as product development. It suggests a role for the original departments as "centers of excellence" or repositories for critical core capabilities or "virtual resources," but not as actual working line units.

5. In the last stage of development, the potential fragmentation of the organization due to the cross-functional teams is dealt with in terms of strategies for accountability, focus, and coordination. This leads to strategies for integrating the organization through human networking in such a way as to build a continual learning capability. These networks are not just informal networks of humans communicating with one another. This capacity is augmented by networks of information processing systems that enable interrelating various knowledge patterns for enhanced capability and competitiveness.

The strategies for human networking and enterprise integration result from the reality that the traditional resources for production—land, labor, and capital—are now augmented by an information and knowledge resource.

It is primarily this that has led to a major need to replace the traditional steep hierarchical structure found in most organizations by cross-functional teams and human networking to enable people empowerment and enterprise integration for enhanced responsiveness and competitiveness. The need is *not* to computerize steep hierarchies. Figures 8.23 through 8.26 indicate the evolution from first- through fourth-generation management. In second-generation management, steep hierarchies are introduced and we show just a simplified representation of one in Figure 8.24. Matrix management, or third-generation management, accomplishes the change in organizational structure to enable horizontal communications through adding additional management complexity. In a sense, this is accomplished in fourth-generation management without the additional management complexity through networking the organization. This involves major use of information technology and the need for integrating information technology products and services into organizational environments.

There has been much contemporary discussion of this augmentation of the traditional resource base with information and knowledge base. The *Coming Post-Industrial Society* [75] was perhaps the first to indicate this shift some two decades ago. A more recent presentation is by Zuboff [76]. She uses the term *informate* to describe the effort of humans in simultaneously working at and on multiple levels of abstraction, each suited to a particular purpose. Such efforts will be prototypical and characteristic of the efforts of many in the emerging knowledge-based networked society. There are a number of useful contemporary works that discuss such topics

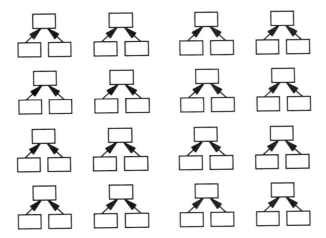

Figure 8.23 Simplified illustration of first-generation management: individual proprietorships made possible by land and labor.

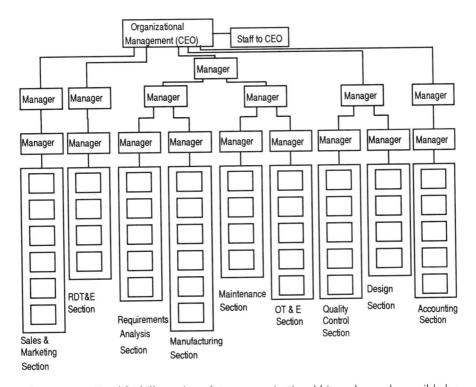

Figure 8.24 Simplified illustration of steep organizational hierarchy made possible by land, labor, and capital.

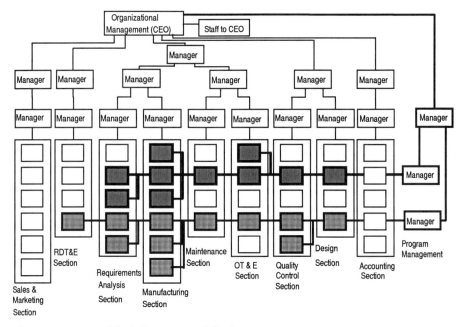

Figure 8.25 Simplified illustration of third-generation management: matrix management introduces horizontal management of programs.

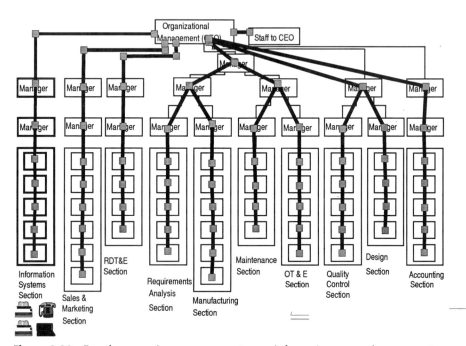

Figure 8.26 Fourth-generation management: one information network structure imposed on steep hierarchy.

as the emergence of top management computer use [77], business design through information technology [78], and managing information technologies in the 1990s [79]. More recent works are concerned with information technology and organizational transformation [80], information technology as an integrating force for such organizational efforts as marketing [81], strategic planning for information technology through information movement and management [82], and how to increase organizational competitiveness and efficiency through use of information as a strategic tool [83]. Peters has denoted the effort to integrate information technology and organizational consideration, and organizational needs for competitive positioning in a rapidly changing environment as *liberation management* [84].

Savage [74] describes five generations of management organizations. The first of these is based on individual proprietorships and resulted from the use of two resources: land and labor. While organizations might take on a hierarchical appearance, they were not steep hierarchies. They did not need to be since the capital available to an individual proprietor would not allow this. In the latter portions of the industrial revolution, large amounts of capital became available. Without major knowledge resources, steep hierarchies naturally evolved as the large organizational model of choice. This represents the second generation of organizational structure. With recognition of the difficulties brought about by steep hierarchies, basically that of coordination across the various functions in the hierarchy, matrixed organizational structures resulted as third-generation management organization structure. These matrixed structures brought about problems in that the notion of one person having more than one boss creates many difficulties. This has often led to the demise of matrix management structures.

Networking is suggested as a fourth-generation management remedy for the dilemmas brought about by steep hierarchies and vertical management. In fourth-generation management, horizontal and vertical communication linkages are established for what was initially the second-generation model of management structural organization. This is not really enterprise integration because the organization is not truly integrated, except in a narrow technological sense by the wires and software that one person uses in interfacing with another. It is really just computerizing a steep hierarchy, with perhaps 10 to 20 layers of management. Savage identifies six issues that generally emerge from fourth-generation management:

1. Ownership of information issues, as information becomes "turf" in a steep functional hierarchy.
2. Managed and massaged information system issues, as various functional units present selective information that best supports their unit.
3. Hidden assumptions imbedded in various software representations of levels of abstractions and associated information presentations.
4. Inconsistent terms and definitions across different applications, which are due to lack of organizational standardization of information architectures and dictionaries.
5. Accountability and social value of information.
6. Organizational information politics.

Some of these are not inherent issues in information technology and networking but are aided and abetted by retention of the steep hierarchy form of management. It would appear that these are very related to and influenced by the organizational cultures we discussed in Chapter 7 and the information cultures examined earlier in the process innovation approach of Section 8.2.3. Figures 8.23 through 8.26 are representations of the first four generations of management structure evolution. Second-, third-, and fourth-generation management involve steep hierarchies. Third-generation management attempts to improve on horizontal communication needs through a matrix management structure, but this superimposes additional management layers and brings about the difficulty of one worker reporting to more than one supervisor. There are communication difficulties as well. Fourth-generation management attempts the needed horizontal communication through technology but does not fully ameliorate the other difficulties we have just cited.

Savage presents a number of illustrations in an attempt to show that the computerization of steep hierarchies, or fourth-generation management, really will not work. He presents five needs, in the terms of a set of interrelated conceptual principles, that form the nexus of early fifth-generation management that will enable the desired transformation.

- *Peer-to-peer networking* is a major need. This involves three major ingredients: technologies, information, and people. Peer-to-peer networking enables communication from any individual in the organization to any other individual without the necessity of having to go through the conventional steep hierarchical structure. It allows people to work together in a cross-functional manner. Far from eliminating hierarchies, this results in a redefinition of the role and function of the hierarchy and a resulting hierarchy that is much flatter than before networking. While there are major hardware and software difficulties in bringing this about, the human and organizational issues are larger and more complex.
- *Work as dialogue* is another important need. This involves listening, visioning, remembering, and using knowledge relative to both process and product.
- The *human time and timing* need is concerned with developing an understanding of past, present, and future patterns such that it becomes possible to see and anticipate future patterns on the basis of experiences and knowledge.
- An *integrative process* across people, technologies, and the organization allows for continuous change and teamwork in the organization, as contrasted with the pattern of unfreezing, change, and refreezing [85], typically in a reactive fashion, that does not support continued improvement over time except at the discrete time instances where refreezing and change occur.
- *Virtual task-focusing teams* is the final major need and results only from satisfaction of the first four needs.

On the basis of these principles, Savage suggests ten pragmatic organizational considerations for enabling fifth-generation management.

1. Develop a technical networking infrastructure that is flexible and adaptable to organizational needs and continual change.
2. Develop a data integration strategy.
3. Develop functional centers of excellence.
4. Develop and expand the organizational knowledge base.
5. Develop organizational learning, unlearning, and relearning capabilities that are continuously updated and rejuvenated.
6. Develop visioning capacities so that the context for judgments and decisions is visible to all through knowledge of strategic plans and organizational objectives, mission statements, and values.
7. Develop behavior norms, a sense of values, a reward structure, and measurements that support task-focusing teams.
8. Develop the organizational ability to identify, support, and manage multiple functional-task teams.
9. Develop the organizational capacity and capability to support the teamwork of teams.
10. Develop virtual task-focusing teams that are formed of suppliers, customers, and appropriate people from within the organization.

The first two are primarily technology-based needs, although there is much need for human interaction with the technologies to be implemented. The last needs have very much to do with people. Those in the middle represent organizational needs. There is no sharp cleavage between technology, organization, and people needs; these were identified in Figure 8.1 as major ingredients for reengineering.

Notably lacking in this work is a very clear explanation of the structure of a fifth-generation organization. It is indicated that the horizontally functional units in the typical organization are wrapped around into a circle, and that there are linkages to customers and suppliers and organizational cognitive connections to knowledge and vision. But, aside from this, no explicit structure is shown. Perhaps it is simply too early in the development of fifth-generation management strategies, purposes, and functions to be concerned with specific organizational architectures. Perhaps it is simply best to let an individual organization adapt to a structure that fits in best with its evolution to the fifth generation.

Denton [86] is concerned with horizontal management and associated refocusing of leadership, culture, and cognizance within the organization. Horizontal management involves much participatory management and people empowerment, as well as the development of a nearly flat pyramid-like structure for an organization that is well focused on cross-functional activities and results.

He suggests a *next organization as customer* (NOAC) strategy that has been used in a number of successful organizations. In this way, every person concerned with an individual process or product line operation within an organization is encouraged to consider those who supply the inputs to that particular process, or part of a process, as if they were suppliers or providers, and those who receive the outputs as if they were customers or users. Thus the identity of suppliers and providers changes as one moves from one process or subprocess to another. It is maintained that considering the next unit to receive the output from any given process phase as if they were customers allows identification of needed communications paths within the organization.

Major objectives in the NOAC effort include identifying needed communication flows within the organization and process change to enable this and associated improvements. The effort is particularly focused on requirements and on being sure that there is conformity between the external or final customer requirements and the plethora of "internal customers" who are identified as the process is traced from the external customer through the front end of the lifecycle phases. Process improvement is obtained by selecting the process phase with the greatest potential for improvement and improving it first. In some cases this will occur through elimination of unnecessary or redundant activities. Measures of effectiveness are determined and improvements implemented in order to enable performance of necessary activities right the first time and such that all activities are in conformance with a meaningful process to ensure final customer satisfaction and internal customer satisfaction as well. Metropolitan Life and Motorola have implemented versions of NOAC and these implementations are discussed in the referenced text.

Denton defines a horizontal management maturity model that is comprised of five steps that indicate various horizontal-maturity gradations with the ultimate being described as a level-1 organization or completely flat hierarchy. Moving up these steps increases individual decision-making responsibility and empowerment from relatively narrow to relatively broad areas. The time span of the decisions at increasing steps is also increased. Figure 8.27 illustrates climbing the steps of the horizontal management ladder until level-1 management is reached. These steps are not necessarily easy to climb. The first step allows worker empowerment over very operational issues such as monitoring quality control charts and determining work breaks. At the second step, schedules are arranged, weekly record keeping takes place, and short-term forecasting is done at the lowest possible level. At step 3, selection of vendors and technologies is accomplished and intermediate range forecasting is done at the lowest possible level. At steps 4 and 5, the hierarchy flattens further as management control decisions, long-range forecasting, and strategic issues are all accomplished at the lowest level.

Denton identifies a number of organizational culture and leadership issues that potentially need to be addressed in order to bring about *employee involvement* (EI), which is indicated as the cornerstone of moving to a true horizontal management organization. The efforts of the Ford Motor Company to bring about EI are described in some detail. It is indicated that horizontal management requires streamlining— through elimination, simplification, and combination ESC—of many workplace efforts and that this can only be accomplished satisfactorily through employee involvement. A number of vertical motivators and horizontal motivators are suggested. Among the horizontal motivators are various TQM-related measurement approaches, the NOAC philosophy, employee stock ownership plans (ESOP), decentralization of almost everything, and participative management. The needed transfor-

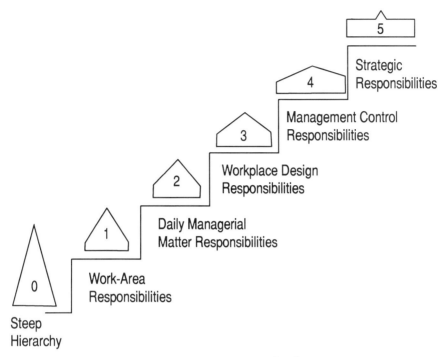

Figure 8.27 Steps in the progression to level 1 management.

mations to bring this about are a reduction in the knowledge gap and use of knowledge incentives across the organization, creation of a sense of full partnership and lines of communication across the organization, fluid leadership based on competency, and much teamwork across an equitably treated workforce.

Notions of horizontal management as an approach to reengineering, or perhaps more appropriately as the result of reengineering, have been suggested by many. We have attempted here to provide a salient overview of two of the major works on horizontal management. Essentially all of these suggest an approach toward creation of a horizontal organization that involves the sort of definition, development, and deployment phased efforts illustrated in Figure 8.28. As we have discussed here, the major precepts in implementing this and other approaches for TQM and strategic reengineering can be summarized as follows:

- Make customer satisfaction the major driver of the organization and the major driver of organizational performance.
- Maximize contact and interaction with customers and suppliers.
- Educate, train, and inform all organizational personnel with respect to knowledge about the organization's mission as well as with respect to general problem formulation, analysis, and interpretation abilities.

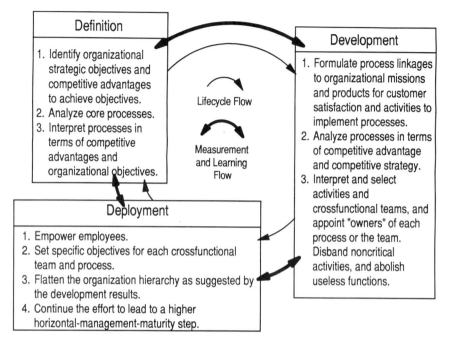

Figure 8.28   Lifecycle phases in implementation of horizontal management.

- Organize cross-functional, and generally multidisciplinary, teams that are self-managing and accountable for their performance responsibilities.
- Use cross-functional teams to manage virtually everything.
- Reward team performance.
- Define the organization's missions and critical objectives.
- Identify the strategic processes and those that are nonessential or redundant as candidates for abolition.
- Organize around processes and not functions or departments.
- Assign a process owner to each process.
- Flatten the hierarchy to reduce unnecessary layers of management and administration and to increase worker empowerment.
- Develop an interactive and proactive measurement system to assist in guiding the development and deployment of the strategy as a results-oriented set of activities.

It is important to note that maximization of short-term, or long-term for that matter, profits is not one of the fundamental objectives or activities. This is also true for all other approaches discussed in this chapter and in Chapter 7. Profit is really an objectives measures. If this is not acknowledged, ultimately the organization suffers, through the short-range perspective that typically results.

Denton identifies Metropolitan Life, Motorola, Aluminum Company of America (ALCOA), Glaxo, and Ford Motor Company as organizations moving in the direction of horizontal management. According to a recent study in *Business Week* [87], AT&T, the Eastman Chemical unit of Eastman Kodak, General Electric, Lexmark International (a former IBM Division), and Xerox are also among the American companies also moving toward a horizontal management structure.

There are many challenges associated with implementation of a horizontal management outlook. Among these are the culture and leadership issues we addressed in our last chapter. These relate to many of the concerns associated with bringing about total quality management [88], such as the implementation of work teams [89,90], which will generally be self-managing, and the implementation of cross-functional purposes to meet organizational performance challenges for competitive advantage through people [91].

8.2.15 Concurrent Engineering

Often, it is desired to produce and field a system in a relatively rapid manner. The lifecycle processes needed to bring this about could indeed be potentially accelerated in time if it were possible to accomplish phases of the relevant lifecycles in a more or less concurrent or simultaneous manner. Concurrent engineering is a systems engineering approach to the integrated coincident design and development of products, systems, and processes [92]. Concurrent engineering is intended to cause systems acquisition, broadly considered to include all phases of the lifecycle, to be explicitly planned in order to better integrate user requirements to result in high quality cost-effective systems and thereby to reduce system development time through this better integration of lifecycle activities.

The basic tasks in concurrent engineering are much the same as the basic tasks in systems engineering. The first step is that of determining what it is that the customer wants. After the customer requirements are determined, they are translated into a set of technical specifications. The next phase involves program planning for development of a product that will satisfy the customer. Often, especially in concurrent engineering, this will involve examining the current process, especially at the systems management or management controls level. This process is usually refined to best deliver a superior quality product as desired by the customer, within cost and schedule constraints.

In concurrent engineering, the very early and very effective configuration of the systems lifecycle process takes on special significance. This is so because the simultaneous development efforts need to be very carefully coordinated and managed or the opportunities abound for significant cost increases, significant product time increases, and significant deterioration in product quality. The use of coordinated product design teams, use of improved design approaches, and careful and critical use of standards are among the aids that can be brought to bear on concurrent engineering needs. These are particularly critical in concurrent engineering because of the group nature and simultaneous nature of the system development effort.

There is much need for a controlled environment for concurrent engineering and for system integration needs as well. This requires several integration and management undertakings.

1. *Information Integration and Management.* It must be possible to access information of all types easily. It must be possible to share design information across the levels of concurrent design in an effective and controlled manner. It must be possible to track design information, dependencies, and alterations in an effective manner. It must be possible to effectively monitor and manage the entire configuration associated with the concurrent lifecycle process.

2. *Data and Tool Integration and Management.* It must be possible to integrate and manage tools and data such that there is interoperability of hardware and software across the several layers of concurrency.

3. *Environment and Framework Integration, or Total Systems Engineering.* It must be possible to ensure that the process is directed at evolution of a high quality product, and that this product is directed at resolution of the needs of the customer or user in a trustworthy manner that is warmly endorsed by the customer. This requires integration of the environment and framework or process of systems engineering.

Concurrent engineering clearly requires much upfront planning such that simultaneous development of subsystems may occur in a trustworthy manner. This requires a potentially larger number of subsystems to be identified such that it is possible to design and develop them in parallel. Compression of the phases of the lifecycle and at least partial parallel accomplishment of some of them are somewhat more problematic. The macroenhancement approaches to system development, especially software system development [1], would appear particularly useful in this regard. These include prototyping as a means of system development, use of reusable (sub)systems, and expert system and automated program generation approaches. Each of these allows, at least in principle, compression of the acquisition lifecycle in a manner that is compatible with acquisition of a trustworthy system.

Through use of approaches such as these, it is hoped to obtain systems that are of (1) high quality, in terms of system performance, suitability, and reliability in a large variety of operational environments; (2) short deployment time, for new product and service designs, and for delivery and maintenance of existing product designs; and (3) low lifecycle costs, for system design, development, maintenance, and retrofit or phaseout.

In a very insightful work, Winner et al. [93] identify three critical activities and a number of technical capabilities that support these.

1. Obtain early, complete, and continuing understanding of customer requirements and priorities. This requires capabilities for obtaining information concerning comparable products, processes, and support. It requires identification of complete and unambiguous information on this new system and product, including support needs. Finally, it requires synthesis or translation

of user requirements into design specifications for the system product and the validation of design specifications.

2. Translate the system requirements and specifications into optimal products and manufacturing and support processes that can be performed concurrently and in an integrated fashion. There are many required capabilities. These include managing information and data concerning the system product and development process; and dissemination of product, process, and support data to the concurrent teams.

3. Continuously review and improve the system product, product line, and support characteristics. This includes intelligent oversight to enable impact assessment of changes and proactive, concurrent availability of current design.

These activities provide a very useful set of critical success factors for the concurrent engineering process. Several recommendations are made that will enhance success probabilities for concurrent engineering efforts.

* There is much needed leadership for change, and this must come from the very top of the organization through executive level commitment.
* Pilot projects may be very advantageous in acceleration of the deployment of appropriate concurrent engineering methodology in a given organization.
* Concurrent engineering should be considered in addition to other approaches for reengineering.
* Education and training for concurrent engineering will be needed across the organization.
* It will generally be necessary to identify and remove a number of barriers to successful implementation of concurrent engineering efforts.

It appears reasonably clear that there is no single, unique best way to approach concurrent engineering. It would appear to be more of a philosophy of and approach to strategic management rather than anything else. Of course, this strategic management needs to be translated into management controls or systems management, and thence to task and operational level effort that results in a system. How a particular organization approaches concurrent engineering will be very much a function of their organizational traditions, leadership, and culture, as we have seen in Chapters 6 and 7. Again, we see that the subjects in Chapters 6, 7, and 8 are very interrelated.

Formally, there is little that is very new in the subject of concurrent engineering. We simply speed things up by doing them concurrently, at least on the surface. But we should be very careful not to dismiss the much strengthened needs for strategic planning and systems management, the major need for attention to processes that are well deployed, and the resulting integration necessary to ensure success in concurrent systems engineering.

Concurrent engineering approaches are also discussed in [94] and [95]. In a recent and first-class work by Carter and Baker [96], it is indicated that success in concurrent engineering depends very much on maintaining a proper balance between four important dimensions of a concurrent engineering environment:

- Organizational culture and leadership and the necessary roles for product development teams.
- Communications infrastructure for empowered multidisciplinary teams.
- Careful identification of all functional and nonfunctional customer requirements, including those product and process facets that impact on customer satisfaction.
- Process and product development.

They identify approaches at the levels of task, project, program, and enterprise to enable realization of the proper environment for concurrent engineering across each of these four dimensions. Each of the four dimensions is associated with a number of critical factors and these may be approached at any or all of the levels suggested. It is suggested that the general equivalent of the matrix in Figure 8.29 be completed both for the present situation and the desired situation. This will enable identification of the needed development areas to ensure definition, development, and deployment of an appropriate concurrent engineering process environment. We show some very hypothetical development needs in this figure. The cited reference pro-

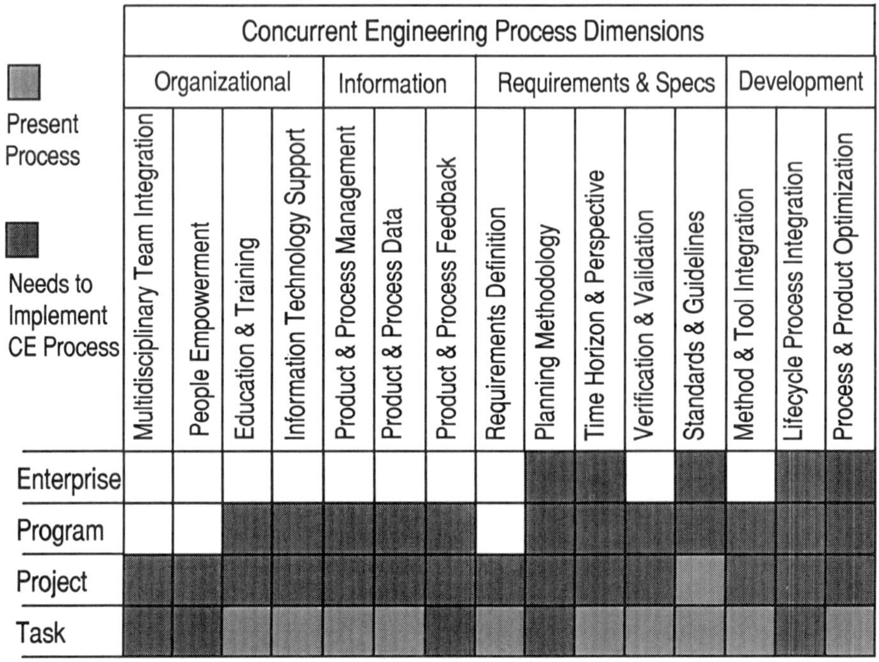

	Concurrent Engineering Process Dimensions														
	Organizational				Information			Requirements & Specs					Development		
	Multidisciplinary Team Integration	People Empowerment	Education & Training	Information Technology Support	Product & Process Management	Product & Process Data	Product & Process Feedback	Requirements Definition	Planning Methodology	Time Horizon & Perspective	Verification & Validation	Standards & Guidelines	Method & Tool Integration	Lifecycle Process Integration	Process & Product Optimization
Enterprise										■	■	■	■		
Program			■	■	■	■	■	■		■	■	■	■	■	■
Project	■	■	■	■	■	■	■	■	■	■	■	■	■	■	■
Task	■	■			■	■	■		■	■	■	■		■	■

Figure 8.29 Hypothetical needs to implement a concurrent engineering process.

vides a wealth of pragmatic details concerning determination of concurrent engineering (CE) process needs.

It is noted that there are often five major roadblocks that exist to impede development of a concurrent engineering process environment.

1. The currently available tools are not adequate for the new CE environment.
2. There is an excess of noninteroperable computers, networks, interfaces, operating systems, and software in the organization.
3. There is a need for appropriate data and information management across the organization.
4. Needed information is not communicated across horizontal levels in the organization.
5. Correct decisions, when they are made, are not made in a timely manner.

Approaches are suggested to remove each roadblock to enable development of a concurrent engineering process. Presumably, this needs to be implemented in a continuous fashion over time, as appropriate for a given organization, rather than attempting a revolutionary or radical change in organizational behavior. A number of worthwhile suggestions to enable this implementation are provided. Three recent references [97–99] provide a number of details concerning the method, tool, and environment integration needed to bring about concurrent engineering.

8.2.16 Integrated Product Development

In many ways, integrated product development (IPD) is an extension of concurrent engineering. Fiksel [100], in a work that focuses on the importance of requirements management, states that concurrent engineering is more accurately known as integrated product development. It is also closely related to the other reengineering approaches we describe here. In particular, both relate very closely to enterprise integration, which we discuss next.

The following definition of IPD seems appropriate.

Integrated product development is a systems management philosophy and approach that uses functional and cross-functional work teams to produce an efficient and effective process for the ultimate deployment of a product that satisfies customer needs through concurrent application and integration of all necessary lifecycle processes.

We see in this many of the same terms that we have already used in this book. IPD involves systems management, leadership, systems engineering processes, the products of the process, concurrent engineering, and integration of all necessary functions and processes throughout the organization, to result in a cost-effective product that provides total quality and customer need satisfaction, generally in a rapid just-in-time fashion.

Thus IPD is an organization's product development strategy. It is focused on results. It also addresses the organizational need for continual enhancement of efficiency and effectiveness in all of its processes that lead to a product or service. There are many focal points for IPD. Twelve are particularly important.

1. A *customer satisfaction focus* is needed as a part of competitive strategy and is the result of a successful competitive strategy.

2. A *results focus* and a *product focus* are needed in order to bring about total customer satisfaction.

3. A *process focus* is needed because high quality competitive products that satisfy customers and result in organizational success come from efficient and effective processes. This necessarily requires process understanding.

4. A *strategic planning and marketing focus* is needed to ensure that product and process lifecycles are fully integrated throughout all organizational functions, external suppliers, and customers.

5. A *concurrent engineering focus* is needed to ensure that all functions and structures associated with fulfilling customer requirements are applied throughout the lifecycle of the product to ensure correct people, correct place, correct product, and correct time deployment.

6. An *integration engineering focus* is needed to ensure that relevant processes and the resulting processes fit together in a seamless manner.

7. A *teamwork and communications focus* is needed to ensure that all functional or multifunctional teams work synergistically and for the good of the customer and the organization.

8. A *people empowerment focus* is needed such that all decisions are made by qualified people at the lowest possible level that is consistent with authority and responsibility. Empowerment is a responsibility and not just an entitlement and entails commitment and appropriate resource allocation to support this commitment.

9. A *systems management reengineering focus* is needed, both at the levels of radical and revolutionary change, as well as for evolutionary change, such as to also result in radical, revolutionary, or evolutionary changes in processes and product.

10. An *organizational culture and leadership focus* is needed in order to successfully accommodate changed perspectives relative to customers, total quality, results and products, processes, employees, and organizational structures.

11. A *methods, tools, and techniques focus* is needed throughout all aspects of the IPD process even though they alone will not bring about success.

12. A *systematic measurements focus,* primarily on proactive measurements but also on interactive and reactive measurements, is needed as we need to know where to go and where we are now, in order to make progress toward getting there.

All of this should bring about high quality, continual and evolutionary, and perhaps even radical and revolutionary, improvement for customer satisfaction. Each of these could be expanded into a series of questions, or a checklist, and used to evaluate the potential effectiveness of a proposed IPD process and team. While our discussion of IPD may make it seem to be an approach particularly and perhaps even uniquely suitable for system acquisition, production, or procurement, it is equally applicable to the products of the RDT&E and marketing lifecycle.

We see that IPD is a people, organization, and technology focused effort as linked together through a number of lifecycle processes by systems management. These are major ingredients for all our efforts here, as we suggested in Figure 8.1. The major result of IPD is the ability to make optimum decisions within available resources and to execute them efficiently and effectively in order to achieve three causally linked objectives:

To integrate people, organizations, and technology into a set of multifunctional and networked product development teams.

To increase the quality and timeliness of decisions through centrally controlled, decentralized, and networked operations.

To completely satisfy customers through quality products and services that fulfill their expectations and meet their needs.

The bottom line is clearly customer satisfaction through quality, short product delivery time, reduced cost, and improved performance and functionality. Equally supported by IPD are organizational objectives for enhanced profit, well-being of management, and a decisive and clear focus on risk and risk amelioration.

Figure 8.30 illustrates a suggested sequence of steps and phases to establish an IPD process. As with other efforts, this embodies the definition, development, and deployment triage we have used so often in this book. As the implementation of the detailed steps in these phases is relatively standard, we will not describe them further here.

Appropriate references to IPD include [101] and [102]. At this point, IPD is a relatively new concept used primarily within the U.S. Department of Defense and there are few widely available references on the subject. It is closely related to corporate information management and enterprise information integration, and we now look at these approaches for systems reengineering.

8.2.17 Enterprise Information Integration and Corporate Information Management

Corporate information management (CIM) and enterprise integration through information technology, which we denote as enterprise information integration (EII) and development approaches, focus on the role of information technology in supporting development. The Center for Information Management, Defense Information Systems Agency (DISA), has been chartered to support the Director of Defense Infor-

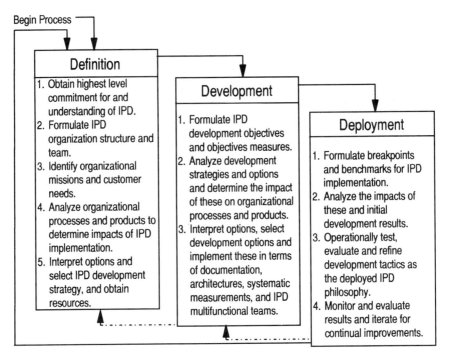

Begin Process

Definition
1. Obtain highest level commitment for and understanding of IPD.
2. Formulate IPD organization structure and team.
3. Identify organizational missions and customer needs.
4. Analyze organizational processes and products to determine impacts of IPD implementation.
5. Interpret options and select IPD development strategy, and obtain resources.

Development
1. Formulate IPD development objectives and objectives measures.
2. Analyze development strategies and options and determine the impact of these on organizational processes and products.
3. Interpret options, select development options and implement these in terms of documentation, architectures, systematic measurements, and IPD multifunctional teams.

Deployment
1. Formulate breakpoints and benchmarks for IPD implementation.
2. Analyze the impacts of these and initial development results.
3. Operationally test, evaluate and refine development tactics as the deployed IPD philosophy.
4. Monitor and evaluate results and iterate for continual improvements.

Figure 8.30   A simplified process to implement IPD.

mation (DDI) by providing information management technical services to the DoD community. These services are an integral part of the CIM program. The CIM program represents an effort to streamline organizational operations and processes to support definition, development, and deployment of high quality, cost effective, standard information systems.

Five support efforts are considered essential for CIM.

1. CIM provides assistance to functional managers in identifying better ways of doing business, in part by providing standard methods and tools for developing improved business methods and practices that are tied to quantifiable measures of performance.
2. CIM promotes efficiencies and standardization in information technology and software engineering through appropriate tools and methods.
3. CIM assists in integrating common and standardized information systems within each functional area, and across functional areas, of an organization.
4. CIM promotes the use of open systems standards, as discussed briefly in Chapter 6, to allow use of commercial off-the-shelf (COTS) products and vendor neutral commercial products and to facilitate open competition for services. This should facilitate porting of application among platforms and enable the emergence of applications operating in common environments.

5. CIM efforts should assist in planning for and managing development of an efficient and effective information technology infrastructure. Such reengineering technologies as benchmarking are suggested for these efforts.

The CIM effort is intended to be customer oriented and to provide support for development and implementation of improved business practices and information management capabilities. The ultimate aspiration is enhanced mission capability with reduced costs.

The scope of the CIM effort is large and includes the following:

- Standard methods and tools for improved business practices.
- Standard methods and tools for information engineering, software engineering, and infrastructure engineering.
- Standardizing information engineering, data administration, reuse, and software engineering practices.
- Integrating common information systems within and across functional areas.
- Identifying and promoting open systems standards.
- Providing wide scope and common system acquisition frameworks.
- Planning and engineering of a full service utility that will provide technical support to customers on a fee-for-service basis.

Thus it seems that an inferred definition of CIM might be the following:

Corporate information management is an activity that connects humans across the organization in order to facilitate access by appropriate people, in a timely and cost-effective manner, to appropriate information. This requires information access and infrastructure to ensure pertinent information integration and decision support for enterprise management.

The CIM initiative appears based on the premise that there are two fundamental processes in modern organizations, one each for converting raw material into products and converting data into information.

The major objective of the CIM initiative is to provide support for information technologies upholding the production function. While this is appropriate, the major relations between organizational leadership and culture, processes innovation needs, and information support concerns also need to be considered and in a major way. As stated, the major focus in the CIM effort appears directed at the product and single-process level and improvements in these through information technology based supports. While this is fully appropriate, even greater benefits may result from considerations directed at the level of systems management and with respect to organizational leadership and cultural issues as well.

In more recent efforts [103], the CIM initiative has been broadened to include more of a focus on strategic and organizational issues. The resulting effort has been named *enterprise integration* (EI) and is intended to align the major elements of the

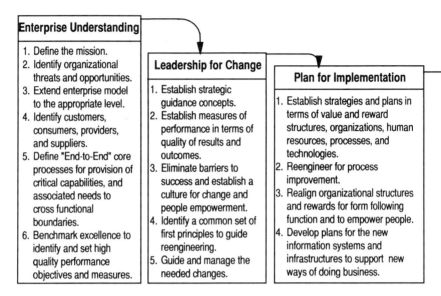

Figure 8.31 The lifecycle phases for enterprise integration.

CIM model and prepare the way for implementing improved information technology capabilities on a common infrastructure of platforms, software, communications, and applications. An enterprise roadmap is suggested. This is comprised of a five-phase lifecycle for bringing about enterprise information integration. Figure 8.31 represents the key aspects of this lifecycle. There is intended to be much feedback and iteration across the various steps shown for each of the five major phases and an *integrated computer-aided manufacturing definition* (IDEF) software-based modeling approach is used in the referenced document to display a plethora of possible interconnections among these elements to yield an activity model for this lifecycle.

The activities and critical core processes of the DoD have been described in an enterprise model. This model is comprised of four major activities, 15 supportive core processes, and 54 procedures that result in successful products from the processes. The major activities and core processes are as follows

Establish policies and plans
  Establish policies
  Determine requirements
  Develop plans
  Allocate resources
Acquire assets
  Manage acquisition process
  Conduct research, development, test and evaluation
  Produce assets

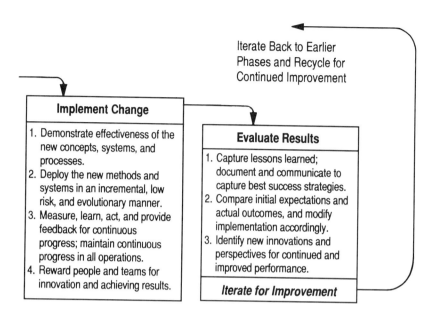

Iterate Back to Earlier
Phases and Recycle for
Continued Improvement

Implement Change

1. Demonstrate effectiveness of the new concepts, systems, and processes.
2. Deploy the new methods and systems in an incremental, low risk, and evolutionary manner.
3. Measure, learn, act, and provide feedback for continuous progress; maintain continuous progress in all operations.
4. Reward people and teams for innovation and achieving results.

Evaluate Results

1. Capture lessons learned; document and communicate to capture best success strategies.
2. Compare initial expectations and actual outcomes, and modify implementation accordingly.
3. Identify new innovations and perspectives for continued and improved performance.

Iterate for Improvement

Provide capabilities

    Manage assets through appropriate allocations

    Maintenance and support of assets

    Provide administrative services

    Embody, train, and develop unit capabilities and assess readiness

Employ forces

    Constitute operational forces

    Provide operational intelligence

    Conduct operations

    Sustain operations

Understanding the enterprise is very much enhanced by understanding this enterprise model and expanding it as needed to accommodate the other needs that are associated with this phase and identified in Figure 8.30.

There are a number of "end-to-end" processes that will need to be managed across functional and organizational boundaries at step 5 in the first phase of effort. Six core processes were identified in the referenced documents. The purposes of these processes are as follows:

• Conduct strategic and operational planning and deploy the plans as operations.
• Raise forces for an approved program of personnel, equipment, supplies, and facilities.
• Maintain force readiness before force deployment.

- Provide deployed forces and associated training, transportation, and force integration.
- Sustain operations in the areas of deployment.
- Return and restore forces to the initial state after the end of the deployment effort.

Clearly, the lifecycle process suggested for enterprise integration is very thorough, at least in a conceptual fashion. It embodies many of the other approaches to "reengineering" that we have discussed in this chapter, as well as the quality management and leadership and culture efforts discussed in Chapters 6 and 7. Volume II of [103] concludes with a very fitting summation: "The journey to the future never ends."

8.2.18   Product Reengineering

Reengineering at the level of product has received much attention in recent times, especially in information technology and software engineering areas. This is not a subject that is truly independent of reengineering at the levels of either systems management or of a single lifecycle process. In this final subsection concerning contemporary reengineering approaches, we examine some facets of product reengineering.

As we noted earlier, much of product reengineering is very closely associated with reverse engineering to recover either design specifications or user requirements. This is followed by refinement of these requirements and/or specifications and the forward engineering to result in an improved product. The term reverse engineering, rather than reengineering, was used in one of the early seminal papers in this area [104] concerned with software product reengineering. In this work, as well as in a more recent chapter on the subject [105], the following efforts represent both the taxonomy of and phases for what we denote here as *product reengineering:*

1. *Forward engineering* is the original process of defining, developing, and deploying a product or realizing a system concept as a product.

2. *Reverse engineering,* sometimes called inverse engineering, is the process though which a given system or product is examined in order to identify or specify the definition of the product either at the level of technological design specifications or system or user level requirements.

   (a) *Redocumentation* is a subset of reverse engineering in which a representation of the subject system or product is recreated for the purpose of generating functional explanations of original system behavior and, perhaps more importantly, to aid the reverse engineering team in better understanding the system at both a functional and a structural level. There are a number of redocumentation tools for software available and some of these are cited in [105]. One of the major purposes of redocumentation is producing new documentation for an existing product, where the existing documentation is faulty and perhaps virtually absent.

(b) *Design recovery* is a subset of reverse engineering in which the redocumentation knowledge is combined with other efforts, often involving the personal experiences and knowledge of others about the system, that lead to functional abstractions and enhanced product or system understanding at the level of function, structure, and even purpose. We would prefer to call this deployment recovery, development recovery (which would include design recovery), and definition recovery, depending on the phase in the reverse engineering lifecycle at which the recovery knowledge is obtained.

3. *Restructuring* involves transformation of the reverse engineering information concerning the original system structure into another representation form. This generally preserves the initial functionality of the original system or modifies it slightly in a purposeful manner that is in accord with the user requirements for the reengineered system and the way in which they differ from the requirements for the initial system. For our purposes, the terms deployment restructuring, development restructuring, and definition restructuring seem to be appropriate disaggregations of the restructuring notion.

4. *Reengineering* is, as defined in these efforts, equivalent to redevelopment engineering, renovation engineering, and reclamation engineering. Thus it is more related to maintenance and reuse than the other forms of systems management and process reengineering that we have discussed in this chapter. Reengineering is the recreation of essentially the original system in a new form that has improved structure but generally not much altered purpose and function. The nonfunctional aspects of the new system may be considerably different from those of the original system, especially with respect to quality and reliability.

Figure 8.4, which illustrates product reengineering, involves essentially these six activities.

We can recast this by considering a single phase for definition, for development, and for deployment that is exercised three times. We then see that there is a need for recovery, redocumentation, and restructuring as a result of the reverse engineering product obtained at each of the three basic phases.

This leads us to suggest Figure 8.32 as an alternative way to represent Figure 8.4 and as our interpretation of the representations used in [104] and [105]. These discussions utilized a three-phase generic lifecycle of requirements, design, and implementation. In this representation, implementation contains some of the detailed design and production efforts of our development phase and potentially less of the maintenance efforts that follow initial fielding of the system. The restructuring effort, based on recovery and redocumentation knowledge obtained in reverse engineering, is used to effect deployment restructuring, development restructuring, and definition restructuring. With these restructured products, which might well be considered as reusable products, we augment the knowledge and results obtained by detailed consideration of potentially augmented requirements. These augmented requirements are translated, together with the results of the restructuring efforts, into the outputs of the reengineering effort at the various phases to ultimately result in the reengineered product.

For the most part, this is the perspective taken on reengineering in a recent

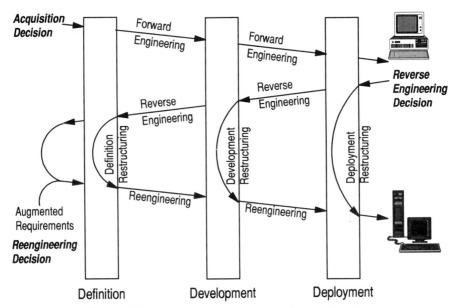

Figure 8.32   Expanded notion of product reengineering.

definitive reprint book on software reengineering [106], especially in the lead article by the editor of this work [107], which takes an inherently transformational view of product reengineering. This reprint book is concerned with the major ingredients needed for software product reengineering as summarized in Figure 8.33.

There are three basic classes of transformational views.

1. *Nonprocedural views* are metalevel views, such as decision tables, event trees, attribute trees, data schemata, user requirements, and system specifications. These do not represent views of the actual entity but rather a view of a view of the entity or, in other words, salient characteristics of the entity. A nonprocedural view is a purposeful view.

2. *Procedural views* contain direct information about procedures or representations, or information intimately associated with this information. Source code and the objects and entities of object-oriented languages are procedural views. A procedural view is a functional view.

3. *Pseudoprocedural views,* or architecturally oriented views, contain perspectives of both procedural and nonprocedural views. Hierarchy charts, structural models, data flow diagrams, entity-relationship diagrams, and Petri nets are examples of pseudoprocedural views. A pseudoprocedural view could also be called a structural view.

We can also have views that are derived from analysis of one of the three basic view categories. Arnold [107] denotes these as analysis views. For the most part, purposeful views or nonprocedural views are associated with the definitional phases of

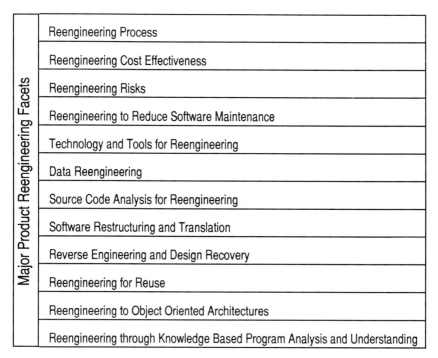

Figure 8.33 Major product reengineering issues.

the lifecycle for product acquisition. They concern user requirements and technological specifications. Functional or procedural views tend to be associated with the very end of the development phase of the lifecycle and the deployment phase when systems may be thought of in terms of their input/output characteristics. Pseudoprocedural, or architectural or structural, views tend to be associated with the earlier phases of system development. One of the major purposes of both forward and reverse engineering, and tools that support these, is to enable transformation from one view to another such as to ultimately obtain a functionally useful product.

Arnold [107] indicates several potential uses for and characteristics of product reengineering. These, which are neither mutually exclusive nor collectively exhaustive, include the following:

Reengineering may help reduce an organization's risk of product evolution through what effectively amounts to reuse of proven subproducts.

Reengineering may help an organization recoup its product development expenses through constructing new products that are based on existing products.

Reengineering may make products easier to modify for purposes of accommodating evolving customer needs.

Reengineering may be a catalyst for automating product maintenance.

Reengineering may be a catalyst for application of new technologies, such as CASE tools and artificial intelligence, to system acquisition.

Reengineering is big business, especially considering the major investment in legacy systems that need to be updated and maintained.

In short, reengineering provides a mechanism that enables us to understand systems better, such that we are capable of extending this knowledge to new and better systems. Thus it enhances both understanding and improvement abilities. Reengineering is accompanied with a variety of risks that are associated with processes, people, tools, strategies, and the application area for reengineering. These risks can be managed using the methodologies discussed in Chapter 3 and the metrics discussed in Chapters 4 and 5.

A number of authors have suggested specific lifecycles that will lead to a decision to reengineer or not to reengineer a product and, in support of a positive decision, enable a product reengineering lifecycle [108,109]. There are a number of needed accomplishments. These include the following:

1. Initially, there exists a need for formulation, assessment, and interpretation of definitional issues associated with the technical and organizational environment. These issues include organizational needs relative to the area under consideration, and the extent to which technology and the product or system under reengineering consideration support these organizational needs.

2. Identification and evaluation of options for continued development and maintenance of the product(s) under consideration are necessary, including options for potentially outsourcing this activity.

3. Formulation and evaluation of options for composition of the reengineering team, including insourcing and outsourcing possibilities, are necessary.

4. Identification and selection of a program of systematic measurements that will enable demonstration of cost efficiency of the identified reengineering options and selection of a chosen set of options are required.

5. The existing legacy systems in the organizations need to be examined in order to determine the extent to which these existing systems are functionally useless at present and in need of total replacement, functionally useful but with functional and nonfunctional defects that could potentially be remedied using product reengineering to create renovated systems, or systems that are fully appropriate for the current and intended future uses.

6. A suite of tools and methods to enable reengineering needs to be established. Method and tool analysis and integration are needed in order to provide for multiple perspective views across the various abstraction levels (procedural, pseudoprocedural, and nonprocedural) that will be encountered in reengineering.

7. A reengineering process for product reengineering needs to be created on the basis of the results of the earlier steps. This will provide for the reengineering of complete products or systems, and for incremental reengineering efforts that are phased in over time.

8. There must be major provisions for education and training such that it becomes possible to implement whatever reengineering process eventuates.

This is more of a checklist of needed accomplishments for a reengineering process than it is a specification of a lifecycle for the process itself. Through perusal of this checklist, we should be able to establish an appropriate process for reengineering in the form of Figures 8.4 or 8.32

There are several needs that must be considered if a product reengineering process is to yield appropriate and useful results.

1. There is a need to consider long-range organizational and technological issues in developing a product reengineering strategy.

2. There is a need to consider human, leadership, and cultural issues, and how these will be impacted by the development and deployment of a reengineered product as a part of the definition of the specifications for the reengineered product.

3. It must be possible to demonstrate that the reengineering process and product are, or will be, cost effective and of high quality, and that they support continued evolution of future capabilities.

4. Reengineered products must be considered within a larger framework that takes into account the potential need for reengineering at the levels of systems management and organizational processes as it will generally be a mistake to assume that technological fixes only will resolve organizational difficulties at these levels.

5. Product reengineering for improved postdeployment maintainability must consider maintainability at the level of process rather than at the level of product only, such as would result in the case of software altered through rewriting source code statements. Use of model-based management systems or code generators should yield much greater productivity, in this connection, than rewriting code at the level of source code.

6. Product reengineering must consider the need for reintegration of the reengineered product into existing legacy systems that have not been reengineered.

7. Product reengineering should be such that increased conformance to standards is a result of the reengineering process.

8. Product reengineering must consider legal issues associated with reverse engineering.

The importance of most of these issues is relatively self-evident. Issues surrounding legality are in a state of flux in product reengineering, in much the same way as they are for benchmarking. They deserve special commentary here.

It is clearly legal for an organization to reverse engineer a product that it owns. Also, there exists little debate at this time on whether inferring purpose from the analysis of existing functionality of a product and without any attempt to examine the architectural structure or detailed components that comprise the existing product, and then recapturing the functionality in terms of a new development effort (the so-called black box approach), is legal. Doubtlessly, it is legal. Major questions, however, surround the legality of "white box" reverse engineering in which the

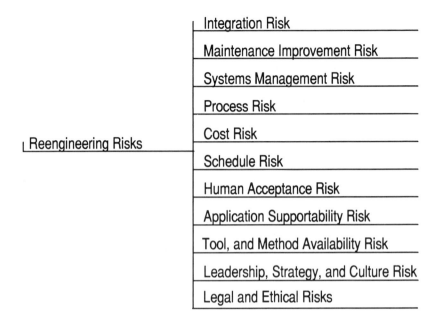

Figure 8.34 Some product reengineering risks.

detailed architectural structure and components of a system, including code for software, are examined in order to reverse engineer and reengineer it. The major difficulty appears to surround the fair use provisions in copyright law, and the fact that fair use provisions are different from those associated with the use of trade secrets for illicit gain. Copyrighted material cannot be a trade secret since the copyright law requires open disclosure of the material that is copyrighted. In particular, software is copyrighted and not patented. So trade secret restrictions do not apply. There is a pragmatist group that says white box reengineering is legal and a constructionist group that says it is illegal [110,111]. Those who suggest that it is illegal argue that it is not the obtaining of trade secrets that is illegal, but rather the subsequent use of these for illicit gain. These issues will be the subject of much debate over the near term.

A number of potential risks are important in product reengineering. Arnold [112] has identified many of these product reengineering needs in the form of risks that must be managed during the reengineering effort. These risks are associated with a variety of factors for product reengineering, as suggested in Figure 8.34.

- *Integration risk* is the risk associated with having a reengineered product that cannot be satisfactorily integrated with, or interfaced to, existing legacy systems.
- *Maintenance improvement risk* is the risk that the reengineered product will exacerbate, rather than ameliorate, maintenance difficulties.

- *Systems management risk* is the risk that the reengineered product attempts to impose a technological fix on a situation where the major difficulties are not need for greater support but need for organizational reengineering at the level of systems management.

- *Process risk* is that associated with having a reengineered process that might well represent an improvement in a situation where the specific organizational process in which the reengineered product is to be used is defective and in need of reengineering.

- *Cost risk* is associated with having major cost overruns in order to obtain a deployed reengineered product that meets specifications.

- *Schedule risk* is associated with having schedule delays in order to obtain a deployed reengineered product that meets specifications.

- *Human acceptance risk* is the risk associated with obtaining a reengineered product that is not suitable for human interaction, or one that is unacceptable to the user organization for other reasons.

- *Application supportability risk* is that risk associated with having a reengineered product that does not really support the application or purpose it was intended to support.

- *Tool and method availability risk* is associated with proceeding with reengineering a product based on promises for a method or tool, needed to complete the effort, which does not become available or which is faulty.

- *Leadership, strategy, and culture risk* is that associated with imposing a technological fix in the form of a reengineered product, in an organizational environment that cannot adapt to the reengineered product.

Clearly, these risks are not mutually exclusive, the risk attributes are not independent, and the listing is incomplete. For example, we could surely include legal risks. We can use this as the basis for a multiattribute type utility assessment that could be a part of the model-based management system or a decision support system [113] design that supports risk assessment and management for product reusability.

8.3 SUMMARY

In this chapter, we have considered a number of issues relative to systems reengineering. We indicated that reengineering can take place at either, or all, of the levels of *product, process,* or *systems management.* Reengineering at any of these levels is related to reengineering at the other two levels. Reengineering can be viewed from the perspective of the organization fielding a product as well as from the perspective of the customer, individual or organizational, receiving the product. From the perspective of either of these, it may well turn out to be the case that reengineering at the level of product only may not be fully meaningful if this is not also associated with, and generally driven by, reengineering at the levels of process and systems management. For an organization to reengineer a product when it is in

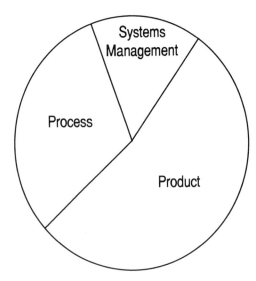

Figure 8.35   Hypothetical distribution of resources to implement systems reengineering at the levels of product, process, and systems management.

need of reengineering at the levels of systems management and/or process is almost a guarantee of a reengineered product that will not be fully trustworthy and cost efficient. An organization that contracts for product reengineering when it is in need of reengineering at the levels of systems management and/or process is asking for a technological fix and a symptomatic cure for difficulties that are institutionally and value related. Such solutions are not really solutions at all.

Figure 8.35 is a hypothetical representation of potential need for reengineering at the levels of product, process, and systems management. While it may well be the case, as suggested in the figure, that product reengineering may occupy much of the resources, the combined total of resources needed for systems management and process reengineering may not be insubstantial. What the figure does not show is the fact that resources expended on product reengineering only, and with no investigation of needs at the systems management and process levels, may well not be wise expenditures—from either the perspective of the organization producing the product or the one consuming it.

In an insightful study, Hall, Rosenthal, and Wade [114] indicated that organizations often squander resources on solutions that look very promising but that fail to produce long-lasting results of value for the organization. Four major ways to fail are identified.

1. Assigning average performers to the reengineering effort, often because the more valuable people are needed for other more important efforts, will guarantee mediocre performance of the reengineered product or process.
2. Measuring the reengineering plan and activities only, and not the results, will often produce deceptive measurement results.

3. Allowing new and innovative ideas for reengineering to be squelched through opportunistic politics and extreme risk aversion will preserve the status quo rather than encourage implementation of beneficial activities.

4. Failing to communicate wisely and widely during implementation will almost always frustrate success.

To this list, we might add failure to obtain real commitment from the highest levels of the organization for the reengineering effort. It might be argued, of course, that this leads to such things as assignment of average and mediocre performers to the reengineering effort. These authors also offer five factors said to enhance success at reengineering.

1. Set aggressive reengineering performance targets in terms of results.

2. Commit a significant portion of the CEOs time to the reengineering effort, especially during deployment of reengineering operations.

3. Assign a very senior executive to head the reengineering effort, especially during deployment.

4. Perform a comprehensive review and analysis of customer needs, organizational realities, strategic economic issues, and market trends as a prelude to reengineering.

5. Conduct a pilot study and prototype the reengineering effort in order to obtain results useful both to refine the reengineering process and to enhance communications and build enthusiasm.

This study was based primarily on organizational, or systems management, reengineering efforts. However, there are clear implications in these suggestions for all three types of reengineering effort.

In an insightful article, Venkatraman [115] identifies five levels for organizational transformation through information technology. We can expand on this slightly through adoption of the three levels for reengineering we have described here and obtain the representation shown in Figure 8.36 through 8.38. These figures show our representation of these five levels: two for organizational reengineering, two for product reengineering, and one for process reengineering. Organizational reengineering is generally revolutionary and radical, whereas product reengineering is usually evolutionary and incremental. Process reengineering may be at either of these extremes.

Venkatraman notes technological and organizational enablers and inhibitors that will affect desired transformations at both evolutionary and revolutionary levels of transformation. The technological enablers include increasingly favorable cost–effectiveness trends for various information technologies and enhanced connectivity possibilities. Technological inhibitors include the lack of currently established standards that are universally accepted and the rapid obsolescence of current technologies. Organizational enablers include managerial awareness of the need for change and leadership. Organizational inhibitors include financial limitations and manage-

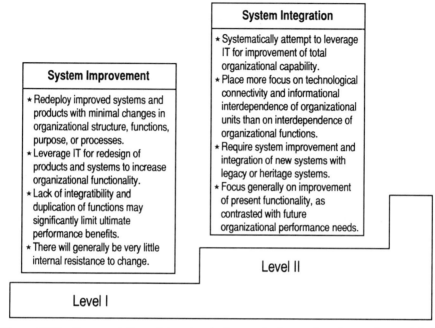

Figure 8.36   Representation of two levels for product reengineering and associated characteristics.

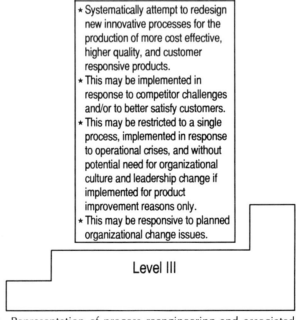

Figure 8.37   Representation of process reengineering and associated characteristics.

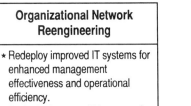

Figure 8.38 Representation of two levels for organizational reengineering and associated characteristics.

rial resistance to change. While both product reengineering and organizational reengineering desires will ultimately lead to change in organizational processes, changes for the purpose of producing a product with greater cost–effectiveness, quality, and (external) customer satisfaction will generally be different from and more limited in scope than those made for the purpose of improvement in internal responsiveness to satisfaction of present and future customer expectations.

Top–down directed changes, from level V to lower levels, are often directed at capability and effectiveness enhancement. Efforts directed from level I up are generally concerned with efficiency enhancement. It is generally at the level of improved processes that enhancement in efficiency and effectiveness may both be realized. It is generally the case that organizations should develop strategy first, then determine appropriate processes, and then choose information technology and other products that are most appropriate. There are exceptions, however, and an interesting case study is described by Yetton, Johnson, and Craig [116] of an organization with a high organizational learning capacity and a mature approach to risk management in which, incremental adoption of information technology, was a driver of strategic change.

So, change can be initiated at any of these levels. Systems management deals with appropriate changes at all three levels, with efficiency and effectiveness, and also with the explicability and equity issues necessary to bring this about and to ensure a better tomorrow. It involves a number of perspectives and has roles for a great many professionals. Some of these are illustrated in Figure 8.39. This figure shows some of the many roles and identities associated with systems engineering

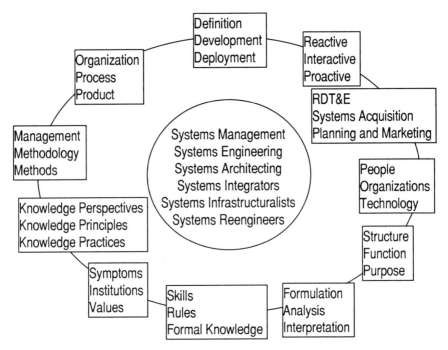

Figure 8.39   Some of the roles for and facets of system management.

and systems management which enable, and which are enabled by, successful reengineering [117–118].

REFERENCES

[1] Sage, A. P., and Palmer, J. D., *Software Systems Engineering,* John Wiley & Sons, New York, 1990.

[2] Rekoff, M. G. Jr., "On Reverse Engineering," *IEEE Transactions on Systems, Man, and Cybernetics,* Vol. SMC 15, No. 2, Mar. 1985, pp. 244–252.

[3] "Software Engineering Glossary," *IEEE Software Engineering Standards,* IEEE Press, New York, 1991.

[4] *IEEE Standard for Software Maintenance,* P1219/D14, IEEE Standards Department, New York, 1992.

[5] Davenport, T. H., and Short, J. E., "The New Industrial Engineering: Information Technology and Business Process Redesign," *Sloan Management Review,* Vol. 31, No. 4, Summer 1990, pp. 11–27.

[6] Davenport, T. H., *Process Innovation: Reengineering Work Through Information Technology,* Harvard Business School Press, Boston, MA, 1993.

[7] Hudak, G. J., "Reengineering the Systems Engineering Process," *Proceedings of the National Council on Systems Engineering Annual Meeting,* Alexandria, VA, Aug. 1993, pp. 105–112.

[8] Brackett, J. W., and Pyster, A. B., "High-Level Software Synthesis," *Proceedings of the National Council on Systems Engineering Annual Meeting,* Alexandria, VA, Aug. 1993, pp. 207–214.

[9] Hammer, M., "Reengineering Work: Dont Automate, Obliterate," *Harvard Business Review,* Vol. 68, No. 4, July 1990, pp. 104–112.

[10] Hammer, M., and Champy, J., *Reengineering the Corporation: A Manifesto for Business Revolution,* Harper Business, New York, 1993.

[11] Harrington, H. J., *Business Process Improvement: The Breakthrough Strategy for Total Quality, Productivity, and Competitiveness,* McGraw-Hill Book Co., New York, 1991.

[12] Quinn, J. B., Paquette, P. C., and Doorley, T., "Technology in Services: Rethinking Strategic Focus," *Sloan Management Review,* Winter 1990, pp. 79–87.

[13] Quinn, J. B., Paquette, P. C., and Doorley, T., "Technology in Services: Creating Organizational Revolutions," *Sloan Management Review,* Winter 1990, pp. 67–78.

[14] Quinn, J. B., Paquette, P. C., and Doorley, T., "Beyond Products: Service Based Strategies," *Harvard Business Review,* Vol. 68, No. 3, Mar. 1990, pp. 58–68.

[15] Quinn, J. B., *Intelligent Enterprise: A Knowledge and Service Based Paradigm for Industry,* Free Press, New York, 1992.

[16] Davenport, T. H., Eccles, R. G., and Prusak, L., "Information Politics," *Sloan Management Review,* Vol. 34, No. 1, Fall 1992, pp. 53–65.

[17] Rockart, J. F., and DeLong, D. W., *Executive Support Systems: The Emergence of Top Management Computer Use,* Dow Jones–Irwin, Homewood, IL, 1988.

[18] Raiffa, H., *The Art and Science of Negotiation,* Belknap, Cambridge, MA, 1982.

[19] Neale, M. A., and Bazerman, M. H., *Cognition and Rationality in Negotiation,* Free Press, New York, 1991.

[20] Kennedy, G. (Ed.), *Field Guide to Negotiations,* Harvard Business School Press, Boston, MA, 1994.

[21] Johanson, H. J., McHugh, P., Pendlebury, A. J., and Wheeler, W. A. III, *Business Process Reengineering: Breakthrough Strategies for Market Dominance,* John Wiley & Sons, Chichester, UK, 1993.

[22] Schoemaker, P. J. H., "When and How to Use Scenario Planning: A Heuristic Approach with Illustrations," *Journal of Forecasting,* Vol. 10, 1991, pp. 549–564.

[23] Schoemaker, P. J. H., "How to Link Strategic Vision to Core Capabilities," *Sloan Management Review,* Vol. 34, No. 1, Fall 1992, pp. 67–81.

[24] Strebel, P., *Breakpoints: How Managers Exploit Radical Business Change,* Harvard Business School Press, Boston, MA, 1992.

[25] Camp, R. C., *Benchmarking: The Search for Industry Best Practices That Lead to Superior Performance,* Quality Press, American Society for Quality Control, Milwaukee, WI, 1989.

[26] Liebfried, K. H. J., and McNair, C. J., *Benchmarking: A Tool for Continuous Improvement,* HarperCollins Publishers, New York, 1992.

[27] Watson, G. H., *The Benchmarking Workbook: Adapting Best Practices for Performance Improvement,* Productivity Press, Cambridge, MA, 1992.

[28] Watson, G. H., *Strategic Benchmarking: How to Rate Your Company's Performance Against the World's Best,* John Wiley & Sons, New York, 1993.

[29] Rockart, J. F., "Chief Executives Define Their Own Data Needs," *Harvard Business Review,* Vol. 57, No. 2, 1979, pp. 81–93.

[30] Rockart, J. F., and Bullen, C. V. (Eds.), *The Rise of Managerial Computing,* Dow Jones–Irwin, Homewood, IL, 1986.

[31] Watson, G. H., Bookhart, S., et al., "Applying Moral and Legal Considerations to Benchmarking Protocols," Appendix 2 in *Planning, Organizing, and Managing Benchmarking: A User's Guide,* American Productivity and Quality Center, Houston, TX, 1992.

[32] Porter, M. E., *Competitive Strategy: Techniques for Analyzing Industries and Competitors,* Free Press, New York, 1980.

[33] Porter, M. E., *Competitive Advantage: Creating and Sustaining Superior Performance,* Free Press, New York, 1985.

[34] Porter, M. E., *The Competitive Advantage of Nations,* Free Press, New York, 1990.

[35] Sage, A. P., *Economic Systems Analysis: Microeconomics for Systems Engineering, Engineering Management, and Project Selection,* North-Holland/Elsevier, New York, 1983.

[36] *The State of Strategy,* Harvard Business Review Paperback 90082, Harvard Business School Press, Boston, MA, 1991.

[37] Porter, M. E., *On Competition and Strategy,* Harvard Business Review Paperback 90079, Harvard Business School Press, Boston, MA, 1991.

[38] Thomas, R. J., *New Product Development: Managing and Forecasting for Strategic Success,* John Wiley & Sons, New York, 1993.

[39] Abell, D. F., *Managing with Dual Strategies,* Free Press, New York, 1993.

[40] Rumelt, R. P., Schendel, D. E., and Teece, D. J. (Eds.), *Fundamental Issues in Strategy: A Research Agenda,* Harvard Business School Press, Boston, MA, 1994.

[41] Thomas, Philip R., *Competitiveness Through Total Cycle Time,* McGraw-Hill Book Co., New York, 1990.

[42] Bower, J. L., and Hout, T. M., "Fast-Cycle Time Capability for Competitive Power," *Harvard Business Review,* Vol. 66, No. 6, Nov. 1988, pp. 110–118.

[43] Schmenner, R. W., "The Merit of Making Things Fast," *Sloan Management Review,* Vol. 30, No. 1, Fall 1988, pp. 11–17.

[44] Stalk, G. Jr., "Time—The Next Source of Competitive Advantage," *Harvard Business Review,* Vol. 66, No. 4, July 1988, pp. 41–51.

[45] Stalk, G. Jr., and Hout, T. M., *Competing Against Time: How Time Based Competition is Reshaping Global Markets,* Free Press, New York, 1990.

[46] Meyer, C., *Fast Cycle Time: How to Align Purpose, Strategy, and Structure for Speed,* Free Press, New York, 1993.

[47] Roussel, P. A., Saad, K. N., and Erickson, T. J., *Third Generation R&D: Managing the Link to Corporate Strategy,* Harvard Business School Press, Boston, MA, 1991.

[48] von Hippel, E., *The Sources of Innovation,* Oxford University Press, Oxford, UK, 1988.

[49] Howard, W. G. Jr., and Guile, B. R., *Profiting from Innovation: The Report of a Three Year Study from the National Academy of Engineering,* Free Press, New York, 1992.

[50] Smith, P. G., and Reinertsen, D. G., *Developing Products in Half the Time,* Van Nostrand Reinhold, New York, 1991.

[51] Millson, M. R., Raj, S. P., and Wilemon, D., "A Survey of Major Approaches for Accelerating New Product Development," *Journal of Production Innovation Management,* Vol. 9, No. 1, 1992, pp. 53–69.

[52] Robertson, T. S., "How to Reduce Market Penetration Times," *Sloan Management Review*, Vol. 35, No. 1, Fall 1993, pp. 87–96.

[53] Anthony, R. N., *The Management Control Function*, Harvard Business School Press, Boston, MA, 1988.

[54] Shank, J. K., and Govindarajan, V., *Strategic Cost Management: The New Tool for Competitive Advantage*, Free Press, New York, 1993.

[55] Venkatesan, R., "Strategic Sourcing: To Make or Not to Make," *Harvard Business Review*, Vol. 70, No. 6, Nov. 1992, pp. 98–107.

[56] Prahalad, C. K., and Hamel, G., "The Core Competence of the Corporation," *Harvard Business Review*, Vol. 68, No. 3, May 1990, pp. 60–74.

[57] Stalk, G., Evans, P., and Shulman, L. E., "Competing on Capabilities: The New Rules of Corporate Strategy," *Harvard Business Review*, Vol. 70, No. 2, Mar. 1992, pp. 57–63.

[58] Meyer, M. H., and Utterback, J. M., "The Product Family and the Dynamics of Core Capability," *Sloan Management Review*, Vol. 34, No. 3, Spring 1993, pp. 29–48.

[59] Lacity, M. C., and Hirschheim, R., "The Information Systems Outsourcing Bandwagon," *Sloan Management Review*, Vol. 35, No. 1, Fall 1993, pp. 73–86.

[60] Lacity, M. C., and Hirschheim, R., *Information Systems Outsourcing: Myths, Metaphors, and Realities*, John Wiley & Sons, Chichester, UK, 1993.

[61] Benjamin, R. J., and Blunt, J., "Critical IT Issues: The Next Ten Years," *Sloan Management Review*, Vol. 33, No. 4, Summer 1992, pp. 7–19.

[62] Boynton, A. C., Jacobs, G. C., and Zmud, R. W., "Whose Responsibility is IT Management?" *Sloan Management Review*, Vol. 33, No. 4, Summer 1992, pp. 32–38.

[63] Pine, B. J. II, *Mass Customization: The New Frontier in Business Competition*, Harvard Business School Press, Boston, MA, 1993.

[64] Pine, B. J. II, Victor, B., and Boynton, A. C., "Making Mass Customization Work," *Harvard Business Review*, Vol. 71, No. 5, Sept. 1993, pp. 108–119.

[65] McCutcheon, D. M., Raturi, A. S., and Meredith, J. R., "The Customization-Responsiveness Squeeze," *Sloan Management Review*, Vol. 35, No. 2, Winter 1994, pp. 89–99.

[66] Day, G. S., *Market Driven Strategy: Processes for Creating Value*, Free Press, New York, 1990.

[67] Mintzberg, H., "The Rise and Fall of Strategic Planning," *Harvard Business Review*, Vol. 72, No. 1, Jan. 1994, pp. 107–114.

[68] Mintzberg, H., *The Rise and Fall of Strategic Planning*, Free Press, New York, 1994.

[69] Dertrouzos, M. L., Lester, R. K., and Solow, R. M., *Made in America: Regaining the Productive Edge*, MIT Press, Cambridge, MA, 1989.

[70] Thurow, L., *Head to Head: The Coming Economic Battle Among Japan, Europe, and America*, Morrow, New York, 1992.

[71] Cohen, S. S., and Zysman, J., *Manufacturing Matters: The Myth of the Post-Industrial Economy*, Basic Books, New York, 1987.

[72] Harmon, R. L., and Peterson, L. D., *Reinventing the Factory: Productivity Breakthroughs in Manufacturing Today*, Free Press, New York, 1990.

[73] Brandin, D. H., and Harrison, M. A. *The Technology War: A Case for Competitiveness*, John Wiley & Sons, New York, 1987.

[74] Savage, C. M., *Fifth Generation Management: Integrating Enterprises Through Human Networking,* Digital Press, Burlington, MA, 1990.

[75] Bell, D., *The Coming Post-Industrial Society: A Venture in Social Forecasting,* Basic Books, New York, 1973.

[76] Zuboff, S., *In the Age of the Smart Machine: The Future of Work and Power,* Basic Books, New York, 1988.

[77] Rockart, J. F., and DeLong, D. W., *Executive Support Systems: The Emergence of Top Management Computer Use,* Dow Jones–Irwin, Homewood, IL, 1988.

[78] Keen, P. G. W., *Shaping the Future, Business Design Through Information Technology,* Harvard Business School Press, Boston, MA, 1991.

[79] Harvard Business Review Editors, *Revolution in Real Time: Managing Information Technologies in the 1990s,* Harvard Business School Press, Boston, MA, 1990.

[80] Morton, M. S. S. (Ed.), *The Corporation of the 1990s: Information Technology and Organizational Transformation,* Oxford University Press, New York, 1991.

[81] Blattberg, R. C., Glazer, R., and Little, J. D. C. (Eds.), *The Marketing Information Revolution,* Harvard Business School Press, Boston, MA, 1994.

[82] Boar, B. H., *The Art of Strategic Planning for Information Technology,* John Wiley & Sons, New York, 1993.

[83] McGee, J., and Prusak, L., *Managing Information Strategically: Increase Your Company's Competitiveness and Efficiency by Using Information as a Strategic Tool,* John Wiley & Sons, New York, 1993.

[84] Peters, T., *Liberation Management: Necessary Disorganization for the Nanosecond Nineties,* Knopf, New York, 1992.

[85] Fishbein, M., and Azjin, I., *Belief, Attitude, Intention, and Behavior,* Addison-Wesley, Reading, MA, 1975.

[86] Denton, D. K., *Horizontal Management: Beyond Total Customer Satisfaction,* Lexington Books, New York, 1991.

[87] Editors of *Business Week,* "The Horizontal Cooperation," *Business Week,* Dec. 20, 1993, pp. 76–81.

[88] Grant, R. M., Shanu, R., and Krishnan, R., "TQM's Challenge to Management Theory and Practice," *Sloan Management Review,* Vol. 35, No. 2, Winter 1994, pp. 11–24.

[89] Manz, C. C., and Sims, H. P. Jr., *Business Without Bosses,* John Wiley & Sons, New York, 1993.

[90] Katzenbach, J. R., and Smith, D. K., *The Wisdom of Teams,* Harvard Business School Press, Boston, MA, 1993.

[91] Pfeffer, J., *Competitive Advantage Through People,* Harvard Business School Press, Boston, MA, 1994.

[92] Rosenblatt, A., and Watson, G. F., "Concurrent Engineering," *IEEE Spectrum,* July 1991, pp. 22–37.

[93] Winner, R. I., Pennell, J. P., Bertrand, J. P., and Slusarczuk, M. M. G., "The Role of Concurrent Engineering in Weapons System Acquisition," Institute for Defense Analyses Technical Report R-338, Dec. 1988.

[94] Nevins, J. L., and Whitney, D. E. (Eds.), *Concurrent Design of Products and Processes: A Strategy for the Next Generation in Manufacturing,* McGraw-Hill Book Co., New York, 1989.

[95] Shina, S. G., *Concurrent Engineering and Design for Manufacture of Electronics Products,* Van Nostrand Reinhold, New York, 1991.

[96] Carter, D. E., and Baker, B. S., *Concurrent Engineering: The Product Development Environment for the 1990s,* Addison-Wesley, Reading, MA, 1992.

[97] Andrews, C. C., and Leventhal, N. S., *FUSION—Integrating IE, CASE, and JAD: A Handbook for Reengineering the Systems Organization,* Prentice-Hall, Englewood Cliffs, NJ, 1993.

[98] Kronlof, K. (Ed.), *Method Integration: Concepts and Case Studies,* John Wiley & Sons, Chichester, UK, 1993.

[99] Schefstrom, D., and van den Broek, G. (Eds.), *Tool Integration: Environments and Frameworks,* John Wiley & Sons, Chichester, UK, 1993.

[100] Fiksel, J., "Computer Aided Requirements Management for Environmental Excellence," *Proceedings of the National Council on Systems Engineering Annual Meeting,* Alexandria, VA, July 1993, pp. 251–258.

[101] Hunt, V. D., *Reengineering: Leveraging the Power of Integrated Product Development,* Oliver Wright Publications, Essex Junction, VT, 1993.

[102] *Air Force Material Command Guide on Integrated Product Development,* May 25, 1993.

[103] Office of the Secretary of Defense, ASD (C³I), "The DoD Enterprise Model Volume I: Strategic Activity and Data Models; Volume II: Using the DoD Enterprise Model—A Strategic View of Change in DoD," U.S. Department of Defense, Jan. 1994.

[104] Chikofsky, E., and Cross, J. H., "Reverse Engineering and Design Recovery, A Taxonomy," *IEEE Software,* Vol. 7, No. 1, Jan. 1990, pp. 13–17.

[105] Cross, J. H. II, Chikofsky, E. J., and May, C. H. Jr., "Reverse Engineering," in Yovitz, M. C. (Ed.), *Advances in Computers,* Vol. 35, Academic Press, San Diego, CA, 1992, pp. 199–254.

[106] Arnold, R. S. (Ed.), *Software Reengineering,* IEEE Computer Society Press, Los Altos, CA, 1993.

[107] Arnold, R. S., "A Road Map Guide to Software Reengineering Technology," in Arnold, R. S. (Ed.), *Software Reengineering,* IEEE Computer Society Press, Los Altos, CA, 1993, pp. 3–22.

[108] Ulrich, W. M., "Re-engineering: Defining an Integrated Migration Framework," in Arnold, R. S. (Ed.), *Software Reengineering,* IEEE Computer Society Press, Los Altos, CA, 1993, pp. 108–118.

[109] Olsem, M. R., "Preparing to Reengineer," *IEEE Computer Society Reverse Engineering Newsletter,* Dec. 1993, pp. 1–3.

[110] Samuelson, P., "Reverse Engineering Someone Else's Software: Is it Legal?," *IEEE Software,* Vol. 7, No. 1, Jan. 1990, pp. 90–96.

[111] Sibor, V., "Interpreting Reverse Engineering Law," *IEEE Software,* Vol. 7, No. 4, July 1990, pp. 4–10.

[112] Arnold, R. S., "Common Risks of Reengineering," *IEEE Computer Society Reverse Engineering Newsletter,* Apr. 1992, pp. 1–2.

[113] Sage, A. P., *Decision Support Systems Engineering,* John Wiley & Sons, New York, 1991.

[114] Hall, G., Rosenthal, J., and Wade, J., "How to Make Reengineering Really Work," *Harvard Business Review,* Vol. 71, No. 6, Nov. 1993, pp. 119–131.

[115] Venkatraman, N., "IT-Enabled Business Transformation: From Automation to Business Scope Redefinition," *Sloan Management Review,* Vol. 35, No. 2, Winter 1994, pp. 73 –88.

[116] Yetton, P. W., Johnson, K. D., and Craig, J. F., "Computer Aided Architects: A Case Study of IT and Strategic Change," *Sloan Management Review,* Vol. 35, No. 4, Summer 1994, pp. 57–68.

[117] Petrozzo, D. P., and Stepper, J. C., *Successful Reengineering,* Van Nostrand Reinhold, New York, 1994.

[118] Hamel, G., and Prahalad, C. K., *Competing for the Future,* Harvard Business School Press, Boston, MA, 1994.

Index